SELLING

Principles and Methods

SELLING

Principles and Methods

SELLING
Principles and Methods

The Irwin Series in Marketing
Consulting Editor Gilbert A. Churchill, Jr. *University of Wisconsin, Madison*

SELLING
Principles and Methods

Carlton A. Pederson
Late Professor of Business Management
Graduate School of Business
Stanford University

Milburn D. Wright, Ed.D.
Late Dean and Professor of Marketing
School of Business
San Jose State University

Barton A. Weitz, Ph.D.
Professor of Marketing and
J. C. Penney Eminent Scholar
University of Florida

1988
Ninth Edition

IRWIN
Homewood, Illinois 60430

Cover photo: Michael Stuckey/Comstock, Inc.

This book was set in Times Roman by Carlisle Communications Limited.
The editors were Jeanne M. Teutsch, Eleanore Snow, Ethel Shiell, and Merrily D. Mazza.
The production manager was Irene H. Sotiroff.
The designer was Michael Warrell.
The drawings were done by Precision Graphics.
R. R. Donnelley & Sons Company was the printer and binder.

ISBN 0-256-03644-6

Library of Congress Catalog Card No. 87–81434

Printed in the United States of America

2 3 4 5 6 7 8 9 0 DO 5 4 3 2 1 0 9 8

Preface

We are going through a turbulent period in the business community. Domestic and international competition is increasing; firms are merging, acquiring other firms, and divesting divisions; new technologies are replacing traditional methods of conducting business relationships; products are becoming more complex; and customers are demanding more service, support, and lower prices.

These changes in the business environment indicate that salespeople will play an increasingly important role in business activity. Salespeople are ideally suited to help customers deal with complex problems and an uncertain environment. Few businesses will survive these turbulent times without an effective salesforce.

However, salespeople will need to develop greater skills to meet the challenges of this dynamic business environment. They will have to learn how to use lap-top computers, modern telecommunication, and the latest psychological and communication principles.

This edition emphasizes the excitement and rewards of selling careers. Twenty selling scenarios have been added to the text to illustrate the selling principles presented. In the scenarios, real salespeople talk about problems they confronted and how they used creative approaches to overcome these problems.

In addition, changes have been made in this edition to help future salespeople meet the challenges of our dynamic business environment. An additional chapter on adaptive selling (Chapter 7) has been added, and the discussion of communication principles related to adaptive selling has been expanded. More illustrations are provided of techniques for asking questions, probing for information, and listening actively. Examples of interpreting nonverbal cues and using nonverbal communications are incorporated throughout the text.

In Chapter 17, a variety of new communication methods that make selling more effective are discussed. Telemarketing, direct mail, and telephone selling received more discussion.

This book is dedicated to Dr. Milburn D. "Mel" Wright who passed away before this edition was completed. While many changes have been made in this edition, the features that Mel and Bud Pederson emphasized since the first edition are preserved. The easy-to-read writing style is complemented by an attractive layout and useful illustrations. Actual business examples are used throughout the text, and a how-to approach is emphasized. These features have made Pederson, Wright, and Weitz an important vehicle for educating future salespeople over the last 37 years.

My family has a long tradition in selling. My grandfathers sold merchandise in their retail stores. My father traveled the Midwest selling overcoats to major retailers. He made a lot of friends among his customers and had a rewarding business career. My aunt Mollie sold high-fashion garments for Bonwit-Teller well past the traditional age of retirement. My uncles, Jack, Milton, and Paul, have all worked in sales for most of their lives. These family members have all reaped the rewards—both personal and financial—that come to effective salespeople.

None of my family members went to college. They did not even take selling courses. But times have changed. Colleges, universities, and community colleges are now the source of supply for sales trainees. It is vital that future sales representatives obtain a basic foundation of knowledge in the field of selling before they enter specific on-the-job training programs or establish their own sales organizations. The purpose of this book is to supply the educational materials and experiences that will prepare men and women for their entry into the exciting and rewarding field of selling.

We are indebted to many users of the previous editions for suggestions made to improve this revision. Special acknowledgment is due the following professors, who carefully reviewed the eighth edition and provided critiques on the text material and organization: Don McColum, Portland Community College; James Boespflug, Arapahoe Community College; Edward J. Mayo, Western Michigan University; Clyde E. Harris, Jr., University of Georgia; and William D. Henley, Auburn University.

Finally, I would like to thank Kathleen Brown, Jhinuk Chowdhury, and Mona Chowdhury for their assistance in preparing this edition.

Barton Weitz

Acknowledgments

The authors wish to express their sincere gratitude to the following companies for their generous contributions to the ninth edition:

AM International, Inc.

American Airlines Inc.

American Management Association

American Telephone & Telegraph Company

Bank of America

Blyth Eastman Dillon & Co., Inc.

Bristol Laboratories

Burroughs Corporation

Carnation Company

Carter, Hawley, Hale Stores, Inc.

Chrysler Corporation

The Coca-Cola Company

Colgate-Palmolive Co.

Connecticut Mutual Life Insurance Company

Control Data Corp.

Crown Zellerbach Corp.

Dictaphone Corp.

Dow Chemical Company

Dukane Corp.

E. I. duPont de Nemours & Co.

Eastman Kodak Co.

The Emporium/Capwell

Federated Department Stores

The Firestone Tire & Rubber Co.

FMC Corporation

Ford Motor Co.

General Electric Corp.

General Foods Corp.

General Telephone & Electronics Corporation

The Goodyear Tire & Rubber Company

Gulf Oil Corp.

Hart Schaffner & Marx

Hewlett-Packard Co.

International Business Machines Corporation

International Harvester Co.

Johnson & Johnson

ix

Kaiser Aluminum & Chemical Corp.

Lever Brothers Co.

Lily Tulip Cup Division of Owens-Illinois, Inc.

R. H. Macy & Co., Inc.

The Maytag Co.

McKesson & Robbins, Inc.

Merck Sharp & Dohme Division, Merck & Co., Inc.

Metropolitian Life Insurance Co.

Mutual Benefit Life Insurance Company

NCR Corporation

New York Life Insurance Company

A. C. Nielsen Company

Ortho Pharmaceuticals Corp.

Otis Elevator Company

The Pacific Telephone & Telegraph Co.

Paine, Webber, Jackson & Curtis Inc.

Paper Mate Division, The Gillette Company

Penn Mutual Life Insurance Company

J. C. Penney Company

Perrygraph Division, Nashua Corporation

Personal Finance Company

Procter & Gamble Co.

Provident Mutual Life Insurance Company

The Royal Bank of Canada

Safeguard Business Systems Corporation

Sears, Roebuck & Co.

SKF Industries

Sperry

Standard Oil Co. of California

Standard Register Co.

State Farm Insurance Companies

Technicolor Audio-Visual Systems

3M Company

Toledo Scale Company

U.S. Rubber Company

U. S. Steel Corporation

Wear-Ever Aluminum, Inc.

Westinghouse Electric Corporation

Xerox Corporation

Zenith Radio Corporation

Contents

Part II
Knowledge and Skill Required for Successful Selling

I

The Field of Selling

Part I provides an introduction to the nature of personal selling. In Chapter 1, we define personal selling and discuss the role of personal selling in the firm's marketing program, the importance of personal selling to our society, the opportunities and rewards of selling careers, and the future of personal selling. Chapter 2 focuses on the duties and activities of sales representatives, while Chapter 3 emphasizes ethical and legal responsibilities.

1

Personal Selling: Its Nature, Its Role, and Its Rewards

Some questions answered in this chapter are:

- Why is selling an exciting and challenging job?
- What is selling?
- Why should someone learn about selling even if they do not plan on taking a selling job?
- What is the role of personal selling in a business firm? In society?
- What are the employment opportunities in selling?
- What are the rewards in a selling career?
- What are the future trends in selling?

This chapter focuses on the nature, role, opportunities, and rewards of personal selling. We will see what effect selling has on the development of the American economy and how important creative selling is to our future economic progress.

THE CHALLENGE AND REWARDS IN SELLING

In addition to pay and promotion opportunities, selling offers excitement and challenges. Sharon Snowden sells word processing systems for Lanier Business Products. Before taking a job with Lanier, she was the top salesperson for the largest distributor of Sharp photocopiers in the United States and made more than $7,000 a month. When asked why she went into sales after teaching school for several years, she said, "I wanted more freedom to set my own schedule, to grow and be rewarded based on performance rather than seniority." Her sales philosophy is "never sell price. I sell service, reliability, and the fact that our company is honest and sound. I love sales. It's the ultimate challenge."[1]

Many people like Sharon do not want to spend long hours behind a desk. They prefer to be outside, moving around, and meeting people. Selling is ideally suited for people with these interests—the typical salesperson contacts dozens of people each day. Most of these contacts are challenging new experiences, and through these contacts, the individual builds valuable experiences. By providing real and continuing service to many customers, the salesperson also builds a large group of loyal friends. Salespeople reap another reward of successful selling: They establish self-confidence and prove to themselves that they will always be able to hold their own in a highly competitive environment.

Selling also offers unusual freedom and flexibility; it is not just a 9-to-5 job. Many salespeople can allocate their own time. They do not have to report in or punch a time card. Long work hours may be required some days, while there may be few demands other days. In addition, salespeople have the freedom to determine what they do during a day. They can decide which customers to call on, when to do paperwork, and when to look for new customers.

Salespeople are like independent entrepreneurs. They have a territory to manage and few restrictions on how to manage it. Due to this freedom, their success or failure is largely a result of their own skills and effort. Because of the independence granted salespeople, they must be self-motivated.

THE NATURE OF SELLING

Everyone has been exposed to personal selling. Some common selling experiences include:

Buying a suit in a clothing store.

Making a purchase at a friend's Tupperware party.

Taking a demonstration ride in a new car and deciding to buy the car.

---

[1]Donald J. Moine, "Going for the Gold in the Selling Game," *Psychology Today,* March 1984, p. 39.

Buying a calculator after seeing a clerk demonstrate one in a campus bookstore.

These aspects of personal selling are familiar to most people, but they are only a small sample of the wide variety of selling activities salespeople perform. Some less visible but more representative selling activities are:

A SmithKline Beckman salesperson telling a doctor about the benefits and side effects of a new drug.

A Xerox sales representative analyzing a customer's office copying needs and proposing a copier with automatic sorting and stapling.

A Procter & Gamble salesperson helping a store manager arrange an end-aisle display.

A sales team from Boeing making a presentation to Northwest Airlines about increased profits to be gained from purchasing Boeing 767 aircraft.

The first set of examples is more familiar to most people because it describes sales activities directed toward consumers. The second set of examples deals with selling to professional, commercial, trade, and industrial customers. While the second set of examples is less familiar, it is more representative of the work salespeople do. Sales made to consumers are less than 20 percent of sales activity in the United States; four times more selling activity is directed toward professional and industrial customers.[2] Selling Scenario 1–1 illustrates the nature of selling to industrial customers.

Thus, most people are exposed to a narrow, atypical group of selling activities. Unfortunately, this limited exposure to selling created a misconception of what salespeople are like and how they do their job. For example, a survey of college students taken 20 years ago revealed these impressions:

Salespeople must lie and be deceitful to succeed.

Salesmanship brings out the worst in people.

Selling benefits only the seller.

Salesmen are prostitutes because they sell all their values for money.

Selling is no job for a man with talent and brains.[3]

---

[2]*Statistical Abstract of the United States 1982* (Washington, D.C.: U.S. Government Printing Office).

[3]Donald L. Thompson, "Stereotype of the Salesman," *Harvard Business Review,* January–February 1972, pp. 20–29.

Selling Scenario 1–1

THE $2 BILLION MAN

 Making a $2 billion sale may seem like something to get really excited about, but the man who did it, Keith Bergstrom, while certainly pleased, appears as low-keyed and conservative as, well, the company for which he works.

Bergstrom, 42, has been with Boeing for 20 years, and has what is considered a "typical" sales background in this business: a B.S. in electrical engineering, another in industrial engineering, and an MBA. He's been in the sales department for eight years and for the past five has been in direct line sales (selling airplanes).

It is a highly competitive business that keeps him away from Seattle 30 percent of the time, but one in which sales only develop over a period of time. "My first presentation of the Boeing 757s to Northwest was in January 1980," he explains. "They announced the purchase of that type—the first one—in November 1983."

Toward the end of the negotiation for the $2 billion order, Bergstrom says that he probably spent more time in Minneapolis (Northwest's headquarters) than in Seattle.

He freely gives credit to others for this and other sales, saying that his job is "to orchestrate a campaign, to draw in the people you need in a sales effort—analytical talents, engineering talents, management talents."

Still, he says, he takes a leadership role because of his background on the airliner. "On major accounts, I should be the most knowledgeable person about that airline in a broad sense than anybody else at Boeing," he says.

Despite the complexity of the product he sells and his educational background, Bergstrom says he has "no problem" with being called a salesman. After all, that's what he is, which is evident when asked if he expects to sell any planes to Northwest sometime soon. His answer: "You never know!"

Source: Reprinted from Bill Kelly, "How to Sell Airplanes, Boeing-Style," *Sales & Marketing Management*, December 9, 1985, p. 34.

But times have changed and so has this negative stereotype. As the business environment shifted from a seller's market to a buyer's market, salespeople and business firms embraced the marketing concept—that is, they began to emphasize satisfying customer needs. Based on recent surveys, most college students now believe that sales jobs are challenging, creative, intellectually rewarding, a good use of a college education, and have a high degree of professionalism.[4]

---

[4]Alan J. Dubinsky, "Recruiting College Students for the Sales Force," *Industrial Marketing Management,* Winter 1980, pp. 37–45; and "On Campus, Selling Is Still A Tough Sale," *Sales & Marketing Management,* August 16, 1982, pp. 58–59.

Marketing Concept and Modern Selling

The business environment has changed dramatically since World War II. Low-cost transportation, mass communication, and increased domestic and international competition have forced companies to adopt the marketing concept.

Today's companies no longer rely solely on local markets. With low-cost transportation and modern communications, U.S. firms can compete effectively in global markets. While this has increased the potential market for U.S. companies, it has also increased the competition they face. U.S. manufacturers now compete against European and Japanese companies as well as traditional domestic ones.

With mass communication, companies can educate consumers about their products at a low cost. TV messages can be delivered at less than one tenth of a cent per person per exposure.

Thus, the modern customer has a wider range of alternatives to consider than the customer at the turn of the century. In addition, many of these alternatives have special features tailored to specific customer needs. Businesses can no longer operate under the premise, "If we can make it, the customer will buy it." Customer needs and competition play a central role in the success of modern business.

This orientation of modern business is embodied in the marketing concept. Professor Phillip Kotler defines the *marketing concept* as:

> a management orientation that holds that the key task of the organization is to determine the needs and wants of target markets and to adapt the organization to delivering the desired satisfactions more effectively and efficiently than its competition.[5]

Practice of the marketing concept means that all departments in a business, not just the marketing department, are oriented toward satisfying customer needs. Engineers design products that customers want, not products that engineers are interested in designing. Production builds the products that people need, not those they can manufacture easily. Salespeople sell products that satisfy customer needs, not those that are easiest to sell or that pay higher commission. This modern sales approach is exemplified by the instructions John H. Patterson, founder of NCR (National Cash Register), gave to his sales force: "Don't talk machines. Don't talk cash registers. Talk the customer's business."[6]

The marketing concept also points to the need to replace high-pressure, deceptive sales tactics with a customer-oriented approach. Salespeople may be able to deceive customers into buying products that do not meet their needs *once*. Yet in time, the customers realize they were deceived

---

[5]Philip Kotler, *Marketing Management,* 4th ed. (Englewood Cliffs, N.J.: Prentice-Hall, 1981), p. 31.

[6]"NCR's Radical Shift in Marketing Tactics," *Business Week,* December 8, 1973, p. 102.

and that the product is not satisfactory, and they place future orders with competitors. So salespeople who are successful in the long run help customers solve their problems, rather than pressuring them into buying whatever is available.

What Is Selling?

A sales executive of a large corporation was asked the question, What is selling? He replied, "To me, selling is the act of merchandising your goods or products at a profit." Other definitions in selling textbooks are:

> Selling is the process of inducing and assisting a prospective customer to buy goods or services or to act favorably on an idea that has commercial significance for the seller.[7]

> The act of persuading another person to do something when you do not have, or cannot exert, the direct power to force the person to do it.[8]

The Definitions Committee of the American Marketing Association has given considerable thought to defining the various terms used in the field of marketing. The committee defined *selling* as "the personal or impersonal process of assisting and/or persuading a prospective customer to buy a commodity or a service or to act favorably upon an idea that has commercial significance to the seller."[9]

The above definitions, however, are not complete. They do not emphasize that the sales process should provide mutual, continuous satisfaction to *both* the buyer and the seller. A sales representative who depends on emotional appeals and high-pressure tactics to force a sale has no place in modern selling. Enlightened sales organizations practice the marketing concept and stress that personal selling brings long-term satisfaction to the company, the sales representative, and the customer.

Selling, then, should be defined as *the process whereby the seller ascertains, activates, and satisfies the needs or wants of the buyer to the mutual, continuous benefit of both the buyer and seller.*

Our definition of selling stresses that influence and persuasion are only a part of selling. Selling also involves helping customers identify problems, supplying information on potential solutions, and providing after-the-sale service to ensure long-term satisfaction. Robert Taaffe, described in Selling Scenario 1–2, illustrates the benefits of emphasizing customer satisfaction.

---

[7]Ferdinand F. Mauser, *Selling: A Self-Management Approach* (New York: Harcourt Brace Jovanovich, 1977), p. 8.

[8]Frederic A. Russell, Frank H. Beach, and Richard H. Buskirk, *Textbook of Salesmanship,* 10th ed. (New York: McGraw-Hill, 1978), p. 3.

[9]Ralph S. Alexander and the Committee on Definitions of the American Marketing Association, *Marketing Definitions: A Glossary of Marketing Terms* (Chicago: American Marketing Association, 1960), p. 21. This definition includes advertising, other forms of publicity, and sales promotion as well as personal selling.

Selling Scenario 1–2

ROBERT TAAFFE OF XEROX

At 29, Robert Taaffe is making between $40,000 and $50,000 a year. He is one of the 6,700-member domestic sales force for Xerox. After getting an MBA degree from Adelphi, Mr. Taaffe started as a geographic representative in New York. He made between $14,000 and $18,000 selling small copy machines door-to-door. He would take the elevator to the top of a building and work his way down. "I never called beforehand. I didn't want to give them a chance to say no without even seeing me." Most of his sales to doctors, lawyers, and store owners were completed in an hour. However, his most memorable sale, to the accountants for John Lennon and Yoko Ono, was held up for weeks because "Yoko had to make the decision, and she was off someplace."

Mr. Taaffe has moved up the sales ladder. He is now specializing in the top-of-the-line Xerox copiers that cost more than $100,000 each and make up to 500,000 copies per month. Now each sale involves dozens of trips to the client and can take several months to complete.

The term *consultative selling* is used to describe Mr. Taaffe's approach. Product and customer knowledge gained through months of training have replaced skill on the golf course or ability to handle one's whiskey as the key elements in making a sale.

Source: Adapted from Steve Lohr, "How Companies Sell to Companies," *New York Times*, December 7, 1980.

Everyone Sells

This text presents personal selling as it relates to the activities of salespeople. But the principles of selling are useful for all people, whether they work in businesses, in not-for-profit organizations, or at home. Influencing people is an important aspect of all interpersonal relationships. Thus, hermits may be the only people in our society who do not need to apply the principles of selling.

Children soon learn the most effective way to sell their parents on a trip to the circus. As college students, they use more refined techniques to convince their parents that they need a car at school. As young graduates, they confront a more important sales job—selling themselves to an employer. To do this effectively, they go through the same essential steps used in making a sale (discussed in Chapters 8 through 13). They identify potential employers. They analyze the needs of the potential employer and the strong points in their background. Then they develop a presentation to demonstrate how their capabilities are compatible with the employer's needs. During the interviews, they answer questions and provide additional information. This is selling at a personal level.

All of these people
are selling
something.

George W. Gardner

© Jock Pottle 1983/Design Conceptions

Charles Gatewood/The Image Works

Jeffry W. Myers/Stock, Boston

An increasing number of people are studying selling even though they do not plan on selling as a career. They recognize that almost everyone in business uses certain principles of selling in everyday work. Aspiring executives are eager to sell themselves to associates, superiors, and subordinates; the accountant uses selling to present a new cost control program to the production employees; the engineer uses selling to present a research budget for approval; the industrial relations or personnel executive uses sales techniques to handle negotiations with a union.

People in nonbusiness situations also practice the art of selling. Ministers encourage people to come to services, political candidates ask for votes, members of the Sierra Club lobby against off-shore drilling, United Fund volunteers solicit donations. People who are skilled at influencing the actions of others are usually the leaders in our society.

Personal selling is a vital part of a free enterprise economy. Selling provides a valuable role for society as a whole and for the individual company. In the next two sections, we review each of these roles.

Alexander R. Heron described the importance of the sale in the following words:

> The ultimate sale has become the measure of the success of every enterprise from the mine or farm to the travel bureau. That ultimate sale is the incentive for the discovery of oil, the efficient layout of the factory, the reduction of costs of extraction, conversion, and distribution. It is the all-powerful governor of the levels of profits, investments, production, and employment.[10]

Heron, who spent most of his business career in the field of industrial relations, emphasized that management must carry to the workers the vital truth that if there is "no sale" there is "no job."[11] Clearly, salespeople are the key actors in the sales transaction.

SELLING'S ROLE IN THE FIRM

Personal selling is the key element in the marketing programs for most companies. The marketing activities of a firm are composed of four components—product, price, place (distribution), and promotion. These components, illustrated in Figure 1–1, are known as the firm's marketing mix.

Selling and the Marketing Mix

The elements in the promotion component are advertising, sales promotion, packaging, publicity, and personal selling. These elements communicate the benefits of the firm's products to its customers. Most people think advertising is the most important element in marketing communications programs. However, this impression is incorrect. As Figure 1–1 shows, U.S. firms' annual expenditures on personal selling exceed $140 billion—more than 50 percent larger than their annual expenditures on advertising. Chapter 18 discusses how other elements in the promotion component affect personal selling.

Personal selling plays an important role in all firms—even companies like Procter & Gamble that spend over $900 million a year on TV advertising. While advertising informs consumers about P&G's products, salespeople make sure the products are available and properly displayed on the shelf when consumers go to the store to buy them. All marketing people at P&G must spend significant time in the field with salespeople. This illustrates the importance of selling in companies that are heavy advertisers like P&G.

---

[10]Alexander R. Heron, *No Sale, No Job* (New York: Harper & Row, 1954), p. ix.
[11]Ibid., p. 7.

FIGURE 1–1
1986 Estimated
Expenditures on
Promotional
Elements by U.S.
Companies

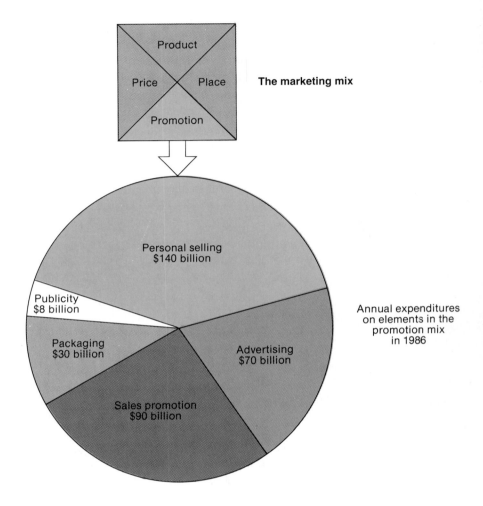

The marketing mix

Annual expenditures
on elements in the
promotion mix
in 1986

Importance of Selling for Industrial and Consumer Goods

But personal selling is more important in some industries than others. A study by Professor Jon Udell points out these differences. Udell surveyed marketing executives in 485 successful companies that produce industrial goods and consumer durables and nondurables. He asked the executives to allocate a total of 100 points across six activities in proportion to the relative importance of the activity to the company's communication effort. The results, shown in Table 1–1, indicate that personal selling is the most important activity for all types of products. But it is relatively more important for industrial goods compared to consumer goods.

Why is this so? To answer this question, consider the nature of the products and the buying process associated with them. Typically, industrial products are technically complex, and a great deal of knowledge is required to use them effectively. Since the purchase of an industrial prod-

Table 1–1   Relative Importance of the Elements in Marketing Communications

| | Producers of | | |
Communication Activity	Industrial Goods	Consumer Durable	Consumer Nondurable
Sales management and personal selling	69.2%	47.6%	38.1%
Broadcast media advertising	.9	10.7	20.9
Printed media advertising	12.5	16.1	14.8
Special promotional activities	9.6	15.5	15.5
Branding and promotional packaging	4.5	9.5	9.8
Others	3.3	.6	.9
Total	100.0%	100.0%	100.0%

Source: Jon G. Udell, "The Perceived Importance of the Elements of Strategy," *Journal of Marketing*, January 1968, p. 38.

uct usually has a significant impact on the firm's operation, the purchase decision involves a number of people. They have to analyze the implications of the decision and study the alternatives. And this, of course, takes time.

A survey by *Factory* magazine found that an average of 11.9 people are involved in industrial purchase decisions. And to reduce the risk of a poor choice, they normally take as long as five months to decide.

On the other hand, purchases of consumer nondurables, such as packaged goods and grooming aids, are not very important decisions. Choosing a breakfast cereal is not that critical, so people don't spend much time weighing the alternatives. The purchasing process for consumer and industrial goods is described in more detail in Chapter 4.

Mass media advertising is the most effective method for informing consumers. Typically, consumers need only a small amount of information to make purchase decisions for products such as breakfast cereal, dog food, or canned fruit. A one-minute ad on TV can provide the needed information at less than 1 cent per person. It would cost over $100 for a salesperson to provide the same information.

Because it is more flexible, personal selling is more effective than advertising when the consumer needs a lot of information and assistance to make a decision. And industrial customers need *much* more. Salespeople can develop and deliver unique presentations for each customer. They can answer questions on the spot and adapt their presentations to the needs of the specific customer. On the other hand, advertising is very inflexible. Ads consist of a predetermined message that cannot be changed, so they don't meet the needs of an industrial customer. Thus, advertising plays a much smaller role in marketing communications for industrial products. The nature of the various marketing communication vehicles is discussed in more detail in Chapter 18.

SELLING'S ROLE IN SOCIETY

Salespeople play an important role in providing goods and services that improve the well-being of all people. They make products more valuable, solve problems facing businesspeople, and help develop new products.

Salespeople Increase Product Value

You may know that the manufacturing process adds value to a product, but did you know that selling also adds value? In the production process, companies add value to raw materials by assembling them to provide a more useful product—a finished product that does a better job than the raw material in satisfying customer needs. The form of the finished product provides more utility or value to the customer. Thus, the production process is said to provide form utility. Personal selling affects the three other types of utility—place, time, and possession.

To illustrate this, consider an Apple personal computer. It is sitting on the shelf of a warehouse in Santa Clara, California. Is this computer going to satisfy your needs for a computer? No! The computer is only valuable to you if it is available, where you want it (place utility), when you want it (time utility), and you own it (possession utility). Salespeople play an important role in providing these utilities.

Without the work of Apple salespeople, their computers would not be available in the local store when you are ready to buy one. The salesperson in the store increases the value of the computer by showing you how to use it to solve your problems. Finally, the salesperson handles the negotiations and paperwork for transferring the title of the computer to you.

Salespeople Solve Problems

Salespeople have become the problem solvers in the business world. A railroad's recent experiences show the importance of salespeople in improving efficiency. The railroad had problems scheduling its operation. At the railroad's request, IBM assigned four salespeople to study the problem. The salespeople spent three years examining every operation of the railroad. They rode the line, worked in the dispatcher's office, and inspected the switchyards. Based on their analysis, IBM designed and installed a $13.5 million computer-directed communications system to run the trains. Then the salespeople trained railroad staff to use the system. Before the system was installed, only 10 percent of the railroad's cars were used because dispatchers couldn't locate them all. Now dispatchers can tell where every car is in an instant.

Salespeople Help Develop and Introduce Innovations

Salespeople also play an important role in the development and diffusion of new products and techniques. Salespeople are in a unique position to observe customer needs. They can see when a number of their customers have similar problems. With market research information from their salespeople, companies are in a better position to develop new products to solve these problems. For example, Bell Labs developed a novel tech-

Table 1–2   Outlook for Sales Occupations

Sales Job	Estimated Employment, 1982	Estimated Percent Growth, 1982 to 1995
Insurance agents and brokers	361,000	25%
Manufacturers' sales workers	414,000	15
Real estate agents and brokers	337,000	33
Retail trade sales workers	3,367,000	27
Securities sales workers	78,000	36
Wholesale trade sales workers	1,093,000	30
	5,650,000	

Source: *Occupational Outlook Quarterly*, U.S. Department of Labor, Bureau of Labor Statistics, Spring 1984, p. 17.

nique for making reliable, electrical connections by simply wrapping wire around a special terminal. Gardner-Denver Company, through its sales force, secured a contract to build the equipment for Western Electric. It obtained a license from Bell Labs for the design and is now a major supplier of this equipment to the electronics industry.[12]

Over the last 50 years, a vast number of new products and services have been developed—computers, central air conditioning, television, airplanes, frozen foods, mutual funds, overnight mail delivery, and stereo records. Contrary to Ralph Waldo Emerson's dictum, when you invent a better mousetrap, people *don't* beat a path to your doorstep. People, in general, are reluctant to adopt new ideas and innovations. First, they must be educated about the new product or service. Someone needs to explain how to use it and what its benefits are. The more complex the product is, the more information and help customers need before they decide to purchase the product. Because salespeople are an important source of such help, they play a vital role in improving social welfare through the adoption of new products and services.

OPPORTUNITIES IN SELLING

Selling offers many employment opportunities. About 6 million people are employed in sales work. Thus, 1 out of 16 workers in the United States is a salesperson. Nontechnical sales was listed by the Department of Labor as one of the 40 occupations with the highest growth projections through 1995. A breakdown by sales job and projected growth is shown in Table 1–2. The expected growth rate varies for different sales jobs, but the growth for every sales job is higher than the national average. The Department of Labor anticipates that there will be ample career opportunities in sales throughout the decade.

---

[12]Eric Von Hippel, "Successful Industrial Products from Customer Ideas," *Journal of Marketing*, January 1978, pp. 39–49.

Employment Opportunities

The number of minority and women salespeople is increasing dramatically. From 1970 to 1980, the number of white male salespeople increased 3.8 percent, while white female salespeople increased 121.2 percent, black males by 100.1 percent, black females by 146.8 percent, Hispanic males by 77.9 percent, and Hispanic females by 181.2 percent.[13]

Opportunities for Women   Women have always been in sales. But before 1970, most women in sales were real estate agents, retail sales workers, or Avon ladies. This situation is changing rapidly. More and more women are pursuing sales careers in all industries, including computers, steel, drugs, lumber, and other industries that used to be male-dominated. The life insurance industry has been aggressively seeking more saleswomen. In 1971, only 2 percent of the new insurance salespeople were women. By 1978, women represented over 12 percent of the new recruits in the life insurance industry.[14]

Women may have some distinct advantages over men in sales. First, there is the novelty factor. Because saleswomen are still unusual in some industries, customers frequently are interested in meeting them and remember them better. But getting through the door is only a small part of successful selling. The second advantage women have relates to their selling skills.[15] Women, in our society, have been socialized to be sensitive to people around them and adapt their behavior to their surroundings. As you will see in this text, these qualities are important to the success of a salesperson. Karen White, a sales representative for Letraset, a manufacturer of graphics arts products, illustrates these skills when she commented:

> As a woman, I think I am more perceptive to emotional reactions—which client is a "down-home" type, which is "all business," which is in a bad mood. Some men think they can just go in there and be a good old boy. It doesn't always work.[16]

While women may have some advantages, they also face some unique problems.[17] Three areas in which problems faced by women differ from those faced by men are travel, customer relations, and working relations.

---

[13]"Women and Minorities Get into Sales," *Sales & Marketing Management,* July 4, 1983, p. 31.

[14]"The Industrial Salesman Becomes a Salesperson," *Business Week,* February 19, 1978, p. 104.

[15]Rayna Skolnik, "A Woman's Place Is on the Sales Force," *Sales & Marketing Management,* April 1, 1985, pp. 34–37.

[16]Georgia Dullea, "The Saleswoman, Not Just in Retail and Housing, Hits the Road for Industry," *Marketing Times,* September–October 1981, p. 37.

[17]For a more detailed discussion of the problems and how to overcome them see, Barbara Pletcher, *Saleswoman* (Homewood, Ill.: Dow Jones-Irwin, 1979).

More and more women are pursuing sales careers in all industries.

"Mom is it true that mothers used to stay home all day and keep house?"

Reprinted by permission of *Sales & Marketing Management* magazine. © 1987.

Most sales positions require some travel. Both men and women share the problem of being away from home, but women may be more vulnerable to the physical dangers that can arise when traveling. However, these dangers can be avoided with a little planning. For example, if one travels long distances by car, make the trip in the early morning before work, rather than late at night after work.

Dealing with customers who are accustomed to interacting exclusively with salesmen may cause some problems. For instance, some male customers feel uncomfortable when a saleswoman invites them to lunch and picks up a check. One saleswoman overcame this problem by suggesting to customers that they "let my company treat us to lunch."

Occasionally, customers tell sales managers that they don't want to be called on by saleswomen. A saleswoman, when confronted with this problem, said, "When a customer tells me he wants to do business with a man, I tell him 'I'm your man.' "[18]

Working relations are an important element to success. Some people in the firm may not accept women in nontraditional roles. For example, secretaries may resent a woman in sales, or a saleswoman may not be given the proper respect. She may be identified as "one of the women in

---

[18]"The Industrial Salesman Becomes a Salesperson," p. 104.

Today there are
many opportunities
for women and
ethnic minorities
in selling.

Courtesy Golas Insurance Agency

Ellis Herwig/Stock, Boston

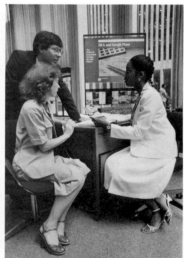

Hazel Hankin/Stock, Boston

the office.'' Perhaps the most difficult problem facing saleswomen is their relationship with their managers. One study has found that managers view saleswomen as more humble, apprehensive, reserved, and home-oriented than salesmen.[19] These potentially biased perceptions can affect pay and promotion opportunities for women. But the bottom line for most managers is results, and women certainly have shown that they can get results.

---

[19]Dan H. Robertson and Donald W. Hackett, ''Saleswomen: Perceptions, Problems, and Prospects,'' *Journal of Marketing*, July 1977, pp. 66–71.

The financial
rewards of selling
vary greatly.

"I'm prepared to offer more money if you'll wear
a tie."

From *The Wall Street Journal*, with permission of
Cartoon Features Syndicate.

Minorities in Selling   Unfortunately, few studies have been done on minorities in selling. However, a study completed in 1970 reported that 48 percent of the companies surveyed employed blacks in sales positions.[20] These salespeople were *not* hired to call on just black customers. Over 75 percent of the black salespeople were assigned to territories that included both black and white customers. Of the companies that did not employ black salespeople, over 50 percent planned to recruit them for sales jobs soon.

Many companies have formal programs for hiring minorities. These programs include a definitive statement from top management, long- and short-term goals, and minority advisory panels to help implement the programs. The motivation for hiring minorities in sales is expressed by Herbert Barnett, former chairman of the board of PepsiCo, Inc: "Our motives are not altruistic; we hire blacks because it's plain good business sense. We find they are good workers, good managers, and dedicated employees."[21]

REWARDS IN SELLING

Financial Rewards

The financial rewards of selling vary greatly. They depend on the skill and sophistication needed. For example, industrial salespeople normally are paid more than consumer product salespeople because the industrial selling process is more complex and difficult. The average salary in 1986 for different types of salespeople is shown in Figure 1–2.

However, these average salaries can be misleading. It is not unusual for a salesperson to make over $75,000 a year. For instance, experienced salespeople for a manufacturer of top-quality women's shoes make be-

---

[20]Robert F. Vizza, "Experiences in Recruiting, Hiring and Retaining Blacks for Sales Positions," *The Sales Executive,* September 11, 1970, pp. 7–10.

[21]Ibid., p. 8.

FIGURE 1–2
Annual Compensation in 1985 for Salespeople Compensated by Salary Plus Incentives

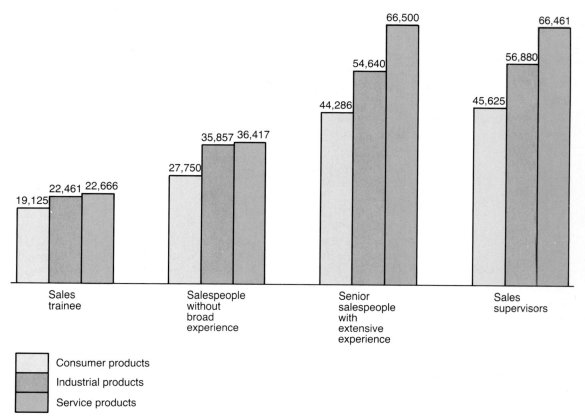

Source: "1986 Survey of Selling Costs," *Sales & Marketing Management,* February 16, 1987, p. 56.

tween $90,000 and $100,000 per year and only work nine months a year. Two of the firm's salespeople who made only $55,000 were fired because they were not selling enough to stores in their territory.[22] Sometimes, in fact, the top salesperson in a company makes more than the chief executive officer.[23]

Promotion Opportunities for Salespeople

It is impossible to generalize about the one best background or spawning ground for managers. Managers in the electronics industry probably have a different background from managers in food-processing or life insurance companies.

---

[22]Richard T. Hise, *Effective Salesmanship* (Hinsdale, Ill.: Dryden Press, 1980), p. 35.

[23]Some specific examples of high-paid salespeople are presented in James O'Hanlon, "The Rich Rewards of the Salesman's Life," *Forbes,* October 16, 1978, pp.155–58.

Many studies have attempted to determine which qualifications are most important for success in top management positions. Some important qualities are personal drive, good judgment, ability to get along with people, persuasiveness, flexibility, creativeness, and intellectual capacity.

In general, people attracted to the sales field are strong in these characteristics to begin with. Because their work demands it, they also develop new skills in human relations. So a large and growing number of business concerns are giving their sales and marketing executives a stronger voice in major company policy decisions.

The effectiveness of sales training as a preparation for top responsibility is best shown by a recent study reporting that 28 percent of the presidents of 1,000 leading firms had marketing experience.[24]

Corporate executives clearly recognize the importance of selling experience. Frank Cary, former chairman of the board of IBM, gave the following advice to those who had ambitions of becoming chairman and president of IBM:

> It's hard to find a better start than sales because you get thrown into contact with a great variety of situations and problems to solve. So I would recommend the sales track to anybody. I think it is a very good one.

While selling can launch a corporate career, many entrepreneurs began in sales before starting their own firms. Figure 1–3 describes the sales background of people who developed well-known consumer products.

Two Career Paths in Selling

The excitement and challenge of selling is so rewarding to some salespeople that they do not want to be promoted. They prefer selling to managing people. Many companies recognize that some excellent salespeople either do not want to become managers or do not have the skills to be managers. To accommodate these salespeople, companies establish two career paths for new salespeople.

As shown in Figure 1–4, a junior salesperson can receive more pay and recognition through promotions to managerial positions or through promotions within the sales rank. Each promotion along the managerial path means responsibility for larger budgets and supervising more people. Promotions along the sales path mean responsibility for larger and more important customers and more challenging sales situations. Typically, compensation is similar at the same level along each path.

Syntex, a pharmaceutical company, has a Professional Development Program with the following five growth levels along the sales path: (1) representative, (2) professional medical representative, (3) certified medical representative, (4) territory manager, and (5) senior territory manager.

---

[24]"S&MM Marketing Newsletter," *Sales & Marketing Management,* June 4, 1984, p. 29.

FIGURE 1–3
Entrepreneurs Who
Started in Sales

Adolphus Busch—Anheuser-Busch Beer

Left an inheritance by his father, Busch went into business for himself selling brewers' supplies. It was through this business that he met and married the daughter of Eberhard Anheuser. Busch then bought interest in Anheuser Brewing and went on to make substantial strides in improving its sales. He proved to be a spectacular salesman in that he was aggressive and made wide use of posters, pocketknives, trays, and other novelty items to promote sales.

Roy Halston Frowick—Halston Fashions

He began as a salesman of women's hats while still attending Indiana University and became a major designer of women's fashions.

Marcel Bich—Bic Pens

Bich began his career by selling flashlights door to door in Paris. Later, he went on to develop inexpensive, reliable, disposable products such as ballpoint pens, cigarette lighters, and razors.

Dr. William Scholl—Dr. Scholl's Foot Care Products

A skilled shoemaker, William "Billy" Scholl advanced from apprentice to cobbler-salesman in just one year. While on the job he realized a need for improved foot care for his customers. He developed and proceeded to sell what he called the Foot-Eazer, an arch support. An unorthodox salesman of his time, he used the skeleton of a human foot to capture the attention of the store owner and explain the merits of his Foot-Eazer.

Adolph Coors—Coors Beer

Coors began his career as a beer salesman in the mining towns of Front Range, Colorado. He went on to become the owner and namesake of one of the largest beer manufacturers in the nation.

Henry Heinz—Heinz Ketchup

As a teenager in Sharpsbury, Pennsylvania, he made money selling his own bottled horseradish to local grocers.

Mary Kay Ash—Mary Kay Cosmetics

Left on her own by divorce, Mary Kay supported herself and her three small children by selling cleaning supplies at in-home demonstrations. She went on to form Mary Kay Cosmetics, a direct sales cosmetics company.

William Coleman—Coleman Camping Equipment

To pay his way through law school, Coleman took a job as a traveling typewriter salesman. While on the job he discovered a powerful gasoline-powered lamp in Brokton, Alabama. He purchased the rights to the lamp and marketed them as Coleman Arc Lamps, starting him on the path to becoming a multimillionaire via the Coleman Company.

FIGURE 1–4
Dual Career Paths in Sales

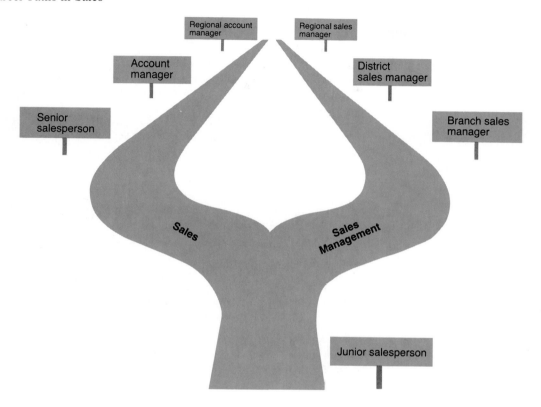

To attain level 3, a salesperson must pass the Certified Medical Representative Institute's basic program, which takes about 2½ years. Salespeople who achieve level 3 are given such responsibilities as working with new salespeople and assisting district managers.[25]

Drawbacks in Selling

Although there are many advantages in selling, it has some undesirable aspects. Sales jobs are physically and psychologically demanding. It is not unusual for salespeople to work 10 to 12 hours a day or 60 to 70 hours a week. Driving in traffic, sleeping in motels, and staying mentally alert during eight sales calls in a day can make these long hours even more difficult.

In addition to these physical hardships, the nature of sales jobs is psychologically demanding. Psychological problems arise from the nature

---

[25]"Syntex Helps Them Choose," *Sales & Marketing Management*, October 6, 1980, pp. 11–12.

Selling has its
drawbacks.

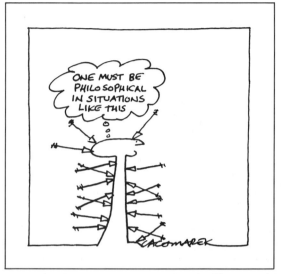

Reprinted by permission from *Sales & Marketing Management*
magazine. © 1980.

of the relationships salespeople have with their customers and their companies. Fortunately, most prospects are understanding, and sales interactions are generally pleasant and productive. But some prospects can
be rude and insulting to salespeople, taking out their own personal or job-
related problems on the salespeople. In these situations, it can be difficult
for a salesperson to be understanding and not become upset. Even friendly
prospects will not always buy all the products offered. Only one salesperson is going to get the order; several are not. Some customers will
refuse to see salespeople because they feel uncomfortable about telling
the salespeople that they lost the order. Successful salespeople must learn
to deal with rejection and not take lost orders personally.[26] In Selling
Scenario 1–3, Bill Razzouk, a vice president of Federal Express, talks
about overcoming a rejection to make his most significant sale.

Salespeople are in a unique position. They span the boundary between
their company and their customers. Because they occupy this boundary-
spanning role, they are often in the middle of conflicts between their
company and its customers. These conflicts arise because the needs of
customers and employees in the salesperson's company may differ. For
example, a customer may need quick delivery. When the salespeople
communicate this need to the production manager, they may be told that
special-delivery requests cannot be met because these special requests
will disrupt the smooth running of the production department. The salesperson must resolve the conflict between the customer's need for quick

---

[26]Larry McMahon, "Taking the Sting Out of Selling!" *Sloan Management Review,* Fall
1981, pp. 3–11, discusses how sales managers can help salespeople deal with rejection.

Selling Scenario 1–3

A LONG DRIVE TO THE TOP

When asked to describe his most unforgettable experience in selling, Bill Razzouk, vice president for electronic product sales at Federal Express, described the following situation:

The most significant sale I made was back in 1971. I was a new sales rep for Xerox, and my job was to sell large duplicating machines to garment manufacturers, which use them to print tags to keep track of piecework. The machines leased for $2,500 a month, while the Linotype machines they were currently using went for only $35 a month.

One day, I called on the purchasing agent at Garland Manufacturing in Monroe, Georgia. He had no hint of what I was talking about, and he politely escorted me out the door and told me not to come back. On the 50-mile drive back to Atlanta, I was feeling pretty down, trying to think of what to do next.

When I got back, I called the vice president of operations and asked for 10 minutes of his time. Unfortunately, the only time he could meet me was on a Saturday, which happened to be New Year's Day. I guess he was trying to test if I was serious. Well, I drove the 50 miles back to Monroe through the snow and showed him a 10-minute presentation, telling him about the increased productivity he could get from the duplicators, which would also improve the quality and sales of his goods. I spent two hours with him, and he asked me to come back later with a proposal. When I went back, the same purchasing agent that threw me out was there, but this time he wasn't saying much. They wanted to try out the system for 30 days. A month later, the agent actually called me back. Not only did they keep the machine, they bought two more!

I was only 22 at the time, and the lesson I learned was not to be afraid to go right to the top. That helped me to become Xerox's number one garment-industry salesperson, and the next year, I sold 230 percent of quota.

Source: Reprinted from "Strange Tales of Sales," *Sales & Marketing Management*, June 3, 1985, pp. 43–54.

delivery and the production manager's need to reduce cost by reducing special-delivery requests.

Other role conflicts can arise because the demands of the salesperson's supervisor and family may differ. The supervisor might want the salesperson to work longer hours, while the family may want the salesperson to spend more time at home.[27]

---

[27]See Neil M. Ford, Orville C. Walker, Jr., and Gilbert A. Churchill, Jr., "The Psychological Consequences of Role Conflict and Ambiguity in the Industrial Salesforce," in *Marketing: 1776–1976 and Beyond*, ed. Kenneth L. Bernhardt (Chicago: American Marketing Association, 1976), pp. 403–8.

PERSONAL
SELLING IN
THE FUTURE

The environment in which businesses operate is changing dramatically. At the same time, the costs of selling are increasing. For example, the weekly expenses (meals, lodging, automobile) for the typical salesperson were only $339 in 1975. By 1985 the weekly expenses had increased 114 percent to $726.[28] These trends suggest that the nature of selling will change in the future.

Professionalism
and Training

The impact of some changes in the business environment has been discussed previously. Heightened competition due to improved production techniques, transportation, and communications led to development of the marketing concept. Other trends are increases in customer knowledge, product complexity, the number of new products, and consumer activism. These suggest that companies will place more emphasis on selling in the future. Salespeople are ideally suited to advise customers about complex products. But companies will need to respond to this new environment. They must spend more money to train salespeople, and salespeople must achieve a higher level of professionalism.

Sales Training   New products are the key to success for most companies. Typically, 50 percent of a company's sales are related to products developed during the previous five-year period. Due to the growing electronic industry, these new products are more and more complex. Even some children's games are based on sophisticated electronics.

Companies recognize the need to educate their salespeople to sell new and complex products. Application engineers and sales representatives must have adequate training to do an effective job of matching customer needs with their products. Over $5 billion a year are spent for sales training in the United States. In 1985, the average training cost for *each* industrial product salesperson was $26,670.[29] IBM has a multimillion-dollar budget for training both its salespeople and customers. The company spends over $50,000 initially to train a new computer salesperson. Avon has recently purchased 17,000 video cassette recorders to assist in field training its 500,000-member sales force.

Professionalism in Selling   Salespeople will need to develop a more professional attitude to meet the increasing challenges of selling to knowledgeable customers. R. S. Wilson, former executive vice president and sales manager of the Goodyear Tire & Rubber Company, said, "The distinguishing mark of a professional is the constant aspiring toward perfection." He illustrated this point in the following words:

---

[28]"S&MM 1986 Survey of Selling Costs," *Sales & Marketing Management,* February 17, 1986, p. 11.

[29]Ibid., p. 82.

> The Professional sales representative is a person who is constantly studying to improve proficiency. I am thinking of a surgeon whom I know well who personifies to me the Professional attitude. I met him at lunch one day not long ago and he told me he was leaving by plane that afternoon for Dallas. Why? He had read in one of the Medical Journals of a surgeon in Dallas who had performed a delicate cheekbone operation in a manner that was new to him. He immediately called the Dallas surgeon on the telephone and found he was to perform such an operation the next day, so he dropped everything and left by plane to watch the operation and learn a new technique. This friend of mine was 56 years old when this incident occurred, and to the end of his career he will go on studying and practicing to improve his proficiency. He is a true Professional.[30]

Wilson defined the professional salesperson as (1) one who is constantly studying to improve his or her proficiency; (2) one who recognizes that there is no substitute for hard work; (3) one who, above all else, maintains his or her self-respect, integrity, and independence; and (4) one who puts true value on his or her services.[31]

When one thinks of professionals in terms of the factors described above, it is obvious that many sales representatives today are not true professionals. But in a number of selling fields, certain sales representatives do meet all or most of the requisites of the professional. Some life insurance companies, for example, have comprehensive programs for selecting and training new sales representatives. A course of study is also prescribed for those who are to qualify as CLUs (chartered life underwriters). The American College of Life Underwriters, an independent nonprofit educational institution, awards the diploma and registered CLU title. This college has had a major impact on development of professional sales representatives in the field of life insurance.

It is encouraging to note that the standards of behavior have improved rapidly in the past few years. There is greater acceptance of the concept that successful selling means providing lasting benefits to both buyer and seller.

Computers and Telecommunications

To counteract the rising costs of selling, companies are increasing the efficiency of salespeople through the use of computers and telecommunications. Computers have been used for some time to design sales terri-

---

[30]R. S. Wilson, *Salesmanship as a Profession* (New York: Goodyear Tire & Rubber Co., 1958), p. 16. This publication is a reproduction of the Parlin Lecture given by Wilson before the Philadelphia Center of the American Marketing Association.

[31]Ibid., pp. 16–17.

Stockbrokers (*top and lower left*) and a mortgage banker (*lower right*) use computers to improve their efficiency.

Monika Franzen

John Maher/Stock, Boston

John Maher/Stock, Boston

Alan Carey/The Image Works

tories, determine the appropriate number of calls to make on customers, and evaluate the performance of salespeople.[32]

During the last five years, salespeople began using computers to improve their productivity. Over 10 percent of the salespeople contacted in a recent survey used a personal computer.[33] Computer uses range from providing information on a sales call to planning daily activities. Ryder

[32]James M. Comer, "The Computer, Personal Selling, and Sales Management," *Journal of Marketing,* July 1975, pp. 27–33.

[33]"PC's Used by 1 in 10 Salespeople, Half of Sales, Marketing Staffs," *Sales & Marketing Management,* June 3, 1985, pp. 116–19.

Rental Trucks developed a model that helps salespeople assist customers in determining the cost trade-off between leasing and purchasing trucks. The salesperson asks the customer questions concerning estimated mileage driven and the type of trucks needed, enters the answers into a portable computer, hits a single key, and reviews the printout with the customer.[34]

Many salespeople have computers at home that can tie into a central computer via telephone lines. In the evening, they identify the accounts they are going to call on the next day. The computer then prints out information about each customer, such as key buying influences, the purchase activity over the last 90 days, credit position, and recent personnel changes and financial performance.

Video presentations now demonstrate complicated products. Thomas Bird, president of Gould, Inc.'s medical products division, indicates, "One of the problems in technical sales is that some salespeople do not exactly convey the message the inventor or manufacturer had in mind when the product was designed." To overcome this problem, Gould spent $200,000 to produce two videocassette presentations and $75,000 to equip its salespeople with VCRs.[35]

Satellite communications are used to improve sales productivity. Hewlett-Packard uses two-way, closed-circuit TV to introduce new products to the sales force and provide fast, economical sales training. Drug companies use closed-circuit TV presentations and telephone selling to inform doctors about new drugs and therapies. We shall take up some of these uses of telecommunications in selling in more detail in Chapter 18.

Will modern telecommunication methods replace salespeople? Most experts say no. Phillip Scott of Foxboro says, "Sure you can show a customer a tape, but I'd be fooling myself if I thought the customer was going to stand up and give the salesperson a sales order because of a tape I made. It's just one part of the sales puzzle."[36] Telecommunications, video presentations, and computers will increase the productivity of salespeople, not replace them. Salespeople will have more time to advise customers and not have to spend time processing paperwork.

SUMMARY

Chapter 1 considers the nature of personal selling, its role in society and the operation of a company, the rewards and drawbacks of selling careers, and future trends in selling. Salespeople engage in a wide range of activities. Most of us are not aware of many of these activities because they

---

[34]Terry Kennedy, "Boost Productivity with Computer Enhanced Selling," *Marketing News,* November 9, 1984, pp. 20–21.

[35]"Rebirth of a Salesman: Willy Loman Goes Electronic," *Business Week,* February 27, 1984, p. 103.

[36]Ibid., p. 104.

are directed toward industrial or commercial customers. The negative stereotype of selling arises because we do not understand what salespeople actually do.

Modern salespeople practice the marketing concept. They use a customer-oriented sales approach to demonstrate how their products can solve customer problems and satisfy customer needs. Consistent with this customer orientation, selling is defined as *the process whereby the seller ascertains, activates, and satisfies the needs or wants of the buyer to the mutual, continuous benefit of both the buyer and the seller.*

Selling plays an important role in society. Salespeople can help develop new products and get them adopted. In addition, salespeople can add value to products by increasing their time, place, and possession utility.

Selling also plays an important role in modern business. Personal selling is the most important aspect of marketing communication programs for industrial and consumer product companies.

As a result, there are many job opportunities in selling. These opportunities will increase over the next 10 years. A sales career has the following advantages: financial rewards, the chance to get ahead, intellectual challenges, and the freedom to arrange one's everyday activities. But there are some drawbacks to a sales career, too. Selling is demanding, both physically and psychologically.

Business trends indicate that the role of selling will become more important; there will be more emphasis on sales training, and the level of professionalism in selling will rise. There will also be a greater effort to increase the efficiency of salespeople through the use of computers and telecommunications.

QUESTIONS AND PROBLEMS

1. Do you think that going to college is useful for a sales career? Why or why not?

2. The manager of a retail store selling personal computers asks you if he should hire more salespeople or do more advertising. What would you recommend and why?

3. In this chapter, the importance of selling to society and individual business firms is stressed. If selling is so important, why do some salespeople have such a negative image?

4. How would you respond to the following observations by a friend:
   a. "I wouldn't be a good salesperson because I'm not much of a talker."
   b. "I couldn't be a salesperson. I just can't try to make people buy something that they don't need."

5. Compare and contrast the four definitions of selling mentioned in this chapter.

6. Some outstanding salespeople are poor sales managers. Why? Compare and contrast the skills needed to succeed in sales and sales management.

7. What should you consider in deciding if you have the abilities and desire for selling?

8. Would it help society if the large life insurance companies decided to eliminate all their sales representatives and sell life insurance by mail order at a lower quoted cost to the consumer?

9. What are the advantages and disadvantages of seeking a beginning job in sales as compared to accounting? Banking? Purchasing?

10. Do you believe that the comptroller of a company should have a basic knowledge of how to sell? Why?

PROJECTS

1. Write a report on the impact of the salesperson in our free enterprise economy.

2. Review several copies of *The Wall Street Journal* and write a report summarizing information that appears in the *Journal* that would be useful to:
    a. A farm equipment sales representative.
    b. An investment securities salesperson.
    c. A real estate agent.

3. Survey your friends and summarize their feelings about selling as a career.

CASE PROBLEMS

Case 1–1   David Bettman Contemplates a Sales Career

David Bettman is a sophomore at Piedmont Junior College. He started talking with a group of his friends about his selling course.

Joan Kelly: Why are you taking that selling course?

David: Well, I have been thinking about what I would like to do when I graduate. I thought I would like to go into sales. So I took the course to see what it was all about. Frankly, I am really excited about the course.

Sally Kemp: But selling is a real "dog-eat-dog" business. I don't think I am aggressive enough to hack it in sales.

Joan Kelly: But you sure won't get bored. You meet new people all the time. Each sales call is different. I can see why David is excited about the course.

Sally Kemp: But David has a terrible poker face. He blushes whenever he tries to hide the truth. How can you succeed in sales if you're as transparent as David?

Joan Kelly: I don't know. I think David could learn to control his feelings more with experience.

Sally Kemp: How about the work load? On the road all the time. No time for family life.

Joan Kelly: At least you would have an exciting job. Who wants a 9-to-5 job sitting behind a desk! And think of all those weekday afternoons that you can take off and go sailing!

Sally Kemp: People don't respect salespeople. I'd be ashamed to tell my friends I was a salesperson.

Questions

1. How would you reply to each of these negative statements?
2. What could you tell David Bettman to help him understand why his friends view selling so differently?

Case 1–2   IBM—The Story of Bill Frech—Sales Representative, IBM Office Products Division*

For a typical account of how a person can join and work for the IBM Office Products Division, we went over the records of a number of the IBM sales representatives throughout the United States.

This is the story of Bill Frech, a young man who has started a rewarding sales career in St. Louis with the Office Products Division of IBM. Yet when he was planning his future, he had never even considered sales.

"I Never Wanted Any Part of Sales."

It was one career he didn't want.

Why Bill Frech changed his mind about IBM selling may also change yours.

Two years ago Bill Frech was 22 years old and a liberal arts major at the University of Missouri. Like many college seniors, Bill was not certain what he wanted to do. He had to choose a career. But what?

He had talked to a number of companies, but nothing aroused his interest. "I want something challenging," he said.

Bill had paid most of his college expenses by waiting on tables, washing dishes, and working in construction. One summer, he had even managed a restaurant. Before that,

he had worked part time while attending high school in Columbia, Missouri. After graduation, he had spent six months in the Army. But this experience did not make choosing a career any easier.

And college didn't help, either. Bill had started at the University of Missouri as a business administration major. But he later changed his major to liberal arts. That's when he met Sandy, an art student. At the end of Bill's junior year, they were married, and she took a job as an art teacher while Bill was getting his degree. Together they tried to solve the problem of his career.

"I'm Not the Selling Type.
I'm No Extrovert."

Three weeks before graduation, an old friend, Russell Rose, dropped in for a visit. He was very interested in Bill's problem. Russ explained that he was now a sales representative for the St. Louis branch of IBM's Office Products Division. He was enjoying his job, working hard, and being well paid.

"I know you've never considered sales, but there's a selling job open in our office, and I think you're the right kind of man for it."

---

*Adapted by permission of the International Business Machines Corporation.

"Who wants to sell?" asked Bill, remembering the despair of Willy Loman in *Death of a Salesman.* "It's the salesperson's job to smile—to use tricks and gimmicks. He forces people to buy. And outside of a little money, what does he ever get out of selling?"

Bill spoke of the bad image some salespeople have, the monotony of the work, and the lack of security.

"Besides," he added, "I'm not the selling type. I'm no extrovert."

"Being an extrovert or an introvert isn't the point," Russ said. "IBM selling needs people who are problem solvers. We're not door-to-door drummers. Our aim is to be professionals—to know our prospects' problems and show how our products solve them. The result is my job is satisfying and interesting. The pay is good, and I feel secure."

Bill was not so much persuaded by the words as by Russ's manner. Still he had doubts. Was selling for him? Could he succeed on his own? Would he be compromising his principles?

His wife, Sandy, had a point. "A job doesn't change your principles. You do. I think people with high principles bring more to any job and get more out of it."

"I Wasn't Sure, but I Asked for an Interview."

Bill also talked to other sales representatives and to people in other fields. He began to piece together a picture of a salesperson who was totally different. It supported the picture Russ had painted of the IBM sales representative as a professional, someone businesspeople could turn to for advice and help in solving problems and getting their work done more efficiently. And Bill was surprised to learn that a good, hardworking IBM sales

representative earned considerably more than other workers in the United States.

Still, was sales for him? "I wasn't sure, but I asked for an interview." Within a week, he was seated across the desk from "Ship" Atwater, office products branch manager in St. Louis.

Ship is youthful and dynamic. Like all office products branch managers, he has risen through the sales ranks. He understands the doubts and uncertainties that a young person can have about selling.

A formal interview quickly became a friendly conversation.

"A Troubleshooter, Marketing Expert, and Executive Rolled into One."

Ship asked Bill for his frank opinion of selling. Bill spoke honestly, and as he did, Ship saw many of the qualities that IBM looks for in a young person. Ship then began to explain that today's salesperson is a new kind of individual—a troubleshooter, marketing expert, and executive rolled into one. And to do this effectively, the salesperson has to know and understand the customer's business.

"One of the key concepts in today's approach to selling," explained Ship, "covers the whole area of paper flow—from the origin of an idea to its finished typed form. At IBM we call this *word processing.*

"When someone dictates a report, has it typed, reviews it, changes it, and then has a final version prepared, he or she is processing words.

"Processing words as efficiently and economically as possible is a real problem. Let me give you some background. During a 12-year period, the number of professional and technical people—idea originators— increased by 87 percent. At the same time, the number of secretaries, stenographers, and typists who support these professionals went up only 49 percent. In terms of words alone, administrative costs have skyrocketed.''

"But more paperwork means more business and profits, doesn't it?" asked Bill.

"Yes, if the paperwork flows efficiently. But that doesn't always happen, because people and office equipment have been added without system. Manufacturing, for example, has had to face these problems. For instance, if you are producing cars on an assembly line, and there is a demand for more cars than your line can produce, you don't always build a new assembly line to meet the new demand."

"Why not?"

"Then You're Really Selling a Solution to a Problem."

"It may increase the cost per car. So instead, you carefully study your assembly line and expand production by modifying that line with new equipment, new procedures, and new people, at minimum cost."

"So you use this approach in offices?"

"That's right. The cost of processing words can represent anywhere from 40 to 90 percent of administrative time and expense. This is where we come in. We make an analysis of actual versus potential paperwork production and devise a system integrating people, equipment, and training that can process words more efficiently and economically.

"And when we can prove to top executives that an IBM word processing approach gives them the method, the tools, and the training to save them money and do the job better, they listen."

"Then you're really selling a solution to a problem?"

"Exactly. The administrator buys the idea because it's a modern approach to his

or her problems. And selling an idea, Bill, is challenging work."

"I Had to Admit the Job Sounded Challenging."

Still questioning sales, Bill asked, "Do you have a management training program at IBM?"

"Yes, there are a number of management training programs available. But to start, we believe sales is the best management training program we have," answered Ship. "Most of our managers and top executives come up through sales. Starting in sales, you'll be managing your own territory from the beginning, and you'll be getting valuable exposure to other businesses. Managing people is easier after that initial responsibility."

Ship introduced Bill to some of the other people in the office. They went out to lunch together, and Bill felt these were the kind of individuals he would like to work with. "I had to admit the job sounded challenging," he said. His attitude had certainly changed.

Shortly after, when Ship called to offer him a job, Bill accepted.

"At Sales School, You Begin to Get the Idea You Can Be a Salesperson."

The Office Products Division Sales School in Dallas is staffed with instructors who not only have proved themselves to be among the best salespeople in the country, but also have the ability to train others. The school was established to give all new people the benefit of the best IBM experience.

Bill attended seminars that outlined the marketing programs for the products he would be selling.

He learned how market analysis, product planning, specialized marketing, advertising, sales promotion, and a host of other resources worked together to give him the product to sell and the means to sell it. He learned that, in the entire marketing structure, he and the other sales representatives were the key to the success of the division. Nothing happened unless they did their job.

And they were taught their job. They learned all about the various products, how they were built, and what they were meant to do. They learned to give presentations and make demonstrations to all levels of management.

It was an intensive school, and Bill had never worked harder. But he enjoyed it. "At Sales School, you begin to get the idea you can be a salesperson."

"There Are Trained Selling Experts to Assist You."

Back in St. Louis, Bill was given a quota and assigned his own territory. As he expected, his first day was a frightening experience. He was not sure he could use his skills. But he soon realized that there was little cause for worry. "There are trained selling experts to assist you," is how Bill puts it.

Ship was there to help—and so were the assistant branch manager and the field manager. They made calls with him.

Afterward, they discussed his calls and made suggestions. He learned a lot watching these professionals work with his account, and he learned from the other sales representatives. Soon he gained confidence, and he knew when to turn to other specialists.

The IBM customer engineers were always ready to solve technical problems before a sale or to follow up with service after the sale was made.

Bill also learned to work with the marketing support representative, who usually had business teaching experience and had also been trained in Sales School. These representatives were invaluable in training the personnel who would be using IBM office products. "They very often helped with the actual sale."

Bill had been trained, and he had help. He recognized his problems, and he worked hard. He made his monthly quota.

Bill Frech was on his way.

"Watching Those Products Being Built Makes a Believer Out of You."

After he had been in his territory a short time, Bill was sent back to the second part of Sales School for further training. The instructors took off some more of the rough edges, but Bill had his confidence now. He had sold more equipment than anyone in the class. Now he was eager for the last part of the course, the trip to Lexington, Kentucky, location of one of the Office Products Division's manufacturing plants.

He was amazed at the size of the plant and the number of products produced. He learned that productivity at Lexington is second—quality comes first—built by craftspeople, checked by computer. He now understood why IBM products are superior, and how they help with the job he is doing. When it came to engineering, Bill understood the IBM dedication to excellence.

"Watching those products being built makes a believer out of you," Bill added.

"I Made My Quota. I Made the 'Club.'"

He returned to St. Louis once more and went to work. He made his yearly quota. This qualified him for membership in the Hundred Percent Club, which meets once a year in various cities of the United States. There he met and exchanged views with other employees from all over the country. He got to talk to the division's top management, and he attended meetings outlining new developments in his field.

But a good part of the time was devoted to recreation.

It had been a good year for Bill. He put it this way: "I made my quota. I made the 'Club.' I made money." He also sold more new accounts than anyone in the district, and he was named "Rookie of the Year" in the St. Louis office. Best of all, his son Tyler was born.

"I Was Working Smarter, Not Harder."

In Bill's second year, something happened. "I was working smarter, not harder," he says. He had more time to think. He knew his job and he was more relaxed.

Bill had become more organized. He was budgeting his time and planning his work. His sales and income were far ahead of his first year.

He also got to know the people he was working with much better. "I don't think you could find a finer group of people," he explained. "Each sales representative, with his or her own territory, still realizes that we're all working on the same team."

"Selling is a shared experience," he states.

"A Problem Solver, a Real Professional."

The most important change in his second year, however, came in his dealing with customers. He was establishing sound and lasting relationships.

Peter B. Goelz, vice president and controller of United Van Lines, one of Bill's accounts, expressed it this way: "You like to see a young man like Bill develop. He maintains his composure. He has goals and ambitions. You accept him and go out of your way to work with him." Mr. Goelz believes that Bill is helpful. "He keeps us up to date, because he knows our business—what we're doing, how we use our equipment. He analyzes, points out our paperwork problems, and helps us solve them."

Bill also calls on a number of schools. Arthur Langehennig, superintendent for the school district of Hancock Place, likes to have him call. "Bill's a problem solver. . . . He keeps us informed on equipment and techniques that will help us better prepare our business students for jobs."

Bill Frech had become a real professional.

"I'm on the Right Track."

Today, Bill Frech is extremely pleased with his decision to join the Office Products Division of IBM. His future looks good. The maturity and experience he has gained have brought him respect in his community.

Bill is earning twice as much as many college graduates his age. He is financially secure. His goal is to stay with IBM.

He wants to go as far as he can, enjoy his work and his family.

Looking back over the last two years, Bill smiles at his fears and misconceptions about sales. He realizes he is taking the same road that most IBM management has traveled.

"I'm on the right track," he says.

Questions

1. How do you explain Bill Frech's initial attitude toward sales work?

2. What has happened to change this original attitude?

SELECTED REFERENCES

Bagozzi, Richard P. "Marketing as Exchange." *Journal of Marketing,* October 1975, pp. 32–39.

Bellizzi, Joseph A., and Gene W. Murdock. "Industrial Sales Management in the 1980's." *Industrial Marketing Management,* Fall 1981, pp. 299–304.

Carter, Robert N., and Milton R. Bryant. "Women as Industrial Sales Representatives." *Industrial Marketing Management,* Fall 1980, pp. 23–26.

Churchill, Gilbert, Jr.; Neil Ford; and Orville Walker, Jr. *Sales Force Management: Planning, Implementation, and Control.* 2nd ed. Homewood, Ill.: Richard D. Irwin, 1985.

Crawford, John C., and James R. Lumpkin. "The Choice of Selling as a Career." *Industrial Marketing Management,* Fall 1983, pp. 257–61.

George, William R., and J. Patrick Kelly. "The Promotion and Selling of Services." *Business,* July–September 1983, pp. 14–20.

Kanter, Rosabeth Moss, and Barry A. Stein. "Birth of a Saleswoman." *Across the Board* (The Conference Board Magazine), June 1979, pp. 14–24.

Lacniak, Gene R., and Jon G. Udell. "Dimensions of Future Marketing." *MSU Business Topics,* Autumn 1979, pp. 33–44.

McCarthy, E. Jerome, and William D. Perreault, Jr. *Basic Marketing.* 9th ed. Homewood, Ill.: Richard D. Irwin, 1987.

Meyers, Kenneth A. "The Selling Professional of the 1980's." *Business,* October–December 1982, pp. 44–46.

Shapiro, Benson, and John Wyman. "New Ways to Reach Your Customers." *Harvard Business Review,* July–August 1981, pp. 103–10.

Shook, Robert L. *Ten Greatest Salespersons.* New York: Harper & Row, 1978.

Taylor, Thayer C. "S&MM Special Section: The Computer in Sales and Marketing." *Sales & Marketing Management,* December 9, 1985, pp. 66 + .

2 Duties, Responsibilities, and Qualifications of Sales Representatives

Some questions answered in this chapter are:

- What are a salesperson's basic duties and responsibilities?
- Are all selling jobs the same? What factors differ?
- What do retail, trade, missionary, direct, and capital goods salespeople do?
- What are their jobs like?
- What does it take to be a successful salesperson?
- Are successful salespeople born or made?
- How can people decide which selling job suits them best?

The duties and responsibilities of salespeople are quite different for retail, trade, missionary, and industrial salespeople. All salespeople are responsible to their customers and their companies. They all spend time selling to customers, traveling between accounts, attending meetings, and doing paperwork. But some jobs differ in the amount of field work and technical knowledge required, and the emphasis placed on closing.

In this chapter, we will examine the general nature of and the differences between selling jobs. Then we'll look at the duties and responsibilities of some specific jobs. The chapter ends with a discussion of the skills needed to be a successful salesperson.

THE SALES-PERSON'S JOB

Service to the Buyer

A salesperson's job is to get an order. Yet while getting an order is the practical end result of all good selling, the real objective is to provide service. Selling is a two-way relationship. A sale must benefit both buyer and seller; otherwise a continuous, long-term relationship cannot exist. "Putting over a deal" that does not benefit the buyer is harmful to both buyer and seller in the long run.

This view is a basic element in the marketing concept. And as discussed in Chapter 1, progressive companies throughout the world subscribe to the marketing concept. To implement the marketing concept, many companies do not pay salespeople with commissions because they believe commissions encourage salespeople to use high-pressure selling techniques. For example, the Digital Equipment Corporation (DEC) pays its computer salespeople a straight salary without commissions—and without bonuses for exceeding quotas—because DEC wants its sales representatives to think more about their customers than about their next meal. "Sales representatives are encouraged to meet both the reasonable and unreasonable demands of users, and their performance is measured by customer satisfaction (determined through an annual survey)."[1]

Selling consumer goods, specialty products, and industrial lines requires a long-range selling plan—a plan based on years of association between the buyer and seller. If a sale isn't made on the first call, it may be made on the second or third. Once an initial sale is made, repeat business is the source of big dividends to the company and its sales representative. This opportunity for repeat business is impossible unless the salesperson is honest and sincere in providing service.[2]

Service to the Company

A new salesperson returned to the office after a day's work and reported the sale of three office machines. This was cause for a round of congratulations until the sales manager saw the duplicate order slips. The salesperson had quoted too low a price because excessive allowances had been granted on trade-ins; the discounts had been figured incorrectly; and the new-account reports had not been filled out.

This sales representative served the buyer—perhaps too well—but had failed to serve the company efficiently. The transaction was not profitable to both buyer and seller; therefore, it was not a satisfactory sale.

The marketing concept does not mean salespeople should focus solely on satisfying customer needs. They must also consider the needs of the

---

[1] Bro Uttal, "The Gentlemen and the Upstarts Meet in a Great Mini Battle," *Fortune,* April 23, 1979, p. 100.

[2] For a study on college students' opinions on honesty, see John S. Ewing, "Honesty, Salesmen, and College Students," *Sales & Marketing Management,* May 10, 1976, pp. 73–75.

company. Companies need more than just sales: To survive, they have to have *profitable* sales. If salespeople make unprofitable sales over time, their companies will go out of business. Salespeople must balance the needs of their company and their customers.

Duties and Responsibilities of Salespeople

A salesperson's duties are determined by the type of selling job he or she chooses. The responsibilities of salespeople selling gas turbines for General Electric, soap and detergents for Procter & Gamble, or handbags for Macy's department stores are quite different. But certain basic duties and responsibilities are common to all types of selling, regardless of the company or the product sold. However, the importance of these duties varies for different jobs.

Direct Selling   This includes prospecting for new customers, increasing sales to existing customers, making sales presentations, demonstrating products, quoting price and sales terms, and writing orders. These activities, which are discussed in Part III of this book, are closely associated with selling jobs. But they are only one part of a salesperson's responsibilities.

Figure 2–1 reports the results of a 1985 survey of salespeople. On average, the salespeople worked over nine hours a day; many worked through lunch. Only 26 percent of their time was spent in face-to-face selling. However, 17 percent of their time was spent selling prospects and customers on the telephone. The rest of the day was spent in meetings, traveling, waiting for interviews, doing paperwork, or making service calls. This means that the typical industrial salesperson only spends 609 hours each year in front of customers.

In addition to direct selling, a salesperson's duties include indirect selling and nonselling activities.

Indirect Selling—Promoting Company Goodwill   The salesperson *is* the company to its customers. The salesperson's job is to maintain and improve the company's good name and corporate image.

Advising and Counseling   This involves supplying information to help solve the customer's merchandising, marketing, or management problems.

Handling Complaints   This requires the salesperson to make adjustments or to recommend settlements to the home office.

Attending Sales Meetings   These periodic meetings advise salespeople about new products or policies and stimulate sales activities. Such meetings may take place in the branch, district, regional, or home office.

FIGURE 2–1
How Industrial
Salespeople Spend
Their Time

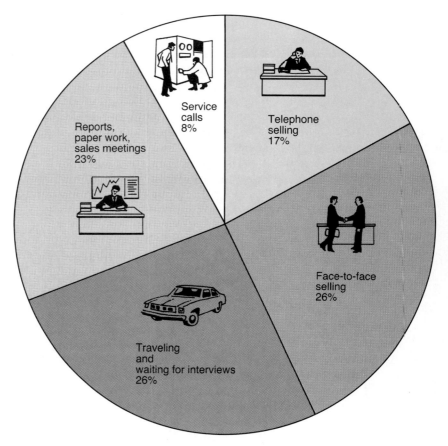

Source: How Salespeople Spend Their Time, Laboratory for Advertising Performance 7023.2
Courtesy of McGraw-Hill Laboratory for Advertising Performance

Nonselling Activities—Reporting   This includes preparing daily, weekly,
and monthly reports. The reports may include information on expenses,
cash, calls made, sales made, miles traveled, competition, business conditions, service rendered, orders lost, and route schedules.

Collecting   Some companies require the salesperson to collect payment
for merchandise sold.

Assisting the Credit Department   Some companies depend on the salesperson to collect credit information and forward it to the home office as
a basis for credit ratings. Other companies give the salesperson full authority for credit.

Organizing   This requires the salesperson to plan routes, to use his or
her time properly, and to systematize all sales efforts.

Working with Management   This requires the salesperson to follow the sales manager's orders. It includes the ability to work enthusiastically without close supervision.

Traveling   If the traveling is local, the salesperson can be home each night. But a salesperson may cover a district in a state, an entire state, a region that includes several states, or the entire nation.

Studying   Salespeople are expected to acquire new knowledge about the company, its products, and its customers' problems. They should also learn about factors that affect business conditions in their territories.

Salespeople can expect to encounter the duties and tasks listed above in most fields of selling. As we shall see in the next section, companies place different emphases on each of these duties and tasks.

CHANNELS OF DISTRIBUTION AND SALES JOBS

Distribution is an important part of a company's marketing program (see Figure 2–2). It includes stocking inventory, handling credit, transporting products, offering an assortment of products, providing service, and selling the products. Because of these activities, customers can buy a wide range of products at convenient locations.

Manufacturers, wholesalers, and retailers distribute their products through channels. The nature of these channels depends on the product sold, the customers' buying habits, the amount of selling and service required, the location and concentration of buyers, and the customs of the trade and competition.

We cannot describe all the distribution channels. But Figure 2–2 shows the principal channels for industrial and consumer products and the position of sales representatives within these channels. The two main channels for industrial products are the first and second channels in Figure 2–2. In the first channel, industrial salespeople employed by the manufacturer sell directly to industrial customers. In the second channel, industrial trade salespeople working for the manufacturer sell to distributors. The distributors' salespeople sell products made by a number of different manufacturers to industrial customers.

The remaining three channels in Figure 2–2 concern consumer products. The third channel shows firms such as State Farm Insurance whose salespeople sell directly to consumers. The fourth channel shows a manufacturer that employs trade salespeople to sell to retailers; salespeople working for the retailer then sell the products to the final consumers. The fifth channel uses an additional level of distribution—manufacturers sell to distributors, who sell to retailers, who sell to consumers.

The role of the missionary salesperson is shown in the fifth channel. This salesperson works for the manufacturer and promotes the manufacturer's products to retailers. But the retailers buy the products from distributors, *not* directly from the manufacturer.

FIGURE 2–2
Sales Jobs and Distribution Channels

Industrial products channels

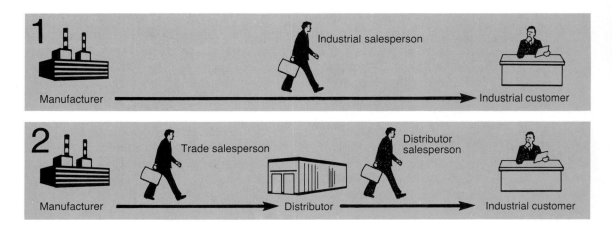

Consumer goods channels

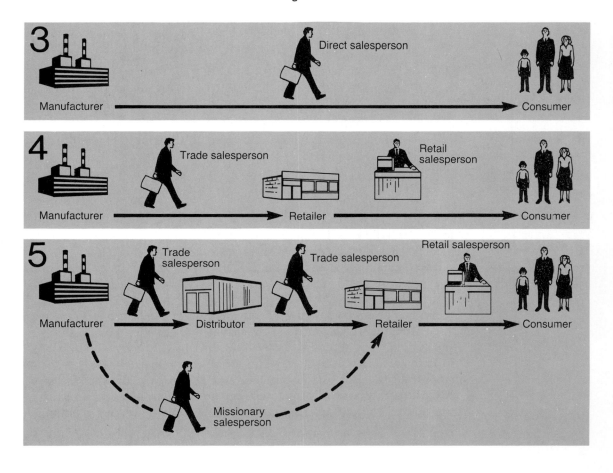

Often independent agents or manufacturers' representatives serve as industrial salespeople, direct salespeople, or trade salespeople. Manufacturers contract with them to do the selling. The agents are independent business owners who are paid a commission by the manufacturer for all products sold. We'll take up the role of a manufacturers' agent later in this chapter (see Selling Scenario 2–1).

DIFFER-ENCES BETWEEN SALES JOBS

There have been many attempts to classify sales jobs. Some systems classify sales jobs based on the following factors:

1. Type of employer—is the salesperson employed by a manufacturer, a wholesaler, or a retailer?
2. Type of customer—does the salesperson sell to industrial companies, wholesalers, retailers, or consumers?
3. Type of product sold—does the salesperson sell industrial or consumer products, capital goods or supplies, tangible products or intangible services?

It is hard to develop a set of categories that would place each type of selling in its own category. Sales jobs are difficult to categorize for two reasons. First, there is a wide variety of sales jobs—from the L'eggs hosiery salesperson who stocks displays in grocery stores to the Westinghouse salesperson who sells nuclear power plants. Second, sales jobs vary in different companies. Procter & Gamble and Colgate-Palmolive salespeople both sell soap to grocery stores. But they have different duties and tasks because each company defines the role of its salesperson in its own way.

The next section takes up some basic factors that account for the differences between sales jobs. Then the duties and tasks of typical sales jobs are described in detail.

Factors in Sales Jobs

Key factors in sales jobs are: (1) the kinds of customers called on by the salesperson, (2) the salesperson's duties, (3) the importance of the purchase decision to the buyer, (4) where the selling takes place, (5) the products or services sold, and (6) the level of closing skills required.

Kinds of Customers—New or Continuing Customers   Some sales jobs involve selling existing customers, and others are concerned with finding new customers. Thus, two types of salespeople sell computer time-sharing services for Xerox Data Services (XDS). Marketing representatives at XDS are responsible for signing up new customers. After using XDS's time-sharing services for six months, the customer is turned over to an account representative. This person has the task of continuing to satisfy the customer's needs and encouraging the customer to use additional services.

There is a wide variety of selling jobs: Here one salesperson sets up an in-store display, another demonstrates office equipment to a team of buyers, and a third shows textile mill samples to a buyer.

© Joel Gordon 1979

Charles Gatewood

Cameramann International, Ltd.

More sales skills are required to sell new prospects than existing customers. To sell new accounts, the salesperson has to look for the customers and then persuade them to try the company's product. Such salespeople must be able to deal with the inevitable rejections that occur during prospecting. Salespeople responsible for existing customers place more emphasis on servicing them than on selling them. Such salespeople do not have to persuade new customers to try a product or service.

The Salesperson's Duties—Selling or Servicing Customers   The main emphasis of some sales jobs is service to customers; other jobs emphasize persuading customers to purchase a product or service. Salespeople concerned with servicing are mainly order takers. They provide information to the buyer and then process the order. For example, most salespeople selling to grocery stores check the stock of their products, arrange the products on the shelves, find out how much new stock is needed, and tell the store manager if inventories are low. Their main task is to help the store manager. On the basis of the salesperson's inventory report, the store manager decides whether to place an order. The salesperson does little real selling.

Some salespeople, however, sell only to the headquarters purchasing departments of large grocery store chains. Such headquarters salespeople spend their time persuading buyers to put a new product on store shelves or to increase the shelf space for old products.

Importance of Buying Decision to the Customer   Consumers and industrial buyers make many purchases each year. Some are important to them, such as the purchase of a home or a computer; others are not crucial, such as the purchase of candy or industrial supplies.

Sales jobs involving important decisions for a customer are quite different from sales jobs involving minor decisions. Let's consider the differences between retail sales jobs in a designer's fashion salon and a stationery department. Buying expensive designer clothes is a big decision for the buyer. The salesperson in the salon spends a lot of time with each customer finding out which styles appeal to the customer and suggesting alternatives. He or she should comment on how the outfits look when tried on. The final task is convincing the customer which apparel to buy. Salespeople with this job in a department store usually develop a loyal group of customers. They contact their customers when new styles arrive and arrange special showings. Often customers develop loyalty to a specific salesperson and may follow the salesperson to another store.

But the salesclerk in a stationery department meets customers who are making unimportant decisions. The customers rarely need information and ask few questions. Such salesclerks simply make the sale easier. They enter it on the cash register, take the money, and put the merchandise in a bag.

Selling intangibles:
These salespeople
are soliciting alumni
in a university fund-
raising phone-athon.

Courtesy of National College of Education

Location of Selling Activity: Field or Inside Sales   Field salespeople perform most of their duties in the customer's place of business or residence.
Inside salespeople work at their employer's location.

Field selling is more demanding than inside selling because the salespeople have to go to the customers. Inside salespeople do not travel or
look for customers. They do not have to arouse a customer's interest in
buying. The customers already have an interest when they contact the
inside salesperson. Inside salespeople play an order-taking role; field
salespeople play a demand-stimulating role.

The Products or Services Sold—Tangible Products or Intangible Services
The product or service to be sold affects the duties and tasks of a sales
job. As we have seen, products like designer clothing involve a bigger
decision for the buyer. Sales jobs for these products are more demanding
and time-consuming.

Also, the benefits provided by a product or service affect the nature
of the sales job. Many products, such as cars, appliances, and computers,
have mainly tangible benefits. Customers can see the styling of the car,
the number of burners on the stove, and the speed with which a computer
analyzes data. Services like life insurance or investment opportunities
offer intangible benefits. It is harder to sell intangible benefits than tangible
benefits because it's not easy to demonstrate intangible benefits to a customer. While it's fairly easy to convince a customer that a car is roomy,
it's harder to demonstrate the benefits of investing in stocks.

Closing Skills   Closing—asking for the order—is perhaps the most challenging aspect of selling. In some jobs, salespeople never close. For ex-

Table 2–1   Questions that Describe Sales Jobs

	Low Creativity		High Creativity
Nature of customer—Does the salesperson contact predominately:	Present customers	or	New prospects
Nature of salesperson's duties—Is the emphasis of the salesperson's duties on:	Servicing customers	or	Persuading customers
Importance of buying decision—How important is the buying decision to the customer?	Not very important	or	Very important
Location of selling acitivity—Do the salesperson's selling activities take place:	Inside the company	or	In the field
Nature of salesperson's duties—Do the products or services sold by the salesperson have:	Tangible benefits	or	Intangible benefits
Closing skills—What level of skills is required to close a sale?	Limited skills	or	Extensive skills

Creativity

ample, pharmaceutical salespeople call on physicians and describe, or "detail," the uses and side effects of new drugs. They do not ask for an order. Impressed by the sales presentation, physicians may prescribe the drugs for their patients. The patients then have to buy the drug at a pharmacy. The physicians do not order directly from the pharmaceutical company.

The Continuum of Sales Jobs

To understand what is meant by the *continuum of sales jobs,* let's look at the questions in Table 2–1. Using the questions in the table, we can decide which jobs are less creative and which are more creative. Then we can line up a number of jobs in the order of their creativity, as shown in Figure 2–3.

At the right side of the continuum in Figure 2–3 are jobs that require a good deal of skill and creativity. These jobs, described by the responses in the right-hand column of Table 2–1, require salespeople to go into the field and call on new customers who can make important buying decisions. Selling involves persuading new customers, not servicing old customers. Salespeople of this type have to promote the intangible benefits of their products, and they must make good use of their closing skills.

At the left side of the continuum in Figure 2–3 are sales jobs that correspond to the responses in the left-hand column of Table 2–1. Such jobs are less creative. Salespeople in these jobs service old customers. But since their customers do not make crucial decisions, fewer closing skills are needed. As we might expect, salespeople at the right side of the continuum usually make more money than those at the left.

The continuum in Figure 2–3 indicates that a missionary salesperson needs more skill and creativity than a department store salesperson. This

FIGURE 2–3
The Continuum of Sales Jobs

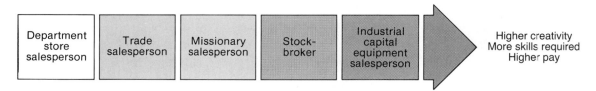

| Department store salesperson | Trade salesperson | Missionary salesperson | Stock-broker | Industrial capital equipment salesperson | Higher creativity
More skills required
Higher pay |

difference between missionary and department store selling is generally
true. But some department store selling jobs are more challenging than
missionary selling. For instance, a sales job in a furniture or high-fashion
clothing department requires a lot of product knowledge and selling skills.
Such salespeople often can earn more than a missionary salesperson. So
the lineup of sales jobs along the continuum in Figure 2–3 is accurate
only in a general sense. Since sales jobs differ so greatly, there are many
exceptions to the job descriptions on the continuum. In the next section,
we will learn about the duties and tasks of some specific sales jobs.

EXAMPLES OF SALES JOBS

Retail Selling

Retail salespeople sell to customers who come into the store. Most customers have already decided they need the product and are "looking
around" to make a purchase. Thus, retail selling, as a rule, involves
servicing rather than selling. Few closing skills are needed.

Yet many retail salespeople have interesting and challenging jobs.
Clothing salespeople often act as fashion consultants for their customers.
Such salespeople must access the physical characteristics of their customers, find out how the garments are to be used, learn how much the
customer is willing to pay, and choose several garments for the customer
to look at. But some retail salespeople are merely order takers. They wrap
up the merchandise and make change.

Retail salespeople also perform many nonselling activities, such as
arranging displays, taking inventory, stocking shelves, and putting prices
on merchandise.

Retail selling experience forms a sound basis for many other selling
and merchandising jobs. It is a valuable training for those who plan to
have businesses of their own; for those who want to become department
heads, buyers, merchandise managers, or other store executives; and for
those who plan to go into advertising.

Some large department stores conduct training programs that prepare
college graduates and others to manage a selling department. Candidates
first gain experience in various selling departments. Then they learn merchandising by observing their superiors and by attending special training
classes. Finally, they may become qualified as managers of selling departments. Chapter 16 discusses retail selling in more detail.

Trade salespeople make regularly scheduled calls on existing customers in a designated territory.

George W. Gardner　　　　　　　　　　　　Cameramann International, Ltd.

Trade Selling

Trade salespeople mainly seek to increase the sales of their company's products by promoting services to wholesalers and retailers. The actual selling is low key. Trade salespeople are not required to find new customers. They make regularly scheduled calls on existing customers in a designated territory. Some specific services of trade salespeople are spelled out in the Carnation Company's list of objectives for a sales call (see Figure 2–4).

There are many job opportunities in trade selling. Procter & Gamble employs over 4,500 salespeople in six separate sales forces. Some of the brands sold by each sales force are: (1) package goods and detergents—Tide, Ivory Liquid, Spic and Span, and Cascade; (2) bar soap and household cleaning products—Ivory Soap, Spic and Span, and Comet; (3) case food—Crisco and Duncan Hines; (4) toilet goods—Crest, Liquid Prell, and Scope; (4) paper products—Charmin and Pampers; and (6) Folger's Coffee. General Foods also has six separate sales divisions. Because of the size of the sales forces at consumer-product firms, there are many chances to get ahead. At Procter & Gamble, most new salespeople receive their first promotion to unit manager in one year.

Many trade salespeople do not work directly for a manufacturer; they work for brokers or wholesalers. Brokers, or manufacturers' representatives, are independent sales agents who do not own or take physical possession of the product. When they get an order from a retailer, they transmit it to the manufacturer who ships the goods directly to the retailer.

FIGURE 2–4
Basic Sales Call
Objectives for a
Carnation
Salesperson

In order of importance:

1. *Secure full distribution of Carnation products.* In a retail chain store, this would entail making certain that all Carnation products authorized or available from their supplier or direct account are stocked. If there is a gap in the retail outlet of authorized items, the primary sales goal would be to have the contact write an order guide for the item.

2. *Maintain adequate in-store inventory.* Assuming complete distribution of all Carnation products, all sales efforts should be made to obtain sufficient product inventory both on the shelf and in the back room. If this is not done, an out-of-stock condition occurs, resulting in lost sales. By selling the contact on adequate back room stock in addition to a sufficient amount of shelf space, these out-of-stocks will not occur.

3. *Insure correct pricing.* The unit prices of both Carnation items and competitive items should be checked to be certain they are in line and competitive with each other. In the case of a chain outlet, the prices of all items are set at headquarters; therefore, your job is to see that all prices on the shelf and on the products are identical to the authorized ones. In an independent outlet, you should make certain the prices of the Carnation products carry the same percent markup as the competitive items.

4. *Obtain best shelf position.* An effort should be made to secure the best possible shelf positions for all Carnation products. In chain stores, sections are frequently set up and authorized by a headquarter merchandising manager, in which case it would be best to contact him regarding merchandising changes. In independent stores, changes are always made at the store level. Only by securing the best shelf positions can you be sure of the maximum "off the shelf" movement.

5. *Build displays.* Market research has shown that 76 percent of all the items purchased in retail grocery stores are the result of a store decision made by the shoppers. This points up the importance of creating "impulse purchases," which are most frequently bought from product displays. Developing and presenting ideas for displays (e.g., tie-ins, promotions, etc.) is, therefore, one of your main objectives for both chain and independent outlets.

6. *Obtain advertising support.* In the case of chains, feature ads are usually set up at headquarters, while the independents set them up at the retail level. Other forms of in-store advertising, such as shelf strips and shelf talkers, should be used whenever possible.

In addition:

1. *Know account's distribution.* Know the products stocked by the direct account, especially those products that are in direct competition to Carnation products. When possible, you should find out how well competitive products are selling in the stores the buyer services. This will, in many cases, reinforce the points in your sales presentation. This communication process is a two-way street since, by giving useful information to the buyer about changing market conditions, you will be building a healthy business relationship based on mutual trust.

FIGURE 2–4
(*concluded*)

> 2. When a favorable decision is reached or is imminent, be prepared to offer suggestions on the size of the order, the retail shelf price, suggested feature prices for ads, displays, shelf position locations, and any other information you can anticipate the buyer might request. Try to avoid replying, "I'll have to check on that and call you back." Our customers expect us to be the authority on Carnation products and merchandising ideas.

Larry Lodish (center) points out features of Stanley Furniture during a training session for retail salespeople (see Selling Scenario 2–1).

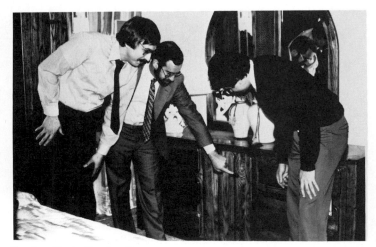

Courtesy Stanley Furniture Company

Brokers are paid a commission on all orders they get. Most of them work in a small geographic region. For example, Food Enterprises of Pennsylvania employs 19 salespeople in the Philadelphia area. Some of the products they represent are Welch's grape juice, Gino's frozen pizzas, and Libby's canned fruit.

In contrast, wholesalers or distributors own the goods they sell. They buy from the manufacturers and resell to retailers or industrial companies. Thus, wholesalers carry out warehousing and billing functions as well as selling. The activities of a manufacturers' representative for Stanley Furniture are shown in Selling Scenario 2–1.

Trade salespeople sell industrial as well as consumer products. Industrial trade salespeople call on industrial distributors. While trade salespeople for consumer products help retailers promote their products, industrial trade salespeople concentrate on training and assisting the distributor's salespeople.

Selling Scenario 2–1

LARRY LODISH—A MANUFACTURERS' REPRESENTATIVE

Larry Lodish and his two partners own GCL Associates—the exclusive agent for Stanley Furniture Company in New York City, Long Island, and northern New Jersey. As an independent agent, GCL receives a commission on all Stanley Furniture sold in the territory, and it pays all sales expenses. In addition to the three partners who sell furniture, GCL employs three people who do order processing, inside selling, and customer service.

After graduating from Miami University in Ohio, Larry took a job in sales with the Simmons Bedding Company. He left Simmons Bedding, worked as the manager of a large retail store, and then joined GCL. At GCL, he calls on independent furniture stores, large department stores such as Bamberger's, Gimbels, and Macy's and chain stores such as Levitz's. He attempts to persuade buyers to stock and display Stanley Furniture. However, he does more than just sell to buyers. He also holds sales meetings in the stores to teach the retail salespeople how to sell Stanley Furniture—he describes the key features of the furniture and the customer benefits provided by these features. In addition,

he advises store managers how to display and promote the furniture—which sets should be displayed on the floor and where they should be located to increase sales.

Larry also manages the distribution of Stanley Furniture in his territory. Each department or furniture store wants to offer products different from its competitors. For example, two competing stores will not both carry Stanley Furniture. So Larry must decide which stores he should target his sales efforts toward and which stores will not be part of a qualified distribution program.

Twice a year, Larry goes to the furniture show in High Point, North Carolina. At the show, he demonstrates the new Stanley products to his customers and other furniture dealers. He also reviews his selling experiences and needs with Stanley management. For example, the furniture stores he calls on in part of his territory sell a lot of large china cabinets with many shelves. These cabinets are popular with Italian and Orthodox Jewish families in Brooklyn. Larry's suggestion that the company make a larger china cabinet for this market has increased sales for both Stanley and GCL.

Missionary Selling

Missionary salespeople work for manufacturers. Their principal objective is to encourage users of the product to purchase their company's products from distributors or retailers.

The classic example of missionary selling is detail salespeople who work for pharmaceutical companies. Detail salespeople call on physicians

This missionary salesperson is encouraging farmers to plant a new type of soybean.

Steve Leonard/Click, Chicago

and describe the benefits and side effects of drugs. Seventy-four percent of physicians contacted in a recent survey indicated that detailers or direct mail were their first source of information about new drugs.[3] Detailers attempt to get the doctor to prescribe the drug for patients. If they succeed, their company will receive orders from local pharmacies where patients have their prescriptions filled. The job description for a pharmaceutical salesperson is shown in Figure 2–5.

Industrial trade salespeople often do missionary selling. In addition to encouraging distributors to stock more products made by their company, industrial trade salespeople also call on end users. During these calls, the salespeople demonstrate the advantages of their product and stimulate end users to place an order with the distributor.

Direct Selling

Direct salespeople sell goods and services directly to ultimate users. Some familiar companies employing direct salespeople are Mary Kay Cosmetics, Avon, and Tupperware. Direct selling is challenging because salespeople contact consumers in the field and often must stimulate an interest in the product in addition to persuading the consumer to buy it. The most challenging direct selling jobs involve the sale of intangible services, such as insurance or investment securities.

---

[3]Louis J. Haugh, ''Detailers—Salesmen Who Don't Sell,'' *Advertising Age*, February 13, 1978, pp. 67–68, 70.

FIGURE 2–5
The Pharmaceutical
Representative

Nature of Work

Salespeople who work for pharmaceutical companies provide information on their company's products to physicians, pharmacists, and other people licensed to provide medical services in their territory. They call on four to eight doctors and three to six pharmacists each day. Usually their calls are made without an appointment.

When calling on doctors, the representative's aim is to get the doctors to write prescriptions for drugs supplied by his or her company. Often the representative has to wait until the doctor is available. Then the representative spends between 10 and 15 minutes "detailing" two or three pharmaceuticals to the doctor. Usually the company decides which drugs are to be presented and how to present them. The presentation includes an accurate representation of the symptoms for which the pharmaceutical is effective, how effective it is, and possible side effects. Doctors consider these presentations an important source of information about new products.

Even though the company provides a general outline of the presentation, the representatives need to tailor their presentation to the doctor's specialty and special interests. Representatives may supplement their presentation with product literature and samples.

Pharmacy calls are made to provide information to the pharmacists, to check stock, to encourage the use of special counter and window displays, to sell special promotions, and to check on credit and delinquent payments. Pharmaceutical representatives may also call on staff physicians and nurses in hospitals, health departments in industrial companies, and dentists.

Requirements

While prior experience is usually not required, a bachelor's degree is desirable, and some background in pharmacy or the life sciences is helpful. Work experience in a pharmacy, retail store, or direct selling is desirable.

Pharmaceutical representatives need to be well groomed, personable, energetic, and enthuasiastic. They should be good planners and time managers as well as able to think and talk clearly and concisely.

Training

Newly hired representatives usually receive disease and product information over a four- to six-week period at their territory office and the company's home office. In addition to this technical information, they take a thorough course in presentational and selling skills. A variety of modern sales training techniques is used.

Selling Commercial and Industrial Goods

The most creative sales jobs involve selling capital goods. These sales jobs are high on all the factors described in Table 2–1. Since capital good purchases are made infrequently, salespeople usually have to approach new customers. The selling job requires persuading customers who are making an important buying decision in a field setting. In selling capital goods, salespeople need to demonstrate both immediate tangible benefits and future intangible benefits. Because many people are involved in a purchase decision for capital goods, a salesperson needs to close the sales many times. Figure 2–6 describes a typical day for a Xerox copier salesperson. Chapters 6 and 15 give a more complete description of capital goods purchasing and selling.

QUALIFICA-TIONS FOR SUCCESS IN SALES

For the last 60 years, people have written books and articles about the determinants of success in sales. ''Perhaps no other occupation has been subjected to quite so much amateur analysis and pseudopsychology as personal selling, without moving one step closer to an understanding of the problems and influences involved.''[4]

Professional researchers have been unable to determine which personality traits or individual characteristics (age, sex, etc.) are needed to be a successful salesperson. A recent review of studies of the last 20 years concluded that *no* set of characteristics ensures sales success or failure. While some studies found that good salespeople are aggressive, other studies reported that aggressiveness is not related to sales success. Some studies showed that sociability is related to sales performance, but other studies found no such relationship.[5]

One reason researchers have not found the profile for the perfect salesperson is that sales jobs are so different. As the job descriptions in the previous section show, the characteristics and skills needed for success in trade selling are quite different from those needed for success in selling capital goods.

In addition, the customers a salesperson calls on are all different. Some customers like to interact with an aggressive salesperson, while others are turned off by aggressive behavior. Some customers are all business and want formal relationships with salespeople. But other customers may look forward to chatting with salespeople in an informal way. Thus, the hard-driving or back-slapping personality will not succeed with all customers. There is no magic formula for selling that works on all sales jobs or with all customers.

Although there is no one personality profile for the ideal salesperson, successful salespeople are hard workers and smart workers. They are emotionally mature, dependable, and knowledgeable.

Working Harder

Most salespeople work in the field with no direct supervision. Under these conditions, it is tempting to get up late, take long lunch breaks, and stop work early. But successful salespeople do not succumb to these temp-

---

[4]V. R. Buzzotta, R. E. Lefton, and Manuel Sherberg, *Effective Selling through Psychology* (New York: John Wiley & Sons, 1973).

[5]Barton A. Weitz, ''Effectiveness in Sales Interactions: A Contingency Framework,'' *Journal of Marketing*, Winter 1981, pp. 85–103.

FIGURE 2–6
Typical Day for a
Xerox Copier
Salesperson

If you are selling low-volume equipment (desktop copiers and duplicators), you are responsible for your sales coverage, time, and budget. You have marketing and service support, but you are expected to work independently, without constant direction.

Your day is devoted primarily to customer contact. Potential customers may phone the branch and ask to see a Xerox representative. More likely, however, you will acquire customers by making appointments or by "cold calling"— visiting businesses to meet the firm's decision makers, discussing their needs and offering solutions to their problems. As part of your position, you will make product presentations, either at the branch office or at the customer's firm. You will also spend time on the telephone, following up leads, arranging appointments, and speaking with managers in a variety of businesses and organizations.

If you are selling high-volume equipment (large copying systems), a typical day will see you set and keep appointments with present and potential customers, coordinate the activities of support personnel, maintain the needed records of your accounts, and manage other administrative activities.

As a sales representative, you will spend much of your time dealing by telephone with decision makers at your assigned accounts. You might investigate account problems, present proposals analyzing the results of a study you completed, or confirm that your customer's office layout and electrical system can accommodate new equipment. You will also have present and potential customers visit the branch office, where you can demonstrate Xerox equipment.

Coordinating the activities of support personnel involves directing the efforts of employees skilled in specialized areas such as high-volume equipment and consultative studies. You will also be responsible for maintaining account records that detail customer needs, the decision makers in the customer's organization, financial criteria, and other important factors in the buying process. Because your accounts will often be large and complex, with many separate departments and locations, up-to-date records are essential to the efficiency of your marketing efforts. Other administrative tasks you will coordinate include processing customer orders for equipment, documenting special pricing agreements, and processing requests necessary to relocate equipment.

In working with customers in either selling situation, you will need to solve a number of problems. What Xerox product best fits the customer's needs? How does this product compare with the competition? Should the machine be purchased or leased? What is the total cash outlay—and per copy cost—for the machine and its service? How should the product be financed? Where should the machine be placed for maximum efficiency? What training is needed for employees? How can Xerox products fit future needs?

You will also have a number of customer support activities, such as expediting deliveries, checking credit, writing proposals, and training customer employees in the use of the product. You might also refer customers to other Xerox sales organizations and make joint calls with representatives from these organizations.

Source: Reprinted with permission from *Xerox: Opportunities in Sales.*

Selling Scenario 2–2

PROLONGED NEGOTIATIONS

 Kathleen Garcia, director of sales for the Ramada Inn at Fisherman's Wharf in San Francisco, describes her most memorable sale:

I would say that my greatest sale was when I renegotiated our contract with Woodside Management, a corporate travel agency, for a guaranteed production program. It guarantees us payment whether or not rooms are filled. Before, we just offered them a straight corporate rate. The circumstances surrounding this particular sale are something I'll never forget.

In March of 1984, I was two months pregnant. I went to Woodside to discuss various programs. I had to show them that Ramada had changed from being a tour and travel inn to a hotel serving the corporate and commercial markets. I had to try to convince them that they'd be right to choose us.

We were up against another major hotel chain, Marriott, which had just opened across the street, and I had to do a lot of research to show them what we could do for them that Marriott couldn't. In August, we finally signed the contract, which is worth about $300,000 a year to us, and raised our sales by 70 percent. By that time I was seven months pregnant, and I think the fact that I was still working so hard helped me earn the respect of the people I was selling to.

Source: Reprinted from "Strange Tales of Sales," *Sales & Marketing Management,* June 3, 1985, p. 43.

tations. They are "self-starters" who do not need the fear of a glaring supervisor to get them going in the morning or to keep them working hard all day. The law of averages holds for most sales jobs: The more calls you make, the more orders you get.

In addition to working hard, salespeople need to be persistent. Most customers are not sold on the first call. Many sales, like the railroad computer system, take several years and thousands of calls before an order is placed. In Selling Scenario 2–2, Kathleen Garcia describes how hard work paid off.

Working hard is particularly important in trade and missionary selling. Because these selling jobs emphasize servicing rather than selling customers, selling skills are not as important as being there and being dependable.

Working Smarter

Spending long hours on the job is not enough. Salespeople must spend their time efficiently. They need to maximize the time they spend contacting customers and minimize the time they spend traveling and waiting for customers. To do this, salespeople must organize and plan their work—a subject discussed in more detail in Chapter 17.

A key to working smarter is practicing the marketing concept—being responsive to a customer's needs. To be responsive to a customer's needs, the salesperson needs to be a good communicator. Talking is not enough. The salesperson has to listen to what the customer says, ask questions that uncover problems and needs, and pay attention to the responses. The successful salesperson also realizes that the same sales approach does not work with all customers—it must be adapted to each selling situation. The salesperson must be sensitive and flexible enough to make those adaptations during the sales presentation. Chapters 6 and 7 discuss these ideas in more detail.

Finally, working smarter also means learning on the job. Successful salespeople continually improve their skills by analyzing their past performance. They learn from their mistakes.

Emotional Maturity

To succeed in selling, people need to have the maturity to accept themselves and have confidence in their capabilities. They also need to respect their customers and not become offended when they do not get an order. The orders will come in the long run if the salesperson does not become defensive.

Salespeople are active people who are often under a lot of pressure. They may find it difficult to be patient with customers. When a customer blames the salesperson for a late delivery or a defective product, the salesperson has a natural reaction to strike back at either the customer or a coworker. Successful salespeople have the emotional maturity to restrain this instinctive response and solve the problem.

Dependability

In some selling, such as used-car sales, the salesperson rarely deals with the same customer twice. However, this book deals mainly with selling situations in which the customer and salesperson have a continuing relationship. The salespeople are not just interested in what the customers will buy tomorrow but also in getting orders in the years to come.

Customers develop long-term relations only with salespeople who are dependable. If a salesperson says the equipment will perform in a certain way, he or she had better make sure the equipment performs that way! If it doesn't, the customer will never rely on that salesperson again.

Honesty and integrity are an important part of dependability. In the long run, customers will know who they can trust. Ethical sales behavior is such an important topic that the next chapter is devoted to it.

Technical Product Knowledge

In most sales jobs, the salespeople need to know how the product works, what it can do, and how the features of the product relate to customers' needs. Though many sales jobs for high-technology products require an engineering background, 30 percent of the sales representatives hired by

IBM to sell computers have a liberal arts undergraduate degree. And Hewlett-Packard hires many business majors to sell computers.

In those technical selling jobs that do require a person with an engineering degree, a major responsibility of the salesperson is to solve technical problems for the customer.

Are Salespeople Born or Made?

On the basis of this discussion, we can see that the skills required to be a successful salesperson can be learned. People can learn to work hard, to plan their time, and to adapt their sales approach to their customers' needs. They can also master the technical aspects of their products. Research has shown that innate characteristics, such as personality traits, sex, and heights, are largely unrelated to sales performance. In fact, companies show their faith in their ability to teach sales skills by spending over $5 billion each year on training programs.

However, research shows that people who learn to be effective salespeople, who work smart and hard, are intrinsically interested in the sales job itself. They don't sell simply for the money or promotion opportunities. They like to sell and are motivated to master the art and science of selling. Salespeople who are motivated only by money do not develop into effective salespeople.[6]

In Selling Scenario 2–3, the number one Toyota salesperson in the United States discusses the factors that made her so successful.

CHOOSING A CAREER IN SALES

This chapter points out the responsibilities, duties, and qualifications needed for many types of selling. People considering a sales career should evaluate themselves in light of these requirements. As the candidates think about which line of selling to go into, they should follow the procedures described below:

1. Decide whether a sales career offers the chance to fulfill personal goals in life. No one should become a salesperson if they are not already sold on the advantages of a sales career.

2. Decide whether to sell products or services. The products to be sold may be machines, equipment, supplies, or other tangibles; the services may be insurance, investments, advertising, or other intangibles. Some people prefer to work with tangible products; others welcome the challenge of selling ideas.

3. Decide whether to sell to customers on a one-call basis or to sell accounts on a continuing basis. Some products are sold once, and there is no need for service or for another contact

---

[6]Barton Weitz, Mita Sujan, and Harish Sujan, "Knowledge, Motivation, and Adaptive Behavior: A Framework for Improving Selling Effectiveness," *Journal of Marketing*, October 1986, pp. 174–91.

DEBRA SCHEPPER—NUMBER ONE

Debra Schepper is the number one Toyota salesperson in the United States. In 1983, she sold 1,300 Toyota vehicles. The owners of Toyota of Dallas were so impressed they bought her a gold necklace with a large number "1" and 13 diamonds— one for each hundred vehicles she sold. In the following interview, she discusses her secrets.

Q: What prompted you to get into the car business?

A: If you'd asked me when I was 18 if I was ever going to sell cars, I would have laughed. I'm not really a car nut. There are some salesmen who can tell you the engine size of the 1962 Chevy and who won this race or that one. That doesn't appeal to me. The car business is a people business, and you meet so many different kinds of people. That's what keeps me interested.

Q: Is it important to believe in the product you sell?

A: Very important. A born salesman can sell almost anything, but I'm not like that. There's a part of me that's a natural-born salesperson, but I couldn't sell anything I didn't believe in. I just don't think it would come across right.

Within a model line, I sell more the cars that I like best. I think the Corolla is a great value, and my attitude apparently comes through to the customer because I sell more of those than any other model.

Q: As a salesperson who's not an automotive buff, how do you keep up on product technology?

A: I use a lot of Toyota sales materials and talk to the mechanics about new products. When a new model comes out, for example, they can tell you more than you'd learn if you went to a new-car showing. You also can learn a great deal by just getting in and out of the cars, looking things over, and driving them. You can retain more through visual contact than through reading books.

Q: What are your strong points?

A: I have a lot of energy, and I think the effort I put forth is worth more than a lot of the knowledge that somebody else might have. I'm also honest and that's important to the customer. A lot of customers fear going to a dealership and getting the hard sell.

I'm not high-pressure; it just wouldn't fit my looks to go in there and try to bulldoze somebody. Times are changing and people don't accept high pressure anymore.

That's why the car salesmen with the white plastic belts, white shoes, and diamond pinkie rings are not around anymore. The hard-sell approach might have worked great in the 1950s and early 1960s, but not with the knowledgeable consumer of today.

Q: Are there any special touches you use that surprise customers or impress them enough to turn the sale?

A: First of all, if there's a husband and wife I talk to the wife, someone most men in the car business totally ignore. They figure, "She doesn't have the final decision; she's just picking the color. I'm going to sit here and talk turkey with the guy and find out what the bottom line is."

But whether you want to believe it or not, the women in the United States handle the money. They know how much their last electric bill was, and they know what they can afford. They can make or break a sale for you.

More and more women who come to our dealership have read the consumer reports and done research. Many women in the marketplace are single heads of households and they've got to be taken seriously. That's one reason why women in the car business do so well—they can relate more to women customers.

Q: Do you think you have any advantage as a female salesperson?

A: There are good and bad points about women in the car business. Once you get a male customer to take you seriously and make him realize you know what you're talking about, then you're okay.

Women do have a few things going against them. Salespeople work so many hours that married women often get complaints from their husbands about never being home, and single women often get frustrated because they want to have more time to socialize. But the women who do work through these things are usually exceptional.

Q: If you were training a new saleswoman, what would you tell her to do?

A: First and foremost, to act professionally. There's nothing that bothers me more than to see some giggly girl on the showroom floor. I'd also tell her to be patient, as confidence comes with experience. The more you deal with problem customers or questions that catch you off guard, the better you become.

I've seen it happen with new salespeople. For example, their hands get all sweaty and they come running frantically into the store and say, "I've got this guy and he wants to test-drive this car and there's another car behind it." They're so nervous.

It took me a few years to develop confidence. About three years ago, I had this customer who was a Grade A know-it-all. He wasn't satisfied with my answer to one of his questions and said, "Well, sister, you'll never make it in this business." I rarely lose my temper, but I looked at him and said, "Buddy, I have made it."

Salespeople can choose from a wide variety of selling careers.

with the buyer—at least for many years. Such sales may involve real estate or construction materials. Other products require servicing and replacements, or the users may need advice and help in maintaining, selling, or using the products. These products may include industrial machinery, office equipment, or merchandise. Some salespeople like to influence different buyers to close each sale; others prefer to work closely with customers and to serve them over a long period.

4. Decide whether to sell to manufacturers, distributors, or household consumers. Manufacturers need parts, supplies, equipment, raw materials, and other products to manufacture their goods. People who sell to manufacturers may have only a few accounts, and the sales volume may be large. Distributors who need goods for resale may be wholesalers, retailers, independent operators, or members of a chain group. Those selling to distributors may handle many accounts; their work may vary from routine assignments to highly creative selling. Salespeople selling to household consumers have many

Prospective salespeople must decide whether a sales career offers the chance to fulfill personal goals.

"Tell me about yourself, Kugelman — your hopes, dreams, career path, and what that damn earring means."

From *The Wall Street Journal,* with permission of Cartoon Features Syndicate.

accounts and evening appointments, and they may need boundless energy.

5. Decide whether to sell in a limited geographic area or to sell wherever there are market opportunities. People who limit themselves to a specific area and are unwilling to move as promotions and opportunities become available automatically narrow, and often eliminate, a wide range of selling jobs. For example, a manufacturers' representative whose products are distributed nationally would make little progress if he or she always declined new assignments in distant territories.

6. Finally, explore the present and future opportunities of a specific industry or job opening. In assessing this, the candidates should also consider the financial and nonfinancial benefits.

A salesperson's job may vary, then, according to the conclusions reached about the decisions listed above. Another factor might be the standards set by a specific company. Finally, salespeople should periodically review this checklist to determine if their job still meets their goals.

SUMMARY

Chapter 2 examines the duties and responsibilities of different sales jobs and the qualifications needed to be a successful salesperson. In practicing the marketing concept, salespeople must not forget they have a responsibility to their company as well as to their customers.

The specific duties and responsibilities of salespeople depend on the type of selling job; however, most salespeople engage in other tasks besides direct selling. These extra tasks may include promoting company goodwill, handling complaints, attending sales meetings, assisting the credit department, reporting, and traveling.

Sales jobs can be classified as to the type of employer, the type of customer, and the type of product. There is such a wide variety of sales jobs that two jobs may differ even though they fall into the same category, according to these classification schemes.

Other factors to be considered in describing sales jobs are the nature of the customer, the salesperson's duties, the importance of the buying decision to the customer, the place where the selling occurs, the kind of product, and the closing skills required. Retail, trade, missionary, direct, and capital goods selling differ on these factors.

Researchers and practitioners cannot determine personality traits or other characteristics that lead to selling success. But some typical behaviors are associated with successful salespeople. Such people are hard and smart workers. They are emotionally mature, responsive to individual customers, and dependable. Some sales jobs also require substantial technical knowledge about the product.

QUESTIONS
AND
PROBLEMS

1. In selling a computer, would you approach the purchasing agent differently than the manager of the data-processing department? Why and how?

2. How important is creativity in a selling career? Is creativity more or less important to a salesperson than to an accountant or an engineer?

3. Using the questions in Table 2–1, evaluate the level of creativity in retail, trade, missionary, direct, and capital goods selling.

4. Assume that you are considering the following sales jobs: (1) sales representative for a large national prescription drug company; (2) salesperson for a major department store; (3) sales representative for a national company that sells sophisticated machine tools and equipment to large manufacturers. List advantages and disadvantages for each of the job opportunities.

5. The Bayview Music Store is a local retail store that sells radios, pianos, sheet music, instruments, and music supplies. Mr. Cleff,

the owner, would like to have his six salespeople make a self-analysis of their jobs to improve their efficiency in selling. He asks you to draw up a simple checklist in question form to enable each salesperson to determine the effectiveness of his or her work. Prepare a series of questions to help the salespeople check on themselves and their jobs.

6. Why does a person in sales need to be more of a self-starter than a production worker or computer programmer?

7. What type of sales position would you like? Are you qualified for that job? Why?

8. Assume you are a sales manager and that you need to recruit someone for the sales positions listed below. For each position, list the different qualities you would want in a sales recruit:
    a. New car salesperson.
    b. College textbook salesperson.
    c. Salesperson selling calculators to a distributor.
    d. Used-car salesperson.

9. Analyze yourself. List your strengths and weaknesses. Do you belong in sales? Why or why not?

10. How do you think the training programs for a sales job in a department store, for a sales job with a pharmaceutical company, and for a sales job as a stockbroker would differ in terms of length and content?

PROJECTS

1. Make a survey of the materials in your college placement and career counseling office to determine the following:
    a. The number and kinds of firms recruiting at the college for sales positions.
    b. The personal qualifications the firms are looking for.
    c. The duties and responsibilities of the salespeople who are hired.
    d. The company training programs available to new salespeople. Summarize your findings.

2. Conduct a survey of selected business firms in your community. Interview the personnel managers, and collect data on the requirements for employment in sales. Report your findings and conclusions.

3. Application blanks used by many companies have space for the sales applicants to list their college extracurricular activities. Prepare a paper showing how the personal qualities companies are looking for may be utilized in student activities.

CASE PROBLEMS

Case 2–1   The Jackson Paint Company

The Jackson Paint Company does business on a national scale and has a regular sales force that calls on independent wholesale and retail paint dealers. The company handles a complete line of nationally advertised paints and paint supplies.

It plans to introduce a new line of insecticides, weed killers, and other nonpaint products during the next year. The sales manager is undecided as to whether the new line should be introduced through the company's regular outlets by the present sales force or whether it should be introduced by a group of specialized missionary sales representatives who will devote their entire efforts to introduction of the line.

You have applied for a position with Jackson Paint, and the sales manager promises to give you the job if you can come up with some recommendations on the pros and cons of using the methods described above.

Questions

1. What are the advantages and disadvantages of each method?
2. What are some other possible methods of introducing the new products?
3. What is your recommendation?

Case 2–2   The Atlanta Outing Company

The Atlanta Outing Company has had considerable success in merchandising thermos bottles, picnic jugs, insulated picnic boxes, and insulated picnic bags.

Sales representatives are expected to perform a variety of jobs. Calls are made on retail drug, hardware, automotive, and grocery outlets.

Recently the Atlanta Outing Company decided to interview at college and university placement bureaus to recruit sales representatives. In arranging an interview date with a placement office, the company was informed it would be desirable to file a copy of its job description for sales trainees along with a copy of the personal requirements for the sales job. The sales executive for the Atlanta Outing

Company forwarded the following job description to placement officers.

Questions

1. Prepare a statement of the personal requirements to fit the job description. This statement will accompany the job description to be forwarded to college placement officers. Identify each personal requirement (such as age) that you believe is important and write a paragraph explaining each requirement.
2. Will the Atlanta Outing Company succeed in recruiting college or university graduates? Why?
3. List 8 or 10 factors that are important to you when selecting a career job. Arrange the factors in order of importance.

Job Description: Merchandising-Sales Trainees

Field trainee merchandising-sales representative for the Atlanta Outing Company.

After three weeks of training to provide company background, general policies, product knowledge, marketing information, sales procedures, and practices, the sales representative will be assigned to his or her home area, which will be the headquarters city for the divisional supervisor (New York, Pittsburgh, Atlanta, Chicago, Dallas, San Francisco).

Fifty percent of the trainees' time will be spent making merchandising calls on retail stores in the drug, hardware, automotive, department, and grocery fields. During such calls the representative will be obtaining survey information about the distribution, pricing, and product acceptance of our products, as well as those of competitors; building effective counter and window displays of our products out of stock; establishing sales tests for new products and/or packaging; where possible, selling replacement turnovers orders for handling through local distributors.

Twenty-five percent of the trainees' time will be devoted to assignments by the divisional supervisor. These assignments will include checking prospective accounts; inspecting defective merchandise for large customers; assisting the supervisor at dealer trade shows; traveling with the supervisor a minimum of one day per month to observe sales activities in all types of accounts to learn as much as possible about distribution, merchandising, advertising, and selling of our products.

Fifteen percent of the trainees' time will be spent on market and consumer research projects, as directed by the home office. This will include trade and consumer interviewing to obtain information on new products, marketing, and distribution problems.

After proving their aptitude and ability to handle the above activities, the trainees will devote 10 percent of their time to servicing and selling smaller distributor accounts, as assigned by the divisional supervisor.

Approximately 90 percent of all work will be accomplished within the metropolitan trading area of the trainees' home location. Ten percent will be accomplished in smaller towns within a radius of 100 miles. When trainees are working outlying sections, a supervisor's car will be used and full expenses paid.

Compensation will be on a straight-salary basis, commensurate with background, education, and future potential offered. Out-of-pocket business expenses will be fully paid. No company car will be provided.

SELECTED REFERENCES

Buzzotta, V. R., and R. E. Lefton. "What Makes a Sales Winner?" *Training and Development Journal,* November 1981, pp. 70–77.

Coleman, Daniel. "The New Competency Tests: Matching the Right People to the Right Jobs." *Psychology Today,* January 1981, pp. 35–46.

Dubinsky, Alan J., and William A. Staples. "Are Industrial Salespeople Buyer Oriented?" *Journal of Personal Selling and Sales Management,* Fall 1981, pp. 12–19.

Greenberg, Herbert, and Jeanne Greenberg. "The Personality of a Top Salesperson." *Nation's Business,* December 1983, pp. 30–31.

McManon, Larry. "Taking the Sting out of Selling." *Sloan Management Review,* Fall 1981, pp. 3–14.

McMurray, R. N. "The Mystique of Super-Salesmanship." *Harvard Business Review,* March–April 1961, pp. 57–66.

Moine, Donald J. "Going for the Gold in the Selling Game." *Psychology Today,* March 1984, pp. 37–44.

Moncrief, William C. "Selling Activities and Sales Position Taxonomies for Industrial Salesforces." *Journal of Marketing Research,* August 1986, pp. 261–70.

Newton, Derek A. "Get the Most out of Your Sales Force." *Harvard Business Review,* September–October 1969, pp. 130–43.

"PA's Examine the People Who Sell to Men." *Sales & Marketing Management,* November 11, 1985, pp. 38–41.

Weitz, Barton A. "Effectiveness in Sales Interactions: A Contingency Approach." *Journal of Marketing,* Winter 1981, pp. 85–103.

3 Legal and Social-Ethical Responsibilities of the Salesperson

Some questions answered in this chapter are:

- Why is there an increasing concern for legal and ethical issues in selling?
- What laws govern the behavior of salespeople?
- Can verbal statements made by salespeople be legally binding?
- Why do salespeople need to develop their own code of ethical behavior?
- What ethical responsibilities do salespeople have to themselves, their customers, and their companies?
- Do salespeople have any ethical responsibilities to their competitors?
- Will ethics get in the way of the successful salesperson?

In the last 10 years, international and domestic bribery and mortality in business and government have been common news topics. Business activities have been investigated by the Federal Trade Commission, the Securities and Exchange Commission, the Justice Department, and various congressional committees.

Part of this increasing concern over legal and ethical issues is due to the changing nature of the marketplace. Products are more complex, and the terms of sale are more complicated. Fifty years ago, businesses dealt mainly with their neighbors. Now most sales are made to strangers. And growing international competition means more transactions are made between people of different cultures. Obviously, there is far more chance for honest differences of opinion.

Changes in business practices have also resulted in an increased attention to ethical issues. As a result of the growth of the marketing concept, businesses are trying to establish long-term, mutually satisfying relationships with customers. It is hard to imagine how this can occur if salespeople engage in unethical practices. Salespeople cannot build customer loyalty if they use high-pressure, deceptive sales tactics.

The legal issues discussed in the first part of this chapter are concerned with things salespeople should not do. The laws and regulations define and penalize sales behaviors that are not in the best interest of society.

For most situations, there are no laws to govern behavior, but still there is some question about what is right. In such situations, philosophies of ethical and social responsibility, which are taken up in the second part of this chapter, should provide a higher standard. The Caterpillar Tractor Company's Code of World-Wide Business Conduct says: "The law is a floor. Ethical business conduct should normally exist at a level well above the minimum required by law."[1]

LEGAL ISSUES[2]

The activities of American salespeople are affected by three forms of law—statutory, administrative, and common law.

Statutory law is based on legislation passed by either the state legislatures or Congress. The main statutory laws concerning salespeople are the Uniform Commercial Code and the antitrust laws. There are also local laws and ordinances that affect door-to-door salespeople.

Administrative laws are set by city, county, state, and federal regulatory agencies. The Federal Trade Commission is the most active agency in developing administrative laws that concern salespeople. The Securities and Exchange Commission regulates stockbrokers, while the Food and Drug Administration regulates pharmaceutical salespeople.

Finally, common law grows out of court decisions. Precedents set by these decisions fill in the gaps where no law exists.

Uniform Commercial Code

The Uniform Commercial Code (UCC)[3] is the legal guide to commercial practice in the United States. The code was drafted in 1952 when the high level of interstate commerce necessitated uniform business laws across the states. The final version appeared in 1958. The UCC has been adopted

---

[1]Fred T. Allen, "Corporate Morality: Is the Price Too High?" *The Wall Street Journal,* October 17, 1975, pp. 1, 17.

[2]Some material from C. Robert Patty, *Managing Salespeople* (Reston, Va.: Reston Publishing, 1979), was used in developing this section.

[3]Len Young Smith and G. Gale Robertson, *Business Law—Uniform Commercial Code,* 3rd ed. (St. Paul, Minn.: West Publishing, 1971).

by all the states except Louisiana. Some specific provisions from Section 2 of the code are discussed below.

Agency   An agent is a person who acts in place of his or her company. Typically, salespeople are authorized agents of their company. This authorization to represent the company does not have to be in writing. A salesperson is a spokesperson and a legal representative because the company knowingly and without objection allows the salesperson to act as its agent.

Sales versus a Contract to Sell   The UCC defines a sale as "the transfer of title to goods by the seller to the buyer for a consideration known as the price."[4] Thus, a sale is made only when title passes from the seller to the buyer.

A sale is different from a contract to sell. Anytime a salesperson makes an offer and receives an unqualified acceptance, there is a contract. The UCC also distinguishes between an offer and an invitation to negotiate. A sales presentation is usually considered to be an invitation to negotiate. However, if a salesperson quotes specific terms and the customer accepts, the contract may be binding.

Oral versus Written Agreements   Oral agreements between a salesperson and a customer are as binding as written agreements unless the Statute of Frauds applies. The Statute of Frauds, adopted by the English Parliament in 1677, describes the types of contracts that are enforceable only if they are written. Similar statutes have been adopted by individual states. Written agreements are normally required for sales over $500.

In general, sales agreements should be in writing. But, salespeople must be careful when signing agreements because they are the legal representatives of their companies.

Obligations and Performance   When the terms of a contract are agreed on, the salesperson and the customer must perform according to those terms. Performance must be in "good faith." This means both parties must perform according to commonly accepted industry practices. Even if the salesperson misrepresents the product, his or her company has to meet the terms of the contract.

Title and Risk of Loss   A sale is not completed until title passes from the seller to the buyer. The question of title is most important when goods are shipped to the seller. If goods are shipped FOB (free on board) destination, the seller has title until the goods are received at the destination.

---

[4]Ibid., p. 497.

Any loss or damage during transportation is the responsibility of the seller. The buyer assumes this responsibility and risk if goods are shipped FOB factory. Similarly, the UCC is explicit in defining when title passes for goods shipped COD and for goods sold on approval or consignment.

Warranties and Guaranties   A warranty is an assurance by the seller that the goods will perform as represented. Sometimes a warranty is referred to as a guaranty. The UCC distinguishes between two types of warranties—expressed and implied. An expressed warranty is an oral or written statement by the seller. An implied warranty is not actually stated but is an obligation imposed by law. For example, if products are sold using oral or written descriptions rather than samples, there is an implied warranty that the products are of average quality. There is also an implied warranty that products purchased from a seller are appropriate for the purposes stated by the buyer.

Problems with warranties often arise when selling to a reseller. The ultimate user, the reseller's customer, may complain to the reseller. The reseller, in turn, tries to shift the blame to manufacturer. Salespeople often have to investigate and resolve these problems.

Legal Restrictions on Trade Selling[5]

The Sherman Antitrust Act of 1890, the Clayton Act of 1914, the Federal Trade Commission Act of 1914, and the Robinson-Patman Act of 1936 prohibit unfair business practices that may lessen competition. The federal laws and court decisions that interpret these laws define illegal business practices. Most of the unfair practices described in this section arise when salespeople are selling to the trade—wholesalers and retailers. Figure 3–1 lists rules for avoiding legal problems. Perhaps the most important is the last rule. If in doubt, talk to the company lawyer.

Exclusive Arrangements   An exclusive arrangement is a requirement by a seller that the buyer (a wholesaler or retailer) only resell its products and not resell products offered by competitors. Exclusive arrangements are legal under some circumstances and illegal under others. When the seller's product has a very high market share or the reseller has a very high market share in an area, exclusive arrangements will reduce competition and are probably illegal. However, exclusive arrangements are usually legal when there is significant competition for the seller's product.

Interference with Competitors   Some ways in which a salesperson can interfere unfairly with a competitor's business are:

---

[5]See Louis W. Stern and Adel I. El-Ansary, *Marketing Channels,* 2nd ed. (Englewood Cliffs, N.J.: Prentice-Hall, 1982), pp. 364–99.

FIGURE 3–1
Rules Related to
Antitrust Laws

1. Don't discuss with customers the price your company will charge others.
2. Don't attend meetings with competitors (including trade association gatherings) at which pricing is discussed. If you find yourself in such a session, walk out.
3. Don't give favored treatment to your own subsidiaries and affiliates.
4. Don't enter into agreements or gentlemen's understandings on discounts, terms, or conditions of sale; profits or profit margins; shares of the market; bids or the intent to bid; rejection or termination of customers; sales territories; or markets.
5. Don't use one product as bait for selling another.
6. Don't require a customer to buy a product only from you.
7. Don't forget to consider state antitrust laws as well as the federal statutes.
8. Don't disparage a competitor's product unless you have specific proof that your statements are true. This is an unfair method of competition.
9. Don't make either sales or purchases conditional on the other party making reciprocal purchases from or sales to your company.
10. Don't hesitate to consult with a company lawyer if you have any doubt about the legality of a practice. Antitrust laws are wide ranging and subject to changing interpretations.

Source: Reprinted from the January 27, 1975, issue of *Business Week* by special permission, McGraw-Hill, Inc.

1. Trying to get a competitor's customer to break a contract.
2. Confusing market research studies by buying stock from a store.
3. Tampering with a competitor's merchandise.

Tie-In Contracts   A tie-in occurs when a buyer is required to purchase a product in order to purchase another product. For example, a customer who wants to buy a piece of machinery can be required to buy supplies needed to operate the machinery or a distributor who wants to stock a product can be required to carry the seller's full line of products only if it can be shown that such a policy does not reduce competition. Tie-in contracts are legal only under limited conditions, such as when two products are made to be used together and one product will not function properly without the other. Tie-ins are also legal when a company's reputation depends on the proper functioning of some equipment, so a service contract can be tied into sale of the equipment.

Reciprocity   The concept of reciprocity—"you scratch my back and I'll scratch your back"—is discussed in more detail in Chapter 15. In general, reciprocity agreements are illegal only if one company forces another company to join in the agreement. Reciprocity is legal when both parties mutually consent to the agreement.

Resale Price Maintenance   At one time it was legal for companies to establish a minimum price below which their distributors and retailers could not resell their products. Now, all forms of price fixing—setting either a minimum or maximum price—are illegal. However, some states still have laws that prevent a reseller from selling below its costs.

Conspiracy and Collusion   It is illegal for competitors to make an agreement that reduces competition by setting prices or dividing territories. Thus, two competing salespeople cannot agree to divide a territory.

Conspiracy covers an agreement made before the sale; collusion relates to the sale itself. An example of collusion would be two car dealers agreeing not to discount prices on certain models.

Refusal to Deal   Sellers can select their retailers and distributors based on their judgment. They can also announce, in advance, the circumstances under which they refuse to sell to dealers.

Incentives to Reseller's Employees   One sales practice considered unfair is providing special incentives to induce a reseller's salespeople to push products. For example, salespeople for a cosmetic manufacturer may give cosmetics salespeople in department stores commissions based on sales of their products. Such special incentives are called "spiffs," or push money. They are legal only if the employer of the salespeople is aware the incentives are being offered. And the same incentives must be offered to salespeople working for all competing resellers.

Commercial Bribery   Kickbacks, or commercial bribery, is the practice of paying a customer's employee to purchase from the payer. This practice is considered unfair competition. In one case, 30 to 40 salespeople and 6 managers were suspended for 15 days because they kicked back liquor to relatives.[6] However, it is often hard to tell a legitimate business gift from a bribe. Is a $15 bottle of liquor to a $5,000-a-year customer a gift or a bribe?

Fraud and Misrepresentation   The Federal Trade Commission Act states it is illegal to misrepresent products. Fraud or willful misrepresentation does not have to be shown. Misrepresentation of significant facts can enable the customer to nullify a contract and even sue for damages.

---

[6]"Punishing Salesmen for Kickbacks," *Sales & Marketing Management*, April 11, 1977, p. 12.

However, the concept of permissible puffery makes it difficult to determine what misrepresentation is. *Permissible puffery* is defined as an expression of mere opinion by the salesperson. It does not purport to be a representation of fact.

Price Discrimination   The Robinson-Patman Act was passed because of considerable pressure exerted by independent wholesale and retail groups for additional protection against chain stores' aggressive merchandising tactics.

The major objective of the act is to forbid price discrimination in interstate commerce that will injure competition. The act does not apply to sales within a state. But most states have passed similar laws that apply to intrastate sales. Other types of sales not covered by the Robinson-Patman Act include the following: sales in which price differentials do not prevent competition or injure competitors of the seller, the buyer, or customers of the buyer; and sales made to special buyers such as governmental units, exporters, and nonprofit institutions (for example, schools, hospitals, churches, and cooperatives).

Although the Robinson-Patman Act forbids price discrimination, it does not describe in detail what price discrimination is. But a number of court decisions have made it clear that illegal discrimination exists when a seller gives unjustified special price or discount concessions or special services to some customers and not to others. To justify a special price or discount, the seller must be able to prove that price differentials are the result of (1) differences in the cost of manufacture, sale, or delivery; (2) changes in the quality or nature of the product or in market conditions; or (3) an attempt to meet equally low prices of competitors.

Because of the Robinson-Patman Act, salespeople must treat all their customers the same. If they offer a price discount or special service to one customer, they must offer it to all customers. But different prices can be charged if the cost of doing business with the customer is different. For example, a customer who buys in large volume can be charged a lower price than a low-volume customer if the manufacturing and shipping costs for the high-volume customer are lower.

The Robinson-Patman Act also prohibits payment of any special allowances to a dealer unless the allowances are made available to other competing dealers. However, allowances can be offered to all retailers in one region of the United States, but not offered to retailers in other regions, because typically retailers only compete within regions.

Legal Issues
Related to
Direct Selling

The focus of efforts to legislate or regulate marketing practices is shifting. In the first half of this century, efforts were directed toward protecting competition, assuming that keen competition would improve consumer welfare. Now government activity is focusing on protecting consumers

Door-to-door
solicitations for
charity are also
regulated by local
ordinances.

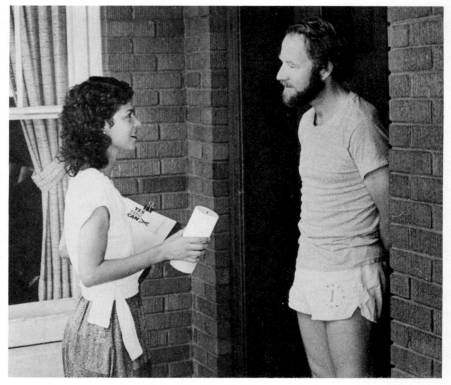

S. A. de Jesus

directly. Some laws regulating the behavior of salespeople who deal directly with consumers in stores and door to door are discussed in this
section.

Local Ordinances   In many metropolitan areas, municipal ordinances restrict the activities of door-to-door salespeople. These ordinances are
often called *Green River ordinances* because the first legislation of this
kind was passed in Green River, Wyoming, in 1933.

According to this first ordinance, it was illegal to solicit door to door
without the householder's prior permission. Since then, ordinances have
been passed restricting phone solicitations; the time of day when solicitations can be made; solicitation on holidays; and solicitation at homes
that post ''No Soliciting'' signs.

State constitutional provisions, state laws, local ordinances, and state
court decisions related to door-to-door selling vary widely. Salespeople
should check the local ordinances of the city where they plan to sell.

Doorstep Identification   A common complaint against direct salespeople is they use deceptive or misleading tactics to get in the door. Salespeople may say they are conducting a survey, taking a poll, or giving away merchandise to influential citizens.

A number of states have passed laws requiring salespeople to identify the purpose of their call right away. Some laws even require them to hand the prospect a card with the name of the salesperson and the company.

Cooling Off   In reaction to public dissatisfaction with the tactics used in direct selling, the Federal Trade Commission and most of the state legislatures have adopted "cooling-off" rules. The basic purpose of these rules is to allow buyers to review the decisions they made during a sales presentation in their homes. These rules state that a notice of cancellation must be given to the buyer. A sale can be canceled by a written notice mailed to the seller within three business days after the transaction. The FTC regulation requires that the information in Figure 3–2 be included on the first page or next to the signature of any contracts.

Cooling-off rules apply only to retail sales calls made outside the seller's regular place of business. Many statutes exempt sales under $25.[7]

Most new salespeople just want to make sales calls. They are quite naive about the legal complexities of their jobs.

Even though there are many legal considerations, few salespeople say or do things that result in a court suit. A salesperson is not expected to know the fine points of the law. Clearly, salespeople should never set themselves up as experts in legal issues. Yet it is important for a salesperson to understand the issues that might arise and to know when to seek legal advice.

ETHICAL AND SOCIAL RESPONSIBILITY

Salespeople are often exposed to situations where the appropriate behavior is unclear. For example:

> Should you sell cigarettes or alcoholic beverages if you think these products are health hazards?
>
> What should you do if a customer asks for free tickets to a basketball game?
>
> Should you tell a good customer how much and which type of material a competitor is ordering?
>
> Is it all right to use high-pressure, manipulative tactics if you know your product is best for the customer's need?

---

[7]For an evaluation of the effects of the cooling-off rule, see W. L. Shanklin and H. G. King, "Evaluating the FTC Cooling-off Rule," *Journal of Consumer Affairs,* Winter 1977, pp. 101–6.

FIGURE 3–2
Cooling-Off
Regulations

You, the buyer, may cancel this transaction at any time prior to midnight of the third business day after the date of this transaction. See the attached notice of cancellation form for an explanation of this right.

The "attached notice of cancellation" form must read as follows:

Notice of cancellation
(enter date of transaction)
_____
(date)

You may cancel this transaction, without any penalty or obligation, within three business days from the above date.

If you cancel, any property traded in, any payments made by you under the contract or sale and any negotiable instrument executed by you will be returned within ten business days following receipt by the seller of your cancellation notice, and any security interest arising out of the transaction will be canceled.

If you cancel, you must make available to the seller at your residence, in substantially as good condition as when received, any goods delivered to you under the contract or sale; or you may if you wish, comply with the instructions of the seller regarding the return shipment of the goods at the seller's expense and risk. If you do make the goods available to the seller and the seller does not pick them up within 20 days of the date of your notice of cancellation, you may retain or dispose of the goods without any further obligation. If you fail to make the goods available to the seller, or if you agree to return the goods to the seller and fail to do so, then you remain liable for performance of all obligations under the contract.

To cancel this transaction, mail or deliver a signed and dated copy of this cancellation notice or any other written notice, or send a telegram, to *(Name of seller)* at *(address of seller's place of business)*, no later than midnight of _____
(date)

I hereby cancel this transaction.
_____
(date)

                                        _____
                                        (buyer's signature)

Note: This statement must appear on the first page of the contract or on the receipt.

Should you put the cost of a hotel room on your expense account even though you stayed at a friend's house during your business trip?

Should you sell a product to a customer even if you know there are better products for the application?

Is it ethical to tell a customer the bad points about a competitor's product?

If your supervisor suggests that you pad your expense account to make some extra money, should you do it?

Should you give preferential treatment to some customers?

Businesses try to
establish long-term,
mutually satisfying
relationships with
customers.

Marc PoKempner/Click, Chicago

Should you tell a customer about a problem with your
product even if the customer doesn't ask about it?

While laws often provide guides for conduct, many situations are not
covered by the legal code. These issues should be covered by the salesperson's own ethics.

The term *ethics* is easy to define but hard to relate to everyday events.
Ethics is "the principles of conduct governing an individual or group."
But determining those principles is difficult because what one person
thinks is right, someone else may consider wrong. Also, the principles
change over time. Some years ago advertising by doctors and lawyers
was thought to be a breach of professional ethics. Today it is accepted
and common.

Even though there are no absolute standards, salespeople need to develop their own code of ethics. If they have no clear idea of right and
wrong, their companies and customers cannot trust or depend on them.
And they will affect their own self-image and personal satisfaction.

Salespeople also need a sense of social responsibility. Ethics and social
responsibility are not the same. Ethics are the individual's concepts of
what is right and wrong. Social responsibility refers to the individual's
obligations to society in general. For example, some salespeople believe
it is unethical to offer discounts indiscriminately because their employers
trust them to get the highest price possible. But it might be argued that

offering price discounts whenever possible is socially responsible since this makes products less expensive to society.

Social responsibility and ethics are important for salespeople. Since salespeople have a lot of freedom on the job, they do not have help readily available to guide their behavior. They have to rely on their own standards and their own interpretations of social standards. Some factors to consider in developing such standards are discussed in this section.

Your Personal Philosophy

Social-ethical responsibilities in the marketplace have their birth in the personal philosophy of each salesperson. His or her behavior is directly related to personal beliefs, habits, and attitudes. No matter how many "codes of ethics" are developed by trade associations and professional organizations, high ethical standards will not be achieved unless each salesperson bases his or her behavior on a sound personal philosophy. That philosophy should include a priority of responsibilities that places the interests of the company above self-interest and the interests of society above the interests of the company. In Selling Scenario 3–1, a senior vice president of sales and merchandising recalls a test of his integrity as a young sales manager.

The personal philosophies of salespeople are built on specific social and ethical responsibilities to (1) themselves, (2) their customers, (3) their competitors, and (4) their company. Each of these areas is discussed below.

Your Responsibilities to Yourself

The salesperson's first duty is to abide by his or her own ethical standards. During selling interactions, salespeople are often tempted to act against their own standard of conduct. The pressure to make a sale may be so great that the salesperson considers being dishonest in order to close a sale.

Compromising on ethical standards to achieve short-term gains can have adverse effects in the long run. First, salespeople who compromise their principles lose self-respect and confidence in their own ability. They begin to think they can make sales only if they are dishonest. Second, a short-term compromise makes it hard to develop a good reputation with customers. Once customers know a salesperson is untruthful, they will hesitate to deal with the same person again. They may even tell their friends in other companies.

A salesperson's responsibility begins when he or she selects a company. Salespeople should not work for companies whose products conflict with their own standards. Before taking a sales job, a person should also investigate the company's procedures and selling techniques. Many companies have drawn up ethical policies for their salespeople. (See Figure 3–3 for an outline of the ethical policy of Merck Sharp & Dohme.) These policies should be kept in mind when choosing an employer.

Selling Scenario 3–1

MAINTAINING YOUR INTEGRITY

 Alan Lesk, senior vice president, sales and merchandising for Maidenform, recounts his most unforgettable sales call:

It was my first call as a district manager in Washington, D.C., in 1970. One of the major department stores there was not doing a lot for business with Maidenform, and we were looking to get some more penetration in the market. Surprisingly, the sale took only two sales calls.

The first person I approached was a buyer. He was completely uncooperative. On the way out of the store, I popped my head into his boss's office and we set up a meeting with some higher level executives later in the week.

So there I was, a young kid facing a committee of nine tough executives, and I had to make my presentation. I was in the middle of my pitch when the executive vice president stopped me. He told me this was going to be a big problem, about $500,000, and

asked me point-blank, how much of a rebate I was willing to give him to do business with the store, over and above the normal things like co-op ad money. He was actually asking me for money under the table!

I had to make a decision fast. I stood up and said, "If this is what it takes to do business here, I don't want anything to do with it." I then turned to walk out the door, and the guy started cracking up. I guess he was just testing me to see what lengths I'd go to in order to get my sales program into the store.

This one incident taught me some very important things: You can't compromise your integrity, and you can't let people intimidate you. But most important, don't lose your sense of humor. Needless to say, we got the program into the store, and today, we do more than $2 million worth of business a year with it.

Source: Reprinted from "Strange Tales of Sales," *Sales & Marketing Management,* June 3, 1985, p. 46.

Your Relations with Your Customers

Recently a wave of "consumerism" has swept the country. It is evident at all levels of government and business, including the White House; federal, state, and local governmental bodies; trade associations; and private companies.

Some businesses view consumerism as a threat to the free enterprise system. Others have accepted this new movement as a challenge to do a better job.[8] More and more companies are forming consumer advisory panels to consider and take appropriate action on legitimate consumer

[8]See Frederick E. Webster, Jr., "Does Business Misunderstand Consumerism," *Harvard Business Review,* September–October 1973, pp. 89–97.

FIGURE 3–3
Example of a
Company's Ethical
Policy

Statement of Professional Responsibility of
Merck Sharp & Dohme Professional Representatives

Preamble.   The Merck Sharp & Dohme field organization strives at all times to adhere to the spirit and letter of the law. The following principles express the Merck Sharp & Dohme professional representatives' commitment to a high level of ethical conduct in the service of physicians, pharmacists, and other health care professionals.

Section 1.   Physicians, pharmacists, and other health care professionals should receive as complete and accurate information about Merck Sharp & Dohme products as is appropriate to their role in health care delivery. Professional representatives will discuss product information in strict conformance with the labeling that has been approved or permitted by the Food and Drug Administration. Physicians, pharmacists, and other health care professionals will be offered a copy of the current product circular for each product discussion initiated by the representative.

Section 2.   During product discussions, contraindications, warnings, precautions, adverse reactions, dosage, and administration, as well as advantages and usefulness, should be discussed according to the physician's knowledge of the product. Professional representatives must always provide fair balance in their communications with physicians.

Section 3.   Discussions about competitive products should not be initiated unless specific instructions are issued by the company; however, when asked, professional representatives may provide such information, limiting their statements to that information contained in the most current product circulars for the products discussed.

Section 4.   The privacy of the physician-patient-pharmacist relationship should be respected at all times. Professional representatives may not examine prescription files or other documents that provide information about an individual physician's prescribing practices.

Section 5.   Scientific or medical educational materials supplied by Merck Sharp & Dohme may be given to health professionals for information, education, or service. Professional representatives shall not, however, provide gifts, premiums, or prizes to physicians, pharmacists, medical students, or other health care professionals either as a direct or indirect offering in return for the prescribing, use, or dispensing of Merck Sharp & Dohme products.

Section 6.   Samples and complimentary packages of prescription products may be distributed in reasonable quantities to physicians authorized to prescribe drugs. Professional representatives must obtain a signed request for the drugs from the physician.

Section 7.   Proper care must be exercised at all times to keep prescription drugs out of illicit or inappropriate channels of distribution. Professional representatives are fully accountable for the security and proper disposition of all drug samples.

Section 8.   The honesty and integrity of professional representatives must not be compromised. They may not, therefore, accept compensation of any kind from any party other than Merck Sharp & Dohme for the distribution and sale of pharmaceutical products. Adherence to these standards by professional representatives supports the safe, knowledgeable, and effective use of Merck Sharp & Dohme products in the practice of medicine and pharmacy.

Source: From Statement of Professional Responsibility of Merck Sharp & Dohme Professional Representatives, January 1, 1976. Provided by Merck Sharp & Dohme.

Consumer advocates Ralph Nader and Kathleen Conkey with their 1983 report on the U.S. Postal Service. Rising consumerism is a challenge to business to do a better job.

United Press International

grievances. Salespeople and/or sales managers are often asked to serve on these panels to provide firsthand information on the needs and desires of consumers.

In order to fulfill their duties to customers, salespeople must:

1. Sincerely believe in the modern concept of selling, which includes long-term benefits to both the buyer and seller.
2. Be willing to sacrifice short-term gains for long-term mutual benefits.
3. Treat all customers alike in terms of prices and services.
4. Respect the confidences of each customer when dealing with other customers.
5. Maintain high ethical standards at all times.

Bribes, Gifts, and Entertainment   Commercial bribery generally goes beyond the normal lunch or entertainment given to purchasing agents. A

Some companies
maintain private
boxes such as this
to entertain
customers at sports
events.

United Press International

number of specific issues on customer relations are discussed in the following sections. As mentioned above, bribes and kickbacks are illegal
under FTC regulations and most state laws. In fact, the Internal Revenue
Service does not allow money paid for bribes to be deducted as a business
expense. Ethical issues are involved in determining what is a legitimate
gift and what is a bribe. To avoid these problems, many companies forbid
employees to accept gifts from suppliers. As president of Avis, Robert
Townsend sent out the following note before holidays:

> There is nothing wrong with having personal friendships with
> representatives of those companies with whom we do
> business. However, this cannot be permitted to extend to the
> giving or receiving of gifts.
>   It is therefore against our policy for any employee to
> accept from any company or representative of a supplier
> company with whom we do business any gifts of value,
> including cash, merchandise, gift certificates, weekend or
> vacation trips. This means, of course, returning any such gifts
> which may be delivered to your home or office.[9]

But many companies do not have a policy against receiving gifts. And
there are unethical employees who will accept and even solicit gifts, even
if their company has a policy against such a practice. Most sales managers
do not think such traditional gifts as lunch, dinner, or tickets to a sporting
event are unethical. But standards vary across industries. Cash, "elaborate" entertainment, vacations, and the provision of prostitutes are generally regarded as beyond the bounds of propriety. Table 3–1 shows the
results of a survey of the attitudes and policies of purchasing managers.

---

[9]Robert Townsend, *Up the Organization* (New York: Alfred A. Knopf, 1970), p. 66.

Table 3–1   Ethical Practices and Purchasing Managers

Practices	Percent Replying Definitely Yes or Probably Yes		
	An Ethical Problem?	Have Stated Policy Now?	Want a Stated Policy?
1. Acceptance from a supplier of gifts like sales promotion prizes and "purchase volume incentive bonuses."	83%	71%	89%
2. Giving a vendor information on competitors' quotations, then allowing him to requote.	77	55	86
3. Acceptance of trips, meals, or other free entertainment.	58	70	83
4. Preferential treatment of a supplier who is also a good customer.	65	45	68
5. Discrimination against a vendor whose salespeople try to deal with other company departments directly rather than go through purchasing.	35	38	62
6. Solicitation of quotations from new sources, when a market preference for existing suppliers is the norm, merely to fill a quota for bids.	23	37	59
7. To a supplier, exaggerating the seriousness of a problem in order to get a better price or some other concession.	68	28	57
8. According special treatment to a vendor who is preferred or recommended by higher management.	65	28	56
9. Attempting to avoid a cancellation charge when the cancellation involves an order already being processed by the source.	40	22	52
10. Allowing personalities—like of one sales representative or dislike of another—to enter into supplier selection.	63	24	46
11. Use of the company's buying power to obtain price or other concessions from a vendor.	22	29	46
12. To obtain a lower price or other concession, informing an existing supplier that the company may use a second source.	34	26	42
13. Seeking information about competitors by questioning suppliers.	42	19	34

Source: Reprinted by permission of the *Harvard Business Review.* Figure from "Ethical Problems of Purchasing Managers," by William Rudelius and Eugene A. Buchholz, *Harvard Business Review,* March–April 1979, pp. 8–9. Copyright © 1979 by the President and Fellows of Harvard College; all rights reserved.

A good rule is to provide limited entertainment at most. Bribery is not only poor ethics, but it can also be bad business. Lavish spending on food, drink, and entertainment is a poor substitute for high-quality selling. Sales won this way are usually short-lived. Salespeople who are known as "easy marks" may be blackmailed before being given orders. Customers who can be bribed are likely to switch their business when a better offer comes up. In a specific situation, salespeople might use this guideline: When in doubt, don't provide it.

Divulging Confidential Information   In the course of their calls, salespeople are often exposed to confidential company information (schedules, costs, patented designs and methods, etc.). Since customers are often competitors, a salesperson may be tempted to exchange such information for an order. But this can backfire. Once a salesperson gets a reputation for loose talk, no one, not even the customer who was offered the information, will trust the salesperson again. As a result, the salesperson will not get the information needed to make an effective sales presentation.

Your Relations with Competitors

Do salespeople have a responsibility to their competitors? Yes, even if it is only indirect. Making false claims about a competitor's products or sabotaging a competitor's efforts is clearly not ethical. This behavior can backfire, too. When customers detect such practices, the reputation of a salesperson and his or her company may be damaged.

Another tactic involves criticizing competitors to make the salesperson's own products look better. While there is always a temptation to downgrade competitors, this approach does not usually succeed. Customers assume that salespeople are biased, so they discount negative comments about competing products. Some customers may be offended by these comments. If they have bought those products in the past, they may regard the comments as a criticism of their own judgment.

Your Relationships to Your Company

If salespeople are true professionals, they put the interests of their company above self-interest. They may have to make short-term sacrifices at times, but in the long run, they will benefit both the company and themselves.

Salespeople are often tempted to cut corners on ethical standards. They have considerable freedom in the field, and supervision is usually thin. A few of the most common temptations include padding expense accounts, working at less than capacity, faking customer call reports, and withholding sales until a sales contest period. Some representatives agree with competing salespeople to divide a territory or to fix prices. Others hoard information that may benefit other salespeople in the company, fail to use new tools and techniques provided by the company, and get orders with lavish entertainment or gifts rather than effective selling.

Use of Expense Accounts   Most companies give their salespeople enough travel and entertainment allowances to cover their business expenses. But other companies do not always provide enough funds. In these cases, salespeople pad their expense accounts in areas covered by the company to make up for inadequate coverage in other areas. Salespeople may also

Entertaining customers at tea is a fashionable and legitimate business expense.

Steve Leonard/Click, Chicago

use their expense accounts to add to what they perceive as inadequate income.

Such use of expense accounts is unethical. If salespeople cannot live within company policies, they have only two ethical choices: (1) to persuade the company to change its compensation or expense policy, or (2) to find another job.

Controlling expenses doesn't mean the salesperson should be miserly. The following suggestions should help keep expenses in line:

1. Eliminate unnecessary car expenses by planning calls in advance.
2. When communicating with the home office, don't rely solely on the phone. An airmail letter, a night letter, or a telegram may do just as well.
3. Eat plenty of good food but not always in the most expensive restaurants.
4. Stay in clean, comfortable, and respectable hotels. But it's not necessary to have the best room in the best hotel.
5. Do a moderate amount of entertaining.
6. While on the road, maintain the same standard of living and appearance as you do at home.

Switching Jobs   A salesperson also has an ethical responsibility to an employer when changing jobs. Companies invest a lot of money training salespeople, and the salespeople are often given advance information on new products and practices. Over a period of time, salespeople also build up customer knowledge and goodwill. Some salespeople may take advantage of this situation when they accept a job with a competitor.

Proselyting has been common in the sales field for many years. But recently, more companies have taken the position that they will not try to hire away another company's salespeople.

Successful sales representatives in leading companies are prime prospects for offers from other companies trying to increase their market share. IBM, for instance, has provided a large number of sales representatives for other companies in the computer and business machines field. This is one of the prices of leadership.

A salesperson may have good reasons to change jobs. If the salesperson becomes dissatisfied with the company, he or she should discuss the reasons with a superior. Before making a change, the salesperson should give the company reasonable notice. On leaving, the salesperson should not take along confidential information, such as customer files.

SUMMARY

This chapter discusses the legal, social, and ethical responsibilities of salespeople. These responsibilities are increasing in importance because of the growth of business operations and the marketing concept.

Statutory law, such as the Uniform Commercial Code and the antitrust laws, affects the activities of salespeople. Administrative law, such as the Federal Trade Commission rulings on unfair business practices, also has an effect on these activities. But many issues that confront salespeople are not covered by law.

Salespeople need to develop their own ethical standards so they can determine what is right and wrong. If they don't have such a standard, they will lose their own self-respect and the respect of their company and customers. Strong ethics are also good business. Over the long run, salespeople with a good sense of ethics will succeed more than those who do not let ethics get in their way.

Salespeople's ethical standards should define their responsibilities to themselves and their relations with their customers, companies, and competitors. Relations with customers include a limit on entertainment costs and care not to disclose confidential information. Salespeople must be careful how they criticize the products of competitors. Finally, salespeople have to have a standard for dealing with their own companies in such matters as expense accounts and job changes.

Many companies have ethical standards that describe the behavior expected of their salespeople. In considering possible employers, salespeople should take these standards into account. But they should also develop their own standards since many situations may not be covered by the company codes.

QUESTIONS
AND
PROBLEMS

1. What features of the selling job make a salesperson more susceptible to unethical behavior?

2. What effects would relaxation of antitrust laws have on salespeople? Would this be good or bad?

3. Why do most retail stores disapprove of their buyers' receiving gifts from vendors?

4. Give an example of unethical sales behavior of which you are aware. Why do you consider this behavior unethical?

5. If you believe that a competitor's salesperson has been making unethical remarks about your product to customers, what should you do?

6. Some cities have passed ordinances prohibiting door-to-door soliciting or selling. What is your reaction to such ordinances? Under what circumstances would you favor door-to-door selling?

7. What is the best way to eliminate unethical practices in a salesperson's relationship with an employer?

8. How can a salesperson handle a buyer who wants a payoff?

9. Jim Hanson is a sales representative for a plastics manufacturer. His company has always had a policy of uniform prices for all customers. One of his customers, the Hoffman Department Store, always tries to bargain for special prices because of its large volume of purchases. Several times, Mr. Hoffman threatened to give his business to a competitor unless Jim agreed to a special price concession. Jim checked Mr. Hoffman's proposal with his sales manager, and the sales manager told him to make the concession. Jim had previously sold a similar order to another customer at a price about 10 percent higher than the Hoffman price. What responsibility, if any, does Jim have to his other customer? What are the long-term implications?

10. Assume you are a loan officer in a bank and one of your customers has a large balance in an account prior to the date when personal property taxes are due. If this balance remains at tax time, it will be subject to a sizable tax. Should the loan officer suggest that the customer withdraw the money until after tax time? This procedure would not be illegal, and the customer might consider the suggestion a service.

PROJECTS

1. Arrange to interview a local salesperson. Try to determine the following about the salesperson:
   a. Knowledge of the local, state, and federal laws that govern sales behavior.
   b. Perceived need for new laws or changes in the existing laws related to personal selling.

       c. Perceptions regarding the frequency and nature of unethical behavior by:

          (1) Customers.

          (2) Competitive salespeople.

2. Call the local Better Business Bureau, Chamber of Commerce, or Federal Trade Commission office. Ask for written or verbal descriptions of the local regulations governing the behavior of salespeople.

3. Find some recent issues of the *Journal of Marketing,* and read the section titled "Legal Developments in Marketing." Cite several legal decisions that have implications for salespeople and describe how these decisions affect sales behavior.

CASE PROBLEMS

Case 3–1   Childwear, Inc.

J. R. Fredricks received his BA in June 1980 and joined Childwear as a sales trainee. He expected to work for six to nine months as a trainee and then to be assigned to a sales territory.

Childwear was a large manufacturer of children's wear with annual sales in excess of $20 million. It employed 25 salespeople who were paid a straight commission of 6 percent. They all reported to the national sales manager, Susan Hoyt.

In November 1980, Ed Davis, the salesman covering the Atlanta territory, died suddenly. Davis was a long-time employee of Childwear and had a good reputation for his selling abilities. When news of his death reached headquarters, Hoyt asked Fredricks to take over the territory. She went on to explain that she was going on a four-week business trip to Europe and would be unable to introduce Fredricks to the territory.

During his first two weeks in the territory, Fredricks visited most of its key customers. He made several sales and

opened some new accounts. After this success, he felt confident enough to meet with the buyer for his largest account, Don Black of the Kiddie World chain. The previous year, Kiddie World had ordered $80,000 in merchandise. Fredricks arranged a dinner date with Black and was anxious to present the new spring line and to establish rapport with this key customer.

The dinner meeting went well. After some social conversation, Fredricks presented the new line and asked Black what he thought of it. Black said he was impressed but he was also considering two competitive lines. After Fredricks explained how Childwear's line was superior, Black told Fredricks that Ed Davis had given him a $500 bonus before each season. Black said, "I hope we can work together the way Ed and I did. There are a lot of good lines and a lot of good salespeople, but Ed was something special."

What would you do if you were in J. R. Fredricks' position?

Case 3–2   Evaluating Ethical Aspects of Selling Behaviors*

For each of these situations, evaluate the salesperson's action and indicate what you think the appropriate action should be:

1. A salesperson picks up an order at a customer's plant but forgets to turn it in to the order processing department. After a few weeks, the customer calls to complain about the slow delivery. The salesperson realizes the order has not been turned in and immediately submits it. Then the salesperson returns the customer's call and says the slow delivery is due to a mistake in the order processing department. The salesperson lays the blame on the order processing department because if the truth were known, future relationships with the customer might be jeopardized.

2. A company solicits bids from several suppliers of a specific electrical component. After submitting a bid for his company, the salesperson is contacted by the purchasing agent. The purchasing agent states he has been pleased with products purchased from the salesperson in the past. He wants to give this new business to the salesperson, but his bid of $1,000 is too high. The salesperson then persuades his company to lower their bid.

3. A customer gives a salesperson a suggestion. The salesperson does not turn in the idea to her company, even though the company policy manual states that all customer ideas should be submitted with the monthly expense report. Instead, the salesperson quits her job and starts her own business using the customer's suggestion.

4. A cosmetics manufacturer begins a program of providing extra incentives to retail clerks in the cosmetics department. The salespeople for the cosmetics company are instructed to contact retail clerks and offer them $1 for each item they sell from the manufacturer's product line. The company instructs the salespeople not to mention this program to the management of the retail stores.

5. Mary Wilson, a retail salesclerk, uses a sales technique that enables her to increase her sales significantly. When customers are shopping for various items, Mary takes the item they seem to favor and immediately wraps it up. She then asks the shoppers if they need anything else. Mary has found that most shoppers will buy the item that has been wrapped.

6. A salesperson selling small business computers is asked by a customer if the computer has software for an inventory control system. The salesperson states an inventory control software package is

---

*Several of these situations were suggested by examples in Ferdinand F. Mauser, *Selling: A Self-Management Approach* (New York: Harcourt Brace Jovanovich, 1977), and R. D. Nordstrom, *Introduction to Selling* (New York: Macmillan Publishing, 1981).

available as part of the standard software system that comes with each unit. The salesperson has answered the question truthfully, but has failed to mention that the inventory control software is only useful in a few special situations.

7. A business major is being considered for a sales job. During the interview, the sales manager indicates that company officials want to meet the student's husband before offering the student a job. Such a meeting is necessary because the company believes a salesperson's family can be helpful in influencing customers during social events.

8. The "custom of the trade" is that competitive firms submit bids based on specifications provided by the buyer. Then the buyer places an order with the firm offering the "lowest" bid. After a salesperson submits a bid, the purchasing agent calls the salesperson and indicates his bid is $100 too high. The buyer asks the salesperson to submit another bid at a price $100 lower.

9. A student interviews for a job. The job is attractive, but the salary is about $2,000 lower than other sales jobs. When the student tells the interviewer about the low salary, the interviewer says, "You can pick up about $50 a week by padding your expense account."

10. In Latin America, it is considered normal to give a cash payoff to customers who do a favor for a salesperson. A young, inexperienced salesperson is given the responsibility for sales in a Latin American company. When a buyer confronts the salesperson with a demand for a cash payoff in return for a large order, the salesperson complies.

SELECTED REFERENCES

Aaker, David A., and George S. Day. *Consumerism.* 3rd ed. New York: Free Press, 1981.

Brenner, Steven N., and Earl A. Molander. "Is the Ethics of Business Changing?" *Harvard Business Review,* January–February 1977, pp. 57–71.

Caywood, Clarke, and Gene R. Laczniak. "Ethics and Personal Selling: *Death of a Salesman* as an Ethical Primer." *Journal of Personal Selling and Sales Management,* August 1986, pp. 81–87.

Dubinsky, Alan J.; Eric N. Berkowitz; and William Rudelius. "Ethical Problems of Field Sales Personnel." *MSU Business Topics,* Summer 1980, pp. 11–16.

Ferrell, O. C., and K. M. Weaver. "Ethical Beliefs of Marketing Managers." *Journal of Marketing,* July 1978, pp. 69–73.

Finn, David W., and William C. Moncrief. "Salesforce Entertainment Activities." *Industrial Marketing Management,* Fall 1985, pp. 227–34.

Goodwin, James R. *Business Law: Principles, Documents, and Cases.* Homewood, Ill.: Richard D. Irwin, 1980.

Kertz, Consuelo L. "Keeping Legal." *Sales & Marketing Management,* October 11, 1982, pp. 53–55.

Levy, Michael, and Alan Dubinsky. "Identifying and Addressing Retail Salespeople's Ethical Problems: A Method and Application." *Journal of Retailing,* Spring 1983, pp. 46–66.

Sack, Steven. "The High Risk of Dirty Tricks." *Sales & Marketing Management,* November 11, 1985, pp. 56–59.

———. "Treat the Customer Right—Or Else." *Sales & Marketing Management,* January 13, 1986, pp. 63–64.

———. "Watch the Words." *Sales & Marketing Management,* July 1, 1985, pp. 56–58.

II Knowledge and Skill Required for Successful Selling

Part II provides information needed to be a successful salesperson. Chapter 4 focuses on customers—their reasons for buying and their buying process—while Chapter 5 centers around the salesperson's company and products. Chapters 6 and 7 examine communication principles used in successful selling.

4 Buyer Behavior and the Buying Process

Some questions answered in this chapter are:

- Why is it important to study buyer behavior?
- What is the difference between selling to ultimate consumers, resellers, and industrial customers?
- How do individual buyers and organizations make purchase decisions?
- What factor affects these purchase decisions?
- How much and what kind of information about customers are needed to sell effectively?

To apply the marketing concept, salespeople need to know what their customers are like and how they make purchase decisions. The more salespeople know about their customers, the better able they will be to "help the customers buy." To develop individualized selling strategies directed toward customer needs, salespeople should have a thorough knowledge of customer buying behavior.

TYPES OF BUYERS

Buyers can be grouped in many different ways. One method is to divide them into ultimate consumers, resellers, and industrial customers. This classification is useful because these groups have very different buyer behaviors and thus require different selling approaches.

Ultimate Consumers

Ultimate consumers purchase products for use by themselves or their families. Clothing, self-improvement lessons, and sports equipment are examples of products individuals consume. The decision to buy these products is generally made by the persons who will be using them. In such cases the salespeople need to be concerned only with the needs of these persons.

Many products are purchased to maintain the well-being of a household. Such products include food, shelter (purchasing or renting a house), and risk reduction (insurance). In such cases all members of the household receive the benefits of the products purchased, and several members may be involved in the purchase decision. For this reason the salesperson must consider the needs of each individual in the household.

Resellers

While consumers buy products for their own use, resellers buy products with the intention of reselling them. For example, the sportswear buyer in a department store who buys blouses from a manufacturer does not wear the blouses, but resells them to the ultimate users. Similarly, a buyer for an electronic distributor purchases electronic components for resale to manufacturers.

Resellers are an important part of a channel of distribution that stretches from the manufacturer to the ultimate users. There are many different types of resellers. Among the more common types are retailers, such as department and grocery stores, distributors, wholesalers, and jobbers.

When selling products to resellers, the salesperson must realize the reseller will buy only those products that ultimate consumers or industrial customers want to buy from them. If there is no demand for products from ultimate consumers or industrial customers, the salesperson will not be able to sell the products to the reseller. As a result, the salesperson must not only satisfy the product needs of the immediate customer, the reseller, but must also be aware of how to satisfy the product needs of the reseller's customers.

When resellers make decisions to buy products, they are usually interested in the services provided along with the products. They would like the manufacturer to help them sell the products by providing advertising assistance, training their salespeople, setting up point-of-purchase displays, and stocking the product on shelves. Often the salesperson provides these services.

Buyers can be classified as ultimate consumers, resellers, or industrial customers.

Peter Franzen

Chuck Keeler, Jr./Click, Chicago

W. A. Bladholm

Industrial Customers

Industrial customers purchase products for use in their design and production efforts, such as machinery and test equipment, and products for use as components in the manufacturer's products. Many people are involved in the typical industrial purchase decision. Engineers examine the product's technical performance; quality control people evaluate its reliability; and purchasing agents consider its price and delivery.

Industrial purchases are often very important to the company. The people who make these decisions spend a long time evaluating alternatives. Formalized decision procedures are often used. These procedures require that specific steps be taken to find and evaluate alternatives. A number of individuals must approve the final decision.

The complexity of the industrial purchase decision means a salesperson must be able to work with a wide range of people. In selling a new packaging material to a food processor, a salesperson might deal with advertising, product development, legal, production, quality control, and customer service people in the customer's company. The salesperson must know both the technical and economic benefits of the product. And salespeople must coordinate all the areas of *their own firm* to assist in making the sale. The salesperson works with engineering to provide the performance needed by the customer, with production to meet the customer's delivery needs, and with the business office to set financial terms.

FIGURE 4–1
The Buying Decision Process for Individuals

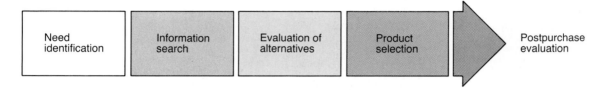

THE
DECISION
PROCESS OF
BUYERS

This section focuses on buying behavior of individuals. Multiple-person decision-making aspects are considered in the following section. However, the information on individual decision making is needed to understand industrial buying behavior because people, not companies, make purchase decisions.

People usually purchase a product only after prior thought or action. Their purchase decisions typically involve several steps. Consider a person's decision to buy a personal computer. First, the person realizes that schoolwork or office work would be easier if a computer were available. Then the person might talk to friends about their computers. A trip may be made to the library to read a *Consumer Reports* article on personal computers. Several computers might be examined in a store. Finally, the person buys one. After using the computer on some problems, the person evaluates the degree to which the computer satisfies his or her needs.

This purchasing scenario suggests that salespeople cannot understand their customers' buying behavior merely by looking at past purchasing decisions. Salespeople must know how and why their customers make purchasing decisions. What are the customers' needs? What information have the customers obtained? What stores have they visited? What products have they seen? With knowledge of these aspects of the buying process, salespeople can influence purchase decisions.

The buying process can be represented as a sequence of steps people go through in solving a buying problem.[1] The steps in this process are shown in Figure 4–1.

Need
Identification

The buying process is triggered by needs, desires, and wants that give rise to an urge or drive to take some action. People recognize that a need or want is unsatisfied when their desired level of satisfaction differs from their present level of satisfaction. Tension builds. It is reduced when the consumers act to satisfy the need.

---

[1] A complete discussion of the buying process can be found in James Bettman, *Information Processing Theory of Consumer Choice* (Reading, Mass.: Addison-Wesley Publishing, 1978).

Effective selling is based on providing what the customer needs.

But we don't *want* a poignant comment on the hopelessness of the human condition. We want a pretty picture to hang in our living room!"

From *The Wall Street Journal,* with permission of Cartoon Features Syndicate.

Types of Needs   Needs or buying motives can be classified into two types: (1) functional and (2) psychological. This classification is based on the notion that some products are purchased because of their intrinsic characteristics, while others are purchased because they satisfy psychological needs.

Functional needs are directly related to product performance. For example, a consumer with a need to decorate a wall may purchase paint and a paintbrush. The purchase is based on the expectation that these products will satisfy the need. Industrial customers generally make purchases to satisfy functional needs. When salespeople believe that functional needs are stimulating the buying process, they should stress the practical and operational aspects of their products.

Psychological needs are associated with the gratification that customers receive from purchasing or owning products. When products are purchased to satisfy psychological needs, functional product characteristics are of secondary importance. For example, a sports car may be purchased to enhance the consumer's self-image as an adventurous, free-spirited person. The functional need of providing transportation may be only indirectly related to the purchase. In this situation the salesperson might want to emphasize the use of the car by adventuresome people in auto races rather than the car's reliability and dependability.

Frequently, functional needs are referred to as *rational,* and psychological needs are termed *emotional.* These labels suggest that people who buy products to satisfy psychological needs are acting irrationally. Is it irrational for people to buy sailboats so they can socialize with members of the local sailing club? Is it irrational to buy expensive clothes if it makes you feel important? Perhaps any action taken to improve satisfaction should be regarded as rational, even if the action only increases psychological satisfaction.

In fact, people buy products to satisfy both functional and psychological needs. A person may buy a sports car to satisfy psychological needs, but the sports car will also satisfy a functional one—transportation.

The Hierarchy of Needs   Another well-known classification of needs was developed by psychologist Abraham Maslow.[2] Maslow suggested that the first and most basic needs are such physiological needs as thirst, hunger, and sleep. These needs must be satisfied for a person to survive. The second group of needs is safety and security. The third group is the need for love and belongingness—for family and friends. The fourth group is the need for esteem and status—for self-respect and the respect of others. The highest-order needs are the needs for self-actualization. These are the needs of people to achieve everything they are capable of achieving.

Maslow proposed that these groups of needs are hierarchical, as shown in Figure 4–2. This means that people are motivated to satisfy lower-order needs before they try to satisfy higher-order needs. Since physiological needs are the most basic, people will attempt to satisfy them before they attempt to satisfy safety and security needs. People are not interested in love and affection when they are hungry or have no shelter. When people have satisfied their lower-order needs, they will be motivated to satisfy the higher-order needs of self-esteem and self-actualization.

Even though needs are hierarchical, Maslow recognized that several groups of needs can motivate behavior at the same time. But the relative importance of the higher-order needs will be related to the degree of satisfaction of the lower-order needs. If the lower-order needs are largely unsatisfied, their satisfaction will be most important to the person. If the lower-order needs are largely satisfied, higher-order needs will be more important.

Maslow's theory is a useful guide for salespeople. It indicates which types of needs might be more important to specific customers. It provides some clue about what the consumer's "hot button" is.

Figure 4–3 lists some key words related to each of Maslow's needs and shows how these words can be used to sell pens.

---

[2]Abraham Maslow, *Motivation and Personality* (New York: Harper & Row, 1954).

FIGURE 4–2
Maslow's Hierarchy
of Needs

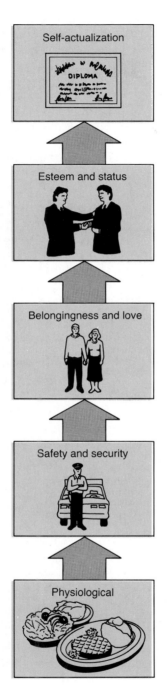

FIGURE 4–3 Sales Appeals for Pens Based on Maslow's Need Hierarchy

Need	Examples of Unsatisfied Need (To Be Avoided)	Examples of Satisfied Need (To Be Cultivated)
Physiological	Hunger Sickness Inconvenience Discomfort	Healthy Comfortable Pleasure Ease
	Examples: EASE of replacing an ink refill. Physical COMFORT when holding pen.	
Safety and security	Worry Danger Loss Fear	Guarantee Safety Assurance Stability
	Examples: Our national advertising ASSURES you that your customers will be presold on Paper Mate pens. Paper Mate GUARANTEES all damaged goods will be replaced at no cost to you.	
Belonging and love	Criticism Misunderstanding Embarrassment Rejection	Acceptance Popularity Compliment Attention
	Examples: Your customer will COMPLIMENT you on your attractive display of Paper Mate pens. Your stock of Paper Mate pens will bring a lot of ATTENTION to your store.	
Self-Esteem	Failure Inadequacy Ignorance Guilt	Pride Prestige Recognition Confidence
	Examples: The PRESTIGE image of your store will be upheld by the display of felt-tip pens. Customers have a high level of CONFIDENCE in the operation of Paper Mate pens.	
Self-Actualization	Boredom Dependence Uselessness Inhibition	Creativity Growth Openness Sensitivity
	Examples: The co-op advertising program will give you an opportunity to show your CREATIVITY With the profits you make from our pens, you will realize your GROWTH objectives.	

Conflict of Needs   Most buyers find that not all their wants and needs can be gratified. Needs compete for satisfaction. The need to be socially accepted may conflict with the need to save money. The need for recreation may conflict with the need to study. A person may have a very high-quality need, a latest-style need, and an economical-price need. It's not likely that all three needs can be satisfied by buying any one product. The buying decision will be delayed until this buyer can resolve the conflict.

Typically, buyers must make trade-offs among conflicting needs. For example, they may decide to satisfy one need and neglect another, or they may satisfy both needs in part. Trade-offs among needs are considered in the discussion of multiattribute models later in this chapter.

Recognition of Needs   Buyers must recognize an unsatisfied need before it can motivate their purchasing behavior. Often people do not realize they have unsatisfied needs. In these situations salespeople can help potential customers recognize their needs and then demonstrate how the products will satisfy those needs. Salespeople promote need recognition in two ways. First, they can give customers information about products, and the customers can use this information to identify unsatisfied needs. Second, salespeople can examine the customer's situation and demonstrate that unsatisfied needs exist.

However, salespeople and other marketers *cannot* make people buy products they do not want. The potential customer must recognize the need before any sale can be made. Salespeople can raise the buyer's level of need awareness and perhaps increase the desire to satisfy needs. But salespeople can only influence buyer behavior; they cannot control it.

Information Search

Once buyers recognize a need, they will search for ways to satisfy it. They may search for information about alternatives quickly or over a long time. When stock is low, a purchasing agent may simply look up the address of a reliable vendor used in the past. However, when faced with the need for a new vendor, the purchasing agent may begin an extensive search. A number of vendors may be asked to submit proposals and samples. Other companies purchasing from these vendors may be asked to describe their experiences with them.

Amount of Information Search   The search for information is costly. It requires time and effort. How much information is sought depends on the benefits the consumers expect to get from the information. People who have had little prior experience in using or buying a product will spend more time searching for information because they feel uneasy about making a quick decision. They will also spend more time when the purchase decisions are very important. Buyers who are making a large purchase will spend a lot of time and effort to make sure they have evaluated all the alternatives. For instance, consumers who plan to buy a car often spend a lot of time collecting information about different models. They may visit several dealers and talk with friends who own different models. On the other hand, when buying a breakfast cereal, the information search is usually limited to a quick review of the family's past favorites.

Sources of Information   Customers have two major sources of information: internal and external. Internal sources refer to information possessed by the person. This is information stored in the consumer's memory, such as the names of different brands, awareness of how members of the family or the company feel about the brands, or the person's own attitude toward the brands.

Buyers are exposed to a vast amount of information about commercial products. Each person sees over 500 advertising messages each day.[3] In addition, consumers get information about products from friends and acquaintances. One of the most important sources of consumer information is past experience with the products. Even if consumers remember only a small fraction of the information they are exposed to, they have an extensive internal information bank to help them make buying decisions.

Yet buyers may want to collect additional information for several reasons. The information stored internally may be out of date. If the consumer bought a TV set a long time ago, he or she may want to learn about the new models. He or she may also believe the internal information is not adequate. The purchase decision may be so important that additional information needs to be collected. In some industrial purchasing situations, buyers are required to get additional information. They may be required to get bids from three vendors before they can place an order.

There are a larger number of external sources of information. Some of these sources are readily available—for example, books, magazines, and department store catalogs. Industrial buyers usually have access to extensive data files. Other external sources of information may require more effort. A consumer may visit the library to look at a *Consumer Reports* issue on the product, or examine the product at several stores, or ask friends for their opinions. Similarly, industrial customers may request current information from various suppliers.

Salespeople are an important source of information for ultimate consumers, resellers, and industrial customers. Good salespeople give the prospects the exact information needed—information about how a product will satisfy their needs and the product's advantages and disadvantages. But buyers will seek information from salespeople only if they believe the salespeople are knowledgeable and trustworthy. They will not seek information from salespeople who, they believe, have little knowledge about the products they are selling or the needs of the customers. If customers think salespeople do not have their interests at heart, they will not believe what the salespeople tell them. For these reasons, salespeople are effective only if they are perceived as credible sources of information.

Evaluation of Alternatives

After collecting information about alternatives, customers review the information, evaluate the alternatives, and select the alternative that best satisfies their needs. This evaluation process can be represented by a

---

[3]Stewart Britt, Stephan Adams, and Alan Miller, "How Many Advertising Exposures per Day?" *Journal of Advertising Research,* December 1972, pp. 3–10.

Table 4–1   Information about Typewriters

Typewriter Characteristics	Brands		
	Alpha	*Beta*	*Delta*
Purchase price ($)	300	600	900
Consumer Reports reliability rating	Very good	Very good	Excellent
Weight (pounds)	9.5	15.3	16.2
Size (cubic inches)	600	975	1,100
Maximum typing speed (words per minute)	80	120	100
Appearance of type	Average	Very good	Excellent
Distance to nearest service center (miles)	20	10	2
Warranty (months)	6	12	12

multiattribute model. The model will be discussed in detail because it provides a framework for developing sales strategies.

The multiattribute model is based on the idea that buyers view a product as a collection of attributes or characteristics. Buyers evaluate a product by considering each characteristic and determining how it will help satisfy their needs. Consider Jane Stewart, a student who plans to buy a typewriter. She narrows her choice to three brands—Alpha, Beta, and Delta. Some of the information collected about these brands is shown in Table 4–1. Note that the information collected goes beyond the physical characteristics of the product to include the service provided and the warranty offered. This demonstrates that buyers consider a wide range of characteristics in evaluating a product.

Jane mentally processes the "objective" information she has collected and forms beliefs about the performance of each typewriter on a series of dimensions. Each dimension combines several objective characteristics. Purchase price, warranty, and availability of service are considered when forming a belief about economy. Her beliefs on the various dimensions are represented in Table 4–2 as ratings on a 10-point scale. Because of Alpha's low weight and small size, the student forms the belief that it is a very portable typewriter. This is represented numerically by giving Alpha the best rating—10—on portability. Beta and Delta have the same poor ratings on portability. Considering price, reliability, and warranty, the student believes Alpha to be the most economical. But Alpha is also the most difficult to service because the nearest service center is 20 miles away. These belief ratings illustrate the trade-offs that consumers must make. No one product will have the best performance on all dimensions. No one product will satisfy the consumer's needs on all dimensions. Delta is poor on economy, but its appearance is very good. Beta has a very high rating on typing speed but a low rating on portability.

Table 4–2 Beliefs about Performance of Typewriters

	Brands		
Performance Dimensions	Alpha	Beta	Delta
Economy	10	6	2
Portability	10	3	3
Typing speed	4	9	6
Appearance of typed copy	4	7	10
Ease of service	2	6	9

With this set of beliefs, how does Jane select a typewriter? Her eventual decision depends on the relationship between her beliefs about performance and her needs. Trade-offs must be made. Jane needs to consider how important each attribute is to her and the degree to which she is willing to sacrifice poor performance on one dimension for good performance on another dimension.

Product Selection

In selecting among the three typewriters, Jane forms an overall evaluation of each typewriter. This evaluation is based on how important the typewriter's performance on each dimension is in terms of satisfying her needs. Since this particular student has little money, she sees economy as the most important dimension. Portability is also important because she wants to use her typewriter in the college library and at home. She is not a good typist so typing speed is not very important to her.

Each person has a unique set of needs, and the importance of each dimension varies for different people. For example, the supervisor of a university typing pool is very interested in typing speed. The supervisor's salary and promotion are based on how fast manuscripts and papers are typed. Since spare typewriters are on hand, the speed of service is not too important. Portability is unimportant because the typewriters are never moved. Economy is also unimportant. In this school, the purchasing agent, not the typing pool supervisor, is concerned with price.

The importance a consumer places on a dimension can also be shown on a rating scale ranging from 10 for very important to 1 for very unimportant. The importance weights for the student and the supervisor are shown in Table 4–3 along with their beliefs about performance discussed above. The most important dimension for the student is economy (10 weight), and the least important is typing speed (1 weight). The supervisor places the most importance on typing speed (9 weight). Economy and portability are equally unimportant to the supervisor.

In this example, the student and the supervisor have the same beliefs about the performance of the products. They only differ in terms of their importance weights. In general, customers differ on both beliefs and importance weights.

Table 4–3   Information on Which Overall Evaluations Are Based

Dimensions	Importance Weights for:		Brand Beliefs		
	Student	Supervisor	Alpha	Beta	Delta
Economy	10	1	10	6	2
Portability	9	1	10	3	3
Typing speed	1	9	4	9	6
Appearance of typed copy	6	8	4	7	10
Ease of service	5	6	2	6	9
Supervisor's overall evaluation of each brand			100	182	193
Student's overall evaluation of each brand			228	168	158

Basis for Evaluating Products   Often the buyer's overall evaluation of a product is related to the sum of the performance beliefs weighted by the importance weights. For this reason the student's overall evaluation of Alpha would be the importance of economy times the belief about the brand's performance on economy plus the importance of portability times the brand's performance on portability, and so on. Jane's overall evaluation or score for Alpha would be:

$$
\begin{aligned}
10 \times 10 &= 100 \\
9 \times 10 &= 90 \\
1 \times 4 &= 4 \\
6 \times 4 &= 24 \\
5 \times 2 &= \underline{10} \\
&228
\end{aligned}
$$

The overall evaluations or scores for the three brands, using the student's and the supervisor's importance weights (needs), are shown at the bottom of Table 4–3. The student evaluates Alpha the highest and would probably purchase it. The supervisor prefers Beta and Delta over Alpha. Since Delta has a slightly higher evaluation, the supervisor would probably choose that brand.

In fact, only a few people go through such a mathematically involved process to make a purchase decision. If you ask people how they decided on a brand, they will *not* tell you they listed the important dimensions, wrote down their importance weights and performance beliefs, performed multiplications and additions, and finally picked the brand with the highest score. However, scores calculated this way can be good indicators of the brands buyers actually purchase. Although the multiattribute model does not describe the actual purchasing process, it is a good model of the process. Customers make choices as if they were using multiattribute models.

While consumers may not use multiattribute models in a formal way, industrial customers often do. Industrial customers often develop scores for each vendor they are considering by rating the vendor's performance on the critical dimensions and then weighting the dimensions to arrive at an overall score.

Vendor and Product Evaluations by Industrial Customers   Many organizations use a formal method to evaluate potential vendors. Typically, each vendor is rated numerically on a number of dimensions. Among the dimensions commonly used are labor situation, quality control, financial condition, plant utilization, spending on research and development, age of equipment, and delivery performance.

For example, National Can uses the following factors and weights to evaluate vendors:[4]

Factor	Weight
Competitive pricing	0.8
On-time delivery	0.9
Quality	0.9
Emergency assistance	0.9
Communications	0.4
Technical service	0.4
Cost reduction suggestions	0.5
Inventory (stocking) program	0.3

A new vendor is then rated on each factor from 0 ("absolutely unacceptable") to 5 ("excellent—top 10 percent of all suppliers"). The rating for each factor is multiplied by the factor weight to find a total score. A total score of 18 or higher qualifies a vendor as a preferred supplier; a 10–17 score is acceptable; 5–9 indicates a marginal supplier; and 0–5 is unacceptable.

Similar methods are used to evaluate alternative products and proposals. Among the most important criteria for evaluating industrial products are performance, service, and price—generally in that order of importance. However, the importance attached to a factor depends on the phase in the buying process, the type of buying decision, and the type of person who is being sold.[5]

Performance   A product is purchased only if it meets the customer's needs. A product that is lower in price but does not provide the necessary performance has no value to the customer.

---

[4]Somerby Dowst, "You Can't Rate Vendors in a Vacuum," *Purchasing,* October 10, 1979, pp. 79–84.

[5]See William A. Dempsey, "Vendor Selection and the Buying Process," *Industrial Marketing Management,* Spring 1978, pp. 257–67.

Service   Industrial customers expect service. This is particularly true in purchases of heavy equipment. Prepurchase service starts with an analysis of the customer's needs. This analysis should demonstrate to the customer that the salesperson understands the problem and is proposing a useful solution.

Postpurchase service includes installation of the equipment, training of operators, and equipment maintenance. A recent survey of purchasing agents reported that of the purchase contracts for heavy equipment 88 percent included installation requirements; 75 percent, operator training; and 38 percent, maintenance.[6]

Another aspect of service is dependability of supply. Purchasing agents must be able to count on the delivery dates quoted by a supplier. If the supplier's delivery is very late, the customer may be unable to produce its products and meet its delivery commitments. A major responsibility of the salesperson is to make sure the customer is receiving the service needed.

Price   Obviously, customers want to satisfy their needs at the lowest possible cost. They want the lowest-priced product that will meet their requirements. However, comparing the prices of alternative products is often complicated. In addition to the basic cost of the equipment, the customer must consider the cost of accessories, installation costs, freight charges, estimated maintenance costs, and operating costs, including the cost of energy.

Life-cycle costing is an important concept in industrial marketing. Using this method, the cost of the product is calculated over its useful life.[7] The salesperson can often show that a product with a higher initial cost will have a lower overall cost. An example of life-cycle costing is shown in Table 4–4.

Implications for the Salespeople   How can salespeople use multiattribute models to influence their customers? To begin with, the models indicate what information customers use to make decisions. Salespeople need the following information to influence their customers' decisions:

1. The brands customers are considering.
2. The product dimensions or characteristics customers are looking for.
3. The customers' rating of each product's performance on each dimension.
4. The weights customers attach to each dimension.

---

[6]Somerby Dowst, "Capital Buying: One Strike and You're Out," *Purchasing,* March 8, 1979, p. 59.

[7]Roger Brown, "A New Marketing Tool: Life Cycle Costing," *Industrial Marketing Management,* Summer 1979, pp. 109–13.

Table 4–4 Example of Life-Cycle Costing

	Product A	Product B
Power consumption per year	150,000 kwh	180,000 kwh
Life of machine	10 years	10 years
Initial cost	$ 35,000	$ 30,000
Power cost at $0.03/kwh for 10 years	45,000	54,000
Operating and maintenance cost at $3,000/year	30,000	30,000
Life-cycle cost	$110,000	$114,000

Note: A more thorough analysis would consider the present value of future costs and the tax implications.

With this knowledge salespeople can use several sales strategies to influence the customer's decision. First, salespeople must make sure their product is included in the brands being considered. Then they can try to change the customer's overall evaluations by altering the values in the customer's decision matrices. Some sales strategies for doing this are as follows:

1. Increasing the rating for your product.
2. Decreasing the rating for a competitive product.
3. Increasing or decreasing an importance weight.
4. Adding a new dimension.[8]

The first strategy involves altering the consumer's belief about your product's performance—increasing your product's performance rating. If you were selling the Beta typewriter to the typing pool supervisor, you could base sales strategies on the decision matrix shown in Table 4–5. From that matrix, you would realize that Delta is the main competition because its overall evaluation is closest to that of your product. Then you might try to convince the supervisor that your typewriter has greater performance on an important dimension. For example, you might show that Beta is extremely fast, so the supervisor should give it a 10 rating and not a 9. A small change in the performance belief on a dimension important to the customer will result in a large change in the customer's overall evaluation. In this case the supervisor's overall evaluation of Beta would go up 9 points. You would not spend time trying to influence the supervisor's opinion about the typewriter's economy. A 1-unit change in the performance rating on economy would change the supervisor's overall

---

[8]See Harper Boyd, Michael Ray, and Edward S. Strong, "An Attitudinal Framework for Advertising Strategy," *Journal of Marketing,* Summer 1972, pp. 27–33, for a discussion of how multiattribute attitude models can be used in developing advertising messages.

Table 4–5   Typing Pool Supervisor's Decision Matrix

Dimensions	Supervisor's Importance Weights	Supervisor's Performance Beliefs about:	
		Beta	Delta
Economy	1	6	2
Portability	1	3	3
Typing speed	9	9	6
Appearance of typed copy	8	7	10
Ease of service	6	6	9

evaluation by only 1 unit because of the low importance placed on this dimension.

Another sales strategy would be to decrease the performance rating for your competitor. This is often dangerous. Customers do not like salespeople who say bad things about the competition. They like salespeople who say good things about their own products.

Changing the customer's importance weight is still another sales strategy. You increase the importance of dimensions on which your product performs better than the competition and decrease the importance of those on which it performs worse. For example, the Beta typewriter salesperson might try to persuade the supervisor to place more importance on economy by demonstrating that more typewriters could be bought if a more economical model were purchased. If the salesperson could get the customer to increase the importance of economy by 3 units (to a weight of 4), the supervisor's overall evaluation of Beta relative to Delta would go up 18 points. Similarly, the salesperson might try to get the supervisor to place less importance on ease of servicing by emphasizing the availability of a spare typewriter. If the salesperson can reduce the importance placed on servicing, the relative evaluation of the Beta typewriter will increase.

In summary, multiattribute models indicate what salespeople should know about their customers. These models also indicate some good sales strategies, such as increasing the performance rating on important dimensions and increasing the importance of dimensions on which your product performs well.

Postpurchase Evaluation

The purchase decision process does not end once customers choose a product. Customers must still decide whether they have made a wise choice. Most consumers make their postpurchase evaluations informally. They use the product, decide whether they like it, and store this information in their memory for future use. Industrial customers often have a very formal postpurchase evaluation. The users complete a written evaluation that is distributed to other members of the organization.

After customers purchase products, they usually cannot return them even if they are dissatisfied. But dissatisfied customers can affect salespeople in other ways. They may decide not to purchase products from the same salespeople again. Such decisions might have a large effect on the performance of industrial salespeople because they usually have long, continuing relationships with their customers.

Dissatisfied customers can also tell other people (for example, friends or co-workers) not to buy the product.

Salespeople play an important role in reducing customer dissatisfaction. Part of this effort begins before the sale is made. If salespeople see that customers are fully aware of the capabilities of the products they are buying, dissatisfaction will be minimized. If customers receive reliable information before the purchase, they will achieve the level of satisfaction they expected.

Salespeople can also minimize dissatisfaction by helping people use the products they buy. Often customers become dissatisfied when they don't know how to get the most out of their purchases.

Types of Purchase Decisions

For each purchase decision, individuals generally go through the five stages in the buying process shown in Figure 4–1. However, each purchase decision is unique in terms of the time spent and the activities undertaken at each stage. The following are three types of buying situations:[9]

1. Extensive problem solving.
2. Limited or routine problem solving.
3. Automatic response.

The relative importance of the five buying stages depends on the type of buying situation.

Extensive Problem Solving   Individuals face extensive problem solving when they think their decision involves a great deal of uncertainty or risk. This usually happens when the purchase involves satisfying an important need, when the product is expensive, and when the customer has little product knowledge.

Risk is subjective. The amount of risk in a purchase decision is the amount the buyer perceives, and it may or may not be related to the risk that really exists. You as a salesperson may not believe a given decision is very risky, but if customers think so, they will act like it.

Buyers perceive many kinds of risk. Financial risks are associated with purchases of expensive products. Physical risks can be important if con-

---

[9]John Howard, *Marketing Management,* 2nd ed. (Homewood, Ill.: Richard D. Irwin, 1963).

sumers believe the products may affect their health. Social risks may develop if buyers believe the product will affect the way others think of them. Psychological risks arise when the product affects the customer's self-image.

When people perceive a purchase decision as risky, they try to reduce the level of risk with extensive problem solving. In such situations, buyers become information seekers. Since they have had no experience with the product class and know little about it, they do not have a well-defined set of alternative models to consider, or dimensions for evaluating the alternatives. Customers in such situations will usually consider a number of alternatives. The salesperson can help reduce the perceived risk by providing buyers with information and by helping them evaluate alternatives.

Limited Problem Solving   Limited problem solving describes the purchasing behavior of people who have had some prior experience with the product. They need less information. In such situations, buyers will probably buy a brand they have used before. When selling in such situations, try to reinforce the customers' buying pattern if the customers are buying your products. If they aren't, try to introduce new information to break the established pattern.

Automatic Response Behavior   When the purchasing behavior of customers is automatic, it is because they have already decided on the specific brand that best satisfies their needs. When the need arises, they automatically buy that brand. They don't seek additional information or consider new alternatives. Such decisions are usually of little importance. Advertising is the main way to market such products.

INFLUENCES ON THE BUYING PROCESS[10]

Individuals tend to behave in the same way when faced with similar circumstances. This tendency or predisposition leads to some consistency in behavior. Knowing these predispositions helps salespeople predict what their customers will want and which products they will buy. Two major factors that contribute to people's predispositions are their personal characteristics and the influence of groups they associate with.

Personal Characteristics

Each person has hundreds of characteristics. Some that are useful in determining a customer's predispositions are discussed below.

Demographic Characteristics   Demographics are vital statistics describing people, such as sex, age, marital status, number of children, race,

---

[10]For a detailed discussion of factors influencing the buying process, see William F. Wilkie, *Consumer Behavior* (Reading, Mass.: Addison-Wesley, 1985).

Every customer is different.

Michael Weisbrot/Stock, Boston

Michael Weisbrot/Stock, Boston

Cameramann International, Ltd.

Jack Spratt/The Image Works

Mike Tappin

Camerique/H. Armstrong Roberts

education, and geographic location. These characteristics indicate certain buying predispositions. For example, people in New England are predisposed to buy different clothing from what southerners buy. Consumers living in the country need cars more than people living in New York City. Married couples with young children buy life insurance more than elderly single people do.

It is relatively easy for a salesperson to determine a customer's demographic characteristics. But the relationship between these characteristics and buying tendencies is not strong. Be careful not to prejudge customers from their demographics. For example, many products traditionally purchased by men are now being purchased by women. The trend will continue as the role of women in society continues to change.

Socioeconomic Characteristics   Customers can be categorized into social classes on the basis of their income, education, and occupation. Typically, customers with higher incomes are in higher social classes. However, this is not true for certain occupations. For example, college professors and ministers have low incomes but high educational levels and high-status occupations. For this reason they are in a higher social class.

In some situations social class can be used to predict a customer's buying process. Social class is a good predictor of the types of clothing and furniture purchased. As compared to consumers in low social classes, consumers in high social classes are generally exposed to more product information and can evaluate more alternatives when making a purchase decision.

Personality   Personality is defined as a consistent set of responses individuals have to their environments.[11] For example, the cautious and methodical person will react cautiously and methodically in most situations.

The personality theory most commonly used in selling is the trait theory. It is based on the notion that each individual's personality can be described by the degree to which he or she possesses specific traits. These traits include extroversion, agreeableness, emotional stability, and conscientiousness.

Some suggest that salespeople rate buyers' various traits. However, ratings may not be useful when making a sales presentation because it is very difficult to accurately determine a customer's personality.

Buyers can be nervous and agreeable at the same time. They can have characteristics of both the extrovert and the introvert—be poorly dressed, yet have a large bank account; be pleasant, yet buy very deliberately; be

[11]See Harold Kassarjian, "Personality and Consumer Behavior: A Review," *Journal of Marketing Research,* November 1971, pp. 409–18, for a more detailed discussion of personality and consumer behavior. A thorough discussion of personality theories can be found in Walter Mischel, *Introduction to Personality,* 3rd ed. (New York: Holt, Rinehart & Winston, 1980).

cautious and suspicious when buying some products and impulsive when buying others; be procrastinators at one time and enthusiastic and confident at other times; be friendly today and disagreeable tomorrow; and be skeptics when buying products they are well acquainted with and dependent customers when buying products they know little about.

Self-concept   Customers may have several different concepts or images of themselves. Some people believe customers buy products to match their self-concept. Thus, the salesperson must realize which image or self-concept the customer is trying to match. The four types of self-concept are:

1. Real self—the customer's actual personality, thoughts, needs, and behavior patterns.
2. Self-image—the customer's perception of his or her real self.
3. Ideal self—the image the customer would like to portray to others.
4. Looking-glass image—the image the customer believes other people have of him or her.

Salespeople should direct their presentations to the customer's self-image rather than the salesperson's perception of the customer's real self.

Psychographics   Psychographics is a way to describe a person's lifestyle as it applies to his or her buying behavior.[12] These lifestyle descriptions include the consumer's activities, values, needs, interests, opinions, purchasing behavior, and personality. Since these variables are directly related to buying behavior, marketers are emphasizing psychographics more than personality profiles. Part of a psychographic profile of 1,000 purchasing managers is shown in Figure 4–4.

The Use of Individual Characteristics   The success of customer relations depends on how well the salesperson understands customers. Understanding customers is difficult because of the problems involved in placing people into exclusive categories. Personality and demographic variables supposedly simplify the salesperson's job of classifying prospective buyers. But many of these schemes make unfounded claims. Human reactions are too varied for quick, easy, and accurate classification into types.

Despite all evidence to the contrary, many still believe there are shortcuts in the process of analyzing human beings. They think facial or other

---

[12]For a complete discussion of psychographics, see William Wells, "Psychographics: A Critical Review," *Journal of Marketing Research,* May 1975, pp. 209–14. For the use of psychographics in advertising, see Peter Bernstein, "Psychographics Is Still an Issue on Madison Avenue," *Fortune,* January 16, 1978, pp. 73–75.

FIGURE 4–4
Psychographic
Profile of Purchasing
Managers

Favorite nonbusiness publications are *Time, Reader's Digest, Newsweek,* and *Sports Illustrated.*

They think the federal government is to blame for the biggest problems facing the country—inflation, oppressive taxes, unemployment.

55 percent classified themselves as conservative, while only 10 percent classified themselves as liberals.

Over 70 percent stay late or take work home occasionally or often.

Favorite leisure activities are sports followed by hunting/fishing/hiking, reading, handicrafts, and music.

70 percent are active in business and professional organizations, and 65 percent are active in their church.

In terms of reading preference, most read either fiction or history.

98 percent of the respondents were male. The typical respondent had 2.8 children, 2 cars, 2 TV sets, 2.5 grandchildren, and presently lived within 440 miles of his/her birthplace.

85 percent of the respondents had been outside the United States, and 70 percent are occasional travelers.

83 percent of the respondents still drink; however 38 percent used to smoke and gave it up.

58 percent of the purchasing agents have a college degree, and 12 percent have a master's degree.

Most purchasing managers feel that societal forces are having an adverse affect on the family. Some specific problems affecting the family unit are: availability of drugs, TV violence, stress on material values, and difficulty in finding mutual interests among family members.

Source: Somerby Dowst, "He's a Traditionalist and a Solid Citizen," *Purchasing,* April 26, 1977, pp. 49–53; and Somerby Dowst, "Lifestyle Comments Center on the Family," *Purchasing,* May 10, 1977, pp. 89–94.

body features, handwriting, or the stars will help analyze and classify character and personality. Phrenologists, physiognomists, palmists, graphologists, and astrologers earn millions of dollars each year preying on the gullible. A glance at the classified ads in a newspaper will indicate the extent of this pseudoscientific activity.

Still, companies do classify customers to acquaint their salespeople with various consumer types. Use these tools with good judgment and always be aware of their limitations. An example of how Loctite uses psychographic profiles to help salespeople develop effective presentations is described in Selling Scenario 4–1.

Group
Influences

The previous discussion focused on personal characteristics of customers. Yet people do not function independently. Each customer belongs to a number of groups. These groups include a family or living group, social clubs and organizations, business organizations, and other reference groups.

Selling Scenario 4–1

LOCTITE BASES SALES PRESENTATIONS ON PSYCHOGRAPHICS

Loctite, headquartered in Newington, Connecticut, makes adhesives and sealants for industrial markets. Even though Loctite is a leader in its market, in 1983 the company's sales did not increase. To develop a better understanding of its customers, Loctite surveyed them and developed a psychographic profile of the three types of engineers who buy Loctite products.

The survey found that design engineers consider themselves to be innovators, futuristic types, and creative problem solvers. They feel strong pressures to be "right" and not make bad decisions. Hence, they won't respond to appeals to "be innovative," which implies the risk of failure. They don't like to be told they have a "problem," because that implies they've made a mistake. Essentially, they are risk avoiders. Design engineers, therefore, like to see diagrams, charts, and graphs in communications because those create

the impression that the promoted technology is performance-proven and less risky.

In contrast, production engineers, feeling the pressure for performance, are "today oriented" and concerned about making mistakes that have a high financial cost for their companies and high personal cost for them. They, too, avoid risk.

Finally, plant maintenance engineers, who represent important targets for Loctite, consider themselves the unsung heroes of their companies. They see themselves as the fixers who keep things running with creative, expedient solutions to maintenance, repair, and overhaul problems. They're uncomfortable with the "three-piece suit" style of presentation and prefer hands-on demonstrations of products rather than diagrams or graphs explaining performance abstractions.

Source: Adapted from Bob Donath, "What Loctite Learned with Psychographic Insights," *Business Marketing*, July 1984, pp. 100–101.

Groups affect the individual's buying behavior in two ways. First, they provide information. Members of the group communicate with each other, sharing experiences in purchasing and using products. Second, groups can provide a standard of buying behavior. If buyers do not act in accord with the group's standard, the group can apply social pressure to bring their behavior into conformity.

The Family Unit   Perhaps the single most important group to influence the behavior of the individual consumer is the family unit. Often each family member has specific roles in the buying process. These roles usually vary, depending on the type of product being purchased. For example, children may influence cereal or toy purchases. In the past, men assumed a "breadwinner role" and made purchase decisions for household items. These gender distinctions are blurring now that more women are working and becoming heads of households.

Spouses may assume different roles during the buying process. In one study, couples were asked a series of questions about the relative influence each had on the purchase of cars and furniture.[13] From this study it seems that husbands have more influence in purchasing a car, while wives have more influence in purchasing furniture. Yet within a product category, the influence over different aspects of the buying process varies. When buying furniture, for example, husbands have the most influence in initiating the buying process and deciding how much to spend. Wives are most influential in selecting fabrics and colors.

It is important for salespeople to understand the roles performed by family members. This information can help direct the presentation to the appropriate family members at the appropriate stage of the buying process.

Reference Groups   The term *reference group* means a group of people an individual uses as "a point of reference" when making judgments. At one extreme, a reference group could be as small as the number of people in the individual's Bible study group. At the other, a reference group could be as large as a political party, a union, a social class, or even a culture.

Reference groups have substantial influence on consumers. For instance, a doctor may prescribe a drug recommended by physicians at a leading medical school. Reference group influence usually has the most impact on products consumed in a socially visible manner. Reference group influence is probably greater for clothing than for mouthwash.

THE ORGANIZATIONAL BUYING PROCESS

Just as individuals go through a sequence of steps in making a buying decision, there are phases in the organizational buying process. Industrial buying decisions are the result of a complex set of activities. Many people in both the salesperson's organization and the buying organization participate in such decisions. This section discusses the phases of the decision process, the types of buying decisions, and the roles of the various participants in the decisions.

Phases of the Organizational Buying Decision Process

An important study of purchasing decisions in industrial organizations defined the following eight phases in the process:

1. Recognition of a need.
2. Definition of the type of product needed.
3. Development of the detailed product specification.

---

[13]Harry Davis, "Dimensions of Marital Roles in Consumer Decision-Making," *Journal of Marketing Decision,* May 1970, pp. 168–77.

4. Search for qualified sources.
5. Acquisition and analysis of proposal.
6. Selection of a supplier.
7. Selection of an order routine.
8. Evaluation of product performance.[14]

The organizational buying process starts when someone realizes a problem can be solved by purchasing a product or service. This need-recognition phase can be initiated by either external or internal stimuli. Examples of external stimuli might include a salesperson's presentation of a new product or a display at a trade show.

When a production manager concludes his or her factory is not running efficiently, the buying process enters phase 1, as the result of an internal stimulus. A problem is recognized. But this may not lead to a purchase decision. The manager may find the inefficiency is due to poor supervision, unskilled employees, or inadequate organization of the production facility.

However, a production equipment salesperson might work with the manager to analyze the situation. This analysis might demonstrate that efficiency could be improved by purchasing some automated assembly equipment. When this occurs, the buying decision goes through phase 2. In the next phase, the salesperson helps the manager develop detailed specifications. The specifications are used by the purchasing department in phase 4. In phase 5 the salesperson works with people in his or her company to prepare a solicited proposal. Then the salesperson attempts to influence evaluation of the proposals so his or her equipment is selected in phase 6. If the equipment is selected, the salesperson, in phase 7, finalizes the delivery dates as well as terms and conditions for the order with the purchasing manager. The salesperson's job is not done when the order has been placed. The salesperson must work with the production department to make sure the equipment performs well after it arrives. This after-sale support ensures that the salesperson's equipment will get a positive evaluation in phase 8 and thus be considered a qualified source in future decisions.

The steps taken by a car manufacturer to purchase a test stand for engines are shown in Figure 4–5. Can you relate each step in the test stand purchase decision to the eight phases described above?

Types of
Organizational
Buying
Decisions

Differences in organizational buying situations exist just as do differences in individual buying decisions. There are three basic types of buying decisions—a new buy, a straight rebuy, and a modified rebuy. The salesperson must use a different sales strategy for each of these situations.

---

[14]See Patrick J. Robinson, Charles W. Faris, and Yoram Wind, *Industrial Buying and Creative Marketing* (Boston: Allyn & Bacon, 1967).

FIGURE 4–5
Steps in Purchasing an Automotive Engine Test Stand

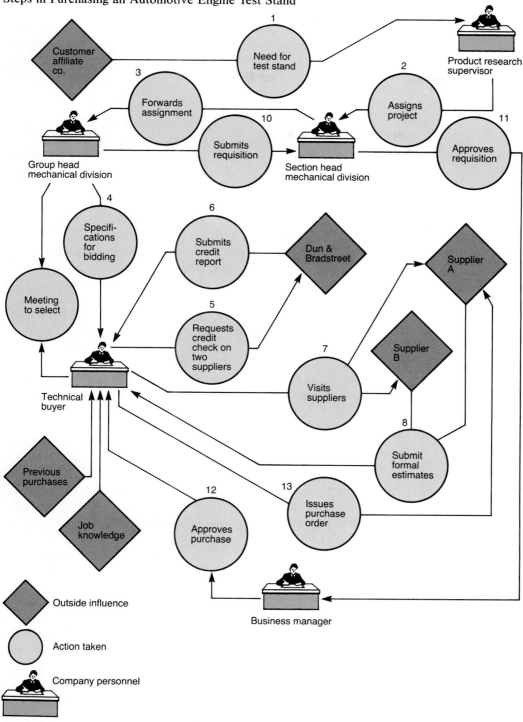

Source: Reprinted by permission of the Motor and Equipment Manufacturers Association from *Marketing Insights,* October 31, 1966, p. 18.

New Buy   A new buy occurs when the customer is purchasing a product that has not been purchased before. An example of a new buy would be a company's purchase of a small computer for automating its manual accounting system. Most purchase decisions involving heavy equipment are new buys. The initial purchases of components or even raw materials are also new buys. In such situations, the purchase decision is quite complex. The customer goes through all eight phases of the buying decision. However, the early phases are usually the most important.

In the new buy situation, the customer's knowledge is limited. Since the product has not been purchased in the past, the customer is open to suggestions. No competitor has an advantage. Such situations give the salesperson an excellent opportunity. The alert salesperson can help the customer define the characteristics of the needed product and develop the purchase specifications.

The salesperson who works with a customer on these early phases has a significant advantage over the competition. The purchase specifications can often be written so competitive products are not able to meet all the requirements at a reasonable price.

The postpurchase evaluation phase is also important in new buy situations. Since the buyers are making a new type of purchase decision, they are interested in evaluating the results of the decision.

Straight Rebuy   In the straight rebuy situation, the customer has already purchased the product a number of times. In fact, the decision may be so routine that it is computerized. When the inventory level of a part reaches a certain level, a purchase order is automatically rewritten. Typically, straight rebuy purchases are triggered by internal stimuli, such as depletion of inventory or recognition of a supplier's poor performance.

The later buying phases are most important for straight rebuy decisions. The needs are easily recognized; specifications have been developed; and qualified sources are well known. If the price and delivery are in line, the company that provided the product in the past will probably continue to get orders. The salesperson whose company is providing the product does not want the customer to consider another supplier. For this reason, the salesperson must make sure the product is delivered on time and meets all the performance specifications.

The salesperson trying to break into a straight rebuy situation faces a tough sales problem. It is hard to persuade a customer to change products when the competition is doing a satisfactory job. In such situations, the salesperson calls on the customer in the hope that the competitor will make a critical mistake. The salesperson can also try to create a modified rebuy situation by getting the customer to reassess needs.

A recent study reported that two to three people in the buying company are involved in straight rebuys, while three to seven people are involved in new buys. A straight rebuy takes from one week to seven months, while a new buy takes from seven months to five years.[15]

Modified Rebuy   In a modified rebuy situation, the customer has purchased the product in the past but is interested in obtaining new information. This situation typically occurs when the performance of a previous supplier has been unsatisfactory or when new products become available. In such situations, the salesperson needs to persuade the customer to change the purchase specifications or the list of qualified sources.

Who Makes the Organizational Buying Decisions?

Even in the smallest company, more than one person is likely to be involved in the purchase decision. The industrial salesperson needs to know the names and titles of all the people involved. Frequently, salespeople have detailed files for each customer, including a complete organization chart of the company and the roles each person plays in the decision. This section describes some of the people or groups involved in purchase decisions.

The Purchasing Agent   The person who has the formal buying position in a company is the purchasing agent or buyer. The importance of the purchasing agent in a buying decision varies with the type of decision and the company. Generally, purchasing agents are most involved in the later phases of the decision. They place the order; establish the price, delivery, and financial terms; and monitor supplier performance. Because of their involvement in the later phases, purchasing agents are more important in straight rebuy situations than in new buy situations.

However, purchasing agents may play an important role in all buying situations. They are at the hub of the activities concerning purchase decisions. They know most of the people in the company and what sales opportunities exist. In this way the purchasing agent can be a valuable source of information. The purchasing agent can also serve as an "internal salesperson" representing the salesperson's product to people in the company. Therefore, the salesperson must cultivate contacts in the purchasing department even if other people in the company have more influence over the purchase decision.

The purchasing agent may also serve as a gatekeeper. In some companies, all contacts must be made through the purchasing agent. The salespeople cannot contact a user directly. The interview has to be arranged by the purchasing agent. When the economy is depressed and sales are hard to make, salespeople are tempted to bypass the purchasing

[15]Peter Doyle, Arch G. Woodside, and Paul Mickell, "Organizations Buying in New Tasks and Rebuy Situations," *Industrial Marketing Management,* Winter 1979, pp. 7–11.

agent. One agent's comment on this practice is, "I will warn a vendor once. If he continues, we will not do any business with him."[16]

Purchasing agents are professional buyers. They see thousands of salespeople each year. They have heard a lot of sales presentations and have had many two-martini lunches. They can't be fooled easily. While they are interested in hearing about the benefits of a product, they have no time for idle conversation.

On the other hand, don't be afraid of purchasing agents. They have problems, too. It is often difficult for them to find alternative sources for a product. By proposing new ways of solving problems with products that will reduce costs or increase performance, salespeople can help purchasing agents look good to their supervisors. Purchasing agents appreciate any assistance that will help them save time or effort.

The Users   While the users typically do not make the ultimate decision, they are particularly important in the need-recognition, product-definition, and final evaluation phases. On this account the users are particularly important in new buy and modified rebuy situations. The salesperson can trigger a new buy or a reassessment of a straight rebuy by demonstrating a product's new benefits to a user.

The Influencers   In addition to purchasing agents and users, a number of other people in a company may influence the purchase decision. Engineers may develop specifications. Frequently, quality control and maintenance people determine which vendors are qualified sources. Marketing people may argue that the company's product would sell better if a particular supplier's components were used. The salesperson needs to sell such influencers.

The Decision Makers   It is often difficult to find out who makes the ultimate decision in an industrial purchase. For small, routine purchases, the purchasing agent selects the vendor and places the order. However, for important purchases, a number of people influence the selection. Moreover, several people must approve the decision and sign the purchase order.

In purchases involving new tasks, the decision is made by "creeping commitment." At each phase, small decisions are made. These small decisions result in the choice of one supplier. For example, an early decision concerning the type of equipment that will solve the problem eliminates some potential suppliers from consideration. When specifications are developed, manufacturers that can't meet all the specifications are eliminated. Some potential suppliers may be eliminated because they

---

[16]James Morgan, "Backdoor Selling Is Up—The Economy Down," *Purchasing,* November 21, 1979, pp. 65–68.

Comments by the user(s) of a product can filter back to those who make purchasing decisions and affect a new buying situation.

Monika Franzen

can't meet delivery requirements. For this reason, successful salespeople have to involve themselves in decisions made throughout the purchasing process.

Salespeople also must recognize that different people involved in the buying decision will have different needs and executive criteria. Thus, a different approach may be required to influence each person involved in the purchase decision. Figure 4–6 illustrates how people in various departments in a firm are looking for different things when evaluating a product or service.

INFORMATION NEEDED ABOUT THE BUYER

In order to practice the marketing concept, salespeople must spend a lot of time collecting information about their customers. Instead of developing tricky appeals, good salespeople try to determine what the buyer's needs are. They try to get action by appealing to customer's needs only when they have made a proper investigation and have full confidence the product will fulfill those needs. Salespeople should collect the following information about their prospects before launching into a presentation.

1. The timing of the purchase decision—the stage of the buying process the consumer is in.

FIGURE 4–6
Summary of the
Most Important
Attributes by
Department (ranked
in order of
importance)

Accounting

  1 Offers volume discounts.

  2 Regularly meets quality specifications.

  3 Is honest in dealing.

  3 Answers all communications promptly.

  5 Has competitive prices.

  5 Handles product rejections fairly.

  5 Provides needed information when requested (e.g., bids).

Production Control

  1 Can deliver quickly in an emergency.

  2 Ships products when wanted (i.e., moves up and/or pushes back deliveries if necessary).

  3 Regularly meets quality specifications.

  4 Willing to cooperate in the face of unforeseen difficulties.

  4 Helpful in emergency situations.

Purchasing

  1 Regularly meets quality specifications.

  2 Advises of potential trouble.

  2 Is honest in dealing.

  2 Provides products during times of shortages.

  5 Willing to cooperate in the face of unforeseen difficulties.

  5 Delivers when promised.

  5 Provides needed information when requested (e.g., bids).

  5 Helpful in emergency situations.

Manufacturing Engineering

  1 Delivers when promised.

  2 Is honest in dealing.

  2 Provides products during times of shortages.

  4 Regularly meets quality specifications.

  5 Can deliver quickly in an emergency.

Quality Control

  1 Regularly meets quality specifications.

  2 Is honest in dealing.

  3 Allows credit for scrap or rework.

  3 Provides products during times of shortages.

  5 Has a low percentage of rejects.

FIGURE 4–6
(*concluded*)

Special Machinery Engineering

1 Provides products during times of shortages.
2 Regularly meets quality specifications.
3 Has a low percentage of rejects.
4 Delivers when promised.
5 Is honest in dealing.

Tool Design

1 Is honest in dealing.
2 Has technical ability and knowledge.
2 Handles product rejections fairly.
2 Allows credit for scrap or rework.
2 Invoices correctly.
2 Provides products during times of shortages.
2 Answers all communications promptly.

Source: Stanley D. Sibley, "Interfacing Departments Rate Vendors," *Journal of Purchasing and Materials Management,* Summer 1978, pp. 30–38.

2. The consumer's performance beliefs—the information the consumer has collected about the product.

3. The competition—the alternatives the consumer is considering.

4. The importance of product characteristics—the consumer's needs related to the product.

5. The amount of information the customer possesses about the product and the customer's level of perceived risk in making the purchase decision.

6. Characteristics of the customer—demographics, socioeconomic characteristics, and personality traits.

7. Influences on the customer—family roles, reference groups, and business associates.

8. For industrial buying decisions, the key decision makers, the type of buying decisions, and the stage of the buying process.

WHERE AND HOW TO GET INFORMATION ABOUT THE BUYER

Knowledge about a prospect or a customer is usually obtained over a period of time. First impressions may be erroneous. The job of learning about a customer is never-ending, and the good salesperson's ability to size up a customer improves with experience.

Some sources of customer information are discussed in the following paragraphs.

Good salespeople
try to determine the
customer's needs.

Alan Carey/The Image Works

Observe and Listen

In some fields of selling, the salesperson has to gather customer information chiefly by observing the customer. Sizing up a customer may have
to be done on a trial-and-error basis. The customer may give clues, however, as to the treatment expected, and the salesperson learns to recognize
these clues through experience.

If salespeople have no opportunity to gather facts about the customer
in advance of the call, they have to observe carefully. When calling on a
retail merchant, the following clues may help in sizing up the merchant
and the business: the location and appearance of the store, the types of
merchandise and price lines displayed, the brand names featured, the
window displays, the types of salesclerks, the selling methods, and the
types of customer. In addition, some clues may be obtained by observing
the merchant's mannerisms, methods of treating the sales staff, or actions
when waiting on customers.

Given the opportunity, most people like to talk about themselves. The
buyer, being interested in need satisfaction, is likely to make some wants
known through conversation. The good salesperson listens and asks questions to bring out the buyer's motives.

In the course of conversation the prospect may say, "Our friends get
so much more satisfaction out of their new refrigerator than we do from
our old one," or, "Mr. Jones, who plays bridge with us, has a car just
like this model." From this the salesperson may be able to conclude that
pride of ownership, rivalry, or desire for recognition are dominant motives
with this buyer.

The prospect may ask, "Does this car give good gas mileage?" or, "Are repairs expensive on this model?" These questions may indicate that the buyer's dominant need is economy.

The industrial buyer who is interested primarily in dependability or service features may ask, "How long does it take to get repair parts?" or, "Where is your nearest service department?"

Effective listening is an important skill that all salespeople must develop. Listening is an important part of the overall communication process. The lore of personal selling suggests that "if a salesperson was supposed to talk more than listen, he would have two mouths and one ear."

Ask Questions

Obviously, the salesperson's opportunity to size up the buyer is enhanced by observing the buyer's reactions to questions asked. If the proper questions are directed to a purchasing agent, they should yield information on such matters as the purchasing agent's needs, ability to pay, and authority to buy. The conversation will give the salesperson an opportunity to ascertain the purchasing agent's attitude or frame of mind.

Use Records

On each call, the salesperson should attempt to gather information about the prospect or customer. These data should be recorded. After a period of time, the information accumulated will be an excellent basis for evaluating the prospect or customer.

If possible, an accurate evaluation of a customer and his or her business should be made before the sales call. At least a tentative evaluation should be made, based on facts obtained up to that point.

Data about the customer that may be useful if properly recorded are: the size and frequency of past orders, the status of the customer's credit, the preferences shown for certain price lines, the nature of the company's correspondence with the customer, the adjustments made, the habits established, and the likes, dislikes, and peculiarities evidenced. Companies usually provide their sales representatives with all of the available data on each customer.

Read Sales Manuals and Training Materials

Some companies supply their salespeople with sales manuals describing various types of customers and accounts. Such manuals are valuable because the material is usually the result of the accumulated experiences with users of the company's products. The manuals include facts about the company's customers that the salesperson could gather only through many years of experience. For example, the manuals may list the common needs of purchasing agents, government representatives, large retail merchants, and various executives of large corporations.

Large retail organizations supply materials on new merchandise and suggestions for selling it. Specific suggestions are given on how to sell various types of customers. Organized discussions may take place at regular or special department meetings. In addition, store training departments may post information sheets on employee bulletin boards.

Obtain Experience

There is probably no substitute for experience as a method for learning about people. Good salespeople are students of human nature. They observe people and their reactions whenever they can. They soon learn people's reactions are endlessly varied; but they also learn that certain habits and reaction patterns are repeated in many customers. While each selling situation is somewhat different, certain similarities will be recognized.

SUMMARY

The buying behavior for individuals and organizations is described in this chapter. A good understanding of buying behavior is essential to the practice of the marketing concept and successful selling.

Customers—ultimate consumers, resellers, and industrial customers—typically go through the following stages when making a purchase decision: (1) need identification, (2) information search, (3) evaluation of alternatives, (4) product selection, and (5) postpurchase evaluation. The buying process begins with an identification of an unsatisfied need. This need can be either functional or psychological. When the need is recognized, buyers search for information from their own experiences and from external sources. This information then is used to evaluate alternatives. The evaluation of alternatives usually involves making trade-offs among conflicting needs. On the basis of these evaluations, the customer purchases a product. However, the buying process is not over when a purchase decision has been made. The postpurchase evaluation affects subsequent purchase decisions.

Customers encounter several types of purchase decisions. Extensive problem-solving decisions arise when buyers face a high-risk decision with little prior experience. Limited problem solving describes decisions that require less information search and risk because the customer has some past experience. Automatic response behavior describes impulse purchases that typically do not involve salespeople.

The buying process is influenced by the personal characteristics of the buyer and group influences that impinge on the buyer. Personal characteristics such as demographics, personality, and psychographics are difficult for salespeople to use effectively because it is hard to determine how to classify a person. Group influences from family members and reference groups can have an important effect on the individual decision maker.

Organizations, like individuals, go through stages in making a purchase decision. The initial stages are most important for decisions on new buys involving products that have not been purchased previously. The later stages are more important for straight rebuys of products that have been purchased frequently.

Many people are involved in organizational buying decisions. While purchasing agents have a formal role in placing orders, other members of the organization are usually involved in the buying decision. The importance of the different types of people depends on the stage of the buying process and the type of buying decisions.

Successful selling requires a knowledge of the buyer's needs, the alternatives under consideration, and the people who will influence the decision. Salespeople can get this information by observing, listening, asking questions, using records, and reading sales manuals and training materials.

QUESTIONS AND PROBLEMS

1. Using Maslow's hierarchy of needs, demonstrated in Figures 4–2 and 4–3, write five statements, one for each group needs, that could be used by a salesperson to sell a $100 fishing rod.

2. Analyze in detail all the decision steps you went through the last time you purchased a suit. How do those steps correspond to the five buying stages shown in Figure 4–1?

3. List the factors people might consider when making the following decisions:
    a. Enlisting in the armed forces.
    b. Buying a videocassette recorder.
    c. Renting an apartment.
    d. Buying a calculator.
    e. Buying a personal computer.
    How would the importance placed on the factors considered in buying a house vary for different groups of consumers?

4. You are a salesperson in a large department store, working in the toy department for the holidays. A customer approaches you and says, "I'd like to buy a toy as a present for my child." What questions would you ask to help the customer reach a buying decision?

5. You have acquired the franchise to sell a portable all-stainless steel home water distiller. The suggested retail price is $135. Why would anyone want a unit that purifies water? Prepare some statements you might use to appeal to a potential buyer.

6. Assume that as a manufacturer's salesperson you are selling various types of office equipment to dealers. The dealers sell the equipment to business firms. Would you be more successful in the eyes of your firm if you stocked all your dealers to the hilt or if you helped your dealers keep the pipeline clear? Would there be a difference between the short-run and the long-run effects of these two approaches? Why? How could you as a salesperson help the dealers keep their stock moving to their business customers?

7. For what reasons might a consumer switch from a routine purchase behavior to an extensive problem-solving behavior? As a salesperson, what would you do to alter a consumer's purchase behavior if the consumer was not purchasing your product?

8. Compare the sources of product information used by industrial customers with the sources of information used by consumers. How do these sources of information and their importance differ for the two groups?

9. Should a salesperson ever try to change the way in which an individual customer makes a purchase decision? Explain.

10. Assume you are calling on a customer for the first time. You have just found out that the customer needs a product like the one you are selling. What questions would you ask in order to learn how to sell your product to the customer?

PROJECTS

1. Arrange an interview with an industrial purchasing agent. Ask the purchasing agent to describe a recent purchase decision. Analyze the decision in terms of the following factors:
    a. Was the decision a new buy, a straight rebuy, or a modified rebuy?
    b. Who besides the purchasing agent was involved in the decision?
    c. What factors were considered in evaluating the different vendors?
    d. Why was the purchase order given to the specific supplier?
    e. What role did salespeople play in the decision?

2. Talk with a salesperson about a significant sale in which he or she is now involved or has just completed. Use the material in the chapter to understand the situation—both the buying process and the selling process. Describe how that material is helpful in understanding the situation. Also, discuss the limitations of the chapter material.

3. Develop a paper on the college student market. Compare the buying habits and student characteristics of 1970 with those of the current year. Summarize the differences you find and state the implications of your findings.

CASE PROBLEMS

Case 4–1   Buying a Motor Home

Shirley and Ray White were thinking about buying a motor home for use on weekends and vacations. Both Shirley and Ray spent a lot of time on their jobs. They believed they were not spending enough time with their children, Chris and Carol. Taking family trips in the motor home would bring the whole family together. One weekend, the entire family visited a large motor-home dealer in Campbell. They approached a salesman seated in the dealer's office.

Ray: Good morning. We're interested in learning more about motor homes. Can you help us?

Salesman: You've come to the right place. We sell more motor homes than any other dealership in Arizona. I've got some paperwork to fill out on the home I just sold. I am sure we have a model for you. Why don't you walk around the lot and see what you like? Here are some brochures.

Shirley   [*walking out the door*]: He doesn't seem very interested in us.

Ray: I guess that's a soft-sell approach. Let's look at that brown and white one over there. It looks like the right size.

Carol   [*inside the third home they had looked at*]: Look. This one has a TV. That's fantastic. Dad, how does the TV work in a motor home?

Ray: I guess it works off batteries. I really don't know how you get all the appliances working when you stop overnight. I hope it's not too complicated to hook up.

Shirley: This really has everything— shower, refrigerator, stove. Looks like there's plenty of room for cooking and eating meals. How do you think the stove works?

Ray: Probably natural gas. I wonder how long a tank of natural gas lasts. I hope you don't have to fill it up all the time.

Salesman   [*entering motor home*]: Well, how do you like this one? We really have a good deal on this model. It's

usually $15,000, but it's reduced to $14,000 this month.

Shirley: Where do you sleep in this one? How many can sleep in it?

Salesman: You can squeeze in six people, I think. The bed folds down there and there. By the way, we are also giving a full tank of gas with a purchase. That's 50 gallons.

Ray: This home is really big. I bet it's difficult to drive.

Salesman: No. It's a breeze. Have you ever driven a truck?

Ray: No!

Salesman: Oh! Don't worry. You'll get used to it. By the way, this model is really economical to run. It gets 10 miles to the gallon. Most motor homes get only 8.

Ray: I just don't think we're ready for a motor home yet. I guess we'll just stay in motels on our trips.

Salesman: You really should consider this model more. You can save a lot of money on vacation with a motor home. No motel costs. Do your own cooking. No restaurants.

Ray: Well, we'll think about it. Thanks for your time.

Questions

1.   What does each member of the family want in the motor home?

2.   Did the salesman know what the family wanted?

3.   Was the salesman a good listener?

4.   What questions would you have asked if you were selling the motor home?

5.   Rewrite this interaction as it would have occurred if you were the salesperson.

Case 4–2   Indiana Steel

One of Indiana Steel's most important customers is the John Elk Company, a small manufacturer in Mason City, Iowa. Elk buys a special steel alloy in the form of preweighed forgings from the Indiana Steel Company. Elk then casts the alloy into heavy-duty moldboard plow bottoms and sells these to International Cultivator, a large tractor manufacturer.

Unfortunately for Tom Torrance, the Indiana Steel salesman who deals with the Elk Company, a competitor is offering the same forgings at a lower price than Indiana's—$17 as opposed to $19.50. Indiana's price reflects several recent reductions that have been passed on to the customer. These were made possible by technical innovations. At the present price, the profit margin for Indiana is rather low. Tom's performance is evaluated on the basis of profits, not just sales. Therefore, he cannot simply undercut the competitor's price. Furthermore, because of recent wage hikes, the price of the forgings will be increased to $21 within the next year.

Tom knows the competitor has never produced this particular alloy to these specifications before. He figures Elk will probably have to pay the competitor nearly $100,000 for the retooling and additional equipment needed to produce these forgings. Although Elk's buyer has not admitted this, he has expressed some doubts about the competitor's ability to meet the specifications. On the other hand, other materials purchased from the competitor have proved satisfactory.

Since International Cultivator is Elk's largest customer, Elk cannot afford to lose the moldboard contract. International Cultivator is developing a new 24-bottom plow, the largest ever made. In light of the large size of the moldboard contract, Torrance believes Elk may give some of the business to the new competitor, despite the risks involved.

Torrance has called Indiana Steel's vice president of marketing. The vice president OK'd a price cut to $17 if that was the only way to keep the business.

Questions

1. What should Torrance's strategy be in negotiating with Elk's buyer?
2. What factors should he keep in mind?

Case 4–3   Scents Unlimited—A Role-Playing Exercise

Background

Scents Unlimited, a 15-year-old manufacturer of perfumes and related toiletry items, is launching a new line called Kiss. Kiss represents a significant departure from the prior marketing practices of Scents Unlimited. From its highly successful inception in the mid-1960s, the company has aimed its products toward well-to-do women in the 18-to-35 age bracket. In keeping with the deluxe image of its products, Scents' prices have been higher than the industry average. In response to a recent problem of excess production capacity, Scents' management has developed the following strategy, which is also expected to expand its market and increase profits.

Kiss, the new line, is a low-priced fragrance the company is aiming at lower-to middle-income women between 25 and 50 years of age. It will be distributed exclusively in supermarkets.

Although this method of distribution is somewhat novel in the industry, the test market results were highly encouraging, and Scents Unlimited believes the decision to stock this new product will prove profitable for the supermarket.

Scents Unlimited has chosen Shoprite Markets as its sole distributor in the Midwest because Shoprite has a reputation for innovation in the retail grocery field.

Instructions for a Scents Unlimited Sales Representative Role

Your sales presentation should include the following points:

Presenting the new fragrance.

Describing the target market.

Emphasizing that the supermarket industry in general is expanding into nonfood items. The profit potential for Shoprite is great—the cost to Shoprite is $2.00 per 4-ounce bottle, and the suggested retail price is $3.95, so the markup will be nearly 100 percent, which is higher than on most supermarket items.

Shoprite will have exclusive distribution rights in the Midwest.

You will undertake a broad mass-media advertising campaign to support the launching of Kiss.

Your company will set up, stock, and service the display, which will include samples.

You will require a display area of 2 feet by 3 feet by 5 feet high.

Be prepared to handle the objections of the buyers and convince them of the benefits of adding this new item to their stock.

Instructions for Shoprite Buyers

(Instructor will provide.)

Instructions for Student Observers

After the role play is completed, the class will analyze the interaction of the role players by considering the following questions:

1. How did the seller find out the customer's needs?
2. What benefits were introduced? How?
3. How did these benefits answer the customer's needs?
4. How credible was the seller?
5. What nonverbal cues did you observe in the interaction? What was the meaning of these cues?
6. How did the seller adapt to the customer during the presentation?

SELECTED REFERENCES

Crow, Lowell E., and Jay D. Linquist. "Impact of Organizational and Buyer Characteristics on the Buying Center." *Industrial Marketing Management,* February 1985, pp. 49–58.

Kern, Richard. "Demographic Roundtable '85." *Sales & Marketing Management,* October 28, 1985, pp. 32–48.

Oh, Tai K. "Selling to the Japanese." *Nation's Business,* October 1984, pp. 36–38.

Sheth, Jagdish N. "A Model of Industrial Buyer Behavior." *Journal of Marketing,* October 1973, pp. 50–61.

Webster, Frederick E., Jr., and Yoram Wind. *Organizational Buyer Behavior.* Englewood Cliffs, N.J.: Prentice-Hall, 1972.

Weitz, Barton. "Relationship between Salesperson Performance and Understanding Customer Decision Making." *Journal of Marketing Research,* November 1978, pp. 501–10.

Wells, William. "Attitudes and Behavior: Lessons from the Needham Lifestyle Study." *Journal of Advertising Research,* February/March 1985, pp. 40–44.

Westbrook, Robert A., and William C. Black. "A Motivation-Based Shopper Typology." *Journal of Retailing,* Spring 1985, pp. 78–103.

Zeithamel, Valerie A. "The New Demographics and Market Fragmentation." *Journal of Marketing,* Summer 1985, pp. 64–75.

Zotti, Ed. "Thinking Psychographically." *Public Relations Journal,* May 1985, pp. 26–30.

5

The Company, Its Products, Competition, and Policies

Some questions answered in this chapter are:

- Why is knowledge so important?
- What specific information do salespeople need to know about their company, its products, and its policies?
- Why do salespeople need to know information about their competitors?
- Why is it important to sell benefits, not just features?
- What do salespeople need to know about pricing? Discounts? Credit?
- How can salespeople acquire the information they need?

Modern selling is based on facts. Salespeople cannot depend on fast talking, a pleasing personality, and a bag of tricks to produce profitable sales.

In addition to a thorough knowledge of customer needs and the buying process, salespeople must have factual information about the company, its products, its competition, and its policies to represent the company effectively and demonstrate how the company's products and services can benefit customers.

KNOWLEDGE
AND
SUCCESSFUL
SELLING

There is a direct relationship between sales production and the knowledge a salesperson possesses. On the basis of this knowledge, the salesperson supplies appropriate facts to customers and meets the claims of competitors. Such knowledge gives salespeople confidence and enthusiasm and helps them gain the trust and respect of their customers.

Customers
Demand Facts

Customers today demand more and more information about the products they buy. In most cases they are eager to ask advice of the salesperson. His or her statements are regarded by the buyers as those of an expert, someone with authority.

In many fields of selling there is greater competition each year. More new products appear on the market, the products are more complex, and companies are expected to supply more services of a varied nature to satisfy customer needs for information. As a result, successful salespeople must have enough information at their disposal to satisfy such demanding buyers.

Buyers Trust
Well-Informed
Salespeople

The key to successful selling is gaining the buyers' trust. By becoming a reliable source in one area, a salesperson can win acceptance in another. For example, salespeople who are able to cite facts about their company's growth or trademark are respected as individuals who "know what they're talking about." As a result, buyers will be apt to believe the salespeople's statements in other areas, such as the company's products or competitive conditions. It's not enough just to give facts about the company and its products; the customers have to be willing to *believe* what the salespeople say.

Knowledge
Develops
Personal
Confidence

In addition to making selling easier, having a thorough background of product and company information will enable salespeople to acquire confidence in themselves and their company. It will help them develop a sense of loyalty and a feeling of being a member of a team. To sustain interest in any field, a salesperson needs to have a thorough understanding of "what makes the company go" and of what company policies are. Enthusiasm and interest cannot be developed on the basis of meager information.

Salespeople must sincerely believe they have services or products that will benefit the users. Knowledge is the basis for this belief. They can have little self-confidence unless they have thoroughly explored the merits of their products or services and those of their leading competitors.

Salespeople who have prepared themselves with full knowledge of their company, its products, and competitive products do not fear competition—*they welcome it*. They know they have the answers.

The salesperson is a member of the company team.

Chicagoland Citibankers.

The best part of the Citi at your front door is the Citibanker at your front door.

• Because they live in Chicagoland, these Citibankers are committed to bringing you money center services faster and more efficiently.

• Citibankers are authorized to make substantial loan commitments—on the spot.

• Citibankers know your business—and your company. Because they're Chicagoans, they understand the distinctive character of Chicago business. And are sensitive to your company's needs.

• Citibankers use their time constructively—and yours. They appreciate the time they spend with you. It's a "get it done" type relationship.

• Citibankers will keep you informed of changes affecting your business. And help you take full advantage of the latest economic and financial conditions.

• These Chicago Citibankers are just part of an organization geared to get results—promptly. It's a service business (that's why more than 500 Citibankers live and work in the Chicago area). And Citibankers never forget it.

• The Citibankers at your front door are ready to work with your local banks to help your company expand across the country, or around the world.

Because they're local, Citibankers can deliver a full range of money center services right to your office. Including a controlled disbursement service that can get daily check clearings to you by 10AM EST.

For more information on how the Citi at your front door can help your company, call your local Citibanker.

© 1983 Citibank, N.A. Member FDIC   *200 S. Wacker Drive

CITIBANK✚CITICORP®
The Citi at your front door.

WHAT SPECIFIC INFORMATION IS NEEDED?

A salesperson needs a lot of information about his or her company, its products, and its competitors. This kind of information will vary depending on a number of factors. Among them are the kind of selling, the products themselves, the traits of the customers, and the complexity of the company. To gain a working knowledge of all these factors, salespeople in large firms may need many years of on-the-job training and sales experience. In smaller companies salespeople can expect to gain this information in an informal way over a period of time.

Company Performance and Capabilities

Growth and Development   Company histories often provide information salespeople can use in their work. Useful items in a company history might tell who founded the company as well as when, where, and for what reasons. There might be details about the size of the early plants, early experiences in financing and selling, the dates new products were added, the origin of trademarks or trade names, and people who have played an important role in the company's growth.

In many situations salespeople can secure an advantage by using facts about the company's competitive position. For example, a salesperson who can advise a buyer that the company ranks first in sales will give the buyer confidence in the company's capabilities. Let's take the case of a customer who says, "I'm satisfied with our present products. I see no reason to make a change." An effective answer might be, "Company X is a fine company. But last year our firm sold three times as many units as our nearest competitor. Customers want our products. A recent survey of the industry showed that our products were requested by trade name more than any competing products. Let me explain what this can mean to you."

Production and Service Facilities   Every salesperson needs to know about the company's plant capacity, production schedules, and other relevant data. What value do products have for customers unless the company can deliver them in the right quantity and at the right time?

Frequently a buyer will consider a company's extra services in deciding to place an order. He or she may reason, "If all brands are alike in construction and performance, what other benefits does this company offer me to buy their product?" Some companies help new dealers decide on the right location for their stores. They are prepared to help plan the store layout and select store fixtures. They may even offer to provide hiring and training programs as well as help sell the new product and maintain records. If a sales representative can say, "We have well-trained people who will call on you and service our machines," they have an important extra selling point. A company can offer its customers other services that help strengthen the sales message. It might, for example, supply advertising pieces, ship orders from its branch offices or warehouses, or carry out research on behalf of customers.

The salesperson's knowledge of specific facts about the product increases the customer's confidence in the salesperson's judgment.

Product Knowledge

A *Purchasing* magazine survey of 1,000 industrial purchasing agents found that buyers rated knowledge of the product line as the most important attribute of a good sales representative.[1] An effective salesperson needs to know how the products are made, what services are provided for the products, and how products interface with related products. Most important, he or she needs to know *how the products will satisfy buyer needs.* Selling Scenario 5–1 shows how George Beattie of American Explosives demonstrates his product knowledge to customers.

How Are Products Made?   Certain buyers may want detailed information on the manufacture of a product such as a man's suit. They may want to be informed about how the raw wool is processed and how the yarn is prepared. In addition, they may believe it helps them sell the suit to know how the fabric is woven and finished before it is made into a suit. They may be curious about the cutting, sewing, and styling of the suit. Other

[1]"The Industrial Salesman: Industrious, but Is He Believable?" *Sales Management,* January 12, 1976, p. 82.

Selling Scenario 5–1

LACK OF PRODUCT KNOWLEDGE CAN BE EXPLOSIVE

Product knowledge helps George Beattie, vice president and sales manager of American Explosives in Hayden Lake, Idaho, make sales and stay alive.

George Beattie was no stranger to danger before starting his selling career recently. His past is a colorful one, including stints in the U.S. Navy during World War II and service as a paratrooper in Korea. Out of uniform, he entered the Colorado School of Mines at age 29 and spent his years before buying his current Du Pont explosives distributorship as a mining consultant and engineer. As the mining industry shrank, troubleshooter jobs became scarce and he sought a way to stay his own man. Selling offered him that opportunity.

Now Beattie lends his expertise to miners. He spends weeks underground "shooting," or detonating, comparison blasts between his product and those of rivals. Descending as deep as 5,000 feet into the silver mine shafts with the mining crews, Beattie stays down for one or two eight-hour shifts a day. In the course of one shift, the miners first drill 1¾-inch holes, called headings, into the rock, then load them with explosives and "shoot" the charge. The shift ends as they sort through and examine the fragmentation and clear it away, called "mucking." Beattie creates a data base, tracking the breakage quality of the competitive explosive, then that of his own product, through the "drill, blast, and muck" of each shift.

"I haven't banged my head in a little while," he says, "and I've only been injured once. I was down in a mine and the rock looked dangerous to me so I ordered the crew out. I went back in to get a drill, and a 6 foot-by-6 foot slab fell on me. It snapped my neck." Co-workers pulled Beattie out, and surgery prevented paralysis. "Unfortunately," says Beattie, "that sort of accident is not uncommon."

Beattie recognizes a likeness between opening a sale and a mine. "Opening a mine is always a financial risk," he says. "There's a point you can't spare the time or money to make absolutely sure it's worth it. You think there's a good grade of ore there, but you don't always have the good answer you'd like. You start cold with a new customer the same way."

On whether his explosives expertise helps him sell his line, Beattie offers an observation on "shooters," and on his own approach. "I have a healthy respect for the explosives, but no real fear. It really is a touch," he says. "I seem to be able to feel how much powder you need for good breakage. Many blasters don't. Let me put it like this," says Beattie, "it's like the difference between a fry cook and a gourmet chef."

Source: Adapted from Mark Thalenberg, "Salesmen Live in Dangerous Territory," *Sales & Marketing Management*, June 3, 1985, pp. 55–56.

buyers of the same product would not want so many details; they may believe the company's name is enough to sell the suit.

To cite another example, the buyer of small business computers may ask for information about the microprocessor used in a certain computer. In addition, he or she may want precise details about its operating system and memory type. If the salesperson can supply answers to *specific* questions, he or she will gain the customer's respect. If a customer asks, "What type of microprocessor does this computer have," an effective response would be, "It has a 32-bit microprocessor manufactured by Intel, the biggest and most trusted maker of this component in the world." It is not enough to state, "It has a very reliable microprocessor."

What Service Is Available?   Any mechanical product will need service. People who buy stocks and bonds or life insurance expect service on their investments to take care of changing needs or shifting economic conditions. Retail dealers also expect varying amounts of service from dealer salespeople.

Purchasers of industrial equipment are vitally interested in service. Efficient servicing insures the manufacturer against costly shutdowns of production lines. A food-processing firm cannot wait for service on food machinery that is processing perishable fruits or vegetables. Nor can the farmer or the trucker afford a delay in the servicing of equipment—time lost means money lost.

In view of these facts, it is not surprising that good salespeople need to know what services their company is willing to offer customers. They also need to understand the terms and costs of such services. A company that can supply dependable, fast service certainly has the edge on its competitors.

In *Purchasing* magazine's 1978 contest to find the top salespeople, all the winners were chosen because of the unusual efforts they made to service their buyers. Here are some of the examples of services carried out by these sales representatives: "One salesperson hired a U-Haul and drove all night to keep a customer's plant running." "[He] digs into *Federal Register* to assess impact of government regulations on his accounts. Came up with uniform unloading procedure that minimizes customer's problems in unloading materials." "Supervises tests in customers' plants— even at 2:00 A.M. Went to bat for buyers to solve winter freeze-up problems."[2] A service-oriented attitude is important in salespeople; it makes it possible for them to solve buyers' problems at any hour of the day.

How Does the Product Relate to Other Products?   Product knowledge and the ability to offer service are not enough. To succeed, good sales-

---

[2]Somerby Dowst, "Top Salesmen Deliver Service, Expertise," *Purchasing*, August 23, 1978, pp. 48–50.

people often need to understand how their products work with other products. When Polaroid salespeople introduce a new type of film, they should know which cameras can use it. In addition, the salespeople ought to have information about similar products of their competitors. For example, will the new Polaroid film also work in some Kodak cameras?

Salespeople can also use information about related products to satisfy customers' needs. For example, they might be able to suggest a combination of products and services. Often salespeople help their customers obtain the financing they need to buy the new equipment. Such help is offered to make the sale; salespeople do not sell the financial service themselves.

Knowledge of Competitive Products

Salespeople need knowledge of more than just their company and its products. Since they come up against competitors in the marketplace, they have to be able to compare their own products with those of competitors.

Boat salespeople must know how their boat compares with competitors' boats for water skiing, fishing, racing, picnicking, or just cruising. They may have to compare their boat on such features as safety and construction as well as discuss the relative merits of wood, aluminum, cement, and plastics. They may also require detailed comparative data on motor horsepower, gearshifts, electric starters, and remote steering controls.

People who sell dictating and transcribing equipment will probably gather competitive information on ease of operation, convenience in use, size or compactness, versatility, and dependability.

Table 5–1 shows how one large corporation provides a comparison with competition when submitting a written proposal to a prospect. Buyers are interested in the competitive features of a product only to the extent that these features will benefit them. It's not enough to know a product is novel and different; the differences must be translated into advantages to the user. For example, companies in the airfreight business sell this method of transportation in terms of what it will mean to the shipper. Obviously, speed is essential for airfreight. What does this mean to the shipper? It means profits from extra value and extra sales when perishable products are involved; it means more sales and increased company prestige when fashion goods are involved; it means extra sales when newspaper distribution is involved.

To meet the competition, a salesperson has to respond to competitors' claims. However, salespeople should try to present a positive picture when comparing their products with competitive products. Emphasis should always be placed on the superior points or features of the salesperson's products rather than on any negative aspects of competitive products.

Table 5–1   Comparison of Product Features

Feature	Present Copier	Proposed System
Speed:		
Rated speed	10 per minute	40 per minute
Warm-up	None	None
First copy	15 seconds	8 seconds
Flexibility:		
Copy on:		
1. Plain cut-sheet bond paper	No	Yes
2. Digital letterhead	No	Yes
3. Gummed labels	No	Yes
4. Transparencies	No	Yes
5. Colored stock	No	Yes
6. Copying bound volumes	Only for volumes up to one-inch thick	Yes, books of any thickness
7. Copying on both sides of paper	No	Yes
Capacities:		
1. Paper tray capacity	625 8½ × 11 copies per roll	2,000 sheets
2. Toner capacity	16,000 copies	16,000 copies
3. Productivity*	10 copies per minute; manual feeding and manual sorting	40 copies per minute; automatically feeds originals and sorts finished copies

*Productivity refers to personnel who have increased their output by doing unproductive chores (copying, sorting, changing originals) much more rapidly and then returned to their more productive duties.

Courtesy of Xerox Corporation

We can best understand this strategy by examining a typical statement about a competitive product. Instead of saying, "Company X's machine has a very poor record on maintenance," it would be better to state, "Our machine has lower maintenance costs than any comparable machine on the market. Records show that our maintenance costs are 10 to 15 percent lower than those of our nearest competitor."

Tearing down a competitor doesn't strengthen a sales presentation. In fact, it may weaken the sales representative's message and be an injustice to the salesperson, the company, and the industry.

Company Organization and Personnel

Salespeople need to coordinate their activities with many departments and individuals in their company. A simple activity like processing a customer's order depends on the activities of many departments in addition to the sales department. The order must be processed by the credit department, the accounting department, and the traffic department. It may require the attention of other departments as well. A salesperson should know the routine every order must follow and who is responsible for each activity in the routine. The salesperson can then make the proper contacts to expedite an order, adjust a complaint, or explain a shipping delay.

In addition, salespeople must know who to contact in the service department when a service problem arises, who to contact in engineering when they need technical information to answer customer questions, and who in accounting handles special billing requests. Successful salespeople build a large and often informal network of information and decision-making sources in their companies.

FEATURES, BENEFITS, AND ADVANTAGES

Knowledge of product features is not enough. To be an effective salesperson, you must know what your customers' needs are, what benefits they are seeking, and how *your product's features will satisfy their needs*.

Translating Features into Benefits

Buyers are not interested in facts about the product or the company unless these facts help solve the buyers' wants or needs. The salesperson's job is to supply the facts, and then point out what these features mean to the buyer in terms of *benefits*. One field sales manager criticized his sales representative by saying, "You have what I call the 'salesman's curse': you know your product better than you know how your customers' businesses can use it."[3] Successful salespeople need to know how their products will benefit the customers.

Figure 5–1 illustrates the features and benefits of a Flair pen manufactured by Paper Mate that buyers will be interested in.

As mentioned previously, customers typically consider a set of competitive products when making a purchase decision. Thus, salespeople need to know more than the benefits provided by their products. They need to know how the benefits of their products are superior to the benefits of competitive products. Figure 5–2 shows how the features of MacGregor golf clubs offer advantages over alternative golf clubs and how these advantages are translated into superior benefits for the customer.

PRICING, DISCOUNTS, AND CREDIT POLICIES

Knowledge of pricing, discounts, and credit policies is important because salespeople are often responsible for quoting prices. Since salespeople are authorized agents of their companies, these quotations are legally binding.

In addition, salespeople often have some flexibility with regard to the price and terms quoted to customers. While a salesperson can make some adjustments to meet customer demands or competition, these adjustments may affect his or her compensation. Many compensation programs are

---

[3]Mack Hanan, "The Three C's of Selling: A Sure Cure for the 'Salesman's Curse,' " *Sales & Marketing Management*, May 10, 1976, pp. 70–72.

FIGURE 5–1
Features and
Benefits of Flair Pen

Features	Benefits
Best-selling porous pen	Flair produces sales and profits for everyone in the trade because most porous pen users are satisfied with its performance.
Snap seal cap; nonbreathing plastic	Minimizes loss from dry-out and offers the economy of longer writing life. Insures longer shelf life and lessens stock-keeping worries for the retailer.
Nylon bonded tip	Stays sharp unlike softer materials and produces uniform lines throughout the life of the ink supply.
Point guard	Users get extended writing life that produces sharp, neat, more legible writing.
Scientifically contoured grip	A consumer choice for writing ease and comfort.
Broad color selection	Allows the consumer to "write the way you feel" and produces extra retailer profits through the sales of additional colors.
National TV advertising	The trade enjoys a "no-cost" partnership in attracting customers.
Unconditional guarantee	Flair performs as expected or Paper Mate replaces. No one loses.

based on the profitability of a salesperson's sales, so concessions on price or terms can reduce a salesperson's income.[4]

Pricing Terms

Among the most common expressions used in quoting price are list price, net price, guaranteed price, FOB price, FAS price, and CIT price. Each of these price terms is discussed in this section.

List price is the quoted or published base price (usually in catalogs or price lists), from which buyers may receive discounts. *Net price* is the price buyers pay after all discounts and allowances are subtracted. Many customers focus on net prices because they make it easier to compare potential suppliers.

---

[4]See P. Ronald Stephenson, William L. Cron, and Gary L. Frazier, "Delegating Pricing Authority to the Sales Force," *Journal of Marketing*, Spring 1979, pp. 21–28.

FIGURE 5–2
Selling Product Benefits

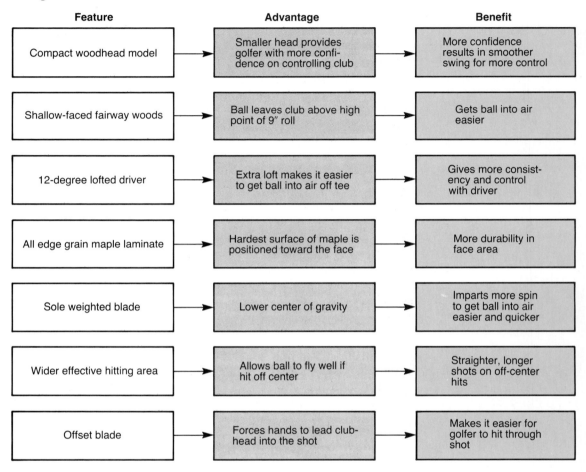

During periods of falling prices, resellers are concerned about losing money on their inventory. For example, Texas Instruments may sell calculators to a department store at $15. If it decreases the wholesaler price to $10 before the store can sell its inventory, the store will suffer an opportunity loss of $5 per calculator. To encourage resellers to place larger orders, manufacturers may offer to protect the resellers' inventories with a guaranteed price. So in the example above, if Texas Instruments offered such a guarantee to the department store, it would refund $5 for each calculator still in inventory. It would be the salesperson's responsibility to verify the inventory and initiate the refund request.

Price quotations usually specify who pays the transportation costs. When an *FOB* (free on board) price is quoted, the seller agrees to load the goods on board a truck, freight car, or ship at the seller's factory. Such products as coal, lumber, and automobiles are usually priced at FOB mine, mill, or factory. There are a great many variations in the use of the term FOB, including the following: (1) "FOB destination"—the seller assumes the responsibility for transportation costs to the buyer's place and the responsibility for loss or damage while the goods are in transit; (2) "FOB (shipping point) freight allowed"—transportation costs are assumed by the seller, but responsibility for the goods ceases when the goods are delivered to the transportation company; (3) "FOB (shipping point) freight equalized"—this term is used by the seller when a competitor has a more favorable freight cost as a result of being located nearer to the buyer. The seller assumes the difference in the freight rates and thus is able to meet competition.

FAS (free alongside ship) is used in quoting prices on overseas shipments. The seller agrees to pay the transportation charges necessary to get the goods within the reach of the ship's loading cranes. The title to the merchandise is transferred to the buyer at this point.

CIF (cost, insurance, and freight) is used in export selling. Such a price quotation includes the cost of the goods to the buyer, all freight and drayage costs to the seaport, ocean freight charges, marine insurance, and fees to land the goods at the foreign port. Unless otherwise stated, the title to the goods passes when the seller turns them over to the common carrier.

Credit Terms and Financial Discounts

Most U.S. sales are made on a credit basis with certain discounts allowed for early payment. A common discount is 2/10, n/30 (2 percent in 10 days, net in 30 days). This means the buyer may deduct 2 percent if the bill is paid within 10 days from the date of invoice. Otherwise the full amount must be paid within 30 days. Another common discount is 2/10 e.o.m., which means the customer can take a 2 percent discount if payment is made within 10 days after the first of the following month. Buyers frequently request deferred datings on their invoices as an extra form of discount.

Trade Discounts

When a manufacturing company sells its products to resalers, it will usually allow trade discounts, depending on the function performed by these buyers. The manufacturer may offer the wholesaler a trade discount of 55 percent of the list price to the ultimate consumer. If the manufacturer also sells directly to a large retailer, the retailer may be quoted a trade discount of 40 percent of the list price to the consumer. Trade discounts provide a sufficient margin to cover the costs of the services rendered by the various middlemen and to provide the middlemen with a fair profit.

Most companies classify their customers according to the trade discounts they are allowed. However, certain customers may operate both as wholesalers and retailers. In such cases, it may be difficult for the salesperson to determine which trade discount to quote.

Quantity Discounts

The purpose of the quantity discount is to pass on to the customer or consumer the savings resulting from the handling, delivering, and billing of large orders.

Quantity discounts may take the form of single-order discounts or period discounts. A typewriter company, for example, may quote a 5 percent discount on a single order for three typewriters, a 10 percent discount on a single order for four typewriters, and a 15 percent discount on a single order for five or more typewriters. In addition, the company may have a time or period quantity discount plan whereby a discount of 15 percent is allowed on all typewriters purchased during a year or a six-month period.

Promotional Allowance

Manufacturers often offer special allowances if resellers agree to promote their products. For example, Clorox may offer a special discount to grocery stores if they agree to offer a special price for Clorox liquid bleach, advertise the special price in the local paper, and permit the Clorox salesperson to construct an end-aisle display of Clorox products.

The Salesperson's Responsibility for Credit

A company's credit policies are usually established by the credit department after consultation with the sales organization. Some companies delegate the entire credit responsibility to the credit department. Others give the individual salesperson considerable authority in administering the credit policies. The Standard Oil Company of California, for example, emphasizes the importance of the sales representative in administering the company's credit policies as follows: *"The application of any credit policy rests finally with the representative of the Company who actually talks with the customer.* The results of these conversations have a direct effect on profitable selling, and the outcome depends not only on what you say but how you say it."

When a salesperson's compensation is based on total sales volume, there may be a tendency to make sales that do not result in a profit to the company. Recognizing this factor, most companies have changed their sales compensation plans so compensation is related to the profits derived from an order.

Experience shows that it is good business to pass up sales to poor credit risks. When a sale is lost, the company sacrifices the potential profit. But when a sale is made to a poor credit risk, the company may lose not only the profit but also the cost of the goods delivered.

Relations with the Credit Department   Friction often develops when a credit department refuses credit to a salesperson's customer. Since salespeople are generally optimistic, they tend to be somewhat liberal in evaluating a customer's credit position. The credit manager, on the other hand, is usually less optimistic and stricter in the interpretation of the company's credit policies. Differences of opinion are bound to occur. But the credit manager and the salesperson should realize that complete cooperation and understanding of each other's problems will result in greater long-term profits for both the company and the salesperson.

Salespeople must be honest in all their dealings with the credit department and must do everything possible to keep it informed on conditions in their territories. If salespeople give the credit department complete factual information on all their customers, the credit department should be equally cooperative in working out special credit and collection problems.

Collecting Credit Information   The salesperson is in an excellent position to obtain current information on the financial condition of customers. When the credit department combines this information with the information from reporting services, the company will have a fairly accurate picture of the credit position of individual customers.

The salesperson usually asks potential customers to send complete financial statements to the credit department. The salesperson also supplies information on such items as management's ability, owners' habits and local reputation, local business conditions, location and identity of the store or plant, bank and credit references, and evidence of the financial status of the business.

When calling on old customers, sales representatives should be on the lookout for danger signals that indicate unfavorable changes in the customers' credit standing. The New York Credit Men's Association suggests sales representatives review the following points to discover credit indicators for the credit department:

a. Are there any indications the customer has been buying heavily from one house?

b. Have any of the customer's accounts with other creditors been placed in attorneys' hands for collection?

c. Is the customer becoming loose in personal habits? Is the retailer drinking or indifferent in handling customers?

d. Is there any evidence the customer is getting ready to sell or close with the intention of quitting business?

e. Is there any indication the customer is letting business run down—that is, allowing stock to deteriorate?

    f. Has the customer guaranteed the paying of obligations incurred by some friend or relative?

    g. Is a strike pending in the community's principal plant or industry?

    h. Is the customer doing too much credit business?[5]

The salesperson may also run into unhappy customers who feel antagonistic toward the company's credit department. The salesperson should try to discover the reasons. If the company has erred, the credit department should be given the facts so it can take the necessary steps to reestablish cordial relations.

Informing Customers   Credit policies and terms must be clearly explained to each customer at the time of the sale to avoid later misunderstandings. If special credit arrangements are made with trade acceptances, drafts, notes, and installment sales contracts, the salesperson should be certain customers understand the exact amount of their payments and when they are due. Salespeople should tell customers the advantages of taking quantity discounts even if the customer has to borrow to do so.

When discussing credit and collection policies and terms with customers, a high degree of tact and diplomacy is needed. At times it is necessary to obtain personal or confidential information. In this case, indirect questions and careful observation often succeed without offending or embarrassing customers. When direct questions are necessary, care should be taken to explain that similar credit information is required of all customers. If salespeople are sincere and honest in all relations with customers, they should have little trouble securing the necessary credit information.

Collecting Delinquent Bills   If sales representatives have collection responsibility, they should not be apologetic about asking for money. Successful salespeople know that most customers respect a courteous but firm stand on collections. This kind of personal contact also makes it harder for the customer to refuse payment. In addition, the salesperson is in a position to know all of the details of the bill or invoice and should be able to make collections with less annoyance to the customer. Finally, the salesperson knows that if collections are not made promptly, the customers' orders may be held up and sales may suffer.

An example of using the telephone to collect an overdue account is given in Chapter 18.

---

[5]Research and Survey Committee, *Suggested Outline for Preparing a Credit and Collection Manual for Salesmen* (New York: New York Credit Men's Association), p. 7.

Annual reports are a good source of information for the salesperson.

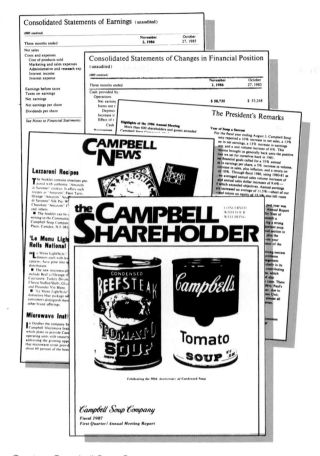

Courtesy Campbell Soup Company

WHERE AND HOW IS INFORMATION SECURED?

There is no shortage of facts about the company, its products, and its competitors' products. A continuous, well-organized plan for collecting material will keep a salesperson abreast of all new developments.

Information about the Company and Its Products

Information about the company and its products is available from the following sources: work experience, sales training programs, company sales and service manuals, sales meetings and conventions, plant visits, research and testing department bulletins, company employees, company publications and handbooks, company advertising and sales literature, trade association magazines and reports, labels on products or their containers, and customers.

In many of the larger, well-organized corporations, where formal training is considered an important activity, much of the necessary information about the company and its products is presented to trainees. Some companies also require their trainees to spend 90 days or more in purchasing operations.

Yet salespeople cannot learn all they need to know from a training program or from any one source. Learning about the company and its products is a continuous activity—*the process never ends.*

Most companies use refresher courses, sales conferences, bulletins, and other devices to keep their experienced sales representatives up to date. In addition to the organized training programs prepared by the companies, salespeople are expected to use initiative in adding product information. They may read association magazines and reports, observe customers' experiences, and converse with company employees. Some companies prepare manuals or handbooks for sales representatives to keep for ready reference.

The company's annual report provides such information as the names of directors, the names of members of the executive committee, the names and titles of the company's officers, and a report on business activities for the past year, as well as a comment on what the future may hold. The report of business activities usually includes such topics as improvement and expansion programs, new plant facilities, product improvements, product demand, current markets, scientific developments, service and supplies, sales and service training, advertising, employee relations, wages and employment, employee welfare, personnel changes, finances, earnings, and plans. The annual reports are usually condensed and easily understood, so they are excellent sources to use.

Information about Competitors and Their Products

Information about competitors' products may be obtained from competitive advertising and sales literature, trade association magazines and reports, company research and testing department bulletins, sales meetings and conventions, customers' experiences with competitive products, and claims of competitive salespeople. Independent laboratories may be sources of competitive data. Material can usually be obtained from testing companies for a fee.

Probably one of the best and most direct ways to gather needed data is to question users of competitive products. In this way a salesperson can find out what has sold them on the products. Observation also pays dividends. By observing empty containers, it is easy to identify the company's chief competitor. In a dealer's store, a salesperson can observe display advertising, listen to the sales talk of the retail salespeople, or investigate which products are on the dealer's shelves.

In some fields of selling, it may be helpful to "shop" (buy or price competing goods or services) at the outlets of competitors to learn product's sales features. If the article is inexpensive, the salesperson may buy it and test it to have firsthand information for comparison.

SUMMARY

To be successful, salespeople need to know their company, its products, its competitors, and its policies. Salespeople need this knowledge to satisfy the information demands of their customers, to earn the confidence of their customers, and to build self-confidence in their abilities.

Salespeople should acquire specific information about the history of their company and their company's production and service facilities. Product knowledge is particularly important. Salespeople need to know how the products are made, what service is available, how the product relates to other products, and how the product will meet customer needs. To demonstrate how products will satisfy customer needs, salespeople must relate product features to specific customer benefits. In addition, salespeople should be aware of how their products compare to products offered by competitors.

Knowledge of pricing, discount, and credit policies is important because salespeople are often responsible for implementing these policies. Salespeople need to understand a wide variety of pricing and discount terms so they can quote prices and compare quotations made by competitors. In addition, salespeople are intimately involved in credit decisions. Their income is affected by bad debts. They are used as a source of information about customer credit and may even be used to collect bills.

QUESTIONS
AND
PROBLEMS

1. Which is more important in making a sale—knowledge of the product or knowledge of the customer? Explain.

2. Find the annual equivalent rate of interest earned by buyers who qualify for cash discounts under the following terms: 1/10, n/30; 2/10, n/60; 3/10, n/60; 2/15, n/30.

3. Is it always a good idea to encourage buyers to order a large quantity in order to get a better quantity discount? Why?

4. You are selling a replacement product for carbon paper—it won't rip or tear; it won't wrinkle or curl; and it won't strike through like carbon paper. One of these polyester sheets will make 100 copies. List these product features in terms of buyer benefits.

5. The hot tub is usually made of redwood, is either round or oval, and is from three feet to five feet high and from three feet to eight feet in diameter. It can be installed indoors or outdoors. A heater is used to keep the water between 104 and 115 degrees. The basic price is $1,500. Optional accessories are available. Why would anyone want to buy such a tub?

6. As a salesperson in a large department store, where are you most likely to find information on the products you sell? How will a thorough knowledge of your merchandise help you?

7. Why is it insufficient to *describe* the product's benefits?

8. Improve the following statement, "Mr. Buyer, our new inventory control system [feature] will assure you of prompt deliveries [benefit]."

9. Henry Downs, a manufacturer's representative, sells footballs, basketballs, volleyballs, and other rubber products to sporting goods dealers. His firm is known throughout the country as the leader in the merchandising of rubber sporting goods. In what facts about the company would the owner of a sporting goods store probably be interested? Identify the facts, and show why the retailer would be interested.

10. The list price for men's shirts is $20. Your company offers trade discounts of 20 percent and 30 percent to wholesalers and retailers, respectively. If the shirts are ordered in quantities greater than 4 dozen, wholesalers receive an additional 5 percent quantity discount. A wholesaler places an order for 12 dozen shirts. What does the wholesaler pay?

PROJECTS

1. What benefits could a buyer of the following products obtain?

Customized van	Home video game
Microwave oven	CB radio
Food processor	Solar heating system
Facsimile transmission system	Home computer
Smoke detector	Videocassette recorder

2. Choose a product you plan to buy soon. Shop for it at four stores that carry the product. Where do you plan to buy it, and why are you planning to buy the particular brand you have chosen? Be sure to include all the factors that influenced your decision. Submit the analysis, using an appropriate business report form.

3. Send in for the latest annual report of a major corporation. What information in it would be useful when selling the company's product? How would you use that information? Be specific.

CASE PROBLEMS

Case 5–1   Radio KLOK

Bob works for Radio KLOK, which is located in a city of about 85,000. Four stations of a strictly local nature have come on the air in the last three years, and Bob's station is one of this group. The city is only 50 miles from a city of 600,000 and only 45 miles from one of 400,000. The trading area the local stations hope to reach contains a population of between 300,000 and 350,000, exclusive of the population of the two larger cities.

Advertising over a local station is a relatively new experience for the owners of local retail stores and industries. Bob knows it will be necessary to sell them on the advisability of using local radio as an advertising medium, and he must also sell them on KLOK as the station to use.

Bob discovers that none of the four stations has been able to collect sufficient data to "prove" to the prospects that it is profitable for them to use the medium. However, surveys are under way to collect the necessary information. The stations have been pioneering in the area, and they have found it difficult to sell time.

Questions

1. What facts about the company or station could be useful in Bob's presentation? What should he say about competitors?

2. What buying motives may be used to convince a merchant that local radio advertising is desirable? Illustrate.

Case 5–2   Storter Drug Company

Jennie Wren, a sales representative for the Storter Drug Company, calls on a number of customers in Tampa, Florida. One of her customers, Mr. Sparrow, has been in the retail drugstore business for a very short time. He is operating his store on a fairly small working capital.

The Storter Drug Company has established a maximum credit limit of $2,000 for the Sparrow Company. Terms of sale are 2 percent 10 days, net 60 days. Sparrow hopes to develop a strong credit rating.

Ms. Wren is responsible for calling on drugstores to obtain competitive information and to get distribution of all designated Storter products. She is also responsible for making collections and submitting reports to the credit manager.

In a recent discussion with Mr. Sparrow, Ms. Wren decided to encourage him to take advantage of the available cash discount terms. Mr. Sparrow's initial response was that he was short of working capital and couldn't see any benefit to him or to her company if he took the discounts.

Questions

1. How would taking the discount help Mr. Sparrow?

2. How would taking the discount help the Storter Drug Company?

3. Make an analysis of whether the Sparrow Company could gain by borrowing the money to take advantage of the discount terms.

Case 5–3   Premium Oil Company

The credit department of Premium Oil Company has published a booklet on credit information for members of its sales organization. The following dialogue included in the booklet describes a situation in which Frank Barnes, a sales representative, is calling on Jim Brown, a customer, who owns a large dairy ranch. Brown has been given a temporary extension of credit, and he now wants to stay on a 60-day basis.

Frank Barnes   [*area representative*]: Good morning, Mr. Brown, I put that barrel of Animal Fly Spray on the rack where you wanted it.

Jim Brown   [*customer*]: Thanks, Frank. I'll be needing it this afternoon, so I'm glad you got here.

Frank: I knew you wanted to use it. That's why I made it a point to stop this morning.

Brown: I've got to hand it to you, Frank. You've never disappointed me on a delivery.

Frank: Thanks, Mr. Brown. By the way, I have your statement here. It's for $230.

Brown: How much is the oldest month?

Frank: It's $125, but could you make the check for both months this time?

Brown: No, just the oldest month like I've been doing. Isn't that OK? I'll bet you'd be satisfied if all your accounts paid in 60 days.

Frank: Well, hardly, Mr. Brown. Our business or any business has to collect promptly to pay its bills just the same as you. That's why we have 30-day terms. Besides, it wouldn't be fair to ask my other customers to pay every month and then let you take two months. You wouldn't like it if we were regularly giving our other customers twice as long as we give you to pay.

Brown: Maybe I wouldn't. But if your company doesn't think I'm good for that much money, I don't know as how I want to keep on trading with them.

Frank: The amount you owe isn't the question at all. It's just a matter of payment in line with our regular terms—the same terms we use with all our customers. In fact, I'll gladly deliver to you right now any products you want even though they might add up to several times the amount you now owe for two months' deliveries.

Brown: Why all the fuss today? I've been paying you this way for months.

Frank: That's right—remember it was some six months ago when you had to lay out some extra money for hay you asked me if it would be OK to skip paying that month. I don't think either one of us had in mind then that it would become a permanent paying plan.   .

Brown: No, perhaps we didn't. But regardless of that, I can't pay both months now. I could borrow the money, but if you make me do that I'll buy from someone else.

Frank: I'm not asking you to do that, Mr. Brown, but let's go back over this situation. You paid me right on the dot for a long time, and there was never any question about payment. Then one day about six months ago you asked me to let you skip paying that month, and you'll recall I told you the company was willing to help you out with a temporary extension. You really don't mean that as a direct result of my granting you a favor you would buy from some other oil company, do you?

Brown: No, I guess that wouldn't be right. But I can't pay $230 this month, and I don't want to have to borrow from the bank at this time of year, particularly since I'm all clear with them.

Frank: It was a help to you when we gave you the extension. Let's see if we can't again figure out something that will help you. How about this? The 60-

day balance is $125—you planned on paying that today. That leaves a balance of $105. Let's set that figure aside as our problem to solve. Suppose we divide it three ways—could you add the one third, $35, to your regular check today and then do the same thing next month and the month after that? I'd appreciate it if you would.

Brown: Yes. I can do that. Milk production will be higher the next three months.

Frank: That's fine. I'll make a note of it on my copy of your statement [*writing on duplicate statement*]. "Paid 60-day purchases and one third of balance, $35. Will pay $35 next month, plus the 30-day purchases, and the following month will pay balance on statement." Is that right, Mr. Brown?

Brown: That's OK, Frank. Let me borrow your pen and I'll make out this check.

Frank   [*accepting check*]: Thanks very much.

Brown: That's all right, Frank.

Frank: By the way, Mr. Brown, I noticed the oil is low in that 30-barrel. Hadn't I better fill it when I bring out gasoline next week?

Brown: You might as well. I really depend on you to see that I have the oil and gas I need around here.

Frank: OK. Thanks again. I'll see you sometime next Tuesday.

Brown: So long, Frank.

Questions

1. Could Frank Barnes handle this situation better? If so, how?
2. What sales techniques did Barnes use effectively during the interview? Discuss each technique and indicate why it is helpful.

SELECTED REFERENCES

Britt, S. H., and V. M. Nelson. "Marketing Importance of the First Noticeable Difference." *Business Horizons*, August 1976, pp. 38–40.

Crow, Lowell E., and Jay D. Linquist. "Buyers Differ in Evaluating Suppliers." *Industrial Marketing Management*, July 1982, pp. 205–14.

Dowst, Somerby. "Capital Buying: One Strike and You're Out." *Purchasing*, March 8, 1978, pp. 59–63.

Flavey, John J. "The Myths of Sales Training." *Sales & Marketing Management*, April 3, 1978, pp. 40–43.

Fox, Howard W. "Credit Matrix Aids Vendor Analysis." *Purchasing*, February 8, 1978, pp. 56–57.

Holden, Jim. "Winning Control over the Buyer and Competition—Strategy and Tactics." *Industrial Marketing*, December 1982, pp. 28–36.

Hopkins, David S. *Training the Sales Force: A Progress Report*. New York: The Conference Board, 1978.

Lehmann, Donald R., and John O'Shaughnessy. "Decision Criteria Used in Buying Different Categories of Products." *Journal of Purchasing and Material Management*, Spring 1982, pp. 9–14.

Sirgy, M. Joseph. "Using Self-Congruity and Ideal Congruity to Predict Purchase Motivation." *Journal of Business Research*, June 1985, pp. 195–206.

6

Communication Principles and Successful Selling

Some questions answered in this chapter are:

- What are the basic elements in the communication process?
- Why are listening and questioning skills important?
- How can listening skills be improved?
- How can probes be used to collect information?
- How do people communicate without using words?

Effective communication plays an important role in all aspects of life. Through the use of communications principles, misunderstandings are avoided and personal relationships improved. Communication skills are particularly important in personal selling, since successful selling is based on communicating product benefits to potential buyers. Communications in selling involves more than telling prospects about the product. It involves an active, two-way exchange of ideas and thoughts.

FIGURE 6–1
Model of
Communication
Process

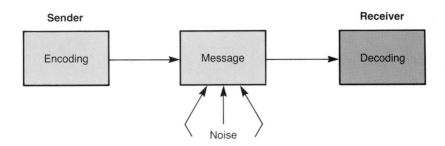

THE COM-MUNICATION PROCESS

The first step in developing communication skills is understanding the communication process. The basic elements in the communication process are the sender, the message, and the receiver. The relationship among these elements is shown in Figure 6–1.

The process begins with the sender—the source of messages to be communicated. In the context of personal selling, the sender is a salesperson. However, in more general terms the sender can be anyone who wishes to communicate an idea, such as a political candidate, a college professor, or a minister. The sender has some thoughts and ideas he or she wishes to communicate to the receiver. Since the receiver cannot read the sender's mind, the sender must translate these ideas into words. The sender encodes the ideas into a message and transmits this message to the receiver. This message can be transmitted by voice in a face-to-face interaction, by telephone, or in a written form such as a letter or proposal. Then the receiver must decode the message and try to understand what the sender intended to communicate.

Consider a stockbroker who wishes to tell a client about the benefits of buying stock in General Motors. The stockbroker has a number of ideas about General Motors, which are encoded into the following message: "General Motors is an excellent buy. Its price/earnings ratio is depressed because of high oil prices, but the oil prices will go down soon. OPEC is breaking up." The stockbroker intends to communicate the benefits of buying stock in General Motors, but the client may not interpret this message correctly. To decode the message, the client must be familiar with the terms *OPEC* and *depressed price/earnings ratio*. The client might attempt to understand the stockbroker's intention for the message by asking, "What does depressed price/earnings ratio mean?" Or the client might not want to show a lack of understanding and respond, "I don't think I am interested in buying stocks now."

Factors Affecting Communication Accuracy

Effective communication occurs when the receiver accurately perceives what the sender intended to transmit. When this does not occur, there is a communication breakdown. Three factors can lead to a communication breakdown. First, senders may not encode their ideas accurately. For example, the stockbroker may have wanted to communicate the idea that

Noise in the channel is anything that interferes with communication between salesperson and buyer—like the machine and office personnel here.

Camerique/H. Armstrong Roberts

General Motors is a safe, low-risk investment but failed to express this idea in words. Second, receivers may not accurately decode messages. The stockbroker's client may have interpreted the message "depressed because of high oil prices" to mean all stocks are bad investments now because oil prices are high. Customers can also distort messages to make them conform to their own beliefs. For example, a customer who prefers Savin copiers may interpret the Xerox salesperson's comment, "Xerox makes the finest copiers" as meaning, "Xerox makes the finest copiers, but they are expensive."

Finally, accuracy of communications is affected by noise that occurs while the message is being transmitted. Noise is unintended messages that interfere with the communication process, such as ringing telephones or other conversations nearby. To improve communications, salespeople should attempt to minimize the amount of noise in the environment. Discussions with a customer should be held in a quiet atmosphere, so the customer will pay attention to the salesperson and not be distracted by noise.

Two-Way Communications

Figure 6–1 shows the communication process as a one-way flow of communications. Communications flow from the sender to the receiver. But effective communication involves a two-way flow of information. As shown in Figure 6–2, the two parties in the communication process act as both senders and receivers. Salespeople send messages to customers and re-

FIGURE 6–2
Two-Way
Communications

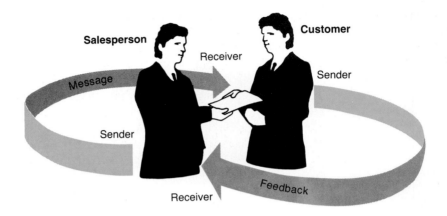

ceive feedback from customers. Customers send messages to salespeople and receive responses.

Consider a salesperson who is demonstrating a complicated product to a customer. At some point in the presentation, a perplexed look comes across the customer's face. The salesperson receives this message and can then ask the customer about aspects of the presentation that need further explanation. The customer's expression provided feedback to the salesperson that the salesperson's message had not been received. The customer then sends messages to the salesperson in the form of questions concerning the operation and benefits of the product.

Two-way communication is essential to the practice of the marketing concept. Without two-way communication, salespeople cannot determine the needs of the customer. In addition, feedback from customers is needed to determine if messages about product benefits are being received accurately. Thus, two-way communication improves the effectiveness and accuracy of communications.

In addition, two-way communication is much more satisfying from the customer's point of view. People enjoy participating in conversations and having an opportunity to express themselves. They do not like being talked to without being able to ask questions or respond. The more customers participate, the more likely they are to sell themselves.

To be effective communicators, salespeople need to adapt their messages to the specific customers they are trying to sell. The messages need to be tailored to the customer's style and needs. Two valuable communication skills that enable a salesperson to adapt effectively are listening and questioning.[1]

---

[1]See Jeremy Main, "How to Sell By Listening," *Fortune*, February 4, 1985, pp. 52–54.

DEVELOP-ING LISTENING SKILLS

Many people believe effective communication is achieved by talking a lot. Inexperienced salespeople often go into a selling situation thinking they have to outtalk the prospect. They are enthusiastic about their product and company and want to tell the prospect all they know. However, a salesperson who is talking is not thinking. Salespeople who monopolize conversations cannot find out what customers need.

Actually, listening is the most critical aspect of effective communications. One study has found that participation in most communications is largely devoted to listening.[2] This study found that the time spent in communications is broken down as follows:

Activity	Percentage of Time Spent
Writing	10%
Reading	15
Speaking	35
Listening	40

People can speak at the rate of only 130 to 160 words per minute, but they can listen to over 800 words per minute. Because of this differential, people often get lazy when listening. They do not pay attention and often can remember only 50 percent of what is said immediately after it is said.

Effective listening is not a passive activity. It is much more than just hearing what the customer is saying. Good listeners project themselves into the minds of the speaker and attempt to feel the way the speaker feels. If a customer says she needs a "conservative" dress, the salesperson needs to listen carefully to find out what the term *conservative* means to this particular customer, how conservative the dress should be, why a conservative dress is needed, and where the customer plans to wear the dress. The salesperson needs to develop a mental image of the customer in the dress. Through effective listening, the salesperson can show the customer her specific needs are being considered in the selection of dresses to recommend.

Effective listeners are actively thinking while they listen. They are thinking about the conclusions to which the speaker is building, evaluating the evidence being presented, sorting out the important facts from the irrelevant facts. In addition, active listening means the listener attempts to draw out as much information as possible. Gestures can be used to

---

[2]Harold P. Zelko, *The Art of Communicating Your Ideas* (New York: Reading Services, 1968), p. 3.

YOU CAN'T LISTEN YOURSELF OUT OF A SALE!

 Ron Willingham describes how listening helped him sell sales training seminars for U.S. Army recruiters.

Upon a referral, I arranged an appointment for 10 o'clock one Tuesday morning with a recruiting commander.

When I walked into his office at 9:50 the Colonel's secretary seated me in his office and told me that he'd be in on time.

At exactly 10 o'clock the Colonel marched in. He shook my hand once, showing no feeling or emotion. Then he sat down in his desk chair and said, "I'll have to be honest with you and tell you that you've probably wasted your time coming all the way out here to see me!"

That was certainly a happy thought!

Without giving me any chance to respond, he went on, "You see, if there's anything we don't need around here it's sales training! I don't want my recruiters running around glad-handing and slapping people on their backs. They're soldiers, not IBM salesmen!"

Ducking his opening shot, I unbuttoned my coat, popped down the lid of my briefcase, crossed my legs and smiled, "Colonel . . . I appreciate your being honest with me."

"How long have you been in the service?" I asked. I found out he'd been in 27 years. "I'll bet you've been in some exciting places! Where all have you been stationed?" He began talking. His gestures were choppy and definite. He loved to talk.

"Where'd you enjoy living the most?" I asked when he ran down. He said Hawaii. He told me that his kids liked to go down to the beach.

"How many children do you have, Colonel?" I found out he had three. Two were boys. The delight of his life.

---

motivate a person to continue talking. Nodding of the head, eye contact, and an occasional "I see," "tell me more," and "that's interesting" demonstrate an interest in and understanding of what is being said.

In Selling Scenario 6–1, Ron Willingham describes how he made a sale by simply listening. Some suggestions for active listening proposed by Xerox Learning Systems are: (1) repeating information, (2) restating or rephrasing information, (3) clarifying information, (4) summarizing the conversation, and (5) tolerating silences.

Repeating Information

During a sales presentation, salespeople should verify information they have collected from a customer. A useful way to verify information is to repeat—word for word—what the customer has said. This technique minimizes chances for misunderstandings. For example:

"How old are they?" They were both graduating from high school that year. They wanted to go to college. It was going to take $10,000 a year to send them. He didn't know how he was going to come up with the money.

"What are their goals?" I asked. He talked . . . and talked. About himself, of course. Never did want to know anything about me. Could've cared less.

He talked for an hour. I occasionally asked a question and . . . listened. Then out of the clear blue sky, he said, "You know . . . some good sales training is exactly what we need!"

Stunned, I tried to compose myself. "Oh . . . how do you feel it would help you, Colonel?"

"Well . . .," he replied, and for the next 15 minutes told me *why* his recruiters needed sales training.

I just listened and let him convince me.

Then I asked him, "Well, when and where would you want to hold these seminars, Colonel?"

In the next three minutes we set up three seminars. All his idea. If I'd tried to "sell" him I'd have been tossed out immediately.

Analyze this story and you'll see that I didn't do a traditional sales presentation. I just asked questions and listened. Had I tried to make a presentation, overcome objections and close I'd have been dead.

Think about it and you'll see that most of my selling took place in the approach and interview!

I sold by listening more than I talked!

Source: From Ron Willingham, "You Can't Listen Yourself Out of a Sale," *Personal Selling Power,* September 1984, pp. 20–21.

Customer: I'll take 15 cases of personal-size Ivory soap and 12 cases of family-size.

Salesperson: Sure, Mr. Johnson. That will be 12 cases of family-size and 15 cases of personal-size.

Customer: Wait a minute. I got that backward. I want 12 cases of personal-size and 15 cases of family-size.

Salesperson: Fine—12 personal and 15 family. Is that right?

Customer: Yes. That's what I want.

Salespeople need to be cautious in using this technique for active listening. Nothing annoys customers more than to have salespeople echo everything they say.

Restating or Rephrasing Information

To verify a customer's intent, salespeople should restate the customer's comment in their own words. This ensures that the salesperson and customer understand one another. For example:

> **Customer:** The service isn't quite what I had expected.
>
> **Salesperson:** I see, you're a little bit dissatisfied with the service we've been giving you.
>
> **Customer:** Oh no. As a matter of fact, I've been getting better service than I thought I would.

Clarifying Information

Another way to verify a customer's meaning is through questions designed to obtain additional information. Such a device will give the salesperson a fuller understanding of the customer's concern. For example:

> **Customer:** Listen. I've tried everything. I just can't get this machine to work properly.
>
> **Salesperson:** Just what is it that the machine doesn't do?
>
> **Customer:** Well, the rivets keep jamming inside the machine. Sometimes two rivets are inserted on top of each other.
>
> **Salesperson:** Would you describe for me the way you load the rivets into the tray?
>
> **Customer:** Well, first I push down the release lever and take the tray out. Then I push that little button and put the rivets in. Next, I push the button again, put the tray in the machine, and push the lever.
>
> **Salesperson:** When you put the tray in, which side is up?
>
> **Customer:** What difference does that make?

This exchange shows how a sequence of questions can give a clearer definition of the problem. By obtaining this information, the salesperson is better able to determine what is causing the problem.

Summarizing the Conversation

Active listening involves mentally summarizing points that have been made. At critical points in the sales presentation, the salesperson should state these mentally prepared summaries. Summarizing provides salesperson and customer with a quick overview of what has taken place and lets them both consolidate the items they've discussed. Summarizing also lets the salesperson change the direction of the conversation. For example:

> **Customer:** . . . so, I told him I wasn't interested.
>
> **Salesperson:** Let me see if I've got this straight. A salesperson called on you today and asked if you were interested in reducing your costs. He also said he could save you about $25 a month. But when you pursued the matter, you found out the dollar savings in costs were offset by lack of service.
>
> **Customer:** That's right.
>
> **Salesperson:** Well, sir, I've got your account records right here. Assuming you are interested in getting more for your dollar with regard to copy costs, I think there's a way we can help you out—without having to worry about any decrease in the quality of service.
>
> **Customer:** Tell me more.

Tolerating Silences

Perhaps this technique is more appropriately titled "Bite your tongue." There are times in a sales presentation when a salesperson needs time to think. Such situations can be triggered by a tough question or by a customer's comments that suggest a complex problem. Customers also need time to think. Because time seems extended during periods of silence, salespeople often believe they need to "plug the gap" by saying something. If they talk in these situations, they often make it hard for customers to find the time to consider the situation. Tolerating silences gives customers time to sell themselves. The following example of setting an appointment demonstrates this point:

> **Salesperson:** What day would you like me to call on you?
>
> **Salesperson:** Silence.
>
> **Customer:** Just a minute . . . let me think about that.
>
> **Customer:** Okay, let's make it on Monday, the 22nd.
>
> **Salesperson:** Fine, Mrs. Quinn, what time would be most convenient?
>
> **Customer:** Hmmm. . . .
>
> **Salesperson:** Silence.
>
> **Customer:** 10:00 would be best for me.

ART OF QUESTION-ING

An essential element in successful communications is learning about a customer's problems and needs. To learn more about customers, salespeople must first persuade them to give them this information. Then the salespeople need to listen to and absorb it. In this section, we'll take up the art of questioning.

There are several reasons why a salesperson should ask questions. First, questioning gets customers to participate in the sales interview. They are encouraged to actively engage in conversation rather than listen to a presentation. This holds the customer's attention and ends up with the customer learning and remembering more about the product. Questioning also shows the salesperson's interest in the customer and his or her problems. Finally, salespeople are able to collect information about customers and test their assumptions by asking questions. Even though a salesperson might have a lot of information about the customer before the sales call, there is no guarantee that the precall analysis has correctly identified the customer's needs. Salespeople can use questions to either confirm or disconfirm their precall analysis.

Guidelines for Questions

Effective questions elicit information to help the salesperson make an effective presentation. Some guidelines for asking good questions follow:

Encourage Longer Responses   Good questions should not be answerable with a simple yes, no, or short response. Such questions just do not get much information from the customer. For example, the question, "Have you heard of our company?" will probably result in a simple yes or no answer. Then the salesperson will have to ask a followup question, such as, "Why haven't you heard of our company?" or "What have you heard about our company?"

A much better question is, "What have you heard about our company?" This will get a longer response from the customer. In addition, asking questions in this manner replaces two questions with one.

Space Out Questions   When salespeople ask several questions, one right after another, customers may feel threatened. They may think they are being interrogated rather than participating in a conversation. Some customers would react by disclosing less rather than more information. For this reason, questions should be spaced out so the customer has time to answer each question in a relaxed atmosphere.

One method for spacing out questions is encouraging prospects to elaborate on their responses. In this way, customers believe they are volunteering information rather than being forced to divulge it.

Ask Short, Simple Questions   Questions that have two or more parts should be avoided. In the face of complex questions, the customer may not know which part to answer, and the salesperson may not know which part has been answered. For example, the question, "How much time do you spend making your annual budget and your sales forecasts?" may yield a response of, "Oh, about three weeks." Does this mean three weeks is spent on both tasks or only on one?

Long questions are hard to remember and to answer. For example, a question such as, "With so many complicated reports to prepare and review, is it difficult for you to determine what your direct material and labor costs are?" can lose the customer's attention. Some customers may be annoyed by long questions that force them to ask the salesperson for clarification.

Avoiding Leading Questions   Questions should not imply an appropriate answer. Such questions are likely to put words into the customer's mouth and not determine what the customer actually thinks. For example, the question, "Why do you think this is a good product?" encourages a positive response and discourages a negative one. Even though such questions may get the responses the salesperson wants to hear, they may mask the customer's true feelings.

Types of Questions

Questions or information probes have three purposes. First, they can be used to collect specific information. Some examples are probes of a directive, evaluative, disadvantage, and consequence nature. Second, questions can be used to maintain the flow of information. Examples of questions that get the customer to continue talking are probes of a reflective, encouragement, and elaboration nature. Finally, questions related to clarifying or understanding a customer's problems are an important aspect of active listening. We will examine all these questions in this section.

Directive Probes or Questions   Directive probes or questions usually start with one of the following five words: who, what, where, how, and why. Responses to directive probes give the salesperson a better understanding of the prospect, the prospect's business, and the present competition. Directive probes ask for factual information and are easy to answer. It is best to begin with directive probes seeking general information that is publicly available. Probes that are too personal or too challenging will make the prospect uncomfortable.

Some examples of directive probes are:

Where do you buy your components now?
Who uses the copier?
What is your policy concerning returns?
Why is the Edgewood plant relocating to Oregon?
How much are you paying for the resistors now?

The responses to directive probes are valuable information that can be referred to when salespeople seek to relate product benefits to customer needs. Frequently, salespeople note important comments made by customers. Note taking shows concern for the prospect's problems.

Evaluative Probes   While directive probes aim to uncover specific facts, evaluative probes are open-ended questions that help the salesperson understand the customer's feelings on a subject. These probes are typically used after directive probes. Some examples of evaluative probes are:

> How do you feel about small cars?
> What advantage do you see in leasing cars?
> How do you feel about increasing your component inventory?

At times, evaluative questions can make customers uncomfortable because they may be reluctant to express their feelings on a subject. In these situations, indirect evaluative questions can be used to get customer reactions. Such questions ask customers to respond to the known views of a third party such as:

> *Electronic News* had a recent article on the increased usage of micro switches. Do you find this to be the case?
> The Apex air conditioner got a good rating in *Consumer Reports*. Do you think it will sell well to your customers?

Disadvantage Probes   These probes ask a customer to articulate a specific problem. For example, a salesperson selling a copier with an advantage in terms of copy quality might use the following disadvantage probe:

> **Salesperson:**   The copier you're using to reproduce these sales proposals uses treated paper, doesn't it?
> **Customer:**   Yes, it does.
> **Salesperson:**   Some of my other customers have indicated to me that treated paper copiers give a gray cast to their copies. Have you experienced that as well?
> **Customer:**   Well, yes, the paper the machine uses isn't the best. It's heavy and doesn't look very good.

Disadvantage probes pose questions so customers can elaborate on problems with their present products. The value of these probes can be seen by comparing the previous conversation with the following conversation.

> **Salesperson:**   The quality of the copies you make of these sales proposals must be very poor. Isn't it?
> **Customer:**   It's OK.

Consequence Probes   When customers realize the disadvantage of their present product, the salesperson can use probes to illustrate the consequences of the disadvantage. Consider the following example of consequence probes:

> **Salesperson:**   How does the lack of copy quality affect you?
> **Customer:**   Well, we don't like it.
> **Salesperson:**   Since the sales proposals go to your customers, is there any chance the impact of the proposals is reduced?
> **Customer:**   Yes, I suppose that could happen.
> **Salesperson:**   Then is it possible that a customer may not have bought your product because of the image those copies projected?
> **Customer:**   That's possible.

Encouragement Probes   This type of probe encourages prospects to reveal further information. Verbal encouragement probes include ''Really,'' ''Uh-huh,'' ''That's interesting,'' and ''Is that so?'' Nonverbal behaviors such as head nodding are also effective encouragement probes.

An example of a sequence of encouragement probes follows:

> **Customer:**   . . . and then this salesperson asked me if I was interested in lower costs than I was getting from Delta.
> **You:**   That's interesting; tell me more about that.
> **Customer:**   Well, he said that at my current usage level, he could save me about $25 a month.
> **You:**   Do continue . . . please.
> **Customer:**   Then came the kicker.
> **You:**   Uh-huh.
> **Customer:**   When I asked about service, the whole picture changed.
> **You:**   I see.
> **Customer:**   In short, they were going to give me a lower cost all right, but they weren't going to give me much in the way of service.

Elaboration Probes   These probes serve the same purpose as encouragement probes; however, elaboration probes are positive requests for additional information rather than simply verbal encouragements. Some examples are:

> Can you give me an example of what you mean?
> Please, tell me more about that.

Reflective Probes   The third type of continuation probe is a reflective probe. Reflective probes are neutral statements that reaffirm or repeat a customer's comment. They allow the salesperson to dig deeper and stimulate customers to continue their thoughts in a logical manner. By using reflective probes, salespeople can respond to customers without agreeing or disagreeing with them. Reflective probes also allow salespeople to show they understand what the customer is saying. If the reflective probe is incorrect, the customer will point out the error.

Some examples of reflective probes are:

> You said you were dissatisfied with your present service?
> So you need the self-correcting feature?

Reflective probes are useful with customers who are angry, upset, or in some other highly emotional state. Often these emotions persist until the customers experiencing them recognize that their emotions are being acknowledged. The technique of reflection does exactly that—it acknowledges the emotional state of the customer. For example:

> **Customer:**   Look, I've just about had it with you, your company, and your machine!
> **You:**   It's pretty obvious you're upset, Ms. Roberts.
> **Customer:**   Of course I am—that's the third time this week the typewriters have gone on the fritz!

By acknowledging customers' emotional states, salespeople let customers know they're being heard. This allows salespeople to focus on the problem causing that emotion, and it usually reduces the level of negative feelings.

Reflective, encouragement, and elaboration probes are examples of neutral probes. The salesperson should continue to use neutral probes as long as they yield pertinent information. But excessive use of neutral probes can cause problems. The salesperson's interest may encourage the prospect to invent requirements that the salesperson's offering cannot meet. When this begins to occur, the salesperson should shift to more directed probes.

COMMUNI-CATING WITH WORDS[3]

There are two ways for people to communicate with each other—verbal and nonverbal. Verbal communication involves the transmission of words either in face-to-face communication, over a telephone, or through written messages. But many messages are communicated without words through such nonverbal means as facial expressions, body movements, or voice intonations. In this section and the next, we'll discuss these two forms of communication in more detail.

When messages are communicated verbally, they are encoded into symbols called words. It is important to realize that words are just symbols and that they have different meanings to different people. The true meaning of words is not in the words themselves or how the receiver interprets the words, it is in the sender's intentions when using the words.

Let us consider a presentation made by a salesperson who is working for a fabric manufacturer. During the presentation the salesperson indicates the fabrics made by the company are of high quality and durable, and their colors are *fast*. But will the prospect know what *fast* means? There are over 30 dictionary definitions of *fast*. Some of these definitions have to do with very different things, including eating habits, running, or behavior on a date. In this case, of course, the salesperson is pointing out the colors will not fade despite frequent washing or dry cleaning.

Each industry has its own trade jargon. A college textbook salesperson must know the meaning of such technical expressions as *test bank, transparency, quarters,* and *instructor's manual*. But salespeople cannot assume all of their customers will be familiar with this trade jargon, so they need to continually check with their customers to determine if their sales message is being interpreted properly.

Words have different meanings in different cultures, and even in different regions of the United States. In England the hood of a car is called a *bonnet*. In Boston, a *milkshake* is just syrup mixed with milk, while a *frappé* is ice cream, syrup, and milk mixed together. The words *ship* and *boat* have very different meanings to sailors.

Characteristics of Words

Words can be either abstract or concrete as well as emotional or neutral in connotation. Concrete words and expressions usually convey more information and are less vulnerable to misinterpretation than abstract

---

[3]See Stewart L. Tubbs and Sylvia Moss, *Human Communications* (New York: Random House, 1974), pp. 109–40.

words. The speed of a printer is communicated more effectively by saying, "This printer types 15 lines per minute," than by saying, "This printer types fast." As we have seen, the abstract word *fast* can be interpreted in many different ways.

Because many words related to politics, gender, and race have strong emotional content, they provoke an emotional response that can inhibit effective communications. Politicians are particularly adept at using words that typically involve a positive emotional response. Who could be against programs such as Truth in Lending, the Fair Deal, or the Right to Work?[4]

Words for Effective Communications

To avoid communications breakdowns, salespeople should not assume everyone understands what they are saying. In addition, they should not assume they understand everything their customers are saying. If there is any doubt about what is being communicated, salespeople should ask their customers to explain just what they mean by a particular expression or statement.

Effective communication is achieved only when salespeople use the communication framework of their customers. Above all, salespeople must use words familiar to the customer. At times salespeople may believe the use of multisyllabic and technical jargon will impress customers, but unfamiliar words usually confuse customers and fail to communicate sales messages effectively. A good communication principle is to use short words and short sentences.[5]

NONVERBAL COMMUNICATIONS

More than two thirds of our communications are nonverbal. Nonverbal communication is basically an unconscious language. People are often not aware of nonverbal signals they are transmitting or receiving. Salespeople need to learn how to read and respond to nonverbal signals sent by customers. In addition, salespeople can increase their effectiveness by using nonverbal communications to transmit messages.

It is frequently difficult to interpret nonverbal signals because such signals vary from culture to culture. For example, Americans typically become uncomfortable if someone invades their personal space, which extends two feet from them in all directions. People engaged in business communications are usually four to seven feet from each other.[6] On the other hand, Spanish people demand less space and like to converse at closer intervals. Because of these cultural differences, an American sales-

---

[4]See John Bremner, "Words for Selling Yourself: Turn Misuse and Abuse into Deft Effective Sparkle," *Marketing Times,* March–April 1981, pp. 40–43.

[5]See Jacob Weisberg, "Watch Your Language," *Sales & Marketing Management,* September 15, 1980, pp. 58–59, for a discussion of avoiding sexist language.

[6]Edward T. Hall, *The Hidden Dimension* (New York: Doubleday Publishing, 1966).

person might misinterpret the attempt of a Spanish customer to move closer to the salesperson.

In addition to cultural differences, many nonverbal cues can be interpreted only by using other evidence. For example, customers may rub their noses because of an itch or because they doubt the information being presented by the salesperson. When verbal and nonverbal signals provide conflicting information, the salesperson needs to dig deeper into the situation. The whole truth is not being told.

Nonverbal Communication Channels[7]

Monitoring nonverbal signals is simplified by scanning the five major channels: (1) body angle, (2) face, (3) arms, (4) hands, and (5) legs.

Body Angle   Back and forth motions indicate a positive outlook, while side to side movements suggest insecurity and doubt. Figure 6–3 shows how body movements directed toward a person indicate a positive regard while leaning back or away suggests boredom, apprehension, or possible anger. Changes in position may indicate a customer wants to end the interview, strongly agrees or disagrees with what has been said, or wants to place an order.

Face   The face has many small muscles capable of communicating innumerable messages. Customers can use these muscles to indicate interest, expectation, concern, disapproval, or approval.

The eyes are the most important area of the face. When people are interested or excited, their pupils tend to enlarge. Thus, by looking at a customer's eyes, salespeople can often determine when their presentations have made an impression. For this reason many Chinese jade buyers wear dark glasses so they can conceal their interest in specific items. In this way the buyers can be more effective in bargaining.

Customers typically avoid eye contact when they are trying to disguise their true emotions. Increased eye contact is an important signal. Information can also be learned by observing skin color and skin tautness. When a customer's face reddens, the customer is signaling that something is wrong. However, a blush can indicate either anger or embarrassment. Tension and anger can be detected by looking for a tightness around the cheeks, jaw line, or neck.

Arms   A key factor in interpreting this channel is intensity. Customers will use more arm movement when they are conveying an opinion. Broader

---

[7]This section and the next section rely heavily on Gerhard Gschwandtner and Pat Garnett, *Non-Verbal Selling Power* (Englewood Cliffs, N.J.: Prentice-Hall, 1985).

FIGURE 6–3
Positive and Negative Body Angles

Cameramann International, Ltd. photos

FIGURE 6–4
Positive and Negative Hand Signals

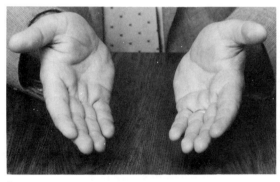 

Cameramann International, Ltd. photos

and more vigorous movement indicates the customer is more emphatic about the point being communicated verbally.

Hands   Some of the many hand gestures are shown in Figure 6–4. Open and relaxed hands are a positive signal, especially if the palms are facing up. Self-touching gestures typically indicate tension; while involuntary gestures such as a tightening of a fist are a good indicator of true feelings.

Legs   When customers have uncrossed legs in an open position as shown in Figure 6–5, they are sending a message of cooperation, confidence, and friendly interest. Legs crossed away from a salesperson suggests the sales call is not going well.

FIGURE 6–5
Positive and Negative Leg Signals

Cameramann International, Ltd. photos

Patterns of Nonverbal Expression

No single gesture or position indicates a specific emotion or attitude. To interpret a customer's feelings, salespeople need to consider the pattern of signals coming from a number of channels. Eight patterns of nonverbal expression are shown in Table 6–1.

Power   The first pattern of nonverbal cues indicates someone who wants to express power, dominance, or superiority. Customers who engage in this type of nonverbal behavior are trying to show salespeople they are taking control.

Nervousness   Customers are indicating they want reassurance when their nonverbal behaviors correspond to the second pattern. This pattern suggests customers are insecure about making a decision.

Disagreement   The third pattern arises when customers are reacting to what they are being told by salespeople. Customers may refrain from shouting, but these nonverbal gestures warn that they are unhappy.

Boredom   Sometimes a sales presentation will be very exciting to one customer and incredibly dull to another. When customers engage in the fourth pattern of nonverbal behavior, they are indicating disinterest. If their attention is not recaptured, their disinterest will turn into dissatisfaction.

Suspicion   When customers suspect salespeople are hiding something or being dishonest, they indicate this belief with the fifth pattern of nonverbal

Table 6–1   Patterns of Nonverbal Expression

	Cues from the Five Channels				
Interpretation	*Body Angle*	*Face*	*Arms*	*Hands*	*Legs*
Power, dominance, superiority	Sitting astride chair Exaggerated leaning over Standing while others sit	Piercing eye contact	Hands on hips	Hands behind neck Hands behind back Steepling (fingertips touching)	Leg over chair Feet on desk
Nervousness, submission, apprehension	Fidgeting Shifting from side to side	Head down Minimum eye contact Constant blinking	Hands to face, hair Rubbing back of neck	Wringing hands Fingers clasped	
Disagreement, anger, skepticism	Turning body away	Negative shake of head Lips pursing Eyes squinting Chin thrusting out Frown	Arms crossed Finger under collar	Fist Finger pointing Hands gripping edge of desk	Legs crossed
Boredom, disinterest	Head in palm of hands	Lack of eye contact Looking at door, at watch, out window Blank stare		Playing with object on table Shuffling papers Drumming on table	Tapping feet
Suspicion, secretiveness, dishonesty	Moving body away Sideways glance Crossing arms or legs with body forward	Avoiding eye contact Squinting eyes Smirking	Touching nose while speaking Pulling ear while speaking	Fingers crossed	Feet pointing toward exits
Uncertainty, indecision	Pacing back and forth	Head down or tilted Biting lip Shifting eyes left and right	Pinching bridge of nose Tugging at pants Scratching head	Pulling neck	Look of concentration while tapping feet
Evaluation	Head tilted slightly Ear turned toward speaker	Slight blinking of eyes Eye squinting Eyebrows raised Nodding	Hand gripping chin Putting glasses in mouth	Putting index finger to lips	Kicking foot slightly

Table 6–1 (concluded)

	Cues from the Five Channels				
Interpretation	*Body Angle*	*Face*	*Arms*	*Hands*	*Legs*
Cooperation, confidence, honesty	Leaning forward in seat	Good eye contact	Putting hands to chest	Open hands	Legs uncrossed
	Sitting far up in chair	Slight blinking	Free movement of arms and hands	Palms toward other person	Feet flat on floor
	Back and forth movement of body	Smile			

cues. This pattern suggests salespeople should provide proof for the causes of the customer's distrust and not get defensive or angry.

Uncertainty   The sixth pattern suggests customers are uncertain or indecisive. Providing more information may reduce their uncertainty. However, customers in this state may need some time to think and ask questions. When salespeople observe these nonverbal cues, they should take a break from their presentation and give the customers time to formulate their thoughts.

Evaluation   Customers indicate they are listening and evaluating a sales presentation when their nonverbal expressions resemble the seventh pattern. When salespeople see this pattern, they can proceed with their presentation.

Cooperation   The eighth pattern indicates customers are relaxed and happy with the salesperson.

Using Nonverbal Communications to Influence Customers

The previous section discussed how salespeople can observe nonverbal behavior to develop a better understanding of their customers. Salespeople also need to use their nonverbal behaviors to communicate more effectively with customers. For example, salespeople should avoid using the "power" nonverbal cues described in Table 6–1. These cues will intimidate customers and make them uncomfortable. On the other hand, salespeople should always strive to use the "cooperation" cues. These cues indicate to customers the salesperson is sincerely interested in helping them satisfy their needs. Figure 6–6 shows how Dan Rather altered his image by changing his nonverbal behavior.

Face   Nonverbal communications are very difficult to manage. Unless a salesperson has an expressionless face, he or she will find that facial reactions can be controlled only with practice. Often facial reactions are

Patterns of nonverbal expression described in Table 6–1.

Boredom, disinterest

Evaluation

Power, dominance, superiority

Nervousness, submission, apprehension

Suspicion, secretiveness, dishonesty

Disagreement, anger, skepticism

FIGURE 6–6
Changing Dan Rather from Public Defender to Public Servant

Before Dan Rather became anchor for "The CBS Evening News" he had won five Emmys and was considered to be the best White House correspondent in the history of broadcast journalism. With his extremely telegenic face, his success as a replacement for Walter Cronkite was inevitable. However, with Dan Rather as anchor, CBS's ratings dropped dramatically.

Viewers were asked why they had this unexpected negative reaction to Rather. The research showed that most people used words in the two left columns to describe Walter Cronkite and used words in the two right columns to describe Dan Rather:

Cronkite		**Rather**	
Warm	Seeks privacy	Cold	Seeks attention
Flexible	Equal	Rigid	Superior
Conciliatory	Relaxed	Aggressive	Tense
Other-oriented		Self-oriented	

The research indicated Dan Rather needed to adapt his body language from that of an aggressive reporter to his new role of a friendly and relaxed anchor.

The following changes were made to successfully alter his image:

Body movements: He used more forward and backward motion to convey drive and energy. He abandoned his highly controlled posture that made him appear rigid and tense.

Facial expression: After some coaching, Rather's face displayed a broader range of emotions, and his rate of smiling increased. He no longer ended broadcasts with serious or stilted expressions.

Eye movement: Too many downward eye movements to read his script made Rather appear to be cold, removed, and concerned only with facts—not with people. By using a TelePrompTer to increase eye contact, he seemed more human.

Arm posture: An increase in hand motion and arm movement gave Rather a more relaxed appearance.

Walter Cronkite
CBS Photography

Dan Rather

Source: Adapted from Gerhard Gschwandtner and Pat Garnett, *Non-Verbal Selling Power* (Englewood Cliffs, N.J.: Prentice-Hall, 1985), pp. 9–11.

involuntary, especially during stressful situations. Lips tense, foreheads wrinkle, and eyes glare without salespeople realizing they are disclosing their feelings to a customer.

Just like muscles anywhere else in the body, the coordination of facial muscles requires exercise. Actors realize this need and attend facial exercise classes to control their reactions. Salespeople are also performers to some extent and need to learn how to use their faces to communicate emotions.

Nothing creates rapport like a smile. The smile should appear natural and comfortable—not a smirk or the exaggerated grin of a clown. To have the right smile, stand before a mirror or a video camera, placing the lips in various smiling positions until finding a position that feels natural and comfortable. Then practice the smile until it becomes almost second nature.

Eye Contact   Appropriate eye contact varies from situation to situation. When talking in front of a group, direct eye contact reflects sincerity, credibility, and trustworthiness. Glancing from face to face or staring at a wall has the opposite effect. However, staring can overpower customers and make them uncomfortable.

Hand Movements   Hand movements can have a dramatic impact. For example, exposing the palm of the hand indicates openness and receptivity, while slicing hand movements are very strong signals and should be used to reinforce only the most important points. Pointing a finger also should be used to reinforce only the most important points. In most cases, pointing a finger should be avoided because it will remind customers of a parent scolding a child. When salespeople make presentations to a group, they often use too few hand gestures. Gestures should be used to drive home a point. But, if salespeople use too many gestures, like an orchestra conductor, people will begin to watch the hands and miss the words.

Posture and Body Movements   Shuffling feet and slumping give an impression of lacking both self-confidence and self-discipline. On the other hand, an overly erect posture, like that of a military cadet, suggests rigidity. When searching for the right posture, salespeople should let comfort be their guide. To get a good idea of what looks good and feels good, a salesperson can stand in front of a mirror and shift his or her weight until tension in the back and neck is at a minimum. Then gently pull the shoulders up and back and elevate the head. Practice walking by taking a few steps, keeping the pace deliberate, not halting. Deliberate movements indicate confidence and control.

Voice Characteristics   Good voice and speech habits are quite important for salespeople.[8] The degree to which a customer receives a salesperson's message depends upon the following vocal characteristics of the salesperson: rate of speech, loudness, pitch, quality, and articulation.

Salespeople should vary their rate of speech. Simple messages can be delivered at faster rates, while more difficult concepts should be presented at lower rates. To avoid monotony, salespeople should learn to vary the loudness of their speech. By changing the loudness pattern, they can indicate that certain parts of their sales presentation are of greater importance.

Articulation refers to the production of recognizable sounds. There are three common causes of poor articulation: (1) a locked jaw, (2) lazy lips, and (3) a lazy tongue. The best articulation is obtained when the mouth is opened by the width of a finger between the teeth. When the jaw is not opened properly, the movements of the lips and tongue are impeded. When the lips are too close together, the enunciation of certain vowels and consonants will be poor.

SUMMARY

In this chapter we've discussed the principles of improving the effectiveness of communication and reducing midunderstandings. The communication process consists of a sender who encodes information and transmits messages to a receiver who decodes them. A communications breakdown can occur when the sender does a poor encoding job, when the receiver has difficulty decoding, and when noise interferes with the transmission of the message.

Effective communication is based on a two-way flow of information. Both parties in the interaction act as sender and receiver at different times. This two-way communication enables salespeople to adapt their sales approach to the customers' needs and communication style. Listening and questioning are two valuable communication skills that enable salespeople to adapt effectively.

There are two modes of communication—verbal and nonverbal. When communicating through words, salespeople must be careful to use words and expressions their customers will understand. Effective communications are facilitated through the use of concrete, neutral words rather than abstract, emotional words.

More than two thirds of communications are conveyed by body messages, facial expressions, and voice characteristics. Salespeople can use nonverbal communications to convey information to customers and to determine which customers are reacting to their sales presentations.

---

[8]For a more complete treatment, see Dorothy Sarnoff, *Speech Can Change Your Life* (New York: Doubleday Publishing, 1970).

QUESTIONS
AND
PROBLEMS

1. Understanding nonverbal communications is more important to salespeople than understanding verbal communications. Do you agree? Why or why not?

2. What does the following body language mean:
    a. Tapping a finger or pencil on a desk.
    b. Stroking chin and leaning forward.
    c. Leaning back in a chair with arms folded across chest.
    d. Sitting in the middle of a bench or sofa.
    e. Assuming the same posture as the person with whom you are communicating.

3. Why is two-way communication preferable to one-way communication?

4. Assume you are a real estate salesperson. Make up three questions about residential houses that are designed to initiate two-way communication with a prospect.

5. Define communications. Can listening habits be a barrier to communication? If so, how?

6. Which communication—verbal or nonverbal—is more believable? Why?

7. Many people do not like to hear the words *sell* or *sold*. Why would you be unlikely to say the following to a friend? "Look at the new personal computer I was *sold* yesterday."

8. How can the personal appearance of a salesperson communicate to a customer?

9. Give two examples of open-ended and closed-ended questions. Why do open-ended questions generally improve communications?

10. It is often said a common outcome of communication is misunderstanding. Do you agree?

PROJECTS

1. Hold a conversation with another person and tape-record it. After the conversation, answer the following questions:
    a. When was each person a source, and when was each a receiver?
    b. What feedback signals did you get during the conversation?
    c. What noise entered this communication?
    d. How carefully did you listen during the conversation? How much of the conversation do you remember? What did you forget?
    e. What nonverbal communications did you detect during the conversation?

2. Make an appointment to accompany a salesperson on a sales call. Observe both the salesperson and the customer and write a report describing their verbal and nonverbal communications.

CASE PROBLEMS

Case 6–1   Communication and Persuasion—A Role-Playing Exercise

Instructions

Role playing provides an excellent opportunity for students to learn and practice selling skills. A role play is a dialogue situation. One student assumes the role of persuader and attempts to persuade the other person (the receiver) to undertake a course of action.

The student playing the receiver role should be an active participant in the dialogue. The receiver should listen to the arguments, make comments, ask questions, and express agreement or disagreement. The receiver should focus on the points made by the persuader and respond to them by assuming the receiver's role. When the receiver feels convinced by arguments presented, he or she should indicate the persuader's point of view has been accepted. Some topics for this initial role playing exercise are:

1. A student who is planning to begin a career in sales tries to persuade another student with different career goals to consider a sales career.
2. A nonsmoker tries to persuade a smoker to stop smoking.
3. A Democrat tries to influence a Republican to vote for a Democratic candidate.
4. An athlete tries to convince a student to attend the next home game.

5. A student tries to persuade another student of the need for more legislation to protect women's rights.

The students in the class should observe the role play dialogue closely and consider the following when the dialogue is completed.

Questions

1. Did the persuader develop rapport with the receiver by establishing a link through common interests or experiences?
2. Did the persuader maintain the receiver's interest throughout the role play?
3. Did the persuader determine what the receiver's needs were?
4. Did the persuader relate arguments to the receiver's needs?
5. Did the persuader monopolize the interaction?
6. Did the persuader listen and respond to the receiver's comments?
7. Did the persuader react to the receiver's body language?
8. Did the persuader use the appropriate voice tone and speed?
9. What significant nonverbal messages were sent during the interaction?

Case 6–2   Polytech Plastics

June Daniels, a sales representative for Polytech Plastics, calls on Jim Goodwin, an optometrist and the owner of Creative Eyewear in Boulder, Colorado. Ms. Daniels is trying to persuade Mr. Goodwin to carry the Polytech line of soft contact lenses in his store.

Ms. Daniels: Jim, I'd like to show you our new line of soft contact lenses. They are really attracting a lot of attention.

Mr. Goodwin: I've heard about them. Only last week I read an article in the *American Ophthalmologist* about some recent studies that showed. . . .

Ms. Daniels: Good! Then you know all about the advantages of soft contact lenses—the better fit, durability, and vision.

Mr. Goodwin: Well, fit is certainly a consideration. But. . . .

Ms. Daniels: It sure is. Customers also appreciate the improvement in vision compared to hard lenses. In fact, the soft contacts are getting a lot of people to switch to contact lenses.

Mr. Goodwin: I can understand that.

Ms. Daniels: We have developed an exciting marketing program to get you to carry our lenses. Our co-op advertising program offers big discounts to optometrists who fit more than 10 pairs of soft lenses a month.

Mr. Goodwin: Co-op advertising program?

Ms. Daniels: I knew you'd be excited. We also can save you a lot of money if you are a large user and qualify for our preferred customer program.

Mr. Goodwin: Sounds good. How have other optometrists been doing with soft lenses?

Ms. Daniels: Just great! Big sales at high margins.

Mr. Goodwin: What do the customers say?

Ms. Daniels: They just love the lenses. No problems. Can I take your order?

Mr. Goodwin: I've got an appointment coming in soon. Could you leave some material that I can look through? I'll get back to you.

Ms. Daniels: Sure. I've got some brochures in my briefcase. Can we set up an appointment?

Mr. Goodwin: Well, business has been really hectic. Let me give you a call. Thanks for stopping by.

Questions

1. Is Ms. Daniels a good listener?
2. What indicates Ms. Daniels has something to learn about communication skills?
3. Rewrite this dialogue to show how Ms. Daniels should have handled this sales call.

Case 6–3   Robertson Office Supply

David Peterson, a salesperson for Robertson Office Supply, has just entered the office of Neal Anderson, the manager of Homemade Crafts. Mr. Anderson is seated behind his large wooden desk, leaning back in his chair with his arms crossed and his feet on the desk.

Mr. Peterson [*walking around Mr. Anderson's desk and extending his hand*]: Good morning, Neal. It's nice to see you. How are you this fine spring morning?

Mr. Anderson [*remains seated; shakes hands*]: Just fine. You're a little late.

Mr. Peterson: Just five minutes. The traffic was awful.

Mr. Anderson [*pulling at his ear and squinting his eyes*]: Well, OK. What did you want to see me about?

Mr. Peterson: I want to show you a new form system we are offering. I think it will really save you some money.

Mr. Anderson [*pursing his lips and shaking his head*]: Before you go any further, let me tell you that we just placed an order for forms with Johnson supply.

Mr. Peterson [*putting his head down and shifting from side to side*]: I'm sorry to hear that. You should have called us up. Our prices have just been reduced by 20 percent.

Mr. Anderson [*uncrossing his arms, leaning forward in his chair, and gripping his chin with his hand*]: You have?

Mr. Peterson [*turning toward the door*]: Well, I guess it is too late if you have already placed the order. Next time give us a chance.

As Mr. Peterson leaves the room, Mr. Anderson sits with his elbow propped on his desk and both hands together in front of his face.

Question:

1. What nonverbal cues has Mr. Peterson missed?

SELECTED REFERENCES

Alessandra, Anthony J.; Phillip S. Wexler; and Jerry D. Deen. *Non-Manipulative Selling.* San Diego, Calif.: Courseware Inc., 1979.

Fast, Julius. *The Body Language of Sex, Power, and Aggression.* New York: Harcourt Brace Jovanovich. 1978.

Funkhauser, G. Ray. "A Practical Theory of Persuasion Based on Behavioral Science Approaches." *Journal of Personal Selling and Sales Management,* November 1984, pp. 17–25.

Goffman, Eric. *The Presentation of Self in Everyday Life.* New York: Doubleday Publishing, 1959.

Grikscheidt, Gary M.; Harold C. Cash; and W. J. E. Crissy. *Handbook of Selling: Psychological, Managerial, and Marketing Bases.* New York: John Wiley & Sons, 1981.

Gschwandtner, Gerhard, and Pat Garnett. *Non-Verbal Selling Power.* Englewood Cliffs, N.J.: Prentice-Hall, 1985.

Harper, Robert G.; Arthur N. Weins; and Joseph Matarazzo. *Non-Verbal Communications.* New York: John Wiley & Sons, 1978.

Kates, Henry E., and Karen W. Crane. *Body Language in Sales.* Indianapolis: Market Builders Library, 1980.

Reeves, Robert A., and Hiran C. Barksdale. "A Framework for Classifying Concepts of Research on the Personal Selling Process." *Journal of Personal Selling and Sales Management,* November 1984, pp. 7–16.

Schein, Edgar H. ''Improving Face-to-Face Relationships.'' *Sloan Management Review,* Winter 1981, pp. 43–52.

Schuster, Camille P., and Jeffrey E. Danes. ''Asking Questions: Some Characteristics of Successful Sales Encounters.'' *Journal of Personal Selling and Sales Management,* May 1986, pp. 17–28.

7
Effective Communications and Adaptive Selling

Some questions answered in this chapter are:

- How does personal selling differ from advertising?
- Why is it important for salespeople to practice adaptive selling?
- What are the different types of social styles?
- How can salespeople adapt their sales approach to customers with different social styles?
- How can transactional analysis be used to improve communications?

This chapter discusses how communications effectiveness is improved by adaptive selling. Two models—the social style matrix and transactional analysis—that can help salespeople adapt effectively are discussed.

IMPORTANCE OF PRACTICING ADAPTIVE SELLING[1]

Comparison between Advertising and Personal Selling

Companies communicate with potential customers in a number of ways, including publicity, packaging, sales promotion, mass media and print advertising, and personal selling (refer to Figure 1–3). However, personal selling is the only marketing communication vehicle in which the marketing message can be adapted to the needs and beliefs of each customer. Salespeople have an opportunity to do "market research" on each customer by asking questions and listening carefully. They can then use this information to develop and deliver a unique sales presentation tailored to be most effective with that customer. In addition, salespeople can observe the verbal and nonverbal behavior of their customers and make adjustments to their presentations.

In contrast to salespeople, advertising managers undertake more formal market research, but are limited to developing ads for broad groups of people (market segments), not individuals. Thus, their communications are tailored toward the typical customer in a segment and not ideally to many of the customers who might view the ad. Advertising managers are also limited in the adjustments they can make in an advertising campaign. While salespeople can make adjustments within minutes, it may take advertising managers months to determine that a campaign is not working and develop a new campaign.

Sales messages are more effective than advertising messages because sales messages can be adapted to each customer. However, companies pay more to deliver their messages through salespeople. The cost per minute for a sales presentation is about $5, while it costs less than one cent to deliver a mass media advertising message to a potential customer.

Adaptive Selling and the Sales Process

Salespeople practice adaptive selling when they alter their sales presentations during a sales call and when they use different presentations for different customers. An extreme example of *non*adaptive selling would be delivering the same "canned" presentation to all customers.[2] In contrast, salespeople are very adaptive when they use a unique approach for each customer and also alter their presentation during each interaction.

The importance of making adjustments is illustrated in Figure 7–1.[3] This diagram indicates a sequence of stages in the sales process, beginning with establishing rapport and credibility and ending with securing commitments and closing the sale. These stages are discussed in more detail in Chapter 10.

---

[1]See Barton A. Weitz, Harish Sujan, and Mita Sujan, "Knowledge, Motivation, and Adaptive Behavior: A Framework for Improving Selling Effectiveness," *Journal of Marketing,* October 1986, pp. 174–91.

[2]Marvin A. Jolson, "The Underestimated Potential of the Canned Sales Presentation," *Journal of Marketing,* January 1975, pp. 75–78.

[3]See Barton A. Weitz, "Relationship Between Salesperson Performance and Understanding Customer Decision Process," *Journal of Marketing Research,* November 1978, pp. 501–16.

FIGURE 7–1
The Selling Process

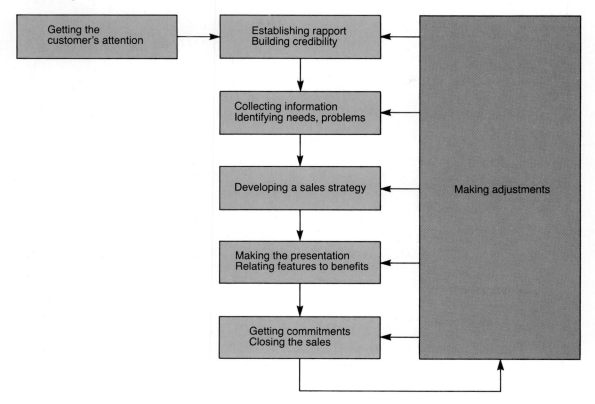

At each stage, the salesperson has an opportunity to make adjustments. By listening to what the customer says and observing body language, the salesperson can determine if the customer is interested in the product. If the customer is reacting favorably to the presentation, no adjustment is needed. But if the customer is not developing enthusiasm for the product, some alteration in the sales presentation is needed. Selling Scenario 7–1 compares the observation powers of Sherlock Holmes to those of successful salespeople.

Salespeople can alter their presentations in a number of ways. During the presentation the salesperson may discover the customer simply does not believe the salesperson has the appropriate product knowledge. Rather than continue with the presentation, the salesperson can redirect his or her efforts toward establishing credibility in the eyes of the customer.

Other adjustments might require collecting additional information about the customer, developing a new sales strategy, or altering the style of the presentation. For example, a salesperson may believe a customer is interested in buying an economical, low-cost motor. While presenting the benefits of the lowest-cost motor, the salesperson discovers the customer

By listening to the customer and observing body language, the salesperson can determine customer interest.

Diane Graham-Henry/Click, Chicago

is interested in the motor's operating costs. At this point, the salesperson can ask some questions to find out if the customer would be interested in paying a high price for a more efficient motor with lower operating costs. On the basis of the customer's response, the salesperson can adopt a new sales strategy that emphasizes operating efficiency rather than the motor's initial price. In this way, the sales presentation is shifted from features and benefits related to a low initial cost to features and benefits related to low operating costs.

An ability to make these adjustments is a crucial element in successful selling. By making these adjustments and practicing adaptive selling, salespeople are exploiting the unique advantages of personal selling over advertising. The social style matrix and transactional analysis are two approaches for assisting salespeople in making these adjustments.

SOCIAL STYLE MATRIX

One of the sales training programs most widely used by corporations is based on the social style matrix developed by David Merrill and his colleagues.[4] Their research uncovered patterns of behavior or social styles that people use when they interact with others. They found that if people adjust to these behaviors in others, they can achieve better relationships. The sales training program based on this research begins with helping trainees understand their own social style and identify their customers'

---

[4]David W. Merrill and Roger Reid, *Personal Styles and Effective Performance* (Radnor, Pa.: Chilton, 1981).

Selling Scenario 7–1

SHERLOCK HOLMES AND SELLING SKILLS

In an episode from *The Memoirs of Sherlock Holmes,* Holmes and Watson return to their Baker Street lodgings to learn from the page boy that a man had called during their absence, waited impatiently for awhile, then departed in a state of agitation, leaving his pipe behind on the table. Holmes picks the pipe up, examines it briefly, and makes the following observations to Watson:

"Now it has, you see, been twice mended: once in the wooden stem and once in the amber. Each of those mends, done, as you observe, with silver bands, must have cost more than the pipe did originally. The man must value the pipe highly when he prefers to patch it up rather than buy a new one with the same money. . . The owner is obviously a muscular man, left-handed, with an excellent set of teeth, careless in his habits, and with no need to practice economy."

So, what has this got to do with selling?

Surely the answer to that question is elementary.

If Sherlock Holmes had not given up his paper route early in life to become a detective, he might well have gone on to become a superlative salesperson. His keen powers of observation would have provided him with so many clues about his prospects' needs, desires, attitudes, and emotions that he would have been able to make effective presentations.

It is no accident that the best salespeople are likely to be people who observe their prospects closely and listen attentively to what they have to say. At the beginning of the sales interview the prospect is always a mystery: there is so much about him or her that is unknown. Unfortunately, at the end of the interview the prospect is still a mystery to many salespeople. The difference between the successful and unsuccessful salesperson is the ability to extract clues from the prospect. Observing and listening are the two best ways to do this. Salespeople should emulate the keen eyes and ears and the analytical approach for which Sherlock Holmes was renowned.

Source: Adapted from Craig Bridgman, "The Power of Observation," *Personal Selling Power,* October 1986, p. 10.

social styles. Then trainees are taught how to make appropriate adjustments in their sales behaviors.

Dimension of Social Style

The two critical dimensions used to understand social behavior are *assertiveness* and *responsiveness.* A third dimension, *versatility,* is discussed in a following section.

Table 7–1 Indicators of Assertiveness

Less Assertive	More Assertive
"Ask" oriented	"Tell" oriented
Go-along attitude	Take-charge attitude
Cooperative	Competitive
Supportive	Directive
Risk avoider	Risk taker
Makes decisions slowly	Makes decisions quickly
Lets others take initiative	Takes initiative
Leans backward	Leans forward
Indirect eye contact	Direct eye contact
Speaks slowly, softly	Speaks quickly, intensely
Moves deliberately	Moves rapidly
Makes few statements	Makes many statements
Expresses moderate opinions	Expresses strong opinions

Table 7–2 Indicators of Responsiveness

Less Responsive	More Responsive
Controls emotions	Shows emotions
Cool, independent	Warm, approachable
Task oriented	People oriented
Uses facts	Uses opinions
Serious	Playful
Impersonal, businesslike	Personable, friendly
Moves rigidly	Moves freely
Limited use of gestures	Gestures frequently
Formal dress	Informal dress
Disciplined about time	Undisciplined about time
Controlled facial expressions	Animated facial expressions
Monotone voice	Many vocal inflections

Assertiveness Assertiveness is the amount of effort people use to influence the thoughts and actions of others. People who are assertive are very direct. They speak out, make strong statements, and have a take-charge attitude. Nonassertive people are usually easy-going and supportive. As a rule, nonassertive people assume an asking role, while assertive people assume a telling role.

Some indicators of assertiveness are shown in Table 7–1. It is important to recognize that these characteristics merely indicate a tendency to be assertive or nonassertive. People's actual behavior can vary in assertiveness in different situations.

Responsiveness Responsiveness is the amount of effort people use to control their emotions when relating to others. Responsive people readily show their emotions. They are friendly, warm, and informal. People who are nonresponsive have learned to control their emotions. As a result, they are usually proper, cool, and formal. Table 7–2 lists some indicators of responsiveness.

Table 7–3 contains rating scales that can be used to rate your own social style. But we need to be cautious in interpreting our own self-rating. Research has found that self-assessments can be misleading because people often do not see themselves the same way others see them. When social styles are assessed for sales training, a trainee's associates are used to determine the trainee's style. Each of the person's associates rates the person, and these ratings are combined to determine the person's communication style.

Table 7–3   Self-Assessment of Social Styles

On the responsiveness scale, total your score and then divide the results by 15.
On the assertiveness scale, give yourself a "1" for every "A," "2" for every "B," "3" for every "C," and "4" for every "D." Total your score and divide by 15. The average score translates into the following rating.

Average Rating	Rating on Assertiveness	Rating on Responsiveness
1.00 to 1.49	A	1
1.50 to 2.49	B	2
2.50 to 3.49	C	3
3.50 to 4.00	D	4

Assertiveness Ratings
I perceive myself as:

Quiet	. . . . .Talkative
D	**C**	**B**	**A**
Slow to decide	. . . . .Fast to decide
D	**C**	**B**	**A**
Going along	. . . . .Taking charge
D	**C**	**B**	**A**
Supportive	. . . . .Challenging
D	**C**	**B**	**A**
Compliant	. . . . Dominant
D	**C**	**B**	**A**
Deliberate	. . . . .Fast to decide
D	**C**	**B**	**A**
Asking questions	. . .Making statements
D	**C**	**B**	**A**
Cooperative	. . . . Competitive
D	**C**	**B**	**A**
Avoiding risks	. . . . .Taking risks
D	**C**	**B**	**A**
Slow, studied	. . . . Fast-paced
D	**C**	**B**	**A**
Cautious	. . . . .Carefree
D	**C**	**B**	**A**
Indulgent	. . . . .Firm
D	**C**	**B**	**A**
Nonassertive	. . . . Assertive
D	**C**	**B**	**A**
Mellow	. . . . .Matter-of-fact
D	**C**	**B**	**A**
Reserved	. . . . Outgoing
D	**C**	**B**	**A**

Responsiveness Ratings
I perceive myself as:

Open	. . . . Closed
4	3	2	1
Impulsive	. . . . Deliberate
4	3	2	1
Using opinions	. . . . Using facts
4	3	2	1
Informal	. . . . Formal
4	3	2	1
Emotional	. . . . Unemotional
4	3	2	1
Easy to know	. . . . Hard to know
4	3	2	1
Warm	. . . . Cool
4	3	2	1
Excitable	. . . . Calm
4	3	2	1
Animated	. . . . .Poker-faced
4	3	2	1
People-oriented	. . . . Task-oriented
4	3	2	1
Spontaneous	. . . . .Cautious
4	3	2	1
Responsive	. . . . Nonresponsive
4	3	2	1
Humorous	. . . . Serious
4	3	2	1
Impulsive	. . . . .Methodical
4	3	2	1
Lighthearted	. . . . Intense
4	3	2	1

Profiles of Social Styles

These two dimensions of social style are used to form a social style matrix (see Figure 7–2). The quadrants in the matrix define four profiles of social styles. Drivers are high on assertiveness (tell) and low on responsiveness (control). Expressives are high on assertiveness (tell) and high on responsiveness (control). Amiables are high on responsiveness (emote) and low on assertiveness (ask). Finally, Analyticals are low on assertiveness (ask) and responsiveness (control).

FIGURE 7–2
Social Style Matrix

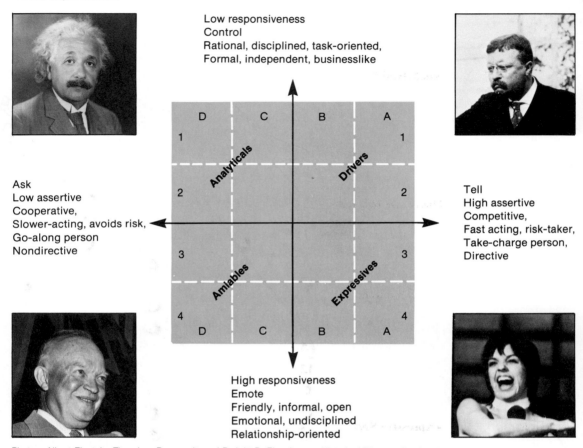

Low responsiveness
Control
Rational, disciplined, task-oriented,
Formal, independent, businesslike

Ask
Low assertive
Cooperative,
Slower-acting, avoids risk,
Go-along person
Nondirective

Tell
High assertive
Competitive,
Fast acting, risk-taker,
Take-charge person,
Directive

High responsiveness
Emote
Friendly, informal, open
Emotional, undisciplined
Relationship-oriented

Photos: Albert Einstein, Theodore Roosevelt, and Dwight D. Eisenhower, Historical Pictures Service, Inc.; Liza Minelli, United Press International.

These four social style types can be related to some well-known personalities. Television commentator David Brinkley, former President Jimmy Carter, and Albert Einstein are in full control of their emotions and very thoughtful. They are good examples of Analyticals. By way of contrast, Liza Minelli, Winston Churchill, and Muhammad Ali are Expressives. While more emotional than David Brinkley and President Carter, they are also take-charge people.

Presidents Eisenhower and Teddy Roosevelt illustrate the difference between Amiables and Drivers. Eisenhower's warm personality and unassuming manner demonstrated a nonaggressive, emotive social style that

led to the "I like Ike" image. In contrast Teddy Roosevelt's slogan—
"Speak softly and carry a big stick"—indicates a nonresponsive, high-
control approach coupled with an aggressive posture. Other examples of
drivers are Barbara Walters and Mike Wallace, while President Gerald
Ford, Mary Tyler Moore, and John Denver are famous Amiables.

Analytical Style   These people are systems specialists who both *ask* and
control. Analyticals are seen as people who ask questions, gather facts,
examine all sides of an issue, and then make a logical decision. They are
best influenced by selling appeals that recognize their technical expertise,
emphasize long-run performance, and offer tangible evidence to back up
the sales claims. Such people like to take time to think about a decision
before they make it.

Driver Style   These people are control specialists who both *tell* and *control*. Drivers are task-oriented people who want to have their own way.
They are self-motivated and like the challenge of nonroutine work. To
influence Drivers, salespeople need to use a direct, businesslike approach
with quick action and followup. The "bottom line" should be emphasized.

Amiable Style   These people are support specialists who *ask* and *emote*.
Amiables are agreeable individuals and good listeners; they usually like
to build long-term relationships. When selling to Amiables sales representatives ought to emphasize such human considerations as the impact
the product will have on the workers' morale at the Amiables' place of
business. Emphasis should be placed on mutual trust, assurance of performance, and minimizing of risks.

Expressive Style   These people are relations specialists who *tell* and *emote*.
Expressives thrive on interpersonal contact, are highly intuitive, and have
a tendency to go with their gut reactions. Expressives are influenced by
sales approaches that place them in the role of an innovator, the first
person to use a new product. Testimonials are quite effective with Expressives. Generally, Expressives make a decision fairly quickly and work
out the details later.

Identifying Social Styles

Some cues for identifying the social style of a prospect or customer are
shown in Table 7–4. Salespeople can learn a lot about their customers by
observing them and looking carefully at the place in which they work. In
addition, simple, straightforward questions addressed to people who know
the prospects can uncover a wealth of information about them. This information can be confirmed or discounted when a meeting occurs between
the prospects and salespeople.

Table 7–4 Cues for Recognizing Social Styles

Analyticals	Drivers
Technical background	Technical background
Achievement awards on wall	Achievement awards on wall
Office is work-oriented, showing a lot of activity	No posters or slogans on office walls
Conservative dress	Calendar prominently displayed
Like individual leisure activities, such as reading, individual sports	Desk placed so contact with people is across desk
	Conservative dress
	Like group activities, such as politics, team sports

Amiables	Expressives
Liberal arts background	Liberal arts background
Office has friendly, open atmosphere	Motivational slogan on wall
Pictures of family displayed	Office has friendly, open atmosphere
Personal mementos on wall	Cluttered, unorganized desk
Desk placed for open contact with people	Desk placed for open contact with people
Casual or flamboyant dress	Casual or flamboyant dress
Like individual leisure activities, such as reading, individual sports	Like group activities, such as politics, team sports

Social Styles and Selling Approaches

What is the best social style for a salesperson? The answer is that no one social style can be characterized as the ''best'' for a given salesperson. Each style has its strong points and its weak points. Driver salespeople are efficient, determined, and decisive, but they may also be perceived as pushy, harsh, and dominating. Some favorable aspects of Expressives are their enthusiasm, dramatic flair, and personable approach, but Expressives can also be seen as opinionated, undisciplined, and excitable. Analyticals are usually orderly, serious, and industrious, but they may be viewed at times as stuffy, impersonal, and uncommunicative. Finally, Amiables are supportive, dependable, and willing, but they can also be undisciplined, conforming, and emotional.

Sales training programs based on the social style matrix emphasize that the objective of salespeople is not merely to present themselves and their product. To effectively communicate with customers, salespeople must recognize the customers' needs and expectations. Salespeople should conduct themselves in the sales interview in a manner consistent with the customers' expectations. Table 7–5 shows how expectations differ for customers who have different social styles.

For example, salespeople interacting with Drivers will be most effective if they are businesslike, inform customers of their qualifications, describe what their product can do, provide documented evidence of the results that can be achieved by using their product, and present a set of options.

Table 7–5 Expectations of Customers with Different Social Styles

Customer's Expectation about:	Customer's Social Style			
	Driver	*Expressive*	*Amiable*	*Analytical*
Atmosphere in sales interview	Businesslike	Open, friendly	Open, honest	Businesslike
Salesperson's use of time	Effective and efficient	Leisurely to develop relationship	Leisurely to develop relationship	Thorough and accurate
Pace of interview	Quick	Quick	Deliberate	Deliberate
Information provided by salesperson	Salesperson's qualifications, value of products	What salesperson thinks and who he/she knows	Evidence that salesperson is trustworthy, friendly	Evidence of salesperson's expertise in solving problem
Salesperson's actions to win customer acceptance	Provides documented evidence, stresses results	Gives recognition and approval	Shows personal attention and interest	Provides evidence salesperson has analyzed the situation
Presentation of benefits	Shows *what* product can do	Shows *who* has used the product	Shows *why* product is best to solve problem	Shows *how* product can solve the problem
Assistance to aid decision making	Provides options and probabilities	Offers testimonials	Provides guarantees and assurances	Offers evidence and service

On the other hand, when salespeople interact with Amiables, they need to be more deliberate, spend time developing the relationship, provide evidence that they are trustworthy, show personal interest in the customer, present why their product will solve the customers' problems, and offer guarantees and personal assurances.

Even though different sales approaches should be used for each customer type, salespeople tend to use the sales approach that is similar to their style rather than their customer's style. For example, a Driver salesperson selling to an Amiable customer will have a tendency to be task oriented, businesslike, efficient, and quick; even though the Amiable customer prefers to deal with a salesperson that is relationship oriented, friendly, nonthreatening, and deliberate. Thus, to be effective with a variety of customer types, salespeople must be able to modify their own style so it conforms to the style of the customer.

Versatility and Style Modification

Versatile salespeople—salespeople who are able to adapt their social style—have a significant advantage over salespeople who cannot adjust their social behaviors. Some indicators of versatility are shown in Table 7–6.

Table 7–6   Indication of Versatility

Less Versatile	More Versatile
Limited adaptability to others' needs	Able to adapt to others' needs
Specialist	Generalist
Well-defined interests	Broad interests
Firm of principle	Negotiates issues
Predictable	Unpredictable
Single-minded	Looks at many sides of issue

Salespeople can increase their versatility by mastering the communication skills discussed in Chapter 6. Through asking questions, listening, and interpreting nonverbal communication, salespeople can collect the customer information needed for effective adaptation.

Another method for increasing versatility is style modification. Salespeople can adjust their social style so it is compatible with the customer's style. For example, salespeople with a Driver orientation need to become more emotional and less aggressive when selling to Amiable customers. An Analytical salesperson must increase his or her responsiveness and reduce assertiveness when selling to an Expressive customer. Some techniques for altering sales behavior in terms of assertiveness and responsiveness are shown in Table 7–7.

Increasing Assertiveness   When dealing with assertive (Driver and Expressive) customers, nonassertive (Analytical and Amiable) salespeople need to simplify and clarify their opinions so they can be understood quickly, volunteer opinions and initiate ideas, and take positions on issues even if it means disagreeing with customers.

Reducing Assertiveness   When assertive salespeople are selling to nonassertive customers, the salespeople should ask questions so the customers will express their opinions, engage in active listening, refrain from interrupting customers, and let the customers assume control of the conversation more often.

Reducing Responsiveness   When responsive (Amiable and Expressive) salespeople encounter nonresponsive (Analytical and Driver) customers, the salespeople need to listen more and talk less, display more self-control, pause and reflect before talking, and acknowledge customers' opinions.

Increasing Responsiveness   When selling to responsive customers, nonresponsive salespeople should admit to their feelings, let their positive feelings come out by paying compliments, engage in more social conversation, and use more informal language and nonverbal communication.

Table 7–7 Adjusting Sales Styles

Reducing Assertiveness	*Reducing Responsiveness*
Ask for customer's opinion	Become businesslike
Acknowledge merits of customer's viewpoint	Talk less
	Restrain enthusiasm
Listen without interruption	Make decision based on facts
Be more deliberate, don't rush	Stop and think
Let customer direct flow of conversation	
Increasing Assertiveness	*Increasing Responsiveness*
Get to the point	Verbalize feelings
Don't be vague or ambiguous	Express enthusiasm
Volunteer information	Pay personal compliments
Be willing to disagree	Spend time on relationships rather than business
Take a stand	Socialize—engage in small talk
Initiate conversation	Use nonverbal communication

TRANSAC-TIONAL ANALYSIS[5]

Transactional analysis (TA), developed by Dr. Eric Berne, is another method for analyzing human behavior and interactions. TA, like the social style matrix, is useful for interpreting the actions of others and avoiding misunderstandings that can lead to a breakdown in communications.

Three Ego States

Transactional analysis proposes that each person has three ego states—the Parent, the Child, and the Adult. An ego state is a mental condition that influences a person's behavior. The potential ego states of people communicating with each other—a salesperson and a customer—are shown in Figure 7–3.

While there may be some overlap between ego states, at any particular time one of the ego states is dominant. However, people can shift from one ego state to another several times during a conversation. Transactional analysis can be used to determine the ego state of the other person in the conversation and to develop a suitable strategy that corresponds to that ego state.

Parent Ego State People in the Parent ego state behave the way their parents acted toward them when they were children. When the Parent ego dominates, people tend to be authoritative, critical, and domineering. They lecture and scold the people to whom they are communicating, they have a preconceived idea of what is right and wrong, and they emphasize rules and do not listen to what the other person is saying. In TA, people

[5]See Eric Berne, *Games People Play* (New York: Ballantine Books, 1978); and Thomas A. Harris, *I'm OK—You're OK* (New York: Harper & Row, 1969).

FIGURE 7–3
Three Ego States

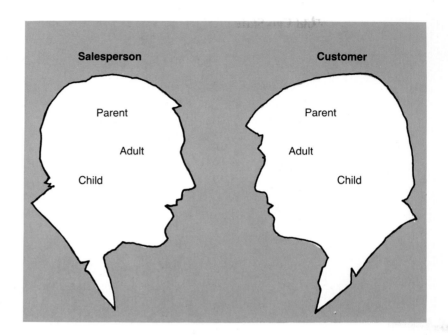

dominated by the Parent ego state are seen to be engaging in "automatic," or nondeliberative, behavior.

Some expressions a person uses when dominated by the Parent ego state are:

> We always do it this way.
>
> It's not right to spend that much for a luxury.
>
> If I were you, I'd tell your company to put a button on the front panel.
>
> We never buy products from Alpha.
>
> I can't depend on you.
>
> Don't tell me what to do.
>
> Your company had better shape up or we will get a new supplier.

Corresponding to these Parent-state statements are nonverbal communications such as a raised voice, pointed finger, pursed lips, folded arms, clicking tongue, and a shaking head.

A salesperson who uses high pressure, dominates the sales calls, and does not listen to the customer is acting under the influence of this ego state. The customer who is highly critical, raises many objections, and tells the salesperson what to do is also acting under the influence of the Parent ego state.

Child Ego State   While the Parent ego state represents the person's conscience, the Child ego state represents the emotional side of people. We need to keep in mind that a child can be either good or bad. When the Child ego state is dominant, the person may be cheerful, happy, curious, and spontaneous. On the other hand, the person may also be selfish or sulky; he or she may throw temper tantrums or seek to avoid the normal responsibilities of life. Like the Parent state, a person in the Child state is seen to be acting automatically.

Some expressions a person may use when dominated by the Child ego state are:

I want that.

You're not going to sell me anything.

Let's talk about it over a drink.

I don't care about your products.

Nonverbal communications are very important in the Child ego state, just as they are important in children who lack well-developed verbal skills. It has been observed that when people are in the Child ego state, their facial expressions tend to change rapidly. They may laugh, whine, giggle, or squirm. As in the Parent state, people in the Child state do not attend to what others are saying.

Adult Ego State   People dominated by the Adult ego state are realistic and rational. They act as mature individuals who make decisions based on facts. Unlike the automatic nature of the Child and Parent states, people in the Adult state act deliberately. Alternatives are thoroughly considered in an orderly manner. They have businesslike attitudes and are interested in exchanging information without becoming emotionally involved.

Some expressions used by a person in the Adult ego state are:

Your product appears to meet our requirements.

When can you deliver the product?

I think we should compare the speed of your drive system to the speed of Acme's system before making a decision.

What companies are using your equipment now?

Here is how our product works.

Effective Communications and TA

During an exchange or "transaction" between two people such as a salesperson and customer, each person is in one of the three ego states. While in one of the three ego states, a person directs communication toward one of the three states of the other person. Some of these transactions are shown in Figure 7–4. For example, a customer in the Parent ego state may direct his or her communication as Parent-Child ("Your product needs to be improved"), Parent-Adult ("What makes you think I want

FIGURE 7–4   Examples of Complementary Transactions

Salesperson's Ego State	Customer's Ego State	
a. Ⓟ ⟵⟶ Ⓟ, Ⓐ Ⓐ, Ⓒ Ⓒ		**Customer:** Your competitor's synthesizer is certainly unreliable. **Salesperson:** Isn't that the truth? I'd never buy it.
b. Ⓟ Ⓟ, Ⓐ Ⓐ, Ⓒ ⟵⟶ Ⓒ		**Customer:** Would you have a drink with me after work? **Salesperson:** I'd love to. I really like being with you.
c. Ⓟ ⟶ Ⓟ, Ⓐ ⟵ Ⓐ, Ⓒ Ⓒ		**Customer:** Your deliveries need to be accelerated or I'm going to cancel my order. **Salesperson:** I'll try to get my company to do better, but it's not my fault.

to buy from Alpha?'') or Parent-Parent (''This is a dog-eat-dog business''). Similarly a salesperson in the Parent state can respond, directing his or her communications to one of the customer's states. For example, a salesperson in the Parent state can respond as Parent-Child (''Don't let another salesperson tell you anything different''), Parent-Adult (''How can you say no to my offer?'') or Parent-Parent (''I don't have to tell you how rough the last six months have been'').

When the two parties are shown diagrammatically, as in Figure 7–4, a transaction is considered complementary if the two directional communication arrows are parallel. For example, in Figure 7–4a, both the salesperson and customer are communicating as Parent to Parent; in Figure 7–4b, they are communicating Child to Child; and in Figure 7–4c, they are communicating Child to Parent. In these cases, the communication is considered complementary and can last indefinitely as long as the parties remain in their present ego states.

Communications can break down whenever the two directional communication arrows are nonparallel, or crossing, as shown in Figure 7–5. Figure 7–5a depicts a case where both the salesperson and the customer are directing communication as Parent-Child. In 7–5b, the salesperson is communicating as Adult-Adult, while the customer is taking a Parent-Child posture. In these two examples, the transaction is noncomplementary, and a breakdown in communication will result.

While transactions such as 7–4a and 7–4b are complementary, these transactions often do not result in effective communication. At times during a sales interaction, salespeople need to respond to the emotions of their customers. Thus, salespeople should assume a Child-Parent or Parent-Child communication style to complement their customers. But to communicate effectively, both the salesperson and the customer typically

FIGURE 7–5   Examples of Noncomplementary Transactions

Salesperson's Ego State	Customer's Ego State	
a.		**Salesperson:** You should buy our typewriter; it's the only one that will do your job. **Customer:** We always use Beta typewriters. They're the only ones that are reliable. You should know that.
b.		**Salesperson:** The self-correcting feature of our typewriters will reduce the time needed to type reports. **Customer:** Speaking of time, you were late for your appointment. You should be on time if you want to make it as a salesperson.

FIGURE 7–6   Adult-Adult Transaction

Effective Communication

Salesperson's Ego State	Customer's Ego State	
		Salesperson: The self-correcting feature of our typewriter will reduce the time needed to type reports. **Customer:** Yes, this typewriter will increase productivity.

must be dominated by the Adult ego state, such as in Figure 7–6. It is difficult to discuss the benefits of products and services with customers who are in the Parent or Child ego states. When customers are in these states, they are concentrating on defending themselves against the salesperson rather than communicating effectively. The salesperson needs to get the Adult ego state of the customer dominant. This is called hooking the Adult.

Hooking the Adult   Effective communication occurs only when both the salesperson and the customer are dominated by the Adult ego state. Thus, to initiate effective communication, a salesperson would have to change the transaction from Figure 7–5b to Figure 7–6. Salespeople must learn how to bring customers back to the Adult state. Often this goal is very difficult to achieve because customers in the Child or Parent ego state may react to salespeople by avoiding them. When this condition arises, salespeople never have the opportunity for a meaningful discussion with customers.

When salespeople do have an opportunity to interact with customers in a Child or Parent ego state, the first principle for the salesperson is to remain in the Adult ego state. While this may not be a complementary transaction, as in Figure 7–5b, it is a necessary step in modifying the situation to an Adult-Adult transaction. The salesperson could make this transaction noncomplementary by shifting to Parent-Child communications.

For example, a salesperson might respond to the customer's comment in Figure 7–5b by saying, "It's impossible for me to be on time for all my appointments. I can't tell how long some calls are going to take or how bad the traffic is going to be." A salesperson who makes such a response has shifted his or her communication from Adult-Adult to Parent-Child. He may or may not win the argument; the salesperson probably will not get the order. Similarly, the salesperson may respond, "I'm really sorry. It's all my fault—I need to show up for my appointments more promptly." In doing so, the salesperson is responding as Child-Parent, making the relationship complementary, but not necessarily effective in getting an order.

The appropriate response for the salesperson would be, "I understand how you feel. Your time is valuable, and I won't let this happen again." This response demonstrates the salesperson understands the customer's feelings and respects the customer's needs.

Listening and expressing understanding during the interaction are the best methods of hooking the Adult. Customers in the Child or Parent state are dominated by emotions. By encouraging such customers to express their emotions, salespeople help them get such automatic responses out of their systems. When customers have a chance to talk about these feelings, they often realize the feelings are automatic and emotional, not rational responses. They can then return to the more rational, deliberate Adult state, and their problems can be handled objectively.

Stroking   An important aspect of maintaining effective communication is stroking. Stroking is making the Child of the person feel good. Some forms of stroking are:

1. Indicating awareness by simply saying "hello" to a person.
2. Making eye contact.
3. Listening to what people say; taking time and letting people finish their sentences.
4. Asking questions.
5. Using names; introducing yourself and using the name of other people as you talk to them.
6. Rewarding people by sending a note saying you appreciate something they have done.
7. Loosening up and using humor.[6]

---

[6]Wagle, John S., "Using Humor in the Industrial Selling Process," *Industrial Marketing Management,* November 1985, pp. 221–26.

SUMMARY   In this chapter, we have emphasized that both effective communication and effective selling are accomplished by salespeople adapting their sales approach to the needs of their customers. Two models used to improve adaptive selling skills are the social styles matrix and transactional analysis.

The social styles matrix defines four social styles—Analytical, Driver, Expressive, and Amiable. Salespeople can determine their social styles and the social styles of their customers by consulting friends and observing verbal and nonverbal behaviors. Selling effectiveness is improved when salespeople adjust their social styles to conform with their customers' social styles. Salespeople need to improve their versatility in terms of increasing or decreasing assertiveness and responsiveness, depending on the customer's nature.

Many people have found that transactional analysis is an effective approach for improving communication. TA suggests that salespeople need to be aware of the ego state indicated by their comments and their customers' comments. Effective communications are achieved when both customer and salesperson are communicating Adult-Adult. Thus, salespeople should attempt to communicate Adult-Adult and "hook" the Adult state of the customer.

QUESTIONS
AND
PROBLEMS

1. A salesperson who is a Driver is preparing to deliver a sales presentation. What suggestions can you make to improve the salesperson's performance during the call?

2. A good salesperson can sell any type of buyer. Do you agree? Why or why not?

3. Potential customers often have more favorable opinions of salespeople who are similar to them. What is the significance of this statement to salespeople?

4. What do you think of the following statement? "Good salespeople need to be aggressive. They need to have powerful voices and a winning smile."

5. If you are an Expressive, what adjustments should you make when selling to an Amiable?

6. Construct a "Crossed Transaction" between a sales representative and a customer.

Sender	Responder	
ⓟ	ⓟ	1. _____
Ⓐ	Ⓐ	2. _____
Ⓒ	Ⓒ	

7. What social styles do individuals listed below display? Why?
   a. Lucy, in "Peanuts."
   b. Diane in "Cheers."
   c. Angela Lansbury in "Murder, She Wrote."

    d. Johnny Carson.
    e. Sharon Gleiss in "Cagney and Lacey."
    f. Eliza Doolittle in *My Fair Lady.*
    g. Bob Newhart in "Newhart."
    h. Charles Bronson.

PROJECTS
1. Listen to a television program and record a conversation that demonstrates "hooking an adult."
2. Make an appointment to accompany a salesperson on a sales call. Classify the customer and salesperson in terms of their social styles—Expressive, Amiable, Driver, or Analytical—and justify your classification.

CASE PROBLEMS

Case 7–1   The Reluctant Shopper

Salesperson: This suit is just perfect for you. You look very dignified in blue, and the style is just what you need on the job.

Customer [*tentatively*]: Well, it is a nice suit.

Salesperson: It sure is. You should buy it right now. These suits are going like hotcakes. You're not going to find anything better.

Customer: Gee, I don't know.

Salesperson: What don't you know about? It's perfect.

Customer: I wish you wouldn't pressure me so much. I like the suit, but I don't know if I need another suit. I have a blue suit now.

Salesperson: Just look in the mirror. Don't you think this suit gives you a real authoritative air? You know you can charge it, and you won't have to pay for it for 60 days.

Customer: I'm just not sure. It's a lot of money.

Salesperson: You really ought to buy this suit.

Customer: I guess I'll think it over, and maybe I'll come back.

Salesperson: OK, but we probably won't have it in stock when you come back.

Questions

1. Analyze this sales interaction using transactional analysis to explain what happened.

2. What should the salesperson have done in this situation?

Case 7–2   Using the Social Styles Matrix to Develop Sales Approaches

Rich Calson

His office is pleasant and really looks "worked in." You notice a couple of file folders on the floor behind this person's desk. There are two, attractive nonbusiness posters (not framed) on the walls. There are also four small framed group photos on the wall. You notice a number of souvenirs on the desk. Chairs are comfortable and casually arranged. An assortment of snapshots is tucked in the frame of a family portrait on the desk.

Sammy Taylor

There are a lot of things on his walls— framed, autographed photos of sports notables, a Chamber of Commerce "citizenship citation," children's colorful crayon drawings, a large newspaper ad with a clever headline. A tennis bag with racquet is propped against a cabinet full of trophies. You count at least eight stacks of papers and magazines. The visitors' chairs are pulled close to this person's desk.

Sandra Conner

Her office has one oil painting and nicely framed prints on the walls. There is a large stack of business periodicals on the credenza behind the desk. The pen and

pencil set on the desk has an achievement plaque with the occupant's name on it. The desk is cluttered with current work, but the rest of the office is well organized. You notice a "to do" list with today's date on it next to the telephone. The desk divides the room in two and separates you from the occupant.

Boris Black

His office is relatively neat. There are some nicely framed diplomas and achievement certificates on the walls. There are two reference posters with helpful business data pinned to the wall nearest the desk. There are several "in-out" baskets, all well labeled. Two chairs are set up so the occupant faces visitors directly across the desk.

Questions:

1. Identify each customer's social style.
2. Outline the approach you would take to sell each customer.

Case 7–3 Exercise in Identifying Ego States

Read each of the statements below. Identify each statement as to the ego state that is talking and determine whether the transaction is complementary or crossed.

1. **Travel agent:** Joe, this is Bud French from Carefree Travel. One of your flight attendants gave my best customer a hard time on her flight home last night. What kind of airline are you guys running, anyway? _____

   Airline salesperson: Hey, what are you yelling at me for? I can't keep an eye on every flight attendant every second! _____

   Travel agent: Maybe you'd better start! I'm going to start using you people as a last resort! _____

   Airline salesperson: Oh, come on, Bud! You're making a big deal over nothing! _____

   Travel agent: It *is* a big deal! Your airline almost lost me a good customer! _____

2. **Manager:** Job review is due next month, John. I'll be taking a close look at you. _____

   Salesperson: I wonder if I can stack up against the others? _____

3. **Traveler:** This food is lousy! _____

   Flight attendant: What is it that you don't like, sir? _____

   Traveler: To begin with, it's ice cold! _____

   Flight attendant: I'm sorry about that, sir. Let me get you a hot one. _____

   Traveler: Thank you very much. ___

4. **Sales rep:** According to many of the companies I deal with, an incentive package that includes a trip to an exotic place seems to motivate their salespeople. _____

   Sales manager: They should be motivated without having fancy trips to shoot for. I work hard because I want to! Why shouldn't they? _____

5. **First friend:** You're 30 minutes late for our tennis game. Why can't you ever be on time? _____

   Second friend: I got here as soon as I could. _____

SELECTED REFERENCES

Bolton, Robert. *People Skills*. Englewood Cliffs, N.J.: Prentice-Hall, 1978.

Bolton, Robert, and Dorothy Grover Bolton. *Social Style/Management Style*. New York: American Management Association, 1984.

Cialdini, Robert B. *Influence, How and Why People Agree to Things*. New York: William Morrow, 1983.

Harris, Amy Bjork, and Thomas A. Harris. *Staying OK*. New York: Avon, 1985.

Ingrasci, Hugh J. "How to Reach Buyers in Their Psychological 'Comfort Zone.' " *Industrial Marketing,* July 1981, pp. 60–64.

James, Muriel, and Dorothy Jonge Ward. *Born to Win*. New York: New American Library, 1978.

Jolson, Marvin A. "Selling Assertively." *Business Horizons,* September/October 1984, pp. 71–77.

Soldow, Gay F., and Gloria Penn Thomas. "Relational Communications: Form versus Content in Sales Interaction." *Journal of Marketing,* Winter 1984, pp. 84–93.

Williams, Kaylene C., and Rosann L. Spiro. "Communication Style in Salesperson-Customer Dyads." *Journal of Marketing Research,* November 1985, pp. 434–42.

III The Sales Process

Part I of this book provided a general introduction to the nature of selling jobs. In Part II, we reviewed the knowledge about customers, products, company policies, and competition, along with the communication skills an effective salesperson needs. In Part III, we discuss the seven steps in the sales process (shown on the next page). Notice the highest step, and the goal of a sales interaction, is to build a long-term relationship—one in which the customer develops loyalty and commitment to the salesperson and to his or her product. Making a sale is just one step toward achieving this goal!

Chapter 8 covers the first step in the sales process: locating potential customers. This initial activity identifies the people most likely to purchase the products or services offered by the salesperson. Steps 2 and 3—planning the sales interview and making the initial contact—are treated in Chapter 9. Chapters 10 and 11 review the methods of making presentations and the characteristics of effective presentations (Step 4). An important aspect of a sales interview, overcoming customers' objections, is treated in Chapter 12 (Step 5). Chapter 13 deals with Step 6, the logical conclusion to a single sales interaction—closing a sale. Finally, the methods for converting a single sale into a long-term relationship (Step 7) are reviewed in Chapter 14.

Seven Steps in the Sales Process

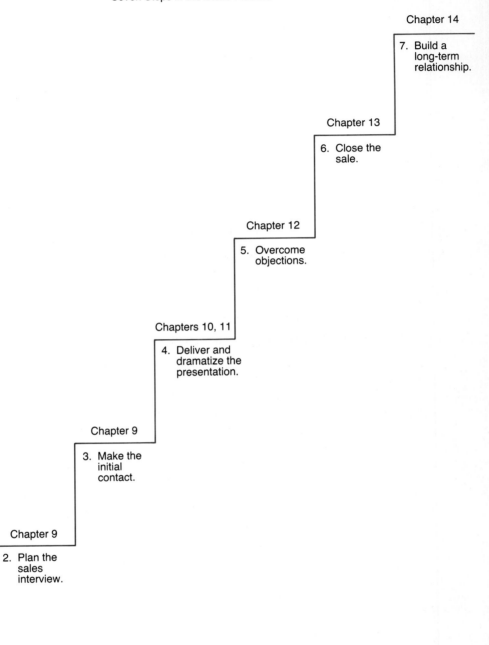

Chapter 14

7. Build a
   long-term
   relationship.

Chapter 13

6. Close the
   sale.

Chapter 12

5. Overcome
   objections.

Chapters 10, 11

4. Deliver and
   dramatize the
   presentation.

Chapter 9

3. Make the
   initial
   contact.

Chapter 9

2. Plan the
   sales
   interview.

Chapter 8

1. Locate
   potential
   customer.

8

Prospecting and Qualifying Potential Customers

Some questions answered in this chapter are:

- Why is prospecting important for effective selling?
- Are all sales leads good prospects? What are the characteristics of a qualified prospect?
- How can prospects be located?
- How can the telephone and direct mail be used in prospecting?
- What are the elements in a prospecting plan, and how should it be developed?
- How can a salesperson overcome a fear of prospecting?

Finding new customers is the first phase of the selling process. This activity is particularly important because sales volume will slip unless new customers are obtained to replace customers lost through relocation, bankruptcy, and solicitation by aggressive competitors.

Seven Steps in the Sales Process

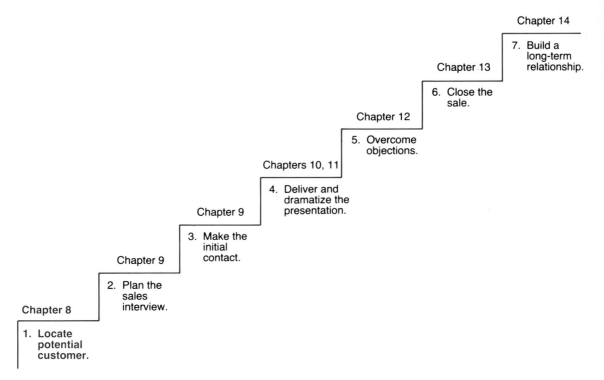

IMPORTANCE OF PROSPECTS

Beginning the Sales Process

Prospecting begins the process of converting prospects into repeat customers. Figure 8–1 shows how the sales process starts when sales leads are used to identify prospects. A suspect is a potential prospect, that is, a person or organization that *might* have a need for a salesperson's products or services. Many suspects will not become prospects because they have no real need for the products or services. If a salesperson determines the suspect *has* a real need for the product, then that person or organization becomes a prospect. The next step is for the salesperson to qualify the prospect to find out if that person has both the ability and the authority to make a purchase.

Once a qualified prospect is located, the selling process begins. The sales process does not end with the first order that converts the prospect into a customer. The goal of all salespeople is to get repeat business—to convert the customer into a repeat customer. Figure 8–1 shows how the sales process rejuvenates itself. Both customers and repeat customers can be sources of new prospects.

Need for Prospects

Having a list of prospects is critical to the success of both experienced and new salespeople. For this reason, acquiring prospects is a continuing process. Today, extensive changes are taking place in population move-

FIGURE 8–1
Converting Sales
Leads into Repeat
Customers

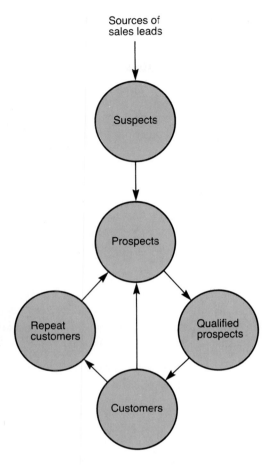

ments, in creation of new businesses and products, in shifting of businesses to new lines, in expansion of old-line companies, and in methods
or channels of distribution. It is estimated these changes result in a 15 to
20 percent annual turnover of customers. Unless a company has a steady
flow of new prospects, it will soon be out of business.

Prospecting is more important in some selling fields than in others. The
life insurance or real estate sales representative who does not have an
effective prospecting plan, for example, usually does not last long in the
business. The New York Life Insurance Company emphasizes the importance of prospecting as follows:

> No one with an ample supply of good prospects ever left the life
> insurance business. As long as the human heart keeps pumping
> blood through the veins, a person continues to live despite all
> other infirmities. As long as prospecting keeps pumping a supply
> of names, a person continues in the life insurance business.[1]

---

[1]*Prospecting Guide* (New York: New York Life Insurance Co., 1975), p. 3.

In these sales positions, a general rule is that it takes 100 suspects to get 50 prospects, to have an opportunity to make 25 presentations, which will result in 12 sales.

Prospecting is important even for salespeople in high-technology products. A recent survey of computer salespeople found that reps who had sales of more than 150 percent of quota did more prospecting than lower performing salespeople. To generate leads, they relied heavily on referrals, business-related articles in newspapers and trade journals, civic meetings, and cocktail parties.[2]

In many types of retail selling, on the other hand, most of the prospecting is done through advertising. Salespeople who can go out and get their own prospects have an advantage over retail salespeople who must wait for customers to come into the store. Some retailers, such as appliance dealers, recognize the importance of an aggressive prospecting system by having salespeople call at homes to demonstrate and sell their products.

CHARACTER-ISTICS OF A GOOD PROSPECT

Some salespeople make the mistake of considering everyone a prospect without first finding out whether they possess the necessary characteristics.

The importance of qualifying prospects is illustrated in a statement made by a vice president of Emery Air Freight Corporation:

> Most sales reps are sitting in lobbies. They're calling on
> wrong accounts. They're calling on accounts that give them
> all the business that they can. They're calling on people that
> they think can make the buying decision when, in fact, they
> do not or cannot make much of it at all. They are efficient in
> talking about what they do—what their company provides—
> but not in how it fills the customer's needs, because they
> haven't probed to find out what those needs are.[3]

Successful salespeople are realists who soon determine how fine a screen should be used in separating suspects from prospects. They discover the most profitable way to distribute time between prospecting and making sales presentations. Naturally, the amount of time spent trying to answer the question "Who is a prospect?" varies for different types of selling. It depends on such factors as the type of product or service, the value of the salesperson's time, and the profit per sale.

The following five questions will help determine who the good prospects are:

1. Does the prospect have a want or need that can be satisfied by the purchase of my products or services?

---

[2]Robert J. Pacenta, John K. Ryans, and William L. Shankin, "High-Tech Can't Forget Sales Prospecting," *Industrial Marketing,* November 1981, pp. 78–79.

[3]"The New Supersalesman: Wired for Success," *Business Week,* January 6, 1973, p. 45.

2. Does he or she have the ability to pay?
3. Does he or she have the authority to buy?
4. Can the prospect be approached favorably?
5. Is the prospect eligible to buy?

Does a Want or Need Exist?

Most sales are made on the basis of primary or recognized needs. The salesperson considers such needs as basic in selecting prospects but also includes as prospects those people who may have unrecognized needs for the salesperson's products. The salesperson should always remember the old adage, "Sell a product to a customer where the product doesn't come back but the customer does." By using high-pressure tactics, sales may be made to those who do not need or really want the salesperson's products. Such sales benefit no one. The buyer will resent making the purchase, and a potential long-term customer will be lost.

Research has not supplied infallible answers to why customers buy, but it has found that there are many reasons. Some customers buy products to satisfy basic practical needs. As pointed out in Chapter 5, customers also buy to satisfy intangible needs, such as prestige or aesthetic desires.

It is not simple, therefore, to choose those prospects who need a salesperson's products or services. Life insurance salespeople often use the telephone to determine the needs of a lead or suspect. Industrial salespeople often have an exploratory interview to determine whether a lead has needs their products can handle. With some product lines, almost everyone is a prospect. For example, Avon salespeople call on all the homes in their territory because virtually everybody uses their products.

Does the Prospect Have the Ability to Buy?

The individual's or company's ability to pay for the products or services helps to separate suspects from prospects. The real estate agent usually tries to find out the financial status of each client to determine which price-range house to show. A client with a yearly salary of $30,000 and savings of $20,000 may be a genuine prospect for a house selling in the $70,000 to 80,000 bracket. An agent would be wasting time, however, showing this client a house listed at $125,000. The client may have a real desire and need for the more expensive house; the client may have the authority to buy the house; the agent may be able to approach the client on a favorable basis; but the client is still not a real prospect for the higher priced house if he or she doesn't have the ability to pay for it.

Industrial companies may subscribe to a rating service such as Dun & Bradstreet or Moody's Industrial. Salespeople can use this service to determine the financial status and credit rating of a lead. Leads can also be qualified using information obtained from local credit agencies, noncompetitive salespeople, and the Better Business Bureau.

Moody's—a source of information about companies.

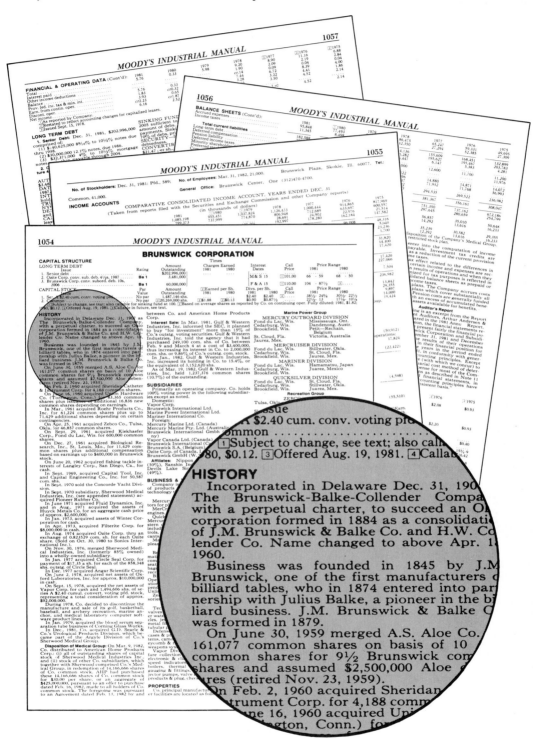

Does the Prospect Have the Authority to Buy?

A suspect may have a real need for a product and the ability to pay for it but may lack the authority to make the purchase. Knowing who has this authority saves the salesperson time and effort and results in a higher percentage of closed sales.

Consider the following experience. A machine tool company planned its advertising and sales efforts on the assumption that its machines were being purchased by production managers. An analysis of coupon and letter inquiries, however, showed that only 10 percent came from production executives. The rest came from engineers (44 percent), purchasing agents (29 percent), and others (17 percent). As a result of this survey, the company redirected its advertising and sales efforts toward engineers and purchasing agents.

Can the Prospect Be Approached Favorably?

Some people may have a need for goods, the ability to pay, and the authority to buy, but still not qualify as prospects because they are not accessible to the salesperson. For example, the president of a large bank, a major executive of a large manufacturing company, or the senior partner in a well-established law firm normally would not be accessible to a young college graduate starting out as a sales representative for an investment trust organization. Getting an interview with these people may be so difficult and the chances of making a sale so small that the sales representative eliminates them as possible prospects.

Is the Prospect Eligible to Buy?

Eligibility is an equally important factor in determining if a person is a genuine prospect. A possible prospect for life insurance may meet all of the other requirements of a real prospect but be unable to pass the necessary medical exam. This one factor eliminates the person as a prospect.

Likewise, if a manufacturer's representative sells exclusively to wholesalers, the representative should be certain the individuals he or she calls on are qualified wholesalers. Another factor that may determine eligibility to buy from a particular salesperson is the geographic location of the prospect. Many companies operate on an exclusively territorial basis. In this case, each salesperson must consider the prospect's location to determine eligibility to buy.

HOW AND WHERE TO OBTAIN PROSPECTS

Prospecting methods and sources vary for different types of selling. A sales representative for commercial chemicals uses a different system than that used by the car, real estate, or life insurance salesperson.

Table 8–1 summarizes how frequently computer salespeople use various sources for prospects and how effective they believe these sources are. Notice that satisfied customers are the most effective sources. Some of the most common prospecting methods are described in this section.

Table 8–1   Source of Prospects for Computer Salespeople

Source	Percentage of Salespeople Who:	
	Often or Occasionally Use Source	*Almost Always Find Source Effective*
Salespeople from your firm (those *not selling* in your line of business)	93%	48%
Referrals from satisfied customers	91	50
Salespeople from your firm (those *selling* in your line of business)	88	24
Engineering departments of potential customers	85	21
Each person you contact during the day	63	25
Responses to your company's ads in trade publications	59	4
Local trade shows	57	8
Civic meetings, cocktail parties, and other social events	49	2
Purchasing departments of potential customers	48	3
Your company's files on firms located in your territory	48	12
Industrial directories	45	8
Business-related articles in newspapers or journals	31	1
Lists bought from list brokers	27	5
Local chambers of commerce	21	5
Professional society meetings	19	1
Discussion with noncompeting salespeople from other firms	9	1

Source: Robert J. Pacenta, John K. Ryans, and William Shankin, "High-Tech Can't Forget Sales Prospecting," *Industrial Marketing*, November 1981, pp. 78–79.

Inquiries

Most companies receive a steady supply of sales leads from their advertising, telephone calls, and catalogues. The importance of these leads as a source of prospects is illustrated by the following comment:

> The exciting truth is that inquiries generated by advertising, direct mail, publicity, trade shows, etc., can and do produce sales. Our experience at Clayton Manufacturing is that at least 45 percent of our inquiries come from prospects who (1) have a real interest in our products, (2) have the necessary decision-making authority to buy them, and (3) intend to purchase the type of product about which the inquiry is made within about eight months.
>
> More than 30,000 inquiries for our basic product lines have been received and processed, and millions of dollars of sales have been identified and recorded that we can prove are directly traceable to advertising inquiries.[4]

[4]Frank S. Hill, "Why Clayton Loves Its Inquiries," *Sales & Marketing Management*, Special Report 117, November 22, 1976, pp. 5–6.

The following example shows how a typical company helps its salespeople find customers. Beckman advertises its digital multimeter in *Electronic Technician/Dealer,* a trade magazine. A reader sees the ad and requests additional information, using a reader service card in the magazine. The ad and the reader service card are shown in Figure 8–2. *ET/D* forwards information about all people who inquire about the digital multimeter to Beckman. Each is sent a cover letter and information about the advertised product and a followup inquiry card (see Figure 8–3). A copy of the inquiry is also sent to the appropriate salesperson. On the basis of his or her knowledge of the territory, the salesperson determines whether a personal followup is appropriate. If the inquirer returns the second inquiry card (frequently called a *bounce-back card*), the salesperson is sent a "qualified" inquiry notification.

The leads are printed on a multiple copy of the form. The salesperson is asked to return a copy of the form with information about the followup of these leads. Some companies prequalify leads before distributing them to salespeople.[5]

Endless-Chain Method

When sales representatives use this method to obtain prospects, they try to get at least one additional prospect from each person they interview. This endless-chain method of prospecting has proved very effective in the sale of such intangible products as educational courses, insurance, and investments. Industrial salespeople also use this method to locate other people in a customer's company who may also need their products.

This simple but effective plan of prospecting produces a continuous supply of good prospects for the salesperson who is skillful in knowing when and how to ask for names. Some people object to having their names used as a means of opening the door to friends or relatives. Others, particularly those who are enthusiastic over the sales representative's products or services, will not hesitate to provide the names of additional prospects. They may write a letter or card of introduction for the sales representative. A prospect obtained this way is known as a *referred prospect* and is generally considered to be the highest type of prospect.

Figure 8–4 shows a case history of how a life insurance sales representative used the endless-chain method of prospecting to produce $300,000 worth of business within an eight-month period. All the clients shown in the illustration came directly or indirectly as a result of the first referral from an engineer to whom the sales representative had sold a $20,000 policy. This example indicates the wide range of the client's occupational activities. It is also significant to see how one referral from a lawyer was responsible for $115,000 of insurance sales.

---

[5]H. S. Cummings, "Streamlined Sales Management Doubles Customers," *Business Marketing,* March 1985, pp. 100–104.

FIGURE 8–2
Advertisement and
Request for
Additional
Information

Courtesy of SmithKline Beckman

FIGURE 8–3
Cover Letter, Data Sheet, and Salesperson Copy of Inquiry

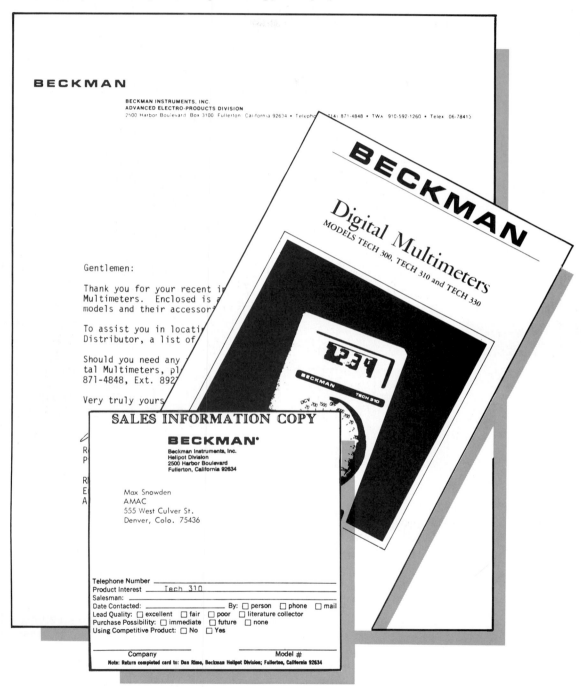

BECKMAN

BECKMAN INSTRUMENTS, INC.
ADVANCED ELECTRO-PRODUCTS DIVISION
2500 Harbor Boulevard Box 3100 Fullerton California 92634 • Telephone (714) 871-4848 • TWX 910-592-1260 • Telex 06-78413

Gentlemen:

Thank you for your recent i...
Multimeters. Enclosed is a...
models and their accessori...

To assist you in locati...
Distributor, a list of...

Should you need any...
tal Multimeters, pl...
871-4848, Ext. 892...

Very truly yours...

BECKMAN
Digital Multimeters
MODELS TECH 300, TECH 310 and TECH 330

SALES INFORMATION COPY

BECKMAN·

Beckman Instruments, Inc.
Helipot Division
2500 Harbor Boulevard
Fullerton, California 92634

Max Snowden
AMAC
555 West Culver St.
Denver, Colo. 75436

Telephone Number _____
Product Interest _____ Tech 310 _____
Salesman: _____
Date Contacted: _____ By: ☐ person   ☐ phone   ☐ mail
Lead Quality: ☐ excellent   ☐ fair   ☐ poor   ☐ literature collector
Purchase Possibility: ☐ immediate   ☐ future   ☐ none
Using Competitive Product: ☐ No   ☐ Yes

_____   _____
        Company   Model #
Note: Return completed card to: Dan Rime, Beckman Helipot Division; Fullerton, California 92634

FIGURE 8–4
Example of ''Endless-Chain'' Method of Prospecting

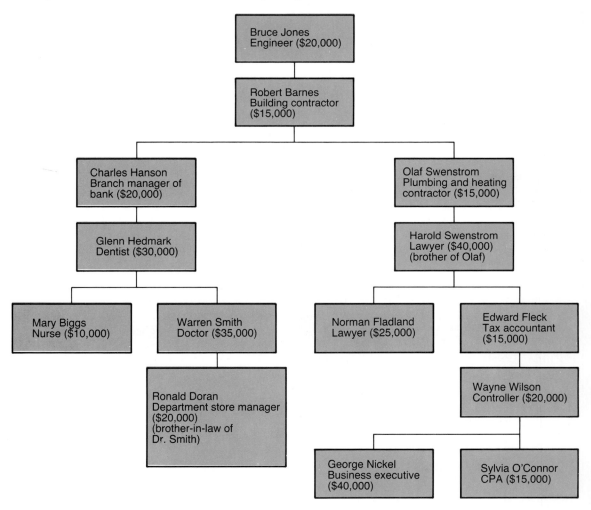

Center-of-
Influence
Method

This prospecting plan is a modification of the endless-chain method. The salesperson cultivates people in the territory who are willing to supply prospecting information. Whenever possible, well-known, influential men or women are cultivated as centers of influence.

In industrial sales situations, the centers of influence are frequently people in important departments not directly involved in the purchase decision, such as quality control, equipment maintenance, and receiving. The salesperson keeps in close touch with these people over an extended period, solicits their help in a very straightforward manner, and keeps them informed on sales that result from their aid.

The Penn Mutual Life Insurance Company recommends the following approach for its new sales representatives when calling on a center of influence:

> Mr. Brown, I have made what I believe to be a mighty fine connection with a real future for me. I am at present taking the training course of the Penn Mutual Life Insurance Company, but I am doing no selling as yet. As I expect this to become my life work, I am anxious to build a permanent and substantial clientele.
>
> You can help me to this extent, if you will. My job is to get before people in a favorable light. Who is the most promising young married man you know?[6]

Centers of influence can be very productive for the salesperson in a number of ways. They provide information about potential prospects, and they help the salesperson make appointments by introducing their friends or acquaintances personally or through the use of cards, letters, or the telephone.

The sales representatives who have the greatest success with the center-of-influence method of prospecting are those who provide the right kind of service to their customers. Influential people have little use for the sales representative who puts self-interest above the prospect's interest. However, they are happy to assist the salesperson who represents his or her company in a professional manner.

Public Exhibitions, Demonstrations, and Trade Shows

Many companies display or demonstrate their products at automobile shows, business machine shows, trade association and professional conventions, and state or county fairs. Sales representatives are present to demonstrate their products to inquiring visitors.

Trade shows are an important source of prospects who are not reached regularly by salespeople. A recent survey found that 83 percent of the people with buying influence who visited manufacturers' exhibits had not been called on by the manufacturers' sales representatives during the year before the show.[7]

At most trade shows, the salesperson's primary function is to qualify prospects for future followup. Typically, the salesperson has only 5 to 10 minutes with a prospect. The marketing manager of Minnesota Rubber instructs his salespeople "to dispense with the small talk used in field selling and get down to the business of qualifying the prospect immediately." To that end, he provides a checkoff form for qualifying buyers.[8]

---

[6]*Prospecting* (Philadelphia: Penn Mutual Life Insurance Co., 1975), p. 9.

[7]William Mee, "Who Visits Your Booth and Why," *Sales & Marketing Management,* August 20, 1979, pp. 64–66.

[8]"Minnesota Rubber Gets Leads Bouncing," *Sales & Marketing Management,* August 20, 1979, p. 78.

Trade shows are an
important source of
prospects for
salespeople.

Brian Seed/Click, Chicago

Lists

Individual sales representatives need to develop prospect lists of their
own by referring to such sources as public records, classified telephone
directories, chamber of commerce directories, newspapers, club membership lists, and professional or trade association membership lists. Secondary sources of information in public libraries can be useful. For example, there are industrial trade directories for most states. Figure 8–5
shows pages from the *New York State Industrial Directory.* The geograph-
ically arranged list of companies provides prospects for an office equipment salesperson whose territory includes Nassau County. A salesperson
selling small motors could use the list of companies manufacturing electrical household appliances in New York state. Salespeople should become
familiar with the information applicable to their business. A list of some
useful secondary sources is shown below:

1. Guides and bibliographies
   Encyclopedia of Business Information Sources, 3rd ed.
   (Detroit: Gale, 1976); 2 vols.
   Guide to American Directories, 9th ed. (Coral Springs, Fla.:
   B. Klein Publications, 1975).
2. National directories:
   Middle Market Directory, annual (New York: Dun &
   Bradstreet).

FIGURE 8–5
Pages from *New
York State
Industrial Directory*

Poor's Register of Corporations, Directors, and Executives,
annual (New York: Standard & Poor's).

3. Trade directories:
    Macrae's Blue Book, annual (Springfield, Ill.: Charles C.
    Thomas); 5 vols.

    Thomas Grocery Register, annual (New York: Thomas).

    Thomas Register of American Manufacturers (Endicott, N.Y.:
    Thomas-Newell).

    U.S. Industrial Directory, annual (Stamford, Conn.: Cahners); 4 vols.

4. Trade associations:
    Encyclopedia of Associations (Detroit: Gale, 1976).

FIGURE 8–6

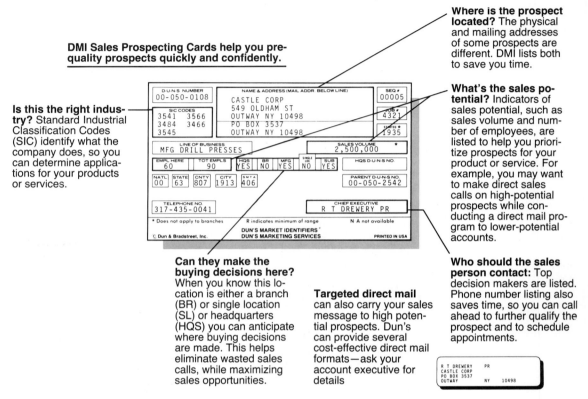

DMI Sales Prospecting Cards help you pre-quality prospects quickly and confidently.

Where is the prospect located? The physical and mailing addresses of some prospects are different. DMI lists both to save you time.

Is this the right industry? Standard Industrial Classification Codes (SIC) identify what the company does, so you can determine applications for your products or services.

What's the sales potential? Indicators of sales potential, such as sales volume and number of employees, are listed to help you prioritize prospects for your product or service. For example, you may want to make direct sales calls on high-potential prospects while conducting a direct mail program to lower-potential accounts.

Can they make the buying decisions here? When you know this location is either a branch (BR) or single location (SL) or headquarters (HQS) you can anticipate where buying decisions are made. This helps eliminate wasted sales calls, while maximizing sales opportunities.

Targeted direct mail can also carry your sales message to high potential prospects. Dun's can provide several cost-effective direct mail formats—ask your account executive for details

Who should the sales person contact: Top decision makers are listed. Phone number listing also saves time, so you can call ahead to further qualify the prospect and to schedule appointments.

Courtesy of Dun & Bradstreet

Dun & Bradstreet also provides prospecting cards from its files for a fee (see Figure 8–6 for an example).

Friends and Acquaintances

In many fields the salesperson's friends and acquaintances serve as an important source of prospects. This is particularly true in selling insurance or cars. The Guardian Life Insurance Company of America analyzed where its successful agents secured their prospects. The results of this analysis are shown in Table 8–2.

New insurance sales representatives usually start building their prospect lists with the names of friends and neighbors. They add to this list the names of those to whom it will be possible to secure a favorable introduction from a mutual acquaintance. Every possible source of new and old acquaintances is explored. The sales representatives think back to their school associates; they join social, fraternal, religious, civic, and professional organizations or clubs; they list the names of persons to whom they pay money—the milk carrier, the grocer, and the doctor; they

Table 8–2 Where Successful Agents
Secure Their Prospects

Source	Percent
Old general acquaintances	35
Old associates	4
Recommended or introduced	39
Office leads	11
Newspapers and lists	4
Advertising and circulars	2
Cold-canvass	5

Source: Guardian Life Insurance Company of
America, *The Guardian Training Program for
Successful Selling*, sec. 3, "Prospecting," p. 3.

An automobile salesperson's friends and acquaintances are important prospects.

Cezus/Click, Chicago

try to recall the names of former co-workers; and they list the names of people they have met through sports or recreational activities.

Cold-Canvass Method

If a product has widespread demand among most of the people or companies in a territory, the salesperson may resort to the cold-canvass method of prospecting. He or she calls on every individual or company belonging to a certain group. No advance information as to the needs or financial status of each of these suspects is available. The salesperson relies on the law of averages to provide sales. Past experience may indicate that one sale will result from every 10 calls. This ratio varies, depending on the company and the salesperson.

The cold-canvass method has been used extensively for a long time. The H. J. Heinz Co. was launched in England by cold canvassing. Henry John Heinz, the company founder, made his first major sale in England after a cold call on "the largest house supplying the fine trade of London and suburbs and even shipping."[9]

Cold canvassing does waste the salesperson's time because many suspects have no need for the product or no ability to pay for it. Yet this disadvantage is offset by the complete territorial coverage that often results in sales to people who would otherwise be neglected.

Some companies use a selective type of cold canvass they refer to as a *cool canvass*. In this plan, a complete canvass is made of each person within a classification. A car salesperson, for example, may secure a list of all the doctors in the community and may then make a complete canvass of them.

One of the commercial airlines has its sales representatives "blitz" a certain area of a city by calling at every building to solicit business. During these calls, the sales representatives pass out folders and seek the aid and goodwill of everyone in a business concern from the receptionist to the manager.

Other Sources of Prospects

Some other sources of prospects are as follows:

1. *Salespeople for noncompetitive but related products.*
2. *Personal observation.* Many salespeople find prospects by regularly reading trade journals, business publications (such as *Business Week* and *The Wall Street Journal*), and the local newspaper and by just keeping their eyes open when they drive through their territory.
3. *Sales associates or spotters.* In selling cars, "sales associates" or "spotters" are sometimes used to do missionary prospecting work. The associate provides information concerning potential prospects. If the salesperson makes a sale, the associate is compensated.
4. *Group prospecting.* Many companies that sell such products as aluminum ware, cosmetics, kitchen utensils, and jewelry rely on group prospecting to stimulate sales. The sales representative might work with women's clubs by providing mass demonstrations to members. Each club receives a premium for its part in arranging the demonstration. Another method is to compensate a person for holding a party in his/ her home.

---

[9]Robert Alberts, "Those 57 Varieties of Selling Know-How," *Marketing Times,* May–June 1974, pp. 20–23.

USING
DIRECT
MAIL FOR
PROSPECT-
ING

The use of direct mail for prospecting is illustrated by the sales experiences of the president of a large data-entry equipment company:

> Inforex president Mike Harvey's aversion to cold calls began on the first day of his sales career, as an IBM account representative in 1962. "I became interested in marketing," he recalls, "and kept all the secretaries in the branch office busy typing the direct mail pieces I created to screen out the poorest prospects." In his second year he went 400 percent over quota and was made president of the 100% Club, IBM's elite group of supersellers.
>
> Later, he was transferred to a Chicago branch and given the local universities as an account responsibility. "A university is really a hundred separate customers," he notes, "because each department can buy something." Making the rounds in person didn't appeal to him. His solution that time was a weekly newsletter, complete with an inquiry form and eyecatching typefaces, that told department heads what was new in their fields. "It worked beautifully," he claims.[10]

PROSPECT-
ING BY
TELEPHONE

Telephone prospecting has been used effectively to sell life, health, and accident insurance, cars, investments, and other products and services. Records show that from five to eight good prospects may be secured out of each 100 phone calls made when prospecting for life insurance and health-and-accident customers. Good salespeople have closed between 40 and 50 percent of the prospects secured in this manner.

One real estate salesperson found it profitable to call firms that were planning to hire new employees from other cities. The salesperson secures the name of the new employee and then writes offering the services of the real estate company in locating a new home. This system has paid dividends from contacts with schools, colleges, chain stores, and branches of nationwide organizations. If the salesperson maintains close enough contact with the appropriate sources of information, the information may be secured before it is published in newspapers and becomes available to competitors. Many such contacts can be made quickly by phone.

It may be appropriate to try to complete the sale by phone when selling some products or services, but most products require a personal contact to close the sale. The salesperson should usually use the phone to locate and qualify prospects and then arrange to call and deliver the sales presentation.

The following steps are involved in telephone prospecting: (1) developing a plan, (2) making an opening statement, (3) asking qualifying questions, (4) delivering a sales message, and (5) requesting an appointment.

---

[10]Thayer Taylor, "New Marketing Input for Inforex," *Sales & Marketing Management,* July 9, 1979, p. 34.

Extensive planning is needed for telephone prospecting.

Hazel Hankin/Stock, Boston   Alan Carey/The Image Works

Planning for Telephone Prospecting

Extensive planning is needed for telephone prospecting. Prospects will participate in a phone conversation for only a limited time, so salespeople must make every word count. Idle conversation takes valuable time that could be spent qualifying the customer or persuading the customer to make an appointment. Since it is easy for customers to terminate telephone conversations, salespeople must be especially careful to maintain customer interest and involvement.

A telephone prospecting plan begins with developing a list of prospects and establishing criteria for qualifying them. Before picking up the phone, the salesperson needs to develop a plan for the conversation. This plan should include preparing an opening statement, a set of questions for qualifying customers, a sales message, and a request for an appointment.

It is often useful to develop a written text for the telephone call and keep it near. This text can give the salesperson more confidence and ensure a smooth-flowing conversation. Practicing the text will greatly improve its effectiveness. An excellent practice method is to rehearse the prospecting text with a tape recorder. In reviewing the recorded rehearsal, attention should be paid to the delivery.

Introductory Statement

Introductory remarks are very important. During the first 20 or 30 seconds, salespeople need to introduce themselves and their company and then create some interest in the customer. The introduction should include the prospect's name, the salesperson's name, and the name of the salesperson's company. By mentioning the prospect's name, salespeople can make certain they have contacted the correct person. In addition, some rapport is established by using the prospect's name. Examples of introductory statements are illustrated below:

> Hello, Mr. Jones. [*pause*] I am Doug Lane of the First National State Bank.
>
> Mr. Jones? [*pause*] My name is Lane. Doug Lane of the First National State Bank.

In the second illustration, the salesperson's last name is mentioned twice, and the name of the salesperson's company is emphasized. This increases the chances that the prospect will remember these two critical points.

Establishing Rapport

Right after the introduction, there should be a lead-in statement that establishes some rapport or link between the salesperson and the customer. Perhaps the best lead-ins are mentioning a reference from a third person. For example:

> Mr. Jones? [*pause*] My name is Lane. Doug Lane of the First National State Bank. I was with Ron Levy at Levy Grocery yesterday, and he mentioned that you might be interested in some of the new financial services we are offering.

Other lead-ins are based on mail that has been sent to the prospect or on recognition of a recent event concerning the salesperson's or the prospect's company. Examples of these lead-ins are as follows:

> Last week, we sent you a brochure describing our new financial services. Have you had a chance to read it?
>
> Did you see our four-page spread on our new financial services in *Business Week?*
>
> I just read an article about your new expansion in the Cleveland *Plain Dealer.* Our bank is expanding also.

Even if the prospects say they have not read the brochure or seen the ad, they have begun to participate in the conversation. The next step is to get the prospect's interest.

Creating Interest

The lead-in statement is used to attract the prospect's attention. Now the salesperson needs to give the prospect a reason to continue the conversation. A benefit statement often generates interest. Here's an example:

> Our financial planning services can increase your interest earnings by 30 to 50 percent.

Precall research on the prospect can help determine which benefits are likely to be appealing. It may be necessary to deliver a short, two- or three-sentence sales presentation at this time, but the salesperson must be careful not to provide too much information. Prospects may be reluctant to grant appointments if they feel fully informed by the telephone conversation.

Qualifying the Prospect

After getting the prospect interested in the product, the salesperson should ask a few questions to qualify the prospect before requesting an appointment. Information gained in this way will indicate whether additional time should be spent on a sales call. For example, the salesperson might ask:

> Our financial planning services are designed for retailers with annual sales greater than $10 million. Are your sales in that range? How much of your sales are made with credit cards?
>
> What type of budget plans have you made for this investment?
>
> Would you be able to tell me who in your company will be responsible for signing the purchase order?
>
> Is there anyone else besides yourself who will have a say in buying this product?
>
> Will you be needing immediate delivery?
>
> What other companies are you considering?

Requesting an Appointment

After qualifying the prospect, the salesperson closes the conversation by requesting an appointment. When requesting an appointment, the salesperson should indicate that the interview will be brief. Specific times for the appointment should be proposed. For example:

> I'd like to meet with you for a few moments to show you how our services relate to your business. Could I see you for 30 minutes this Thursday or Friday morning?

Another approach is to assume that the interview has been granted by asking, "Is Thursday or Friday morning better for you?" This approach should be used only when there is some basis for making the assumption.

For example, the customer may indicate significant interest in obtaining more information during a lengthy phone conversation.

If the salesperson is successful in getting an appointment, the conversation should be terminated quickly. Since the sale will not be made over the phone, there is no point in prolonging the conversation, as this just increases the chance that the prospect will reconsider granting the appointment. In concluding the conversation, salespeople should assure the prospect they will be there on time by saying:

> Thank you, Mr. Jones. I'll be at your office this Friday at 2:00 P.M. Good-bye.

Chapter 18 provides additional information on telephone communication techniques. Approaches to be used in making appointments are discussed in more detail in Chapter 9.

HOW TO GET THE MOST OUT OF PROSPECTING

After sales representatives separate the suspects from prospects, they make a careful analysis of the relative value of each prospect. This grading of prospects, or establishing of a priority list, produces increased sales and results in the most efficient use of time and energy.

Qualify and Evaluate Prospects

Many companies conduct extensive research studies to determine what distinguishes a good prospect. These characteristics are used as measuring sticks for prospects. The New York Life Insurance Company, for example, uses an evaluation formula based on six factors: age, number of dependents, approximate income, acquaintance, accessibility, and economic status. Each prospect is given a point score on each of the six factors as well as a composite point rating.

Other companies use additional methods to qualify prospects. Office machine and equipment sales representatives often qualify their prospects through questionnaires. It is often necessary to study the practices of certain potential customers. The findings are used to qualify prospects for the specific kinds of machines and equipment that serve their needs.

Countless other methods of qualifying prospects are used in other types of selling. Whichever method is used, it is essential to make an effort to segregate prospects so the maximum amount of time can be spent making sales presentations to prospects who are likely to purchase.

Have an Organized Prospecting Plan

The person who does not have an orderly prospecting plan is a slave to confusion, frustration, and chaos. Inexperienced salespeople frequently rattle around in their territories, jump from one spot to another, and waste considerable time between calls. Successful and experienced sales representatives, on the other hand, almost always have efficient systems for recording, studying, and using their prospect information.

Keep Good Records   The information and the type of prospect file needed vary by types of business. Most large companies have developed prospecting systems and standard prospect cards for their sales representatives to use. The extent to which these systems and cards are used can determine the success or failure of individual sales representatives.

The New York Life Insurance Company has an excellent system for organizing and filing its standard prospect cards so the sales representatives have the necessary information available on each prospect. This system, which the company calls the *Automatic Secretary,* divides the prospect file into four sections: (1) the master prospect and policyholder card file, (2) the tickler file, (3) the center-of-influence file, and (4) the district or zone file.

The cards in the master prospect and policyholder card file are filed alphabetically. They contain sufficient information so they may be used as prospect cards and also as policyholder cards after the prospects have purchased policies.

The tickler file provides the names of prospects and policyholders to be seen each month and the specific days of the month on which they should be seen.

The center-of-influence file helps the sales agent cultivate his or her centers of influence.

The district or zone file cards are used to segregate the names of prospects and policyholders by geographic areas. These cards are very useful for sales agents who cover a number of towns or several well-defined sections of a large city.

Most industrial salespeople keep a file card for each customer and each prospect. They complete a form after each contact is made. An example of a form used by an electronic distributor is shown in Figure 8–7. The salespeople also put other information into the file that might be useful in converting the prospect into a customer. This information might come from local newspaper or trade magazine articles, annual reports, and data sheets on the prospect's products.

Though these are more detailed than those used in other types of selling, some kind of prospecting record is essential in every type of selling. In selling cars, it is especially important to keep good prospecting records because sales commissions are often allocated to the salesperson who files the first prospect card on a customer.

Set Quotas   Most effective prospecting plans include weekly and monthly quotas for new prospects. In the long run, goals for obtaining the names of new prospects are just as important as profit and sales goals. The continuous profitable operation of a territory or area depends on a steady

FIGURE 8–7
Prospect Contact
Form for an
Electronic
Distributor

ELECTRONIC COMPONENT INC.

Prospect Contact Form

Date *3/20/86*

Name of Contact *Jack Barry*   Telephone Number *(714) 833–1340*

Company *AL Labs*   Type of Business *Instrument Mgr.*

Address *2305 Campus Dr., Hinsdale, Chicago*

Position *Purchasing Agent*

Contact Needs *Interested in quick delivery; needs second source for metal h/m capacitors*

Present Suppliers *Wylie, Hamilton–Avnet*

Credit Rating *A.A.*   Annual Sales *$3M*

Annual Purchases of Components *$200 K*

Types of Components Purchases

_____ low precision resistors	_____ RAM's
___✓___ precision resistors	___✓___ microprocessors
___✓___ potentiometers	_____ LCD's
___✓___ metal film caps	_____ LED's
_____ MOS memory	_____ bi-polar IC's

Result of Visit *Still trying to get parts from Wylie*

Follow Up *Call in two weeks*

flow of new prospects. Quotas remind the salesperson of the importance of keeping a constant lookout for new names to fill the prospect pipeline.

Evaluate Results   One of the greatest dangers in prospecting is the tendency to "ease off" in locating new prospects as soon as the prospect file contains a substantial number of names. Names alone are not enough. Prospect files must be checked periodically to eliminate the deadwood and to make sure the best possible factors are being used to evaluate prospects.

Experiment with New Methods   Analysis may show that the present system is not producing enough prospects or the right kind of prospects. Sales representatives may, for example, depend entirely on referred names from company advertising or from the service department. These two sources may not supply enough names to produce the sales volume desired. The use of other prospecting methods, such as the cold canvass, lists, the endless chain, or the center of influence, should then be considered.

Frequently a new salesperson calls on potential customers who have never been called on. A predecessor may have eliminated these prospects for one reason or another or may never have thought of calling on them. In this way the new salesperson with new prospecting methods can uncover an additional source of sales volume.

Follow-through   One of the most common complaints from sales managers is that salespeople do not follow through on prospect leads. An insurance company branch manager followed a policy of asking each sales representative to provide a list of 50 of the best prospects at the beginning of each month. The names of these prospects were recorded on visible index cards, and a color-tab system was established to show the action taken on each prospect during the month. Photographs of each sales representative's card file were taken at the beginning and end of the month to show the overall progress made on the 50 key prospects during that month.

The salesperson may call a prospect several times without getting any positive action. He or she must then use judgment as to whether the prospect merits additional time and effort. Too frequent calls may cause the prospect to become resentful and thus kill all possibilities of a sale. There is no simple solution to this kind of problem. The salesperson needs judgment, tact, diplomacy, persistency, and ingenuity to know the exact extent to which he or she should follow through. This skill is gleaned from actual selling experience.

Overcoming a Reluctance to Prospect[11]

People have a stereotype of salespeople as responsible, bold, adventurous, and somewhat abrasive. The view that salespeople are fearless is more fiction than fact. Salespeople often struggle with a reluctance to prospect and this persists no matter how well they have been trained and how much they believe in the products they are selling. While many people are uncomfortable when they initially contact other people, call reluctance can be a career-threatening condition for salespeople. In Selling Scenario 8–1, John Paul Jones of Monsanto tells how a snowstorm forced him into a prospecting situation that turned out to be extremely profitable for his company.

Cause of Call Reluctance   Research shows that call reluctance is not simply a fear of failure or a fear of rejection. Some reasons for call reluctance are:

1. Unwillingness to take social risks.
2. Tendency to overanalyze situation, which leads to underactivity.
3. Fear of humiliation.
4. Fear of group presentation.
5. Fear of being seen as exploiting of friends or family.
6. Unwillingness to accept career choice resulting in embarrassment when associated with selling.
7. Reluctance to intrude on people.
8. Fear of contacting affluent prospects with high social status.

Dealing with Call Reluctance   The following procedure is recommended for overcoming call reluctance among newly hired salespeople.

1. Listen to the excuses other salespeople give to justify their call-reluctance behavior.
2. Identify the excuses you use to avoid making calls.
3. Engage in role-playing exercise to experience how it feels to be free of call reluctance.
4. Have a supporting partner accompany you when contacting two strangers (prospects).
5. Make two more calls on strangers without the supporting partner.
6. Reenact the last two calls in a role-playing exercise in front of a group.
7. Set specific goals for prospecting activity.

---

[11]Based on George W. Dudley and Shannon L. Goodson, "Fear of Prospecting: The Psychology of Call Reluctance in Salespeople," *Training*, September 1984, pp. 58–68.

Selling Scenario 8–1

THE SNOWBALL PROSPECT

John Paul Jones, senior territory manager for Monsanto, describes an unusual prospecting circumstance that led to a major sale.

It was 1967 and I had been in sales for about three years. I was servicing western New York state. I was driving down the road in the middle of a terrible snowstorm on my way to a prospective client. I'm a native Floridian, so I was not prepared for that climate, and I was almost forced off the road. In desperation, I pulled into the parking lot of the Alliance Tool & Die Company to wait out the storm. While I was sitting there, I decided to go inside and see what local business conditions were like. I wasn't trying so much to make a sale as to maybe pick up a few leads.

I went in and introduced myself to the manager and told him I'd been in Rochester six months and that the weather here stinks. I asked him if he needed a lot of plastic materials. He said no, but asked me what product I was pushing. I told him nylon and he told me that the chemical products division office of General Motors across the street was looking for nylon for about 18 different applications. He gave me the name of a person to speak to.

To get there, I had to walk because of the weather. It was about 4 P.M., and the person's receptionist told me he had a lot of appointments that day, but many of them canceled because of the snow, and he might see me. He did.

Before I even took a seat, he asked me if we had the capacity to make 2- to 3-million pounds of nylon a year. Without blinking an eye, I said yes, even though I wasn't sure. He then told me that GM had to develop a special grade of the material and that we were just about six months behind our competitors. So I had to go back to our R&D people while our competitors were making inroads.

Six months later, one of them pulled out of the competition because they didn't have the capability to take this on for the long term, and in the next 12 to 14 months another also dropped out.

It took us a year to develop the product in the lab. But with two rivals dropping out, we eventually became the second source of supply for this material (Du Pont became the first), which was used for the automobile emission control devices that were mandated by the Environmental Protection Agency.

So a situation that I was forced into by a snowstorm turned out to be one of Monsanto's major products in the late 60s and early 70s.

Source: Reprinted from "Strange Tales of Sales," *Sales & Marketing Management,* June 3, 1985, p. 46.

SUMMARY

Locating prospective customers is the first step in the sales process. New prospects are needed to replace old customers lost through plant relocations and employee turnover.

Not all sales leads qualify as good prospects. A qualified prospect has a need that can be satisfied by the salesperson's product, has the ability and authority to buy the product, can be approached by the salesperson, and is eligible to buy.

There are many methods for locating prospects. Companies provide leads to salespeople through their advertising. Salespeople can obtain leads through their customers by using the endless-chain and center-of-influence methods. Industrial prospects are located through trade shows, directories, noncompeting salespeople, and simply by cold canvassing. Finally, friends and acquaintances are important sources of leads. Both direct mail and telephoning can be used to improve prospects.

Effective prospecting requires development of a plan. This plan hinges on keeping good records, setting quotas, and evaluating the results of prospecting effort. It is important to test new prospecting methods.

QUESTIONS
AND
PROBLEMS

1. If you were a salesperson for the following companies, how would you develop a prospect list?
   a. A manufacturer of private light airplanes.
   b. A travel agency specializing in group tours.
   c. A manufacturer of heavy equipment for road construction.
2. Robert Eppler is a real estate salesperson in a city of approximately 150,000. He believes a successful prospecting plan involves the following three basic steps: (1) an analysis of each residential property listing to determine its main selling features, (2) a plan for securing an adequate number of prospects, and (3) a system for qualifying the prospects.
   a. What selling features of residential properties, such as size of lot and number of rooms, is Mr. Eppler likely to look for in making his property analysis?
   b. What are some common sources from which Mr. Eppler may secure prospects for homes?
   c. What information should Mr. Eppler obtain on his prospects to qualify them properly?
3. The company you represent carries a full line of sophisticated office equipment, including electronic calculators, word-processing equipment, and small business computers. How would you develop a list of business, industrial, and institutional accounts? What information would you collect to screen the prospect list for potential customers?

4. What information should a salesperson collect to qualify prospects for:
   a. A uniformed guard service?
   b. Sponsorship of a Little League baseball team?
   c. Paper for computer output.

5. Salespeople should forget prospects who do not qualify. Comment on this statement.

6. Assume you are starting a career as a stockbroker. Develop a system for rating prospects. The system should contain several important factors for qualifying prospects and scales to rate the prospects on these factors. Use the system to rate five of your friends.

7. Assume that you are a sales representative for a national manufacturer that sells a wide variety of business machines. You have heard that the Tanner Manufacturing Company (which employs 3,500 employees and does an annual business of $38 million) is planning to install a new production and cost control plan that includes a complete cost accounting system. Your company has a new machine designed specifically for cost control work. It is being used by a number of large manufacturing companies in your territory. The cost of the machine is $10,000.

   How would you go about making an appointment with a representative of the Tanner Manufacturing Company? Would you attempt to see the president? The controller? The chief cost accountant? The purchasing agent? Why?

8. A paper-products sales representative uses the following approach when in doubt as to whether a certain executive has the authority to buy: "Mr. Smith, my presentation will take approximately 15 minutes of your time. I realize that your time is valuable, and therefore I want to be sure that you are the person with whom I should talk. I would appreciate your frank comments. Are you the one I should see on paper packaging or does another executive have responsibility for the purchase of this product?"

   What is your reaction to this approach? Why?

9. In industrial sales situations, several people are influential in making the purchase decision. Suppose you had just completed an interview with an industrial prospect and believed you should contact other people in the company. How would you raise the subject with the prospect?

10. Suppose you phone a prospect to make an appointment for a personal interview. When the secretary answers the phone, you say, "Mr. Welsh, please; Joe Herbert calling." Assume the secretary says, "What do you wish to talk to Mr. Welsh about?" What answer would you give? Assume you answer and then are told Mr. Welsh is too busy to see you. What would you say?

PROJECTS

1. Assume you have just been appointed advertising manager for your college or university student paper. What would you do to develop the most successful prospecting plan for obtaining advertisers?

2. Write a sales letter designed to induce a prospect to send an inquiry on your product requesting a salesperson to call. Prepare a second letter designed to encourage the prospect to phone in an order. Prepare some guidelines for the people who will be answering the phone.

3. Assume you are a sales representative for the U.S. Steel Corporation and you call on industrial companies, engineering construction firms, and large building contractors. Also assume you are working in one of the following geographic areas: Cleveland, Philadelphia, Atlanta, Chicago, St. Louis, New Orleans, Denver, San Francisco, or Seattle. Take one week to review local newspapers, magazines, and other available public information and write a report assessing the available information in terms of its value for prospecting purposes.

CASE PROBLEMS

Case 8–1   Climatron, Inc.

Two young college graduates organized Climatron, Inc., soon after they graduated. The company obtained an exclusive sales agency for a national brand of home air-conditioning units. The units included both portable air conditioners, which could be moved from room to room, and larger units, which could be installed in windows or walls.

The two young owners, Mr. Lewis and Mr. Hall, received their degrees in mechanical engineering. While in school, they became interested in the air-conditioning field and decided to enter this type of business after graduation. Between their junior and senior years in college, they worked to earn money and to obtain business experience. Lewis worked for a sheet-metal and heating company doing a combination of office work and sales work. Hall worked for a retail appliance company doing outside sales work.

During the last semester of their senior year in college, Lewis and Hall spent all of their spare time investigating the air-conditioning business. They talked with the distributors of a number of the most popular air-conditioning units and wrote to several manufacturers to inquire about the possibility of obtaining a franchise for certain territories in Texas.

After considerable negotiation, they were successful in obtaining the franchise to sell the Star brand air-conditioning units in El Paso, Texas. The owners put up a limited amount of capital, rented a small combination warehouse and display room, hired a part-time office clerk, and ordered a few units to use for display and demonstration purposes. They decided to concentrate on the sale of units that would be installed in the windows or walls of houses or office buildings. The average home-installation unit was priced to sell for approximately $900.

Lewis and Hall believed there was a good market for air-conditioning units in the El Paso area but realized they would have to conduct a hard-hitting sales program if their business was to be successful. One of their first problems was to obtain a list of prospects.

Questions

1. What prospecting methods should Lewis and Hall use?

2. What factors should they use in evaluating their potential prospects?

3. What methods, if any, may be used to determine whether their potential prospects have the necessary qualifications?

Case 8–2   Alicia Maxwell—Hubbard-Jones, Inc.

While Alicia Maxwell attended college, she worked at a large supermarket full time during the summer and part time during the school year. After graduation from college, Ms. Maxwell accepted a position as a sales representative for Hubbard-Jones, Inc., a well-known company selling a line of delicatessen foods, relishes, preserves, and meat products to retail groceries and supermarkets. Hubbard-Jones carried a full line of meat products and also featured a popular brand of TV frozen dinners.

Ms. Maxwell had a successful career as a sales representative for Hubbard-Jones and was promoted to a branch manager's position in the central New York region. In this capacity, she was responsible for a number of salespeople, and she also made calls on large customers with multistore operations. One of her toughest assignments was to get the Hubbard-Jones line of products into the National Supermarkets chain, which operated approximately 50 supermarkets in her region. Neil Sundby, vice president of National, was the key person to see in getting the Hubbard-Jones products into National. Alex Joseph, president of Hubbard-Jones, had called on Sundby on several occasions but had never been successful in getting his line of

products introduced into National Supermarkets.

When Ms. Maxwell called on Sundby for the first time, Sundby was friendly, but he made it quite clear that National had no intention of stocking Hubbard-Jones products in its stores. Ms. Maxwell made several followup calls on Sundby but was unsuccessful in convincing Sundby of the advantages of substituting Hubbard-Jones products for the line now carried by National or of adding Hubbard-Jones products.

Although somewhat discouraged by her first efforts to "crack" the National account, Ms. Maxwell was challenged by the situation confronting her and was determined to get some of the National business.

Questions

1. If you were Alicia Maxwell, what plan of action would you follow to get your products accepted by National Supermarkets?

2. Would you continue to call on Sundby, or would you call on someone else at National? If you did call on someone else, what strategy would you use?

Case 8–3   **Qualifying Suspects**

You have just graduated from college and today is the first day of your job as a real estate salesman. Your boss, Mr. Hunt, has assigned you your first task: to sell a $100,000 split-level house to one of six prospects: Jones, Antonelli, Schwartz, Murphy, Delgado, or Washington.

The Jones family consists of Mr. and Ms. Jones, who are in their late 20s, and two young children. Mr. Jones is employed by a large multinational corporation in lower management. Ms. Jones works part time as a bank teller. The family's combined income is $19,000 a year, and they intend to make a down payment of $7,000 on the house. According to Mr. Hunt, the Joneses have been after him to find them a suitable home.

Mr. Antonelli, age 35 and single, is a self-employed attorney with an income of $36,000 a year. Mr. Antonelli is looking for a spacious home that is easy to maintain. He is willing to make a down payment of $35,000.

Mr. and Ms. Schwartz are nearing retirement. Mr. Schwartz is a professor at a nearby university, and Ms. Schwartz is an administrative assistant at a small publishing firm. Their youngest daughter recently graduated from the MBA program at a well-known university. Their household income is currently about $40,000, and they are seeking a smaller home for their retirement. The Schwartzes' intended down payment is $37,500.

Mr. and Ms. Murphy, who are in their mid-20s, own and operate an insurance brokerage office. Their income is $31,000, and their intended down payment is $31,000. According to Mr. Hunt, the Murphys are seeking a home that can also be used as an office for their business.

Mr. Delgado is a middle manager with a large oil company. His salary is $56,000 a year. Ms. Delgado is a homemaker. The Delgados are in their mid- to late 30s, and they have three children between the ages of 4 and 10. Their intended down payment is $20,000. Mr. Hunt commented that the Delgados are looking for an adequate amount of living space.

Mr. Washington is an electrician with an income of $25,000 a year. Ms. Washington is a bookkeeper who earns $13,000. Although they have no children, the Washingtons intend to have a child within two years, at which time Ms. Washington will resign from her job. The Washingtons are willing to make a down payment of $30,000. Mr. Hunt commented that the Washingtons have already turned down several possible houses for relatively minor reasons.

The split-level house has three bedrooms, two baths, and a one-car garage. It is on a 6,500-square-foot lot and is located within a convenient distance of schools, a shopping center, and a downtown area.

Mr. Hunt has suggested that before contacting the prospects you draw up a graph. On the horizontal axis write the four analytical criteria: *need or desire, economic stability, eligibility to buy,* and *authority to buy.* On the vertical axis write the names of the prospects. For each criterion write a "+" if the prospect meets the criterion, a "−" if the prospect doesn't meet it, or a "0" if you aren't sure.

Question

1. How would you rank the prospects? Why?

SELECTED REFERENCES

Blickstein, Steve. "How to Find the Key Buying Influence." *Sales Management,* September 20, 1971, pp. 51–54.

Collins, Robert H. "Microcomputer Systems to Handle Sales Leads: A Key to Increased Salesforce Productivity." *Journal of Personal Selling and Sales Management,* May 1985, pp. 77–83.

Deutscher, Terry; Judith Marshall; and David Burgoyne. "The Process of Obtaining New Accounts." *Industrial Marketing Management,* Fall 1982, pp. 173–81.

Feldman, Laurence P., and Gary M. Armstrong. "Identifying Buyers of a Major Automotive Innovation." *Journal of Marketing,* January 1975, pp. 47–53.

Goodman, Gerson. "Filling Holes with Cold Calls." *Sales & Marketing Management,* February 5, 1979, pp. 46–47.

"Managing Sales Leads: Order from Chaos." *Sales & Marketing Management,* June 6, 1983, pp. 59–83.

Scanlon, Sally. "Striking It Rich with Industrial Ads." *Sales & Marketing Management,* June 18, 1979, pp. 39–44.

Seif, Donald R., and Steve Roberts. *The Prospector—A Professional Sales Management Data Base.* Atlanta: Executive Data Systems, Inc., 1983.

Skolnik, Rayna. "Where There's Smoke, There's a Prospect." *Sales & Marketing Management,* April 5, 1982, pp. 65–66.

"Trade Shows: Where Prospects Call on You: A Special Report." *Sales & Marketing Management,* August 28, 1979.

9

Planning the Sales Presentation and Getting the Right Start

Some questions answered in this chapter are:

- Why should salespeople plan their sales presentations?
- What information do they need to plan their presentations?
- What elements should be included in the plan for a sales call?
- How should appointments be made? Objections handled?
- What is the appropriate dress for a salesperson?
- How should the initial approach be made?

There is a great temptation for a salesperson to call on a prospect or customer without planning what to say and how to say it. It is easy to depend on spur-of-the-moment thinking. A few talented individuals may get by with this approach, but most salespeople will benefit from preparing their presentations in advance. This chapter will discuss precall planning as well as how to make a good impression during the initial approach.

Seven Steps in the Sales Process

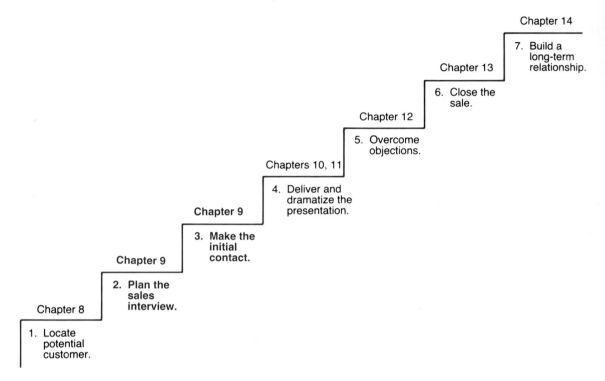

PLANNING THE PRESENTATION

Most salespeople agree that advance planning of the sales interview is essential to success in selling. Such planning has many advantages. It saves the time of the buyer and the seller; it helps the beginning salesperson; it ensures an effective presentation; and it increases sales volume.

Why Plan the Sales Presentation?

Saves Time of Buyers and Sellers Buyers respect a salesperson who delivers a well-prepared presentation. Purchasing agents want the salesperson to get down to business so they can function as professional buyers. As James B. Emerson, a marketing consultant, says:

> Your prospect is busy and highly organized. Frankly, he expects you to be equally businesslike. Your presentation should be brief and to the point, your samples geared to the prospect's probable needs: those you discovered during your homework on his company.[1]

The salesperson should remember that the buyer's time is valuable. If the salesperson can make an intelligent analysis of the needs and wants

---

[1]James B. Emerson, "How to Conserve Your Prospect's Time for Fun and Profit," *Sales & Marketing Management,* March 14, 1977, p. 80.

of each buyer and then, through a well-organized and well-planned presentation, show how the company's products or services fill those needs, the salesperson is likely not only to make a sale but also to win the buyer's respect and confidence.

Aids Beginning Salespeople   Most salespeople feel a certain amount of tension when they first call on prospects. This tension is especially noticeable when they don't know exactly what to say or how to say it. A well-planned presentation can relieve this strain and help boost the salesperson's confidence.

Many large companies have developed standard sales stories based on the experiences of their most successful salespeople. Considerable time and effort are spent in developing each phase of the sales presentation so it flows smoothly from one sales point to the next. All customary objections are anticipated, and carefully worded answers are formulated for the salesperson's use. Often engineering or production department representatives are called in to provide technical information for use in planning the sales story. This type of sales planning is invaluable to the new salesperson.

Ensures Effective Presentation   Planning the sales presentation in advance ensures against ineffective interviews and lost sales. If a salesperson does not plan what to say, he or she is likely to ramble, backtrack, omit important sales points, or exaggerate. This results in lost sales and a waste of valuable selling time. In many respects, the salesperson is like a public speaker. Anyone who has talked before an audience recognizes the necessity for planning exactly what to say and how to say it.

Increases Sales   Careful advance planning of which price line to show first will give the salesperson a chance to trade up to the higher-priced merchandise during the sales interview. To illustrate, if the salesperson's product has three price lines, attention will normally be focused on the medium-priced line first. It is then possible to move up or down, depending on the needs and desires of the customer. Generally, it is much easier to trade up to higher-quality and high-priced merchandise than it is to trade down.

The following illustrates the results of a sales call made with inadequate planning:

Salesperson: Good morning, Mr. White. I'm Bob Thompson, the new sales rep for McNeil Clothing.
Customer: My name is Waits, not White.

> **Salesperson:**   Oh! I'm sorry. I should have asked your secretary to spell your name when I called to make an appointment. I want to show you our new fall line. It is ideally suited for the growing teenage market.
>
> **Customer:**   Most of our customers are middle-aged. I don't want to attract teenagers to my store. They make a lot of noise and bother the older customers.
>
> **Salesperson:**   Well, we also have a line for the middle-aged market. Here's some photographs of the items in the line. (Reaches into his pocket for a package of cigarettes.) Would you like a cigarette? This has really been a tough day.
>
> **Customer:**   I don't smoke, and smoking really bothers me. The smell gets into the clothing in our store. Please don't smoke.

By not planning this sales call, the salesperson has already encountered several embarrassing situations. Because of this poor start, it is unlikely a sale will be made on this call.

Planning a sales call includes collecting information about the prospect or customer, analyzing this information to set objectives for the sales call, and outlining the sales presentation that will be used to achieve those objectives. The outline of the presentation includes illustrating how the product will satisfy the customer's needs, identifying potential objections that might arise, and developing responses to these objections.

Obtaining Precall Information

Often the difference between making and not making a sale depends on the amount of "homework" done by the salesperson before making the call. The more information the salesperson has about the customer, the higher the probability of making a sale. However, the salesperson must be aware of the costs involved in collecting information. At some point, the time and effort put into collecting information become greater than the benefits obtained.

Salespeople should acquire precall information about both the individual customer and the customer's company. Clearly, when a salesperson has been calling regularly on a customer, there is no need to collect a lot of additional information. The salesperson's records and notes from prior calls will be adequate to prepare for the sales call. But in making an initial call on a prospect, considerable effort should be spent on collecting precall information.

Information about the Individual Customer   Useful information about a customer can be obtained by answering the following questions:

1. What is the customer's name? How does he or she pronounce the name?
2. What is the customer's family status? Is he or she married? Does the customer have children? How old are they? Where do they attend school?
3. What is the customer's formal education? What schools were attended, degrees earned? Is the prospect currently enrolled in an educational program?
4. What are the customer's hobbies? Does he or she play golf or tennis, follow specific sports, read current novels, or engage in other interests?
5. To what organizations or clubs does the customer belong?
6. What is the customer's attitude toward salespeople in general, toward the salesperson's company, toward products offered by the salesperson's company and competitors?
7. What are the customer's job aspirations, attitudes toward risk, and self-confidence in decision making?

This information can be used to develop rapport with a customer and to tailor the presentation to fit his or her needs. For example, during the initial stages of a sales call, a salesperson can establish a relationship with a customer by discussing such mutual points of interest as hobbies or families. Information about the customer's attitudes toward the salesperson's company and products is useful for identifying potential objections that might be raised during the sales call and planning responses to those objections.

Information about the Customer's Organization   Answers to the following questions provide useful information about the customer's organization.

1. Is the organization in manufacturing, wholesaling, or retailing? How large is the organization? What products or services does it provide?
2. What types of customers does the organization sell to? What are the benefits sought by the organization's target market?
3. Who are the organization's primary competitors? How do the competitors differ in their business approach?
4. What is the volume of the organization's purchases in the product category? Does the organization buy from several suppliers or only one supplier? Why?
5. Why does the organization buy from its present suppliers? Is it satisfied with them? Why or why not?

6. Who is involved in the purchase decision for the product category? How do they fit into the formal organizational structure? The informal organizational structure? Who is most influential?
7. What current problems are facing the organization?
8. What policies does the organization have regarding salespeople, sales visits, purchasing, and pricing?
9. What is the organization's position? How good is its credit?

After obtaining information about the individual customer and the customer's organization, the salesperson can begin to plan the presentation. An illustration of precall planning and research is shown in Selling Scenario 9–1.

Setting Specific Objectives

The first and most important step in planning the sales presentation is to set objectives for the call. Specific objectives should be established for every sales call. The objectives should be aimed at obtaining action by the customer. The plans should be made in terms of what the customer should do, not what the salesperson will do. Finally, the objectives should be measurable so the salesperson can easily determine if his or her objectives were accomplished.[2]

Merely stating that the objective for a call is to make a sale is insufficient. There are many steps involved in the customer's decision-making process and many activities salespeople need to undertake as they guide customers through the process. Specific objectives that will lead to a sale should be established for each call.

Consider the following example. Tom Reynolds, a salesperson for General Electric Major Appliances, is preparing to call on Jim Dunlop, owner of Kitchen Kubboard. Kitchen Kubboard presently carries GE clothes washers, dryers, and dishwashers. While Dunlop is selling a lot of washers and dryers, dishwasher sales are disappointing because he stocks only the lowest priced model offered by GE.

Tom Reynolds states his objectives for the sales call using the sales call organizer shown in Figure 9–1. His first objective is to have Dunlop place a fill-in order for washers and dryers. Then, he wants to get Dunlop to stock the entire GE line of dishwashers—not just the low-priced model. His third objective is to have Dunlop place newspaper ads featuring GE washers and dryers over the next 90 days. Finally, Reynolds would like to demonstrate a new line of compact microwave ovens and encourage Dunlop to place an order for the microwaves.

---

[2]From Porter Henry, "Who Needs to Plan?" *Sales Management*, June 24, 1974, pp. 26–27.

Selling Scenario 9–1

PLANNING AND PERSISTENCE

 Jim Gibbons, president of the Manufacturer's Agents National Association, discusses his most memorable sale.

My greatest triumph occurred around 1961, when I was representing a small bearings manufacturer in Wisconsin whose salesmen had been tossed out of an industrial heating and air conditioning manufacturer's plant. Their bearing requirements were substantial—on the order of $300,000 a year—and with considerable effort, I was able to discover exactly where the problem was and sit down and renegotiate the contract. This was not a major account at this time, but it did have a lot of potential.

The reason I was able to renegotiate the contract had to do with some really in-depth research I did at the company. In this case, it wasn't the vice president of purchasing who had the beef, but an engineer who happened to be one of the last people on the totem pole. He had very little clout title wise, but management listened to him.

I had to start with the purchasing people and work my way through the company from there. Over a period of four or five months, I did a lot of detective work to find the right person. Along the way, I met a lot of engineers who were skeptical, but never the right guy. Finally, I located the engineer who was causing the problem. We sat down and totally re-engineered the bearings, which actually ended up increasing the price a little.

As a result, the manufacturer sent me a big medal and a certificate, and I brought them about $1 million worth of business by satisfying both my principal and their customers. This happened very early in my career, and I'm glad it did because it taught me the importance of being persistent.

Source: Reprinted from "Strange Tales of Sales," *Sales & Marketing Management,* June 3, 1985, p. 42.

Reynolds has prioritized his objectives using the following logic. Dunlop always places a fill-in order for washers and dryers, so it will be easy to accomplish the first objective. Getting Dunlop to carry the full line of dishwashers will be more difficult to accomplish. Dunlop presently sells the Kitchen-Aid dishwasher line to customers who want a high-performance, expensive dishwasher. Stocking the entire GE dishwasher line will mean dropping the Kitchen-Aid line. Dunlop needs to schedule his advertising to get the co-op advertising support before the program runs out, so the third objective should be easily achieved. Finally, if the situation seems right, Reynolds will begin the process of getting Dunlop to stock GE's compact microwave ovens. This will require a major selling effort, since Dunlop does not carry microwave ovens at this time.

FIGURE 9–1

CALL ORGANIZER & WORK SHEET

Customer ___Kitchen Kubboards___ Date _9/14/86_ | Followup

Person(s) Seen ___Jim Dunlop___

_____

Objectives	Results
Fill in order for washers and dryers. Increase inventory by 50%. #1	Order # 93681. Boosted inventory by 30%.
Schedule newspaper ads for next 90 days. Co-op will run out. Need to build store traffic. #3	Will blitz ads in October. I agreed to come in with a factory demonstration for customers on Saturday. Will call and let me know which Saturday.
Stock high-end dishwashers. Emphasize trading customers up to increase dishwasher sales. Improved delivery due to redesign. #2	Order # 93682 for three B5 x 31's and three B5 x 41's. Need to hold a training session for salespeople.
Stock GE compact microwave ovens. Growth in product category. #4	Jim thinks margins on microwaves too low. Need to get examples of profits being made by other dealers.

Developing the
Presentation
Plan

After establishing the objectives for a sales call, the next step is developing a plan to achieve these objectives. This plan includes an outline of how the product will provide the benefits sought by the customer and supporting evidence that proves the product will provide those benefits.

Benefits and Supporting Evidence   Consider Reynolds' second objective. To prepare a presentation to accomplish this objective, Reynolds reviewed the information he had on Dunlop's sales of dishwashers and compared Dunlop's dishwasher sales to the sales of other appliance stores. Based on this information, Reynolds decided to stress the benefit of increasing dishwasher sales by being able to easily get customers to trade up from the lowest priced to the more expensive GE models. To support this benefit, Reynolds demonstrated how appliance stores in other cities had increased dishwasher sales by carrying a full GE line.

In addition to selecting a key benefit and providing supporting evidence, Reynolds needs to anticipate potential objections the customer might raise. For example, Dunlop might have purchased the higher priced models from GE several years ago, but switched to Kitchen-Aid because GE's delivery was slow. Reynolds must prepare a response to the potential objection. Faced with this objection, he might say:

"I am sorry that you had a bad experience with our delivery in 1984. We had some problems with the supplier for special microswitches and redesigned the units so they use standard microswitches, which are readily available from a number of sources."

An example of a detailed precall planning work sheet used by stockbrokers is shown in Figure 9–2.

Finally, salespeople need to have at hand supporting brochures and information on ordering, pricing, credit terms, and delivery. The salesperson can lose an order by making the customer wait for this crucial information.

Mental Role Playing   Role playing can be used effectively to prepare for a sales presentation. Salespeople should review their sales plan, memorize the major point to be made, imagine the setting in which the interaction is to take place, and mentally go through the interchange that will occur.[3] By mentally rehearsing the sales call, the salesperson will feel more comfortable and confident when making the actual presentation.

Keep
Records—
Preparing for
Next Sales Call

At the completion of a sales call, the salesperson should begin to plan for the next call with the customer. This means recording the information learned during the call and the results of the call.

By reviewing this information, the salesperson can gain some insights

---

[3] "Are You Ready? Here's Mind Control," *Sales Management,* May 1972, p. 12.

FIGURE 9–2
Precall Work Sheet

Client _____   Needs: Product(s) to be presented:
Investment: ☐ Current income   General _____
   Experience _____   ☐ Short-term growth   _____
   Capital _____   ☐ Long-term growth   Specific _____
   Attitude _____   ☐ Other _____   _____

Initial need statement

I plan to: 2. Refer to the general product.
1. Restate the client's need(s).
                                                _____

_____   3. Relate a general product benefit to need(s).

_____   _____

Presentation

I plan to:

1. Refer to the specific product. _____   4. Relate specific product benefits. _____

_____   _____

2. Probe for knowledge or attitude.   _____

3. Mention specific product features. _____ _____

_____   5. Pause or open probe to verify acceptance.

Close

I plan to close by:
1. Restating general products benefits ac-   2. Restating specific product benefits accepted by the client.   cepted by the client.

_____   _____

_____   _____

_____   3. Requesting a commitment to: _____

_____   _____

Proof

Sources I could cite about this product are:_____

_____

_____

Possible objections

My client's objections might be: _____   I'll use these benefits to handle the objections:

_____   _____

_____   _____

_____   _____

_____   _____

into which approaches have worked in the past and which have been unsuccessful.

Figure 9–1 shows how Tom Reynolds recorded the results of his call on Kitchen Kubboard. Dunlop placed an order to increase the inventory level of washers and dryers and placed advertisements; however, the increase was less than Reynolds' objective. In addition, Dunlop ordered some higher priced GE dishwashers. Reynolds noted he needs to provide training for Dunlop's salespeople on the new GE dishwashers. Finally, Dunlop indicated some interest in the microwave ovens but was not ready to place an order.

In addition to the information previously mentioned about the customer and the customer's organization, the salesperson should note observations that might be useful, such as:

> Plays racquetball during lunch on Tuesdays and Thursdays.
> Tired after lunch.
> Doesn't like jokes.
> Very concerned with on-time delivery.
> Husband teaches marketing at Fresno State.

MAKING AN APPOINTMENT

Advantages of Making Appointments

Many sales managers insist their salespeople make appointments before calling on prospects or customers. They have found from experience that working by appointment saves valuable selling time. One large sales organization estimated that advance appointments increase the effectiveness of their sales force by at least one third.

Appointments dignify the salesperson. The prospect or customer is more likely to be open-minded toward the salesperson who makes an appointment as compared to the one who "just happened by." Appointments get the sales process off to a good start by putting the salesperson and the prospect on the same level—equal participants in a legitimate sales interview. Appointments also increase the chances of seeing the right person.

How to Make Appointments

Experienced sales representatives use different methods to contact individual customers. They have found through trial and error that a certain method of making an appointment works well with a regular customer but may be entirely ineffective with a new prospect. They have also found that knowledge of many different methods and techniques of making appointments is extremely helpful in obtaining sales interviews. Some of the basic principles and techniques of making appointments are discussed below.

Seeing the Right Person   Many salespeople complete an effective sales presentation only to find they have been talking to the wrong person—someone who does not have the authority to make a purchase. New sales representatives are prone to this mistake. Often they are so enthusiastic

Cultivating barriers
gets the salesperson
to the authorized
buyer.

"I won't see any underlings. I want to speak directly to Grandma."

From *The Wall Street Journal*, with permission of Cartoon Features Syndicate.

about their product and so eager to give their presentation they do not use sufficient care to see that their appointment is with the person who has the authority to buy.

To illustrate, a paper salesperson for years called mainly on printers. After a careful analysis of sales records and the sales potential, the salesperson concluded the territory was not producing maximum sales volume. Many sales were lost because the printers lacked the authority to specify the brand of paper used by their clients. The sales representative solved this problem by contacting the printers' sales representatives and finding out from them which clients normally specified a certain brand of paper when they gave their orders to the printers. The sales representative then contacted these persons and explained the merits of the company's products to them.

Any salesperson whose product or service fills a customer's need should not hesitate to request an appointment with the right person—the person who has the authority to say yes or no.

Frequently, however, no one person has the sole authority to buy a product. The salesperson may first be required to obtain the approval of representatives of the line organization or of an operating committee. A forklift salesperson, for example, found he had to see the safety engineer, the methods engineer, the materials-handling engineer, and the general superintendent before he could sell the product to a certain manufacturing company. In this case, the salesperson should try to arrange a meeting with the entire group.

Making an advance
appointment
increases the
salesperson's
effectiveness.

Henley & Savage/Click, Chicago

Some companies that sell technical industrial products, such as tools, have found it practical to have factory experts periodically accompany salespeople. In advance of the expert's visit to the territory, the salesperson maps out a schedule of interviews with key prospects. It is usually easier to get an appointment with these key people when they hear a factory expert will be present to explain the new technological changes in the product and the industry.

Calling at the Right Time   Much has been written about the best time of day for sales interviews. Certain salespeople claim the best time to see prospects is right after lunch, when they are likely to be in a pleasant mood. Others try to get as many appointments as they can during the early morning hours because they believe the prospects or customers will be in a better frame of mind early in the morning. There is little agreement on this subject, for obviously the most opportune time to call will vary with customers and types of selling. The salesperson who calls on wholesale grocers, for example, may find from experience that the best time to call is from 9:00 A.M. to 11:00 A.M. and from 1:30 P.M. to 3:30 P.M. A life insurance agent, on the other hand, may discover the most productive calls are made in the evening between the hours of 7:00 P.M. and 9:00 P.M., when there will be a chance to meet with both husband and wife.

For most types of selling, the best hours of the day are from approximately 9:00 A.M. to 11:30 A.M. and from 1:30 P.M. to 4:00 P.M. This is particularly true for sales representatives who call on business executives because the executives generally like to have the first part of the day free to read their mail and answer correspondence and the latter part of the day free to read and sign their letters.

Although the above hours may be the most favorable, this does not mean a salesperson should restrict appointments to these hours. Each salesperson soon learns what hours and what days are most favorable for each customer.[4]

Cultivating Subordinates   Busy executives usually have one or more subordinates whose function is to plan and to schedule interviews for their superiors. These "barriers," as they are sometimes called by salespeople, often make it rather difficult to see the boss. A secretary usually feels responsible for conserving the superior's time; therefore, he or she is eager to discover the true purpose of each salesperson's visit before granting an interview with the boss.

A salesperson should go out of his or her way to treat all subordinates with respect and courtesy.

A rule for success used by Bob Schiffman, one of the top 100 Cadillac salespeople, is as follows:

> To do business with the boss, you must sell yourself to everyone on his staff. I sincerely like people—so it comes naturally to me.
>
> I treat secretaries and chauffeurs as equals and friends. Ditto switchboard operators and maids. I regularly send small gifts to them all. An outstanding investment.
>
> The little people are great allies. They can't buy the product. But they can kill the sale. Who needs influential enemies? The champ doesn't want anyone standing back throwing rocks.
>
> In many cases, all you do is treat people decently—an act that sets you apart from 70 percent of your competitors.[5]

Using the Telephone to Make Appointments   Salespeople can save many hours by phoning to make appointments. While all of us have used telephones since childhood, many people have developed bad habits that reduce their effectiveness when talking over the phone. For example, the mouthpiece of the telephone should always be held in front of the mouth, not under the chin. Don't put fingers over the mouthpiece, and make an effort to talk distinctly, not too loudly or too softly.

Some steps for making appointments over the phone are:

1. Get ready, both physically and mentally. Have your appointment book and other necessary information in front of you.

---

[4]See "When Can Salesmen Call? At Most Plants, Anytime," *Purchasing,* September 29, 1983, pp. 21–22.

[5]Bob Schiffman, "Confessions of a Cadillac Salesman," *Marketing Times,* May–June 1979, p. 24.

2. State customer's name and pause.

3. State your name and the name of your company.

4. Ask if this is a convenient time for the customer to talk with you. This inquiry demonstrates courtesy and helps ensure you will have the customer's full attention.

5. Pause to give the customer time to respond.

6. State the purpose of your call.

7. Pause.

8. Make a brief presentation to get an appointment. Often this presentation involves stating the source of a referral or following up on an inquiry.

9. Overcome any objections.

10. Close.

11. Express your appreciation, restate the appointment time, or keep the door open for a future appointment.

12. Update your records with information learned from the call.

13. Send a letter confirming the appointment.

An example of a telephone approach for making an appointment is shown in Figure 9–3.

FIGURE 9–3
Example of
Telephone Approach

1. State customer's name.	Hello, Mr. Walker? [pause]
2. State your name.	This is Glen Scott with Gamma Industries.
3. Check time.	Did I call at a convenient time or should I call later? [pause]
4. State purpose and make presentation.	I'm calling to let you know about our new office copier. It has more features than the present copiers and could be a real money saver.
	I noticed you recently inquired about our copiers.
5. Close.	Could you put me on your calendar for 30 minutes next Monday or Tuesday?
6. Show appreciation, restate time, or keep door open.	Thank you, Mr. Walker. I'll be at your office at 9:00 A.M. on Tuesday.
	or
	I appreciate your frankness, Mr. Walker. I'd like to get back to you in a couple of months. Would that be all right?

Objections are the reasons a potential customer might have for not granting an interview. The goal of the telephone call is to set up an appointment, not to sell the product. Therefore, in addressing the objection, the salesperson should use the objection itself as a reason for granting an appointment. Figure 9–4 shows some appropriate responses to common objections to making an appointment encountered by Xerox copier salespeople.

Frequently when a salesperson calls for an appointment, the prospect may ask certain questions about the product or service. If this happens, the salesperson should refrain from giving a sales presentation over the telephone. The purpose of the call is to obtain an appointment and not to make a sale.

Some salespeople have their secretaries make telephone appointments for them. They believe this gives them greater prestige in the mind of the prospect or customer. If the secretary is unable to obtain an appointment, the salesperson may make a second call using a different approach.

The use of tricky subterfuges to obtain appointments has no place in modern selling. If the salesperson selects prospects carefully in terms of their product needs, it should not be necessary to conceal the purpose of the visit. At times, the salesperson may have to use determination, persistence, and ingenuity to obtain interviews; but he or she should never resort to deceitful or dishonest tactics.

Waiting for the Appointment

Some sales managers instruct their sales representatives that, in normal circumstances, they should not wait for any prospect for more than 10 minutes. There are exceptions to this rule, of course, depending on the importance of the customer and the distance the salesperson has traveled.

When a salesperson requests an interview, the receptionist may merely say, "I'll tell Mr. Jones that you are here." After the receptionist has had a chance to check with Mr. Jones, the salesperson should ask the receptionist or secretary approximately how long it will be. If the waiting period is excessive and the salesperson has another appointment, it may be advisable to explain this tactfully and to ask for another appointment. Usually the secretary will either try to get the salesperson in to see his or her superior earlier or will make arrangements for an appointment later.

Every salesperson must expect to spend a certain portion of each working day waiting for sales interviews. Successful salespeople make the best possible use of this time by working on their reports, studying new product information, planning and preparing for their next calls, and obtaining additional information about the prospect.

MAKING A GOOD FIRST IMPRESSION

The first few minutes a salesperson spends with a prospect often make or break a sale. If the first impression is favorable, the prospect is usually willing to listen. A negative first impression, on the other hand, sets up a barrier that may never be hurdled. The success achieved during the first

FIGURE 9–4
Responses to
Objections
Concerning
Appointments

Objection *From a secretary:*	Response
I'm sorry but Mr. Wilkes is busy now.	What I've to say will only take a few minutes. Should I call back in a half-hour or would you suggest I set up an appointment?
We already have a copier.	That's fine. I want to talk to Mr. Wilkes about our new paper flow system design for companies like yours.
I take care of all the copying.	That's fine, but I'm here to present what Xerox has to offer for a complete paper flow system integrating data transmission, report generation, and copiers. I'd like to speak to Mr. Wilkes about this total service.
From the prospect:	
Can't you mail the information to me?	Yes, I could, but everyone's situation is different, Mr Wilkes, and our systems are individually tailored to meet the needs of each customer. Now, . . . [benefit statement and repeat request for appointment].
Well, what is it you want to talk about?	It's difficult to explain the system over the telephone. In 15 minutes I can demonstrate the savings you get from the system.
You'd just be wasting your time. I'm not interested.	The general objection is hiding a specific objection. The salesperson needs to probe for the specific objection with: Do you say that because you don't copy many documents?
We had a Xerox copier once and didn't like it.	Probe for the specific reason of dissatisfaction and have a reply, but don't go too far. The objective is to get an appointment, not sell a copier.

Source: Courtesy of Xerox Corporation.

few minutes of an interview depends a great deal on the appearance, poise, and ingenuity of the salesperson and on the sincere interest shown in the prospect and his or her problems.

Many salespeople make a poor impression without realizing it. They may know their customer's needs and the product they are selling, but they overlook seemingly insignificant things that can create negative impressions. For example, sloppy dress, shopworn samples, and dog-eared brochures, a messy car, and a notebook bulging with little pieces of paper can suggest the salesperson does not care about details and will not follow up on commitments.

Entering a Room

Customers develop impressions by simply observing how a salesperson walks into the room. A brisk pace, lengthy stride, and erect posture demonstrate confidence. Shuffling feet and walking with the head down demonstrate a lack of self-confidence.

Handshake

Salespeople should not extend their hand to a customer, particularly if the customer is seated. Shaking hands should be the customer's choice. If the customer offers a hand, the salesperson should respond with a firm but not overpowering handshake. Everyone remembers the feeling one gets when shaking hands with someone that has no grip, or sweaty palms, or a grip of steel. The impression is often lasting and negative.

First Few Words

The salesperson's opening statement is an important aspect of creating a good first impression. Salespeople need to develop a short opening, about 15 words long, that will motivate customers to listen attentively and stimulate their desire to hear more. The customer's name should be used in the opening statement. Dale Carnegie, a master at developing relationships, said a person's name is "the sweetest and most important sound" to that person. Using a person's name is an indication of respect and a recognition of the unique qualities of the person.

APPEARANCE

A neat and well-groomed appearance is a most valuable asset to a salesperson. Good taste in dress, knowing what to wear and what not to wear, is a characteristic every salesperson should acquire. Salespeople shouldn't be walking fashion models, but should dress in a manner that will make a good first impression on their prospects. If clothing distracts from a sales presentation, the salesperson is overdressed. Proper attire and grooming give the salesperson additional poise and confidence during the first interview with a prospect. Some suggestions for effective attire follow.[6]

---

[6]See John T. Molloy, *Dress for Success* (New York: Peter H. Weyden, 1975); John T. Molloy, *The Woman's Dress for Success* (Chicago: Follett, 1977); and Jeffrey A. Trachtenburg, "Executive Suit," *Forbes,* March 26, 1984, pp. 191–94.

Salespeople know that using a person's name is an indication of respect and a recognition of the person's unique qualities.

Reprinted by permission of *Sales & Marketing Management* magazine. Copyright 1985.

Dress Like the Customer

The appropriate dress style varies depending on a person's occupation, social status, age, physical size, and location. Some useful clues about the appropriate dress for salespeople can be gained by observing their customers. Salespeople should attempt to match the dress of their typical customers. If they achieve this objective, they will blend in with the customers. Customers will find it easier to develop rapport with the salespeople because they will see them as being similar.

Salespeople should avoid dressing more stylishly or expensively than their customers. While such a dress style might give the salesperson more authority, it may also make a customer uncomfortable and defensive.

Wear Classic Styles

Unless a salesperson works in the fashion industry, high-fashion clothing should be avoided because it is too expensive, goes out of style too quickly, and does not look professional or businesslike. But classic dresses, suits, and accessories are always in style.

Hints for Men The suit is the focal garment in business dress, particularly when interacting with upper-middle-class decision makers. Take care in choosing the color, material, fit, and accompanying garments and accessories. In general, darker suits give a more authoritative image; lighter colors create a friendlier one. Pinstripes convey the most authority, fol-

In general, salespeople should dress conservatively. But sometimes, like the truck saleswoman and the feed salesman here, it is better to dress like the customer.

H. Armstrong Roberts

Cezus/Click, Chicago

Courtesy Yale Industrial Trucks
of Southern California, Inc.

Courtesy Ralston Purina

lowed in descending order by solids, chalk stripes, and plaids (which must be very subtle). Natural fibers such as wool (or wool-polyester blends that look and feel like wool) are preferable. They wear better and look better than most synthetics. Cottons and linens, while comfortable, wrinkle too easily.

The fit of the suit is also important. The pant waist should fit slightly above the navel and horizontal to the ground. Plain-bottom cuffs should break in front and be longer in back than in front. Turned-up cuffs should be horizontal to the ground and the same length both back and front. Jacket sleeves should come within five inches of the base of the thumb.

White-on-white patterns and solid white shirts create the most effectiveness and credibility, but blues and other pale pastels are also popular.

Shirts, as a rule, should be lighter than the suit, and the tie darker than the shirt. Shirt stripes should always be close together, clearly defined, and of one coordinating color on a white background.

Ties are important indicators of the salesperson's status, credibility, and personality. A good rule is to wear suits and shirts in basic colors and let the tie provide the accent color. For example, the accent color for a navy suit and white shirt can be provided by a striped red and navy tie. The tie tip should come just to the belt buckle, and its width should harmonize with the width of the suit lapels. The standard tie length is 55 or 56 inches; and to make a good knot, a tie must have added material sewn into it. Bow ties give off negative signals and tie pins and clasps are currently out of style. Silk is the best choice for tie material—it looks elegant and wears well. Polyester or a combination blend must *look* like silk to be effective. Wool or cotton is acceptable, too. Acetate or rayon tends to look cheap, however; and linen should be avoided because it wrinkles so easily. Solid ties with solid suits look good. Other acceptable tie patterns include polka dot, rep, club, Ivy League, repeating diamond, paisley, and basic plaid.

As for accessories, the less jewelry worn, the better. Stay away from bracelets and pins, and wear simple and small cuff links. Shoes should be black, brown, or cordovan, in lace-up, wingtip, Gucci-type buckle, or all-leather slip-on styles. Never wear shoes with multiple colors, platforms, or high heels with business dress. Most belts are acceptable. Buckles should be small, clean, and traditional. Attaché cases are positive symbols of success.

Hints for Women In 1977 when John Molloy wrote his *Dress for Success* books, businesswomen were advised to wear only very conservative navy or gray suits, tailored blouses, and string ties. They were entering professions (like selling) that were dominated by men, and they had to give clear signals they were serious about their jobs and were members of the company team. In those days, the more women looked like men in these "uniforms," the more easily they were accepted in the business world.

Today, thanks to those pioneers, women just beginning their careers have the luxury of dressing with more flair and style while still maintaining a dignified, professional look. Women in business can now send signals that they are good at—and relaxed about—their jobs and that they know the difference between business and private life.

John Molloy's more recent research shows that a tailored suit is still the best choice for a woman bent on success. Other research shows that in 1985, women bought 24 million suits, compared to 16 million in 1980. So, although standards have relaxed, skirted suits for business and professional women are still "in."

Today a good business wardrobe still starts with navy, black, and gray suits worn with light-colored blouses. But you can also add suits in more cheerful shades, wool or silk dresses with jackets, and blazers with co-ordinated skirts. As with menswear, women's suits look and wear best in natural fibers or in blends that look and feel like natural fibers. Women should choose a suit whose jacket and skirt length complements their figure size and height and that is stylish without being so trendy it will look dated in a short time.

Women's blouses have much more variety than men's shirts in color, style, and fabric. Cotton and silk are the best fabric choices—and they are much more professional looking than sheer polyester or slithery silk imitations. Keep blouses businesslike, feminine but tailored, soft but not see-through, plain or with small prints.

Choose shoes and hose to complement the costume. Black, brown, navy, or cordovan are always acceptable shoe colors. Tailored, classic pumps, slings, and gillies with one-inch or one-and-a-half-inch heels (especially if the job requires a lot of walking) combined with neutral or color-coordinated hose look both professional and feminine. But fishnet or patterned hose, ankle straps, chunky loafers, and trendy boots are best left for after-hours wear.

Accessories like ties, scarves, simple pins, gold chains, and plain watches can make even a plain, dark suit look dressy and businesslike. Chunky jewelry and clanking bracelets are "out." Silk scarves, especially, can add flair and a touch of color, if they are tied or draped attractively. Scarves are becoming more popular and acceptable today than the so-called power ties that were formerly a required part of the "uniform."

The businesswoman's hairstyle should meet many of the same criteria as her clothes: subtle, formal, comfortable, and easy to care for. Hair length is not an issue, but she must demonstrate effective management of it.

General Hints   Business clothes project an image of the salesperson, the salesperson's company, and the product. Salespeople will feel most comfortable if they use their own natural style plus some common sense. Keep in mind that standards of acceptable business dress vary in different areas of the country, and adapt clothing style accordingly. Consider corporate culture, too: how do the executives of the company dress, and what image does this project? And finally, remember the customers. The salesperson's business dress should make both him or her and them comfortable.[7]

---

[7]Sources for the preceding sections include "Dressing for Success Isn't What It Used to Be," *Business Week,* October 27, 1986, pp. 142–43; "Suit May Not Be Best Way To Top," *New York Times,* November 4, 1985, pp. 1, D–4; Esther B. Fein, "Redefining Office Style," *New York Times,* March 3, 1985, Sec. 6, Part II, pp. 64, 140; and M. B. Fiedorek and D. L. Jewell, *Executive Style: Looking It, Living It* (Piscataway, N.J.: New Century Publishers, Inc., 1983).

Plan before Buying Clothes	Before buying business clothing, salespeople should review their entire wardrobe. Clothing should be separated into basic colors—black or gray, brown, and navy—and the outfits assembled for each basic color. Only buy clothing that will increase the number of different outfits that can be assembled in a basic color.
Don't Overspend on One Item	The customer's impression of a salesperson depends on the salesperson's overall appearance. Wearing an expensive designer suit will not offset the negative impression caused by old, unattractive shoes.
Use Clothing to Complement the Body	Before buying clothing, salespeople should analyze their bodies. Clothing should be used to camouflage liabilities. For example, because large men sometimes appear too authoritative, they may frighten customers. For this reason large, authoritative men should avoid clothing that makes them look even more authoritative, such as dark, pinstripe suits.

SUMMARY

This chapter stresses the importance of planning the sales presentation and getting the right start. Developing a precall plan saves time for both salespeople and customers. In addition, planning helps salespeople organize the sales presentation, ensures that key points will not be omitted, and increases sales effectiveness.

To develop an effective plan, salespeople first need to collect information about the individual customer and the customer's company. The next step is to set specific objectives for the sales call. Finally, salespeople must develop a plan for the actual sales presentation. The plan for the presentation includes the benefits to be emphasized and the evidence provided to support the benefits. After organizing a presentation, salespeople should practice it by mentally rehearsing their own comments and the anticipated comments of the customer. When the sales call is over, salespeople need to begin preparing for future calls by keeping complete and accurate records.

As a general rule, salespeople should make appointments before calling on customers. In this way, the salespeople can be sure they will talk to the right person.

There are a number of methods for making appointments. Perhaps the most effective technique is the straightforward telephone approach. This includes stating the salesperson's name, establishing a link with the prospect or customer, stating the purpose of the call, and asking for an appointment.

The first minutes salespeople spend with customers are crucial. Salespeople need to make a good first impression through their appearance and poise. A good rule is to dress in a style similar to the customer's dress style. The salesperson's initial remarks are aimed at gaining the customer's interest and attention.

QUESTIONS
AND
PROBLEMS

1. The first few seconds of the salesperson's interview with the customer are critical. Why?

2. Why is it desirable to make appointments before visiting a customer? Under what circumstances might it be unnecessary to make appointments?

3. How would you react to salespeople who dress just the way they want to when making a sales call because they believe no one has the right to tell them what to wear?

4. Why should a salesperson try to make a good impression on a customer's subordinates?

5. Evaluate the following objectives for a sales call:
   Objective 1:
   Show and demonstrate the entire line of grinding wheels.
   Objective 2:
   Have the customer order one dozen grinding wheels, models 1001, 4014, and 5511.
   Objective 3:
   Have the customer promise to test our grinding wheels during the next two weeks.

6. Evaluate the following statement: "Arriving on time is not as important as making a good presentation."

7. Should a salesperson attempt to bypass a receptionist? What are the potential advantages and disadvantages of this approach?

8. You have an appointment to see a purchasing agent at 2:00 P.M. You arrive at 1:55 P.M. The receptionist tells you the purchasing agent is busy with a telephone call. What should you do at 2:20 P.M. if the receptionist has not called you yet?

PROJECT

1. Assume you are a sales representative for an automobile dealer that sells an economy car. You are calling on the purchasing agent of the Electro Corporation for the purpose of selling Electro a six-car fleet that can be used by its sales representatives. Secure the necessary product information from a local automobile dealer and then prepare a script—for use in a role-playing demonstration in class—outlining your sales interview for the Electro purchasing agent.

CASE PROBLEMS

Case 9–1   **The Anderson Company**

The Anderson Company produces and distributes business forms for almost every office and business need. The company's main office is in Chicago. Its products are sold through regional and district offices in the United States and Canada. Sales representatives are usually assigned to specific geographic areas. However, in some larger cities they are assigned certain key customers.

Alan Beebe, a salesman in the Philadelphia area, has been with the company for 30 years and is planning to retire in 6 months. In general, he has done a fairly good job in his territory, but his sales during the last year have been somewhat spotty. One of the largest business concerns in Beebe's territory, the United Manufacturing Company, has never given any business to the Anderson Company. Beebe has made regular calls on the purchasing agent but has never been able to obtain an order for Anderson business forms. The purchasing agent has told Beebe on several occasions that it is impossible to give the Anderson Company any business because United Manufacturing has entered into an exclusive agreement for all printing work with a local concern, the American Printing Company. Beebe has heard indirectly that the sales representative of the American Printing Company is a close friend of the purchasing agent.

Ralph Monroe has been a sales representative for the Anderson Company for eight years. He has worked three years for the company in the Chicago area, and during the last five years he has been in the San Francisco area. Monroe, an excellent sales representative, has a fine background in office systems and methods work. The Eastern regional sales executive has told Monroe he will take over Beebe's territory in Philadelphia when Beebe retires. Plans call for Monroe to work with Beebe in the Philadelphia area during the last six months of Beebe's service. When the sales manager told Monroe of his new assignment, he said he wanted Beebe to introduce Monroe to the regular customers in the new territory. In addition, he said, "Ralph, I want you to concentrate on getting some business from the United Manufacturing Company. There is no reason why we shouldn't be getting some of that business. I told Beebe that I wanted you to spend whatever time was necessary to break that account open for us."

Questions

1. Assume you are Monroe. What steps would you take in attempting to get some business from the United Manufacturing Company?

2. Whom would you see? If you call on the purchasing agent, how will you get around the objection of the exclusive agreement with the American Printing Company? How can you win the support of the purchasing agent?

Case 9–2 High Energy Inc.—Making an Appointment

Let's assume you are Alvin Jones, a salesperson for High Energy, a small technology firm that has invented a process for creating energy out of a common mineral. You believe the major oil firms will be interested in your firm's discovery. Your first "cold call" is on H. K. Quibble, executive vice president of Ohio Oil. How should you approach Mr. Quibble's secretary? Pick the statement that is most likely to succeed and justify your choice.

1. Good morning. I'm Alvin Jones of High Energy Inc. I would like to meet Mr. Quibble.

2. Good morning. I'm Alvin Jones of High Energy Inc. We have recently developed a product that will revolutionize the energy industry and completely alter energy consumption for decades to come. It's a product Mr. Quibble will desperately want to see. When will he be available?

3. Good morning. You will recall my appointment with Mr. Quibble. I am Alvin Jones.

4. Good morning. I am Alvin Jones. Mr. Quibble will be interested in learning about our new product, which we have recently sold to Indiana Oil.

5. Good morning. I am Alvin Jones of High Energy Inc. I have a matter of great interest to Mr. Quibble and would like to discuss it directly with him.

The secretary doesn't think much of the opening and attempts to brush you off. You are certain Mr. Quibble is in, but the secretary says, "Mr. Quibble is away on a business trip today." What is your best response and why?

1. When can I see Mr. Quibble?

2. Where can I contact Mr. Quibble? This matter is of such importance that Mr. Quibble will not want to wait.

3. I'll wait for Mr. Quibble in case he returns today.

4. Is tomorrow morning better?

5. I'd like to get in touch with Mr. Quibble again, after I discuss this product with some of the competition.

The secretary thinks there is enough merit in what you are saying to send you to one of Mr. Quibble's subordinates, Mr. Smart, director of research and development. How should you respond? Why?

1. Thank you; that will be OK.

2. Thank you, but I insist on speaking with Mr. Quibble.

3. This technique is of such significance that Mr. Quibble will want to hear about it firsthand.

4. I'll speak to Mr. Smart, but I would prefer to talk with Mr. Quibble.

5. Mr. Smart is more knowledgeable about this technique, but he has no power. I would prefer to speak with Mr. Quibble, rather than waste your time and mine.

Case 9–3   ICM Typewriter Division—A Role-Playing Exercise

The following role play is a means of practicing and evaluating the student's ability to secure interviews with prospects over the phone. One student plays the role of salesperson, and five others play the roles of purchasing agents. The information defining the roles is presented below.

ICM Inc. is the leading producer of premium office products, including typewriters, copy machines, and computers. For example, its Speedtouch brand of typewriter is widely recognized as the best made. Likewise, ICM's prices are high, reflecting the superior quality of the product.

ICM is interested in selling typewriters to a wide variety of firms. Its chief competition is Washington Writers Inc., an ambitious firm that offers typewriters of slightly lower quality but is highly competitive with regard to price and speed of delivery.

Marie Nichols

Ms. Nichols began working with ICM Typewriter Division in the mid-1970s. She soon established herself as ICM's leading salesperson in the Northeast. She devotes about five hours per week to telephone prospecting and from experience knows that to do a good job of prospecting she must begin the telephone conversation by *identifying* herself and ICM; attract the *interest* of the prospect; establish rapport with the prospect, *make the prospect comfortable;* make certain the prospect has the *authority* to make a purchase; convince the prospect that a face-to-face *interview* will be beneficial.

Purchasing Agents

Joe Murphy: Selectronics, Inc. Selectronics manufactures components for TV sets. The firm has recently received a major contract with a large TV producer and is planning a move to larger, more comfortable offices in Philadelphia. Mr. Murphy, somewhat introverted, is an exceptionally sharp purchasing agent.

Peter Stevens: Now Chemicals, Inc. In the past, Now Chemicals has purchased office equipment of somewhat lower quality than ICM is offering. However, there has recently been a change in the executive personnel at Now Chemicals, including the purchasing agent, Mr. Stevens. Mr.

Stevens, new at his job, is ambitious, but very wary of salespeople.

Rebecca Smith: US Can Company, Inc. Ms. Smith was promoted from the secretarial ranks to the position of purchasing agent. Ms. Smith is quite conservative (she expects to retire in 18 months), reflecting a philosophy that is consistent with US Can. US Can is a very large corporation whose cash position is good, but the firm has tended to economize in the past.

Alan Horowitz: Ajax Elevator Co. As office manager of this small- to medium-sized firm, Mr. Horowitz's duties include purchasing as well as managing the day-to-day affairs of the Ajax office. Ajax Elevator Co. was founded by Mr. Horowitz's brother-in-law and has grown solidly over the years. Ajax seems like a good prospect.

Juan Torres: Downtown Medical Group. Mr. Torres is director of administration of this clinic, which includes 20 doctors of various specialities. Mr. Torres has recently graduated with a BBA degree in accounting.

In the role play, Marie Nichols calls each of the five purchasing agents and attempts to arrange an interview. Ms. Nichols uses the above-mentioned plan: She identifies herself; she interests the prospect; she makes the prospect feel comfortable, developing rapport; she makes certain the prospect has sufficient authority; she persuades the prospect to grant an interview. The purchasing agents respond as they normally would in real life, given the information in their roles.

SELECTED
REFERENCES

Curtis, Carol E. "Tailoring the Corporate Woman." *Forbes,* February 16, 1981, pp. 47–48.

Fahner, Hal. "Call Reports That Tell it All." *Sales & Marketing Management,* November 12, 1984, pp. 50–53.

"How to Dress to Get Ahead." *Glamor,* July 1985, p. 170.

Johnson, Mark. "How Computerization Can Organize a Sales Force: A System That Makes Planning Easy." *Business Marketing,* December 1985, pp. 98–100.

King, Ronald H., and Martha B. Booze. "Sales Training and Impression Management." *Journal of Personal Selling and Sales Management,* August 1986, pp. 51–60.

Levin, Mortimer. *The Executive Look and How to Get It.* New York: AMACOM, 1979.

Swan, John E., and Robert T. Adkins. "The Image of the Salesperson: Prestige and Other Dimensions." *Journal of Personal Selling and Sales Management,* Fall/Winter 1980–81, pp. 48–56.

Tuthill, Mory. "A Change of Image Can Change Your Future." *Nation's Business,* November 1980, pp. 74–77.

"Two Views of Those Vital 30 Seconds." *Sales Management,* October 23, 1972, p. 31.

10 Delivering the Sales Presentation

Some questions answered in this chapter are:

- What are the basic sales approaches?
- What are the advantages and disadvantages of the various types of sales presentations?
- What steps in the sales process are associated with the need satisfaction and problem solution sales approaches?
- How can salespeople approach customers, develop rapport, and increase source credibility?
- Why is it important for salespeople to "read" body language?

In view of the millions of sales transactions completed each day, it is little wonder that various types of sales presentations are used. In certain types of selling, memorized canned presentations produce the highest sales volume. In other types, unstructured presentations are more effective. This chapter describes the basic approaches to personal selling and the type of sales presentation associated with each approach.

Unstructured interviews or presentations aimed at recognizing and solving customer problems are the most exciting and challenging sales situations. The activities and skills required in these sales presentations are discussed in more detail in this chapter.

Seven Steps in the Sales Process

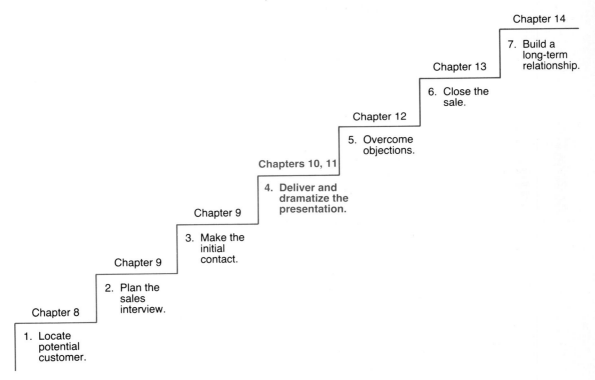

APPROACHES TO PERSONAL SELLING

The four major selling approaches are (1) stimulus-response, (2) mental states, (3) need satisfaction, and (4) problem solution.[1] These approaches are described in this section.

Stimulus-Response Approach

Psychological experiments show that subjects will respond in a predictable manner when exposed to a specific stimulus. When subjects are rewarded for correct responses, the responses may become automatic.

Salespeople using the stimulus-response approach concentrate on saying the right thing (the *stimulus*) at the right time to develop a favorable *response* from the prospect. A standard memorized sales presentation is used to ensure the right points are made at the right time. Knowing how prospects normally respond to certain stimuli helps salespeople build a sequence of favorable responses.

---

[1]See Robert F. Gwinner, "Base Theories in the Formulation of Sales Strategies," *MSU Business Topics,* Autumn 1968, pp. 37–44.

The major disadvantage of this approach is that people often do not respond in the expected way. When this happens, the salesperson is thrown off track and may not be able to complete the presentation.

The stimulus-response approach is most appropriate in simple, straightforward selling situations such as selling a vacuum cleaner in a home. The approach is also useful when selling time is limited, as in selling (detailing) pharmaceuticals to a doctor.

Mental States Approach

The mental states approach is based on a slogan coined by E. St. Elmo Lewis in 1898: "Attract attention, maintain interest, create desire, and get action." This formula suggests that a prospect goes through a logical sequence of mental states in any buying situation. The salesperson's first task is to present sales appeals that will capture the prospect's attention. Then the salesperson must plan and deliver the sales story in order to advance the buyer from one mental state to another until the sale has been completed.

Although the mental states theory of selling is widely accepted, it has shortcomings. During a sales presentation, it is impossible to know when attention stops and interest starts, or when interest stops and desire starts. In fact, most experienced salespeople agree that they do not think about the various mental states when making their presentations. Another disadvantage of the mental states theory is that it puts the emphasis in the wrong place. Salespeople who follow this four-step plan may overemphasize their side of the story to get attention and interest, instead of adapting themselves to the buyer's desires, needs, and wants.

Despite the weaknesses of the mental states theory, it has the advantage of encouraging salespeople to plan their sales presentations. Because of its simplicity, it has been widely accepted.

Need Satisfaction Approach

The discussion of customer behavior in Chapter 4 emphasizes that people buy products to satisfy needs and solve problems. The need satisfaction approach uses the prospect's need as the logical starting point for the sales presentation. A salesperson using this approach first determines the customer's need. After securing the prospect's agreement the need exists, the salesperson offers a solution to satisfy the need.

The major advantage of this approach is that it forces the salesperson to practice the marketing concept. The emphasis is on satisfying the customer's needs, not on the product or service being offered. The salesperson must analyze the sales process from the buyer's viewpoint. The presentation is planned and the selling points organized to answer such questions as: What are the prospect's real needs and wants? How will my product benefit the buyer? How can I best guide the prospect's thinking so a decision to buy my product will be made, thus solving the buyer's problems and satisfying the buyer's wants?

Problem solving
with the customer
enhances sales
potential.

David Aronson/Stock, Boston

The need satisfaction approach is designed for more experienced and sophisticated salespeople. Salespeople using this approach must understand the psychology of communication and persuasion. They must also spend time and effort to determine the prospect's needs and to demonstrate how their product satisfies those needs. Because of the experience and time required by this approach, it is typically used when the product and the customer are rather sophisticated. For example, the need satisfaction approach is often used in selling insurance, stocks and bonds, farm machinery, and industrial products.

Problem Solution Approach

The problem solution approach combines the need satisfaction approach with the scientific method for solving problems. Like the need satisfaction approach, the problem solution approach begins with the salesperson identifying the prospect's need. The salesperson then helps the customer list possible alternative solutions and evaluate the advantages and disadvantages of each alternative. Finally, the salesperson works with the customer to select the best alternative. In using this approach, the salesperson builds a relationship with the customer that resembles a consultant-client relationship.

The problem solution approach places greater demands on the salesperson's time and skills than the three other approaches. It is typically used in industrial sales of technical products and services.[2]

---

[2]For a discussion of the limitations of need satisfaction and problem solution selling, see Dan T. Dunn, Claude A. Thomas, and James L. Lubowski, "Pitfalls of Consultative Selling," *Business Horizons,* September/October 1981, pp. 59–65.

Conclusion

In this section, we have emphasized the advantages and disadvantages of different selling approaches. However, each of the selling approaches recognizes that buyers must be considered in developing a sales presentation. The stimulus-response approach assumes salespeople must stimulate specific needs in their customers, while the need satisfaction and problem solution approaches emphasize probing customers to uncover their needs. Most sales presentations involve a blend of these approaches. At some points in the presentation, a stimulus-response approach might be appropriate, while a problem solution approach might be more effective at other points. For example, the use of an attention-getting approach at the beginning of the presentation is consistent with mental states approach. On the other hand, probing for information during the presentation is an important aspect of the need satisfaction approach.

TYPES OF SALES PRESENTA-TIONS

The three basic types of sales presentations are (1) the standard memorized presentation, (2) the outlined presentation, and (3) the program presentation. The first two types are used in the stimulus-response and mental states selling approaches. The third type is used in need satisfaction and problem solution selling. The three types are described below.

Standard Memorized Presentation

The standard memorized sales presentation is a carefully prepared sales story that includes all of the key selling points arranged in the most effective order. The presentation is usually developed after a careful analysis of the sales stories of the most successful salespeople. The best features and sales points from the various presentations are incorporated into a standard sales story, which is then memorized.

Sixty years ago John H. Patterson, president of the National Cash Register Company, originated the standard sales presentation. He visited the company's sales agencies and had a stenographer take down the sales conversations of the best NCR sales representatives. The talks were analyzed, and a standard sales story was developed. All sales representatives were required to use this standard presentation and demonstration. A tremendous increase in sales resulted, and soon many other companies standardized their sales techniques and demonstrations.

There is considerable disagreement among sales managers as to the merits and demerits of the standard memorized sales talk. Many managers insist every salesperson memorize the entire sales talk and deliver it word for word. Others believe salespeople should memorize a standard sales story but be free to adopt it to suit their own personalities. Still other managers are bitterly opposed to any standard memorized presentation.

Some of the major arguments for and against the standard memorized sales presentation are given below.

Advantages   The main advantages are:

1. It ensures the salesperson will tell the complete and accurate story about the company's products and policies.
2. It encompasses the best techniques and methods used by the most successful salespeople.
3. It helps the new and inexperienced sales representative.
4. It eliminates repetition and saves time for both the salesperson and the buyer.
5. It guarantees the most effective presentation by having the sales points arranged in a logical and systematic sequence.
6. It provides effective answers to all possible objections that may be raised by the prospects, and thus gives the salesperson additional confidence.
7. Since most salespeople tend to standardize their sales talks anyway, why not standardize on the "one best way"?

Disadvantages   The main disadvantages of the standard memorized sales talk are:

1. It is inflexible and artificial, and it tends to make a robot out of the salesperson. As a result, he or she loses enthusiasm and originality.
2. It cannot be used in types of selling in which the salesperson makes regular calls on customers.
3. It discourages or prevents the prospect from participating in the sales conversation. This keeps the salesperson from discovering the true needs and wants of each prospective buyer, and the sales story tends to become a monologue.
4. The salesperson who relies on a memorized presentation often finds it difficult to get started again after being interrupted by the prospect.
5. Its use is not practical when many products are sold.

Conclusions   The success or failure of a standard sales talk depends to a great degree on the ability of the person delivering it. A competent person can use a memorized sales talk so skillfully the prospect doesn't suspect it is a canned presentation. On the other hand, an inferior salesperson may sound phony.

For certain types of selling, such as door-to-door selling, the standard memorized sales talk has proved effective. It has also been of great help to beginning salespeople in other types of selling. Many individuals memorize a sales story and later modify it to fit their particular personalities or speaking styles. In this way, they derive most of the benefits of the standard presentation and are able to deliver their sales talks in a free and natural manner.

Perhaps the chief weakness of the standard memorized sales talk is that it encourages salespeople to talk too much about the products or services without paying proper attention to the wants or needs of prospective buyers. If a product has a universal demand, this may not be a serious objection. But if the product is designed to fit many different needs, it's essential to consider each buyer's specific needs and wants. Too many salespeople who use a standard memorized sales talk disregard the interests and desires of their prospects. There is no quicker way to create ill will.

In general, it is not advisable to use a standard memorized sales talk if a person can't adapt the sales story to the prospect and make it sound informal. It should not be used when calling professional buyers, when selling a complete line of products, or when making regular calls on customers.[3]

Outlined Presentation

The outlined presentation differs from the standard memorized presentation in that it is more flexible and need not be memorized. It usually consists of a systematically arranged outline of the most important sales points. It may also include the necessary steps for determining the prospect's needs and for building goodwill at the close of the sale.

Sales representatives often memorize certain parts of their presentations, such as a standard introduction, standard answers to the most common objections, and a standard close. These memorized portions then become a part of their outlined presentations. Through skillful use of the memorized parts, the sales representatives gain many of the advantages of a complete standard memorized presentation, but they still keep the interview flexible and informal.

Some companies provide their sales representatives with suggested outlines for each product. Others provide general instructions on the techniques of developing sales outlines, but rely on the salesperson to develop the individual sales presentation.

Examples of Sales Presentation Outlines   A manufacturer of electric ranges provides each retail salesperson with an outlined selling guide. The main points in the illustrated selling guide are:

1. *Open your presentation by calling attention to overall beauty, style design, finish, and fixtures.*
    Hard, smooth porcelain finish holds its natural luster.
    Easy to keep clean.

---

[3]See Marvin A. Jolson, "Should the Sales Presentation Be Fresh or Canned?" *Business Horizons,* October 1973, p. 85.

Fiberglass insulation holds oven heat and keeps kitchen cool.
Sturdy, all-steel, one-piece unit construction eliminates drawer
jamming or fixture rattling.

2. *Focus attention on surface units.*
Surface units are faster, safer, and easier to clean.
Can depend on uniform penetrating heat.
No dangerous fumes or flames.
No soot on walls or cooking utensils.
Can prepare entire meal in deep-well cooker—ideal for soups,
stews, and french fries—handy at canning time—convenient
for sterilizing baby's bottle.

3. *Explain the controls.*
Efficient controls make cooking a science—always get same
results from same recipe.
Can connect toaster or coffee maker in convenience outlet.
Special thermostat controls preheating of oven.
Automatic timer makes it possible to go shopping while dinner
is baking.
Minute minder is handy for fast cooking operations of
vegetables, eggs, etc.
Entire range surface illuminated by fluorescent lamp.
Pilot light shows when deep-well cooker or surface units are on.

4. *Explain oven and broiler.*
Each shelf has safety stop to prevent accidents when
removing things from oven.
Oven light comes on when door opens.
Extra-heavy insulation holds heat in.
"Positive seal" floating oven door automatically adjusts itself
to keep heat in as oven temperature rises.
No unsightly oven vent—concealed vent takes away excess
moisture and fumes.
Handy waist-high broiler ideal for steaks, chops, and fish—
excellent for toasted sandwiches.
Roomy storage compartments save unnecessary steps.
Drawers roll easily because they are mounted on roller-
bearings.

5. *Stress ease of buying through budget plan.*
Use low-cost slide chart in figuring terms.

The following steps for an outlined sales presentation are recommended
by a national stock brokerage firm:[4]

---

[4]Paine Webber, Jackson & Curtis, *Securities Selling Skills*, unit 3: "Presentation."

Step	Example
1. Restatement of client's needs.	Ms. Blank, last week when we spoke, you emphasized you're looking for an investment that can provide you with long-term growth and reasonable security.
2. General product reference.	One investment that can help you meet these needs is in the communications field.
3. Statement relating general product benefits to the client's needs.	The communications industry has a history of stable growth—the kind of history that represents the reasonably secure, long-term growth you want.
4. Reference to specific product.	The particular company I have in mind is International Television Company.
5. Probe for client's knowledge and attitudes about the product.	How well do you know International?
6. Statement of specific product features.	Two factors that attract our analysts to ITV now are its selling price and its strong balance sheet. ITV is now selling for 10 times its estimated earnings, well below its typical P/E ratio.
7. Statement relating specific product benefits to the client's needs.	With a clean balance sheet, ITV can show profits even in lean years. Its steady growth rate will continue for some time to come. Considering its depressed price now, you can really maximize on your investment.
8. Pause or probe to determine client's acceptance of specific benefit.	How does the growth potential ITV offers sound to you?

Advantages and Disadvantages   The previous illustrations show the great variations in sales presentation outlines. Because of these variations, it is difficult to make an absolute evaluation of the outlined sales presentation. Many of the advantages of the standard memorized sales talk also apply to the outlined sales story. For example, the outlined presentation places the main sales points in the proper sequence; it eliminates duplication and overlapping; it prevents gaps; it forces the salesperson to think of possible objections and to plan appropriate answers; and it serves as a guide for the new salesperson.

The main advantages of the outlined presentation over the standard memorized sales talk are as follows:

1. It is more informal and natural.
2. There is less chance for domination by the salesperson, and therefore the prospect's needs, desires, viewpoints, and opinions are more likely to be considered.
3. It is more flexible.
4. It is easier for the salesperson to get back on track if interrupted.

The main objections to the outlined sales presentation are as follows:

1. The salesperson may not be able to express himself or herself as effectively when speaking extemporaneously.
2. There is a greater chance to be sidetracked from the sales story.
3. The salesperson may not prepare the sales talk as carefully when it is not committed to memory.

Most experienced sales representatives are able to overcome these objections. As they gain experience and confidence, they tend to favor the outlined or program type of presentation over the standard memorized type.

Program Presentation

The program presentation usually consists of a complete written or illustrated presentation developed from a detailed and comprehensive analysis or survey of the prospect's or customer's needs. This type of presentation is used extensively in trade selling, in the sale of industrial equipment and office equipment and supplies, in management consulting work, in the sale of certain types of advertising, and in many similar types of selling.

A complete program presentation normally includes four basic steps: (1) getting permission to make an analysis or survey; (2) making the survey, which includes the gathering and analysis of the facts; (3) preparing the program or proposal; and (4) presenting the program or proposal to the prospect or customer.

Getting Permission to Make a Survey   In order to develop an effective program presentation, the sales representative must first convince prospects or customers of the desirability of making a survey to discover their exact needs or problems. Often the sales representative will refer to similar surveys that have produced substantial savings or gains for other customers. A sales representative of word processing equipment may use case histories to illustrate how surveys helped certain companies find inefficiencies in their practices and save money by installing word processing equipment.

In many instances, a sales representative calls in specialists, such as engineers or systems analysts, to help make the surveys or analyses. This lends prestige to the proposal, and the prospective customer is thus more likely to authorize the fact-finding survey.

Making the Survey   The simplest type of survey consists of a single interview or a short questionnaire that provides the sales representative with a picture of the problems and needs of the prospective buyers. A life insurance sales agent who is trying to plan a comprehensive life insurance program for a prospect normally makes no attempt to sell during the first interview. Instead, all the necessary personal information is obtained about the prospect. The sales representative may then spend hours planning a personalized program that is presented during a subsequent interview. Computers may be used to develop specific personalized programs.

Some surveys, however, are very complex and require the services of many technical specialists or experts. For example, IBM spends thousands of dollars in personnel costs alone to get a single proposal ready for presentation to a prospect.

After the fact-finding or initial research work is completed and all of the facts are obtained, the sales representative, or in some cases the specialist, diagnoses these facts to determine how the company's products or services can best solve the prospect's problems. This analysis serves as the foundation for a definite program proposal.

Preparing the Program   After the facts have been carefully analyzed, a written or illustrated proposal is usually prepared for presentation to the prospect. This proposal normally includes a clear statement of the prospect's problem or need, an effective presentation of the proposed solution to this problem or need, and a description of what the proposed program will cost.

Each proposal or program is tailored to the needs of each prospect or customer. Under certain conditions the sales representative will want to dress up the program presentation by using such visual aids as slides or movies, demonstration models, charts, and portfolios. If the presentation is to be given to a group, it is especially important to make use of appropriate visual aids.

Presenting the Program or Proposal   The final step in a complete program presentation is selling the proposal to the prospect, client, or customer. The success or failure of the entire program presentation hinges on the kind of job the sales representative does in explaining and presenting the proposal. Presentations of this kind demand an unusual amount of advance preparation and practice before the actual interview occurs.[5]

---

[5]See Harold M. Horowitz and Marvin A. Jolson, "The Industrial Proposal as a Promotional Tool," *Industrial Marketing Management,* Spring 1980, pp. 101–9.

Advantages and Disadvantages   The foremost advantages of the program type of presentation include the following:

1. It provides an opportunity to determine the real needs and problems of the prospect. Emphasis is put in the right place—the needs of the buyer.

2. It provides sufficient time to gather and analyze the facts and to prepare the most effective solution to the customer's problems.

3. It provides the opportunity to develop a polished and personalized presentation.

4. It builds prestige for the sales representative and the company. The prospect or customer thinks of the sales representative as a professional assistant who is helping to solve the customer's problems.

5. It eliminates wasted time caused by an excessive number of interviews. The sales representative normally obtains permission to make the survey during the first interview and then presents recommendations during the second interview.

The main arguments against the program type of presentation are as follows:

1. It is time-consuming and therefore expensive. The sales representative or a specialist may spend much valuable time surveying the needs or problems of a potential customer without any guarantee of making a sale.

2. The potential customer may object to having the sales representative make a survey on the ground that the sales representative is biased.

3. In the past, many sales representatives obtained interviews under the pretext that they were making surveys. As a result, many customers are wary of surveys or studies.

Conclusions   This type of sales presentation has gained in popularity in recent years. It is used extensively by experienced salespeople, especially where unit sales are high. Life insurance companies have had very successful experiences with the "programming" type of selling.

Perhaps the greatest advantage of this type of sales presentation is that it emphasizes the problems and needs of the customer. Consequently, there is a greater chance each sale will result in long-term gains for both buyer and seller.

THE SELLING PROCESS

The remaining portion of this chapter addresses the selling process associated with the need satisfaction and problem solution approaches discussed previously. These approaches focus on identifying customer prob-

FIGURE 10–1
The Selling Process

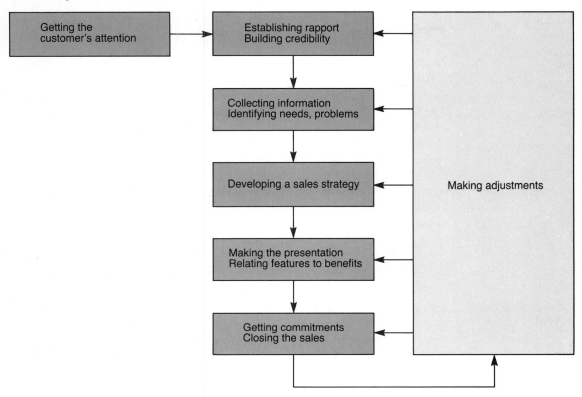

lems and needs and on making a sales presentation to show how the salesperson's product will solve these problems and satisfy these needs. Figure 10–1 provides a diagram of the sales process; a discussion of each step in the process follows.[6]

Getting the Customer's Attention

Time is very valuable to many prospects, and they tend to place a lot of emphasis on first impressions. They concentrate their attention on the first few minutes with a salesperson to determine whether they will benefit from the interaction. In addition to assessing the salesperson's appearance, the first few words the salesperson says set the tone of the entire sales call.

Some ways of opening a sales call are described below. The objective of each approach is to get the prospect's attention and interest quickly. A good approach should contain (1) a positive opening, (2) an indication

---

[6]See Barton Weitz, "Relationship between Salesperson Performance and Understanding of Customer Decision Process," *Journal of Marketing Research*, November 1978, pp. 501–16.

of a benefit to the customer, (3) a statement to get the customer's attention, and (4) some assurance the salesperson will not waste the customer's time. Because each prospect and sales situation are different, salespeople should be able to use a variety of openings.

Introduction Approach   In this approach, salespeople state their name and the name of their company, and they may hand the customer their business card. Handing the customer a business card has the advantage that the customer will know the salesperson's name. Customers may not hear the name because they are busy sizing up the salesperson. But some salespeople think a business card can be distracting and find it is more effective to give their card at the end of the interview.

The introduction approach is the simplest and perhaps least effective way of opening a sales call because it is unlikely to generate much interest. The following is an introduction approach extended to include the topic of the sales call:

> Mr. Smith, my name is John Jones, and I'm with Green Office Supplies. I would like to tell you about our company.

Referral Approach   Using the name of a satisfied customer or a friend is an effective way of beginning a sales call. When a friend's name is used, the prospect will feel obligated to pay attention. Often letters of introduction or testimonials are used in making this approach.

Salespeople should use only the names of individuals and companies they would like the prospect to contact, because prospects often *will* contact these references. Dropping names and stretching the truth concerning third parties are devices likely to backfire.

Some examples of referral approaches are:

> Mr. Smith, I'm here at the suggestion of Mr. McQueen of Philadelphia Products. He thought you would be interested in our new extended financing terms.
>
> Mr. Smith, many people in your business are using our office supply company. Here are some letters they have written about what our service has meant to them.

Question Approach   This approach often consists of stating an interesting fact in the form of a question. The advantage of such a device is it gets the customer's attention, motivates a response, and initiates a two-way communication. The following questions illustrate this approach:

> Mr. Smith, have you ever seen an office copier as small as this one? Do you think it would save a lot of space in your office?
>
> Mr. Smith, what is your reaction to the brochure I sent you on our new copier?
>
> Mr. Smith, if I can demonstrate how you could get a 25 percent savings on copying, would you be willing to invest $100 a month?

Benefit Approach   Perhaps the most widely used way of opening a sales call is the benefit approach, which focuses the customer's attention on a product benefit. To be effective, however, the benefit must be of real interest to the customer. In addition, it should be specific—something the customer can actually realize and something that can be substantiated during the presentation. Some examples of benefit approaches are:

> Mr. Smith, I would like to tell you about a copier that can reduce your copying costs by 15 percent.
>
> Acme has a new line of copiers. You might want to look at it because these copiers are designed for companies with your type of copying requirements. They will make copying documents easier and get the work done sooner.
>
> Your secretary can save an hour a day using this new self-correcting typewriter.

Product Approach   This approach involves actually demonstrating a product feature and benefit. Its advantage is that it appeals to the customer visually as well as verbally. Additional involvement can be realized by handing the product to customers for their examination. Some examples are:

> [*Carrying a 50-pound microcomputer into an office*.] Mr. Smith, you spend a lot of time and money on your accounts-receivable bookkeeping. Let me show you how efficient a computerized system is.
>
> [*Handing a photograph of a computer-controlled milling machine to a production manager*.] How would you like to have this machine in your shop?

Free-Gift or Sample Approach   Customers who are offered free gifts or samples usually feel obligated to listen to the sales presentation. This approach, which is used by door-to-door salespeople, can also be employed in industrial selling. Leaving equipment for a prospect to use on a trial basis is an example. Showing or giving the prospect the sample immediately captures his or her attention. In using this approach, customers may decide to accept the sample, but put it aside to examine it in private later. To minimize the chance of this reaction, the salesperson may wish to offer the sample at the beginning of the call but give it to the prospect at the end of the call. Some illustrations of this approach follow:

> *The clothing salesperson hands the buyer a scarf made out of a new synthetic material.*
>
> [*The retail salesperson sprays perfume on a customer's wrist.*] Doesn't this new perfume have a delightful fragrance?
>
> [*The salesperson places an appointment book on the customer's desk.*] Mr. Smith, I have an appointment book that I hope you will find useful.

Curiosity Approach   This approach arouses interest by making an unexpected comment that appeals to the customer's curiosity such as:

> Mr. Smith, how would you like to get your paper supplies free?
>
> Mr. Smith, would you believe that this new typewriter has a small computer in it, but it's smaller than the typewriters you have now?

Compliment Approach   Most people enjoy being praised or complimented, but there is a danger to this approach. Insincere flattery is often obvious and offensive to prospects. In using this approach, the compliment must be both sincere and specific. The sincerity of a compliment is directly related to its specificity. For example, the compliment, "Mr. Smith, congratulations on the cost savings you achieved through the recent reorganization" is far more effective than, "Mr. Smith, you are really a good businessman." Other examples of the compliment approach are:

> [*Points to trophy in office.*] I see you won the Greenwood Club championship. You must be an exceptional golfer.
>
> You must be proud of your son winning a scholarship to Stanford. He must be quite a student. Their business school is really tops.

I see from yesterday's business section that your company made record profits. Your innovative approaches to office systems have really been effective.

Survey Approach   Salespeople for business equipment manufacturers such as Xerox, IBM, and NCR often approach potential customers by asking for permission to survey the prospect's operations. The information collected in the survey is analyzed and then used as a basis for a program sales presentation discussed previously.

Developing Rapport and Building Credibility

The opening phase of a sales presentation begins when the salesperson walks into the customer's office. The salesperson's body language plays an important role in developing rapport and building credibility.[7]

Expressing Confidence while Standing   When salespeople are standing in front of their customers, they must not appear to be either insecure or overly aggressive. A confident appearance can be achieved by:

- Keeping feet about one foot apart to improve stability.
- Standing at a 45- to 90-degree angle to the customer. Standing straight across from the customer can be perceived as overly threatening.
- Keeping shoulders relaxed and arms off hips.
- Standing between two and four feet from the customer. Standing too close can be seen as threatening, while standing too far away gives an impersonal feeling.

Figure 10–2 illustrates a poor stance and a good stance.

Handshake   Some guidelines for a friendly handshake that improves the rapport are:

- Keep hand in a vertical position. Palms up communicates domination and palms down indicates submission.
- Apply moderate pressure. Avoid the aggressive impression created by a bone-crushing handshake and the insecure impression of a limp handshake.
- Move arm at a moderate pace.
- Pay attention to how the customer returns the handshake.

---

[7]Gerhard Gschwandtner and Pat Garnett, *Non-Verbal Selling Power* (Englewood Cliffs, N.J.: Prentice-Hall, 1985), pp. 105–21.

FIGURE 10–2
Good and Poor
Stances

Cameramann International, Ltd. photos

A good handshake
improves the
rapport.

D. E. Cox/Click, Chicago

Selecting a Seat   The best arrangement for seating is around a small table or at the side of the customer's desk. Salespeople need to be seated so they can observe all five channels of nonverbal communication (see Chapter 6) and show brochures and other visual aids from a comfortable position.

Initial Conversation   Sufficient time to establish a warm and friendly atmosphere should be allowed at the beginning of the sales process. A warm greeting, a friendly smile, and a sincere attitude help create the right climate for a successful presentation. Selling Scenario 10–1 shows how some environments can be distracting for a sales presentation.

Selling Scenario 10–1

PICKING THE PLACE TO MAKE THE SALES PRESENTATION

Lisa Cole, a hospital specialist for Abbott Laboratories, describes how some environments can be distracting for making a presentation.

Selling to the hospital industry is not always different for a woman than for a man. The traditional stereotypes of male doctors and female nurses have been rapidly dispersed in the past decade, and it's very common in urban hospitals to have relatively equal distribution.

On some occasions, however, I have found that being a woman called for a little reshuffling of the schedule. For example, a couple of months ago a doctor expressed an interest in seeing a product I carry. I made arrangements through the proper channels, per hospital policies, to show the product in the unit doctors' lounge the following Monday.

When I showed up with the product, the doctor was rather shocked to discover that I was a woman. I had scheduled the appointment at his request with his receptionist, and she must have referred to me as "the Abbott rep." He was genuinely embarrassed as he explained that the unit doctors' lounge was also the dressing room. I agreed that I knew the product backward and forward—but I had never presented it blindfolded on a Monday morning! After we all had a few laughs, we moved the display and presentation to the general doctors' lounge and it worked out great.

Source: Adapted from Lisa M. Cole, "What Do You Say to a Naked Doctor," *Sales & Marketing Management,* April 1, 1985, p. 40.

Some small talk about current news, hobbies, and the like usually breaks the ice for the actual presentation. Salespeople should use this time to establish links between their customers and themselves. Customers are more receptive to salespeople with whom they can identify—with whom they have something in common. Thus, salespeople will be more effective with customers when they establish such links as mutual friends, common hobbies, or attendance at the same schools.

In selling complex technical products, it is often important to demonstrate product expertise at the beginning of the sales process. The salesperson can accomplish this by telling the customer about his or her special training or education. Salespeople who have established their expertise will have more credibility when they make their presentations. In Selling Scenario 10–2, Cindy Fleming comments on her efforts to establish credibility with her customers.

Selling Scenario 10–2

ESTABLISHING CREDIBILITY

 Cindy Fleming travels to all the port cities of the United States to sell G. Heileman Brewing's beers to suppliers of foreign ships calling on U.S. ports. She is based at corporate headquarters in Milwaukee and was cofounder of the firm's International Division.

She is the only woman in a beer company in this country who travels to the ports. Moreover, her appearance always surprises prospects. Her low voice leads them to expect someone middle-aged; she's 30. Because she sells beer, people assume that she drinks a lot of it and is shaped accordingly. They don't expect someone who weighs 120 lbs. As a result, she says, "One or two of my customers tested me, to find out what I know. But I know my business as well as my competitors do. When people find out you can handle your business, they don't care if you're male or female."

When Fleming made her first call on one customer in a West Coast port, the former salesman for the territory accompanied her to introduce her. Even though the salesman made it clear that Fleming was taking over the account, the customer directed most of his questions to the outgoing salesman. Fleming acknowledges that the customer's Oriental heritage may have been a factor, and that he may simply have been more comfortable talking to a man. "I made delicate inroads and statements to establish my ground," Fleming says. "I had to explain that I was fully knowledgeable and that I travel to all the ports in the U.S., whereas the salesman had called on only this one port." Thus, her experience was much broader.

Source: Adapted from Rayna Skolnik, "A Woman's Place Is on the Salesforce," *Sales & Marketing Management,* April 1, 1985, p. 35.

Pacing   Donald Moine, a psychologist, has spent considerable time studying how top salespeople build rapport with customers by mirroring the thoughts, tone of voice, speech tempo, and mood of their customers.[8] He found that the best salespeople initially create a receptive mood by playing back the customer's observations, experiences, and behavior. The less successful salespeople either launched immediately into their presentations or confronted the customers with an array of questions.

By pacing their behavior, the successful salespeople are saying: "I am like you. We are in sync. You can trust me." The simplest form of pacing is stating accurate, but somewhat obvious, descriptions of the customer's experience such as, "It's been awfully cold this week, hasn't it?" or, "You say your son is going to Notre Dame in the fall?" By using these

---

[8]Donald J. Moine, "To Trust, Perchance to Buy," *Psychology Today,* August 1982, pp. 51–53.

statements, salespeople form an implicit agreement and bond with their customers.

Another form of pacing is agreeing with a customer's objection and then counteracting the objection. For example, an insurance salesperson may agree with a customer by saying, "Insurance is not the best investment out there," and then go on to say, "But it does have some important advantages over other investments."

The most effective form of pacing has more to do with the form of communication rather than the contact. Successful salespeople tended to match the voice tone, rhythm, volume, and speech rate of their customers. This form of pacing is similar to matching communication styles discussed in Chapter 7.

Collecting Information— Identifying Customer Needs and Problems

When a sales representative plans and delivers a presentation, it is easy to make the mistake of starting with product information rather than with a discussion of prospect's needs. Selling Scenario 10–3 illustrates the extent to which a salesperson went to collect information for a presentation.

The experienced salesperson, however, attempts to find out the prospect's needs and problems at the start of the interview. Attention is then focused on the specific features and benefits that will satisfy those needs.

No matter how strong the temptation is to start the presentation with product information, the salesperson should do so only if he or she is sure of what the prospect's problem or need is. A product-information lead without prior discussion of the problem or need puts the cart before the horse.

The following introduction to the sales process indicates the right and wrong ways to begin the sales interview.

Real estate prospect

Prospect: I would like to look at some medium-priced houses in this area.

Wrong method	*Right method*
Salesperson: That's fine. We have some very nice listings. Now, here's a very good buy that just came on the market. . . .	Won't you sit down, Mr. Prospect? We have some very fine listings, and I'm certain that we can show you something that will meet your needs. If you will tell me a little about the kind of house you have in mind, it will be helpful in selecting the right house for you. How many bedrooms will you need?

Selling Scenario 10–3

PRESENTATION TO SATISFY A NEED

 Lynn Mapes, vice president and associate publisher of *Reader's Digest*, describes a memorable sales presentation.

One day about five years ago, a friend of mine at an advertising agency called to tell me there were some big changes under way at a company we had both worked with for years.

"They're putting carpeting in the halls," he said.

You see, the headquarters of this company had always looked more like a grade school than a corporate front office, complete with linoleum floors and walls adorned with pictures of their numerous plants—in other words, pretty dull. So the fact that they were putting down carpeting was something on the order of radical change.

"What are they putting on the walls?" I asked.

"Pictures that don't look like factories," he said.

This was obviously something serious. I soon discovered that a new president had been named, and among his first official acts was the face-lift at company headquarters. Perfect. This was the kind of innovator I thought would go for a big idea. But before we went in to make our pitch, we did a little research.

I got hold of every story that had ever been written on this guy—from *Ad Age, The Wall Street Journal,* even from their own annual report. I also called his secretary to get a copy of every speech he ever made. From this, we put together a presentation that was basically a distillation of all of the concepts and ideas he had put forth in his articles and speeches. I used this as my opening and quickly worked my way toward the big idea. From the research, it developed that what he wanted was a magazine of his own where he could say just what he wanted to say in his own way. I told him we would do the whole package—writing, designing, setting the type, and even distribution. Because we'd bind it into the *Reader's Digest,* his "magazine" would instantly have a circulation equivalent to the biggest magazine in the world.

After we had finished our presentation, he leaned back in his chair. "You know," he said, "you seem to know more about what we're trying to achieve than anybody I've talked to." Which just goes to show you that if you come at people with ideas *they* formulated, they tend to think you're smart.

Source: Reprinted from "Strange Tales of Sales," *Sales & Marketing Management,* June 3, 1985, p. 45.

FIGURE 10–3
Illustration of
Probing for
Information

Salespersons's Probe	Customer's Response
Directive probe:	
1. What brand of pens do you use?	Surewright
2. Have your office people expressed some concerns about Surewright, such as leakage or skipping?	Not really, although you hear some grumbling.
Reflective probe:	
3. You occasionally hear people grumbling?	We have approximately 300 employees at our headquarters office, you know. Our inventory system is reasonably loose. Any employee can go into the stock room and take a handful of supplies . . .
Encouragement probe:	
4. I see.	. . . we haven't noticed any abuse of this privilege. Employees are taking one or two pens at a time. However, we have noticed that our pens seem to be running out of ink fast.
Elaboration probe:	
5. Can you tell me more about that?	Well, I guess I'm not really sure about the life of the Surewright pens.

Probing for information is a useful technique for identifying a customer's needs. Consider the following example. A sales representative for the Paper Mate Company is making an initial call on a purchasing agent for Quaker Foods.[9] Rather than begin the interview with a description of Paper Mate writing instruments, the representative uses the series of probes shown in Figure 10–3. The process of probing for information is discussed in more detail in Chapter 6.

Developing a Sales Strategy

There are many different features and benefits a salesperson can talk about during a sales presentation. Inexperienced salespeople often spend a lot of time telling customers everything they know about the products. These nondirective approaches are usually unsuccessful. Customers either lose

---

[9]This illustration and the information in Figure 10–3 come from *Personal Progress through Skill Development—Probing Your Prospect, Course 4*. The Paper Mate Selling Process, The Gillette Company, Paper Mate Division.

IBM salespeople
demonstrate how
the product's
features will benefit
the customer.

Cameramann International, Ltd.

interest in the sales presentation or are overloaded with information and
become confused.

Effective salespeople develop a sales strategy. Rather than overload
the customer, they focus the sales presentation on a few product features
and benefits. These specific benefits are selected by analyzing the information collected during the initial stages of a sales call.

The sales strategy must focus on benefits important to the customer—
product benefits that will satisfy his or her needs. It is a waste of time to
talk about benefits of little interest to the customer. For example, if a
physician specialized in geriatric medicine, the salesperson should talk
about how elderly people can benefit from the pharmaceutical. Even if
the pharmaceutical has tremendous benefits for younger patients, a discussion of these benefits will not mean much to the physician.

Making the Presentation— Relating Features to Benefits

The next step in the sales process is implementing the sales strategy. After
identifying the customer's needs and problems, the salesperson needs to
deliver a presentation so the thoughts of the prospect will flow naturally
from the prospect's problem to the salesperson's product. As salespeople
make presentations, they need to recognize that customers have a natural

FIGURE 10–4
Steps in a Sales Presentation

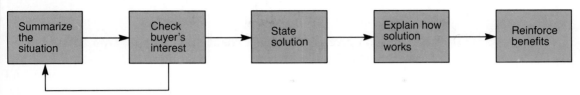

resistance to change. During the presentation, questions will arise in the buyer's mind such as, "Why should I change?" "What's wrong with what I am doing now?" The prospect's thinking must be guided to see the salesperson's product as the solution to a problem or need.

The skilled salesperson maintains a "you-and-your-problem" attitude throughout the sales story. He or she knows the product thoroughly and possesses good judgment in knowing the right amount of product information to give each prospect. The sales presentation has sufficient flexibility built into it to meet the varying problems and need of all prospects. The sales story is a reflection of honest concern for the customer's point of view.

Steps in Sales Presentation   Five steps in making an effective sales presentation are shown in Figure 10–4. The first step, summarizing the situation, lets the customer know you are aware of the conditions confronting the customer, the customer's needs, the limitations facing the customer, and the benefits sought by the customer. For example, a Procter & Gamble salesperson selling Duncan Hines cake mix might summarize the situation facing a grocery store buyer as follows:

> Mr. Dixon, you and I have been working to take advantage of the volume and profit opportunities for cake mixes at this time of year. We have discussed the need to reduce the out-of-stock situations in your store for cake mixes.
>
> Our representatives who call on your stores have just completed a 20-store audit of your cake mix section over the last four weeks. They found 8 of your stores were out of stock on several leading Duncan Hines mixes during every one of the four weeks—and the other 12 stores averaged an out-of-stock every other time we checked.

After summarizing the situation, it is important to check how the buyer sees the situation. The salesperson might say:

> This is how I see the situation. How do you see it?

This question gives the buyer a chance to (1) agree with the summary, (2) give more information about the situation, or (3) disagree with the summary. If the buyer disagrees, the salesperson can use questions and information to find out how the customer sees the situation. For example, Mr. Dixon might say:

> Yes, we have out-of-stock problems on cake mixes, but we just don't have the time to do anything about it.

The salesperson might use one of the following responses to probe for more information:

> Would you expand on that?
> or
> You're concerned about the time it would take.

Having agreed on the situation, the next step in the presentation is to state a solution to the customer's problem and explain how the solution works. For example, the salesperson might say:

> My idea is to suggest that you reallocate the facings in your cake mix department more closely to the sales of each item—without eliminating any sizes or colors. In doing this, you will reduce your out-of-stocks and increase your sales and profits.

Having stated the solution, the salesperson needs to indicate to the buyer he or she has worked out all the details related to implementing the solution. The salesperson should emphasize the solution is practical, answer questions and objectives, and make sure the buyer understands the solution. To continue with the cake mix example, the salesperson would say:

> Here's a chart showing the shelf space and sales for the items in your cake mix department. Notice that Duncan Hines cake mixes

deliver 40 percent of cake mix sales—but have been allocated only 20 percent of the shelf space. On the other hand, you can see that other brands have space out of proportion to their share of sales.

Now, here is a diagram showing the suggested reallocation of Duncan Hines cake mixes in your stores. We've given it 40 percent of the space since it produced 40 percent of the sales. You can easily reallocate the other items according to their sales without eliminating any brand, size, or flavor you are currently stocking.

Getting all the benefits of the revamped section will be easy if you send a copy of your revised diagram to each store manager along with a bulletin such as this one, which I put together to show you how it would work.

Your department heads will be able to rearrange the sections—and we'd be happy to give you help at the store level to get each section reset exactly the way you want it.

After explaining how the solution works, the salesperson reinforces the key benefits the solution provides:

Your revised cake mix sections will look better . . . they'll be easier to restock . . . you will reduce out-of-stocks because the items are displayed more closely to their rate of sale and you will get more sales and profits from the cake mix department. And that's exactly what you said was your objective this quarter.

Selling Benefits Every experienced salesperson has heard the statement, "People buy benefits, not features." However, many salespeople discuss features instead of benefits in their presentations. A benefit is a specific gain the customer achieves from buying a product. In every buying situation, customers are unconsciously asking themselves, "What am I going to get out of this?" Salespeople answer this question by indicating benefits that are personally meaningful to a customer.

Every product has certain key points that make it stand out in comparison to competing products. These points should be highlighted in the presentation and explained in terms of potential benefits to the customer. Customers will buy the products they believe will provide the greatest benefits. They are interested in hearing about product features only to the extent that such features can help solve their problems or satisfy their needs.

Salespeople indicate benefits that are personally meaningful to a customer.

"Just take a look at this onboard computer. It can figure square roots, percentages and the interest rate of your monthly installment."

From *The Wall Street Journal,* with permission of Cartoon Features Syndicate.

The example below illustrates the right and wrong way of stressing key product features.

Selling home insulation
Wrong method

Salesperson: Insul-Wool is outselling all other insulation materials by two to one. It is treated with a new chemical that makes it absolutely fireproof. Our surveys have shown that as much as 40 percent of the heat in non-insulated homes is actually lost through the ceiling. Insul-Wool will stop 95 percent of this loss.

Right method

Mrs. Nelson, I'm sure you will enjoy Insul-Wool in your new home. With children in the home I realize how important it is for you to have it warm throughout each room, especially near the floors. Insul-Wool will provide you with a more even temperature throughout because it stops the loss of the heat that normally escapes through the ceiling. You'll also find, Mrs. Nelson, that your ceilings will stay cleaner much longer if you install Insul-Wool. If your ceilings are not insulated, the air and heat goes through the plaster and before long you will notice lines appearing under each ceiling joist. Our fireproof Insul-Wool will prevent this and thus will indirectly provide you with real savings in reduced painting costs.

FIGURE 10–5
Benefits and
Features for a Brand
of Chinaware

Benefits	**Features**
1. Lasts longer and is therefore less expensive.	1. Hard leadless glaze. Patterns are under the glaze. Body fired at 2600° F. Cup handles are molded into cup body before firing.
2. Stronger.	2. Body fired at 2600° F. Cup handles are molded into cup body before firing.
3. Longer lasting beauty.	3. Translucent. Hard leadless glaze. Patterns are under the glaze.
4. Pride of ownership.	4. Translucent. Patterns are under the glaze. Hard leadless glaze.

A feature is a quality or characteristic of a product. Product features provide benefits to customers. An effective presentation must include both features and benefits. A presentation that includes only features does not answer the question, "What's in it for me?" A presentation that has only benefits does not help the customer understand "how" the benefits will be realized. Features are included in a presentation to assure the customer that the product will provide the benefits. Examples of benefits and features are shown in Figure 10–5.

Getting Commitments—Closing the Sale

The decision to buy should be a gradual one. Most people tend to postpone making decisions, particularly decisions of major importance. It is wise, therefore, for the salesperson to encourage the customer to make many minor decisions throughout the sales interview. This procedure eliminates the need to pile up evidence and obtain a definite yes or no answer at the close of the sales interview. Color or model choices can usually be made early in the sales process. If the salesperson observes the prospect closely, he or she is able to determine the points on which the customer is in agreement. Instead of withholding the order blank and pen until the final stage of the sales interview, most sales representatives prefer to write minor decisions on the order blank as they are made. The final decision thus becomes a natural conclusion to a series of small decisions or agreements.

If the customer is given a chance to make a series of small decisions throughout the sales interview and if a choice is given when each of these decisions is made, closing the sale is greatly simplified. Closing the sale is discussed in more detail in Chapter 13. Figure 10–6 shows an example of using questions to get a sequence of commitments.

Making Adjustments

Perhaps the most crucial activity during a sales presentation is making adjustments. While making a presentation, salespeople need to continually assess the reactions of their customers. By listening to what the customers

FIGURE 10–6
The Use of
Questions to Build
Acceptance

Salesperson: Ms. Campbell, do you prefer all-wool or wool-polyester suits?

Ms. Campbell: I like wool-polyester suits. They seem to hold their shape and not wrinkle as much as all-wool suits. I am looking for a suit for work, and I think wool-polyester holds up better during the day.

Salesperson: I think you're right about the wool-polyesters. The suits you are looking at are really nice. That navy suit has a real classic look, doesn't it?

Ms. Campbell: Yes, it really is nice.

Salesperson: You did say you wanted a suit with a classic look?

Ms. Campbell: Yes, I think that's best for business attire.

Salesperson: And you said that you wear a size 10?

Ms. Campbell: Well, it depends on the cut of the suit. But I think a 10 is probably the right size.

Salesperson: Here are two navy suits with a classic cut in size 10. Which one do you like better?

Ms. Campbell: I think the one on the right is nicer.

Salesperson: I like that one also. Don't you like the stitching around the collar?

Ms. Campbell: That's what attracted me to the suit.

Salesperson: Why don't you just try it on? It will just take a second. The dressing room is right there.

say and by observing their body language, salespeople can determine whether the customers are interested in the product. If customers react favorably to the presentation, there is no need to make alterations or adjustments. But if the customers do not develop enthusiasm for the product, salespeople need to make some changes in their presentation.

To obtain a favorable reaction, salespeople can alter their presentations in many ways. During the sales presentation, the salesperson may discover the customer simply does not believe the salesperson has the appropriate product knowledge. Rather than continue with the presentation, the salesperson should redirect his or her efforts toward establishing credibility in the eyes of the customer.

Other adjustments might require collecting additional information about the customer, developing a new sales strategy, or altering the style of the presentation. For example, a salesperson may believe a customer is interested in buying an economical, low-cost motor. While presenting the benefits of the lowest-cost motor, the salesperson discovers the customer is interested in the motor's operating costs. At this point, the salesperson should ask some questions to find out if the customer would be interested in paying a high price for a more efficient motor with lower operating costs. On the basis of the customer's response, the salesperson can adopt

Table 10–1   Nonverbal Signals for Evaluating Customer Reactions

Channel	Go Ahead: Green	Caution: Yellow	Stop: Red
Body angle	Upright, direct to salesperson	Leaning away from salesperson	Leaning far back or thrusting toward salesperson
Face	Friendly, smiling, enthusiastic	Tense, displeased, superior	Angry, determined, shaking head
Arms	Relaxed, open	Closed, tense	Tightly crossed or thrusting out
Hands	Relaxed, open	Clasped, fidgeting with objects	Fist, pointed finger
Legs	Uncrossed, crossed toward salesperson	Crossed away from salesperson	Tightly crossed away from salesperson

a new sales strategy that emphasizes operating efficiency rather than the motor's initial price. In this way, the sales presentation is shifted from features and benefits related to a low initial cost to features and benefits related to low operating costs.

An important aspect of making adjustments is interpreting customer reactions to the sales presentation. By observing the customer's five channels of nonverbal communication, salespeople can determine how to proceed with their presentations. Table 10–1 shows how salespeople who are sensitive to their customer's body language can read nonverbal cues like traffic signals.[10]

When salespeople observe these signals, they have four alternatives for making adjustments: (1) ignore the signals and continue the presentation, (2) imitate the customer's nonverbal signals, (3) synchronize their body language to the customer's, or (4) begin to send different signals to the customer. If the customer is giving "Go" signals, the salesperson should attempt to synchronize with the customer. When the salesperson also gives Go signals, he or she is providing positive feedback to the customer and displaying confidence.

The salesperson should also indicate Go signals when the customer is expressing "Caution." It is critical that salespeople avoid mirroring the Caution signals of the customer. In addition to Go body language, salespeople should use open-ended questions to draw out the customer's reasons for caution.

When a customer gives "Stop" signals, the chances of making a sale are diminished. To salvage the sales call, salespeople need to refocus the

---

[10]Gerhard Gschwandtner and Pat Garnett, *Non-verbal Selling Power* (Englewood Cliffs, N.J.: Prentice-Hall, 1985), pp. 57–64.

FIGURE 10–7
Do these people project green, red, or yellow signals?

Cameramann International, Ltd. photos

discussion and use open, relaxed gestures. The best way to avoid receiving Stop signals is to deal effectively with Caution signals when they appear. Some examples of body language are shown in Figure 10–7.

SUMMARY

Salespeople employ a wide variety of selling approaches. The stimulus-response and mental states approaches emphasize delivery of a pre-planned presentation with few adjustments made during the presentation. Such approaches tend to work best when inexperienced salespeople are selling simple products. The need satisfaction and problem solution approaches are sophisticated ways of practicing the marketing concept. When using these approaches, salespeople try to identify customer needs and problems and to show how these problems can be solved by the salesperson's product. Such approaches emphasize the benefits of salespeople adapting their presentation to the specific selling solution.

Standard memorized and outlined presentations are used in the stimulus-response and mental states selling approaches. Because these types of presentations force salespeople to plan their presentations, they restrict their flexibility to adapt their presentations. Program presentations are often used effectively in the need satisfaction and problem solution approaches.

When making a sales presentation, salespeople go through the following six steps: (1) establishing rapport with the customer, (2) collecting information about the customer, (3) developing a sales strategy, (4) delivering the presentation, (5) getting commitments, and (6) making adjustments. Perhaps the most important step is making adjustments on the basis of the customer's reaction to the presentation. To make adjustments effectively, salespeople need to develop skills at asking questions, listening actively to customers, and detecting nonverbal signals.

QUESTIONS
AND
PROBLEMS

1. Assume you are a sales representative for one of the major airlines. Your job is to call on business firms in Chicago to sell them on the advantages of shipping their goods by airfreight. In outline form, list the main sales points around which you would build your sales presentation.

2. Ms. Swanson is a sales representative for a leather-goods manufacturer. She makes regular calls on wholesalers and large retailers and carries a fairly complete line of leather products, including luggage, billfolds, briefcases, handbags, and belts. Ms. Swanson has been very conscientious about preparing an effective sales presentation for each of her products. She has found from experience, however, that after she uses the same sales presentation for a certain length of time, she loses enthusiasm and her sales decline. What, if anything, can Ms. Swanson do to overcome this difficulty?

3. Companies often use a two-person selling team to present their products to prospective buyers. In which situations could two-person teams be used effectively? What are the advantages and disadvantages of this type of sales presentation?

4. Assume you are a sales representative for a paper supply house. You sell a number of paper products to retailers and other business concerns. One line of products includes paper napkins and paper drinking cups sold to restaurants and soda fountains. Outline the main sales points you would use in selling paper cups to the owner of a large soda fountain (assuming paper cups are not now used). What sales points would you emphasize in your presentation? How would you start your sales presentation? What would you say to stimulate wants? Would your emphasis be different if you were calling on the owner of a small retail fountain?

5. Evaluate the following approach for getting an appointment: Mr. White, I'm going to be working this work area next week. When can I come by to tell you about our new products?

6. In a selling situation between the salesperson and the prospect, much of what is said is really never heard, and part of what is heard is often misinterpreted by one or both of the parties. What techniques might a salesperson use to improve communication with the prospect?

7. Prepare a list of features and benefits that could be used in a presentation to high school students. The objective of the presentation is to encourage the students to enroll in your college.

8. In selling the following products, what would be a good stimulus statement? What would be the expected response?

      a. A retirement investment program.

      b. A $75,000 vacation home in Florida.

      c. A $25,000 foreign sports car.

9. "The first few minutes in a sales interview may be important to some salespeople, but my selling is different. I only call on a few people whom I know well or have met before." Comment.

10. Assume you are a sales representative for a Volkswagen dealer. You have been asked to contribute ideas and sales product information that could be used in preparing a national magazine ad for a Volkswagen panel truck. What theme and what key points would you suggest?

PROJECTS

1. Outline a presentation to "sell" yourself to a company that has an opening for a salesperson.

2. Observe the selling technique used by a salesperson in a department store. Write a report describing and evaluating the technique.

CASE PROBLEMS

Case 10–1   Food for Less, Inc.

Eleanor Ringel, president of Food for Less, started in the food service business while she was a college student. She was house manager of her sorority, and in this capacity she became aware of the problems fraternities, sororities, and clubs have in providing good food to students at a reasonable cost. Ms. Ringel talked with other house managers about their food service problems and concluded there was an opportunity to provide better food at a lower cost by having one organization serve several eating units. To accomplish this objective, five sororities formed a cooperative organization that purchased their food products.

    The cooperative organization elected Ms. Ringel as its manager and gave her full authority to make its food purchases. Ms. Ringel was very successful, and in this capacity learned a lot about the food service business.

    After graduation, Ms. Ringel decided to go into the food service business on a full-time basis. In 1978, she established Food for Less, which started by providing limited coffee and sandwich service to a number of industrial plants and offices in Denver. Within five years the company had expanded its service to include a complete food service for schools, colleges, hospitals, office buildings, and factories. The company bought food centrally and operated its own commissary and bake shop. In most instances Food for Less employees used the supplies and equipment of the client and prepared, served, and sold the food. Meat was supplied by Food for Less in company-owned trucks. Dairy products were delivered to clients from the closest dairy.

Food for Less operated under different kinds of contracts with its clients. Some contracts were called *limited profit and limited loss contracts,* others were subsidy contracts whereby the company received a guaranteed profit. Contracts ranged in size from a few thousand dollars to over $700,000 yearly. Ms. Ringel utilized effective cost-control methods and was able to provide food service at a cost substantially below what the clients could obtain for themselves.

By 1986 the company had approximately 700 employees in all of its operations. Food service was supplied to many large factories and institutions. Food for Less employed two sales representatives who called on prospective clients to sell the food service. The company also had two food service consultants who worked with the sales representatives and the operating personnel on technical dietary and food problems.

The normal procedure was for the sales representative to call on prospective customers. However, with large accounts, Ms. Ringel and a food service consultant frequently accompanied the sales representative. In some instances a sales representative would work on a single prospect for over a year before a contract was signed.

One day, during a call on a customer, Dave Corbett, one of the sales representatives, was told the American Insurance Company was considering the possibility of having an outside food service company take over its cafeteria food service.

The American Insurance Company had approximately 1,500 employees in its building and a modern cafeteria with the latest equipment. Although the company had operated its cafeteria for the past two years, it was never completely satisfied with the results. The company subsidized the cafeteria, but the employees were still dissatisfied with the food and service.

Questions

1. Assuming you are Dave Corbett, what steps would you follow in attempting to obtain the American Insurance Company account?

2. To what extent should the sales presentation to the American Insurance Company be a team effort? Who should be on the team? If Ms. Ringel participates in the sales presentation, what part should she play?

3. Write a sales presentation to be used in your meeting with the American Insurance Company executives.

Case 10–2   Ray Powers

Ray Powers is a life insurance agent. He used the following approach when calling on Jim Klein, a prospect:

Mr. Powers: Mr. Klein, I'm Ray Powers with Rocky Mountain Life Insurance. Congratulations on your recent marriage. Mr. Samuel Johnson [*Mr. Klein's father-in-law*] said you might

be interested in our financial planning service.

Mr. Klein: I'm glad you called on me, Mr. Powers. My wife and I are just moving into a new house in Paradise Valley. I don't think we can afford any insurance now.

Mr. Powers: I know how tight it can be when you just get married. I've only been married for two years. I just wanted to stop by and meet you and Mrs. Klein. Maybe I can answer some questions you might have about life insurance. Then when you are ready to buy, you will think of me and Rocky Mountain.

Mr. Klein: Well, as long as you understand we are not in the market, I'll get my wife. Nancy, this is Ray Powers with Rocky Mountain Life Insurance. He knows your father.

Mr. Powers: Hello, Mrs. Klein. Your father is one of our policyholders. Everytime I see him, he talks about you and your husband. One of the things you really need is financial security in the future. I just want to take a few minutes to explain how we can provide that security.

Mrs. Klein: Well, if you're a friend of my father's, I guess we can spend a couple of minutes. But we really need furniture for the house now.

Mr. Powers: I understand. [*Addresses himself to Mr. Klein.*] Do you have any life insurance now?

Mr. Klein: No. Why do we need it? We both have good jobs.

Mr. Powers: Yes, but what about children? You need some protection for them if something should happen to you.

Mrs. Klein: We don't plan to have children.

Questions

1. What type of approach did Mr. Powers use?
2. Evaluate the approach. How could it have been improved?

Case 10–3   AstroTravel—A Role-Playing Exercise

AstroTravel, Inc., based in Boston, Massachusetts, organizes and conducts tours, concentrating on Caribbean and Mediterranean cruises and other high-priced, sunny-climate vacations. AstroTravel also offers special-interest tours, including archaeological trips to Central America and Asia Minor. This summer AstroTravel hopes to capture some of the student travel market.

One of the tours AstroTravel has put together for students is a six-week bicycle tour of England. Living and dining accommodations are all prearranged. Hotels are comfortable but not plush. Ten-speed racing bicycles will be provided locally, and riding will average 25 miles per day, with stops at historic sites, museums, castles, cathedrals, and so on. Each group will

consist of 35 to 40 group members as well as 2 guides who are both experienced as bikers and able to explain local history, geography, and culture. Baggage will be transported by bus, and some lengthier parts of the journey will be done by bus. The itinerary includes London, Windsor Castle, Canterbury Cathedral, Cambridge, Bath, the Lake District, York, and the Moors.

Instructions—AstroTravel Sales Representative

Design and deliver a 10-minute sales presentation. Your objective is to arouse student interest in the tour and to induce students to sign a prospect list of those who might like to take the tour.

Instructions—Students

After the presentation, ask questions you have about the tour program and, if you're interested, sign the list. After the role playing is finished, analyze the dynamics of the roleplaying situation with the help of the following.

Questions

1. How did the seller find out the customer's needs?

2. What benefits were introduced? How?

3. How did these benefits answer the customer's needs?

4. Did the customer express skepticism about the benefits offered? If so, how did the salesperson handle this skepticism? Did (s)he offer proof?

5. Did the customer express indifference? If so, how did the salesperson handle it? Did the salesperson elaborate on the benefits?

6. Did the customer express objections or resistance to the product? How did the salesperson handle this situation? How did (s)he minimize perceived drawbacks?

7. How did the salesperson review the accepted benefits and ask for a purchase commitment?

SELECTED REFERENCES

Caballero, Marjorie J.; Roger A. Dickinson, and Dabney Townsend. "Aristotle and Personal Selling." *Journal of Personal Selling and Sales Management,* May 1984, pp. 12–18.

Dubinsky, Alan. "A Factor Analytic Study of the Personal Selling Process." *Journal of Personal Selling and Sales Management,* Fall–Winter 1981, pp. 26–33.

George, William R.; Patrick Kelly; and Claudia Marshall. "The Selling of Services: A Comprehensive Model." *Journal of Personal Selling and Sales Management,* August 1986, pp. 29–38.

Hanan, Mack. "If Your Own Sales Objectives Aren't Working, Try Using the Customer's." *Sales & Marketing Management,* November 12, 1979, pp. 82–85.

Schurr, Paul H., and Julee L. Ozanne. "Influences on Exchange Processes: Buyers' Preconceptions of a Seller's Trustworthiness and Bargaining Toughness." *Journal of Consumer Research,* March 1985, pp. 939–53.

Sokol, G. "The Impact of Consultative Selling." *Training and Development Journal,* November 1979, pp. 34–37.

Spiro, R. L., and W. D. Perreault. "Influence Use by Industrial Salesmen: Influence-Strategy Mixes and Situational Determinants." *Journal of Business,* July 1979, pp. 435–55.

Stevens, C. G. "Anatomy of an Industrial Sales Presentation." *Sales Management,* October 1, 1973, pp. 61–62.

Swan, John E., and Johannah Jones Nolan. "Gaining Customer Trust: A Conceptual Guide for the Salesperson." *Journal of Personal Selling and Sales Management,* November 1985, pp. 39–48.

Warren, M. W. "Using Behavioral Technology to Improve Sales Performance." *Training and Development Journal,* July 1978, pp. 54–56.

Watson, Craig M. "Balancing Dominance: Diagnosing the Buyer-Seller Relationship." *Business Horizons,* September–October 1984, pp. 62–65.

11 Dramatizing the Sales Presentation

Some questions answered in this chapter are:

- Why should salespeople play a role and learn to use multiple-sense appeals?
- Why should the power of effective dramatization be recognized?
- What choices or options are available when choosing visual aids and techniques for dramatization?
- What ways and means are available for the effective use of selling aids?
- What are the secrets of a good product demonstration?

Seven Steps in the Sales Process

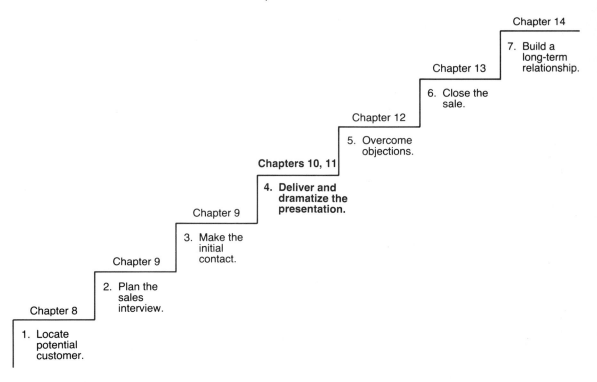

Chapter 14

7. Build a
long-term
relationship.

Chapter 13

6. Close the
sale.

Chapter 12

5. Overcome
objections.

Chapters 10, 11

**4. Deliver and
dramatize the
presentation.**

Chapter 9

3. Make the
initial
contact.

Chapter 9

2. Plan the
sales
interview.

Chapter 8

1. Locate
potential
customer.

THE DRAMA OF SELLING

A well-planned sales presentation provides the necessary organization of the salesperson's materials; in addition, it requires him or her to select the product or service sales features and benefits that are appropriate in a particular sales situation. To ensure maximum effectiveness, the salesperson must plan how best to communicate the sales message.

Next, the salesperson must go over the materials in order to breathe life and vigor into the communication process. Sufficient impact must be created to cause the prospect to *understand* the message, *believe* the message, and *remember* the message. The message must be exciting and convincing enough to motivate the prospect to a favorable action. Webster's dictionary defines *dramatic* as ''full of action, highly emotional; vivid, exciting, powerful—approached from the viewpoint of drama.'' The series of activities designed to facilitate action by the buyer is called *dramatization.*

Each salesperson is expected to inject his or her personality into the sales presentation. No two people are likely to use exactly the same techniques and procedures to put their messages across. Salespeople should ask themselves the following questions: ''How can I use my imagination and resourcefulness to make a vivid impression on my prospect or customer? How can I use my abilities to make my presentation a little different and a little stronger?'' Salespeople with this frame of mind are never completely satisfied with their efforts. They are always trying to do a better and more effective job of selling.[1]

Good Salespeople Are Good Actors and Actresses

Many sales managers have compared good salespeople to good actors. Both salespeople and actors are skillful showpeople; both have parts to play; both live their parts; both dress for their parts; both are sincere and dedicated to their professions; and both attempt to influence an audience. Actors usually have props to help portray their parts more effectively; they practice and rehearse lines tirelessly until they believe they have mastered every action, every tone or inflection of the voice; they strive for perfection. Successful salespeople likewise use props; they attempt to master their parts; they dress appropriately; and they strive to do a better job each time they deliver a sales presentation. Both salespeople and actors are constantly striving to add a personal touch to their parts that will make them different and more successful in their chosen fields of endeavor.

Good Salespeople Use Multiple-Sense Appeals

Five avenues may be used to dramatize sales presentations—the senses of hearing, sight, touch, taste, and smell, which are the *five* channels to the buyer's springs of action. Appeals should be made to as many of these senses as possible.

Studies show multiple-sense appeals increase both learning and retention. It is important for sales representatives to recognize:

We Learn through	We Retain
Taste—1 percent	What we hear—20 percent
Touch—2 percent	What we see *and* hear—50 percent
Smell—4 percent	
Hearing—11 percent	
Sight—82 percent	

Some products can be sold through the use of appeals to all five senses. Others can appeal to a maximum of two or three. When selling candy to a retail merchant, the salesperson may describe its merits—this is an appeal to the sense of *hearing;* or show the candy and invite the merchant to taste it—this appeals to *sight, touch,* and *taste;* if certain candies are aromatic, there is the opportunity to appeal to the merchant's fifth sense—

---

[1]Sherle Adams, ''Liven Up That Presentation!'' *Sales & Marketing Management*, August 16, 1982, pp. 40–42.

smell. On the other hand, salespeople who sell machinery are limited to appeals that affect the buyers' senses of hearing, sight, and touch.

Salespeople should emphasize the sensory system most compatible with the method their customer uses in processing information. Some customers use primarily the visual mode to process information, while others use the auditory mode. By listening to the way customers speak, a salesperson can determine the customer's preferred sensory mode. For example, a customer who comments, "I *see* what you are saying and I can *picture* the product's benefit," is visually oriented. On the other hand, an auditory-oriented customer might say, "I *hear* what you are saying and it *sounds* good to me."[2]

Unless the prospect's interest is secured and maintained, the salesperson has little opportunity to build to a successful close. Few buyers stay mentally awake long enough to be convinced unless multiple-sense appeals are used.

Dramatizing Convinces the Prospect

Buyers who are convinced the product satisfies their needs and who are really prospects, usually buy. Dramatization is convincing when answering objections and closing sales. Few products cannot be dramatized in some way.

Pencil and pad are used to draw diagrams, graphs, and rough sketches, and to figure in order to "prove" a point. When roller bearings were introduced, sales representatives carried sample bearings and a small wooden ruler. The buyer was invited to apply weight to the ruler and push it along the top of the desk. Then bearings were put under the ruler, and the prospect was asked to repeat the experiment. The almost total elimination of friction was evident. This demonstration convinced many prospects that reducing friction in machinery bearings would save power and reduce equipment depreciation.

Computers, along with a great variety of electronic products, have made dramatization possibilities almost endless. An industrial sales representative can create an unforgettable impression when the object is to dramatize the high melting point of an industrial grease by the proof-of-performance technique. Ordinary grease and the company's grease can each be heated in a portable container to show the different melting points. Other product features such as water resistance, rust protection, and noncorrosiveness can also be dramatized.

Colored slides to portray interesting installations of plastic signs have been particularly successful in convincing prospects. Slides are easy to carry, flexible, and inexpensive. Some companies reproduce slides from

---

[2]William G. Nickels, Robert F. Everett, and Ronald Klein, "Rapport Building for Salespeople: A Neuro-Linguistic Approach," *Journal of Personal Selling and Sales Management,* November 1983, pp. 1–7.

A proof-of-performance demonstration is a convincing sales technique. Here the inventor of an air bag leaps from a 115-foot-tall office building to demonstrate (successfully) the use of the air bag in fire rescues from high-rise buildings.

Wide World Photos

original shots taken by the salespeople themselves, since it is always more interesting for salespeople to show installations in their own territory.

The salesperson who wishes to convince the prospect or customer may prove claims by dramatizing what the product will do. If the product won't burn, the salesperson can light a match and try to burn it. If the product won't chip, it's a good idea to bend or twist a sample piece to show that it won't crack or peel. If the product is unbreakable, the representative can drop it or hit it with a hammer to prove the claim. Some type of proof-of-performance demonstration is the most convincing sales technique available to a sales representative because the demonstration has an impact on several senses at the same time.

Dramatizing
Improves
Understanding

Many visual-minded buyers actually lack the power to form clear images from the written or spoken word. For these people the most effective sales approach is a dramatization based largely on visual appeals.

Many product benefits cannot be explained adequately in nontechnical language. In such cases, a verbal explanation may be understood only by buyers with a technical background. But a simple demonstration may *show* other buyers exactly what benefits they can expect.

Insurance companies use a graph to show the prospect's needs and how those needs are to be met. The prospect gets a complete, graphic picture of the insurance program on one page. This picture may include provisions for a cleanup fund, an emergency fund, children's education, special funds, monthly income for the family, and guaranteed retirement income.

Sales representatives for a lithography firm added a new selling tool to enable customers and prospects to visualize more clearly an advertising folder that can be developed with the sales representatives' assistance. This tool is a do-it-yourself kit that enables hotel, motel, and resort operators to produce a colorful brochure. Sample layouts are submitted to the operator, who selects the photographs and prepares copy describing the features and services to be emphasized. Sales representatives carry a library of color shots the operator can use if desired. Once the customer has completed the work-sheet copy of the brochure, the sales representative takes it to the shop for printing. The customer has a complete picture of the brochure before it is printed.''

An old Chinese proverb says, ''Tell me—I'll forget. Show me—I may remember. But *involve* me, and I'll *understand*.''

Dramatizing
Makes a
Lasting
Impression

A product feature that is dramatized vividly creates a strong impression. The customer may almost experience the product's benefits, will remember the claims longer, and is more likely to tell friends about it.

Lasting impressions may be created in many ways. One salesperson steps on the rubber plug at the end of a light cord; another kicks the glass in the door of a microwave oven; still another invites prospects to choose a name or a number from a high stack of cards, and then has the electric sorting machine throw out the card wanted. A salesperson may demonstrate by using the pressure of a feather to activate the keys of a word processor or may invite customers to roll pieces of carbon paper in their hands to prove the carbon won't come off. Whatever method is used, whether it be melting metal without burning insulation materials or immersing paraffin-treated boxes of raisins in water, the prospect is more likely to remember the sales feature if the dramatization is skillfully presented and well timed.

Selling Scenario 11–1

DEMONSTRATING DEMAND

 Bill Blake, former vice president of sales planning and development at Sweetheart Cup, describes how he dramatized a point to get a buyer's attention:

I was selling paper napkins to supermarkets for Hudson Pulp and Paper. This was back in 1951, and in those days, four big chains—A&P, Jewel, Kroger, and National Tea— controlled roughly 80 percent of the market. If you didn't get into these chains, you were out of business. Back then, paper napkins were not taken very seriously. They were thought of as a summer picnic item, and not for the winter months.

For two years, I had called on the buyer at Jewel in Chicago every week. But every time I went to see him, he'd have something different to say about why he wouldn't buy from me. He had a terrific mental block against napkins.

One day, I got an idea. We ran manufacturer's coupons on every box of napkins we sold. People had to bring them to the store to redeem them for a free box, and the coupons eventually came back to us. So I got hold of all the coupons, put them into big bags, and dumped hundreds of them on his desk one day in the middle of winter. Needless to say, he was convinced.

Selling those napkins had to be the biggest sale of my life, because, after selling to Jewel, we went from nothing to 50 percent of the market in Chicago.

Source: Reprinted from ''Strange Tales of Sales,'' *Sales & Marketing Management*, June 3, 1985, p. 43.

Dramatizing Helps the Sales Representative

One manufacturer of menswear accessories believes its salespeople benefit from the company's plan of dramatizing through store demonstrations because this forces the salesperson to deliver an orderly sales talk, familiarizes both the salesperson and the retailer with a completely blueprinted merchandising program, and provides an opportunity to kindle enthusiasm in the people who sell to the consumer.

Salespeople find that a good dramatic presentation also builds confidence in their abilities and products. Successful dramatization requires them to plan and rehearse. They cannot plan and rehearse over a period of time without developing more confidence in themselves and their products.

Dramatization saves time for the seller and the buyer. The sales presentation is reduced to the important points necessary to close the sale. Pictures, actions, and words tell the story more rapidly than do words alone. Time is money to the salesperson. Every sales aid that conserves time is worthwhile. In Selling Scenario 11–1, Bill Blake describes how he dramatized a point to make a memorable sale.

Pharmaceutical sales representatives who call on doctors have found they must tell their story in about five minutes. To persuade the doctors to think about the product and not about their patients for a few minutes, they rely heavily on visual aids, or sales tools, which keep the doctor's mind and eye on the story.

Dramatizing Creates Value

Value is suggested by the manner in which a product is handled. Careful handling gives the impression of value even if no words are spoken. Careless handling implies the product is of little value. A rare painting, an expensive piece of jewelry, or a delicate piece of chinaware "speaks" for itself if the salesperson uses appropriate props, words, and care in handling it.

VISUAL AIDS AND TECHNIQUES FOR DRAMATIZING THE PRESENTATION

In many fields of selling, the company that manufactures or distributes the product supplies effective aids. Xerox, for example, is convinced that using visual aids as a support tool has many advantages. Among the benefits recognized by Xerox are: Visual Aids gain attention, personalize, simplify, clarify, reduce misunderstandings, add importance and emphasis, heighten interest, reinforce verbal stimulus, and professionalize the salesperson's and the company's images.[3]

The following pages show and describe some of the more common visual aids.

Charts and Graphs

These aids are particularly helpful to illustrate relationships and trends. Charts may show advertising schedules, some special details of product manufacture, or typical profit margins. Bars, circles, or squares are frequently used to depict relationships.

The slide chart, as the name indicates, is a chart with movable parts (see Figure 11–1).[4] Usually the parts of the chart can be moved to obtain a quick answer to some problem or to point out some pertinent fact. Slide charts have been developed to describe the best method of removing stains from clothing; to help poultry farmers estimate the cost of eggs; to show how much tile is needed for various areas; to determine the right pump for gallons, pressure, and depth of well; to calculate social security benefits; to compare a company's product with those of leading competitors; to determine the profit on the selling price or cost; to show the conversion of measurements to the metric system; and for many other purposes.

---

[3]Xerox sales training program.

[4]The Perrygraf Division of Nashua Corp. (Los Angeles, California) produces great varieties of slide charts and illustrates them in a 36-page booklet along with 16 short case histories.

FIGURE 11–1
Slide Chart Showing
Engineering
Specifications

Courtesy Perrygraf

Realizing it may cost as much as $7 to type a letter, Dictaphone sales representatives use a pocket-size card to indicate the dollar value of the executive's time when selling their Thought Tank machine (see Figure 11–2).

Photographs, Pictures, and Advertisements

These aids may be supplied individually or incorporated into bulletins or portfolios. They permit a realistic portrayal of the product or service and its benefits.

Photographs are easy to prepare and relatively inexpensive, and photographs of people may be particularly effective. Many companies use photos to illustrate benefits. For example, leisure made possible through savings can be dramatized through photographs of retired people on a ranch, at mountain resorts, or on the seashore. Pictures that are drawn, painted, or prepared in other ways are useful in dramatizing needs or benefits. Real estate brokers rely heavily on photos of properties to help qualify prospects and thereby conserve time and reduce inspection tour expenses.

FIGURE 11–2
Card Used to Show
Value of an
Executive's Time

If You Earn	Every Hour Is Worth	In A Year One Hour A Day Is Worth	Save An Hour A Day Leasing Thought Tank™ For Annual Savings Of	Save An Hour A Day And Pay For A Thought Tank™ Within
$2,000	$1.09	$ 266	$ —	40 months
2,500	1.36	332	39	32
3,000	1.63	398	93	27
3,500	1.91	466	107	23
4,000	2.18	532	173	20
4,500	2.46	600	241	18
5,000	2.73	666	307	16
5,500	3.00	732	373	15
6,000	3.28	800	441	14
6,500	3.55	866	507	13
7,000	3.82	932	573	12
7,500	4.10	1,000	641	11
8,000	4.37	1,066	707	10
8,500	4.64	1,132	773	10
9,000	4.91	1,198	839	9
10,000	5.46	1,332	973	8
11,000	6.00	1,464	1,105	8
12,000	6.55	1,598	1,239	7
13,000	7.10	1,732	1,373	6
14,000	7.64	1,864	1,505	6
15,000	8.19	1,998	1,639	5
20,000	10.92	2,664	2,305	4
25,000	13.65	3,331	2,972	3
30,000	16.38	3,997	3,638	3
35,000	19.11	4,663	4,304	2
40,000	21.84	5,329	4,970	2
45,000	24.57	5,995	5,636	2
50,000	27.30	6,661	6,302	2
75,000	40.95	9,992	9,633	1
100,000	54.60	13,322	12,963	1

What's your time worth?

Based on 244, 7½-hour working days.

PRINTED IN U.S.A.   042

Courtesy Dictaphone Corp.

General Electric has encouraged its dealers to use Polaroid cameras to sell kitchen appliances. Miniature models of kitchens are set up in the home and then photographed to show the prospect how the proposed kitchen will look. Another company has used a similar method to sell office and laboratory furniture.

Copies of recent ads may be used for visual appeal. Detached and covered with cellophane, they can be easily seen while staying fresh and neat.

Sales Manuals and Portfolios

Some sales manuals are used to reproduce standardized sales talks. These manuals are often illustrated with pictures, graphs, cartoons, drawings, and other visual presentations to ensure the use of the right aid at the right time. They are frequently used by direct-to-the-consumer organizations selling such products as cutlery, silverware, and housewares.

Sales manuals are often supplied by companies. Other companies supply their salespeople with the ideas and material they expect the salespeople to organize in an effective manner.

A sales portfolio usually contains only a sales talk, while a sales manual may contain information on many other phases of the salesperson's job. The sales portfolio is usually designed as a guide to the presentation. However, some portfolios are prepared to be read.

Common types of sales portfolios are the easel type, the spiral-bound type, and the binder or zipper-case type.

The easel type is prepared to stand by itself on the prospect's desk or counter. Some larger easel types, which are placed on the floor, are used in selling to a group. The salesperson turns each page after it has been read or used for illustration. The pages are arranged logically so the story unfolds according to plan.

The spiral-bound sales portfolio may or may not be of the easel type. Wire or plastic bindings are commonly used. When not constructed to be used like an easel, this type may be referred to occasionally to supply additional sales features, helps, or suggestions to the prospective buyer or customer.

The binder or zipper-case type is in common use. Material may be labeled by tabs and punched to fit rings in a binder. This type may be referred to often, and it is convenient to carry and use. For example, Toledo Scale Company sales representatives who sell to retail food stores and restaurants "are supplied with selling kits which are zipper-type portfolios with retractable handles and contain detailed illustrative material readily indexed on all of the items themselves."[5]

A large building contractor improved selling efforts by preparing a visual presentation of important facts concerning the business. The portfolio, bound in spiral plastic, contained such information as thumbnail sketches of the company's key employees; a financial statement; a list of special equipment; photostatic copies of letters from satisfied owners of various types of buildings; and pictures of completed industrial plants, apartment houses, stores, supermarkets, and shopping centers. This appeal to the eye tells a story many words and many minutes cannot equal.

Models, Samples, and Gifts

Visual selling aids of this type may be a good answer to the problem of getting and keeping buyer interest. Miniature models are carried when the product is too large or bulky to transport easily. These may be cross-section models, toy models, or working miniature models. Bearings, in-

---

[5]Quoted by permission from a letter from Toledo Scale Co. (Toledo, Ohio).

Bright yellow "Construction Site Service" van used to demonstrate power tools and concrete fastener systems. The product logos shown on this van were widely recognized in the marketplace as trusted, preferred products, and gained attention as well as credibility from the customer.

Courtesy Star Hardware & Supply Company

dustrial equipment, spark plugs, kitchen equipment, and cars are just a few of the products for which models have been prepared.

A large manufacturer of equipment used by such businesses as hotels, meat markets, and restaurants at one time supplied blueprints of layouts for store owners. But it soon became apparent that too few owners could understand blueprints. So the company replaced the blueprints with tabletop miniature models with far more effective results.

An industrial distributor in Birmingham, Alabama, sells to contractors with its Construction Site Service—a four-van fleet in which each van is equipped with an $8,000 inventory and manned by a driver salesperson. The fleet helps the company sell more sophisticated and more lucrative equipment because it enables salespeople to demonstrate on site the company's line of Phillips Drill Red Head concrete anchors and Black & Decker tools.[6]

Some sales representatives carry samples even when the product is large and heavy. National Cash Register salespeople have found it pays to bring along the types of machines they plan to sell. The registers are transported in a station wagon or passenger car. When the prospect is ready for a demonstration, the register is available immediately. Experience has shown that anything can happen if the salesperson gets the interest of the prospect and then must return to the office to get a sample register. It may take several more calls to secure an appointment for a demonstration.

---

[6]"Industrial Newsletter," *Sales & Marketing Management,* September 17, 1979, p. 44.

Samples of the product make excellent sales aids. Foods, candies, paper products, medicines, and books are among the many products that may be sold through the use of samples. The samples may be arranged in a kit or a case for easy carrying.

Samples are frequently used to maintain the prospect's interest and to serve as a reminder for prospects or customers who do not buy at the time of the interview. In selling ethical drugs, for example, salespeople may use a novel container to demonstrate the delayed dissolving action of a drug and then leave the visual with the physician for use as a paperweight. Or an industrial sales representative may use a toy gyroscope to illustrate the quiet performance of a motor and then leave the toy with the buyer as a reminder.

Films, Slides, Cassettes, and Overhead Projectors

Filmstrips, motion pictures, and slides have become common equipment for the salesperson. Films are particularly useful when selling to groups, when selling in a showroom, or when showing the operations of complex machinery in the buyer's office. If sound motion-picture films are used, action is combined with sound and sight to make a forceful impression on the prospect. Motion-picture equipment is heavy and bulky, and motion-picture films are expensive to make. Because of this, filmstrips have been used more extensively.[7]

Films are particularly good for educating distributors and their salespeople. SKF Industries (maker of antifriction bearings) uses sound-slide films for this purpose.

One manufacturer has found that sound filmstrips help sell heavy farm equipment. Sales representatives can take a portable projector, operate it from a car cigarette-lighter socket, and bring a sales message to a farmer in the field. The eight-minute message conserves the time of both the salesperson and the farmer.

Many companies and corporations show films at club and organization meetings. Films of this kind must be more than factual. They should be interesting, and the facts presented should be dramatized.

Slides have been effective selling aids for many companies. One large company, a leader in structural timber sales, found three-dimensional photographs and a viewer convinced prospects that laminated wood treated with waterproof glue was a good substitute for steel. Pictures were taken of construction jobs in which laminated arches were used; slides were made; and sales representatives were provided with three-dimensional viewers to show architects and builders exactly how and where the com-

---

[7]See Steven Mintz, "Whatever the Product, AV Sheds Light on the Sales Message," *Sales & Marketing Management,* January 18, 1982, pp. 64–70. See also "How Industrial Marketers Use Video: Some Examples," *Industrial Marketing,* June 1982, pp. 76, 84–85.

FIGURE 11–3
Portable Unit for Visual Presentation of Sales Message

Courtesy Eastman Kodak Company

pany's product was used. Each salesperson carries about 60 colored Stereo-Realist slides and a battery-lighted viewer to show product applications.

Sound-slide films have been used effectively in selling mutual investment funds. A typical presentation can be made in about 12 minutes.

Products that are too bulky or too fragile to carry can be photographed in color and demonstrated at the flick of a finger through the use of a small automatic projector (see Figure 11–3). Technicolor has Micro-Video Showcase, which effectively communicates the physical layout of facilities in a distant location to prospects interested in commercial real estate. Used by companies such as Coldwell Banker, the presentation can be in full color, sound and action, and shown anywhere, anytime.

For use at retail sales clinics, on a sales call, while selling in showrooms, or at store demonstrations, Technicolor has a slide cassette player/recorder and sound amplification system for putting together a slide and narration show. The equipment is portable and fits under an airplane seat.

An even smaller automatic sound filmstrip projector, which projects sound filmstrips and standard cassette-loaded tapes, is useful for on-the-spot sales activity. It is about the size of a large book and weighs less than eight pounds (see Figure 11–4). Many companies produce small videocassette recorders. Some models weigh only four pounds and are smaller than a desk-top dictionary, while the cassettes are no larger than a deck of cards. These models are easily carried in a briefcase.

FIGURE 11–4
Low-Cost, Small,
Lightweight Sound
Filmstrip Projector

Courtesy Dukane Corporation

A more ambitious dramatization has been prepared by Audio-Visual Laboratories (AVL) through the use of a six-projector, 8½-minute multi-image 3D slide presentation to sell its Eagle II computer to dealers and large corporations. Special glasses must be worn by the viewers. The company comments, "3D creates more excitement about format and uses in new areas for the Eagle II."[8]

Overhead projectors are another effective visual medium. The image projected on a wall can be up to 25 times larger than that on a written page. This can provide more attention and create greater impact. Such a projector is noiseless and simple to operate. Overhead transparencies can be made quickly and inexpensively on either a plain paper copier or an infrared transparency maker. New information, perhaps only available at the last minute, can be written on the transparency with a special marking pen. One model weighs about 17 pounds, fits under an airplane seat, and looks like a briefcase. This medium can be used for presentations to individuals or to groups (see Figure 11–5).

Testimonials

Testimonials are usually in the form of letters written by satisfied users of a product or service. These letters commend the product or service and make it known that the writer believes the product or service to be a good buy. Testimonials are frequently used by advertisers in newspapers

---

[8]"3D Gives New Depth to AVL," *Sales & Marketing Management,* March 15, 1982, p. 21.

FIGURE 11–5
Overhead
Presentation
Projected on Wall

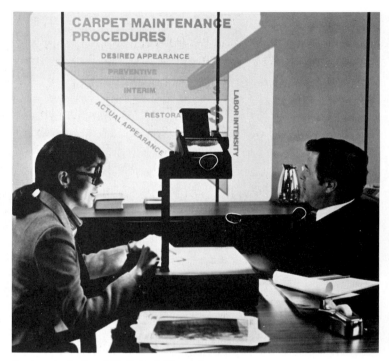

Courtesy Audio Visual/3M, St. Paul, Minnesota

and magazines, and they can be a very effective part of the sales presentation.

Insurance company agents use case histories of claims that report the injuries or disabilities a policyholder has suffered and the benefits the company has paid. A case history usually includes a quotation from a letter written by the policyholder expressing thanks and appreciation for the fair and prompt treatment received. These testimonials may cover many different phases of insurance and may be used in the appropriate spot to prove, support, or illustrate a particular aspect of the presentation.

Company representatives who sell air travel for major airlines have found case histories helpful in dramatizing sales points. American Airlines, for example, reproduces cases that are actual experiences of business firms; they show the variety of problems that can be solved by air travel.

Testimonials are used extensively by progressive sales organizations. There are relatively few products or services for which users are not willing to testify. The effectiveness of a testimonial is determined by the skill with which it is used. In some fields, the testimony of a rival or a competitor of the prospective buyer would end all chance of closing the sale; in other fields, this type of testimony may be a strong factor in closing the sale. Discretion is the key to utilizing testimonials.

Selling Scenario 11–2

CLIMBING MOUNTAINS TO DEMONSTRATE PRODUCTS

 Al Gunther, president of Summit Sports in Boulder, Colorado, demonstrates the quality of his products by mountaineering with customers.

Merchants stocking sporting goods and apparel sold by Al Gunther, president of Summit Sports in Boulder, can rest easy. They can be sure Gunther's goods have been quality-tested.

"I was in southern Russia a few years ago, climbing in the Pamir mountains," says Gunther. "Our team got caught in the worst summer storm in years. We were at 23,000 feet, on an exposed ridge, with 100 mph winds and heavy snowfall. We were there for a couple of days."

Gunther and his party took refuge in their North Face tent, waiting for the tempest to end. "The tent was caving in on one side from the gusts. We were sure we were going to get blown off the mountain," says Gunther, "but the tent even made it through a snowslide that temporarily collapsed one side of it. Without that tent, we would have been dead."

Other climbers were less fortunate. "A German team was on the mountain," says Gunther. "Two members just disappeared about 1,000 feet above us. We rescued the others. They were in very poor shape, due to the storm and poor equipment."

If they are game, Gunther takes clients along on mountainside meanderings, where they can put his wares to the test. "That way, you can really learn about the products," he says. "Together you find features that would not be noticeable without actual field use."

Gunther has built a sales business from climbing contacts. "Selling took me over," he says. "What I found was that I have fun explaining things to people. Before it was a means to an end. Now I spend 90 percent of my time selling."

Gunther notes a sale requires the same sort of preparation as shooting rapids. "You have to scout, planning what to do before you start," he says. "But like shooting rapids, though I know where I want to go, I can't always get there. And everybody takes a spill. You might half-drown, but you can't let it destroy your confidence. You've got to pick yourself up again. That's the challenge."

Source: Adapted from Mark Thalenberg, "Salesmen Live in Dangerous Territory," *Sales & Marketing Management,* June 3, 1985, p. 54.

Product Demonstration

One of the most effective methods of appealing to the buyer's senses is through product demonstration or performance tests. Customers or prospects have a natural desire to prove the product's claims for themselves. Obviously, the proof is much more satisfying and convincing to anyone who is a party to it. In Selling Scenario 11–2, Al Gunther tells how he takes his customers mountain climbing to demonstrate his products.

Product demonstrations are not just a demonstration of how something works. To be effective, demonstrations should prove the product has the capabilities claimed and should enable the prospect to relate those capabilities to the meeting of needs. In addition, demonstrations should permit the customer to become familiar with the product and result in a sale.

A large corporation entering the highly competitive field of plastic covering materials decided to tell its story dramatically. The corporation featured Kalistron, a plastic coating material designed for upholstery and wall-covering uses. The product's unique feature was that color was fused to the *underside* of a clear transparent vinyl sheet, and then a protective flocking was applied. This process made it impossible to reach the color under ordinary conditions. Using a proof-test copy for its advertising, the corporation invited its buyers to scrape, scuff, rub, and scratch the sheeting that protected the color. To dramatize the fact that the color had a long life and was difficult to mar, the corporation prepared a printed card with a swatch of Kalistron on it, a nail file, and instructions on how to try to injure the material. Customers enjoyed the test, and the invitation to "prove it yourself" convinced many people who would have been difficult to convince solely through the use of words.

It is suggested that Schwinn bicycles be sold by inviting prospects to twist an ordinary rim and then a Schwinn Tubular Rim; spin the wheels to see how easily they roll with special roll-bearings; feel the fender braces and note their strength; and stand on the chain guard to see how strong it is.

An enterprising NCR sales representative was having trouble convincing the buyer for a national retailer that NCR could service all of the retailer's scattered outlets. On the next trip to the buyer, the sales representative brought along a bag of darts and a map marked with the chain's hundreds of stores and service locations. The buyer was invited to throw darts at the map, and then find the nearest stores. It was pointed out that the nearest NCR location for service was always within 50 miles. This helped win the company a multimillion-dollar order.

Paper sales representatives sell quality by having prospects hold two sheets of paper to the light and pointing out that in a good grade of paper the fibers are evenly distributed, while in a poor grade of paper uneven distribution produces a mottled effect. To show opacity, they have the customer place a material with black lines on it under the sheet and check for show-through.

A nationally known company manufactures and sells fire extinguishers. Company salespeople—both home-office representatives and distributor salespersons—are trained thoroughly and must become experts in demonstrating techniques for putting out fires. They have little trouble arranging for a demonstration because almost everybody from company presidents to purchasing agents likes to see a good fire. *Showing* how the

Product demonstration: This salesperson is an expert in demonstrating techniques for putting out fires.

Courtesy Ansul Fire Protection

chemical puts out a fire is convincing. Having the prospect take the extinguisher and put out the fire is even more convincing.

Cars provide many opportunities for demonstrations. Salespeople *show* or *demonstrate* as many sales features as possible. Appearance or styling can be shown; comfort and performance can be experienced; and safety can be seen. Power steering, power brakes, air conditioning, and automatic transmissions can be demonstrated effectively. Buyers can *see* or *feel* for themselves, to prove claims about these features. Performance tests give buyers a chance to take the car over rough and smooth roads, into heavy traffic, around sharp curves, and up and down grades. Permitting the prospect to take over the wheel and choose the route adds strength to the demonstration.

Some products can be sold best by getting prospects into the showroom for a "hands-on" product demonstration. Computer seminars are provided for business and personal applications. Prospects can learn about hardware, software, word processing, how to buy a computer, computer terminology, and costs. Sometimes there is no substitute for giving the prospect a chance to operate the product.

While a product demonstration may be used primarily as a closing tool, it can also be used as a prospecting device and proof. As part of the selling process, it offers such advantages as adding visual impact ("Seeing is believing"), acting as the ultimate proof, providing customer involvement, saving time for both the prospect and the sales representative, introducing related equipment, and serving as evidence of a sound professional approach.

Product demonstration is one of the best forms of dramatization.

Words

The principal ways in which human beings communicate, as far as we know, are by physical touch (we make ourselves understood with a tap on the shoulder, a pat on the back, a slap on the cheek, and the ritualistic handshake); by visible movements of some portions of our bodies (pointing a finger, winking an eye, nodding the head, shrugging the shoulders, and smiling, grimacing, or scowling); and finally, by the use of words.[9]

An appropriate choice of words adds strength to any sales presentation. Yet words alone are not as effective as words supported by additional sense appeals. Sometimes intangible services must be sold primarily through the use of words and only secondarily through appeals to other senses. When this happens, it is even more necessary to choose descriptive and meaningful words. Of course, it is important to remember not to talk *more* but to *talk better*—the *quality* of words, not the *quantity,* brings results.

Words are tools. Word artists have the power to be soft and appealing or to be strong and powerful. They can use short words to give strength and force to the presentation or to provide charm and grace. With practice, words may be used like the notes in a musical scale, and the proper mood may be created.

Choose words that have strength or descriptive quality. Avoid such words as *nice, pretty, good, swell,* and *you know.* The salesperson has many choices of words. For example, instead of the word *stingy,* use *penurious, parsimonious, greedy, penny-wise, tight, pinching, scrimping, tightfisted, hardhanded,* or *miserly.* Words of all colors—words soft as fur, hard as steel, and smooth as glass; words that simmer, crackle, or explode; words that sparkle and shine—are available to anyone who spends an extra few minutes preparing a presentation.

Creativity in the use of words is as important to the salesperson as it is to the songwriter or the author. Effective communication is necessary for persuasion, and words are a very important medium of communication. Good salespeople are never completely satisfied with their word power—they are constantly building better vocabularies.

Every sales representative should be able to draw on a set of appropriate analogies to help present a product or service feature. The analogy may be a smile, such as "a savings account is like a spare tire"; or a tongue-pleasing phrase, such as "tired old Ford," "modest plenty of thrift," or "miracle of fruit"; or language that conveys a sensory appeal, such as "smooth as silk," "smooth as glass," or "strong as steel."

The sales representative for a duplicating machine may wish to use such expressions as "clean, crisp copies," "library quiet," "at the push of a button," "one-step processing," "standardize your files," "productivity button," and "standardize all your reports."[10]

---

[9]See *Communications,* Kaiser Aluminum, for a very interesting analysis of problems in communicating.

[10]*Sales Manual,* Xerox Corporation.

Some words that are better to use than others when selling real estate are:

Killer Words	Better Words
Deal	Transaction
Commission	Service fee
Contract	Agreement
Sign here	OK or initial
Salesperson	Counselor
Cheap	Inexpensive
Sell your property	Market your property
Bid	Offer to buy
Down payment	Initial investment
Monthly payment	Monthly investment
Listing	Employment agreement[11]

THE EFFECTIVE USE OF SELLING AIDS

Many of the following suggestions apply to most of the devices discussed in the foregoing pages. However, for illustrative purposes, the "how" of the dramatization is applied mainly to product demonstrations.

Be Prepared

The first requisite of effective demonstration is *knowledge* of the product. Salespeople must *know* to be able to *show*. They must know what the product will do and will not do, how it performs, and what the performance means to the buyer. Only then are they qualified to demonstrate.

But knowledge alone is not enough. Skill must be developed in the demonstration techniques. Therefore, those who wish to present a fault-less demonstration have to practice until they become experts. If the machine demonstrated does not perform as it should because of the demonstrator's awkwardness, the customer is likely to conclude that the machine is not much good or that it is hard to operate. Either conclusion places hurdles in the path of selling.

The car salesperson who cannot find the appropriate controls or switches right away; the industrial machine sales representative who is not quite sure how a particular lever or button is used; the tractor sales representative who cannot shift gears smoothly are placing barriers in the way of the sale.

Before trying to demonstrate, the salesperson should check on two additional points: (1) Has a proper place been prepared for the demonstration? (2) Has the equipment been checked to see that it is in good working order?

---

[11]"Killer Words," *Better Homes & Gardens Real Estate Service*, November, 1979.

A good demonstration uses effective props and is staged to produce just the right effect. Tables, chairs, drapes, lights, and other items may be needed. It is much easier to conduct a demonstration in a showroom than in the prospect's office. A proper setting may make the difference between a good and an ineffective presentation.

Salespeople have learned through bitter experience that there is no substitute for a complete personal check of equipment before a demonstration. If sound films are to be shown, it makes good sense to check the projector, cord, bulbs, and any other parts that can cause trouble. Incidentally, it may be well to make sure that the prospect has outlets available and a room that can be darkened if necessary.

If machines are to be demonstrated, they must be maintained and serviced. No attempt should be made to demonstrate a machine until the salesperson has operated it personally to see it is in good working order. A key that sticks, a lever that is hard to shift, a spring that squeaks, a motor that heats up, or a connection that causes static or shock can ruin otherwise good dramatic presentations.

Control the Demonstration

The most effective demonstrations are those in which the customer is encouraged to participate. This helps get the customer emotionally involved. Many product demonstrations are spectacular when performed by the salesperson alone; but the customer should be allowed to prove personally that the product claims are sound. The salesperson who becomes an exhibitionist instead of a teacher is likely to find that customers are resentful when they realize their skill is no match for the demonstrator's. Not only is it desirable for customers to participate in the demonstration and to experience the results or benefits claimed, but it is also necessary for them to participate in the proper manner and at the most propitious time. To achieve this, the salesperson must have complete control over the demonstration.

To demonstrate effectively salespeople need to plan exactly what they will do and exactly what they expect the prospect to do. Generally, when using such selling aids as pictures, illustrations, and graphics, the salesperson should be careful not to expose the aids too soon. It is usually disastrous to allow the customer freedom to peruse visual sales material during the presentation without any guidance or without attention being focused on the features the salesperson is discussing. Too often customers ignore the salesperson's remarks because they become absorbed in reading captions or looking at pictures that may be unrelated to the remarks.

Many salespeople maintain control of their visual materials by keeping their hands on them and by seating themselves so it is easy for them to turn the pages at the appropriate times. As each point in the presentation is illustrated, the salesperson may point to the visual aid. If individual illustration sheets are used, it is good to present them one at a time and to remove each one when its purpose has been served. The important point to remember is that the selling aids and the sales talk complement each other; to be effective, they have to be coordinated.

Use Sound Principles and Techniques

Successful salespeople make the demonstration an integral part of the presentation. They relate the demonstration to important product features; they appeal to basic buying motives; they *tell, show,* and *sell;* they make the demonstration simple, concise, and easily understood; they get commitments from the prospect after each feature has been demonstrated; and they avoid distractions.

Demonstration Is Part of the Presentation   No attempt should be made to set the demonstration apart as a separate activity in the mind of the buyer. The salesperson who asks permission to conduct a demonstration may be inviting the answer, "Some other time; I'm pretty busy today," or, "I think I understand what the product will do." Most salespeople find they have little trouble conducting a demonstration if they *assume* the buyer is interested. Of course, this assumption is based on the fact that the demonstration has been well prepared and the presentation has paved the way.

If it isn't possible to get the prospect's full attention and he or she seems busy or preoccupied, it would probably be wise to cancel or postpone the demonstration.

Appeal to Basic Buying Motives   Any dramatization of the product should emphasize the major *benefits* that accrue to the buyer through its purchase. The task is to dramatize, through a demonstration or otherwise, the sales features most likely to appeal to the buyer's basic reasons for wanting the product. Dramatizing an interesting sales feature contributes little to closing the sale unless the feature will benefit the particular prospect. Figure 11–6 shows a method for organizing sales materials.

Car salespeople, for example, seldom have enough time, nor can they hold the prospect's interest long enough, to dramatize or demonstrate all the sales features of a new model. They must choose the sales features that make the strongest appeal—the brakes, the beauty, the visibility, the automatic transmission, the pickup, the power steering, or the quietness of the ride. Appeals to safety, economy, comfort, and convenience are common when selling cars. After the appropriate sales features have been demonstrated, the prospect may be invited to drive the car. The salesperson then guides the demonstration through suggestion by asking the driver to stop quickly to test the brakes, or to step on the gas to test the acceleration, or to turn sharply to note the power steering.

Sales representatives for one mutual fund can choose from a library of six sales films. They carefully select the film that focuses on a prospect's

FIGURE 11–6   Method for Organizing Sales Material on Tires

Feature	Benefit	Demonstrate
Low-profile styling of the future with wheel sculptured to complement tire and vehicle	Enhances beauty of car—commands admiration and attention	Place tire next to any tire in your line or, better still, next to tires and wheels now on car; point out increased beauty
Cantilevered construction with four sidewall belts—two on each side	Improved handling, stability, and ride; also in unlikely run-flat emergency, you have superior control	Use cross section to point out sidewall belts and cantilevered construction
Fiberglass tread belts	Doubles puncture and impact resistance over conventional tires and reduces tread distortions at all speeds	Use cross section and/or your selling department tire construction chart—show location of tread belt plies and explain benefit
Rayon cord body with rugged fiberglass tread belts	Over 100 percent more mileage than conventional tires, a smooth ride, and no flat-spot problems	Show cross section of tire and point out how belted construction prevents tread squirming and results in plus mileage
New-concept tread design and more contour featuring more grooves and more siping	Up to 25 percent quicker stopping than conventional tires on wet, slippery pavements	Use cross section or tire itself—point out increased number of lateral grooves and sipes

specific financial objective. The objective may be a college education, retirement, the needs of career women, current income, long-term income, or a profit-sharing plan. Interest and attention are not difficult to secure and hold when the customer's objective has been identified.

The features to be dramatized must be chosen on the basis of each prospect's individual interests. Good judgment and experience help in choosing how many and which features to emphasize, and how to proceed.

Tell, Show, and Sell   This combination of activities results in effective demonstrations. Sales representatives for a large distributor of typewriter ribbons and carbon papers are told to spend only a few moments on the sales talk. Then they are to get a ribbon or a piece of carbon paper into one of the prospect's typewriters or tabulation machines as fast as possible to *show* what the product can do. They keep selling arguments concise and base the strongest appeal on demonstration—on the customer's own equipment.

A sample demonstration, suggested for use by Frigidaire salespeople, requires the use of a grease crayon, a bottle of iodine, a match, and a soft cloth or cleansing tissue. The objective is to use dramatization to prove the advantages of porcelain on the refrigerator, range, washer, and other products. The demonstration may occur like this:

Salesperson: You know, Mrs. Kerns, if there was ever a product that should be well protected it's a washer—for it is constantly exposed to the rusting and corrosive action of water, soaps, and bleaches. But your Frigidaire washer always stays bright because it's protected with Frigidaire Lifetime Porcelain, inside and out.

I can smear it with this greasy crayon . . . [*it is smeared*]. I can douse it with iodine, one of the most penetrating stains known . . . [*it is doused*].

I can even lay a lighted cigarette on it, or burn it with a match [*a lighted match is put on the washer top*]. And even after all this . . .

It will shine as bright as ever, simply by wiping with a damp cloth. I'm sure that's the kind of finish you want on your new washer, isn't it, Mrs. Kerns?[12]

Figure 11–7 shows a portion of a confidential Money Accumulation Plan used to help a prospect identify insurance needs. Accompanying the figure is a graph clearly pointing out the amount of money the prospect will earn by age 65 (see Figure 11–8).

A savings margin per month is supplied by the prospect, and then an insurance program is prepared for that amount of premium.

The prospect's needs are fulfilled by appropriate insurance income from assets and social security income. The needs and resources are all *visually* portrayed. Separate charts are completed that show in detail the social security benefits and returns to be received by the prospect and members of the family; a monthly budget estimator used to help determine the monthly expenses; and a detailed analysis of family assets. Specific insurance recommendations are submitted after this fact-finding interview is analyzed.

When selling is done by means of samples and the customer is given a choice of fabrics or colors, it is best to show one sample (or only a few) at a time. Too many samples and too many demonstrations tend to confuse rather than help the buyer.

Make Demonstrations Simple, Concise, and Easily Understood   Long, complicated demonstrations add to the possibility the buyer may miss the point and salespeople may do a poor job.

Simple demonstrations should show some property of the product or help the prospect draw a pertinent conclusion about the product. Good demonstrations attract attention to sales features and benefits.

---

[12]*The Prospect Meets the Product* (Detroit: Frigidaire Division, General Motors Corp.), pp. 30–31.

FIGURE 11–7
A Visual Approach to Determining Needs

A Money Accumulation Plan

Name _____ Age _____

Plan _____ For $ _____

1. Your financial goals

Goal

	$	

Money to fall back on in emergencies   Money to start a business   Money for children's education
Financial independence at retirement   Money for a vacation home   Money to buy a home

2. A plan
to help you reach your goals

Your increasing cash values*

After ____ years $_____

____ years   _____

____ years   _____

At 65   _____

Less payments to 65 $_____

DIFFERENCE $_____

*Including cash value of dividend additions. The dividend results used in the above figures are merely illustrations of what would be achieved if the latest dividend scale were continued. They must not be considered a guarantee, promise or estimate as to the future. Cumulative figures shown do not allow for any additional interest that might otherwise have been earned.

3. A regular accumulation program

Monthly payments of $_____ make this plan possible.

OPTIONAL FEATURES: □ **Self-completing feature:** With Disability Waiver your premiums are paid for you (after a 4-month waiting period) if you have an accident or illness that makes you unable to work.

□ **Guaranteed insurability feature:** With Additional Purchase Protection, even if you become uninsurable you may buy additional insurance. This privilege could be exercised at age 25, 28, 31, 34, 37 or 40, or when you are married or have a child.

□ **Inflation-adjustment feature:** The Dividend Addition Plan provides steadily increasing death benefits and cash values to counteract or stay ahead of the effects of inflation. The 5th Dividend Option can be used towards providing increased death benefits.

**Financial
Service**

Courtesy Mutual Benefit Life Insurance Company

FIGURE 11–8
Graphic to Support Money Accumulation Plan Presentation

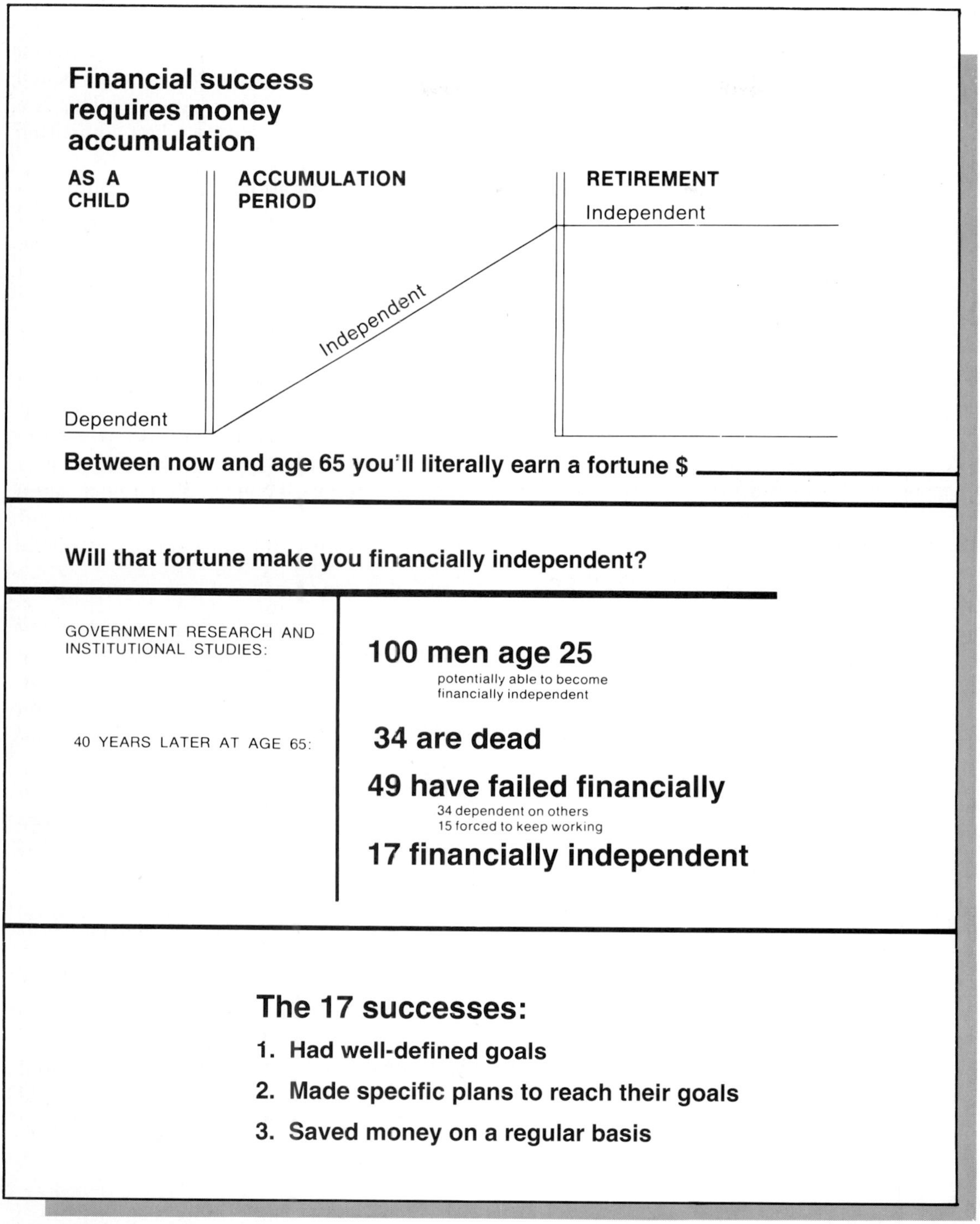

**Financial success
requires money
accumulation**

**AS A
CHILD**

**ACCUMULATION
PERIOD**

RETIREMENT

Independent

Independent

Dependent

Between now and age 65 you'll literally earn a fortune $ _____

Will that fortune make you financially independent?

GOVERNMENT RESEARCH AND
INSTITUTIONAL STUDIES:

100 men age 25
potentially able to become
financially independent

40 YEARS LATER AT AGE 65:

34 are dead

49 have failed financially
34 dependent on others
15 forced to keep working

17 financially independent

The 17 successes:

1. **Had well-defined goals**

2. **Made specific plans to reach their goals**

3. **Saved money on a regular basis**

Adapted from the Mutual Benefit Life Insurance Company brochure

In order to demonstrate the meaning of silver plate, a salesperson may say, "If I were to take this pencil and dip it into some silver, the pencil would come out coated, wouldn't it? You see, the silver covers this pencil much as silver covers the base metal in a silver-plated spoon." This is a simple, easily understood explanation. It could be used when comparing the merits of sterling and plated ware.

Retail tire salespeople for one large corporation are instructed to use a small screwdriver, a piece of chalk, and a smooth tire section to sell tire safety. To emphasize the danger of driving on smooth tires, they rub the smooth tire section against a table, a smooth surface, or the palm of the hand. Attention is drawn to the fact that no traction is left and this could cause the car to slide, especially on wet pavement. The screwdriver is used to remove a piece of glass, a rock, or some other object from the customer's tire, and the spot is circled with chalk. The salespeople then explain that the flexing of the tire while driving could enlarge the cut or bruised area and a blowout could result. These demonstrations are designed to show the customer why tires should be replaced. When new tires are shown, the demonstration involves having the customer rub a disc of ordinary rubber and disc of superrubber on a piece of sandpaper to show the difference in chafing and therefore the extra mileage available from the better tire.[13]

Get a Commitment   After *each* product feature has been demonstrated or explained, a commitment should be secured from the prospect. The salesperson may ask, "Do you see how the machine works? Isn't that easy to operate?" The objective is to find out how well the demonstration is accepted. If prospects agree that the demonstration has proved several sales features, they may be ready to buy.

If the demonstration was poorly conducted or wasn't a natural part of the presentation, the buyer may still be unconvinced. It then becomes necessary to find out exactly why there is some misunderstanding. It is unwise to leave a demonstration until the prospect fully understands.

Avoid Distracting Activities   The physical appearance of salespeople is important when demonstrating a product. Customers evaluate the product and the salesperson by what the salesperson does as well as by what is said. The hands, facial expressions, posture, and mannerisms should not be distractions that will weaken an otherwise effective demonstration.

Salespeople should have clean, neat hands and should keep them out of their pockets; they should handle the product carefully; and they should use their hands skillfully to enhance the success of the presentation. Facial expressions can help or hinder the demonstration. Interest and enthusiasm

---

[13]Courtesy of the Firestone Tire & Rubber Co., Akron, Ohio.

can be shown by facial expressions. Good salespeople look the prospect in the eye while demonstrating and do not allow their gaze to wander about the room. A genuine smile should replace any tendency to frown or to wear a constant grin. Posture is important. Alert salespeople don't slump in a chair, nor do they lean on tables, desks, or chairs. Some personal mannerisms are particularly annoying to a buyer. Rattling coins, swinging a key chain, tapping a foot, smoking, or nudging a prospect can detract from the effectiveness of a demonstration.

SUMMARY

Effective dramatization requires the use of multiple-sense appeals through a well-planned presentation. Dramatization will help maintain interest, convince the prospect, improve understanding, make a lasting impression, and create value for the prospect, as well as contribute to the salesperson's success.

Many visual aids and techniques are available. They should be chosen carefully in relation to the objective desired. Some are better for one-to-one presentations; others are better for group presentations; others are best used when the product is large or complex; and still others may be used to meet heavy competition in a dramatic way.

Product demonstration through performance tests is unusually effective, while the appropriate use of words is indispensable. There is no substitute for being prepared, controlling the demonstration, and using sound principles and techniques.

Show, tell, and sell is the formula used by outstanding sales representatives.

QUESTIONS AND PROBLEMS

1. You are a sales representative for a nationally known maker of ball-point pens. You have an appointment with the office manager of a large firm in the food-processing industry. This is your first call.

    After a short wait, you are ushered into her office. She appears businesslike and pressed for time. You say good morning and introduce yourself.

    Which of the following statements would you select to begin your interview? Why?

    a. I would like to demonstrate to you a Whizzbang product that we are really excited about.

    b. I would like to demonstrate to you a Whizzbang product that offers better quality and color.

    c. I'd like to explore with you how we can reduce the cost of writing instruments. What brand of pens do you currently buy?

2. Studies have shown that there is a need to increase the "listening quotient" of prospects. If prospects tend to hear only about one fourth of what is said to them, what can the sales representative do? Illustrate the value of eye appeals as contrasted to ear appeals.

3. Effective, easily prepared visual aids are the A-frame, which is placed on the prospect's desk, and the easel, which is the same as the A-frame but is usually placed on a three-legged stand for better visibility to a larger group. Under what circumstances would you select different visual aids? When preparing and using an A-frame or easel chart pad, what can be done to make the tool most effective?

4. J. H. Patterson, of National Cash Register fame, trained sales representatives to "talk with their pencils." What are the advantages of using this type of sales aid?

5. It has been said "common words do not have meanings—only people do. And sometimes they don't either." Can you give an example illustrating this observation? What are the implications for a sales representative?

6. A prominent psychologist once made this observation on what salespeople should do with a product: "Weigh it; smell it; taste it; pound it; take it to pieces; put it together; listen to it; squeeze it; shake it; roll it; spread it; pour it; bite it; file it; whittle it; burn it; freeze it; soak it; saw it; cook it; kick it; stop it." What are the implications of this statement?

7. A saleswoman has planned a sales interview to sell sterling silver by developing a sales talk around visual illustrations in an easel portfolio. She has placed the easel in front of her prospect, and she seats herself on the right side. She begins her presentation and gets to the second page of the portfolio when the prospect picks up the portfolio and starts thumbing through it, looking at the pictures and illustrations.

   The prospect says, "Go ahead with your presentation. I can hear you while I glance through your portfolio."
   a. What should the saleswoman do? Explain the reasons for the action you recommend.
   b. How can she dramatize value and other product features in sterling silver forks and spoons?
   c. Suggest ways to dramatize the features of china or crystal glasses.

8. How could you demonstrate the following:
   a. A stereo speaker in a showroom.
   b. A word processor in an office.
   c. Shatterproof plate glass in a factory.
   d. Air conditioning in a home.
   e. A Polaroid camera in a retail store.

9. Farmers understandably like to be shown when it comes to making substantial outlays for farm machines. It is obvious, however, the most enterprising sales representative cannot visit farmer prospects and bring a selection of hay conditioners, harrows, or

other machines. The conventional sales representative relies on word power or on persuading farmers to visit the showroom. Can you think of a better way of making a presentation to the prospect in the home or even in the field where the prospect may be working?

10. Assume you plan a flight demonstration to prove some of the claims you have made for a new-model Piper, Cessna, or Beechcraft airplane. Would the demonstration be any different for each of these three individuals: a nervous person, an economy-minded person, and a performance-minded person? Explain.

PROJECTS

1. Use a book of synonyms and antonyms and see how many words you can identify that are stronger or more descriptive than each of the following: *cheap, pretty, bargain, explain, wonderful, good, neat, swell,* and *nice*. Set up a chart illustrating your findings.

2. Shop several stores for a bicycle, an air bed, a smoke alarm, a home computer, a van, or some other product capable of being demonstrated. Report on the demonstration techniques you encountered. Evaluate the techniques used, and suggest ways to improve the demonstrations.

CASE PROBLEMS

Case 11–1   Sunshine Realty, Inc.

Ted Calhoun owned a real estate office, and he had hired part-time sales agents to sell on a commission basis on weekends. In addition to acting as a broker, Calhoun had qualified for a contractor's license and had built a few homes for speculation purposes. He later invited an insurance agent to join the firm. They soon decided it would be necessary to hire a full-time sales representative for selling real estate.

An ad was placed in the local newspaper, and it was otherwise made known that Sunshine Realty was interested in hiring a young licensed real estate agent. In about three months, they found the person they were looking for.

The new salesperson was asked to suggest techniques that would be effective in increasing real estate sales volume

through a better use of graphics. Calhoun had made no attempt to develop much in the way of selling aids.

Questions

1. Which selling aids should the new salesperson recommend to help dramatize the sale of real estate? What is each selling aid expected to accomplish?

2. How could a sales kit or sales portfolio be used profitably by this real estate salesperson? What records, papers, or materials should be included in the sales kit or portfolio of real estate salespeople so they can sell intelligently? Assume the salespeople would use the sales kit both in the field and at their desks.

Case 11–2   Smoke Alarm, Inc.

A local distributor has offered you the opportunity to sell an early-warning home-fire safety device called SmokeAlert. A generous commission is provided.

SmokeAlert is easy to install and is run by three batteries. It is mounted on the ceiling. It may be used in mobile homes, apartments, summer homes, camper trailers—wherever fire may strike. Depending on the size and layout of the unit protected, it may be desirable to have more than one SmokeAlert for adequate protection.

The device operates on the principle of ionization—slight changes in the air caused by fire or even invisible smoke enter SmokeAlert, and the ionization sensor sounds the alarm. The device is "smart" too—it can be set so heavy cigarette smoke at a party won't cause an alarm, but if a fire starts, SmokeAlert takes over.

Fatal fires in a typical home start in the following areas: living room, den, or family room, 33.8 percent; kitchen, 16.2 percent; basement, 25.7 percent; bedrooms, 12.1 percent; garage, 1.4 percent; and all other, 10.8 percent.

Before deciding to accept this selling opportunity, you plan to investigate and learn how the product might be sold and to whom.

Questions

1. What facts can you assemble about fires in homes—what causes them, their frequency, casualties, and any other pertinent facts?
2. Where might you secure prospects?
3. Prepare some statements you believe will dramatize the need for a SmokeAlert.
4. How can the sales interview be dramatized?

Case 11–3   Thomas Hill Publishing Company

The Thomas Hill Publishing Company includes a highly successful textbook division under the direction of a new editor. This individual has embarked on a new venture designed to tap the increasing demand for adult education, continuing education, and other nontraditional forms of education, as well as the increasing market for "practical" courses.

Thomas Hill has developed video courses in the basic business curriculum, including courses in such subjects as accounting, finance, statistics, and economics. These courses are taped lectures by eminent professors and business leaders from around the country; they include colorful and easy-to-understand animated visual materials such as charts and graphs.

Programmed textbooks, cases, and problems accompany the videotapes, which can be used in "self-teaching" situations on a flexible schedule. The tapes may be checked out for use in more convenient locations than the administering institution, such as homes, libraries, and high schools. The courses are designed for use by people who wish to continue their education but whose family or work commitments prevent them from attending classes at regular hours or at the university. The technique and content of the courses have been judged excellent by an impartial panel of educators.

The cost for the first tape is $500, with a $50 duplicating charge for each additional copy ordered. It is assumed that students will buy the accompanying texts.

Assignment

Write a script for a sales presentation that elicits a buying commitment from the curriculum committee of State University's Business School. Remember, you have the solid reputation of your company behind you. But you must convince the committee there is a need for this individualized, flexible, and yet impersonal teaching method. Furthermore, you must convince the committee that your courses will do an effective teaching job for less money than it would cost to have professors teach at irregular hours in many places. Include the specific approaches you will take to dramatize the presentation.

Case 11–4   KFX Radio Station

KFX is a local radio station in Madison, Wisconsin, a city of 400,000 people. The station was started 25 years ago. James Wensley, its owner and founder, emphasized public service programming rather than entertainment programming. The station's programming was devoted exclusively to local and national news.

During the past year, Wensley sold the station to Tom Campbell. Campbell reviewed the station's ratings and advertising sales and decided to change its programming format. He also hired four advertising time salespeople.

In designing the new format, Campbell used the following research data on the radio listening habits of Madison residents:

Women listen to the radio four hours a day, while men listen two hours a day.

Radio is preferred to television for coverage of fast-breaking news stories.

The KFX all-news format captured an average of 20 percent of the radio audience.

The average age of radio purchasers is 26.

Car radio owners listen to KFX 40 percent of the time when they are driving.

Eighty percent of cars have radios.

The average car owner listens to the radio 30.2 minutes per day.

Radio listeners like to hear sincere, warm, friendly people.

KFX is particularly popular during the summer and winter vacations.

The new KFX schedule is shown below.

Develop a presentation to sell advertising to the following:

1. The promoter of a rock concert.
2. The largest car dealer in the city.
3. A small sporting goods store.
4. A large discount department store chain.

Monday through Saturday

Morning*

12:00–4:00 Classical music
  Host: John Michaels—music host and critic from Los Angeles
4:00–6:00 Call-in question-and-answer format
  Host: Mike Lupin—recently on a national radio show
6:00–10:00 "Good Morning Show"—popular music plus news, weather, and interviews with personalities and local officials
  Host: Jim Jackson—recently host of a similar program on most popular station in Minnesota
10:00–12:00 "Homemaker Show"—information on such subjects as cooking and child rearing.
  Host: Jennifer Fiddler—recently head of a consumer advocate group

Afternoon*

12:00–3:30 Popular music
  Host: Debbie Rudder—host of local TV variety show
3:30–5:00 Rock music
  Host: Mike Evans—recent college graduate
5:00–7:30 "News Roundup"—local and national news
  Host: George Stein—longtime KFX newscaster
7:30–10:00 Call-in comments on current events
  Host: Ward Baxter—host for a similar TV program
10:00–12:00 Popular music
  Host: Kamy Lutz—recently a disc jockey on a Chicago radio station

Sunday

Morning

12:00–6:00 Off the air
6:00–10:00 Religious services (noncommercial)
10:00–12:00 "Newsmakers"—interviews with local and national officials
  Host: Jim Taylor—former University of Wisconsin political science professor

Afternoon

12:00–4:00 "Sport Event of the Week"—a major syndicated event
4:00–6:00 "News of the Week"
  Host: Jim Taylor
6:00–8:00 Dance music
  Host: Debbie Rudder
8:00–9:00 "Wall Street Summary"
  Host: Jim Bettman—financial reporter for a local newspaper
9:00–12:00 Opera music
  Host: John Michaels

KFX Rate Schedule

Class	Time for Spot	Number of Spots Purchased			
		1	10	50	100
AAA (Monday–Friday, 6:00–	60 seconds	$200	$190	$175	$160
10:00 A.M., 3:30–7:30 P.M.;	30 seconds	160	150	140	130
Saturday, 10:00–12:00 A.M.)	10 seconds	100	90	80	75
AA (Monday–Friday 10:00 A.M.–	60 seconds	120	112	105	100
3:30 P.M., 7:30–10:00 P.M.;	30 seconds	100	90	85	80
Sunday, 9:00 A.M.–9:00 P.M.)	10 seconds	60	55	53	50
A (all other times)	60 seconds	85	80	75	65
	30 seconds	72	65	60	55
	10 seconds	45	40	38	35

*Every hour on the hour, five minutes are devoted to national and local headline news.

SELECTED REFERENCES

Adams, Sherle. "Liven Up That Presentation!" *Sales & Marketing Management,* August 16, 1982, pp. 40–42.

Arwady, Joseph W. "Adding Video and Film to Your Presentation." *Business Marketing,* April 1984, pp. 104–8.

"AV Finds Its Niche." *Sales & Marketing Management,* February 2, 1981, special section, pp. 43–55.

"AV Projects a Bright Picture." *Sales & Marketing Management,* January 17, 1983, special section, pp. 47–61.

Bice, D. "Live Presentations Drive Home Point." *Advertising Age,* April 23, 1979, sec. 2, pp. 15–50.

"How Industrial Marketers Use Video: Some Examples." *Industrial Marketing,* June 1982, pp. 76, 84–85.

Kleinberg, Ellen. "How Video Will Change the Sale." *Industrial Marketing,* April 1981, pp. 46–49.

McCall, Chester H. *How to Use the Magic Power of Showmanship.* Englewood Cliffs, N.J.: Executive Reports, 1976.

Moine, Donald J. "To Trust, Perchance to Buy." *Psychology Today,* August 1982, pp. 51–53.

Smith, Homer. "Deliver Your Talk Like a Pro." *Sales & Marketing Management,* March 11, 1985, pp. 130–35.

12 Overcoming Objections

Some questions answered in this chapter are:

- Why do buyers object?
- What objections can be expected?
- When do buyers object?
- What preparation is necessary to answer objections successfully?
- What are some good methods and techniques to use when answering objections?
- Is there a good procedure to follow?

The chapter also provides illustrations of methods and techniques used by salespeople of major companies when answering objections.

Handling objections and closing the sale are the heart of selling. Many sales executives suggest selling has not really begun until the prospect voices objections. They believe many potentially good salespeople are effective only until buyers object—then the salespeople lose heart and consider their efforts to be fruitless.

All salespeople encounter objections during some phase of the selling process. All buyers at some time voice an objection to something that is said or done. In fact, some customers may raise irrational or irrelevant objections that have nothing to do with the product, the company, or the seller. Skill in handling objections is just as necessary as skill in making appointments, in conducting interviews, in demonstrating, or in closing sales. When new salespeople realize buyers' objections are a *normal* and *natural* part of the sales process, they can treat such objections as sales opportunities.

Seven Steps in the Sales Process

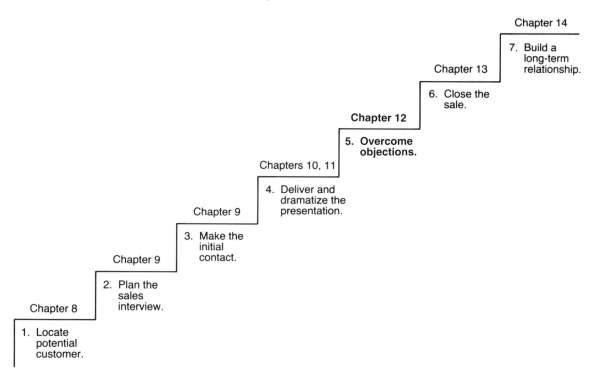

Chapter 14

7. Build a
   long-term
   relationship.

Chapter 13

6. Close the
   sale.

Chapter 12

**5. Overcome
   objections.**

Chapters 10, 11

4. Deliver and
   dramatize the
   presentation.

Chapter 9

3. Make the
   initial
   contact.

Chapter 9

2. Plan the
   sales
   interview.

Chapter 8

1. Locate
   potential
   customer.

WHY PEOPLE OBJECT

Negative Psychological Factors

Every time a prospect voices an objection, he or she is expressing feelings of insecurity common to us all. As has been pointed out earlier in this text, we all fear punishment, pain, loss, and disapproval, and we try to avoid them. One way to avoid them is by not making a decision to buy—we cannot then lose face or suffer the disapproval of others by making a wrong buying decision.[1] The sales representative's task is to help the prospect overcome these fears.

Simply because they are human beings, most buyers harbor some degree of resistance. Attitudes and emotions play a big role in causing buyers to act the way they do.

People are instinctively afraid of strangers. Perhaps this fear is a carryover from our early tribal fears, from a time when strangers meant danger. Buyers may form prejudices and biases. They may, for example, display an irrational dislike of tall people, short people, conservative people, loud talkers, or others. Since ego is the basis for the actions of

---

[1]"Handling Objections," *The Paper Mate Selling Process* (The Gillette Company, Paper Mate Division), p. VI–37.

many buyers, salespeople who do not recognize buyers' need to express their ego can expect many and varied objections, which may seem difficult to understand.

Fear of making a decision because it may be the wrong decision and fear of hurting friends or present sources of supply may be additional negative psychological factors.

The Desire to Get Rid of the Representative

Some prospects voice numerous objections in an attempt to simply dismiss the salesperson. The prospect may not have enough time to devote to the interview, may not be interested in the product or service offered for sale, may not be in the mood to listen, or because of some unhappy experiences may have decided not to face further unpleasant interviews.

These objections may occur when the salesperson is making a cold canvass or is trying to make an appointment. The salesperson who is overaggressive, rude, impolite, or pesty can expect the prospect to use numerous devices to keep the salesperson from making a presentation.

No Money

People who have no money to buy may have been classified as suspects. As indicated in Chapter 8, "Prospecting and Qualifying Potential Customers," the ability to pay is an important factor when qualifying a suspect. An incomplete or poor job of qualifying may cause this objection to arise.

When suspects say they can't afford a product, they may have a valid objection. If that is so, time should not be wasted, and new prospects should be contacted.

Do Not Need Product or Service

This objection also may be valid. Expensive machinery may be designed for handling large volumes of work; if the manufacturer operates on a small scale, there may be no need for the product. Or perhaps the salesperson is selling a collection service; if the retail dealer sells for cash, a collection service is not required.

Legitimate objections will arise when prospective buyers have not been qualified on all the essential characteristics of a prospect.

No Recognition of Need

Salespeople may encounter objections such as, "My business is different," or, "I have no use for your service." If they have qualified the buyer accurately, these objections are evidence that the buyer is not convinced that a need exists. Buyers may be unaware of the benefits of using the product or service. They may have an "unrecognized need."

It is logical to expect a buyer to object if the salesperson cannot establish a need in the buyer's mind. In pioneer selling, for example, selling the benefits of a new and different product, service, or idea is a more difficult task for the salesperson.

Can these customers
afford Gucci?

Alan Carey/The Image Works

Need More Information

Some buyers offer objections in an attempt to get more information. They may not fully understand the presentation, or they may want to receive assurance on points about which they are doubtful.

Buyers who want more information are helping to sell themselves by raising valid objections. They may have already decided they want the product or service, but they may wish to fortify themselves with logical reasons they can use to justify their purchase to others.

There may be a conflict in the buyer's mind. A struggle may be taking place between what emotions dictate and what reason dictates. The buyer may be trying to decide between two competitive products or attempting to choose between buying and not buying. Whatever the struggle, buyers who object in order to get more information are usually interested, and there is always a good possibility they will buy in the end.

Habit or Custom

Buyers' objections are not limited to legitimate objections that cannot be overcome. Human beings are creatures of habit. Once they develop a routine or establish a custom, they tend to resist change. Fear or ignorance may be the basis for not wanting to try anything new or different. Many people resist anything new just because it is new and because they have no related experience to guide them in buying. Others are prejudiced;

FIGURE 12–1
Teaser Objection

Cameramann International, Ltd.

"I can't see how you can charge so much for this product."

they may buy a certain make or kind of product because they have always bought it.

The natural tendency to resist buying a new product or changing from a satisfactory brand to a new one is the basis for numerous objections.

Value Does Not Exceed Cost

Most buyers must sacrifice something in order to buy. The money spent for the product is not available for other things. The choice may be between the down payment on a new car and a vacation trip, or it may be between expanding the plant and distributing a dividend.

Usually, buyers object until they can be sure the sacrifice they are making is more than offset by the value of the product or services they are acquiring. The question of "value received" is often the basis for customers' objections.

COMMON OBJECTIONS

Customers may make objections to tease the salesperson, to avoid making a decision, or because they have misunderstood the salesperson. Other objections are focused on the price of the product, the service offered, the company providing the product, or the salesperson.

Teasing

At times, customers make objections even though the sales presentation has gone well and they are almost ready to place an order. They simply need some additional assurances, such as a friendly summary of the product's benefits.

For example, the customer shown in Figure 12–1 says: "I can't see how you can charge so much for this product." Even though the salesperson may have indicated the additional benefits that justify a higher price, the salesperson needs to restate the benefits using different wording to provide additional assurance. For example, "Our price is higher than company X's. But, the total cost of using our product over its lifetime is substantially lower because we used aged semiconductors to improve reliability."

Salespeople can detect a teaser objection by observing the customer's body language. When a customer's objection is minor, he or she will lean toward the salesperson, smile, and have good eye contact, open arms and hands, and uncrossed legs. Even though teaser objections are minor, they should not be taken lightly. A defensive or overconfident reaction can jeopardize the sale.

Acting Now

Buyers often object to making a decision *now*. In fact, many buyers believe postponing any action is an effective way to say no.

Salespeople expect to hear objections like the following: "I haven't made up my mind," "I want to think it over," "I'd like to talk it over with my partner," "See me on your next trip," "I'm not ready to buy," "I don't want to commit myself," "I think I'll wait a while," "I want to look around," "I'm waiting till my inventory gets down," "I want to turn in the old unit at the end of the season," and "Just leave me your literature—I'll study it and then let you know what we decide."

These objections are evidence the prospect has not been thoroughly sold. The real reason for postponing action may have to do with the price, the product, or one of a number of other problems.

Two types of stalls are passive and active. People who engage in passive stalling probably dislike making decisions. No matter how convinced they are of the product's value, these customers will attempt to postpone making a decision. These people need time to think through their doubts and uncertainties. Reassurance works better than pressure.

Customers who engage in active stalling seem to be favorable toward the product but balk at the last minute. These customers are not indecisive, they just need additional encouragement.

Nonverbal cues can indicate if a customer is passively or actively stalling. Passive stalling is shown by leaning away from the salesperson; tense, puzzled look on the face; crossed legs and arms; and fingers to lips or chin. Active stalling is indicated by leaning forward, friendly look on face, open arms and legs, and open palm gestures.[2] (See Figure 12–2.)

---

[2]Gerhard Gschwandtner and Pat Garnett, *Non-Verbal Selling Power* (Englewood Cliffs, N.J.: Prentice-Hall, 1985), pp. 162–64.

FIGURE 12–2
Passive and Active
Stalls

Cameramann International, Ltd. photos
Passive stall   Active stall

Misunder-
standings

Sometimes objections arise because customers do not understand the salesperson's presentation. The following exchange illustrates a misunderstanding objection:

> **Customer:**   I don't believe this drug will cure my patient's asthma.
> **Salesperson:**   Can you explain what you mean?
> **Customer:**   His asthma is incurable.
> **Salesperson:**   I realize our drug cannot cure asthma. It can only reduce the discomfort of asthma.

Misunderstandings frequently arise when customers are unfamiliar with technical terms, unaware of the unique capabilities of a product, or uncertain about benefits arising from service provided with the product, such as warranties.

Price

Regardless of the price asked for a product, somebody will object that it is too high, "out of line," or higher than that offered by a competitor. Other common price objections are, "I can't afford it," "I can't afford to spend that much right now," "I was looking for a cheaper model," "I don't care to invest that much—I'll use it only a short while," "I can beat your price on these items," "We can't make a reasonable profit if we have to pay that much for the merchandise," "We always get a special discount," and "I'm going to wait for prices to come down."

Though price objections occur more often than any other kind, they may be just masks to hide the real reason for the buyer's reluctance. An illustration of dealing with price objections is discussed at the conclusion of this chapter.

Product

Some common product objections are, "The quality is too poor," "I don't like the design," "It seems poorly constructed," "It is the wrong size," "I was looking for a lighter shade," "I don't think it will wear well," "I don't like the material," and "We prefer printed circuits."

Service

Buyers may be critical of the company's method of making adjustments, its delivery policy, its advisory or consulting staff, its maintenance contract, or the speed with which it makes service calls.

The salesperson who sells industrial machinery or office machines to regular customers may encounter such objections as "I can't get my machines repaired," "It takes too long to get a service person on the job," "Your 'experts' don't seem to know much about our problems," "We don't get maintenance help frequently enough," "Our last purchase was unsatisfactory, and we weren't satisfied with the adjustment," "It took a month for us to get our last order," and "Shutdown time is killing us."

Company

Industrial buyers and retail store buyers are vitally interested in the sales representative's company. It is important for them to be satisfied with the company's financial standing, personnel, business policies, and products.

Some buyers or prospective buyers ask these questions: "Isn't your company a new one in the field?" "Is it true your company lost money last year?" "How do I know you'll be in business next year?" "Your company isn't very well known, is it?" "Who does your designing?" "Can your company give us the credit we have been receiving from other companies?" "How do I know you can deliver on time?" These questions are evidence that the sales representative has a selling job to do.

Salespeople

Some salespeople's personalities may clash with those of their prospects. A wise salesperson knows that everything must be done to adjust his or her manner to please the prospect. However, there are times when it appears impossible to do business with some people. Prospects may object to a presentation or an appointment because they have taken a dislike to the salesperson.

If these prospects are quite candid, they may say: "I don't like to do business with you," or, "You're a pest—I don't have any time for you," or, "You and I will never be able to do business." More commonly the prospect shields the real reason and says: "We don't need any," or, "Sorry, we're stocked up," or, "I haven't time today to discuss your proposition."

Miscellaneous

Objections to price, product, service, company, acting now, and the salesperson's personality are usually the most serious kinds to be raised. However, objections cannot always be classified into these categories. Some additional objections include:

"I always buy from friends."
"My partner must be consulted."
"I'm not interested."
"I'm satisfied with the company with which we now deal."
"I see no reason for taking on another line."
"We have a reciprocity agreement with your competitor."
"We are all stocked up."
"We have no room for your line."
"There is no demand for your product."
"You'll have to see Mr. X."
"My brother-in-law is in the business."

Many of these objections can be handled effectively if the salesperson is prepared to answer them.[3]

WHEN DO BUYERS OBJECT?

If the sales process were to be broken into stages or parts, the salesperson could expect objections to occur at three stages.

Approach

The prospect may object to setting an appointment time or date to allow the salesperson to get started. This is especially true in selling services and ideas. Objections at this stage are not too serious if the prospect has been qualified properly. When using the cold canvass, the salesperson must expect objections at this stage and be prepared to meet them.

Presentation

Objections are usually raised to some points made in the presentation. Such objections may be evidence of the prospect's interest and may actually be desirable. It is easier to sell when the prospects object because the salespeople know where they stand and they are sure they have the prospect's attention and active interest. Some buyers let the salesperson

---

[3]Daniel Caust, "A Plan for Every Customer," *Sales & Marketing Management*, July 7, 1980, pp. 36–37.

deliver the entire sales talk without showing a reaction. In these circumstances, it is difficult to judge the effectiveness of the presentation.

Close

Objections may be offered when the close is attempted. Skill in handling objections is more important at this stage than at any other. If salespeople can answer objections satisfactorily in the first two stages but cannot overcome objections in the close, they will not make a sale. Knowing when objections are likely to occur and what these objections mean helps the salesperson prepare answers in advance so they will be ready for use when the need arises.

If too many objections occur, it is likely that significant selling points are being omitted in the presentation.

PREPARATION REQUIRED TO ANSWER OBJECTIONS

In order to overcome objections, some preliminary work can be done to help guarantee success. There are techniques that have proved successful in handling almost any kind of objection.

Develop a Positive Attitude

To handle objections effectively, there is no substitute for having the proper attitude. Proper attitude is shown by answering sincerely, refraining from arguing or contradicting, and welcoming—even inviting—objections. And by listening!

It is useless to put on a veneer of sincerity; buyers can see through it with amazing ease. If the buyer once gets the idea that the salesperson is talking for effect, it will be almost impossible for the salesperson to regain the buyer's confidence and respect. Sincerity is evidenced as much by the tone of voice and facial expressions as by the actual words spoken.

A successful advertising agency owner states: "I have always tried to sit on the same side of the table as my clients, to see problems through their eyes." The average buyer wants valid objections to be treated seriously. Buyers want their ideas to be respected, not belittled. They are looking for sympathetic understanding of their problems. Real objections are logical to the prospect, regardless of how irrational they may appear to the salesperson.

The salesperson must have the attitude of a helper, a counselor—and an adviser. To do this, it is necessary to treat the prospect as a friend, not a foe. Answering objections should not be a battle of wits. The salesperson's objective is not to win an argument. Arguments create heat and friction, and even when salespeople win an argument, they will probably lose the sale and the customer. A lost sale or customer is too big a price to pay for winning an argument.

There is always the temptation to prove the prospect wrong, to say, "I told you so," or, "I'm right and you're wrong." This kind of attitude invites debate. The salesperson is encouraging, perhaps even forcing, the prospect to defend a position regardless of the merits of the stand taken. Prestige is involved when prospects find their positions bluntly challenged. Most people try to defend their own opinions in these circumstances because they don't want to lose prestige. The sales presentation may then degenerate into a personal duel, which the salesperson cannot possibly win. Arguing with a prospect, contradicting a prospect, or showing belligerence toward a prospect is a negative and unwise attitude.

Real objections are sales opportunities. Ford Motor Company puts it this way, "Objections are signposts guiding you to what's really on the customer's mind."[4] To capitalize on these opportunities, salespeople must show they welcome any and all objections. They have to sincerely and convincingly make the prospect believe they are glad the objection has been raised. This attitude may be shown by remarks such as: "I see just what you mean. I'd probably feel the same way . . . ," "I'm glad you mentioned that, Mr. Atkinson . . . ," "That certainly is a wise comment, Ms. Smith, and I can see your problem . . . ," "If I were purchasing this product, I'd want an answer to that same question . . . ," "Tell me about it. . . ."

The sales representative must convince the buyer that the real objection raised is normal, logical, sensible, important, and deserving of a valid answer.

Truthfulness in dealing with prospects and customers is an absolute necessity for dignity, confidence, and continued relations. Alfred C. Fuller, the original Fuller Brush man, says, "It is the truth that makes men free, not only in their business lives but in their business concepts."[5]

| Anticipate Objections | Salespeople must know that, at some time, objections will be made to almost everything concerning their product, their company, or themselves. It is common sense to prepare answers to the objections certain to be raised because few salespeople can answer objections effectively on the spur of the moment. |

Many companies have drawn up lists of common objections. Effective answers are then prepared, and the salesperson is expected to know the objections and their answers before making sales calls.[6]

---

[4]*Retail Selling Course* (Dearborn, Mich.: Ford Motor Co.), syllabus.

[5]Alfred C. Fuller, *A Foot in the Door* (New York: McGraw-Hill, 1960), p. 175.

[6]See Daniel K. Weadock, "Your Troops Can Keep Control—and Close the Sale—by Anticipating Objections," *Sales & Marketing Management,* March 17, 1980, pp. 102–6.

Successful sales representatives may keep a loose-leaf notebook and record new objections as they are encountered along with any new ideas for handling them. Experience is "money in the bank," and it teaches salespeople which strategies work best with particular types of customers.

When salespeople know an objection is going to be raised and they have good answers ready, they can stop worrying about this particular problem. However, unanticipated or unanswerable objections can easily cause embarrassment and lost sales.

Forestall Objections

Good salespeople, after a period of experience and training, know that certain features of their products or services are vulnerable, are likely to be misunderstood, or are materially different from competitors' products. The salesperson's products may have limited patterns; may have a price that seems to be high; may not be accompanied by cash discounts; may have no service representatives in the immediate area; or may represent a new company in the field.

Some salespeople do such a good job of selling those features that appear at first glance to be obstacles to the sale that buyers change their minds without ever having to go on record as objecting to the feature and then having to change their minds. Other salespeople approach the problem by saying, "I guess you think this product is expensive, don't you? Well, let me show you how little it will really cost you to get the best." Buyers are more willing to change their thinking if they have not already stated a position they believe they must defend.

While not all objections can be forestalled, the major ones can easily be spotted and disposed of during a good sales presentation. Buyers are not likely to raise an objection that has been stated and answered.

Evaluate Objections

Salespeople can make a mistake by treating unfavorable comments about a product as objections. Consider the following exchange:

> **Customer:** "What is this going to cost me?"
>
> **Sales rep:** "Then you're concerned about the value you will receive for the dollar you will spend?"
>
> **Customer:** "No, I want to know what it's going to cost!"

The salesperson should have answered the question honestly and openly. Often, a salesperson selling a higher quality, higher priced product will expect comments and questions about price to be objections.

Objections may be classified as *real objections* and *excuses*. There are probably only two real objections to buying—people have no immediate need for the product or no money with which to buy it. Even these objections can often be handled effectively. The future may bring about a need, and credit may overcome lack of money.

If they do a good job of qualifying prospects, salespeople will encounter more excuses than real objections. But it is important to distinguish between the two because the method of handling them may differ.

An excuse for not buying is seldom stated as, "I don't have any reason—I just don't want to buy." It is more common for the buyer or prospect to give a reason, which may appear at first to be a real objection. "I don't have the money" may actually be an excuse. "I can't use your product" may be an excuse. The tone of voice or the nature of the reason may be evidence that the prospect is not offering a sincere objection.

There is no exact formula to use in separating excuses from real objections. The circumstances will usually be a clue to the answer. In a cold canvass the prospect may say, "I'm sorry, I don't have any money," and the salesperson may conclude that the prospect doesn't want to hear the presentation. However, if a complete presentation has been made, and data on the prospect have been gathered through observation and questioning, the same reason may be a valid one. Salespeople must rely on observation, questioning, their knowledge of why people buy, and their experience to determine the validity of the reason offered for not buying.

Some buyers agree to everything said or make no comment. In these circumstances, if the buyer refuses to buy, the salesperson must uncover the reason. When objections are stated, the salesperson is in a position to answer them; but when they are not stated, it is harder to remove the concealed causes for not buying.

The concealed objections may be brought into the open by observing how prospects react to the sales presentation. Buyers' interest may lag after they hear the price or an explanation of some product feature. The experienced salesperson, seeing these changes in the prospect's attitude, should stop and review the explanation or go through the demonstration again for reemphasis and clarity.

By the manner in which they handle the product, prospects may show they are dissatisfied. They may examine it carefully and then put it aside. This action may imply, "It doesn't look too strong to me," or, "We couldn't sell anything constructed like this," or, "It's the wrong style or color."

It may be appropriate to ask questions when these implications exist. Salespeople may say, "Did you notice the leather lining in that shoe?" Retail store buyers may state an objection at this point or may remark that they did notice the lining. If buyers do not state an objection and there is reason to believe they are not satisfied, salespeople may ask, "What do you think of the lining of that shoe?" If the answer is, "It looks all right to me," the tone of voice will probably be an indication as to how well satisfied they are. More than likely, if the lining is the source of the real objection, buyers will state their objection. Salespeople should learn to ask information-seeking questions and then stop and listen for both obvious and subtle clues.

Open-ended questions that encourage the prospect to *talk more* include: "Would you like to tell me about it?" "Why is that?" "Can we talk more about that?" "Can we explore that further?"

It is important to remember that sales representatives really never sell anybody anything. What they do is *help* a lot of people to *buy*. Help is provided by asking the right kinds of questions—questions that customers and prospects have to ask themselves and answer before they are going to buy.

Good salespeople want to get a reaction from buyers by asking if they understand certain phases of the proposition. As an answer is obtained on each phase, they try to secure agreement on that phase. They thereby accumulate a series of agreements that lead toward a successful close. For example, the sales representative who is trying to sell the prospect on leasing industrial equipment asks: "Do you understand the terms of the lease? Let's take it again point by point. First, we agree to service the equipment within 24 hours after we receive your call. However, in most cases we can handle emergency calls in an hour or two. Are there any questions about this point? Will this provision satisfy your requirements? Second, we agree to replace parts without labor cost to you. That's a fair agreement, isn't it?" If salespeople can get agreement on each point, they eliminate objections that have not been stated. If they fail to secure agreement, the prospect objects, and then the salespeople must answer that objection before going on.

If salespeople try to uncover the real objection and fail, they may admit failure and say to the prospect, "Evidently I have overlooked some aspect in acquainting you with the merits of our products. You still seem to have some doubt in your mind. Do you have a specific question? I believe that I can answer it for you." This procedure may help salespeople get the prospect to state the real objection. Normally, this should be used only as a last resort.

When making repeat calls, it may be inadvisable to try to uncover the real objection during the initial interview. Succeeding calls may afford the opportunity to discover the true reason the prospect is reluctant to buy. Persistence is good only as long as the prospect is gracious about it.

Time the Answer

There are two schools of thought on when to answer a prospect's excuse. Some people think it best to ignore an excuse; that is, unless the prospect mentions it repeatedly. Others believe any reason for not buying should be answered immediately.

The United States Rubber Company makes this recommendation to its distributor sales representatives who encounter the objection, "Your tire is more expensive than other tires":

> From the moment that they [the customers] voice that objection, they want an answer. If you pass over the objection and go on to another portion of your sales presentation, you can be reasonably certain that you have left your customers behind, because they are still thinking of that objection.[7]

Judgment must be exercised in determining whether to ignore an excuse or to answer it immediately. It is always desirable to *recognize* an excuse, whether or not the *answer* is delayed. Otherwise, the impression may be given that high pressure is being applied.

If the reason stated is a real objection, it must be answered immediately. The successful closing of a sale is usually the result of a series of approvals by the customer. So long as a real objection remains unanswered, there is no accumulation of positive responses, making a close more difficult.

Under certain circumstances, it is advisable to postpone answering a valid objection. This may be desirable when price objections occur early in the interview. The technique to be followed is suggested later in this chapter. It is just as important to know when to answer as it is to know what to say.

Build a Skill

A large part of the job of selling is built on skill in the use of techniques and methods. This is true particularly in demonstrating, delivering the sales presentation, answering objections, and closing the sale. Skill can be developed only through much hard work and intelligent practice. The baseball player, golfer, and swimmer know that having knowledge of what to do is not enough. Practice in selling perfects the skill to the point where it is effective, and it then becomes a natural part of the sales representative's equipment.

Some salespeople develop a skill in answering objections by keeping a list of all the objections they encounter. Each objection is written on one side of a three-by-five-inch card, with the answer on the reverse side. They practice the answers until they can state them with ease and conviction. Other salespeople rehearse until they have developed the right tone, the right voice inflection, and the right emphasis for answers to objections. The good salesperson invests whatever time and effort are necessary to make such answers valid and effective.

---

[7]"The Customer Objects," Distributor Training Conference no. 24 (Detroit: United States Rubber Co.), p. 7.

EFFECTIVE METHODS AND TECHNIQUES FOR HANDLING OBJECTIONS

Before discussing specific methods and techniques for overcoming objections, it is necessary to say again that there is no one foolproof method or technique for answering all objections successfully. Some prospects are never going to be convinced.

Good methods and techniques are designed to improve the batting average. That is, more objections will be answered satisfactorily if sound techniques are used. Like a baseball player, a salesperson does not expect to bat 1,000; but good techniques can raise the batting average from .200 to .300, which is a 50 percent increase and may be the difference between a poor producer and a top producer.

In some instances, it may not be wise to spend much time trying to convince the prospect. For example, when an insurance underwriter contacts a prospect who says, "I don't believe in insurance," it may be better to spend the available time calling on some of the vast number of people who do.

Salespeople usually try to supply answers that satisfy prospects and cause them to buy or to handle prospect's objections in such a way that a return call will be welcomed.

Relax and Listen—Do Not Interrupt

One word of caution is necessary when employing any technique—*listen first,* then answer the objection. Allow the prospect to state a position completely. Appropriate questions may help the prospect clarify the objection so there is no misunderstanding. Do not interrupt the buyer to provide an answer even though it may be apparent what objection is to be stated.

Too many salespeople are guilty of conducting conversations somewhat like the following:

> **Salesperson:**   Mr. Clark, from a survey of your operations, I'm convinced you're now spending more money repairing your own motors than you would having *us* do the job for you . . . and really do it *right!*
>
> **Customer:**   I wonder if we are not doing it right *ourselves.* Your repair service may be good . . . but after all, you don't have to be exactly an electrical genius in order to be able to . . .
>
> **Salesperson:**   Just a minute now! Pardon me for interrupting . . . but there's a point I'd like to make right there! It isn't a *matter* of anyone being a genius. It's a matter of having a heavy investment of special motor repair equipment and supplies like vacuum impregnating tanks . . . lathes for banding armatures, boring bearings, turning new shafts.

> **Customer:**   Yeah . . . but you don't understand my point. What I'm driving at . . .
>
> **Salesperson:**   I *know* what you're driving at . . . and I assure you you're wrong! You forget that even if your own workers *are* smart cookies, they just can't do high-quality work without a lot of special equipment. . . .
>
> **Customer:**   But you *still* don't get my point! The idea I'm trying to get off my chest . . . if I can make myself clear on this fourth attempt . . . is this. Our maintenance workers that we now have doing motor repair work. . . .
>
> **Salesperson:**   . . . could more profitably spend their time on plant *troubleshooting!* Right?
>
> **Customer:**   That isn't what I was going to say! I was trying to say that *between* their trouble jobs . . . instead of just sitting around and shooting the bull. . . .
>
> **Salesperson:**   Now *wait* a minute, Mr. Clark. Wait jus-s-t a minute! Let ME get a word in here! If you've got any notion that a good motor rewinding job can be done with somebody's left hand on an odd-moment basis, you got another think coming. And my survey here will *prove* it! Now LISTEN![8]

This type of interruption and attitude is likely to cause a quick end to the interview.

The following six methods have been used successfully in varied fields of selling.

Agree and Counter

This method is often called the *yes-but method*. Its use has been successful because it involves a psychologically sound approach. The edge is taken off an objection when the salesperson appears to agree with the prospect. Prospects expect salespeople to disagree; instead, salespeople who recognize that the objection is offered sincerely will be careful to respect the prospect's view. This avoids a direct contradiction and confrontation. To begin an answer, it is good for a salesperson to agree with the prospect to the extent that the agreement does not weaken the salesperson's position.[9] In Selling Scenario 12–1, Mortimer Adler describes how he acknowledged and overcame a banker's objection to making a loan.

---

[8]*Increase Your Selling Skill* (Pittsburgh: Westinghouse Electric Corp.), sec. 3, pp. 4–5.

[9]For an interesting contrary opinion, see Dan Weadock, "Saying 'Yes . . . but' Is Really No Way to Overcome a Buyer's Objection," *Sales & Marketing Management,* October 15, 1979, pp. 92–96.

Selling Scenario 12–1

PHILOSOPHY SELLS

 Mortimer Adler, philosopher, educator, author, and chairman of the editorial board of the *Encyclopaedia Britannica,* describes how he overcame an objection posed by a banker who was considering a loan to *Encyclopaedia Britannica* for the production of *Great Books of the Western World* and *Syntopicon:*

> The banker came to that meeting highly skeptical of the salability of the product on which the company was spending so much money, and especially skeptical about this strange thing called the *Syntopicon* that threatened to consume more than a million dollars—a lot of money in those days—before it was completed. What good would the *Syntopicon* do anybody that might arouse their desire to purchase the set with the *Syntopicon* attached to it? "I, for example, am interested in buying and selling," the banker said, "and if I went to the *Syntopicon's* inventory of 102 great ideas, would I find one on salesmanship?"
>
> That stumped me for a moment because, of course, the word "salesmanship" does not appear among the names of the 102 great ideas, nor does it even appear in the list of 1,800 subordinate terms that provide an alphabetical index referring to aspects of the 102 great ones. I got over being stumped by asking him a question.
>
> Did he agree that to sell anybody anything one must know how to persuade them to buy what one wanted to sell? He agreed at once. I then clinched the matter by telling him that one of the 102 great ideas is rhetoric, which is concerned with persuasion, and that, if he consulted the *Syntopicon's* chapter on that idea, he would find many extremely helpful passages in that chapter, even though none of the great authors cited there ever used the word "salesmanship."
>
> That was all I had to do to put an end to the banker's qualms about the money being spent on the production of the *Syntopicon.* I had sold him on it.

Source: Adapted from Mortimer Adler, *How to Speak/How to Listen* (New York: Macmillan, 1982).

After agreeing, the salesperson should proceed to mention certain points the prospect either has forgotten or is not aware of. Skill is necessary when introducing the part of the answer followed by *but.* For example, car salespeople may encounter this objection: "I don't like the new automatic transmission on your car." One way to answer is, "You know, Mr. Smith, I felt that way too when I first learned the way it operates, *but* there is really nothing new about it. It is standard for many models that have been on the market for several years." The salesperson has agreed that the reaction of the prospect is logical, but then proceeds to refute the objection by stating there is nothing new about the transmission. In effect, the answer is, "Yes, but you are wrong. It isn't new." The whole purpose of the yes-but method has been defeated.

A better answer to the same objection might be "*Yes*, Mr. Smith, I know exactly how you feel. We all need to accept many new ideas, don't we? *But,* did you know that this transmission is very convenient? Think how handy it would be if you had to stop on an upgrade. Now let me show you some other new features you will like. . . ."

It is not always necessary to use the words *yes* and *but*. The important features of the method are that salespeople recognize the position of the customer who makes the objection, and they then continue by introducing new evidence or a new thought. For example, the objection may take this form: "I think your machines cost too much." An answer might be phrased as follows: "I know you don't want to pay more for a product than you think it's worth. That's why I'm sure you will see that you are getting your money's worth from our machines. You see, the initial expense may be slightly more than for ordinary competitive machines, and this is why. . . ."

Some beginning phrases to use with the yes-but method are:

> I can understand why you feel that way, Ms. Prospect. On the other hand. . . .
>
> Mr. Prospect, there is a lot of truth in what you say. However, have you ever considered this angle? . . .
>
> I would have made that same statement myself two years ago, Mrs. Prospect. Now, let me tell you what I found out. . . .
>
> You know, a customer made that same statement last week, Mr. Prospect. Let me tell you what we finally agreed upon. . . .

Turn Objections into Reasons for Buying

This method is effective when the prospect offers excuses for not wanting to listen to the presentation. It is sometimes called the *boomerang method* of answering objections.

A sales representative calling on the owner of a restaurant has just made a point of the pennies involved in the use of paper cups instead of glassware when serving customers.

The owner may offer an objection such as, "That penny stuff sounds fine, young fellow—until you add it all up. With all the customers I serve every day, I can just imagine my paper cup bill. No, siree!"[10] An effective

---

[10]Adapted from *Successful Selling* (Toledo, Ohio: Lily-Tulip Cup Division of Owens-Illinois), p. 19.

reply and analysis is provided in the company sales manual of a large corporation.

Suggested Reply:	Analysis
1. I know how you feel, Mr. Prospect (*said sincerely, courteously*).	1–2. Consideration for feelings and respect for viewpoint.
2. And you're perfectly right.	
3. That cup bill certainly will add up.	3. Repetition of prospect's own words *add up* appeals to prospect's ego.
4. But then so will your dollar volume! (*Enthusiastically.*)	4–6. The objection is turned into a sales point by citing the benefits of the salesperson's product insofar as it applies to the specific objection made.
5. That is only natural, since a faster service	
6. Will help you serve more people than ever before.	
7. To this increased dollar volume that you'll get from faster service, add the savings of labor, towels, soap, brushes, etc.—savings that come about automatically once glasswashing is eliminated—and I know you'll agree that Lily Cups, far from being expensive, are truly a profitable investment.	7. Repetition of more benefits.
8. You can begin this week to collect the dividends that Lily Cups will pay you.	8. Suggestion that a start be made *now* to collect the rewards of immediate installment.[11]

If the prospect suggests, "I'm too busy to see you," the salesperson may answer, "I know you are a busy man, Mr. Smith, and that's the reason I have called. I have a service that is designed for the use of busy executives." If the prospect remarks, "I can't afford it," the salesperson may be able to show how the prospect cannot afford to be without the product or service.

A prospect may voice this objection, "Your deep freezer is too large—it has too much storage capacity for us." If the salesperson believes the size is appropriate for the buyer's needs, the answer may be: "Yes, Ms. Akin, it would appear that our freezer has some excess storage capacity for your needs. However, I'm sure you realize that one big advantage of owning a deep-freeze unit is that you can store a large supply of frozen foods. You can buy in large quantities, and you can buy during the period of most favorable prices. In other words, what might appear to be extra space is really the feature that provides you the opportunity to save money." To a farmer or a sports enthusiast, extra storage could be an important factor.

This method, when used skillfully, is effective in overcoming reasons for not buying based on the prospect's lack of knowledge.

---

[11]Ibid., p. 20 (adapted).

Ask "Why?" or Ask Specific Questions

This method is often used to separate excuses from real objections. It may also be used to overcome objections.

The inexperienced salesperson may be too quick to answer an objection that seems to be real. If the prospect expresses a major disagreement, the salesperson should ask questions in order to narrow the objection to specific points. Generalized objections are difficult to answer. It is easy to get to the heart of the objection by asking, "Why?" Once the objection is concrete and definite, it can be answered.

For example, the prospect may say, "I don't like to do business with your company." A good answer is, "What is it that you don't like about our firm?" The prospect's answer may indicate that there has been a misunderstanding, and the salesperson can then clear it up. Or, in a retail store the prospect may say, "I don't like the appearance of your stoves." An appropriate question is, "Why do you object to the appearance of our stoves, Mrs. Smith?" The prospect's objection may be to some relatively minor point that can be changed.

Another value of the "why" method, especially in cases where the objection is not too serious, is that some objections do not sound very valid once they have been put into words. The opportunity to talk about an objection gives the prospect a chance to evaluate it. The prospect may conclude, without admitting it, that the objection is inconsequential.

Some salespeople use the "why" method to lead prospects to answer their own objection. For example, the prospect for industrial equipment may say, "I can get a machine much cheaper." A good reply is, "Mr. Brown, what is your basis for buying machinery? Do you base your decision solely upon original cost?" The answer is likely to be, "No, of course I am interested in how long it will last and how well it will do the job." The salesperson may say, "Would you say the machinery you now have in your plant is the least expensive you could buy?" The probable answer is, "No, I guess other makes and models are available at a lesser cost, but we must have machines that will stand up and that will do a job economically and efficiently." Questioning may be continued until the prospect answers his or her own objections. Any attempt, however, to have prospects prove themselves wrong against their will is not likely to result in a sale. People who are *forced* to agree seldom *actually* change their minds.

The question or "why" method is particularly successful in handling the price objection and in helping to close the sale. When the reason for not buying is, "I think your price is too high," a good answer is, "What do you think is a fair price?" or "How much too high?" It may be possible to show how quantity discounts or cash discounts will bring the price to the desired level; or how a model with fewer or different accessories will cost less. Of course, it would be unwise to imply that prices can be reduced just because the buyer thinks they are too high. If a price reduction is not possible through the application of discounts, the salesperson must be able to justify the price differential.

Sometimes it may be best to draw out the customer by asking, "I take it you are concerned over the initial cost of my product because you are not sure whether the cost is justified in terms of what the product can do and, in the long run, how much it can save. Is that a fair statement of your feelings?" This type of question demonstrates a sincere respect for the prospect's objection, and at the same time it offers the sales representative a smooth, logical opening for strengthening the presentation or restating the benefits of the product.[12]

An appropriate question may help make it easier to close the sale. The question may be, "Is that your only objection to our product?" or "Are you willing to buy if I can satisfy you regarding your price objection?" Of course, the tone and manner of asking the question are important.

The questions used to overcome objections are the same types of questions used to collect information. The various types of questions are discussed in Chapter 6 and illustrated below:

Directive question
Why do you prefer the IBM PC to our personal computer?
How much can you save using our electronic typewriters?

Reflective question
You say our computers are not user friendly?

Elaboration question
Can you tell me more about that?

Evaluation question
How do you feel about our warranty?

Admit Valid Objections and Offset

Certain objections raised by the buyer may be valid, and it may be wise to admit such objections and then proceed to show the compensating advantages. This method is similar to the agree and counter method.

A car buyer may say: "I'm not interested in an eight-cylinder car. I'm looking for a good six-cylinder or four-cylinder car because the eights use too much gasoline." A reply may be: "Yes, Ms. Jacobs, eight-cylinder cars often do use more gasoline than six-cylinder or four-cylinder cars. However, just think of these advantages: You will be the owner of a larger, easier-riding car with more reserve power; you'll have more storage capacity; you get more comfort; you'll enjoy a quieter, safer ride; and you are less fatigued on long trips. . . . Don't you believe these advantages are worth a larger expenditure for gasoline?"

The insurance prospect may say, "I want straight term insurance to cover my needs on this mortgage, but your company requires me to buy some ordinary life in order to get mortgage protection." If this is true, little can be done to change the company's requirement, and it is therefore

---

[12]Don Meisel, "Add Salespower! Ask Questions," *Industrial Distribution,* November 1976, p. 64.

necessary to show the compensating features of the policy. For example: "Yes, Mr. Howard, it is true we write a policy that includes a base amount of ordinary life insurance. Let me show you what this means to you— you will have a cash value at the end of 20 years; or you can borrow on your policy; and you will have life insurance when your mortgage is paid for. You will be able to use some money about that time, won't you?"

Almost every product has some advantages and some disadvantages when compared with competing products.

Postpone the Answer

In the early part of a sales presentation, the prospect may raise objections the salesperson would prefer to answer later in the presentation. When this situation occurs, the salesperson should say, "That's a good point. If you don't mind, let's postpone the answer until later. I have some information I am sure will satisfy you." The sales representative may then proceed with the presentation until the point is reached at which the objection can best be answered. The prospect will seldom refuse the request if the sales representative appears to be acting in good faith.

Postponing the answer to a prospect's objection makes it possible for the salesperson to give a more effective presentation. When too much time is spent answering objections, it is hard to make a coherent presentation. The salesperson who is frequently diverted with objections cannot make a strong presentation. Some objections can be answered best when they occur; others can be handled best by delaying the answer. Experience is the sales representative's working capital—draw on it!

Where the objection is really an excuse, postponing an answer provides a chance to classify the reason. If the reason is not stated again later in the presentation, it is probably an excuse.

Deny the Objection

At times salespeople face objections based on incomplete or inaccurate information. The objections should be responded to by providing information or correcting facts as illustrated below:

> **Customer:**   I am not going to buy your chain saws for my store. Phil Jones at Dexter says they break down after a month.
>
> **Salesperson:**   I can understand how you feel. No one wants to carry unreliable chain saws. But don't think Mr. Jones has the correct information on our chain saws. We build the most reliable chain saws in the industry, and we just announced a new, three-year warranty to back up this claim.

The direct denial approach must be used with caution. It is only appropriate when salespeople have facts to back up the denial.

FIGURE 12–3
Value Must Be
Greater than Cost

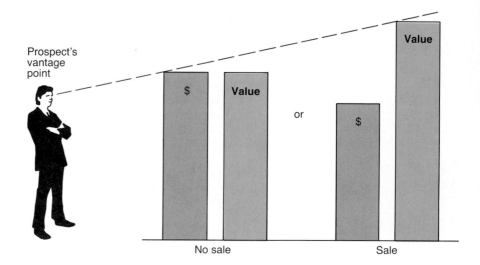

ILLUSTRA-
TIONS OF
COMMON
OBJECTIONS

Price
Objections

A survey of over 1,000 salespeople found that price was the most frequently mentioned obstacle to making a sale. About 60 percent of the salespeople indicated price was the major objection they faced.[13]

Salespeople need to prepare for price objections. Time should not be spent discussing price until the product value has been established. The price a prospect is willing to pay is determined by the value expected. The salesperson should build value to a point at which it is greater than the price asked. This cannot be accomplished, as a rule, during the early stages of the presentation.

If the prospect sees price to be greater than value received, there will be no sale. On the other hand, if the prospect can see value to be greater than price, a sale is a good possibility. This is shown graphically in Figure 12–3.

Price objections are best handled with a two-step approach. First, the salesperson should try to look at the objection from the customer's viewpoint. Some questions that can be used to better understand the customer's perspective are:

Too high in what respect, Mr. Jones?

Would you mind telling me why you think my price is too high?

Could you tell me how much we are out of line?

[13]"What Are the Major Sales Resistances Faced by Salespeople?" Laboratory of Advertising Performance, McGraw-Hill Research, 1979.

We are usually quite competitive on this model, so I am surprised you find our price high. Are the quotes you have for the same size engine?

You say you have a lower bid? I wonder if we are comparing apples with apples. Let's take a minute to find out?

After learning more about the customer's perspective, the next step is to sell value and quality rather than price. All customers are interested in buying cheaper products if they believe they will receive the same benefits. However, many customers are willing to pay more for higher quality when the quality benefits and features are pointed out to them. Many high-quality products are similar in appearance to lower-quality products; thus, salespeople need to emphasize the features that command a price difference.

Just telling customers about quality and value is not enough. Customers must be shown. Top salespeople visually dramatize the quality and value of their products by demonstrating them, by showing test results and quality control procedures, and by using case histories and testimonials.

Value is often provided by intangible features. Some of these features are:

1. Services. Most customers will buy when they see it will be to their advantage to buy, and price alone is not the only advantage. Good service in the form of faster deliveries, technical advice, and field assistance are but a few of the examples that can spell value, savings, and profits to a customer.

2. Company reputation. When a customer is tempted to buy on price alone, salespeople can emphasize the importance of having a thoroughly reliable source of supply—the salesperson's company. It has been demonstrated time and again that quality is measured by the reputation of the company behind it.

3. The salesperson. Customers value salespeople who go out of their way to help them with their problems and promotions— salespeople who keep their word and follow through when they start something. These services are very valuable to customers.

Stalling Objection

Another common objection arises when the customer says, "I want to think it over." One approach for handling this objection is illustrated on the following page:

Customer: I want to think this over. I can't make a decision now! [*Salesperson listens to customer.*]

Salesperson: I understand how you feel. Many of my customers have felt the same way before they decided to buy our product. [*Salesperson offers a softening statement.*] And you probably have several questions you still need to have answered before you make a decision, isn't that right? [*Salesperson rephrases the objection.*]

Customer: Yes, that's right!

Salesperson: Let's make a list of some of them. Which one of these is actually the one that keeps you from going ahead? [*Salesperson moves toward answering the objection and closing.*]

A SUGGESTED PLAN

Salespeople should develop a procedure to follow when answering objections. The following steps can be applied and adapted to most fields of selling:

1. Listen carefully—don't interrupt—let prospect talk.
2. Repeat the prospect's objection. *Make sure the objection is understood.* Ask questions to permit the prospect to clarify objections. Acknowledge the apparent soundness of the prospect's opinion. In other words, agree as far as possible with the prospect's thinking before providing an answer.
3. Evaluate the objection. Determine whether the reason for not buying is a real objection or an excuse. Answer a real objection immediately, if possible. Ignore an excuse or seek more information to identify the real objection.
4. Decide on the methods or techniques to use in answering the objection. Some factors to be considered are the phase of the sales process in which the objection is raised; the mood, or frame of mind, evidenced by the prospect; the reason for the objection; and the number of times the reason is advanced.
5. Get a commitment from prospects. The answer to any objection must satisfy them if a sale is to result. Get them to agree that their objection has been answered.
6. Try a trial close. If an objection is raised when the close is attempted, try to close immediately after answering the objection to the satisfaction of the prospect.
7. Continue with the sales presentation. If the trial close is unsuccessful, continue the presentation until another close opportunity presents itself.

Whenever possible, objections should be answered briefly, and they should not be built into major obstacles by spending an unnecessary amount of time on the answers.

SUMMARY

Handling objections successfully is a vital part of a salesperson's responsibility. Objections are to be expected, even welcomed, and they must be handled with skill and empathy.

Buyers object for psychological and real or imagined reasons. Value received must be established before a buyer is willing to exchange money for benefits. Value may be related to the price, product, or service.

Objections may be offered at any time in the sales presentation, but the greatest skill must be exercised when they occur at the close attempt. Preparation is essential in order to both anticipate and develop effective techniques in overcoming objections. A well-answered objection may provide an excellent opportunity to attempt a trial close. The salesperson's attitude, ability to anticipate, skill in forestalling, insight in separating *real objections* from *excuses,* timing of the answer, and willingness to build a solid skill all are important to the success of the professional salesperson.

Effective techniques are available, and their success has been proven. Sensitivity in choosing the right techniques is vital, and there is no substitute for development of their skillful use. A plan should be developed so nothing is left to chance. As a result, the salesperson will have no surprises when attempting to overcome objections.

QUESTIONS AND PROBLEMS

1. Sales representatives often find it necessary to get through a "screen," such as a receptionist, secretary, or assistant, to reach the decision maker. How would you answer the following objections from a screen:
   a. I'm sorry, but Mr. Harris is too busy right now.
   b. We're cutting back on expenditures.
   c. Could you just leave some literature?
   d. A representative of your company was here recently.
   e. I really don't think we can afford your equipment.
2. Illustrate one way to handle each of the following objections:
   a. During a demonstration the customer says, "You know, I really like your competitor's model."
   b. After a sales presentation the prospect says, "You have a good product. Thanks for your time, and if we decide to buy, I'll give you a call."
   c. After the salesperson answers an objection, the prospect remarks, "I guess your product is all right; but—well, I don't think I need one just now. Thanks a lot."
   d. After a thorough presentation the prospect answers, "No, I'm sorry, we just can't afford it."

    e. After the customer says, "Oh, no! That's really too much money. I've been looking at the same product downtown, and I can buy it at a much lower price."

3. Don Betando spent considerable time working with a prospective buyer. He thought a good order would be forthcoming on his next call. A portion of his conversation with the buyer went as follows:

   Buyer: You know, I like your terms and the styling of your product. But how can I be sure the small parts will hold up and be available?

   Don: We've never had any complaints on the parts, and I'm sure they will be easily available.

   Buyer: You are sure of that?

   Don: Well, I've never heard of any problems.

   The buyer didn't seem convinced, began looking at some of the papers on his desk, and didn't look up.

   Buyer: I'll let you know later what I plan to do. Thanks for dropping by.

   Can you improve on Don's answer? Suggest a more appropriate reply.

4. A common mistake made by sales representatives is to assume a customer's question is an objection. Consider the following:

   Customer: What is this going to cost me?

   Sales rep: Then you're concerned about the value you'll receive for the dollar you intend to spend?

   Customer: No, I want to know what it's going to cost!

   What should the sales representative have done differently?

5. If you believe the prospect isn't giving you the real objection, you may say, "In addition to that, Mr. Prospect, what other reasons have you? Isn't there something else behind your refusal to buy?" What could an answer to these questions accomplish?

6. Salespeople must decide whether to take an objection seriously. If customers make an objection merely because they believe they have to say something or in order to stall, what action should be taken and what dangers are involved?

7. Indicate the appropriate action for the sales representative who encounters the following customer attitudes:

   a. I like the things this copier can do if it really does them. It's kind of hard to believe it'll give me reliable service with all these things that could go wrong.

   b. Let me be plain. Your company's reputation precedes you in this office. I've had more trouble with your machines than you would care to hear.

    c. That sounds fine. But there's really no reason to get rid of the copier I've got. It works well enough for anything I use it for.

    d. I see what you're saying. This machine you're talking about could end up saving us some time and money.

8. You are planning to work part time during the summer, gaining experience through door-to-door selling. You plan to sell food products and are to take over a route and sell quality groceries. The company you will represent guarantees its products, offers credit, provides premiums for buyers, and requires its salespeople to call on customers regularly. Make a list of the objections you may expect to encounter. What can you do to meet these objections effectively?

9. It has been said objections should be anticipated. How could you turn an anticipated objection into a sales point in the following circumstance: You are showing a residence to a potential buyer, and you anticipate the prospect will say the kitchen is too small.

10. With more and more opportunities for people to buy products at a discount, how would you answer prospects who tell you they can buy your product at a discount?

11. The purpose when handling objections is to cause prospects to change their minds without irritating and offending them. Do you believe there are different ways to handle the following kinds of prospects: (1) those who present a point of view; (2) those who have strong opinions; (3) those who have biases or prejudices? How would your technique differ in each case?

12. You have been showing boudoir lamps to a young married couple. The wife wants to replace a lamp she had before they were married. Company is coming for the weekend, and she wants her guest room to look especially nice. She's particularly interested in one of the dainty lamps you have shown. Turning to her husband, she remarks, "Honey, I just love this one!" Her husband says, "Well, if that's what you want, OK. How much is it?"

    You reply, "This one is $89.95." The husband exclaims, "For that little thing!!!"

    What should you say or do?

13. It is generally agreed that it is difficult to determine the *real* reason some customers or prospects habitually refuse to give the real reason. They offer many reasons merely to disguise the true reason. Before a sale can be closed, the exact reason for not buying must be determined, and then it must be answered to the prospect's satisfaction. It does little good to answer excuses satisfactorily because they are not the real hurdles to be overcome. If a customer gives you several reasons for not buying your product, how can you determine whether the real reason has

been stated? What technique would help uncover the real objection?

14. When you make your first sales call on a new prospect, you know one of your major tasks is to reduce the prospect's resistance. Negative psychological factors exist in the minds of all prospects, simply because they are human beings. A knowledge of these attitudes and emotions is certain to help improve your ratio of sales to calls. What are some negative psychological forces that can be anticipated in most buyers? What can be done about them?

PROJECTS

1. Discuss a controversial topic with fellow students or friends—politics, religion, the environment, draft registration, equal rights for women, the nuclear freeze, or some other topic of your choice. Experiment by using a variety of techniques to disagree with the statements they make. Write a one-page report on which techniques were effective and ineffective.

2. Write a 200-word explanation of the need for people to "save face" or what "empathy" means to you.

3. Select a product you intend to buy in the near future. Make a list of the objections you are likely to raise. List the objections in one column and the answers in another.

CASE PROBLEMS

Case 12–1   Pen and Pencil, Inc.

It is Monday morning. You are a sales representative for Pen and Pencil, located in Dayton, Ohio. You have an appointment with Krista Carlson of Ralston Foods, a large user of writing pens in the food industry. This is your first call on Ralston.

Ms. Flair, the receptionist, indicates there will be a wait. When you enter Ms. Carlson's office, she appears businesslike and seems pressed for time. You say good morning and then introduce yourself.

You start your sales interview by saying, "I'd like to explore with you how we can reduce your expenses of writing instruments. What brand of pens do you buy currently?" Ms. Carlson indicates Ralston Foods is using Easywrite pens.

You proceed to question Ms. Carlson about her company's needs and about its evaluation of the Easywrite pen. You take notes, and you provide ample opportunity for Ms. Carlson to explain what experiences she and the company's employees have had with the pens.

It develops that the employees in the Ralston Foods offices have experienced some leakage and skipping of Easywrite pens. On further questioning and allowing plenty of opportunity for Ms. Carlson to talk, you find out Ralston Foods' 300 employees can go into the stockroom and take a handful of supplies whenever they wish. This encourages some employees to take two or three pens at a time—a practice that could be expensive.

To make certain you understand the situation, you attempt to summarize the key problems you and Ms. Carlson have discussed: Orders are being placed more frequently than should be necessary; Easywrite pens occasionally leak and they skip quite often; employees are continually picking up new pens, which costs money. Ms. Carlson agrees this is an accurate summary.

Questions

1. Suggest answers to the following objections that occurred at different times during the sales interview:
   a. Some important things have suddenly come up. Can we make this appointment at another time?
   b. I have too much pressure on me to keep costs down.
   c. Your service has a bad reputation.
   d. I don't care to do business with your firm now.
   e. Look, we have been having considerable success with our present pen for the past three years. Why should we make a change now?
   f. It won't work. I don't think you understand our problem. Our situation is completely different from everybody else's.
   g. That sounds good in theory, but these things never seem to work out in practice. I don't think that idea will work.
   h. Business has been really slow lately.
2. Summarize your philosophy of the best way to answer objections.
3. Distinguish between a "sales interview" and a "sales presentation."

Case 12–2   Florida Farm Supply Co.

Recently the Florida Farm Supply Co. decided to start manufacturing and distributing linings to be used to line crates in which fresh produce is shipped to market. It is important for fresh produce to remain in good condition between the time it's harvested and the time it gets to the consumer.

Prospective users for the linings are large growers of vegetables, such as lettuce, celery, endive, cauliflower, and broccoli, which may be shipped to distant markets. Other potential prospects are packers who buy the produce from growers and repack it; the packers are interested in getting the produce to the market in top condition. A third group of prospects are chain-store buying groups that make volume purchases of produce, pack it, and ship it to their warehouses for retail distribution; these buyers have a big stake in maximum protection. All of these prospects are located in or near the Salinas Valley, the San Joaquin Valley, and the Imperial Valley in California, as well as in Arizona, Texas, and the Northwest.

The Florida Farm Supply Co. has investigated the competition thoroughly and has found a real need exists for a lining that will overcome the difficulties encountered by shippers when using the standard wet-strength papers and the standard waxed papers. Aluminum foil produced by foil manufacturers on the West Coast was introduced to overcome the difficulties mentioned by the shippers. However, upon questioning the shippers, Florida Farm Supply Co. found the following objections were raised about the use of foil as a liner: The foil sheets were difficult to separate and to place in the crates when packers worked rapidly; the foil sheets tended to tear if they were not handled carefully; and the foil sheets, if punctured by sharp corners when the crates were handled, tended to lose some of their effectiveness.

The Florida Farm Supply Co. believed it could manufacture a type of foil sheet that would overcome the difficulties mentioned by the shippers. After considerable experimentation, the company produced an aluminum foil laminated to wet-strength paper. That is, thin sheets of foil were combined with thin sheets of paper to form a lining that conserved the good features of both the paper and the foil. This combination liner could be printed with iceproof and scuffproof inks to provide the shipper with sales appeal and advertising on the crate liners, as well as to provide vastly improved protection.

The main selling features of the new aluminum foil-paper liner are:

1. It keeps contents cool. The foil reflects about 95 percent of all the radiant heat it intercepts, as compared with only 7 percent reflection by brown-paper liner.

2. It helps remove heat from the pack. The thermal conductivity of aluminum foil is high.

3. It decreases collection of moisture on produce. Unloading from cool cars has caused moisture to collect on produce, and this has permitted bacteria to spoil some produce.

4. It prevents penetration of the sun's rays.

5. It prevents evaporation of natural moisture from produce.

6. It decreases the chances of bruising produce.

7. Ice does not penetrate it easily.

8. It is colorful, and it can advertise the packer and be used as a point-of-purchase display by retailers.

The company decided to select its prospects carefully and to attempt to sell only to shippers interested in selling premium-quality produce. The company decided to sell its product through jobbers and, at the same time, to maintain its own sales force to develop and contact prospects and to train and help the jobber sales representatives.

When the company salespeople called on prospects, it became apparent the major objection was price. The liner cost 47 cents per crate, while standard paper liners sold for 28 cents per crate.

Questions

1. As a sales representative for Florida Farm Supply Co., how would you expect prospects to state their objection to the price? What objections are the prospects likely to voice that are really price objections but are not so stated?

2. Suggest some demonstrations, tests, or other selling aids that might be used to overcome the price objection. Illustrate their use.

3. Where should the major emphasis be put when answering the price objection? Illustrate.

Case 12–3   Saginaw Business Products

Tom Celler works part time for Saginaw Business Products. He sells a variety of items both on the floor and in the offices of prospects in the business community. Mr. Celler is paid on a commission basis and has earned considerable supplementary income from his job.

Mr. Celler has had some trouble anticipating and answering objections. Mr. McPherson, the owner, has suggested he should classify the objections of his prospects before attempting to answer them. In addition, he has suggested Mr. Celler should attempt to anticipate the objections many customers might raise. In this way he would not be put in the position of having to answer objections on an impromptu basis.

Mr. McPherson has offered to act in a role-playing situation as an office manager in order to give Mr. Celler an opportunity to practice. Mr. Celler has agreed to try to improve his skill through this method.

It has been agreed that Mr. Celler will attempt to sell dictating equipment and a filing system in two separate practice sessions.

The following statements about the company's automated filing system have been raised as objections for Mr. Celler to analyze:

1. I don't like your visual retriever because I can't be sure I have called the right slide until it arrives.
2. [*Making reference to a lever on the device.*] I would probably get calluses from working that thing all day.
3. [*After a short presentation.*] I think we'll just stick with the inventory control system we have.

The following objections to the use of dictating equipment are to be raised:

1. My work doesn't require it.
2. I've never used it. Why change now?
3. I'd rather have a secretary take dictation.
4. My secretary hates dictating equipment.
5. I tried dictating equipment, but I didn't like it.

Questions

1. How should Mr. Celler classify the objections to the automated filing systems?
2. What suggestions do you have for Mr. Celler after he has classified the objections?
3. Prepare short, effective answers to the objections that might be raised to the use of dictating equipment.

SELECTED REFERENCES

Caust, Daniel. "A Plan for Every Customer." *Sales & Marketing Management,* July 7, 1980, pp. 36–37.

Goldstein, A. *Secrets of Overcoming Sales Resistance: 386 Tested Replies to Objections.* Englewood Cliffs, N.J.: Prentice-Hall, 1969.

Hanan, Mack. "Don't Overcome Objections, Provoke Them." *Sales & Marketing Management,* November 12, 1984, pp. 153–54.

Harrow, Herman. "You Can Disagree without Being Disagreeable." *Sales & Marketing Management,* December 10, 1979, p. 67.

McNutt, George. "Hurdling Toughest Sales Obstacle: State of Prospect's Mind." *Industrial Marketing,* March 1977, pp. 70–73.

Meisel, Don. "Add Sales Power! Ask Questions." *Industrial Distribution,* December 1976, p. 64.

Schurr, Paul H.; Louis H. Stone; and Lee Ann Beller. "Effective Selling Approaches to Buyers' Objections." *Industrial Marketing Management,* August 1985, pp. 195–202.

Weadock, Dan. "Saying 'Yes . . . but' Is Really No Way to Overcome a Buyer's Objection." *Sales & Marketing Management,* October 15, 1979, pp. 92–95.

———. "Your Troops Can Keep Control—and Close the Sale—by Anticipating Objections." *Sales & Marketing Management,* March 17, 1980, pp. 102–6.

13

Closing the Sale

Some questions answered in this chapter are:

■ Why is favorable action important?
■ Why are difficulties encountered when closing?
■ When should a close be attempted?
■ How often should the close be tried?
■ How can sales be closed successfully?
■ What methods and techniques of closing have proved effective?
■ What closing methods are used by major companies?
■ How are closing routines handled smoothly?

The close is not something apart and distinct from the total sales presentation. In fact, the close actually starts with the *beginning* of the sales presentation.

The close is likely to be successful only when the buyer is convinced the purchase is desirable. This conviction comes about when a salesperson talks to a qualified prospect, plans the presentation effectively, develops skill in dramatizing and conveying the sales message, treats the buyer as an individual, appeals to dominant buying motives, and recognizes that the close is an integral part of a well-planned procedure.

Seven Steps in the Sales Process

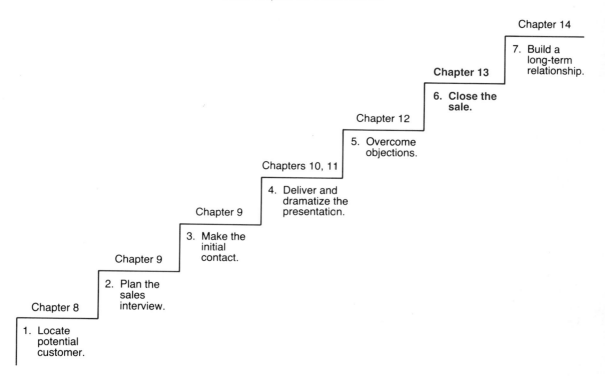

THE IMPORTANCE OF SECURING FAVORABLE ACTION	There are at least two good reasons for becoming an expert at closing sales: First, the close is the ultimate test of sales ability; and second, the income a salesperson receives is usually based on closed sales.

THE IMPORTANCE OF SECURING FAVORABLE ACTION

There are at least two good reasons for becoming an expert at closing sales: First, the close is the ultimate test of sales ability; and second, the income a salesperson receives is usually based on closed sales.

Test of Selling Ability

The true test of the selling ability of salespeople is secured orders. Salespeople may spend months qualifying prospects; they may work long hours and know the product thoroughly; they may speak eloquently and know the customers and their dominant attitudes. But if the salespeople don't get orders, their selling careers will be short-lived.

Sales constitute the final yardstick by which salespeople are measured. Sales may be compared with a quota or may be measured against last month's or last year's figures. Whatever comparison the company makes, it soon becomes evident that success is not determined by the number of interviews secured, or by hours spent in the field, or by the number of goodwill calls made. The employer must ultimately measure success in terms of orders received.

The close is the climax of the sales presentation. It is the point at which the buyer agrees to purchase the product or services. This meeting of the minds of the buyer and the salesperson is the result of a carefully planned procedure. A good salesperson determines what the prospect wants or needs; builds value to a point higher than the price asked; and climaxes the presentation by securing the order. It takes skill, knowledge, and courage to close sales successfully. The close is a challenge.

Relation of Sales Closed to Income

Some companies pay a basic salary plus a commission; others pay on a straight commission basis. Although various compensation plans are used, the salesperson who has the greatest income at the end of the year is almost always the one who closed the greatest number of sales or sold the largest dollar volume.

Companies are constantly looking for men and women who can bring in orders. After salespeople prove they can close, they may be considered for promotion to supervisory or managerial jobs.

WHAT CAUSES DIFFICULTIES IN CLOSING SALES[1]

Wrong Attitudes

Attitudes expressed by speech, mannerisms, body language, or actions may be a hindrance to completing a sale. If salespeople build up a great fear that the close is going to be difficult, this fear may be impossible to hide. It is natural for inexperienced salespeople to be concerned about their ability to close the sale. They know they must close sales to keep their jobs. If the first few attempts to close are unsuccessful, they may believe they *must* close the next sale. When salespeople try too hard to complete the sales presentation—when they feel the pressure—they are likely to do a poor job.

Eagerness to close a sale may be a handicap. The buyer may think the salesperson is inexperienced or has doubts about the product. And this makes the close even more difficult.

Some salespeople display unwarranted excitement when they see the prospect is ready to buy. This may make it difficult to handle the closing routines effectively. If the salesperson appears excited, the sale may be lost even after the prospect has agreed to buy.

Poor Presentation

Some sales executives believe the close is merely a point in the sales presentation that follows automatically from a good presentation. This thought tends to underestimate the need for good closing techniques, but it does point out the need for building up to the close.

Prospects or customers cannot be expected to buy if they do not understand the presentation or are unable to see the benefits of the purchase.

---

[1]See Heinz Goldmann, "The Art of Selling," *Management Today,* September 1977, p. 139, for the results of a survey of training consultants on the major mistakes in closing sales.

Failure to make a good sales talk may be caused by haste in making the presentation. Some company executives estimate the time needed to make an effective sales presentation. If the salesperson tries to deliver a 60-minute presentation in 20 minutes, important sales points may be neglected or omitted.

It may be better to forgo making the presentation than to deliver it hastily. Some salespeople won't try to deliver their sales talk if the prospect will not give them enough time to do it effectively.

A sales presentation given at the wrong time, or under unfavorable conditions, is likely to be ineffective.

Poor Habits and Skills

Closing sales requires skills acquired through constant repetition and intelligent practice. With sufficient repetition and practice, skills become habits. Poorly developed skills can cause inefficient habits. For this reason, the salesperson who expects to close a high percentage of sales must build sound habits.

The habit of talking too much and not listening enough often causes otherwise good presentations to fail. It is just as important to know when to quit talking as to know what to say. Some salespeople become so fascinated by the sound of their own voices that they talk themselves out of sales that have already been made. A presentation that turns into a monologue is not likely to retain the buyer's interest.[2]

WHEN AND HOW OFTEN TO TRY TO CLOSE

Beginning salespeople may ask themselves these questions: "Is there a 'right' time to close?" "How will customers let me know they are ready to buy?" "Should I make more than one attempt to close?" "What should I do if my first close fails?"

When Is the "Right" Time?

The "right" time to attempt a close is when the buyer appears ready to buy. Some say there is one psychological moment in each sales presentation that affords the best opportunity to close, and if this opportunity is bypassed, it will be difficult to secure the order. This is not true. Seldom does one psychological moment govern the success or failure of a sales presentation.

Most buyers make up their minds to buy only when they understand the benefits the purchase provides for them. For some buyers, this point occurs early in the interview, during the first call. For others, it may not arrive until a complete presentation and several calls have been made, and all questions have been answered.

---

[2]Don Meisel, "Add Salespower! Ask Questions," *Industrial Distribution*, November 1976, p. 64.

This prospective buyer's facial expression indicates that he is not yet ready to buy.

This prospective customer's nonverbal signals indicate she is ready to buy.

Cameramann International, Ltd.

Cameramann International, Ltd.

Few buyers *ask* to buy. Buyers usually hesitate to make the decision to purchase until they receive help. Salespeople should make it easy for them to act. When a salesperson believes the buyer understands the proposition and *may* be ready to buy, the right time has arrived. It usually occurs several times in any interview. Failure to recognize one closing opportunity is usually not fatal, but consistently doing so is.

Be Alert for Closing Signals

Customers may indicate they are or are not ready to buy by their facial expressions, by their actions, or by their comments. While these indications are no guarantee the sale can be closed, they should be interpreted as an opportunity to try the close. There are no magic formulas that take the place of good judgment and common sense.

Buyers may not accommodate the salesperson by frowning, looking puzzled, or smiling with satisfaction. Probably the buyer's facial expressions most often indicate he or she is *not* ready to buy. If buyers seem to be puzzled or frown, this may be evidence they are not yet thoroughly sold.[3]

---

[3]For a guide to action see Gerhard Gschwandtner, "Closing Sales via Body Signals," *Marketing Times*, September–October 1982, pp. 12–13.

A customer's actions are often a good indicator of readiness to buy. Some nonverbal signals that indicate a salesperson should attempt to close are:

1. Glancing at, reaching for, or reading the sales contract.
2. Reaching for or casually playing with a pen.
3. When selling in a home, suggesting a move from a living room to a more work-oriented room such as a study.
4. Intently studying a sample or sales brochure.
5. Performing calculations on scratch paper.
6. Placing a restraining hand on the salesperson's arm or shoulder.
7. Resisting a salesperson's attempts to move sales material out of the way.[4]

For example, the prospective buyer of a calculator may get a sheet of figures and operate the machine, or may place the machine on the desk where it will be used. The buyer considering insurance may pick up some literature that has been read previously and give it more thorough study. The buyer of paper may take a sample and again compare it with the stock now being used. The woman shopping for a microwave oven may step back and view the oven from a distance. The industrial buyer may refer to a catalog to compare specifications with competing products. Any of these actions may be *closing signals*. The buyer may be "extending an invitation" to close the sale.

The customer's comments are often the best indications that a purchase is being considered. A prospect will seldom say, "All right, I'm ready to buy. What terms can be arranged?" Customers may indicate, however, that they are about to make a decision (or that they have already made a decision) by asking these questions or making these statements: "I guess it would be better to get a new roof on this building before it rains." "How would we operate while the changeover of equipment is being made?" "Can I pay for the policy on a monthly basis?" "Do you have any facilities for training our employees in the use of the product?" "Do I understand you correctly? Did you say this machine is guaranteed for five years?" "How soon would you be able to deliver the equipment?" "How much will you allow me on a trade-in?"[5]

---

[4]Alan N. Schoonmaker and Douglas B. Lind, "One Custom-made Close Coming Up," *Sales & Marketing Management,* June 13, 1977, p. 6.

[5]For further illustrations of closing signals, see Charles E. Bergman, "Secrets of the Industrial Close," *Sales & Marketing Management,* 1977, special report.

How Often Should the Close Be Attempted?

Relatively few sales are closed on the first attempt, even when the customer plans to buy. Thus, salespeople usually need to close several times during a sales call. Since salespeople will be using multiple closes during a call, they need to develop several different closing routines. Each closing routine used during a call should be different. Repeating the same closing routine is likely to be ineffective.

Since salespeople plan to use several closes during a presentation, the initial attempts are often referred to as *trial* closes. However, the notion of trial closes is misleading. Salespeople should view all closes, whether early or late in the presentation, as attempts to get an order. Salespeople need to use good judgment when determining how often to close.

Some customers make up their minds to buy before anybody calls. They may be sold completely and may be waiting for an opportunity to buy. However, most customers must be sold, and it is the salesperson's job to plan the presentation so as to *create* closing opportunities.[6]

Figure 13–1 illustrates some of the points at which the salesperson may want to try a close. During a sales call, a close should be attempted:

1. Anytime a customer indicates significant interest in the product.
2. Anytime a customer begins asking questions about the product. After answering the question, a close can be attempted. For example, a close can be attempted after a customer says, "Does it come in assorted colors?" or, "You say you will assist us in resetting the shelves?"
3. After the salesperson makes a strong point about the product.
4. After overcoming an objection. For example, a customer may say, "It takes your company too long to deliver." The trade salesperson replies, "Yes, I see timing is important to you. By placing this order now we can be sure the merchandise will be here in time for your ad." After the customer says, "Yeah, I guess you're right," a close should be attempted.
5. When the customer agrees with a major point in the sales presentation. For example, the salesperson tells a retailer, "Other displays like this have increased sales in four weeks." If the customer says, "That certainly would be worth doing," a close should be attempted.
6. When the customer picks up or examines the product, a sales brochure, or the sales contract.

---

[6]Mack Hanan, "The Trick Is to Close by Opening," *Sales & Marketing Management*, September 9, 1985, pp. 157–58.

FIGURE 13–1
Opportunities to Close May Occur at Many Different Times

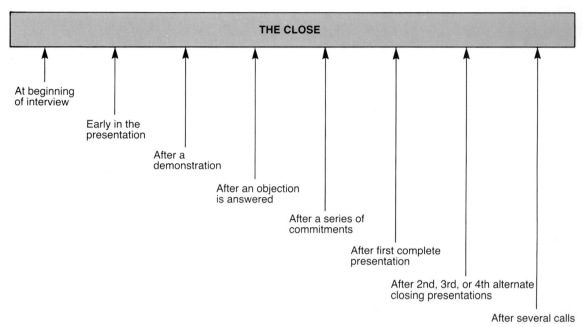

Persistence is a notable trait, but it is only good selling as long as the salesperson's efforts don't antagonize or irritate the prospect. One buyer may willingly accept five or six attempts to close, while another may lose patience after the third.

If the product being sold is highly technical and intensive survey work must precede the presentation, it probably will be necessary to make a rather complete presentation before attempting a close. On the other hand, if the advantages of purchasing are obvious to the buyer, an attempt to close early in the presentation may be acceptable.

What If a Close Fails?

When a close fails, analysis can serve as a basis for future actions. There are many reasons why a close can fail. Salespeople may have attempted to close prematurely; may have misinterpreted a closing signal; may not have made the presentation clearly and forcefully; may have appealed to the wrong buying motives;[7] may have failed to answer an objection satisfactorily; or may have been unskilled in the demonstration. Whatever

---

[7]Mack Hanan, "When Your Salespeople Get a Shot at the Top Man, Don't Let Them Get Shot Down," *Sales & Marketing Management,* July 5, 1982, pp. 102–4.

the cause, the real reason must be uncovered. Only then can salespeople proceed intelligently to eliminate the barriers to the sale.

Probably the most important lesson for the inexperienced salesperson to learn is that when a buyer says no, the sale should not be presumed to be lost. A no may mean "Not now," or, "I want more information," or, "Don't hurry me," or, "I don't understand." "No" should be a challenge to seek the reason for the buyer's negative response.

When a close fails, the salesperson should continue with the presentation and look for another opportunity to close. If the presentation has been completed and several attempts to close have failed, it may be necessary to review parts of the presentation or to question the prospect again to determine the cause of failure.

Actually, failure of a close can prove to be of great value to a salesperson. Often the only way to determine the effectiveness of a sales presentation is by testing—a procedure sometimes known as *taking the customer's temperature*. A close is the salesperson's way to "take the customer's temperature" and thus judge the effectiveness of the sales presentation. The close will let the salesperson know if the customer has been sold and is ready to buy. Or it may tell the salesperson the customer is not ready to buy and why. We can compare a salesperson running a test close to a chef cooking a steak. From time to time the chef may test to see if the steak is ready to serve. It may need to be cooked faster, slower, or a bit longer; or it may need a pinch of salt, pepper, or some other seasoning. The test results tell the chef what needs to be done to prepare the steak to the taste of a particular customer. Because the first two or three tests show the steak is not yet ready to serve, the chef will not give up and throw the steak away. In the same way, the salesperson's close shows him or her what needs to be done to make the benefits of the product or service better known to the prospective buyer. Neither the chef nor the salesperson quits trying after the first test.

HOW TO CLOSE SUCCESS-FULLY

To achieve success in closing sales, salespeople need to master the principles that have made a number of closing techniques especially effective.

Maintain a Positive Attitude

Confidence is contagious. Customers like to buy from people who have confidence in themselves, their product, and their company. Any indication that the salesperson thinks the presentation will not be received favorably or that there is little chance of making a sale is likely to be communicated to the customer. Should this occur, unnecessary barriers are placed between the customer and the salesperson. Enthusiasm and confidence form the necessary background for effective use of any closing technique.

As the presentation is delivered to each prospect, the salesperson's attitude must be, "I will make this sale." It becomes a question of "*How* or *when* will the prospect buy?" not a question of "*Will* the prospect buy?" Whenever salespeople make a sales presentation, they must sincerely and wholeheartedly believe they will succeed. This belief must be evidenced by what they say and what they do, and it should be perceived by the customer.

One successful sales representative describes his attitude as follows: "I approach every interview with the positive attitude that this person is going to buy. I'm not sure what or how much, but I look to every interview ending in a sale."[8]

Is this attitude incompatible with the knowledge that in many fields salespeople lose more sales than they make? How can one maintain this positive attitude knowing the ratio of closes may be only one sale out of every two, three, or four presentations? Simple—we never know *which* prospects will buy. Experienced salespeople know they may sell five or six prospects in a row and then fail to sell the next one or two; they may not be able to detect any pattern in their selling. If we knew in advance which prospects would not buy, it is clear we would decide not to waste our time and theirs.

Any skill is performed best with a positive attitude. The typist who fears errors will make many; the bowler who fears the tenpin is likely to miss it; the ballplayers who know they cannot hit a certain pitcher are likely to get few hits; golfers who know they will miss short putts usually do. So it is with salespeople. If they fear the customer will not buy, the chances are good they'll be right.

Keep Control of the Interview

Control of the interview is necessary in order to create closing opportunities and to permit use of the most effective closing techniques.

If the prospect takes over and keeps the initiative, closing attempts are likely to be fruitless. But if the salesperson has planned the presentation well, it will usually not be difficult for him or her to guide the interview along the lines previously chosen.

The following example illustrates how an experienced salesperson controls the presentation by getting positive feedback throughout. Mary Klein is making a presentation to Phil Strack about a system of office files. Mr. Strack is contemplating a complete renovation of the corporate offices and has been appointed to select functional and decorative equipment. Ms. Klein represents a firm that carries a full line of office furniture, but the focal point of her presentation at the moment is the file system. She believes her system is so distinctive that if she can sell it, she will also sell a lot of desks, chairs, and tables.

---

[8]Gregory M. Genovese, "Observations on Closing Sales," *NYLIC Review,* January 1977, p. 16.

Ms. Klein: . . . and you'll notice how easily these units fit into one another. That's because the lower lip on each unit is designed to slip over the top of the other unit. That makes rearrangement simple, and that was one of the things you wanted, wasn't it!

Mr. Strack: Yes it is. [*Agreement.*] However, I also want some units to be fairly permanent . . . wonder whether these stacking units will hold firmly enough.

Ms. Klein: That's a good point, and there are two good answers to it. First, the stacking units have these little grooves at the back. See how they line up to assure straight stacking? So where flexibility counts, the units will be properly aligned and will stay that way until moved. Now the second part is equally good; we also have units that are permanently stacked . . . look exactly like the modular units, except they're in fixed sizes—two-, three-, and four-drawer sizes. You'll be wanting some of those, too, won't you?

Mr. Strack: Yes, I will. [*Agreement.*] Actually, a majority of the files will have to be that way, but I can see how the modular approach would be beneficial in nearly every office suite. You have a good idea there, Mary.

Ms. Klein: Have you any idea what sort of mix you'd require? For instance, what percent of the total installation would be fixed units, and what percent would be modular?

Mr. Strack: Probably about 80 percent fixed, 20 percent stacking units. I'll have to see.

Ms. Klein: That would work out to your advantage as far as price is concerned, too. The fixed units are less expensive per drawer. Although flexibility and good appearance are uppermost in your mind, I'm sure you won't object to saving a few dollars as well . . . right?

Mr. Strack: Absolutely not. Now, you show these units only in gray and beige . . . pretty standard. What about colors? Deep red, bright yellow, dark mahogany, for instance.

Ms. Klein: If I can get the colors you want, these are the units you'd buy? [*Close.*]

Mr. Strack: I think so . . . if the price is right. [*Agreement.*]

Ms. Klein: Then, lets list the units you need by size and color, and I'll be able to give you a contract price on them. [*Close.*] Now, you'll be needing desks and chairs . . . [*Opening a new sale.*]

Notice that throughout the presentation, Ms. Klein controlled the interaction by providing information and then asking a question. This technique makes Mr. Strack an active participant and keeps Ms. Klein on the right track. It also results in a series of agreements on style, number, and so on. When the issue of colors comes up, Ms. Klein closes, rather than asking another question such as, "What colors do you want?"[9]

Let the Customer Set the Pace

Closing attempts must be geared to fit the varying reactions, needs, and personalities of each buyer.[10] However, this does not mean the buyer should be allowed to control the interview.

Some buyers react very slowly and may need plenty of time to assimilate the material presented. They may ask the same question several times or may give evidence they do not understand the importance of certain product features. In these circumstances, the presentation must be delivered more slowly, and certain parts may have to be repeated. It would be unwise to try a close when it is evident the customer is not yet ready to buy.

All prospects expect salespeople to supply enough information to enable them to evaluate the product properly. The kinds of information and the speed with which the information can be absorbed vary with different prospects. If salespeople know their prospects and customers well, they can judge how to make the presentation at the most effective pace.

Be Assertive, not Aggressive

Professor Marvin Jolson identifies three types of salespeople: aggressive, submissive, and assertive.[11] Aggressive salespeople control the sales interaction but often do not get the order because they prejudge customer needs and fail to probe for information. They are too busy talking to do much listening. Aggressive salespeople respond vigorously. They say, "I can't understand why you are hesitant," but they do not respond to objections.

Submissive salespeople are often excellent socializers. In front of customers, they spend a lot of time talking about families, restaurants, and movies. They are quite effective at establishing rapport, but they do not attempt to control the presentation. They accept the customer's statements of needs and problems, but do not probe to uncover the latent needs.

Assertive salespeople are self-confident. They maintain control by being responsive to customer needs. Rather than aggressively creating new needs in customers through persuasion, they prospect for customers that truly need their products. In order to determine customer needs, they

---

[9]This example is based on George Lumsden, *Closing* (Chicago: Dirtnell, 1984).

[10]See Sally Scanlon, "Every Salesperson a Psychologist," *Sales & Marketing Management,* February 6, 1978, pp. 34–35.

[11]Marvin A. Jolson, "Selling Assertively," *Business Horizons,* September–October 1984, pp. 71–77.

Table 13–1 Differences among Assertive, Aggressive, and Submissive Salespeople

Selling Activity	Selling Style		
	Aggressive	*Submissive*	*Assertive*
Defining customer needs	Believe they are the best judge of customer's needs	Accept customer's definition of needs	Probe for need-related information that customer may not have volunteered
Controlling the presentation	Minimize participation by customer	Permit customer to control presentation	Encourage two-way communication and customer participation
Closing the sale	Overwhelm customer; respond to objections without understanding	Assume customers will buy when ready	Respond to objections, leading to somewhat automatic close

Be assertive, not aggressive, in asking for the order.

"Oh . . . hold it a second . . . at this point my boss says I should ask for the order."

Reprinted by permission of *Sales & Marketing Management* magazine. Copyright 1985.

encourage customers through questioning to provide information. Their presentations emphasize an exchange of information rather than a one-way presentation. Table 13–1 summarizes the differences between assertive, aggressive, and submissive salespeople.

Give the Customer a Chance to Buy

The only reason for making a sales presentation is to *help the customer buy.* It follows, then, that this goal should be kept in mind constantly.

The salesperson must be ready to close when the customer is ready to buy. The customer who says, "This unit appears to be scratched. Do you have others?" may be providing an opportunity to close. It is a mistake to continue with additional sales features when it is apparent the customer is ready to buy. Perhaps the appropriate answer to the question is, "We have the same model in the warehouse. When would you like us to deliver it?"

It is paradoxical that some salespeople give presentations to make sales and then fail to ask for the order. This failure is explained by the fear the prospect will say no. Most people do not like to be told no. The salesperson is likely to rationalize, probably unconsciously, "If I don't ask for the order until I am sure the prospect will buy, then I won't be told no." The fear of asking for the order has lost many sales. One sales representative made many calls on a prospect and was finally able to secure the order. At this point, the salesperson asked the store owner why it took so many calls to get the order. The answer was simple. The prospect replied, "You never asked me to buy until today."

Keep Some Selling Points in Reserve

Sometimes inexperienced salespeople describe and demonstrate all the product's sales points before making their *first* closing attempt. This is a poor practice because if the closing attempt fails, there is little choice but to review the sales points already presented. One or two sales points kept in reserve can add strength and force to succeeding attempts to close.

Seldom do good duck hunters use all of their ammunition on the first flight of high-flying ducks. If they do, they may find to their disappointment that succeeding flights offer better targets. But because their ammunition is now gone, they have lost their best opportunities to bring home the limit. In the same way, salespeople need to keep some sales ammunition in reserve and use it when it is most likely to be effective. One sales manager says, "Hold at least one of the product's advantages in reserve so that prospects will be pleasantly surprised when they find out about it."

Sell the Right Item in the Right Amounts

The chances to close a sale are enhanced when the right product is sold in the right amount.

For example, the life insurance underwriter must be certain a $100,000 ordinary life policy is what the buyer needs or wants before attempting to sell such a policy. The office equipment sales representative must be sure two electronic calculators best fit the needs of the buyer's office work. The paper products salesperson selling to a retailer must know one gross of pencils is more likely to fit the retailer's needs than 12 gross. The chances to close a sale diminish rapidly when the salesperson tries to sell too many units or the wrong grade or style of product.

Salespeople are likely to sell the right product in the right amounts if they keep a service attitude. A large manufacturer of resistance welding machines and equipment, parts, and accessories looks out for its customers' interests by maintaining a production design staff. This staff analyzes the use a customer plans to make of the company's products. Recommendations are then made as to the right number and kinds of machines needed. Sometimes the analysis shows a need for fewer machines than the customer thought. In one case, the company sold a $4,000 machine instead of fulfilling the customer's request for eight $2,000 machines to do the same job.

While the first sale may be smaller if the right product is sold in the right amounts, repeat sales almost always more than make up for a smaller order on the first sale.

EFFECTIVE METHODS AND TECHNIQUES

No method of closing will work if the buyer is not sold on the salesperson, the company, and the product. Closing sales should not require the use of tricky techniques or methods for forcing buyers to do something they don't want to do. Nor should it involve causing prospects to buy something they don't need.

The purpose of studying successful closing methods and techniques is to enable salespeople to *help prospects buy* a product or service they want or need. The buyer may have a need or a want and still hesitate to buy a product, even though it will satisfy this want or need.

One of the salesperson's objectives is to help buyers overcome any fear that the product is not appropriate. For many types of selling, the salesperson must rely on qualifying techniques to determine the appropriateness of the product for the buyer.

Most sales require a sacrifice from buyers. They must sacrifice money for the advantages the product or service provides. Making the decision to spend money for any one product may mean giving up other products. The buyer's sacrifice must be more than offset by the advantages that accrue from purchasing that particular product or service.

There is no one method or technique of closing that can be used successfully in all circumstances. The methods or techniques depend on the product to be sold, the customer to be sold, and the circumstances of the sale. Typically, a salesperson will use several of these approaches during a presentation.

Asking for the Order

Perhaps the most straightforward effective close is simply asking for the order. However, salespeople need to be wary of appearing overly aggressive when using a direct close. The direct close works best with decisive customers who appreciate getting down to business and not wasting time. Often the actual wording of a direct approach assumes the sale is made, such as, "Shall I drop off a case tomorrow?"

Assume the Sale Is Made

In assuming the sale is made, the salesperson is allowing the customer or prospect to follow the line of least resistance. Care should be taken not to create the impression that pressure is being exerted. As is true for all methods of closing, skill in using the method is just as important as knowledge of the method.

The retail salesperson can use this method effectively. The customer may be considering buying a suit. After the sales presentation has reached a point at which an attempt to close is appropriate, the salesperson may say, "Mr. Brown, slip on the trousers too. I will call our tailor to make any necessary alterations." If the customer doesn't object, the sale is probably closed.

The principles involved in giving the customer or prospect a choice have long been recognized. It is important to note that the choice is between two items or among several items. It is never between buying the product and not buying it. The choice is merely *which one* of the products or units is preferred—between ordering one dozen or two dozen, between buying a blue or red one, between model Z and model Y, or between the product alone and the product with accessories. Whichever alternative the customer chooses, the result is an order.

Some questions that can be used in making an assumptive close are:

Which do you prefer, cash or check?

In view of the benefits, can you afford to put off this investment until later?

Would you like to OK this order?

Don't you agree that anything worth having is worth having now?

Your pen or mine?

Would you like it by August 1st or August 15th?

Would you like me to stop by for the check on Monday?

How much of a deposit would you like to leave?

Which color do you prefer?

Will one be enough?

Would you like it gift wrapped?

Will we ship it directly?

Would you prefer early-morning delivery?

Will you be needing accessory items?

Where would you like it installed?

In some fields of selling, the salesperson inventories the customer's stock and prepares an order for the necessary fill-ins. The customer is then asked to approve the order by signing the order sheet. This practice is followed by some sales representatives of Arrow shirts, for example. In other fields of selling in which regular calls are made, the salesperson may ask for information and begin to fill out an order blank. Unless the prospect refuses to give the information, a sale is assumed. When calling on a regular customer, a good way to close the sale is by asking, ''Shall I send this by mail, or do you want me to bring it on my next trip?'' or, ''I'll ship this in the usual manner.''

The actual close must represent a meeting of the buyer's and seller's minds. It should not be assumed the sale has been made until the following conditions exist: The salesperson has a product the prospect wants; the price is right for the prospect; the prospect believes this is the time to buy; and the prospect desires to buy from the salesperson's company.

Build a Series of Acceptances

This method of closing is actually a buildup to the close. But the close is not something apart and distinct from the presentation.

Prospects and customers find it difficult to refuse to buy if they agree the product fulfills their need, the salesperson and the company are reputable, the value received is fair compared with the price asked, and now is a good time to buy.

Some salespeople try to build up a series of yes answers as a basis for the close. For example, the manufacturer's representative who is attempting to sell a dealer on a line of products may ask such questions as these:

Salesperson: These advertisements will appear in *Fortune* and 11 other magazines beginning November 1. They are attractive ads, aren't they?

Customer: Yes, they are very attractive.

Salesperson: These ads should help create store traffic for you, especially if you tie in with your local advertising, shouldn't they?

Customer: Yes, I suppose they will.

Salesperson: Here is a copy of our franchise. You will note that your percentage of markup is higher than that allowed by our competitors. You can use that extra markup, can't you?

Customer: Yes, I certainly can.

Salesperson: You won't need any additional fixtures to display these in your windows. They would make an attractive display by themselves, wouldn't they?

Customer: Yes, I imagine they would.

Salesperson: Your main interests are in a fair profit with a fast turnover. Isn't that true?

Customer: Yes, it is.

Salesperson: If I can show you how these products will turn fast on a small investment, you would be interested, wouldn't you?

Customer: Yes.

This method enables the buyer to make a series of easy decisions. Of course, the last decision in the series is the buying decision.

Many times a no can be the equivalent of a yes. Prospects who answer no may be committing themselves just as strongly as though they were saying yes. For example:

Salesperson: You want to purchase your equipment as economically as possible, don't you?

Customer: Yes.

Salesperson: You don't want to pay any more than you have to for good equipment, do you?

Customer: *No.*

The yes and the no are commitments. Each answer paves the way for further commitments.

Get Decisions on Minor Points

In some fields of selling, decisions on minor points or subordinate points are a good means to a close. Some customers are willing to make minor decisions while they may hesitate to make major ones.

The prospect will usually not hesitate to make a choice of color, delivery date, credit terms, method of shipment, or size. However, some prospects may dislike making the actual decision to buy. Recognizing this, the salesperson should allow decisions on minor points to take the place of a major decision to buy.

The car salesperson may obtain a decision on the customer's preference for a two-door or four-door model; for a black or green color; for stereo and heater accessories; for cash or credit terms; and for black or white sidewall tires. The insurance underwriter may have the prospect designate a beneficiary. The manufacturer's representative may have the buyer choose a method of shipment.

The important principle involved is to get decisions on minor points and not require the customer to make a major decision. This method ties in closely with building a series of acceptances.

Listing the Pros and Cons

This method is sometimes referred to as the *Ben Franklin balance-sheet close* because Ben Franklin described how he used it to make decisions. It has been used with prospects who can't make a decision even though there seems to be no reason for them not to buy. A prospect of this type may be asked to join the salesperson in listing the pros and cons of buying now or buying later; of buying the salesperson's product or that of a competitor; of buying the product or not buying it at all.

This close can start with the following statement:

> You know, Mr. Thacker, the other evening I was reading an article about Ben Franklin. He was talking about making difficult decisions and how anxious he was to reach the right decisions and avoid the wrong ones. I suppose that's how you feel. Well, he suggested taking a piece of paper and writing all the reasons for deciding "yes" in one column, and then listing the reasons for deciding "no" in a second column. He said that when you make this kind of graphic comparison, the correct decision becomes much more apparent.

As the salesperson is telling this story, he gets things started by drawing a T on a plain piece of paper, placing captions on each side of the T and leaving space below for the insertion of specific benefits or sales points. If the product is an Apple computer versus a Compaq computer, the T might look like this:

Benefits of Apple Computer	Benefits of Compaq Computer
1.	1.
2.	2.
3.	3.
Reasons not to buy	**Reasons not to buy**
1.	1.
2.	2.
3.	3.

Then the salesperson suggests, "Let's see how many reasons we can think of for your making a good decision." Then list the benefits (not features) the customer has shown interest in. After listing the benefits, ask the customer to list the reasons he should not take the product.

The balance sheet method can be very effective when done properly. The list of benefits won't always outweigh the objections the customer may have, but almost every time the act of having the customer tell you why he or she should take the product, reinforced visually, has enough power to cinch the deal.

Get a Trial Order

As a last resort or in selling products that are not well known, an attempt to close may be made by encouraging the prospect or customer to order a small number of units on a tryout basis. If the products are useful or if their resale is profitable, larger orders can be expected. If for any reason the products prove unsatisfactory, the buyer has assumed a small risk.

Some salespeople are convinced sales will result if a prospect will give the product a trial. Trial orders may help get a product accepted, especially if it is new.

Certain types of office and industrial equipment are sold on this basis. A unit is installed in the prospect's store or plant and is given a thorough testing under actual working conditions. The trial may be for a few days or a few weeks. At the end of the trial, an attempt is made to close the sale for one or more machines.

The trial-order close is particularly effective when the offer involves no possible loss for the buyer. But this method may be a disadvantage in selling to retailers or wholesalers because the lack of much investment by the buyer may eliminate the need to promote the product. As a result, there may be a tendency for the buyer to give the product little or no attention, and therefore its real value may not be determined.

Make a Special Offer

The danger in this method lies in creating the impression that the first or second offer is not the best one that will be made. Customers or prospects may believe if they put off the purchase a little longer, they may be able to get an even better bargain. They may never feel sure they have secured the best terms possible. It is only natural to think another customer may have secured better terms. In certain fields of selling, it is important to make any concessions available to all competing distributors. The company's name and the salesperson's reputation will suffer if it becomes apparent that a "one-price policy" is not being followed. The company may also be charged with price discrimination.

Some companies promote the sale of their products by offering a special inducement to all buyers who purchase on the first call. This inducement, which is often used in selling direct to household consumers, may be a free accessory; a special price on a storage container; or an extra unit if a certain number of units are purchased. Such inducements are usually offered in an attempt to close the sale immediately. They are usually a part of the regular or standard presentation and are offered to each prospect or customer contacted.

Other companies offer special introductory terms or special advertising tie-in propositions to persuade their dealers to buy a greater volume or in greater variety. The "something extra" or "something-for-nothing" idea is still a strong factor in closing sales.

Use the "What If . . ." or Contingent Method

A sales representative may say, "Mr. Prospect, if I can show you that our copiers will provide you with more accurate work performed at a higher rate of speed and at less cost than do the machines you are currently using, you will want to take advantage of the savings as quickly as possible, won't you?" Most buyers would readily agree that if these facts could be proved, they would be willing to buy.

Another approach may be: "You can see from my explanation that our company has a very attractive offer for the right retail store. I am not sure I can secure an exclusive outlet for your store. *But if it can be arranged,* shall I draw up the contract?'' This close may be used to appeal to some buyers who have difficulty deciding.

People are inclined to want what they cannot have or what they are not sure they can get. Such desires are human weaknesses. If a salesperson takes advantage of them to the detriment of the buyers, sound selling practices are being violated. Such action will result in a loss of reputation and a loss of future sales.

Yet the contingent method can be used if a true uncertainty exists. For example, insurance agents may qualify prospects to the best of their ability before filling out an application. Later, if there is some doubt about the applicant's eligibility, the agent may say: ''The policy we have discussed is exactly what you need. However, there is some doubt that our company will issue the policy. Shall I make an appointment with our doctor for you at 10:00 A.M. tomorrow to see if you can qualify?''

Similar uncertainties may exist when unusual sizes, quantities, colors, or styles are the basis for the close. Sometimes price concessions or special discounts may be the basis for asking for the order.

Emphasize an Impending Event

Some customers may hesitate to buy *now* unless they believe a postponement will cause them to suffer a loss. This fear of a loss is a strong motivating force. The alert salesperson can often close by referring to losses the buyer may sustain because of some impending event. The life insurance agent frequently uses this method. For example, annual premium is determined by age. If the prospect waits to make a purchase, the insurance will cost more for the same coverage. Therefore, it is to the prospect's advantage to buy *now*.

When prices are rising, sales may be closed by pointing out that price increases are pending. The retail store buyer may be particularly eager to take advantage of an appreciation in inventory value. Some companies notify their sales representatives several weeks before price increases take effect. The chance to obtain merchandise that will soon cost more is a strong motivating force.

The real estate salesperson often uses this method to sell building sites and homes. The impending event may be a probable rezoning of residential property to industrial property. It may be the possibility a new school or a new park will be built in the area, or a new subdivision is being planned for an adjacent area. Sometimes the fact that a large national organization is planning to purchase property in an area or an urban redevelopment project is under way will add value to adjacent property.

Other impending events, such as changes in weather, tax rates, or models, may help convince buyers that *now* is the time to buy. When trade-in values on old cars are on the way down, the prospect may lose money by waiting. The chances of an extra dividend or a stock split may make the purchase of stock a good buy *now*. Sometimes the fear of loss caused by waiting to buy causes prospects to purchase such products as roofing, hot-water heaters, refrigerators, and washing machines. The loss may be monetary; or it may be a loss in health, comfort, or convenience to the prospect or the prospect's family.

Obviously, salespeople must be honest in pointing out potential losses. They must also be careful not to predict the future on matters that are extremely difficult or impossible to predict. To say stocks will not go down or real estate cannot possibly decrease in value would be fatal. The method is not intended as a means of exerting high pressure or as a trick way of closing.

HANDLING CLOSING ROUTINES

Closing routines involve getting the buyer's signature on the order blank, as well as performing the activities necessary to terminate the interview satisfactorily.

Getting the Signature

Signing the order is a natural part of a well-planned procedure. The order blank should be accessible, and the signing should appear to be a routine matter. Ordinarily, the customer has decided to buy before being asked to sign the order. In other words, the signature on the order blank merely confirms that an agreement has already been reached. The decision to buy or not to buy should not focus on a signature. If the close was conducted properly, the actual signing is no problem. On the other hand, if the prospect has not decided to buy before the attempt to secure the signature, there is little chance he or she will sign the order.

It is unwise to ask the buyer to "sign the contract." That is, the idea of signing a contract may cause some buyers to feel that they are making a very important decision. If the product has already been sold, this may give the buyer an opportunity to hesitate or reconsider. The salesperson may say, "Just write your name here the way it appears above," or, "While you are writing your name on the line marked by an X, I will be getting together some literature you can use," or, "If you will sign right here, I will see that your order is sent by airmail this afternoon."

The important points to remember are: Make the actual signing an easy, routine procedure; fill out the order blank accurately and promptly; and be careful not to exhibit any eagerness or excitement when the prospect is about to sign.

Confirming the Customer's Choice

In most fields of selling, the close is not the end of a business transaction. A successful close is merely the beginning of a mutually profitable business relationship. A sale is closed successfully if it results in repeat sales.

Customers like to believe they have made a wise choice when they decide to buy. They like salespeople who do not lose interest immediately after the order is signed. Many customers are not always satisfied their decision to buy has been wise.

Experienced salespeople reassure customers that their choice of products or services has been judicious. They may say, "I know you will enjoy using your new office machines. You can plan on many months of trouble-free service. I'll call on you in about two weeks to make sure everything is operating smoothly. Be sure to call me if you need any help before then." Or, "Congratulations, Mr. Jacobs; you are going to be glad you decided to use our service. There is no finer service available. Now let's make certain you get off to the right start. Your first bulletin will arrive Tuesday, March 2." Such remarks as the following may also be appropriate: "You've made an excellent choice. Other stores won't have a product like this for at least 30 days." "This is an excellent model you've chosen. Did you see it advertised in last week's *Time?*" "Your mechanics will thank you for ordering these tools. You will be able to get your work out much faster."

Sales must not only be closed, they must *stay* closed. One good way to keep customers from changing their minds and canceling the order or returning the merchandise is to assure them they have made an intelligent choice.

Show Appreciation

All buyers like to think their business is appreciated, even if they only purchase small quantities. Customers like to do business with salespeople who show that they *want* the business.

Appreciation may be shown by writing the purchaser a letter. This is good practice, and it develops goodwill when the purchase is large or the customer is new. Salespeople should always thank the purchaser personally. Their thanks should be genuine but not effusive.

Cultivate for Future Calls

To be welcomed on repeat calls, salespeople must be considerate of all the parties involved in buying or using the product. They should pronounce and spell all names correctly; make sure the buyer or user gets the service promised; and explain and review the terms of the purchase so there can be no misunderstandings. In addition, they should be sociable and cordial to subordinates, as well as to those in key positions.

If the Prospect Doesn't Buy Now

In many fields of selling, the majority of prospects do not buy. The ratio of sales presentations may be 1 to 3, 1 to 5, 1 to 10, or even 1 to 20. There may be a tendency to eliminate nonbuyers from the prospect list after one unsuccessful call, and in some cases, this may be a sound practice. However, many sales are closed on the second, third, fourth, or fifth calls. It is important to prepare for succeeding calls when an order is not secured on an earlier visit.

Because of the complexity of some products and the number of competitors, the salesperson may not be able to complete the sale after one or two interviews. Instead, a number of tactics might be used: (1) The salesperson might request permission to call again or might offer to demonstrate the product; (2) the prospect might be invited to use the product on a trial basis; (3) the salesperson might conduct a formal survey of ways in which the product would benefit the prospect; and (4) the salesperson might ask the prospect to delay a buying decision until a written sales proposal can be prepared and submitted.

If a close fails, no matter what the reason, the salesperson should take defeat good-naturedly. Salespeople have to learn to be good losers if they expect to call on prospects again. Even if no sale is made, the salesperson should thank the prospects for their time. Arguing or showing disappointment gains nothing.

The salesperson may plan to keep in contact with unsold prospects or customers. This can be accomplished through an occasional phone call, through a followup letter, or by mailing some product literature. In addition, an attempt should be made to analyze the causes for failures to close.

Bring the Interview to a Close

Few buyers are interested in a prolonged visit after a sale is closed. Obviously, the departure cannot be abrupt. The salesperson should take whatever time is necessary to complete the interview smoothly. On the other hand, goodwill is not built by wasting the buyer's time after the business is concluded. Also, there is a risk buyers may change their minds if salespeople prolong their visits unnecessarily.

ANALYZING THE INTERVIEW

Every salesperson loses some sales. Successful salespeople learn from these lost sales by analyzing what happened and make changes in their approach so it won't happen again.[12] A salesperson can try to understand the lost sale by asking:

1. Did I prospect properly? Was the person I talked to qualified to place an order?
2. Did I determine what the customer wanted?
3. Was the customer convinced our price was fair?
4. Did I let the customer talk?
5. Was I outsmarted by the competition?
6. Did I control the sales interview?
7. Did I follow up?
8. Did I ask for the order?

---

[12]E. Ray Bond, "What to Do About That Lost Sale," *Sales & Marketing Management,* April 2, 1984, p. 19.

SUMMARY

Closing the sale starts at the beginning of the salesperson's contact with a customer. A close can succeed only when all facets of the selling process fall into their proper place. We all need to keep in mind the old saying, *"People don't buy products or services—they buy solutions to their problems!"*

A sales representative's income and professional reputation depend on his or her ability to close the sale. All other aspects of selling may be mastered, but if salespeople can't close, they have no future in selling as a career.

Problems in closing can be directly traced to poor habits and skills on the part of the salesperson, deficiencies in attitude, or an inability to make an effective sales presentation. There is no one "right" time to try a close. Salespeople should watch their prospects closely and recognize when to try for a close. There may be many opportunities, called closing signals, during a sales interview, and the salesperson must make use of them as often as this procedure is acceptable to the customer. A no response does not always mean the close has failed. Persistence is required!

Success in closing demands a positive attitude on the part of the sales representative. It requires skill in conducting a sales interview and familiarity with a variety of closing techniques. The customer must be given the opportunity to buy. The salesperson's motto is, *"Ask for the order!"*

Most prospects do not buy on the first attempt at a close. Salespeople must choose from a number of closing methods that have proved effective as sales producers. To achieve success, salespeople need to practice these methods until they are skillful in using them. Experience will dictate which methods are most effective for a particular salesperson in a given sales situation.

Closing methods favored by a number of major companies illustrate techniques that have been profitable for experienced salespeople in today's marketplace. Sales cannot be closed by some magical or miraculous technique if the salesperson has failed to prepare the prospect for buying throughout the presentation. The salesperson should arrange for future calls if the nature of the product sold makes such contact necessary or desirable.

QUESTIONS
AND
PROBLEMS

1. It is said that yes comes as only *one* word, while no may be accompanied by 50 or more revealing words. Suppose you get no to the following attempts to close a sale.

   Prospect: No, I don't think I want to go into that right now—it really doesn't sound practical.

   Prospect: No, we've been buying from (*your competitor*) for a long time. They give us such good service that I don't want to make a change.

   Prospect: No, we'd better not tackle that, our personnel would have to be trained and supervised—the job is just too big.

What three important things could these no statements reveal to you?

2. The most successful salespeople are those who close sales long after they've heard the first, second, and even the third no. Comment on this statement.

3. Analyze the following statement: "You know that when the prospect says no, he or she is saying no to your proposal—he or she is not rejecting you personally." Why is the understanding of this statement vital to sales representatives?

4. "Next to making the sale, the most important thing to accomplish on a sales call is to *leave the door open*. Seldom is a sale made on a single call. That means we have to come back again and again with more of our story. We should leave a sales call with an imaginary welcome mat, with our name on it, on the prospect's threshold—and put there by the client."

   These are the instructions given to sales representatives by Norelco, the manufacturer of a wide variety of office machines.

   Evaluate the statements, and indicate how you might "leave the door open."

5. Salespeople should use simple, familiar words to achieve the greatest impact. Consider the following statement: "When two statements have the same meaning, but the first proposition is in different words from the second one, the two assertions can be considered as indicating the same thing, and for all practical purposes may be considered the same judgment."

   What does this statement mean? Can you simplify it? Say the same thing in fewer words!

6. A sales representative for a manufacturer of industrial machinery believes the best way to get an order is to constantly keep in mind that the order is the goal. Keep your order book very much in evidence when making a sales presentation, and concentrate on timing the request for a signature "on the dotted line." If the order is asked for at the right moment, the prospect will sign the order blank. Is this good selling? What are the strengths and weaknesses of constantly concentrating on getting the prospect's signature?

7. The following close was used by a new salesperson in an attempt to sell to the buyer for a group of stationery stores:

   "Joe, our pen is the number one pen in the writing instrument field. With our display and advertising allowances you can't go wrong."

   "Can we place an order?"

   Comment on this close attempt.

8. You are selling copier/duplicators for office use to businesspeople in your community. After making a presentation you think was rather well done, you request the order and get this reply: "What you say sounds interesting, but I want some time to think it over. I'm sure we'll probably go along with you, but I do need some time to think about it."

   Your answer to the statement is, "Well, OK. Would next Tuesday be a good day for me to come back?"

   Can you improve on this answer? How?

9. Among the more effective ways to close the sale after an appropriate presentation are (*a*) to give the prospect a choice between cash and terms or between a large and a small package; (*b*) to complete the order by beginning to write out the sales ticket and by asking the prospect for the correct initials, name, and address; (*c*) to prewrite the order and hand the written order to the prospect and ask for approval or an OK; and (*d*) to concentrate on one main feature and ask the prospect for the order directly.

   If these attempts to close fail, list at least four contingencies that may motivate the prospect to buy now.

10. A buyer seems to be wavering and can't make a decision. Suppose you approach the close this way:

    Prospect: I don't think I'm ready to buy now.

    Salesperson: Mr. Smith, you're probably as ready now as you'll ever be. If you need any features clarified, I'll be glad to give you the answers. Otherwise, let's get this thing over with.

    Or, try this approach:

    Prospect: Your company is a little steep in price.

    Salesperson: Oh, if that's all that's bothering you, you can just sign right here. There is no company that can beat our price.

    Evaluate the two approaches. Would you use them? When? Why?

11. Draw an analogy between the activities of a salesperson during the close and a base runner in baseball; between the closing activities of a salesperson and a fisherman.

12. One successful salesperson assumes an attitude of indifference toward whether the prospect buys. Does this indifferent attitude help in closing sales? Why? What are the dangers inherent in giving this impression?

13. Assume you are planning to earn extra income while attending school by selling automatic washing machines directly to household consumers. You will represent a local appliance dealer and will be paid on a commission basis. The appliance dealer

requests you to prepare six different closing routines. You are to use your own judgment on the application of each close and on the number of routines to use on any one prospect. What statements would be appropriate when you ask for the order?

14. The Life Insurance Agency Management Association makes this suggestion for use as a final appeal to get the customer to buy now:

   Suppose I walked into your office this morning and said to you, "Mr. Prospect, I have here a 12-pound package of the finest cork the world affords, done up in a strong linen container. Notice the fine, even grain. Notice the strength. Sir, this is 12 pounds of the finest Portugal cork that money can buy. It will cost you just 10 cents a pound. Wouldn't you like to buy it?"

   If I did that, you undoubtedly would say, "What in blazes would I do with 12 pounds of cork?"

   And of course you would be certain you had no use for that cork. But now let us say you were on the wings of a sinking plane, and I came along and offered to sell you this cork—would you want it then?

   Certainly you would. *The trouble is, if you were in such a fix, I would not be there to sell you the cork.*

   There is a fundamental similarity between life preservers of the kind they carry on planes and financial life preservers such as this savings plan—and that is that *each must be secured before it is needed.* When the need is desperate, the time is too late.

   Let's arrange for your financial life preserver while you are still able to get it!

   What do you think of this "cork story" as a final appeal to use in attempting to close a sale? Would you use it? Why?

15. Suppose you are selling a chain saw in your hardware store to an interested prospect. You are nearing the end of your presentation when the prospect says, "Your saw is fine, and I'd like to buy one, but I don't want to put it on an account unless I can pay for it in 60 days without any carrying charges." Company policy prevents you from giving these terms. What would you say?

16. You are selling a built-in dishwasher to a prospect in your store. The prospect asks, "How soon do you think you could install it?" You give the answer, and the prospect says, "What guarantee period do I get?" You answer, "One full year, parts and labor included." Can you think of a better answer than the one given?

17. Do you believe a trial close is helpful to salespeople, even if it fails? Would you recommend they wait until they are positive the customer is ready to make a decision before attempting a close? Why?

18. An old rule used by successful sales representatives has been stated as: "First, tell 'em what you're going to tell 'em; then, tell 'em; and then, tell 'em what you've told 'em."

    Do you believe this rule is sound? Why? Illustrate your answer.

PROJECTS
1. Visit a number of showrooms. They may be for automobiles, personal computers, word processors, exercise or conditioning equipment, furniture, telephones and accessory devices, or other products you may be anticipating buying. Describe the attempts made to "close the sale." Evaluate these attempts and summarize your conclusions.
2. Interview a purchasing agent, a department buyer, or the owner of a small business, and ask for his/her evaluation of the closing routines used by sales representatives who call on them. Write your conclusions in one or two paragraphs.
3. Prepare a one-page article on "The Importance of Body Language in Closing Sales."
4. Prepare a scenario for selling tickets to a college or university activity, or for selling ads for a college publication. Include a series of alternative or optional closing routines. Follow the scenario by actually soliciting orders. Write your conclusions.

CASE PROBLEMS

Case 13–1   Video Records, Inc.

Soon after graduation from college Noel Cantor and Shirley White were seeking opportunities to start a small business. They believed some type of service enterprise would be appropriate, especially one that would not involve a large initial capital investment.

Shirley and Noel had read a lot about business opportunities in various magazines and *The Wall Street Journal*. They had also taken courses in accounting, marketing, selling, management, and communications in their college curriculum.

While in their senior year at college, Shirley and Noel were able to work as "business consultants" for entrepreneurs who requested help managing their small businesses. They had worked as a team

under the direction of a professor, spending a full semester with one company. This experience proved invaluable to them, and whetted their appetites to get into business for themselves.

Noel and Shirley recently participated in several brainstorming sessions at which they tried to identify viable opportunities for a new small business. After discussing a number of opportunities, they believe they have found one that meets their requirements and in which they are willing to risk their time and money. They have concluded that most homeowners and renters do not have an accurate record of all their personal belongings. The loss of possessions through fire, theft, floods, vandalism, or other disasters can strike at any time. Yet it is impossible for most owners to prepare for their insurance companies a complete claim with accurate descriptions and supporting evidence.

Shirley and Noel propose a simple and efficient solution to the owners' problem—a complete recording of all possessions (personal and real) on a *color videotape* with the owners' voice describing the items. This would provide an *audio-visual inventory* at a reasonable cost.

Testing the idea on several home owners, Noel and Shirley have decided to include the following information on the tapes (description and video):

1. A voice introduction identifying the purpose and the date.
2. The exterior of the house, showing outbuildings, landscaping, patios, pool, lawn furniture, and so on.
3. The interior of the house, showing all rooms, hallways, closets, cabinets, and drawers.
4. Pieces of furniture, including antiques or articles of high value that would carry special coverage.
5. Pieces of sterling silver and china to show the patterns; items such as

furs, and oil paintings would be taped separately.

Shirley and Noel plan to call their firm Video Records. They will secure appropriate bonding, insurance, and licensing to protect the firm and its customers. A price structure will be developed for the services and tapes in the following range:

3 hours, minimum charge, including tape	$275.00
Each additional hour	75.00
Duplicate tape	35.00

They estimate three hours should be enough to cover the average residence and its contents. A fixed rate or price will be agreed on before the taping.

Questions

1. Do you believe Noel and Shirley's idea will fly? Why?
2. List four or five benefits that will accrue to customers.
3. What objections should they anticipate?
4. Prepare a series of closes you believe will work.

Case 13–2   Cool Aire, Inc.

For the past two years Cool Aire, Inc. has been promoting the sale of air-conditioning units for use in homes, offices, and stores. The air-conditioning unit is made by a nationally known manufacturer and is considered one of the best premium-quality units on the market. The company's outside sales representatives have attended the factory school maintained by the manufacturer and are well qualified both to service and to sell the unit.

Pat Fraser, one of Cool Aire's sales representatives, has developed a portfolio for use in presenting sales talks to prospects. The portfolio contains pictures of the unit, testimonial letters from satisfied users, technical data on the construction of the unit, and data on cost and maintenance. The portfolio has been helpful in keeping presentations brief and to the point, and at the same time it has enabled Fraser to give a complete sales presentation.

Fraser recently learned that the owner of a women's specialty shop, Ms. Diderot, was considering installing air-conditioning equipment. Fraser gathered as much information as possible on the owner and then made a cold call on Ms. Diderot. Fraser made little progress on the first call, but was able to arrange a second appointment at a more favorable time and under more favorable conditions. On the second call, after 45 minutes, Fraser thought it was time to try for a close. A portion of the conversation that ensued follows:

Fraser: This clean-cut unit with its handsome gray finish certainly blends with your office furnishings, doesn't it, Ms. Diderot?

Ms. Diderot: Yes, it does seem to harmonize with what we have.

Fraser: Not only does it harmonize with your furnishings, Ms. Diderot, but it cools, cleans, and humidifies the air. It will bring in outside air if you wish, provide you with even circulation of air, and all this can be accomplished by the flip of a switch. Best of all, Ms. Diderot, the unit has a very simple mechanism. You'll want good, dependable performance and economy in operation, I suppose.

Ms. Diderot: Why, sure, who doesn't? I want something I can depend on.

Fraser: Well, I'm sure this unit is just what you want. When would you like to get the installation under way?

Ms. Diderot: Well, I don't feel I should air-condition my store just now.

Fraser: Ms. Diderot, I know that when you decide to air-condition your store you'll want our unit. The real question, then, is whether to install the system now or at a later date. Is that right?

Ms. Diderot: I suppose so.

Fraser: Now, let's look over the facts and see if we can determine the answer to the question on *when* to make the installation. Let's do this. . . .

Suppose we draw a line down the center of this piece of paper and make two columns. We'll head the first column "Reasons for Buying Now," and we'll head the second column "Reasons for Buying Later."

In the second column, let's write all your reasons for installing later, and in the first column, let's write all the reasons why it will help your business to install now. Then you can compare the reasons in the two columns and be pretty sure you are making the right decision. How does that sound?

Ms. Diderot: Oh, I don't know. I guess it can't hurt anything. OK.

[Fraser allows Ms. Diderot to state her reasons for installing later, and they are written in column two. Then Fraser completes a much longer list of reasons for acting now and places them in the first column.]

Fraser: We seem to agree there are many more reasons for you to install now than to wait, Ms. Diderot. When do you feel it would be most convenient for you to have the installation made?

Ms. Diderot: Oh, I don't know. I'm still not sure.

Questions

1. Identify the closing techniques used by Fraser. Evaluate the use of the techniques.

2. What additional closing techniques could Fraser use? Illustrate by preparing statements incorporating the use of the techniques.

3. Make a list of statements classifiable as closing signals that Ms. Diderot could have made during the interview.

4. Complete the above interview in a realistic manner.

Case 13–3   Windsor-Jones Cleaning, Inc.

Windsor-Jones Cleaning has developed a process that will reuse cleaning fluid. This process will enable it to market a coin-operated automatic dry-cleaning machine that will clean an eight-pound load of clothing (equal to two dresses, two shirts, and two children's snowsuits) in 45 minutes at a cost of $8.

Windsor-Jones will have at least four competitors. One competitor is launching a national sales program with a sales force of 125. The company will offer a complete building that houses up to six machines. The machine sells for $8,600. Construction of the building will cost approximately $30,000, and a typical complete installation, including six dry cleaners, will cost about $85,000. The company has also constructed a specially built mobile demonstration trailer for use by sales representatives when selling to professional dry cleaners. This company will probably offer the stiffest competition.

Windsor-Jones has been operating six attended centers as a pilot operation. The cleaners are built in banks of eight, costing $45,000, with a common system for recirculating and filtering the cleaning fluid. Plans call for concentrating on selling to present dry cleaners, partly because they already understand the cleaning process and partly to make them allies rather than enemies.

A typical installation for Windsor-Jones will have 16 dry-cleaning machines, 25 to 30 washers, 10 to 15 dryers, and a pickup station for dry-cleaning work done at the cleaner's main plant on items not suitable for the machines. The company does not believe in either unattended centers or one- or two-unit installations. All operators are required to have a "consultant" on hand during operating hours. The centers will represent an investment of $100,000 to $200,000.

Over 300 distributor sales representatives and four factory field representatives for each section of the country have been appointed to assist in all phases of the selling activities. An advertising schedule has been planned through *The Wall Street Journal, Barron's,* and the *Journal of Commerce.* Ad mats are provided for advertising at the local level. In addition, trade publication advertising has been pointed to the commercial dry-cleaning industry.

Windsor-Jones will also provide the owner of a center with floor plans and ad mats, design promotion campaigns on a cooperative basis, and other sales aids, and will arrange for a five-year, easy-term plan with a down payment of 10 percent for financing the center.

Steve Windsor, son of one of the owners, is a distributor for Windsor-Jones in a large midwestern city. He has had thorough training on the merits of his company's product and has had the opportunity to participate in demonstrations of the dry-cleaning machine at state and county fairs. He is completely sold on the "center" idea of merchandising his company's products.

Windsor has been able to secure the interest of an owner of a dry-cleaning plant and has had several visits with him. Recently, Windsor had one of the factory field men accompany him on an interview with the owner.

Questions

1. To what buying motives should Windsor appeal in an attempt to close the sale to the owner of the dry-cleaning plant? Why?
2. List the objections he is likely to encounter.   •
3. Discuss the techniques Windsor might use to close the sale.
4. Prepare one or more closing routines that might be effective.

Case 13–4   Personal Prime Time Audio, Inc.—A Role-Playing Exercise

Facts about the Product and Service

The company sells a pay-per-recording system that works with an FM radio receiver and audio tape recorder.

The system gives the user control over what is heard, when it is heard, and where it is heard.

A catalog provided to the customer lists hundreds of programs. The customer chooses *only* the programs he or she wants and pays only for them.

A small five-inch by six-inch keyboard unit called the Redicoder sits near the radio and tape recorder and facilitates the recording of programs selected by the customer. Programs are broadcast overnight while the customer is asleep. The customer in the morning will have a personalized, commercial-free tape to play back as often as desired, whenever desired, and wherever desired. The unit sells for $99.

A local public broadcasting station, Station KPEP, provides the service for a fee for each program recorded. Programs

include columns from *Business Week,* previews of business and financial news from magazines and newspapers, reviews of movies, feature articles on health, special features for parents, classic science fiction, and albums of music by popular and classical recording artists. As a rule, programs run 10 to 15 minutes daily or weekly (depending on the program); special programs may run 30 to 60 minutes. The cost of the programs varies from $1.50 to $6.00 each, and new programs are being developed regularly.

The Mechanics of Use

Every month the buyer receives a catalog listing hundreds of available programs. The customer chooses the programs he or she wants and then telephones the company programming center where a code number is provided for each program. This code number is entered into the Redicoder placed near the customer's radio. When the program is broadcast, while the customer is asleep, not present, or doing something else, the cassette recorder is automatically turned on; when the program is over, the cassette recorder automatically turns off.

The audio system is easy to install. It can be quickly connected to an FM radio, a tape recorder, and an electrical outlet in the wall.

One good reason for prospects to buy the unit and its service is that the public broadcasting station benefits financially from every program the customer buys. It becomes a form of financial support for the station.

A Description of the Prospects

A retired family couple, Mr. and Mrs. Real Oldtimer.

Ages are 62 and 60, respectively.

They subscribe to a local concert series.

Both have a college background.

They live in a rural area in a home that is paid for.

They participate in area charitable fund-raising activities.

They drive a Volvo and an Audi.

They travel frequently.

Some money is invested in stocks and bonds.

They are gardening and photography buffs.

Mrs. Oldtimer paints pictures in oils and watercolors.

Mr. Oldtimer plays golf.

Both are former teachers.

They have a new video system with a radio stereo receiver, a stereo tapedeck, and a record turntable.

Sales Presentation

Assume you are a sales representative of Personal Prime Time Audio, Inc. From the above material, prepare a scenario and make a presentation to the Oldtimers.

SELECTED REFERENCES

"Closing the Sale." *Sales & Marketing Management,* 1977. A special 20-page report of 10 articles by different authors.

Cronin, Lawrence D. "Help Prospects to Do What They Want to Do." *NYLIC Review,* January 1977, pp. 8–9.

Dichter, Ernest. "Five Ways to Lose a Sale." *Industrial Distribution,* January 1976, p. 83.

Goldmann, Heinz. "The Art of Selling." *Management Today,* September 1977, p. 139.

Gschwandtner, Gerhard. "Closing Sales via Body Signals." *Marketing Times,* September–October 1982, pp. 12–13.

Hanan, Mack. "When the Customer Buys, that's the Time to Start Selling." *Sales & Marketing Management,* March 15, 1982, pp. 96–98.

————. "When Your Salespeople Get a Shot at the Top Man, Don't Let Them Get Shot Down." *Sales & Marketing Management,* July 5, 1982, pp. 102–4.

Hass, Kenneth B. "Listen More to Sell More." *Marketing Times,* July–August 1973, pp. 24–25.

Kahn, George N. "Nosing Your Way into Extra Sales." *Marketing Times,* September–October 1974, pp. 20–21.

Roth, O. B. "Secrets of Closing Sales." Englewood Cliffs, N.J.: Prentice-Hall, 1970.

Scanlon, Sally. "Every Salesperson a Psychologist." *Sales & Marketing Management,* February 6, 1978, pp. 34–36.

Trytten, J. "Salesmanship: 10 Steps for Boosting Your Sales Right Now." (Sales Builders Division) *Sales & Marketing Management,* 1975.

Wilson, John M. *Open the Mind and Close the Sale.* New York: McGraw-Hill, 1953.

Yoho, David. "13 Steps in Closing Sales." *Marketing Times,* September–October 1973, pp. 21–24.

14

Building Future Sales by Servicing Accounts and Developing Customer Relationships

Some questions answered in this chapter are:

- Why is goodwill so valuable?
- What general methods may be used to develop and to keep customers' goodwill?
- What activities will keep the goodwill of prospects who do not buy?
- What activities keep the goodwill of customers who make a purchase?
- What techniques are important to use when handling complaints?
- What guides to handling claims routines are effective?

The relationship between a salesperson and a customer seldom ends when a sale is made. It is becoming increasingly important for salespeople to build long-term relationships with customers so they will select the salespeople's products the next time they buy.

The sale indicates the end of a courtship and the start of a marriage. The quality of the marriage depends on how well the salesperson manages the relationship, how much goodwill the salesperson builds into the relationship.[1]

Future business may be affected by elements beyond the control of any company or its sales representatives. However, one sure way to decrease future uncertainties is to build solid, progressive business relationships with customers. These relationships may be developed through sound customer relations and proper servicing of accounts.

---

[1]Theodore Levitt, "After the Sale Is Over . . . ," *Harvard Business Review,* September–October 1983, pp. 87–93.

425

Seven Steps in the Sales Process

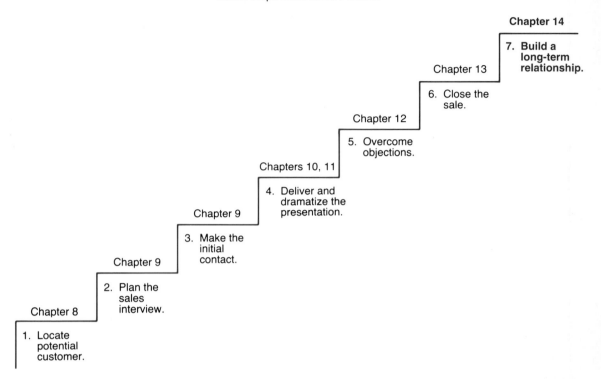

Building goodwill is an activity that enters into every phase of the selling process. Goodwill is built before the sale is made, during the sales presentation, and after the sale is closed. Goodwill is built when prospecting, when demonstrating, when answering objections, when closing the sale, and by servicing the account after the product or service has been purchased.

DEVELOP-ING GOODWILL

The Nature of Goodwill

Goodwill is the value of the feelings or attitudes customers or prospects have toward a company and its products. Those feelings and attitudes may change, depending on customers' reactions to company products and policies. When buyers are satisfied and place more and more confidence in the company, the value of goodwill increases. If the public loses confidence in the company and its products, the value of goodwill decreases and may be wiped out.

Salespeople may view goodwill as the willingness of customers or prospects to give preference to the sales representatives' companies when purchasing products or services. Customers show goodwill when they choose one company's products although several competitors may offer similar products on identical or similar terms. Everything else being equal, buyers prefer to buy from the companies they like best—this is goodwill "at work."

The Importance of Goodwill

Goodwill helps make the first sales and secures repeat sales. Customers who believe in the salespeople and their companies will help attract new prospects and new customers. Salespeople should cultivate their customers because the salespeople benefit directly and indirectly by doing so. The most tangible benefit is increased earnings. Intangible benefits may include development of a wide circle of friends or satisfaction derived from rendering services.

Many salespeople build their prospect lists from names supplied by satisfied customers. The center-of-influence prospecting method used by insurance underwriters is an example of a method based on satisfied customers or friends.

Sellers of tangible goods know that word-of-mouth advertising by a satisfied customer is the best recommendation a product, a company, or a salesperson can receive. Some customers will gladly provide letters of recommendation or testimonials; others may be willing to help demonstrate the product.

Establishing Goodwill

The general methods for developing goodwill include keeping customers' interests paramount, remembering customers between calls, and developing a personal reputation. We shall discuss each of these methods in this section.

Keeping Customers' Interests Paramount Cunning and shrewdness were once considered essential to selling. Today, both customers and businesses know that subterfuge is not conducive to good business relationships. The buyer and the seller realize they can gain most by placing confidence in each other.

In most fields of selling, it is important to have repeat sales. It takes time to know the customer's wants and peculiarities. Therefore, salespeople who plan to be of the most service to their customers must work with them over a period of time.

The kind of customer relations that builds loyal customers who buy again and again requires a better type of salesperson than the one who sells on a one-shot basis.

Goodwill is seldom built on one call. Patience and courtesy are needed to develop long-term customer relations. The customer's attitude toward the salesperson, the company, and the product is the result of actively and positively cultivating customer goodwill.

Goodwill is much like a person's character or reputation. A person can live an exemplary life for many years, but one major breach of accepted custom can destroy his or her reputation—usually forever. Similarly, salespeople can be trusted, respected, and liked because they treat customers fairly; but once a salesperson cheats a customer or gives other evidence of being undependable, the chances of further acceptance by the buyer are practically nil. In order to keep a customer's interest paramount, a salesperson may have to turn down an order that is likely to prove unsatisfactory to the buyer.

Not only must salespeople keep the customer's interest paramount, but also their attitudes toward the customer must be right. Actions alone seldom build friendships if the attitudes behind the actions are not acceptable. The basis for cultivating customers must be rooted in an attitude of service.

Figure 14–1 shows a scale used to measure a salesperson's degree of orientation to his or her customers. We can define *customer orientation* as the habit of keeping the customer's interests paramount in making a sales presentation. Salespeople who think only of making sales are sales oriented rather than customer oriented. Complete the sentences on the scale and see how you score.

Remembering Customers between Calls   Keeping a customer in mind between calls can be an effective way to build goodwill. This remembrance must spring from a desire to help the buyer or from a feeling of friendship. But whatever the reason, the salesperson must be sincere.

In addition to cultivating customers, a salesperson should remember secretaries, gatekeepers, and other influential assistants or associates. Often such people can help a salesperson reach the potential buyer. Sometimes they can supply valuable information to the salesperson on who has the greatest clout in a firm with respect to buying decisions.

Some companies use standard forms to congratulate their customers on birthdays and wedding anniversaries, on the arrival of a new baby, or on some other special occasion. The letter shown in Figure 14–2 is typical of those used by some life insurance underwriters.

The value of such letters depends on the salesperson's ability to make the message personal. A customer shouldn't think the letter is routine and impersonal. A handwritten note at the bottom or in the margin of a letter can add a touch of personal interest. The late Thomas J. Watson, founder of International Business Machines Corp., used to encourage his executives to write notes of congratulation or condolence on their personal stationery. He knew such messages meant more than dictated, typed letters.

Successful methods used by retail salespeople include phoning a customer when new merchandise arrives that might be of interest to the customer; taking special orders to secure the exact merchandise requested

FIGURE 14–1
Customer Orientation Scale

The statements below describe various ways in which a salesperson might act with a customer or prospect (for convenience, the word *customer* is used to refer to both customers and prospects). For each statement, please indicate the proportion of your customers with whom you act as described in the statement. Do this by circling one of the numbers from 1 to 9. The meanings of the numbers are:

1	2	3	4	5	6	7	8	9
True for *none* of your customers (never)	True for *almost none* . . .	True for *a few* . . .	True for *somewhat less than half* . . .	True for *about half* . . .	True for *somewhat more than half* . . .	True for *a large majority* . . .	True for *almost all* . . .	True for *all* of your customers (always)

For example, by circling 6 below, the salesperson has indicated that *somewhat more than half* of his or her customers are asked a lot of questions.

	Never	Always
0. I ask a customer a lot of questions	1 2 3 4 5 6 7 8 9	
	Never	Always
1. I try to give customers an accurate expectation of what the product will do for them	1 2 3 4 5 ⑥ 7 8 9	
2. I try to get customers to discuss their needs with me	1 2 3 4 5 6 7 8 9	
3. If I am not sure a product is right for a customer, I will still apply pressure to get him to buy	1 2 3 4 5 6 7 8 9	
4. I imply to a customer that something is beyond my control when it is not	1 2 3 4 5 6 7 8 9	
5. I try to influence a customer by information rather than by pressure . .	1 2 3 4 5 6 7 8 9	
6. I try to sell as much as I can rather than to satisfy a customer	1 2 3 4 5 6 7 8 9	
7. I spend more time trying to persuade a customer to buy than I do trying to discover his needs	1 2 3 4 5 6 7 8 9	
8. I try to help customers achieve their goals	1 2 3 4 5 6 7 8 9	
9. I answer a customer's questions about products as correctly as I can .	1 2 3 4 5 6 7 8 9	
10. I pretend to agree with customers to please them	1 2 3 4 5 6 7 8 9	
11. I treat a customer as a rival	1 2 3 4 5 6 7 8 9	
12. I try to figure out what a customer's needs are	1 2 3 4 5 6 7 8 9	
13. I try to have the customer's best interests in mind	1 2 3 4 5 6 7 8 9	
14. I try to bring a customer with a problem together with a product that helps him solve that problem	1 2 3 4 5 6 7 8 9	
15. I am willing to disagree with a customer in order to help him make a better decision	1 2 3 4 5 6 7 8 9	
16. I offer the product that is best suited to the customer's problem	1 2 3 4 5 6 7 8 9	
17. I stretch the truth in describing a product to a customer	1 2 3 4 5 6 7 8 9	
18. I begin the sales talk for a product before exploring a customer's needs with him	1 2 3 4 5 6 7 8 9	
19. I try to sell a customer all I can convince him to buy, even if I think it is more than a wise customer would buy	1 2 3 4 5 6 7 8 9	
20. I paint too rosy a picture of my products, to make them sound as good as possible	1 2 3 4 5 6 7 8 9	
21. I try to achieve my goals by satisfying customers	1 2 3 4 5 6 7 8 9	
22. I decide what products to offer on the basis of what I can convince customers to buy, not on the basis of what will satisfy them in the long run .	1 2 3 4 5 6 7 8 9	
23. I try to find out what kind of product would be the most helpful to a customer	1 2 3 4 5 6 7 8 9	
24. I keep alert for weaknesses in a customer's personality so I can use them to put pressure on him to buy	1 2 3 4 5 6 7 8 9	

The scores for items 3, 4, 6, 7, 10, 11, 17, 18, 19, 20, 22, and 24 are reversed, so for these questions subtract the number circled from 9 to get the score. The score for the remaining items is the number circled. Automobile salespeople typically scored from 150 to 160, while industrial salespeople scored from 175 to 185.

Source: Robert Saxe and Barton Weitz, "The SOCO Scale: A Measure of the Customer Orientation of Salespeople," *Journal of Marketing Research*, August 1982, pp. 343–51.

FIGURE 14–2
New Arrival Letter

Metropolitan Life

February 8, 1987

Schedules, schedules!

The new baby is home and doesn't know what "schedule"
means. Sleeping and eating come at the oddest times.

But before long you'll all be sleeping through the night.
Then there'll be the first smile, the first step, the
first word--all this and more on a schedule of baby's
own.

Right now is when you should give serious thought to
another kind of schedule--Metropolitan's insurance
rates for children. These rates are low, because
your child is young.

You should take advantage of these rates to start the
baby out with a sound future. When your youngster
grows up, a strong financial asset will be waiting.

I'll call shortly to tell you about the insurance
plans we offer for your child.

Cordially,

Representative

PAL/cab

Home Office: One Madison Avenue, New York, N.Y. 10010
Head Offices: San Francisco, Calif.; Ottawa, Ontario, Canada

Courtesy Metropolitan Life Insurance Co.

Promotional items keep the company name before the customer.

Cameramann International, Ltd.

by the customer; setting aside merchandise the salesperson believes the customer might want; and following up on merchandise that has been sold.

Many retail stores send individual letters or cards to customers who have recently paid for a major purchase. Such letters usually remind the purchaser that their patronage is appreciated, and that the store hopes they will soon use their charge accounts again (see Figure 14–3). Sometimes special credit ratings are provided for customers of this type. A successful home builder found it pays to send personal letters to recent purchasers to ask if they are satisfied with their new home. Figure 14–4 is a good example of this kind of letter.

Letters sent at Christmas to thank good customers for their patronage during the year have proved effective for some companies. Often an attractive calendar presented at New Year's may help keep the company's name before the customer all year. Figure 14–5 shows a letter used by one company.

Building a Personal Reputation   Many salespeople try to build a personal reputation with their customers and with the community in which the

FIGURE 14–3
A Letter Designed
to Show
Appreciation for
Purchases

Ms. Sue Mee   April 21, 1987
114 High Street
Albany, New York

Dear Ms. Mee:

Patronage such as yours is indeed appreciated, and as
we thank you for your recent purchase, may we ask
you also to accept the enclosed certificate of permanent
credit.

This card is issued only to a very selected list of customers
entitled to maximum credit privileges; and we trust that
you will find it useful not only in immediately identifying
your credit rating in our own store, but also in opening
other retail accounts.

Come in to see us often. New furnishing styles are always
arriving and a cordial welcome awaits you whether or not
you plan to buy.

                            Cordially,

                            LEE BROS.
ML: K   *Marcin Lee*

P.S. Please notify us promptly of any change of address
so that we can give you advance information of any
special events.

FIGURE 14–4
A Letter Designed to Build Goodwill

Mr. David A. Heagerty   April 6, 1987
COAKLEY HEAGERTY COMPANIES
122 Saratoga Avenue, Suite 28
Santa Clara, CA 95050

Dear Dave:

Welcome to a whole new world of carefree living! We know that your new
Centex Home at Spinnaker Cove will afford you a wealth of enjoyment for
years to come.

Although the experience of moving is always difficult, we can assure you
of our diligence to make your "move-in" day go as smooth as possible.
Any items on your "walkthrough" which have not been taken care of by the
time you move in will be repaired and/or corrected as soon as possible.
If there are still items to be taken care of on your walkthrough list,
please be sure our sales office knows where to reach you during the day
to make an appointment for repairs, or if you would prefer, the sales
staff has a form of Key Release that you can sign and then you can leave
a key with them to facilitate entry for repairs or corrections.

Attached you will find your "Warranty Service Request" form. If during
the first year of occupancy in your new Centex Home you need warranty
repairs, please complete this form. We would suggest that you wait for
at least 90 days before sending this form to us. Be sure to include a
telephone number where you can be reached during the day.

One copy of the form is for your records and the rest of the form should
be sent to our Warranty Department, Centex Homes of California, Inc.,
3180 Crow Canyon Place, Suite #145, San Ramon, California 94583. Our
representative will contact you after the form is received to set up an
appointment for the repairs to be made.

NOTHING CAN BE DONE UNTIL WE RECEIVE NOTICE FROM YOU IN WRITING.

Certain items, including appliances, are warranted by the manufacturer
and/or supplier. A list of numbers is attached in the event you have need
of an emergency repair. Please note that unless the repair is an emergency,
you may be charged for the repair service.

Again, we welcome you and wish you a long and happy stay in your new
Centex condominium.

                                         Very truly yours,

                                         CENTEX HOMES OF CALIFORNIA, INC.

                                         Diane I. Hughes
                                         Vice President

DH/jc

Enclosure

Centex Homes
of California Inc
P.O. Box 4160, Foster City, CA 94404 (415) 574-1500

FIGURE 14–5
A Thank-You Letter

> Mr. Ed Friendly   Christmas
> 2 Ridge Road   1987
> Philadelphia, Pa
>
> Dear Mr. Friendly:
>
> One of the greatest pleasures of being in business is the
> privilege of saying "Thank you" to good friends like you --
> and to wish you a Merry Christmas and a Happy New Year.
>
> If it were not for folks like you, there could be no firm like
> ours -- and we are deeply grateful for your patronage.
> It has enabled us to grow, and each step forward has been
> made possible by friendly customers like you.
>
> So at this Holiday Season may we express our sincere
> appreciation for the part you have played in making our
> business what it is today. In the years to come we will do
> our utmost to merit your continued confidence, and it will
> always be a privilege to serve you.
>
> May you and yours have a very Merry Christmas with the
> New Year filled with all the good things of life.
>
>   Sincerely,
>
>   MOSHER SUPPLY CO.
>
>   J. Mosher
>
>   J. Mosher, Sales Rep.

salespeople live. There are many ways to build a good reputation with customers. Some suggestions follow:

1. *Do not reveal confidential information.* The customer should believe he or she can place confidence in the salesperson.
2. *Speak well of other customers and competitors.* A salesperson who talks about other customers makes people think he or she will talk about *all* customers.
3. *Tell the truth even when it hurts.* This may involve stating when merchandise can be delivered, following up on a buyer's

concern, or investigating and making recommendations for credit purposes. Untruths or half-truths are reflections on the salesperson.

4. *Be dependable, considerate, and courteous.* The sales manager of a large steel company recalls how these human qualities can develop goodwill and sales. One day the manager received a big order for steel from a customer. The buyer enclosed a letter explaining this order was an attempt to thank the sales manager for the great courtesy the steel company had shown to the buyer in the past when steel was in short supply.

A grateful retailer named Mr. Smart tells about a salesperson who knew how to sell himself and his company's products. During a conversation, Mr. Smart told the salesperson he was planning to move to a new location. The salesperson offered to help. He not only set up the new department that stocked his product, but he helped move and set up all the remaining departments of the store. Mr. Smart wrote a note of thanks to the sales-person's company. He pointed out that—to him—that salesperson *was* the company and the company should be proud to have such a courteous person in its sales force.

Good relationships are built faster and more soundly by the salesperson who does a "little something extra" for a customer—performing services and doing favors over and above the salesperson's normal responsibilities.

Because of a willingness to provide extra effort, Loren Kennedy of Bay State Abrasive was selected top salesperson in 1978 by *Purchasing* magazine. An example of that extra effort occurred when one of Kennedy's Midwestern customers was in a bind for grinding wheels because of a trucking strike. "Kennedy flew to his Westboro, Massachusetts, plant and picked up a supply. Then he rented a U-Haul truck, loaded it, and drove straight through the night to keep his customer in operation."[2]

Participation in community affairs enhances a salesperson's standing. Some companies place great emphasis on this activity. If the salesperson sells a limited geographic area and lives in the area, membership in a service club, a professional club, and the Chamber of Commerce is a good idea. Participation in United Fund drives or other community activities shows concern for the community. People like to trade with people they know, respect, and trust.

IMPROVING CUSTOMER RELATIONS AND SERVICING ACCOUNTS

The preceding section discussed general ways to build customer goodwill. This section focuses on specific activities for improving relations both with customers who place orders and with those who don't.

---

[2]Somerby Dowst, "Top Salesmen Deliver Service, Expertise," *Purchasing,* August 23, 1978, p. 52.

If the Sale Is Not Made

A salesperson cannot expect to make a sale on every call. The best baseball player averages fewer than 4 hits out of 10 attempts. Figure skaters rarely receive 6.0 evaluations. It is also true that salespeople must expect to lose some sales. However, even when a sale is not made, sales representatives should still try to maintain or increase customer goodwill. In these cases, goodwill is maintained by accepting the customer's decision graciously. If a salesperson tries several closes and the customer is still uninterested in buying, the salesperson should respect the customer's decision. Though disappointed, the salesperson should be polite and cheerful. Parting on a pleasant note leaves the door open for another presentation. The salesperson should thank the customer for the opportunity to make a presentation and then go on to the next call.

The salesperson who has good rapport with a customer might try to learn something from an unsuccessful call. The customer might be asked to evaluate the presentation, to make suggestions for improving it, or to provide a referral to other prospective customers.

Servicing Accounts

Chapters 2 and 5 discussed the importance of repeat sales and the need for postpurchase evaluations. As we saw, the purchasing process is not over when an order is placed. Next, the goods must be received, installed, and used. While this is happening, the customer is making a postpurchase evaluation that can affect future orders and the customer's goodwill.

Just as the purchasing process does not end when the order is placed, the sales process should not end when a sale is made. The salesperson needs to provide followup services to ensure the customer is satisfied with the product. One sales expert says:

> The most important thing I've learned is that selling a man something means doing something for him. Not just describing benefits, but delivering them. In fact, the word I've come to like best is installing: taking out your screwdriver and pliers and actually matching the operating benefit with one of your customer's key processes. This means you don't just take an order; you don't just oversee delivery; you don't just handle complaints. You accept the responsibility for making the benefit happen in the customer's plant. Most important, you make sure the customer realizes he is better off, not because of the benefit per se, but because of you.[3]

The salesperson can ensure benefits happen and continue to happen in the customer's plant by seeing that the right product is delivered on time, by helping during trial periods, and by providing continuing service and information.

---

[3]Mack Hanan, "Learn Something New about Selling? Don't Let It Happen Too Often," *Sales Management,* December 10, 1973, p. 40.

Monitor Order Processing   It is important for the salesperson to prevent delays in the order cycle. Salespeople need to keep track of impending orders and inform buyers when the paperwork is delayed in the customer's plant. If orders are placed directly with a salesperson, they must be transmitted to the factory at once. Progress on orders in process should be closely monitored. Customers need to be informed of anticipated delays so they can plan accordingly.

Shipping delays often occur when customers use outdated information in placing orders. Salespeople can prevent unnecessary delays and mistakes by making sure orders are accurate, complete, and processible. Customers should be provided with the latest data sheets, product information, and descriptions of ordering procedures. All orders should be reviewed for accuracy and completeness.

Fortunately, computers have made the sales representative's job easier. Firms like Joyce Beverages, Max Factor, Goya Foods, Bergen Brunswig, and Coca-Cola have introduced the hand-held terminal for use in the field to provide their sales representatives with a new data-processing tool; other firms have introduced automated order systems.

General Electric Supply Co. facilitates the automatic placement of orders by having customer's terminals talk to its own computer. This boosts the productivity of both the salespeople and the purchasing managers they call on. "As a result salespeople spend less time writing orders and more time talking critical customer problems. Buyers save on ordering and inventory costs, and GESCO profits from sharper insights into customer buying patterns."[4]

Ensure Proper Initial Use of the Product   Customer dissatisfaction often occurs just after a new product is delivered. If customers are not familiar with it, they may have problems installing or using it. They may even damage the product through improper use. Many salespeople visit new customers right after initial deliveries. In this way, they can ensure the correct use of the product; they can also help the customer realize the full potential benefits of the product.

Provide Effective Service   Most products need periodic maintenance and repair, and some mechanical and electronic products require routine adjustments. This offers a chance to show the buyer that the salesperson's interest did not end with the delivery of the product. Salespeople should be able to make minor adjustments or take care of minor repairs. If they cannot put the product back into working order, they must notify the proper company representative. They should check to see that the repairs are made and the customer is satisfied. It's a mistake for salespeople to

[4]Thayer C. Taylor, "G.E. Posts a Sentry to Give Customers Better Service," *Sales & Marketing Management*, December 6, 1982, p. 46.

always pass the servicing job to the company's repair department. By assuming that servicing is not their problem, they run the risk of losing some profitable accounts.

Part of the salesperson's job is getting to know the customer's maintenance and repair people. The salesperson should help speed up parts shipments; in addition, he or she should supply up-to-date service manuals and place the buyer's name on the service mailing list. In this way, bulletins on maintenance and repair reach the proper people. If the service department in a customer's plant is well informed about the product, user complaints fall off dramatically.

Provide Information on the Care and Use of Products   A buyer may be satisfied with the operation of a product. But if it is not operating at maximum efficiency, the wise salesperson will show the buyer how to get more profitable use out of it.

Car salespeople may give buyers a guide that shows how to obtain the greatest satisfaction from the car. This company-prepared booklet may show how to save gasoline, how to get maximum wear from tires, how to cut down repair bills, and how to clean the upholstery. However, merely distributing the booklet doesn't complete the job. The information must be merchandised so the buyer understands it. If buyers don't understand when to service a new car, for example, they may have trouble for years. Even though this may be the buyer's own fault, he or she will blame the company, the product, and the salesperson.[5]

The Ortho Consumer Products Division of Chevron Chemical Co. sells chemicals and fertilizers through its 1,024-page publication *Gardeners' Problem Solver.* Retailers buy the volume to help amateur gardeners identify their plant problems and to recommend Ortho products to cure them.[6]

The O. M. Scott & Sons Co. regularly mails a publication titled *Lawn Care* at no cost to all buyers who ask for it. In this way, Scotts helps gardeners identify weeds and then suggests ways to control them. The publication gives detailed advice and information—with color pictures—on how to plant, water, and care for lawns with the help of Scotts products. Customers who need answers to lawn care problems are given a toll-free number to call. Moreover, customers who claim lack of success with any Scotts product receive a refund on request—with no questions asked!

To be most effective, the salesperson should not wait until the user has had trouble with the product and then point out remedies. The fewer difficulties allowed to occur, the greater will be the customer's confidence in the salesperson and the product.

---

[5]Car manufacturers place considerable emphasis on the care and use of a new car in their training programs for dealer salespersons. Retail stores provide information on how to care for such major items as carpeting and furniture.

[6]"Ortho Sells by the Book," *Sales & Marketing Management,* October 11, 1982, pp. 14–15.

Scotts provides
advice and
information on lawn
care free of charge
to its customers.

Courtesy The O.M. Scott & Sons Co.

Supply Help on Advertising, Sales, and Management Problems   This topic
is discussed more fully in Chapter 18, but it is appropriate to review it at
this point. An industrial buyer or purchasing agent may need help choosing
a proper grade of oil or selecting a suitable floor cleaner. A buyer for a
retail store may want help developing sales promotion ideas. Whether the
buyer needs help in advertising, selling, or managing, good salespeople
are prepared to offer worthwhile suggestions or services.

The salesperson usually prospers only if the buyer prospers. No buyer
is in business just to buy from salespeople. Obviously, unless the buyer
is able to use the product or services profitably or is able to resell the
product at a profit, there is no need to continue buying.

The salesperson who sells to the buyer for retail stores may have to
help merchandise the products. In some stores, the salesperson is expected to supply answers to the following questions: "What must I sell

this product for to realize a 25 percent gross profit?'' ''How can I improve my window displays?'' ''Do you have any suggestions for arranging my stock?'' ''How can I get the most for my advertising dollar?'' ''Can you help me train our salesclerks?''

Lily, a manufacturer of paper containers, offers a booklet titled *The Profitable Art of Merchandising Popcorn* to customers and prospects. The booklet tells how to select, pop, store, and promote popcorn.

Since U.S. Rubber Company recognizes that its sales and profits are directly tied to the performance of individual retailers, the company helps retailers operate at top efficiency. Within the sales area, it has set up a separate department of business-management supervisors whose full-time job is to help small, independent tire dealers. When field sales representatives uncover poor business practices, they offer to bring in a company business expert to help the dealer iron out rough spots. The dealer is usually happy to accept this suggestion. U.S. Rubber reports that the management supervisory program has more than paid for itself in increased orders from new dealers who are both successful and independent.

IBM and Xerox provide a professional product-utilization service to management. This service promotes higher production and lower costs in the office through better utilization of equipment and personnel.

General Telephone & Electronics Corporation (GTE) has prepared a systems approach to help develop and maintain the communications systems of its major accounts. Called MAST (Major Account Service Team), the team is composed of marketing (chairman), engineering, service, supply, and traffic representatives. This interdepartmental approach brings together all skills required to meet the expanding and sophisticated needs of large customers. The team complements regular methods and procedures by making available additional planning and coordination procedures and methods to ''provide major account customers with the service they expect and demand.''[7]

Standard Register promotes a philosophy for success in the highly competitive field of selling business forms to banks, automotive products manufacturers, life insurance companies, and others. Its philosophy is ''the development of a forms management program that makes it a business partner *with,* rather than merely a supplier to, its major accounts.''[8] Customers are shown how to control the costs of buying and using forms by such practices as redesigning existing forms; grouping forms for more economical ordering; keeping records of quantities on hand and on order, and keeping track of the dollar value of the inventory. Standard Register also offers to warehouse the customers' inventory.

---

[7]*GTE Practices,* Marketing Administrative Series.

[8]Rayna Skolnik, ''Standard Register Sells in Top Form,'' *Sales & Marketing Management,* October 11, 1982, p. 49.

Handling customers' complaints quickly and favorably builds goodwill toward the product and the company.

Sue Markson

Opportunities to help the buyer are limited only by imagination and judgment. Progressive companies train their salespeople to be of service. Few companies seeking repeat sales fail to supply some aids to users of their products or services. To be of real service to the buyer and the company, the salesperson should be willing to merchandise these aids. The buyer's problems should be the salesperson's problems.

HANDLING CUSTOMER COMPLAINTS

Adjusting complaints is singled out for special treatment because of its importance in developing goodwill. The goodwill established through cultivating customers is often nullified by shortsightedness in handling customer complaints. Some firms spend thousands of dollars on advertising, but make the mistake of insulting customers who attempt to secure a satisfactory adjustment.

It is well known that the cost of making the first sale is higher than the cost of repeat sales. So it is good business to make every reasonable effort to keep customers in whom the company has invested time and money.

Handling claims gives the salesperson a chance to resell the customer. Many customers don't go to the trouble of complaining. For this reason when a customer does make an effort to secure satisfaction because of disappointment with a product or service, the producing company should

Few customers
welcome surprises!

"I *warned* you that it was going to be a ROUGH estimate, Mr. Withers."

From *The Wall Street Journal,* with permission of Cartoon Features Syndicate.

view this as an opportunity to prove that it is a reliable firm with which to do business.

A recent study prepared for Coca-Cola showed that when a company fails in its dealings with a complainant, the latter will tell as many as 10 people, on average, about the bad experience; those who are satisfied tell only 4 to 5 others. It has also been estimated that for every dissatisfied person who complains, there are 50 more who just stop buying the product.[9]

Despite all the care the manufacturer takes to produce a good product, unsatisfactory products do find their way to the ultimate user or retailer. This is a natural situation. However, it becomes alarming if the unsatisfactory products become too numerous.

Most progressive companies have learned that an excellent way to adjust customer complaints is through personal visits of sales representatives. This means the salesperson may have total responsibility for this portion of the company's public relations. The salesperson who carries this burden must be prepared to do an effective job.

Avoiding Complaints

The best way to handle complaints is to avoid them. Complaints normally arise because the company and/or its products do not live up to the customer's expectations. This can occur for the following reasons: (1) the

---

[9]Significant Trends, "Don't Complain about Complaints," *Sales & Marketing Management,* September 13, 1982, p. 158.

product performs poorly; (2) it is being used improperly; (3) the terms of a sales contract were not met; and (4) the customer's expectations were too high. While salespeople cannot improve product performance, they can affect the three other sources of complaints.

Salespeople should make sure customers have reasonable expectations of product performance. To a large degree, customers base their expectations on the sales presentation. If the salesperson exaggerates the capabilities of the product or the company, the customer will be disappointed and will probably lodge a complaint. Telling the customer there has been a misunderstanding will not satisfy the customer after a complaint is registered. Complaints can be avoided by making an honest presentation of the product's capabilities and eliminating any misconceptions before the order is placed.

Providing after-sales support as described in the previous section will avoid complaints due to late delivery, the delivery of unexpected merchandise, and product misuse.

Complaints cannot be eliminated; they can only be reduced in frequency. The salesperson who knows complaints are inevitable can learn to handle them as a normal part of the job. The following discussion presents a routine and some techniques for responding to complaints.

Encourage Customers to Tell Their Story

Some customers become angry over real or imaginary grievances. They welcome the salesperson's visit as an opportunity to get complaints "off their chests." Other buyers are less emotional in voicing complaints and give little evidence of irritation or anger. In either case, it is imperative to let the customers tell their stories without interruption.

Interruptions will add to the fury and irritation of buyers who are emotionally upset. Reason seldom prevails when a grievance is discussed with an angry person. This makes it almost impossible to arrive at a settlement that is fair to all parties concerned.

The manner in which salespeople treat customers who want to present complaints determines the ease with which adjustments can be made. If salespeople get off to a poor start in the discussion, their chances of developing goodwill diminish rapidly. Customers want a sympathetic reaction to their problems, whether real or fancied. They want their grievances handled in a friendly manner. An antagonistic attitude, or an attitude that implies the customer is trying to cheat the company, seldom paves the way for a satisfactory adjustment.

Good salespeople make it evident they are happy the grievance has been brought to their attention. After the customer describes the problem, the salesperson may express regret for any inconvenience. An attempt should then be made to talk about the points on which there is agreement. Agreeing with the customer as far as possible gets the process off to the right start.

Determine the Facts

It is easy to be influenced by a customer who is honestly and sincerely making a claim for an adjustment. An inexperienced salesperson is likely to forget that many customers make their case for a claim as strong as possible. It is human nature to emphasize the points most likely to strengthen the basis for a request. But the salesperson has a responsibility to the company too. A satisfactory adjustment cannot be made until all the facts are known.

Whenever possible, the salesperson should examine, in the presence of the customer, the article or product claimed to be defective. It's a good idea to have the complaining customer tell and show exactly what is wrong. If the defect is evident, this may be unnecessary. In other instances, it is necessary to make certain the complaint is understood. The purpose of getting the facts is to determine who is at fault.

Experienced salespeople soon learn there are reasons products appear defective when there is actually nothing wrong with them. For example, a customer may complain that paint was applied exactly as directed, but it was necessary to repaint in a short time. So the customer concludes the paint was no good. However, the paint may have been spread too thin. Any good paint will cover just so much area. If the manufacturer recommends using a gallon of paint to cover 400 square feet with two coats, and the user covers 600 square feet with two coats, the product is not at fault if the results are unsatisfactory. Or if an office equipment salesperson sells a duplicating machine that requires special paper, the machine is not at fault if the customer gets unsatisfactory results from a low-grade substitute paper.

In some instances a food product may be frozen although the user has been warned that freezing will spoil it; or leather soles may crack because wet shoes have been placed on a stove to dry; or a battery may fail because it has been used for an extended time without enough water. Complaints about a product cannot be accepted just because the customer says so. It must be determined whether the product was used properly or whether it was abused.

On the other hand, salespeople should not assume that when their products or services fail, it is always the user's fault. They need an open mind to search for the facts in each case. Defective material may have found its way to the dealer's shelves; the wrong merchandise may have been shipped; the buyer may have been overcharged; or the buyer may have been billed for an invoice that was already paid. The facts may prove the company is at fault.

Investigation may prove that neither the buyer nor the seller is at fault. For example, goods can be lost in transit or damaged because of improper handling by the transportation company.

The salesperson may find that both buyer and seller have contributed to unsatisfactory results. Perhaps the buyer failed to follow printed instructions accurately, while the salesperson failed to instruct the buyer about precautions to take when using the product.

Sometimes it is impossible to determine the reason for a failure. Obviously, this creates a problem in attempting to place responsibility.

In this phase of making an adjustment, salespeople must avoid the impression they are stalling. The customer should know the purpose of determining the facts is to permit a fair adjustment; the inquiry is not being made in order to delay action.

Provide a Solution

After the customer's story is told and the salesperson helps place the responsibility, the next step is to take action.

Company policies vary, but many assign the responsibility for settling claims to the salesperson. Other companies require the salesperson to investigate claims and recommend settlement to the home office. The proponents of both methods have good arguments to justify them. Some companies maintain that salespeople are in the best position to make adjustments fairly, promptly, and satisfactorily. Others believe that when salespeople are permitted to only recommend a course of action, the customer is assured of attention from a higher level of management. Therefore, the action taken is more likely to be accepted by the customer. Companies holding the latter view also claim that for many technical products the salesperson is not qualified to make a technical analysis of product difficulties. It is probably better procedure to require salespeople to do the job where possible.

Whatever the company policy, the customer wants quick action and fair treatment and wants to know the reasons for the action.

Nothing is so discouraging to a customer as having action postponed indefinitely. While some decisions may take time, the salesperson is expected to expedite action. The opportunity to resell customers may be lost if the time lapse is too great—even though action is taken in their favor.

Most customers are satisfied if they receive fair treatment. But it is not enough for the treatment to be fair; customers must be *convinced* it is fair. Decisions that are fair to the customer and to the company are a potent factor in building goodwill.

Customers are seldom convinced of the fairness of a decision unless the reasons for reaching it are explained to them. It may be necessary for the salesperson to review the guarantee provided with the product. Or it may be desirable to explain the company's policy and to state why it is followed.

Sometimes salespeople are inclined to take the customer's side and to suggest the customer is being treated unfairly by members of management. This is poor procedure. It does not make a friend of the customer and causes the customer to lose faith in both the salesperson and the company. Moreover, it is poor policy to blame someone else for the action taken. The salesperson who is trusted with making an adjustment or recommendation should shoulder the responsibility. Any disagreement on the action taken should be ironed out between the salesperson and the home office staff. When the action is reported to the customer, it must be stated in a sound, convincing manner.

The action taken may vary with the circumstances. Some possible settlements when a product is unsatisfactory are:

1. Replace the product without cost to the customer.
2. Replace the product, and charge the customer for labor or transportation costs only.
3. Replace the product, and share all costs with the customer.
4. Replace the product, but require the customer to pay part of the cost of the new product.
5. Instruct the customer how to proceed with a claim against a third party.
6. Send the product to the factory for a decision.

Occasionally, customers make claims they know are unfair. Although they realize the company is not at fault, they still try to get a settlement. Fortunately, there are relatively few customers of this type.

It is dangerous to assume that a customer is willfully trying to cheat the company. He or she may honestly feel that a claim is legitimate even though it is clear to the salesperson that the company is not at fault. It is well, then, to proceed cautiously. If there is any doubt, the salesperson should proceed as though the claim were legitimate. If the salesperson is convinced that a claim is dishonest, there are two ways to take action. First, he or she can give the buyer an opportunity to save face by suggesting that a third party may be to blame. For example, if it is apparent that a machine has not been oiled for a long time, a salesperson may suggest, "Is it possible that your maintenance crew neglected to oil this machine?" Most buyers, especially those making an unfair claim, grab at any straw that would help them save face by placing the blame on someone else. In these circumstances, it may be possible to refuse an adjustment and still keep the customer. Second, the salesperson can unmask the fraudulent claim and appeal to the customer's sense of fair play. This procedure is likely to cause the loss of a customer. In some cases, the company may be better off without that customer. But the customer should not be alienated if there is any chance of continuing sound business relationships.

Answers to the following questions affect the action to be taken:

1. What is the dollar value of the claim?
2. How often has the customer made claims?

3. What is the size of the account?
4. How valuable is the customer?
5. How will the action taken affect other customers?
6. How successful is the salesperson in presenting facts and placing responsibility?

Follow through on Action

A fair settlement made in the customer's favor helps resell the company and its products or services. The salesperson has the chance to prove what the customer has been told for a long time—that the company will devote time and effort to keeping customers satisfied.

When the salesperson has authority only to recommend an adjustment, care must be taken to report the facts of the case promptly and accurately to the home or branch office. It is the salesperson's responsibility to act as a buffer between the customer and the company. After the claim is filed, contact must be maintained with the customer to see that the customer secures the promised settlement.

It is the salesperson's responsibility to educate the customer in order to forestall future claims. When a claim is settled to the customer's satisfaction, this is a fine time to make some suggestions. The retail salesperson may remind the user to keep the tennis racket in a press or may caution the wearer to follow directions washing wool socks. The industrial sales representative may provide a new set of directions on how to oil and clean a machine.

Some big businesses have built great names by following the slogan "The customer is always right." Within reason, this should be the attitude displayed by salespeople who plan to cultivate customers and to build goodwill for the company and themselves.[10]

A Suggested Guide

The following suggestions are helpful when a salesperson is expected to handle claims:

1. Listen carefully, sympathetically, and without interrupting.
2. Express regret for any inconvenience suffered.
3. Reassure the customer that the company wants to do what is fair.
4. Talk about those points upon which there is agreement.
5. Inquire, investigate, and examine to get the facts.
6. Try to get agreement on responsibility for the difficulty.
7. Take action as promptly as possible.

---

[10]In a talk, Jack I. Straus, former chairman of the board, R. H. Macy & Co., Inc., said, "I say if we are right and the customer is wrong, but we can't convince her, settle the matter promptly in her favor."

Table 14–1   Actions That Affect Relationships

Positive actions	*Negative actions*
Initiate positive phone calls	Make only call-backs
Make recommendations	Make justifications
Use candid language	Use accommodative language
Use phone	Use correspondence
Show appreciation	Wait for misunderstandings
Make service suggestions	Wait for service requests
Use "we" problem-solving language	Use "owe us" legal language
Get to problems	Respond only to problems
Use jargon or shorthand	Use long-winded communications
Air personality problems	Hide personality problems
Talk of "our future together"	Talk about making good on the past
Routinize responses	Fire drill/emergency responsiveness
Accept responsibility	Shift blame
Plan the future	Rehash the past

From Theodore Levitt, "After the Sale Is Over. . . ," *Harvard Business Review*, September–October 1983, pp. 87–93.

8. Educate and resell the customer to forestall future claims.
9. Follow through to see that the action promised has been taken.

When making adjustments, the salesperson is acting as a public relations representative for the company. Few companies prosper and grow if customer relations are poor.

Complaints and Customer Satisfaction

Although complaints are always a sign of customer dissatisfaction, the absence of complaints doesn't mean customers are happy. Customers probably voice 1 in 20 of their complaints. Complaints may be made only when dissatisfaction is high. A buyer in a big corporation may not be aware of what is happening until product users blow their stacks. Lower levels of dissatisfaction will hurt sales. Salespeople should continuously monitor customers' levels of satisfaction and perceptions of product performance.

SUMMARY

Salespeople can create future sales and keep their current customers from buying from the competition by servicing accounts properly and by cultivating customers through a sound program of customer relations. Goodwill is a valuable asset that can be reported in a dollar amount on the company balance sheet. Actions that build relationships are summarized in Table 14–1.

Goodwill or ill will is generated from the beginning of the sales representative's contact with a customer or prospect. To build goodwill, the

Top Left: Customer returns defective board to salesperson at lumber company and shows receipt as proof of purchase.

Top Right: Salesperson listens to complaint, examines defective board, and discusses it with customer.

Bottom Left: Salesperson cuts new board to customer's specifications.

Bottom Right: Customer accepts replacement board. The complaint has now been settled to satisfaction of both customer and lumber company.

Sue Markson photos

customer's interests must override any tendencies to merchandise shoddy products or to secure sales solely for a profit. Customer benefits and company benefits are inseparable.

Customers appreciate a salesperson's attention or remembrance between sales calls, whether it be to recognize important events, thank the customer for an order, provide help or service for products already in use, or settle any problem of logistics or misunderstandings. Nothing is more important for the sales representative than a good reputation.

Servicing customer accounts properly is an important factor in building goodwill. Customer attention should not cease when an order is secured. It is vital to monitor the orders and make certain the products or services serve the customer properly. Use of a computer can help discharge this responsibility. Some buyers may appreciate assistance or suggestions in managing their businesses. The salesperson should try to be seen as a business partner of the customer rather than just as a supplier.

Probably few opportunities exist to develop goodwill comparable to those provided by the proper handling of customer complaints. Poorly handled complaints open the door for the competition to move in. Unfortunately, only a small percentage of customers who are dissatisfied bother to complain. But word of mouth is still an important avenue for spreading goodwill or ill will.

Sales representatives ought to encourage and permit the unhappy customer to tell his or her story completely, fully, and without interruption. A sympathetic attitude to a real or an imaginary product or service failure cannot be overemphasized. After facts are determined, the solution should be implemented promptly and monitored by the sales representative to ensure that action is taken.

Different solutions are appropriate depending on the seriousness of the problem, the dollar amount involved, and the value of the customer's account. A routine should be developed to make certain every step is followed for handling complaints fairly and equitably.

QUESTIONS AND PROBLEMS

1. How can a salesperson lose by overselling a customer?

2. Explain how the "art of listening" can be applied to a customer who makes a complaint. What can the application of this art accomplish?

3. One way to maintain good relations with customers in the service field is to recognize and adjust to changes. What changes do you see taking place in the service field?

4. If the company can't deliver an item on the date promised by the sales representative who sold it, what should the sales representative do?

5. A solid basis for any business that wishes to build goodwill in a community is to "do more than is expected." How can this be done?

6. A successful business executive has been quoted as saying, "It hurts, but it's true: unless your salespeople have a working knowledge of customer service, they may wind up giving away the store." What are the implications of this statement?

7. You have been asked by the general manager of a large department store to spend some time locating points of customer irritation in the store. The store is proud of its name and is eager to maintain the goodwill it has built over the years. Make a list of the common customer complaints that may help destroy goodwill.

8. Evaluate the effect on customer relations for a real estate agent if the agent's secretary answers the telephone by asking every caller: "Who is calling?" "What is the call about?" "Could I have someone else help you?"

9. Should a salesperson handle all complaints so the customers are completely satisfied? Explain.

10. The soundest philosophy for building goodwill may be summed up in these words: "It's the little things that count." Identify six or eight "little things" a salesperson could do that will cost little or nothing, but may be extremely valuable in cultivating customers.

11. What is your reaction to the statement, "The customer is always right"? Is it a sound basis for making adjustments and satisfying complaints? Can it be followed literally? Why?

12. Many customers become irritated when they take their cars to a garage for servicing. As the sales manager for a local car dealer, you believe your service department can help keep old customers and get new ones. What suggestions would you make to the manager of the service and parts department to build goodwill through good customer relations?

13. Consumers today have almost unlimited expectations with regard to the products and services they buy. What reasons can you give for these attitudes? What are the implications of these attitudes for goodwill development?

PROJECTS

1. Reflect on a recent purchase you have made in a department store. How would you rate the salesperson in terms of postsale activities? Did he or she develop goodwill? Why or why not? What services were provided? Was your level of expectation concerning the product's performance appropriate? Prepare a written report on your observations.

2. Talk to several buyers or purchasing agents in the community. Find out whether they receive gifts from companies they do business with. Get their reactions to the purposes and values of gift giving and receiving between buyers and sellers. Write your conclusions.

3. Contact the office of the local Better Business Bureau. Secure copies of its pamphlets, interview the manager if possible, and learn as much as possible about its operation. After talking with a merchant who belongs to the BBB, prepare a report that describes why the merchant belongs to the BBB.

CASE PROBLEMS

Case 14–1   Handling Complaints

Frank Furter is a sales representative for a manufacturer of industrial supplies. He reports directly to the branch manager in the local district. Since Furter's territory is not large, he can visit the branch office at least every other day. It is customary for Furter to spend two afternoons each week in the branch office.

For the past several months, the home office has had problems meeting its promised delivery dates. This had led to some irritated customers, and of course, the situation does not help make sales or win friends.

One afternoon while Furter is in the branch office, the phone rings and an irate customer is on the line.

> **Customer:**   Look, you know how badly we need those supplies I ordered some time ago. Well, this morning I got a flip notice from your outfit in the mail telling me there will be another delay in the delivery date—the *third* such notice, mind you.
>
> Frankly, Frank, I don't think I can depend on your company's delivery dates any more. And if you think you're going to get any more orders from me, you're nuts.

Questions

1. What action should Furter take?
2. What recommendations could he make to the home office to prevent this type of situation from causing trouble again?
3. What should Furter guard against in his discussion with this customer?

Case 14–2   East Coast Air Lines, Inc.

East Coast Air Lines, Inc., with headquarters in southern Florida, is one of the oldest passenger airlines in the United States. The corporation is proud of its reputation as a safe, efficient carrier.

A special analysis of plane reservations revealed that some business executives with a long experience of flying with East Coast were no longer on its reservation lists. East Coast knows these executives must be flying with a competitor or using other means of transportation.

In order to win back as many of them as possible, East Coast's management has instructed its sales representatives to call on all business executives who travel extensively and who are no longer flying with East Coast.

Ed Burda, who has been with East Coast for three years as a sales representative, selected the owner of a small chain of department stores, August Moon, as his first contact. Burda made an appointment with Moon, and the following interview took place.

> **Burda:**   Thought I'd stop around to see you, Mr. Moon. Haven't heard your name mentioned lately.
>
> **Moon:**   And you won't hear my name mentioned around your place again either. I'm through traveling with East

Coast Air Lines. I'm sick and tired of being kicked around by your outfit. The last time I flew your line, I couldn't locate my baggage for over a week, and when you did return it, it was all bashed in.

Burda: How long ago did this happen?

Moon: The last incident was seven months ago. East Coast seems to have a complex on baggage. You either lose 'em or crush 'em. I've read your ads about having the world's fastest and most modern airlines. I've often thought that you probably have the world's most modern baggage smashers.

Burda: Oh, it can't be as bad as all that!

Moon: You don't think so, eh? You ought to be on the receiving end of a damaged piece of luggage—corners bashed in, skin peeled off, handle ripped away. And you say, "It can't be as bad as all that."

Burda: Well, of course, we are terribly sorry about it, and we are trying to cut down on that sort of thing.

Moon: I've heard that line before, but I haven't enough baggage to keep testing that statement. Moreover, you people just can't get a plane out of here on time. I have six buyers who travel by air at least once a month. I've told them to take your competitor.

Burda: Say, those new L-1011's of ours can beat anything they have to offer.

Moon: Says you, Mr. Burda. My buyers take a DC-10 scheduled out of here one hour and a half after your great L-1011—and as a rule they beat the L-1011 to its destination, usually because of your delayed departures. Hotels won't keep rooms; we miss connections; oh, it's just not worth it.

Burda: Well, Mr. Moon, we are trying to cut down on delays. We are learning more about maintaining our larger equipment, and we feel that we are making headway.

Moon: I'm fed up with East Coast, and I'm not going to give you any more tries—not until you can really sell me that things are actually different. You haven't done a very good job so far.

Ed Burda concluded the interview by saying he would certainly appreciate the opportunity to show that East Coast's service was all it was advertised to be.

Another East Coast sales representative, Russ Hodges, was the luncheon speaker for a local Rotary Club when the club celebrated Aviation Day. He talked about the operations of East Coast Air Lines in particular and about aviation problems in general. After the speech one of the Rotarians, Pete Morley, congratulated him and said he enjoyed the talk. During the conversation Hodges learned that Morley was a former East Coast Air Lines customer but had become disgruntled and was no longer flying with East Coast.

Hodges decided to call on Morley. The following conversation took place about one week later.

Hodges: Mr. Morley, it's kind of you to give me a hearing on your complaints with East Coast.

Morley: Well, I felt I owed it to you after the way I criticized your company at our club the other day. You made a darn good speech; but when I thought about my experiences with East Coast, I got somewhat irritated.

Hodges: Tell me about the experience that is making you fly with our competitor.

Morley: It wasn't *one* experience. It was a lot of the same old stuff over and over again. It was the repetition that got me down. I've used East Coast since the DC-3s, and I've always thought the world of your management—and to such an extent that I'm a stockholder. And I don't invest my money without thoroughly investigating and knowing the company.

Hodges: I'm sorry that you feel the way you do about our company, Mr. Morley. Specifically, what did you experience?

Morley: Essentially, I'm a short-haul commuter. The last time I flew East Coast, I had trouble getting a reservation. Although a round trip reservation was finally confirmed, when I checked in at my destination, your agent said they had no record of it. I'll bet I spent 20 to 30 minutes at your ticket counter trying to get the reservation straightened out. They never did find any record of it, and finally sold me space on a flight that left an hour later. But an hour with you fellows seems to be very unimportant.

All of which reminds me about the time I was on a short flight of only 35 minutes, but we spent 45 minutes at the airport while your agents ran up and down the aisle counting heads and doing a lot of talking in the rear of the cabin. You waste more time in ticketing and boarding. You ought to be able to solve that kind of problem.

And besides, there're those equipment delays. If you're going to be delayed several hours, tell us. You may lose my business that day, but I'll be back sooner than if you keep stalling me off 15 minutes at a time. There's no point my taking a plane for an hour's flight if I have to hang around an airport for an hour waiting for a delayed departure.

Hodges: You know, Mr. Morley, if it weren't for the fact that we are getting those problems licked, I'd say you were justified in using other transportation.

Morley: Getting them licked, how—how?

Hodges: In the first place, we have recently installed a new reservations system that is geared to our current needs. Under this setup, we can usually confirm your going and return space immediately. You make only one call. *One call does it all.*

In addition, we have installed a new loading procedure that has been extremely well received. And it's especially pertinent in your case as a commuter. If you have been ticketed before going to the airport, and you have no luggage, you only need to wait for the loading announcement to enplane. That's a real time-saver and a convenience to the commuter passenger, isn't it, Mr. Morley?

Morley: Yes, you're right. That boarding idea sounds great, and your "one call" is an answer to a traveler's prayer if it only works.

Hodges: It works, all right. How about giving us a chance to prove it?

Morley [*laughing*]: How about those delays? My sales representatives, unlike me, are long-haul passengers. They are using your competitors whenever possible, and your competition is doing better by them too.

Hodges: Well, I'm not going to deny we've had delays with our big planes. Naturally, it takes a while for our maintenance personnel to get the know-how of new equipment. When we introduced our DC-7s and -8s we had the same trouble, but we beat the problem. The same holds for our new L-1011's, but we are beating that one too. The record isn't perfect yet, but we are way ahead of where we were only three months ago. How about giving us another try?

Morley: And then have another piece of luggage crushed? All airlines are tough on baggage, but East Coast is near the top.

Hodges: I'll admit we haven't got an enviable record on that score. We have been putting on a campaign all over our system to eliminate damaged baggage. Management is trying its best to clean up that problem. If you will fly East Coast, I'm sure you will find an improvement on that point too.

Morley: Well, you seem confident things are better. I'll tell you. I'm planning a short trip in about 10 days. I was going to use your competition, but I might try East Coast again. I'll call you as soon as I determine the exact date.

But let me warn you, this is only a trial. I'm not going to advise my sales representatives to travel with your company again until I see some real results. You've told me a good yarn—now we'll see.

Hodges: Thank you, sir. That's a fair arrangement. I'll call you early next week to learn if you have set a definite date for your trip.

Questions

1. What do you believe to be the specific weaknesses and strengths of Burda's interview?

2. What strengths and weaknesses did you observe in Hodges' interview?

3. Which of the two sales representatives did the better job? Why?

4. What do you believe airlines must do to improve their profit patterns?

SELECTED REFERENCES

Berry, D., and C. Suprenant. "Defusing the Complaint Time Bomb." *Sales & Marketing Management,* July 11, 1977, pp. 40 ff.

Blanding, W. "Customer Service: Believe It or Not, Errors of Omission Do More Damage than Any Other Kind." *Sales & Marketing Management,* September 17, 1979, pp. 112–14.

———. "Customer Service Can Make or Break You in More Ways than One." *Sales & Marketing Management,* June 6, 1978, pp. 110 ff.

Cron, R. L. *Assuring Customer Satisfaction: A Guide for Business and Industry.* New York: Van Nostrand Reinhold, 1974.

"GE's Len Vickers." *Sales & Marketing Management,* June 3, 1985, pp. 66–68.

Jackson, Barbara Band. "Building Customer Relationships that Last." *Harvard Business Review,* November–December 1985, pp. 120–28.

O'Connor, John F. "What Happens When One Purchasing Pro Got Mad as Hell." *Purchasing,* January 13, 1983, p. 24.

"Ortho Sells by the Book." *Sales & Marketing Management,* October 11, 1982, pp. 14–15.

"Pulling Sales and Service Together—An Exclusive S&MM Survey." *Sales & Marketing Management,* October 9, 1978, pp. 82 ff.

Rosenblum, S. "10 Secrets of Better Sales Letters." *Sales & Marketing Management,* May 16, 1977, pp. 36–38.

Sabath, E. "How Much Service Do Customers Really Want?" *Business Horizons,* April 1978, pp. 26–32.

Taylor, Thayer C. "G.E. Posts a Sentry to Give Customers Better Service." *Sales & Marketing Management,* December 6, 1982, pp. 46–50.

Woods, Bob. "The Sales Force Gets a Helping Hand." *Sales & Marketing Management,* December 6, 1982, pp. 50–55.

IV
Special Applications of Selling Principles

This section considers special selling environments—selling to industrial and trade customers and selling to consumers in a retail setting. Chapter 15 covers unique aspects of industrial and trade selling including making presentations to groups and supporting distributors. Chapter 16 examines the implications of selling in retail stores.

15

Industrial and Trade Selling

Some questions answered in this chapter are:

- How do industrial, trade, and retail selling differ?
- What do purchasing agents consider when they make buying decisions?
- What are the characteristics of successful industrial salespeople?
- How do trade salespeople stimulate derived demand?
- What are effective methods for selling to a group of people?

Most consumers have frequent contact with retail salespeople in department stores. Behind each retail salesperson is an army of trade and industrial salespeople. These salespeople are involved in selling the things that go into the products sold in the department store.

For each dollar spent at the retail level, $4.50 is spent by various wholesale and manufacturing companies.[1] The following example shows the size of industrial and trade sales relative to retail sales. Let's consider a $15 calculator that might be purchased in a store. To make the calculator, the manufacturer bought $5 of processed materials, such as plastic and electronic components. In addition, capital equipment was purchased to mold the plastic, assemble the components, and test the calculator. The manufacturer sold the calculator to a wholesaler for $10. The retail store purchased the calculator from the wholesaler for $12. In this example, $27 in sales to manufacturers and wholesalers results in a $15 sale at retail.

---

[1]*Statistical Abstract of the United States, 1978* (Washington, D.C.: U.S. Department of Commerce).

Industrial salespeople sell many different products to company buyers who need the items in order to sell their own goods or services.

David Aronson/Stock, Boston

Mike Tappin

Cameramann International, Ltd.

NATURE OF INDUSTRIAL AND TRADE SELLING[2]

Who Are Industrial and Trade Salespeople?

Industrial salespeople sell goods and services to industrial companies. Traditionally, industrial customers were defined as manufacturing companies that acquire products and services in order to provide their own products and services. However, this traditional definition of industrial customers is often broadened to include governmental and institutional customers. Governmental customers include many municipal, state, and federal agencies. The federal government of the United States is the largest purchaser of goods and services in the world.[3] Institutional customers include hospitals, universities, school districts, utilities, and research laboratories. In this chapter, industrial selling is defined as *selling to manufacturing, governmental, and institutional customers*.

---

[2]For a comprehensive treatment of industrial marketing, see Robert W. Haas, *Industrial Marketing Management,* 2nd ed. (Boston: Kent, 1983). A more advanced discussion can be found in Frederick E. Webster, Jr., *Industrial Marketing Strategy* (New York: John Wiley & Sons, 1979).

[3]See Ronald L. Schill, ''Buying Process in the U.S. Department of Defense,'' *Industrial Marketing Management,* Fall 1980, pp. 291–98.

Figure 15–1   Examples of Companies Selling to Both Industrial Customers and Consumers

Type of Company	Products Sold to Industrial Customer	Products Sold to Consumers
Fireman's Fund (insurance)	Group insurance plans	Individual life and automobile insurance policies
Cleveland Electric Illuminating Co. (utility)	Energy for manufacturing companies	Energy for private homes
Boise Cascade (wood products)	Lumber for construction	Lumber for do-it-yourself home repair
International Harvester (motorized vehicles)	Fleet trucks to transportation companies	Trucks to individual farmers
Texas Instruments (electronics)	Calculators for office use	Calculators for home use

Trade salespeople sell products to wholesalers and retailers. These middlemen purchase products for resale. The resellers add value to the products by making them readily available, by providing credit, and by supplying information.

Many firms sell products to both industrial customers and consumers. Their sales to consumers are made directly or through resellers. A salesperson working for such a company usually is assigned to only one of the two markets. Examples of companies selling to both types of customers are shown in Figure 15–1.

What Are Industrial Goods and Services?

Industrial products are classified as heavy equipment, light equipment, components and subassemblies, raw and processed materials, supplies, and services. The successful seller of these products and services must be both a skilled salesperson and a technical specialist.

Heavy equipment comprises construction equipment used to build roads, buildings, and machinery, such as locomotives, turbines, machine tools, and computers. Such equipment is often designed to meet the needs of a particular customer. Companies usually treat the purchase of heavy equipment as a major investment decision. They often borrow money to purchase such equipment. For this reason, the purchase of heavy equipment has a significant financial impact.

Heavy equipment is often referred to as *capital equipment* because it is treated as a capital asset. The depreciation of the asset is considered a production cost.

Light equipment includes such items as hand tools, cash registers, instruments, and small motors. Both heavy and light equipment are used in the production process. Light equipment has a lower price and a shorter expected life than heavy equipment. It is typically available in standard sizes from several manufacturers.

Components and subassemblies are items that become part of a company's final product. Some examples are gauges, semiconductors, plastic parts, and hardware. The cost of subassemblies and components directly affects the cost of the company's products. Thus, companies are very concerned about the price of these items. Another important consideration is uninterrupted availability. If companies cannot get the necessary components, they cannot make and sell their own products. To get low prices and assure availability, industrial customers encourage competition among suppliers. Frequently customers will not buy a component unless a "second source," that is, an alternative supplier, is available. Development of new suppliers is an important activity for purchasing agents. Often companies are faced with "make-or-buy" decisions on components and subassemblies. They must decide whether it is best to make parts themselves or to buy them from a vendor.

Raw and processed materials are the basic or processed materials of the land and sea. Raw materials include logs, iron ore, crude oil, and fish. Lumber, steel, and chemicals are examples of processed materials. Very few firms sell raw materials. Raw materials are typically traded in markets. Their prices are set by the force of supply and demand. Processed materials are usually available from several sources. The materials themselves are not differentiated. Suppliers of processed materials compete on the basis of the services they offer, such as fast delivery, the available range of sizes and forms, and applications assistance.[4]

Maintenance, repair, and operating (MRO) supplies include cleaning supplies, grinding wheels, paper products, and office supplies. MRO supplies are used by an organization as part of its normal operations. They do not become part of the finished product. The items have a low unit price and are purchased frequently. Often, an annual agreement is negotiated with a supplier. In the agreement, the company guarantees to purchase a specific quantity over the contract period. The supplier then provides the item at a reduced price.

Services include all intangibles purchased by an organization, such as insurance, banking, consulting, and shipping. It is very difficult to develop purchase specifications for services. The quality of services is hard to measure. Services depend greatly on the people who deliver them. For this reason, the people responsible for delivering a service are often responsible for selling it.[5]

---

[4]See Elizabeth J. Wilson, "A Case Study of Repeat Buying a Commodity," *Industrial Marketing Management,* August 1984, pp. 195–200.

[5]Most of this chapter deals with selling products. Information on selling industrial services can be found in Warren Wittreich, "How to Sell/Buy Professional Services," *Harvard Business Review,* March–April 1966, pp. 73–78, and Christian Gronroos, "An Applied Theory for Marketing Industrial Services," *Industrial Marketing Management,* Fall 1979, pp. 45–50.

How Do Industrial, Trade, and Retail Selling Differ?

Like all salespeople, industrial and trade salespeople must convince the customer that their products and services will satisfy the customer's needs. Certain characteristics of industrial and reseller markets make them different from consumer markets. The following general characteristics are important to salespeople:

Geographic Concentration   The distribution of consumer product markets and consumer product reseller markets is related to the distribution of the population. In contrast, industrial markets are highly concentrated. There are often great distances between markets in the same industry. For example, companies in the electronics industry are concentrated in Boston, New York City, the San Francisco Bay Area (Silicon Valley), and Los Angeles. Over 50 percent of all U.S. manufacturing is done in seven states: New York, California, Pennsylvania, Illinois, Ohio, New Jersey, and Michigan. Less than 2 percent of the U.S. manufacturing firms account for over 50 percent of industrial sales. Thus, the industrial salesperson usually deals with a few customers in a restricted geographic area.

Derived Demand   The demand for the products sold by industrial and trade salespeople is derived rather than direct. This means the amount of a customer's purchases depends on the demand for the customer's products. For example, the number of Ford cars consumers buy determines how many tires Ford will purchase from a tire manufacturer. Because demand is derived, the salesperson must understand the needs and buying habits of the ultimate customer as well as the immediate customer. Sometimes salespeople can stimulate the demand for their products by directing their efforts toward the ultimate customer. Procter & Gamble salespeople set up in-store displays so consumers will buy more of their products. When consumers buy more, the supermarkets will place more orders with Procter & Gamble salespeople.

Complexity of the Buying Process   As discussed in Chapter 4, the typical industrial sale is much larger in both dollars and units than the typical consumer sale. The purchasing decisions of industrial companies frequently affect company performance. Many people get involved in the decisions. Companies use highly trained, knowledgeable purchasing agents to make the decisions. The purchasing agents work with engineers, production people, and business analysts to evaluate the technical and economic aspects of purchasing decisions. *Factory* magazine found that an average of 11.9 people, not including the purchasing department, are involved in a purchase decision.

These extensive evaluations and negotiations occur over a long period. The average time required to complete an industrial purchase is over five months. During that time, the salesperson must make many calls to gather information and get the order. The importance of contacting the right decision makers is demonstrated in Selling Scenario 15–1. While getting

Selling Scenario 15–1

ICE WATER FOR BREAKFAST

 Joseph Schmelzer III, president, Equipment, Inc., a Jackson, Mississippi construction and material handling equipment dealer describes his most rewarding sales experience.

My most rewarding sale was my first experience in sales, when I was 15 years old. I was selling Black & Decker industrial tools, construction equipment, and Igloo watercoolers to builders at job sites.

This particular sale happened in 1963 in the small town of Flora, Mississippi. Being the son of the owner of the company, I drove the delivery truck. One day, my dad told me to go ahead and try to sell some equipment. We sold things like pins for fastening concrete to woodframe houses, sheet studs, and other standard building supplies, in addition to tools and the Igloo line. We were sort of a one-stop shop, a place where you could get just about anything you needed.

I called on one builder and tried to sell him some tools. Unfortunately, he didn't need them. Next, I tried to sell him some steel scaffolding. He didn't need that either. Then I tried to sell him some concrete pins—no sale. By this time, I could see he was trying to get rid of me. The last thing I could think of to sell him were the portable watercoolers, and he told me that they were no good without ice water in them. This gave me an idea.

The next morning, I got up at 5:30 and went to get ice to put in the coolers. I showed up at the job site at 7 A.M. with the ice still intact. I don't think he expected to see me at that time of the morning. Well, to make a long story short, he ended up buying two coolers—as well as all his other supplies—from me.

This was the first, and definitely the most rewarding, sale of my career, even though yesterday I closed a deal for some automated guided vehicle systems and other materials handling equipment. In 25 years, I went from $15 water coolers to $850,000 worth of equipment in a single sale.

Source: Reprinted from "Strange Tales of Sales," *Sales & Marketing Management,* June 3, 1985, pp. 44–45.

past the purchasing agent in this situation worked, this approach can result in poor relationships.

The complexity of the industrial purchase decision means a salesperson must be able to work with a wide range of people. In selling a new packaging material to a food processor, a salesperson might interact with advertising, product development, legal, production, quality control, and customer service people in the customer's company. The salesperson must know about the technical and economic benefits of the product. In addition, salespeople must coordinate all areas of *their own firm* to assist in making the sale. The salesperson works with engineering to provide the performance needed by the customer, with production to meet the customer's delivery needs, and with the business office to set financial terms. Trade salespeople must often coordinate cooperative ad campaigns in addition to checking on delivery and financial terms.

Long-Term Customer-Salesperson Relationships   In industrial and trade selling, the salesperson and the customer are dependent on each other. The salesperson needs the customer's orders to meet sales objectives. But the customer needs the salesperson to make sure the product is delivered when it is needed and that repair parts and service are provided. Because of this interdependence, obtaining a specific purchase order is only one point in a long-term relationship between the industrial salesperson and the customer. In contrast, in retail selling the salesperson-customer relationship often ends after the sale.

The following comments by Jim Ferguson, a purchasing agent at IG Technologies, illustrates how relationships develop:

> A couple years ago I couldn't get corrugated boxes from the big companies. One company stood by me and got me the boxes. Now the market has changed, and the big companies are coming in and say they can save me $20 by switching. Their salesmen tell me I'm not doing my company justice because I won't save it money. But the other guy was there when I needed the boxes. And the market will change again.[6]

Team Selling

Team selling is becoming more common in industrial selling. The products are so complex that one salesperson cannot be an expert on all facets of the buying process. To handle complex industrial purchase decisions, companies frequently assign a group of people to sell and service a key account. The team includes people familiar with the viewpoints and concerns of key decision makers in the customer's organization.[7]

Each member of the selling team works with a member of the buying decision makers. For example, the production specialist on the selling team is matched with production people in the buying organization. An account manager has to coordinate the efforts of the sales team.

Boeing uses team selling for passenger airplanes. When an airline is considering the purchase of new aircraft, Boeing sends 20 to 30 people to the airline's headquarters. The team consists of specialists in financial analysis, aircraft maintenance, airline scheduling, marketing, forecasting,

---

[6]"PA's Examine the People Who Sell to Them," *Sales & Marketing Management,* November 11, 1985, p. 41.

[7]See Dan T. Dunne, Jr., and Claude A. Thomas, "Strategy for Systems Sellers: A Team Approach," *Journal of Personal Selling and Sales Management,* August 1986, pp. 1–10.

Sales teams from
Boeing help
configure planes to
meet customers'
needs.

Courtesy Boeing Commercial Airplane Company

and engineering. Each of these specialists works with counterparts in the
airline. Frequently, members of the Boeing sales team are at the airline
headquarters for months while the purchase decision is being made.

Some customers are so important to a company that they maintain a
permanent sales and service team at the customer's location. ATTIX (the
AT&T division responsible for selling the long-distance telephone network) has a team of 50 people at General Motors Corporation. Members
of the team periodically fly from Detroit to various GM plants throughout
the United States.

Multilevel Selling

Multilevel selling is a special type of team selling. A multilevel sales team
consists of people from various levels in the selling company who call on
their counterparts in the buying company. For example, the seller's chief
executive officer (CEO) calls on the buyer's CEO. The seller's vice president of finance sees the buyer's vice president of finance. And account
managers call on people at their own level in purchasing and engineering.[8]

---

[8]For a discussion of selling at different levels in an organization, see William S. Staples
and John T. Coppett, "Sales Presentations at Three Company Levels," *Industrial Marketing
Management,* Spring 1981, pp. 125–28.

THE PUR-CHASING AGENT

While many people are involved in the purchasing decisions of distributors, retailers, and industrial companies, professional purchasing agents, or buyers, usually handle the buying process. This section addresses some of the unique activities of purchasing agents.

Value Analysis

In the late 1940s, General Electric introduced a problem-solving method known as *value analysis.* Its objective is to reduce costs and still provide the necessary level of performance. In other words, value analysis is a method for helping the company make the "best buy."

Usually members of the purchasing department do the value analysis. When complex parts or products are examined, technical experts from engineering, production, or quality control may be part of a team making the analysis. They begin by examining the product's function. Then they ask questions to see if changes can be made in the design, materials, or construction of the product to reduce the product's cost but not its performance. A value analysis uses questions like these:

Can the part be eliminated?

If the part is not standard, can a standard part be used?

Does the part have greater performance than is required?

Are unnecessary machining or fine finishes specified?

Can a similar item in inventory be specified?

How can the industrial salesperson use value analysis? A properly planned sales presentation using value analysis is a good way to get a buyer to consider a new product. This technique is particularly useful when customers are satisfied with present suppliers (straight/rebuy situations). In such situations, the purchasing agent will consider a new supplier only if doing so will achieve a significant new benefit. Through value analysis, the salesperson can convince buyers that their needs have changed, and they should consider a new supplier. Customers expect salespeople to make cost-saving suggestions.[9]

Value analysis can be applied to such mundane products as washroom supplies—hand towels and toilet paper. The Scott Paper Company makes premium quality products. To sell their products at a high price, Scott salespeople have to prove the products are worth the extra money. Using value analysis, the salespeople help purchasing agents determine how much it costs to use the product, rather than how much the product costs. They focus on the price per use and the number of dries per case of paper towels rather than on the price per case. Scott even designs its own paper

---

[9]"Help Vendors Board the VA Bandwagon," *Purchasing,* May 29, 1980, pp. 94–95.

towel dispensers to reduce the number of refills needed and thus reduce maintenance labor costs.[10]

Purchasing Contracts

Much of today's purchasing takes place under contracts that reduce the purchase decision to routine clerical activities. In other words, purchase contracts lead to straight rebuy decisions.

Two common types of purchasing agreements are the *blanket purchase order* and the *annual purchase agreement*. The blanket purchase order is often used when low-cost items, such as MRO supplies, are bought frequently.

Under a blanket purchase order, the buyer contracts with the supplier to accept delivery on a specified quantity at a specified price over a specified period of time. A purchase order is issued when the contract is made. When the items are needed, a release form is issued, authorizing the vendor to make a shipment. This type of contract minimizes the number of formal purchase orders.

Under an annual purchase agreement, the supplier agrees to provide parts at a specified discount schedule over the contract period. As the company buys more parts, it qualifies for lower prices.

Purchasing contracts tend to "lock in" organizations to their present suppliers. For this reason, it is advantageous for salespeople to conclude long-term contracts with customers. On the other hand, it is hard for salespeople to sell to customers that have contracts with competitors.

Reciprocity

Reciprocity is a special relationship in which two companies agree to buy products from each other. Such relationships are fairly common in industrial markets. For example, an electronic components manufacturer may buy test equipment only from companies that use its components in making their test equipment. There are some good reasons why companies buy from their customers. The interrelationships caused by reciprocal dealings can lead to greater trust and cooperation between the companies.

Attempts at reciprocity can result in ill will between companies. The procedures for monitoring a reciprocity agreement may become very complex. For example, a company may decide to buy from a customer only if the customer's prices are identical to those of the competition. In some cases, companies may threaten customers. They may indicate they will buy from a customer only if the customer agrees to buy from them.

The use of reciprocity varies from informal arrangements to formal agreements that include systems for keeping track of purchases. Formal agreements tend to reduce price competition. For this reason, most pur-

---

[10]"Smart Suppliers Use VA to Catch the Smartest Buyers," *Purchasing,* May 29, 1980, pp. 100–102.

chasing agents dislike reciprocity.[11] Reciprocity agreements that substantially lessen competition can be illegal. Thus, the salesperson must use caution when discussing such deals.

Purchasing Policies

Formal company policies often control a purchasing agent's activities. For example, a company may insist on receiving competitive bids from at least two suppliers before placing orders over $10,000. Or specific people in the company may have to approve purchase orders of specified amounts. An engineer, for example, may be able to purchase up to $1,000 worth of equipment. But his or her supervisor may have to approve purchases of more than $5,000; purchases of over $10,000 may require the department manager's approval. For this reason, salespeople have to know company policies that control both the steps and the people involved in purchasing.

Increasing Importance of Purchasing Agents[12]

The environment of industrial firms, which began to change rapidly in the 1970s, has continued to change in the 1980s. The major changes include shortages in raw materials such as oil and precious metals, rapidly increasing costs for raw materials, and increased competition from international companies and deregulated industries.

Because of these changes, companies are under pressure to control the cost of purchased goods and minimize inventories. Purchasing departments and their managers are being upgraded in organizational status. Major firms, including Du Pont, Sperry Rand Corp., and Kaiser Aluminum, have elevated the director of purchasing to the level of vice president. Many organizations are combining their purchasing, transportation, inventory control, and various other functions into an all-encompassing materials management department.

In view of these changes, purchasing managers are upgrading their skills and using computers. The National Association of Purchasing Management (NAPM) has a rigorous certification program that requires a minimum of three years of experience and a formal education that includes courses in quantitative techniques; candidates must pass four examinations. Many companies use computers to keep track of inventory levels and production requirements, lists of qualified buyers, and outstanding quotations. The computers also report on the status of orders that have been placed, records of delivery, and the performance of vendors. Each

---

[11]Monroe Bird and C. Wayne Sheppard, "Reciprocity in Industrial Buying and Selling: A Study of Attitudes," *Journal of Purchasing,* November 1973, pp. 26–35.

[12]See Gregory D. Upah and Monroe M. Bird, "Changes in Industrial Buying: Implications for Industrial Marketers," *Industrial Marketing Management,* Winter 1980, pp. 117–21; and Larry Guinjpero and Gary Zenz, "Impact of Purchasing Trends on Industrial Marketers," *Industrial Marketing Management,* Winter 1982, pp. 17–23.

Figure 15–2   What Purchasing Agents Like, Don't Like, and Hate

The Good	The Bad	And the Ugly
"Honesty"	"No followup"	"Wise-ass attitude"
"Lose a sale graciously"	"Walking in without an appointment"	"Calls me 'dear' or 'sweetheart' (I am a female)"
"Admits mistakes"	"Begins call by talking sports"	"Gets personal"
"Problem-solving capabilities"	"Puts down competitor's products"	"Doesn't give purchasing people credit for any brains"
"Friendly but professional"	"Poor listening skills"	"Whiners"
"Dependable"	"Too many phone calls"	"Can't believe what he says"
"Adaptability"	"Lousy presentation"	"Wines and dines me"
"Knows my business"	"Fails to ask about needs"	"Plays one company against another"
"Well prepared"	"Lacks product knowledge"	"Pushy"
"Patience"	"Wastes my time"	"Smokes in my office"

Source: "PA's Examine the People Who Sell to Them," *Sales & Marketing Management*, November 11, 1985, p. 39.

morning, the purchasing agent logs onto the computer from a desk-top terminal to obtain information on new material requirements and potential delivery problems. The purchasing agent can search the vendor files and pick out which vendors should receive requests for quotations. In requesting quotations, there is little human intervention. Requests are prepared on a word processor and sent to the vendor. Some systems automatically place orders with vendors when inventories reach a critical level.

Because of these changes in purchasing procedures, industrial suppliers need to improve the skills of their salespeople. In turn, salespeople must learn to deal with the new needs of purchasing agents for information. All other things being equal, companies that upgrade their salespeople will be in the best position to sell to modern purchasing agents.

CHARACTERISTICS OF TOP INDUSTRIAL SALESPEOPLE

Recently, *Sales & Marketing Management* asked purchasing agents the importance of various qualities.[13] Over 90 percent of the purchasing agents surveyed indicated reliability/credibility, professionalism/credibility, and product knowledge were either extremely or very important. Basically, purchasing agents value salespeople who practice the marketing concept—who are thorough and follow through with commitments and are willing to go to bat with their firms for their customers. Purchasing agents' likes and dislikes are summarized in Figure 15–2.

Each year, *Purchasing* magazine invites its readers—purchasing agents—to nominate salespeople for selection as the top 10 salespersons of the year. Some of the top salespeople in 1986 are described in Figure 15–3.

_____
[13]"PA's Examine the People Who Sell to Them," *Sales & Marketing Management*, November 11, 1985, pp. 38–41.

FIGURE 15–3
The Top 10
Salespeople

Tom Barkley

Petter Supply Co., Paducah, Kentucky. He is an expert at finding parts to help his customers. For example, he located a critically needed wire rope in a local marine supply shop to keep a chemical company's salt conveyor system from going down.

Jack Callahan

Callahan Chemical Co., Palmyra, New Jersey. He works with buyers' production departments in suggesting alternate materials and new manufacturing processes. "Responds immediately to problems."

George E. Davis

Seneca Steel Division, Gibraltar Steel Corp., Buffalo, New York. "When you give him a project, you know that you'll get an answer or an update. You don't have to see him to know he's on your side." For example, he suggested material change to cold-rolled steel to ease postpurchase cleaning, priming, and painting.

Henry F. Dial, Jr.

Kerr Glass Manufacturing Corp., Richmond, Virginia. He assists on technical problems ranging from bulk palletizing of glass bottles to development of tamper-evident closures on consumer goods, such as pharmaceutical products. "Aware of our product direction and general business trends, and communicates them to his company's management." He gets credit for $500,000 in annual savings for one customer.

D. V. "Woody" Marshall

Reliance Electric Co., Cleveland, Ohio. Although he doesn't have a technical degree, he's logged time in engineering and has done work on prototypes in the field. He's also always available, at home or at work.

Thomas J. Nagle

Babcock and Wilcox, Tubular Products Division, Lisle, Illinois. He arranges for speedy deliveries to help customers quote on short-leadtime business or get out of stockouts caused by their own forecasting errors. "He is the standard by which I judge all the other sales reps who call on me."

Jerry Phillips

East Texas Containers, Tyler, Texas. He provides the kind of service that makes every buyer feel special. "We might as well be his only customer."

Paul D. Schaefer

KCS Industries, Milwaukee, Wisconsin. He gets special praise for developmental work with pressure-sensitive labels, assuring that they stay applied to a broad variety of materials under unusual conditions of heat and cold.

FIGURE 15–3
(*concluded*)

> **Terry Simokat**
>
> Burlington Air Express, San Diego, California. He has been instrumental in setting up computerized links that give customers direct-access tracing and auditing. "Always truthful!" stresses one customer. "I can go to sleep on overnight shipments after hanging up the phone with him," says another.
>
> **William Walsh**
>
> Westech Sales, Mountain View, California. He uses VA techniques to find cost-reduction opportunities in both his principals' and customers' plants. "Always willing to assist all departments," says a buyer whose firm netted $200,000 from such suggestions.

Source: "And the Top Ten Salespeople Are. . . ," *Purchasing*, October 23, 1986, pp. 17–18.

TRADE SELLING— STIMULATING DERIVED DEMAND

A main function of trade salespeople is helping retailers, wholesalers, and distributors sell their companies' products. By providing promotional services, salespeople can stimulate their customers' demands. Case 15–2 in this chapter illustrates a sales call by a Carnation trade salesperson.

Promotional Aids

We shall now discuss a few important promotional activities of salespeople.

Training Aids Some companies provide retailers and distributors with a lot of help training salespeople. This can take the form of films, bulletins, publications, manuals, demonstrations, and other sales aids. Figure 15–4 shows pages from a brochure provided by Procter & Gamble to educate retailers about Pert Plus shampoo. Companies can handle the training in a number of ways—through the regular sales representatives, through specialists from the main office, or through training specialists who conduct programs at the factory or home office.

Such aids can help the salesperson increase the retailer's and the distributor's turnover, resulting in greater sales. Training aids are often an important factor in closing sales and opening new outlets.

Special Sales Aids Some companies help retailers and distributors plan and conduct special sales promotions. For many salespeople, this display of interest in the retailer's welfare is a strong selling point. This type of aid can result from a cooperative analysis of the retailer's sales problems. On the basis of the analysis, appropriate sales-stimulating activities can be recommended.

These activities may take many forms: They may include development of a direct-mail campaign or of a newspaper, radio, or TV ad promotion; they may involve new store signs or other means of identification; and

FIGURE 15–4

Pages from an Education Sales Aid Used by Procter & Gamble Salespeople

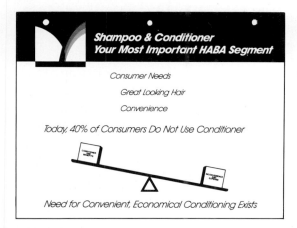

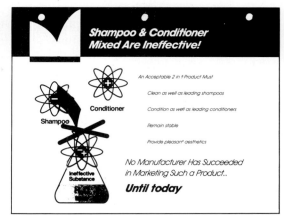

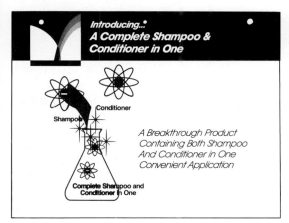

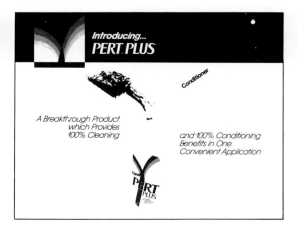

Courtesy The Procter & Gamble Company

they may include participation in trade shows or commercial and industrial exhibits. Sometimes demonstrators come to retail stores, and sampling campaigns are inaugurated. At other times, there are sales contests and consumer contests; premiums, novelties, stickers, tags, and labels may be used.

Point-of-Purchase Display Aids There is constant competition among sales representatives to place their companies' display aids in the most desirable spot.

These display aids may include charts, graphs, pictures, signs, window displays, counter displays, floor displays, banners, and wall hangings. They may involve the use of baskets, bins, racks, price cards, stands, and other devices.

An appropriate shelf display of products is important to manufacturers because of the relationship between the kind of display and its location and the number of sales. Salespeople can greatly increase sales with attractive display aids, if they can persuade the retailer to place the aids in preferred spots.

Management Aids   So far we have spoken of aids designed to help secure immediate sales for the retailer or dealer. In addition, some companies provide management aids for the dealer. These aids aim to develop good-will by helping the store owner reduce expenses. This should result in additional sales for the company.

Some management aids help the retailer remodel the store and improve arrangement of merchandise. Others improve stock control and introduce better methods of accounting, credit, and collection. Still others improve procedures and plans for hiring and compensating salespeople.

Selling the Promotion Program

A sales presentation in trade selling should include the use of company advertising and sales promotion aids. As a result, sales are likely to be easier and quicker.

The trade salesperson must first decide if the company's advertising and sales promotions might interest the buyer. If so, the salesperson should use pertinent data as one of the sales presentation features. If the buyer's interests focus on other sales features, good judgment suggests placing the emphasis where it is most likely to result in a sale.

Many salespeople who sell direct to the ultimate user have portfolios containing full-sized copies of recent company ads in leading magazines. These ads may be shown to the prospect at the beginning of the interview as a technique for starting the sales talk. Or they may be referred to, as needed, to reemphasize some of the product's sales features. To some buyers, a product gains prestige from national advertising.

To other buyers, sales promotion aids may be a major concern. These buyers may be more interested in the merchandising aids than in the price of the product. A single effective merchandising aid may cause some buyers to decide to do business with the sales representative. Figure 15–5 shows pages from a brochure that outlines a promotional program for Pert Plus shampoo.

The buyer is entitled to a clear, definite explanation of the benefits of the company's program. It's not enough to say, "We carry on an extensive advertising program in national magazines." The sales representative should point out the company's advertising schedules, quoting the names of specific magazines, their circulation, the date of their appearance on the newsstands, the cost involved, the theme or appeal used, and what this advertising means to the dealer. Copies of proposed ads and company-prepared schedules should be shown.

FIGURE 15–5
Pages from the Promotional Program for Pert Plus Shampoo

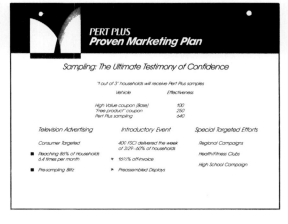

Courtesy The Procter & Gamble Company

If a national network or a local station is used for company advertising, the salesperson must be able to answer such buyer questions as: Who listens to the program? How effectively does the program sell? What can I do to cash in on the company advertising? How much will it cost me? What help does the company offer?

Examples of successful promotions with retailers in other cities would be interesting and convincing if the circumstances were similar. Samples of scripts prepared to advertise the store and for use right after the company program would be effective.

If the company has prepared store display aids or other dealer helps to increase sales of the product, these aids should be described in detail; illustrations and samples should be shown. The salesperson needs to

FIGURE 15–6
Sales Aid for Head & Shoulders Shampoo

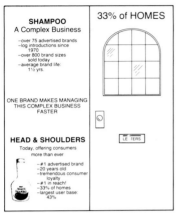

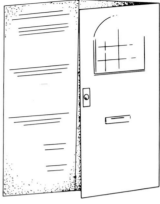

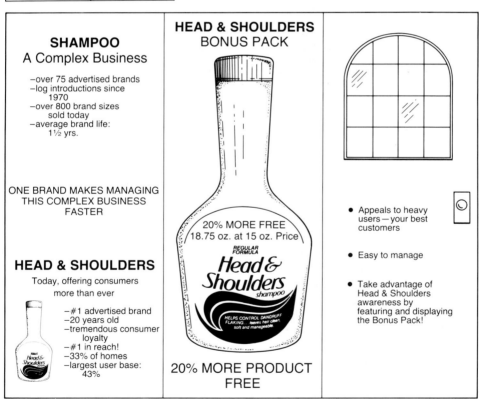

discuss such factors as cost, appearance, effectiveness, accessibility, installation, and timeliness. Often, salespeople will develop their own sales aids to discuss these factors. An example of a sales aid for Head & Shoulders shampoo is shown in Figure 15–6.

GROUP SELLING[14]

Industrial and trade salespeople often make sales presentations to groups of people rather than to individual buyers. This is particularly true in selling to food retailers. Committees make 90 percent of all buying decisions for grocery store chains.

The principles stated in previous chapters are applicable both when an industrial salesperson makes a presentation to an individual in face-to-face selling or to groups. This section discusses additional points to keep in mind when making group presentations.

Selling to Groups versus Individuals

In selling to an individual, the salesperson first determines the individual's needs and then develops a sales presentation to show how the salesperson's product will satisfy those needs. For example, if a salesperson finds that a production manager is interested in the reliability of a drill press, the salesperson can use this information to show that the drill press has a high-reliability design.

In selling to a group, it is not possible to determine the needs of each person and to deliver a separate presentation to him or her. In addition, selling to a group provides additional pressures and complications. The salesperson cannot observe and respond to all the body language signals that indicate how members of the group are reacting to the presentation.

Finally, it is hard to close sales at a group meeting. Since its members rarely agree on all aspects of the sales presentation, they will need time to resolve their differences. Usually, the salesperson must contact some individuals after the meeting to respond to unanswered questions.

In making group presentations, the salesperson must realize the group has an effect on each member as well as on the salesperson. People who are self-confident in a face-to-face situation may be at a loss before the opposing opinions of a group.

Planning a Group Meeting

The salesperson initiates a group sales presentation by making a presentation to an individual. The purpose of this meeting is to persuade that person to schedule a group presentation. Most group presentations are made in a conference room in or near the purchasing department.

Before the group presentation, the salesperson should attempt to contact each member of the group. In the premeeting contacts, the salesperson attempts to learn each person's needs, interests, opinions, and preferences. The salesperson also tries to determine which participants have the most influence on various aspects of the purchase. If a leader can be identified, the salesperson should try to sell him or her before the meeting. It is important to have a strong ally when making a group pre-

---

[14]Much of the material in this section was based on Gary M. Grikscheit, Harold C. Cash, and W. J. E. Crissy, *Handbook of Selling: Psychological, Managerial and Marketing Bases* (New York: John Wiley & Sons, 1981), pp. 228–39.

sentation. But the salesperson must also realize that the group atmosphere can change an individual's opinions and beliefs. Sometimes even a strong ally may not support the salesperson at the group meeting.

Classifying Group Members

Researchers have found that members of a group tend to assume a role or function. Some of them strongly wish to solve the problem facing the group. Referred to as *energizers,* these individuals become upset at any distraction since they want the group to work exclusively on the problem. Others—the *pacifiers* who want to keep all members of the group happy— try to handle any disagreements that arise. Figure 15–7 describes some common roles assumed by group members.

At the meeting, the salesperson should try to classify each member in terms of the role he or she plays. On the basis of this classification, the salesperson can formulate a strategy for using the group member in the meeting. For example, the salesperson might determine that one of the group members is an informer—a knowledgeable individual who tends to offer ideas and facts to the group. The salesperson should call on the informer when new ideas are needed, but should avoid that person when enough good ideas have been presented. Figure 15–7 also shows the different strategies to use with people in different roles. The group leader may often present a difficult problem for the salesperson by assuming the monopolizer's role. The salesperson wants to make sure the leader is convinced by the presentation, but does not want to offend other group members by directing too much attention to the leader. It is also important for the salesperson to realize the leader can be influenced by the group's reactions.

Getting Participation

In making a presentation to a group, the salesperson should involve most members in the discussion. Group members taking an active role pay more attention to the presentation. They also become committed to any group decision.

Salespeople can increase participation by stating that they do not want to make a speech but to exchange ideas. Questions and comments should always be encouraged at a presentation. In addition, the salesperson should listen carefully to the comments of group members and show a sincere interest in their views. Finally, it's a good idea to tolerate even poorly developed or opposing views, particularly at the start of the meeting. If salespeople criticize a group member early, other group members may be reluctant to express their opinions.

Salespeople cannot depend on voluntary participation by group members. They must direct questions to specific individuals rather than to the group in general. But they should avoid calling on a shy person, particularly early in the meeting. That person may feel embarrassed, and other group members may resent the salesperson. At the start of the meeting,

Figure 15–7   Roles and Strategies for Group Members

Role	Description	Strategy for Handling People in Role
Monopolizer	Speaks at every opportunity; needs to be center of attention; a take-charge person.	Reduce eagerness to participate by avoiding eye contact; do not recognize desire to participate.
Informer	Knowledgeable; offers ideas and facts to group.	Recognize when new ideas are needed; avoid when enough good ideas have been presented; call on attacker to refute ideas of informer that are contrary to group objectives.
Questioner	Inquiring; cautious; seeks additional information from group members and salesperson.	Call on when more depth of discussion is needed; use to clarify points that salesperson does not understand.
Developer	Worrier; adds own information to comments made by group; seeks relationships.	Avoid when trying to wind up discussion; call on when more depth is needed.
Energizer	Keeps meeting moving; stimulator; task-oriented.	Call on when salesperson needs to get the discussion on the right track.
Clarifier	Analyzer; gets to key issues; summarizes comments; points out need for additional information.	Use to summarize issues.
Pacifier	Gentle; emphasizes areas of agreement; maintains good relationship among group members.	Use to resolve differences of opinion; bring into discussion when disagreements arise.
Follower	Me-too; agreeable; remains passive.	Use to reaffirm points.
Attacker	Hostile; aggressive; criticizes others' ideas; sarcastic; irritating.	Use to comment on unfavorable ideas; only recognize when the relevant information has been presented.
Joker	Immature; makes light of all ideas; doesn't take problem seriously.	Use to break up tension.
Withdrawer	Inhibited; silent; avoids participation.	Do not attempt to stimulate participation.

Adapted from Gary M. Grikscheit, Harold C. Cash, and W. J. E. Crissy, *Handbook of Selling: Psychological, Managerial, and Marketing Bases* (New York: John Wiley & Sons, 1981), pp. 589–600.

it is best to ask for facts rather than opinion. Most people are reluctant to express opinions to people they do not know well.

Another way to encourage participation is by developing interaction among group members. When responding to a question, the salesperson should try to include in the reply group members other than the questioner. This can often be done by asking another member to answer the question. But the salesperson should use this technique only if he or she *knows* what the response will be. By encouraging interaction among group members, the salesperson gets the group to sell itself—to recognize that the advantages of the proposal or product offset its disadvantages.

Visual aids are particularly important for group presentations.

Camerique/H. Armstrong Roberts

Let's consider the salesperson who has made a presentation on a digital readout subassembly for an FM tuner. The production manager comments that the readout will cost more than the present mechanical dial. The salesperson can then ask the design engineer whether the readout will make the tuner more reliable. Next, the marketing manager is asked whether the more reliable new feature will justify a higher price. A favorable response from the marketing manager will overcome the production manager's objection.

Controlling the Meeting

In addition to making the presentation, the salesperson needs to encourage and control interactions within the group. Such interactions include the salesperson's interactions with each group member and interactions among group members. Control of group meetings is accomplished by monitoring and evaluating each member's responses. This can be done by maintaining eye contact, by observing facial reactions and body movements, and by encouraging comments and questions.

Visual aids and demonstrators are particularly important for group presentations. They focus the attention of group members on key points and help the salesperson demonstrate product features and benefits.

It is a good idea to bring another salesperson when making a group presentation. The other salesperson can observe reactions to the presentation and, on the basis of these observations, can interrupt to present appropriate information that has been neglected. Such interruptions also give the presenter a break.

SUMMARY

Industrial salespeople sell goods and services to industrial companies; trade salespeople sell products to wholesalers and retailers; and retail salespeople sell goods and services to ultimate consumers. While most people are more familiar with retail selling than industrial selling, there are more industrial and trade salespeople than retail salespeople.

Industrial, trade, and retail selling differ because the marketplaces differ. Industrial markets are highly concentrated in a few urban areas, while the location of retail markets is directly related to the distribution of the population. In addition, the industrial purchasing process is quite complex. Many people are involved in purchase decisions, and decisions frequently take a long time. Because of the complexity of industrial purchasing, industrial companies frequently use team selling and multilevel selling approaches.

The industrial buying process is usually managed by a professional buyer, or purchasing agent. Purchasing agents use value analysis to reduce costs while providing the necessary level of performance. When selling to purchasing agents, salespeople must be aware of purchasing policies, the nature of purchasing contracts, and reciprocity relationships.

A critical element of trade selling is helping retailers, wholesalers, and distributors sell products made by the salesperson's company. Trade salespeople use a wide variety of promotional aids to stimulate derived demand.

Industrial and trade salespeople frequently make sales presentations to groups of people. Selling to groups is different than selling to individuals. When selling to a group, a salesperson cannot respond to each group member's needs. In addition, it is difficult to close a sale in a group meeting.

To be effective at group presentations, salespeople need to make precall contacts with group members. It is useful to classify members during the presentation and then call on specific types of members during the various stages of the meeting. Salespeople must encourage group members to participate as well as control the flow of the meeting.

QUESTIONS
AND
PROBLEMS

1. Who has the more difficult job—the industrial salesperson or the industrial purchasing agent? Why?

2. What are the implications of multiple buying influences for the industrial salesperson?

3. What types of point-of-purchase displays would be effective for promoting desk-top calculators? Personal computers? House paint?

4. How does value analysis help the industrial salesperson?

5. How might selling to government agencies differ from selling to industrial organizations?

6. Purchasing agents often do not have the same degree of technical knowledge as salespeople or users of the products. This difference

in knowledge can create tension between the purchasing agent and the salesperson. What can a salesperson do to reduce this tension?

7. Why does management place pressure on purchasing agents to buy from the lowest-priced manufacturer? Why might a purchasing agent ignore this pressure and place an order with a higher-priced supplier?

8. The industrial and retail markets differ in a number of ways. What effects do these differences have on the sales presentations made in these markets?

9. If you are making a formal presentation to a group, and a member of the group asks a question that has nothing to do with the presentation topic, how would you handle the situation?

10. How does selling to industrial agents differ from selling to wholesalers?

PROJECTS

1. Arrange an interview with an industrial purchasing agent. Ask the purchasing agent to describe a recent purchase decision. Analyze the decision in terms of the following factors:
   a. Was the decision a new buy, a straight rebuy, or a modified rebuy?
   b. Who besides the purchasing agent was involved in the decision?
   c. What factors were considered in evaluating the different vendors?
   d. Why was the purchase order given to the specific supplier?
   e. What role did salespeople play in the decision?

2. Write a paper on industrial purchasing agents. In the report, answer the following questions by either interviewing a purchasing agent or consulting a textbook on purchasing:
   a. What are the important qualifications of a purchasing agent?
   b. What are the problems of the job?
   c. What do purchasing agents do during a typical day?
   d. Who do purchasing agents interact with in their jobs?

3. Locate the purchasing office at your school. Get permission to observe a sales call. Write your observations concerning the salesperson's presentation and selling techniques and the buyer's reactions.

CASE PROBLEMS

Case 15–1   HAB Distributors

Bill Marks is a sales representative for HAB Distributors, a pharmaceutical wholesaler. His customers include all the major hospitals in the Chicago area. One of them is Metropolitan Hospital, a public institution under pressure to cut costs.

Bill has experienced difficulties trying to convince Metropolitan's chief purchasing agent that HAB's travel-size toothbrush should be bought in bulk. Bill wants this item to be included in the toilet supply kit furnished to each patient. The kit already contains soap, hand lotion, a plastic pitcher, a tumbler, and a tabletop tub for sponge bathing.

The hospital purchasing agent has argued that the toothbrushes are not essential. Many patients bring their own, and those who don't can ask for a regular-size toothbrush from the hospital pharmacy. The purchasing agent claims that including even this small item would add too much to the patient's bill.

Question

How can Bill convince the purchasing agent that this item should be added to the kit?

Case 15–2   Presentation for Carnation's 22-Ounce Coffee-mate Size*

Carnation Company is one of the largest manufacturing and marketing companies in the food industry. Beginning as an evaporated milk company in 1899, Carnation has diversified into many areas of the food industry, including pet foods, canned tomato products, instant products, dehydrated and frozen potatoes, fresh milk, ice cream, and entrée items. Coffee-mate nondairy creamer is included in the family of Carnation instant products, along with such products as Carnation Instant Breakfast, Carnation Instant Milk, Carnation Hot Cocoa, Carnation Breakfast Bars, and Slender diet foods.

Each Carnation sales representative is assigned a geographic territory. The representative is responsible for selling all Carnation products to supermarkets and wholesalers (jobbers and distributors) in the territory. An important duty of the representative is to get all the grocery stores in the territory to stock new Carnation products. This is a difficult task because shelf space is limited. Large supermarkets can carry only 2,000 to 8,000 of the 50,000 food and nonfood products offered by manufacturers like Carnation.

This is why for every new product stocked, the store must discontinue stocking another product.

A few years ago Carnation Company introduced a 22-ounce size of Coffee-mate nondairy creamer. The product was introduced as an extension of the Coffee-mate line, joining the 3-, 6-, 11-, and 16-ounce sizes. It was marketed as the most economical size for the heavy user of powdered creamers. The following presentation is an example of a typical new-product sales call.

Background for the Sales Call

Blair Market is an independent grocery chain with four stores in Chicago. The chain has been in operation for 10 years and has developed a loyal, upper-middle-class clientele. Blair is planning to open a fifth store in two months.

Planning the Sales Presentation

Jim Jackson, the Carnation salesperson, wants to present Carnation's new promotion on the 22-ounce Coffee-mate to Bill

---

*Mary Fishburn, an assistant brand manager at Carnation, and Jim Heerwagen, director of sales training, assisted in preparing this example of a sales call.

Hansen, the buyer for Blair Market. Using this promotion, Jim hopes to accomplish the following objectives:

1. Get the 22-ounce Coffee-mate on the shelf in all Blair markets.

2. Increase the total shelf space Blair allocates to its coffee creamer section (in which Coffee-mate resides).

3. Get a better position for Coffee-mate within the coffee creamer section.

Blair currently carries four Coffee-mate sizes (3, 6, 11, and 16 ounces). Bill rejected the new 22-ounce size when it was presented five months ago by Jim's predecessor. At that time, he said he didn't have room for another product in the creamer section. In preparation for his call on Bill, Jim reviewed the details of the new Coffee-mate promotion, drew diagrams of Blair's present coffee creamer display section and his proposed reorganization, and pulled together some industry data on coffee creamers. After planning his presentation, Jim made an appointment to see Bill early Thursday morning. Blair's buyers see vendors only on Thursday from 9 A.M. to 3 P.M.

Jim begins his conversations with Bill by discussing an area of the grocery business that allows him to pay Bill an honest compliment and also bring up the purpose of the call. This time he chatted about the new Blair Market that would be opening soon. Then he made an easy transition to Coffee-mate.

Jim: Hi, Bill. How are you?

Bill: I'm fine, Jim. Busier than ever, though [*looking at his watch*].

Jim: I can imagine—especially with all the details of finishing up the new store. I took my boss out to the new location yesterday to show him the site. He was quite impressed.

Bill: Thanks. That store will be a beauty. But like you said, there's still a lot of work left to do. What do you have for me today?

Jim: I want to talk about both our new promotion on the 22-ounce Coffee-mate and the overall merchandising of your coffee creamer section. Since you'll be reviewing all your current merchandising diagrams for the new store, I thought this would be a good time to make some suggestions.

Bill: There isn't much more we can do with the creamer section. We've always done as well as can be expected with creamers. I see no reason to change now. Like I told the Carnation sales rep before you, the creamer section is packed. Everything there now is moving OK.

Jim: Well, I've read some interesting material lately about the section that I knew you'd want to hear. In fact, I've got a couple of questions for you—call it a quiz. And I bet you'll be surprised by the answers.

Bill: OK.

Jim: How would you compare coffee to creamers in terms of profit?

Bill: We sell about 20 times more coffee than creamers. So I'd say coffee's about 20 times more profitable.

Jim: That's what most people think. Actually, an independent research agency has found that coffee sales are about 19 times greater than creamer sales. But the profit margin on creamers is three times as high. So coffee sales are only six times as profitable as creamer sales. And creamers are really growing. Look at this chart [*see Exhibit 1*]. Nondairy creamers are used in almost one quarter of all creamed cups. Dollar

EXHIBIT 1
Sales Growth in
Product Category

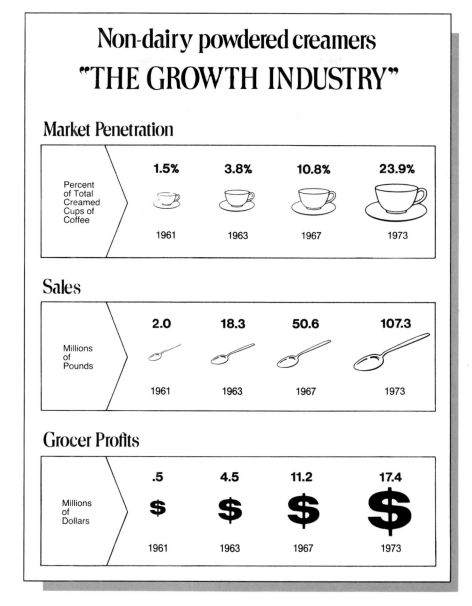

Non-dairy powdered creamers
"THE GROWTH INDUSTRY"

Market Penetration

Percent of Total Creamed Cups of Coffee	1.5%	3.8%	10.8%	23.9%
	1961	1963	1967	1973

Sales

Millions of Pounds	2.0	18.3	50.6	107.3
	1961	1963	1967	1973

Grocer Profits

Millions of Dollars	.5	4.5	11.2	17.4
	1961	1963	1967	1973

sales are increasing 30 percent annually [*see Exhibit 2*].

Bill: That's news to me. What's the next question?

Jim: What size creamer is showing the greatest growth?

Bill: Well, since you've already told me that you're here for a 22-ounce

promotion, I think you've given the answer away. But I would have said the 16-ounce size.

Jim: Right. The 22-ounce Coffee-mate was responsible for 90 percent of the industry growth when it was in test market. It got between 10 and 17 percent share in the four test markets

EXHIBIT 2
Growth in Coffee-
mate Sales

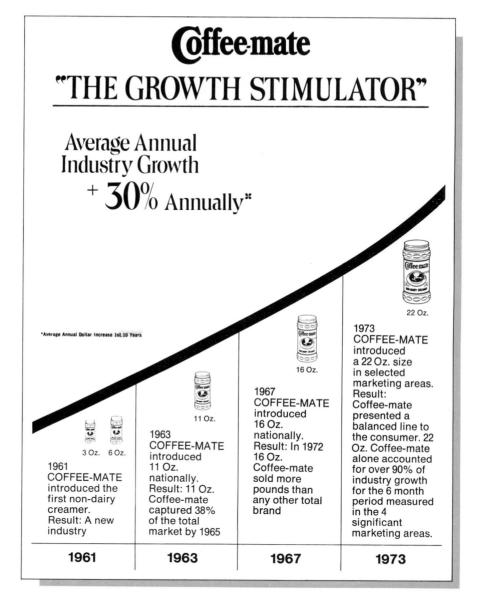

[*see Exhibit 3*]. So you really can't afford not to at least examine some alternative approaches for the creamer section.

Bill: OK. OK. I'm convinced I need to listen—but don't get your hopes up too high.

Jim: I've got two areas I want to talk about. First, our promotion on 22-ounce Coffee-mate. The promotion is great, and the timing is perfect for your new store. I know that you'll be running all sorts of specials then. I want 22-ounce Coffee-mate to be one

EXHIBIT 3
Test Market Results

22 OZ.
Coffee-mate®

enjoyed immediate success
ar.d achieved the following
market shares:

District	Share
P_1	10.3
J	15.7
C	17.0
P_2	10.1

WHY?

- **The right size** for all heavy
  coffee creaming occasions · For the heavy user
  family · For the office · For all social gatherings

- **The right time** to coincide with
  increased powdered creamer acceptance and usage

- **The right brand** with demonstrated
  consumer preference and maximum grocer
  profit dollars

of them. Second, I want to show you some ideas I have for reorganizing the creamer section.

Bill: OK, I'm listening.

Jim: The Coffee-mate promotion is one of our best ever. We have great ad and display allowances, coupons, and even a consumer premium.

Bill: Coupons! Coupons are more trouble than they're worth! They slow down the checkers and are a pain in the neck to administer.

Jim: I thought you might say that, so I took some extra time to find out what they are really worth to you as a retailer. It turns out the best coupon users are exactly the customers you want to attract to your stores. They are in the 24 to 49 age group, fairly well educated, and affluent. That describes your clientele. You are presented with a high sales volume opportunity when we blanket an area with coupons—and we'll be using local newspapers for this coupon.

Bill: Tell me more about the promotional allowances. What do I have to do to qualify for the allowance?

Jim: The promotion begins in eight weeks. That's perfect timing for your opening. We will be offering an allowance totaling $2.50 per case of 12 jars of 22-ounce Coffee-mate. The allowance has two parts. You will qualify for $1.50 per case if you advertise in your newspaper. The other part of the allowance requires that you display Coffee-mate. You'll get $1 for each case displayed during the promotional period.

Bill: That sounds good. Can I make money on this size? Can you give me an idea of what my competitors normally sell this size for?

Jim: No problem. I've already worked up some numbers showing your profit at various suggested retail prices.

Bill: How will the allowances be handled?

Jim: Once I have verified the ad and

noted the number of cases displayed, I will write you a check. The promotion is one of our best ever. We have great ad and display allowances, coupons, and even a consumer premium.

Bill: But displays take a lot of time to set up, and time means money.

Jim: I'll set up the displays. That's part of my job. But even without my help, a Coffee-mate display is well worth the time it takes to build. Displays stimulate impulse buying and reduce out-of-stocks when you've got a special promotion going. And we have found that even when there is no price reduction, a Coffee-mate display increases sales by 250 percent. A display and a special reduced price will ensure terrific sales.

Bill: You said you've worked up some numbers? Let's look at them.

Jim: As you can see, $1.70 is a great price to advertise. Markets around here are charging $1.80. At $1.70, with both allowances taken into consideration, you'll be making over 25 percent net profit on each case you sell. And talking dollars, if you display 100 cases, your profit margin will be $516 [*see Exhibit 4*].

Exhibit 4   22-Ounce Coffee-mate Profit Review

Regular case cost (packed 12 jars per case)	$17.74
Promotional allowances:	
Advertise/price reduction	(1.50)
Display allowance	(1.00)
Net case cost	$15.24
Unit cost (Net cost ÷ 12)	$ 1.27
Suggested retail price	$ 1.70
Case profit margin: (Retail price − [Net cost × 12])	$ 5.16
Gross profit: ([Retail − Unit cost] ÷ Retail)	25.2%

Bill: The numbers look good. You said there will also be a consumer premium and national advertising. Tell me about those parts of the promotion.

Jim: I've got a flier on the consumer premium to show you. We'll be offering an eight-cup automatic filter drip coffee maker for $15 less than the regularly advertised price. All your customer needs is a label from a 22-ounce Coffee-mate jar. I'll have stack-cards and tear-off pads to use in your stores to illustrate the coffee maker and explain the details. Filter drip coffee makers are really increasing in popularity. There should be a lot of consumer interest.

As for our advertising campaign, Coffee-mate has always been the leader in creamer advertising. We do about 80 percent of all the industry advertising. We'll be demonstrating that we're the leader again with a new Coffee-mate advertisement entitled "Good Coffee." It will be airing soon on local TV. This campaign will keep the Coffee-mate name firmly in the mind of the consumer. I have a storyboard of the segments of the commercial to show you. We think it's a winner.

So now you tell me, what do you think of the 22-ounce promotion?

Bill: The promotion looks terrific. It's certainly one of the most complete I've seen in a long time. But I don't think I can get another size of Coffee-mate on the shelf. The creamer section is packed. If I put every new product pitched to me in my stores, I'd have to clear the shelves completely every month.

Jim: I know you have shelf space problems. The new 22-ounce size allows Carnation to present a complete selection of sizes to the consumer. For big families the new size offers convenience and economy along with enough product to last a while even if used frequently and in large amounts. It's also a popular size for use in offices, coffeebreak areas, and other business places where coffee is served throughout the day. Proof of its popularity comes from its success since its introduction. The 22-ounce Coffee-mate accounted for over 90 percent of industry growth in the six-month period measured when the product was in test market. And since the 22-ounce size was introduced, it's captured 14.3 percent of the market. You can't ignore that kind of success, Bill.

Bill: I agree that the product looks like a real winner. But I just don't have room for another creamer. If I take on 22-ounce Coffee-mate, I'll have to discontinue something else. I think the creamer section is in pretty good shape now.

Jim: That leads me into the other topic I want to discuss with you, the overall merchandising of your creamer and coffee sections.

First, I think you should seriously consider enlarging the total creamer section by expanding into the coffee section. This would give us room for both the 22-ounce size and increased creamer inventories.

There are several important reasons why you should do this. First, powdered creamer sales have been growing dramatically since the product was introduced. But you have not expanded the creamer sections accordingly. Meanwhile, coffee sales are going down. They have declined 16 percent during the same period.

Bill: I hadn't realized that the creamer increases and coffee declines were so dramatic! Obviously I'm running the risk of creamer out-of-stocks.

Jim: That's my next point. In the four months I've been on the account, you've run out of at least one Coffee-mate size on five different occasions. I've taken some snapshots of the section on the Mondays that I do my store checks. You can see for yourself that after the peak creamer buying days of Wednesday through Saturday your sections are a disaster area. You're losing out in two areas: customer satisfaction and profits. There are two reasons why you're running out of Coffee-mate. First, as I've already pointed out, your creamer section overall is not large enough to support the product category. Second, within the creamer section, you're not allocating space by market share. Although Coffee-mate is the biggest selling creamer in the Chicago area, your shelf allocation does not reflect that fact.

Bill: I guess I haven't been keeping track of the section carefully enough—mainly because it is so small.

Jim: Well, there's still more information to review. We've already talked about the profitability of creamers compared to coffee nationally. Obviously, some coffee types are less profitable than others. Supermarket studies have shown that because of consumer resistance to higher prices, consumer demand has dropped off for three-pound cans of coffee. You can probably drop one or more brands of three-pound coffee to make room for more creamer inventories without adversely affecting profit or customer

satisfaction. Let's review your sales figures on three-pound coffee to see if your stores show these same trends. What do you say?

Bill: Agreed. And if you're right, then we will drop some coffee lines and expand the creamer section.

Jim: And bring in 22-ounce Coffee-mate?

Bill: And bring in 22-ounce Coffee-mate. Let's look at those sales figures now. *[Bill pulls out the sales figures book and turns to the coffee and creamer section.]* You're right about the three-pound coffee pulling its weight. I carry 15 different items, and it looks as if I can drop at least 5 of those without anyone noticing—at least, none of my customers will notice.

Jim: The next step then is to figure out how much Coffee-mate to bring in and to write up an order. My suggestion is that we plan on a 100-case display plus 2 cases of shelf stock in each store. That adds up to 510 cases total.

Bill: That's an awful lot of Coffee-mate.

Jim: You're going to need that much to ensure enough stock to get through the promotion. At $1.70 per jar, you'll make over $500 on each display. That's 25 percent for every jar sold.

Bill: OK. You certainly seem to be able to back up your suggestions with hard facts, so I'll take a chance on it.

Jim: Terrific. Bringing in the new size of Coffee-mate will mean expanding the creamer section. I'd like to review some merchandising moves with you that will ensure your getting the most out of reorganizing the creamer section.

Bill: OK. Let's see what you've got. *[Jim produces a merchandising diagram of the Blair Market creamer section as it is now organized.]*

Jim: Right now you've got the creamers positioned next to the coffees. That works well. But the products are arranged on the shelf by size. That minimizes the impact of the section overall. Research has shown that a section set by size tends to lose its identity. The category gets lost among the thousands of other items in the store. Let me show you a diagram I've drawn for the section. *[Jim produces another diagram.]*

First, set the creamer section horizontally across the shelf by brand rather than size. The majority of shoppers are looking for a specific brand. Setting the section in a block by brand makes it easier for them to find what they want. And the section overall has a better chance of catching the eye of impulse buyers.

Next, set Coffee-mate on the eye-level shelf. Coffee-mate at eye level increases both its own sales and those of the private label brand you carry. Buyers can see the price differential between Coffee-mate and the private label right away. The two brands really aren't in direct competition. Coffee-mate attracts users who want the highest quality creamer. Private label purchasers don't believe that the difference in quality is great enough to justify the price differential.

Finally, make sure the number of facings allotted to each brand represents that brand's fair share of the market. [Facings are the jars or packages on the front line of the shelf.] This will help ensure that enough of each creamer brand is bought. It lessens the chances of out-of-stocks.

Bill: Sounds like you guys are really getting scientific about shelf organization.

Jim: We have to! The grocery business is a big business. If we just guess about things, we could lose millions of dollars. And that loss is not just Carnation's loss. You'll feel part of it, too. Bad shelf placement or product mix causes the consumer to buy elsewhere.

Jim: We've covered a lot of ground this morning. The next step involves your signing this Coffee-mate order to your wholesaler. *[Bill signs the order.]* As soon as I get an estimated arrival date for the Coffee-mate, we can plan the specific dates for setting up the displays and making the changes in the creamer and coffee sections that we've agreed on.

Bill: Fine.

Jim: Thanks again for the time you've spent with me today. Good-bye.

Questions

1. How would you evaluate Jim Jackson's presentation? What are the strong points in the presentation?

2. Assume you were the Carnation salesperson and Bill Hansen of Blair made the following objections. How would you handle each of these objections?

    a. I don't have enough time to talk to you about rearranging the creamer section.

    b. I've tasted Coffee-mate, and I don't like it. We don't need more of it in the store.

    c. I don't have the stock clerks available to rearrange the shelves at this time.

    d. I think my private brand should be at eye level. That's the one I make the most margin on.

3. What would you do if Bill doesn't want to buy on this call?

Case 15–3   Presentation of the IBM Copier III*

Robert Steele, the office manager for Electronic Data Products, received several complaints from his office staff about the poor copies obtained when using the copying machine. Although he called the manufacturer and had the copier serviced, the complaints continued. Mr. Steele saw an ad for the IBM Copier III on television. He called the IBM office in Century City the next morning and left a message for his IBM account representative, Denise Popper. She returned his call after lunch and made an appointment to see him the next morning.

During the sales call, Ms. Popper presented the key features of the IBM Copier III, using the sales brochure. Mr. Steele described some of the complaints he had been receiving. After Ms. Popper assured Mr. Steele these problems would not occur with the Copier III, she asked him to describe how the copier is used at EDP.

Mr. Steele said a large number of people at EDP used the copier. The typical application was for three copies to be made of each of three originals. About 32,000 copies were made per month.

Ms. Popper then asked if she could speak to some of the office staff who had been having problems with the present copier. Mr. Steele introduced her to Mary Quaint and Tom Robbins. Ms. Quaint and Mr. Robbins described the problems in detail. Ms. Popper then made arrangements to demonstrate the Copier III. She invited Mr. Steele, Ms. Quaint, and Mr. Robbins to walk down the street to an account of hers

that had a Copier III. Mr. Steele declined the invitation but encouraged the other two to go with her. Ms. Popper called the account, Sun Battery, and arranged to have its machine demonstrated.

When they arrived at Sun, Ms. Popper introduced Ms. Quaint and Mr. Robbins to the people who used the copier. She then demonstrated the unique advantages of the Copier III, stressing the design aspects that improve copy quality. During the demonstration, Ms. Quaint told Ms. Popper that EDP was a very cost-conscious company. Mr. Steele's supervisor would not spend more for a copier even if it did produce better copies.

After the demonstration Ms. Popper returned to the office and asked Mr. Clifford to help her prepare a proposal for EDP. Mr. Clifford is the copier specialist in the Century City office. In a week, Ms. Popper delivered the following proposal to Mr. Steele. She went over it with him, making the following points while directing attention to the numbered spots on the pages of the proposal (see Exhibit 1).

Questions

1. Evaluate the proposal prepared by Mr. Clifford. Should there be more discussion of the technical design for high-quality copying? Is there too much detail on the financial aspects?

2. How should Ms. Popper follow up the presentation to Mr. Steele?

3. How would you use the proposal when making the presentation to Mr. Steele?

---

*Jerry Clifford, a copier specialist for IBM, assisted in preparing this presentation.

Exhibit 1

① The six advantages of the Series III over your present copier are consistent high-quality copies, simplicity of operation, versatility, productivity, simplicity of maintenance, and low cost.

Mr. Robert Steele
Electronic Data Products
10031 Wilshire Blvd.
Los Angeles, California 90024

Thank you for your interest and your evaluation of the IBM Series III Copier/Duplicator. This proposal is designed to assist you with the analysis of your copier needs.

As you know, any copier is significant to your word processing distribution system because your personnel depend on it to produce quality copies quickly. In addition, you've indicated the following considerations to be of major importance in evaluating copiers:

Consistent copy quality
Simplicity of use
Versatility
① ➝ Productivity
Simplicity of maintenance
Low cost

These considerations are discussed in detail in the following proposal. I believe that after you have thoroughly evaluated the IBM Series III Copier/Duplicator, you will accept nothing less than the high performance and versatility it offers.

Thank you for providing the information necessary to prepare your analysis. Prices quoted herein are firm for a period of thirty (30) days from the date of this letter and are subject to applicable taxes.

Sincerely,

Denise Popper
Account Representative
Office Products Division

DAP/eat
Attachments

Page 1

Exhibit 1
(*continued*)

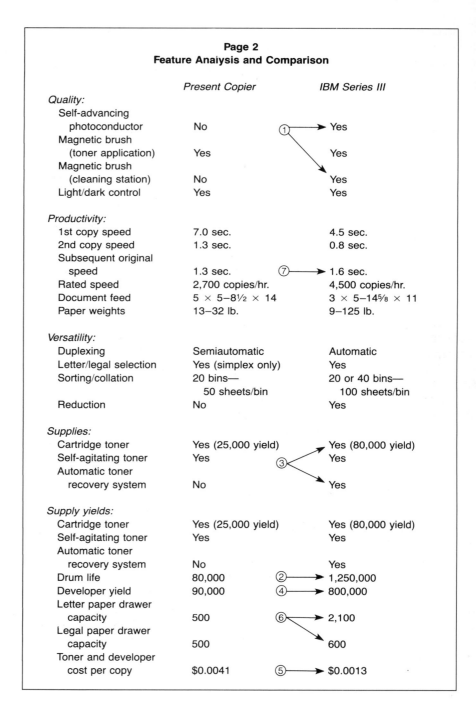

Page 2
Feature Anaiysis and Comparison

	Present Copier	IBM Series III
Quality:		
Self-advancing photoconductor	No	① → Yes
Magnetic brush (toner application)	Yes	Yes
Magnetic brush (cleaning station)	No	Yes
Light/dark control	Yes	Yes
Productivity:		
1st copy speed	7.0 sec.	4.5 sec.
2nd copy speed	1.3 sec.	0.8 sec.
Subsequent original speed	1.3 sec.	⑦ → 1.6 sec.
Rated speed	2,700 copies/hr.	4,500 copies/hr.
Document feed	5 × 5–8½ × 14	3 × 5–14⅝ × 11
Paper weights	13–32 lb.	9–125 lb.
Versatility:		
Duplexing	Semiautomatic	Automatic
Letter/legal selection	Yes (simplex only)	Yes
Sorting/collation	20 bins—50 sheets/bin	20 or 40 bins—100 sheets/bin
Reduction	No	Yes
Supplies:		
Cartridge toner	Yes (25,000 yield)	Yes (80,000 yield)
Self-agitating toner	Yes	③ Yes
Automatic toner recovery system	No	Yes
Supply yields:		
Cartridge toner	Yes (25,000 yield)	Yes (80,000 yield)
Self-agitating toner	Yes	Yes
Automatic toner recovery system	No	Yes
Drum life	80,000	② → 1,250,000
Developer yield	90,000	④ → 800,000
Letter paper drawer capacity	500	⑥ → 2,100
Legal paper drawer capacity	500	600
Toner and developer cost per copy	$0.0041	⑤ → $0.0013

Exhibit 1
(continued)

① The IBM Series III has a self-advancing photoconductor and magnetic brushes for both toner application and cleaning. These are patented technologies that guarantee consistent high-quality copies. The self-advancing photoconductor is a method for continuously adjusting the copying drum. This ensures that the copying drum will be in adjustment during its entire life.

② Notice that the Series III drum has a lifetime of over 1 million copies. Your present copier has a lifetime of only 80,000 copies. This means that you have to change the drum in your copier 10 times as frequently as you would change the drum of the Series III. Also, without the self-advancing photoconductor, the drum on your present copier probably goes out of adjustment after 40,000 copies. Half of your copies are going to be of less than the best quality.

③ The Series III has a unique automatic toner recovery system. Each toner cartridge lasts for 80,000 copies. That's three times as long as the lifetime of a cartridge for your present copier.

④ The developer yield on the Series III is almost 10 times as great as the yield on your present copier.

⑤ That's why the toner and developer costs for the Series III are only 30 percent of the costs for your present copier. The higher yield for toner and developer also means fewer operator interventions, less time waiting for the copier to be serviced.

⑥ The paper bins on the Series III are four times as large as the bins on your present copier. This also reduces the number of operator interventions.

⑦ Notice that the copying speed is much faster for the Series III.

The cost savings are summarized on this page. I have broken down the savings into hard and soft dollars. The hard dollars are out-of-pocket expenses, while the soft dollars are savings in employee time. ① Notice that the savings in hard dollars total over $100 per month. On the next page, the calculations supporting this figure are shown.

Page 3
Executive Summary of Total IBM System

	For 32,000 Copies
Hard-dollar savings:	
Present copying costs, including supplies	$1,302.90
IBM copying costs, including supplies	$1,190.60
Difference ①⟶	$112.30
Soft-dollar savings (people costs at $10/hr.):	
Present copier monthly hours, 16.78	$167.80
Series III monthly hours, 12.34	$123.40
Difference	$44.40
Total hard-dollar difference	−$112.30
Total soft-dollar difference	−$44.40
Total *monthly* IBM system cost difference	−$156.70
Total *annual* cost difference	−$1,880.40

Exhibit 1
(*continued*)

① The monthly service charge for the Series III and the rental charge for the 20-bin collator are slightly higher than the charges for your present copier.

② But look at the savings you get in the copying charge.

③ We worked through all the numbers based on your usage rate of 32,000 copies per month. The savings are about $110 per month. That's $1,350 per year in hard, out-of-pocket dollars. In addition, there are savings in less time spent making copies. I have summarized these savings on the next page.

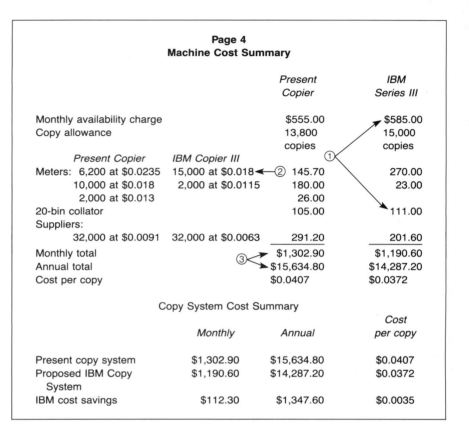

Page 4
Machine Cost Summary

		Present Copier	IBM Series III
Monthly availability charge		$555.00	$585.00
Copy allowance		13,800 copies	15,000 copies
Present Copier	*IBM Copier III*		
Meters: 6,200 at $0.0235	15,000 at $0.018 ◄─②	145.70	270.00
10,000 at $0.018	2,000 at $0.0115	180.00	23.00
2,000 at $0.013		26.00	
20-bin collator		105.00	111.00
Suppliers:			
32,000 at $0.0091	32,000 at $0.0063	291.20	201.60
Monthly total		$1,302.90	$1,190.60
Annual total		$15,634.80	$14,287.20
Cost per copy		$0.0407	$0.0372

Copy System Cost Summary

	Monthly	Annual	Cost per copy
Present copy system	$1,302.90	$15,634.80	$0.0407
Proposed IBM Copy System	$1,190.60	$14,287.20	$0.0372
IBM cost savings	$112.30	$1,347.60	$0.0035

① Using your estimates of three originals per trip and three copies per original, we came up with the following estimates.

② We also assumed an average hourly wage of $10 for the people making the copies.

Page 5
Productivity Analysis (at 32,000 copies per month)

		Present Copier	IBM Series III
Rated speed		45 copies/min.	75 copies/min.
		2,700 copies/hr.	4,500 copies/hr.
Throughput speed		Yes	Yes
Average three copies, three originals			
1st original	1st copy	6.5 ④→	4.5
	2nd copy	1.3 ③→	0.8
	3rd copy	1.3	0.8
2nd original	1st copy	1.3	1.6
	2nd copy	1.3	0.8
	3rd copy	1.3	0.8
3rd original	1st copy	1.3	1.6
	2nd copy	1.3	0.8
	3rd copy	1.3	0.8
Total time		16.9 sec. ⑤→	12.5 sec.

Exhibit 1
(concluded)

③ The Series III has a much faster speed on the second and third copies.

④ It is also much faster on the first copy of the first original.

⑤ As a result, 25 percent less time is spent on each trip.

⑥ This means about $40 per month in soft-dollar savings.

Facts:

Average monthly volume	32,000 copies
Average run length	3 copies ← ①
Average number of originals per trip	3 copies ← ①
Trips to copier per month	3,555
Average hourly wage	$10 ← ②

	Present Copier	IBM Series III
Copying time per month	16.78 hrs.	12.34 hrs.
Soft dollars per month	$167.80 ⑥ →	$123.40

Note: This is not a price quotation. It is an analysis, based on copier usage assumptions that may vary from your actual circumstances. As a result, minor variations may occur in the price calculations. For an explanation of these variations, contact your IBM Marketing Representative.

Thus you can see that the Series III has fewer operator interventions, a cost saving of over $1,000 per year, and a 25 percent increase in productivity. The maintenance costs are also much lower. The toner and developer have a long lifetime. It is so easy to add paper to the Series III that even a casual user can do it. There is no reason to call a key operator.

Page 6
Simplicity of Key Operator Maintenance

Elimination of call key operator light

Paper misfeeds:
Casual users clear most misfeeds.

Cartridge toner:
One cartridge yields approximately 80,000 copies, reducing the frequency of adding toner.

Other:
Add paper (or casual users can add paper).
Assist casual users when necessary.
Mail meter card.

SELECTED REFERENCES

Becherer, Richard C.; Fred W. Morgan; and John P. McDonald. "The Dimensionality of the Industrial Sales Job Characteristics." *Journal of Personal Selling and Sales Management,* May 1985, pp. 54–63.

Dempsy, William A. "Vendor Selection and the Buying Process." *Industrial Marketing Management,* Summer 1978, pp. 257–67.

Doyle, Peter; Arch G. Woodside; and Paul Mickell. "Organizations Buying in New Task and Rebuy Situations." *Industrial Marketing Management,* Winter 1979, pp. 7–11.

Ferguson, Wade. "A Critical Review of Recent Organizational Buying Research." *Industrial Marketing Management,* Summer 1978, pp. 225–30.

Hakansson, Hakon, and Bjorn Wootz. "A Framework of Industrial Buying and Selling." *Industrial Marketing Management,* Winter 1979, pp. 28–39.

Hutt, Michael D.; Wesley J. Johnson; and John R. Ronchetto, Jr. "Selling Centers and Buying Centers: Formulating Strategic Exchange Patterns." *Journal of Personal Selling and Sales Management,* May 1985, pp. 33–40.

Johnson, Wesley J., and Thomas V. Bonomo. "Purchase Process for Capital Equipment and Services." *Industrial Marketing Management,* Summer 1981, pp. 253–64.

Kennedy, Anita M. "The Complex Decisions to Select a Supplier: A Case Study." *Industrial Marketing Management,* February 1985, pp. 45–55.

Laczniak, Gene R. "An Empirical Study of Hospital Buying." *Industrial Marketing Management,* Winter 1978, pp. 57–62.

Narus, James A., and James C. Anderson. "Industrial Distributor Selling: The Roles of Outside and Inside Sales." *Industrial Marketing Management,* February 1986, pp. 55–62.

Reichard, Clifton J. "Industrial Selling: Beyond Price and Persistence." *Harvard Business Review,* March–April 1985, pp. 127–33.

Robertson, Jack. *Selling to the Government.* New York: McGraw-Hill, 1979.

16 Retail Selling

Some questions answered in this chapter are:

- How does retail selling differ from industrial and trade selling?
- What are the rewards, duties, and responsibilities of retail selling?
- What knowledge and skills are required to be successful in retail selling?
- How are the concepts described in Chapters 9 through 14 applied to retail selling?

This chapter focuses on how the basic personal selling concepts are applied to retail selling. Retailing is the largest industry in the United States, employing one in every seven workers. The industry is intensely competitive, exciting, and fast changing. Many new forms of retail stores such as warehouse clubs, off-price merchants, and computer stores have arisen in the last few years. Retailers must constantly seek the right merchandise at the right price for their customers, whose preferences can shift with breathtaking speed. Their performance is monitored at every step by those customers; failures are easily and quickly identified.

These days retailers are especially concerned about the service provided to customers and the store environment—the display of merchandise and that elusive quality ambiance. Salespeople play a critical role in these two areas.

Retailing takes many different forms.

Alan Carey/Image Works

H. Armstrong Roberts

H. Armstrong Roberts

NATURE AND REWARDS OF RETAIL SELLING

Nature and Scope

Retail selling has many faces. Selling to the customer in a retail store may involve no more than standing or sitting at an electronic cash register and totaling customer purchases, bagging the merchandise, and accepting cash, a check, or a credit card in payment. Some stores provide help for the bagging and for carrying the purchases to the customer's car. Little or no expertise in merchandise characteristics or selling skills is expected of the salesclerk.

On the other hand, some retail stores place high demands on their salespeople. This is especially true for selling high-fashion merchandise, home decorating services, appliances, cameras, stereo equipment, and personal computers.

One major difference between retail selling and industrial/trade selling is that the retail salesperson's customers usually come to the store to shop for products and services that will satisfy their needs. Retail salespeople typically do not seek out their customers. However, there are some exceptions. Direct salespeople selling cosmetics (Avon, Mary Kay), encyclopedias (Encyclopaedia Britannica), cleaning products (Amway), and insurance contact customers in their homes.

Industrial and trade salespeople who call on customers and do their own prospecting may be more selective in deciding how to spend their time with various prospects after they have qualified the prospects. The

Retail outlets are
providing many new
services.

SEARS MAIL ORDER

Spring
Fashions

"I would like to order a pair of overalls and 10
shares of AT&T!"

From *The Wall Street Journal,* with permission of Cartoon
Features Syndicate.

retail salesperson must give attention to everyone who comes into the
store, even though many of these people have no intention of buying or
cannot buy. It is important, therefore, for retail salespeople to have the
necessary skills to decide which people are really potential buyers and
which are merely "shoppers" or "lookers." The retail salesperson may
have several customers to serve at the same time, and this requires unusual
tact and skill. In contrast, sometimes there are no customers to serve.
This situation causes some retail salespeople to become bored or frustrated.

Retail selling tends to be more confining than many other sales jobs.
But it provides security and the opportunity for the salesperson to associate with other employees and to participate as a citizen in community
activities.

Retail salespeople represent the largest number of salespeople in the
United States. Approximately 3,367,000 sales workers were employed in
retail trade in 1982. This total is composed of about 1,367,000 males and
about 2,000,000 females. In addition there were about 400,000 males and
over 2,400,000 females engaged in clerical work in the retail trades in
1982.[1] Openings for retail trade salespeople far outnumber openings for
other sales workers.

---

[1]U.S. Department of Labor, "Employment and Earnings," January 1983, pp. 160–62.

Most people who
work in retailing
begin their careers
as salespeople in a
store.

Cameramann International, Ltd.

Rewards

There are many opportunities and rewards for individuals who succeed in retail selling. Chances for promotion are very good, and in many instances experience in retail selling provides an excellent background for people to go into business for themselves.[2]

Most people who work in retailing begin their careers as salespeople in a store. This sales experience gives the new employee an understanding of customer buying patterns and store operations. In fact, the selling activity is so important to successful retailing that many retailers require their executives to spend some time each month selling to customers in their stores.

The normal career path for retail salespeople is to cycle between positions in store management and merchandising management. Figure 16–1 shows that the first promotion of executive trainees and salespeople is to either assistant buyer or department sales manager. An assistant buyer may be promoted to buyer, and the next promotion would be to a store management position—assistant store manager responsible for merchandising. A department sales manager may be promoted to assistant store merchandising manager or move to merchandising management as an assistant buyer.

At one time, the most attractive positions in retailing were in merchandising management. However, the number of merchandise manage-

---

[2]See Delbert J. Duncan, Stanley C. Hollander, and Ronald Savitt, *Modern Retailing Management,* 10th ed. (Homewood, Ill.: Richard D. Irwin, 1983), pp. 3–94, for a description of retailing and retailing opportunities in the United States; and William R. Swinyard, "The Appeal of Retailing as a Career," *Journal of Retailing,* Winter 1981, pp. 86–97.

FIGURE 16–1
Career Progression
in Retail
Management

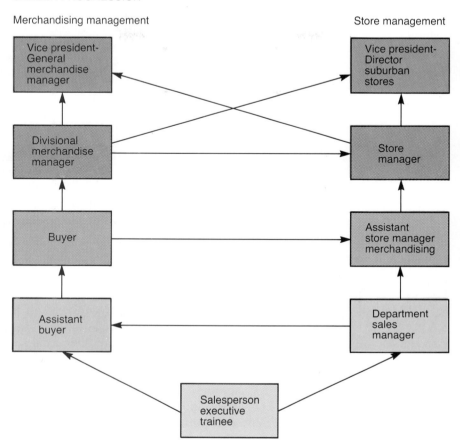

CAREER PROGRESSION

Merchandising management   Store management

ment positions in retailing has been declining due to recent mergers and
the use of computers to analyze sales. As personnel needs in merchandising decrease, store management is becoming a more important factor
in retailing.

Financial Rewards   The starting salaries for new employees in the retailing field have traditionally been lower than in most industries. For a
typical nonmanagement trainee, the pay is likely to be close to the government minimum wage. This has often caused the most competent young
people to accept positions in industries where starting salaries are higher.

However, many young people looking for future opportunities rather
than high starting salaries recognize the tremendous challenges in retailing
for aggressive individuals who are willing to work hard and accept responsibilities. The financial rewards for successful people in the retailing
field can be very substantial. Department managers, merchandise man-

agers, and store managers often earn from $25,000 a year to over $100,000 a year, depending on the size of the store and the method of compensation.

The financial rewards for retail salespeople who do not go into management positions can also be very substantial, especially for those who build a loyal clientele. Selling Scenario 16–1 describes how one salesperson built a clientele.

Nonfinancial Rewards   Retailing is an exciting field. The retail salesperson is constantly exposed to a wide variety of new products, styles, and merchandising techniques.

The professional retail salesperson gets real satisfaction from matching the wants and needs of customers with the new products of his or her company. Retail selling also provides other nonfinancial rewards. It means having security, getting satisfaction out of building a loyal personal following, and developing a clientele with a wide range of individual interests.

DUTIES AND RESPONSIBILITIES OF RETAIL SALESPEOPLE

The retail salesperson is the person between the manufacturer and/or wholesaler and the ultimate consumer. In this capacity, the retail salesperson must satisfy the specific needs and wants of the consumer and at the same time make a reasonable profit for his or her establishment.

The duties of retail salespeople are as different as the merchandise they sell. In selling such items as furniture, electrical appliances, or clothing, the sales workers' primary job is to create an interest in the merchandise. They may answer questions about the construction of an article, demonstrate its use, and show various models and colors. In some stores, special knowledge and skills may be needed to sell merchandise. For example, in a pet shop the retail salesperson must know how to care for and feed animals.

In addition, the salesperson may be required to make out sales and charge slips, receive cash payments, give change and receipts, and handle returns. They exchange merchandise and keep the work area neat. In small stores, salespeople may help order merchandise, stock shelves or racks, mark price tags, take inventory, and prepare displays.[3]

Securities salespeople, known as *registered representatives, account executives,* or *brokers,* perform another type of retail selling. Such salespeople offer financial counseling. They devise portfolios that may include securities, life insurance, tax shelters, and annuities. They also offer advice on buying and selling securities and relay orders to buy or sell securities. Dean Witter Reynolds has stockbrokers in a number of Sears Roebuck stores. Some J. C. Penney department stores and Kroger su-

---

[3]U.S. Department of Labor, "Occupational Outlook Handbook," Bulletin 2200, April 1982, pp. 249–54.

THE IMPORTANCE OF NAMES

For Richard Ciotti, the name of the game is names. Names lead to sales, and that's a subject he's an expert on. In 1985 this merchandising specialist at the Langhorne, Pa., J.C. Penney store racked up an extraordinary $778,815 in furniture sales, making him the top All Star in J.C. Penney Co.

It was an appropriate and hard-earned reward. Richard has been selling furniture at the Langhorne store since it opened 13 years ago, steadily building up a faithful clientele who return to him over and over again for their furniture needs.

In fact, the name of Richard Ciotti has become a household word in more than a few Langhorne homes. Customers ask for him by name and even phone ahead to see if he'll be working that day before they come in. Often, he finds, customers who wander into the department on the days he's not there will wander back out, later returning to place their orders when he is in. They want Richard.

Why? Superb service is one answer. Richard goes to unusual lengths to see that his customers are satisfied in every respect. He makes a special point of following up on purchases to verify that delivery was safe and prompt, to get any necessary repairs done, and to offer suggestions for further purchases. Yet customers remember his name also because Richard knows the importance of names himself. He uses them to build sales.

The most crucial of all names, he says, are the customers'. "I always try to remember their names and make a point of greeting them by name. In fact, I must know a couple of hundred customers' names. It really makes them feel you're taking a personal interest in them and their needs. They're not just a face in the crowd.

"By making them feel important, you're complimenting them. Then they return the favor by remembering *my* name when I give them my business card."

The second most important name, Richard says, is J.C. Penney's. "I sell the J.C. Penney name all the time. It's on our furniture, and I tell customers that it's their assurance of quality.

"One, it means the furniture was made to our high construction and design standards. Two, they can order similar merchandise or complete a set wherever they may move later on, since there'll almost always be a J.C. Penney store nearby. And three, we back up our furniture, with top-notch guarantees and service if anything goes wrong—again, wherever they may be living."

It's not a hard sell, he finds. The J.C. Penney reputation is strong, and once he associates the furniture with the name, he puts customers in a buying mood. Afterwards they leave the store with two names in mind—his and J.C. Penney's.

That's a powerful combination that has written Richard Ciotti's name high among the stars.

Source: *You and the JC Penney Company,* Spring 1986, pp. 8–9.

A branch bank
in a Kroger
supermarket.

Cameramann International, Ltd.

permarkets have counters where a bank or thrift institution sells saving
certificates and insurance.[4]

Travel agents perform a type of retail selling. They have the know-how
and information needed to make travel arrangements, keeping in mind
the customer's tastes, budget, and other requirements. As a rule, wholesale trade selling is in many ways like retail selling. But there is a greater
stress on outside salespeople, and sales are made to resellers.

The responsibilities of retail salespeople fall into three basic categories:
responsibilities to the customer, to the company, and to themselves.

Responsibilities to Customers

Today's consumers are the best educated and most sophisticated in history. They expect the store and the salesperson to be responsive to their
needs. They want to be treated fairly, and they want to be fully informed
about the products they buy.

Various consumer groups have recently pressured manufacturers and
retailers for full disclosure about what the consumer is buying, how it will
work, and what the actual finance charges are. Manufacturers have made
considerable improvements in their advertising, packaging, and labeling
to provide consumers with accurate product information.

Customers still want to talk to someone about their specific needs and
how products will fulfill those needs. First, the retail salesperson has to
listen to customers to determine their needs. Next, he or she has to follow
up with a full explanation about the products offered. Customers who

---

[4]*The Wall Street Journal,* March 24, 1983, p. 1.

have the opportunity to be heard and who are properly informed by the salesperson are happy customers.

Responsibilities to Store Management

The retail salesperson is management's representative with the customers. The image created by the salesperson becomes the store's image in the eyes of customers. The retail salesperson has the responsibility to inform customers on the store's policies and practices. He or she should also inform management on what customers are buying and not buying. One of the most important functions of the retail salesperson is to provide current information to buyers and department managers on the wants and needs of customers. In large stores, this function is likely to be computerized.

Personal Responsibility

Retail salespeople have a responsibility to themselves to use their full capacities at all times. For the person who continues to learn about merchandise, about new selling techniques, about competition, and about new trends in retailing, a career in retailing can be exciting and rewarding.[5]

Successful retail salespeople have a responsibility to themselves to maintain a positive and pleasant attitude at all times, no matter how irritating a customer may be. Personal composure provides rich rewards in the long run.

REQUIREMENTS FOR SUCCESS IN RETAIL SELLING

If people are to succeed in retail selling, they must be proficient in the following areas: (1) knowledge of company policies and practices, (2) knowledge of company's and competitors' merchandise, (3) human relations skills, (4) selling skills, and (5) conceptual skills. In addition, they should be marketing oriented and possess the drive and the competitive spirit necessary for success.

Most large retail stores provide extensive and up-to-date training programs for sales personnel. These programs contribute a great deal to success in selling.

Knowledge of the Company— Its Policies and Practices

It is important for retail salespeople to have a thorough knowledge of the company's or store's background and of its credit, exchange, and delivery policies.

Knowledge of Company or Store   When a customer is making a buying decision, he or she should know that the company or store will guarantee

---

[5]Career information is available from National Retail Merchants Association, 100 West 31 Street, New York, N.Y. 10001.

the quality and performance of the product. If the salesperson is knowledgeable about the company's history, the following comment may be important to the customer: "We have been in business in Kansas City for 50 years and have always followed a policy of 'satisfaction or your money back.' "

If the store has a reputation for leadership in style or fashion, the salesperson should know this and should convey this message to customers. If a salesperson works for a large company with many stores, he or she might refer to the company's advantages in making large-scale purchases that result in savings to customers.

Salespeople who work in large department stores should have up-to-date knowledge on the location of other departments and on what merchandise they carry. If special promotions are featured in other departments, the salesperson should call this to the attention of customers.

Knowledge of Policies and Practices   Knowledge of credit policies and practices is also essential for the retail salesperson. If the store provides delivery services, the salesperson should be able to tell customers exactly when their merchandise will be delivered.

Certain products such as appliances, stereos, and TV sets carry a manufacturer's warranty. The salesperson should know what merchandise carries warranties and should inform the customer of what is required to be sure a warranty is in effect.

Knowledge of Merchandise

The first principle of selling is to know the merchandise from A to Z. In this way, the salesperson can match the values of the products to the needs of customers. It is not enough to say, "This camera is very good, and the price is low." The customer expects and deserves specific information on the camera's special features, how it compares with competing products, and what personal benefits it will bring the customer. The retail salesperson must understand why his or her merchandise is superior to that of competitors. This understanding must be conveyed to the customer.

If salespeople are fully informed on the merchandise, they will be better able to answer price-versus-quality questions. Customers aren't interested in such general statements as: "This is an outstanding value; we are selling a lot of it." They would prefer specific information on the product and its benefits.

It is essential for a salesperson to offer detailed comparisons of different brand products. This is especially the case in highly competitive areas, such as selling computers and word-processing products. It's also true in selling videotape recorders, stereos, and copiers. ComputerLand, the world's largest computer retailer, recently doubled its training staff to raise the level of in-store expertise. The aim is to improve all aspects of selling computers—from basic selling techniques to the ability to translate

Demonstrating an
NEC personal
computer at a
ComputerLand
store.

Cameramann International, Ltd.

technical jargon into language that even computer-shy customers can understand.[6]

Salespeople cannot assume customers will see the true value in the merchandise. The salesperson must emphasize the merchandise's positive points until its value to the customer becomes greater than its price.

Customer Orientation

Most successful salespeople have a keen perception of the feelings of others. They have a high degree of empathy for the behavior and attitudes of customers and shoppers. They know selling is a two-way street and both the customer and the salesperson are human beings. They realize the need to listen to a prospective client; they are prepared to ask questions that encourage him or her to talk. In doing so, the salesperson automatically has a rapport with the customer. As a result, the customer will pay more attention to the salesperson's presentation.

Customers continue to patronize stores that they know from experience have friendly and pleasant salespeople. This is because customers prefer salespeople who really want the store's products to meet the customers' needs.

[6]"ComputerLand Takes a Bigger Byte," *Sales & Marketing Management*, January 17, 1983, p. 28.

Store and personal goodwill is built in the long run by fair treatment, prompt service, and a high degree of integrity on the part of all store personnel.

The president of a nationally known retail store indicates the importance of service in these words:

> I think it is clear that the secret of success in retail
> distribution is concern for the customer. Anything that
> detracts from that objective is fatal. Retailing is a service
> industry. It succeeds or fails depending on how successfully it
> meets the test of service—above all, the vital point of
> *personal* contact. If retail contacts are pleasant, easy, and
> satisfactory, not only will a sale take place but a great many
> future sales as well. This vital service is a function of
> retailing that cannot be automated out of existence. *The
> customer is our business.*[7]

In such fields as women's ready-to-wear and men's clothing, successful retail salespeople build goodwill and a personal following by sending cards or making telephone calls when a new item comes in that the salesperson believes would be particularly attractive to a certain customer. Often, salespeople keep records on each customer's present wardrobe and future needs to plan future sales (see Figure 16–2).

A method of building goodwill when the salesperson is selling cars, appliances, or other big-ticket products is to make followup calls or inquiries to find out if the customer is happy with the purchase. This not only builds goodwill but also frequently results in additional sales to the customer and/or prospect referrals.

SELLING SKILLS AND RETAILING

Separate chapters take up the special skills required in all types of selling (see Chapters 8 through 14). This section will emphasize selling skills that apply particularly to retail selling. These skills include approaching customers, selecting merchandise to show, selling benefits, presenting merchandise, selling add-ons, serving several customers at once, handling objections, and closing the sale.

Approaching Customers

In many types of selling that involve prospecting, salespeople can obtain information about prospective customers before the first interview. This helps the salesperson decide the best approach. But in retail selling, the situation is quite different. The prospective customer may be a stranger; the salesperson may have only a few seconds to size him or her up. The first spoken words and friendly smile are most important in retail selling.

---

[7]From a speech by the chairman of the board, R. H. Macy & Co.

Figure 16–2 Wardrobe Planning Chart

Occupation _____ Name _____

Store Charge _____ Address _____

Other Charge _____ Phone: Business _____

Home _____

WARDROBE PLAN

ITEM	SIZE	SHOULD HAVE	HAS	NEEDS				COMMENTS
				NOW	LATER	COLOR	STYLE	
SUIT								
SPORT COAT								
SLACKS DRESS CASUAL								
SHIRTS DRESS SPORT								
TIES								
OUTERWEAR DRESS CASUAL RAINCOAT								
SWEATERS								
SOCKS DRESS CASUAL								
SLEEPWEAR PAJAMAS ROBE								
ACCESSORIES BELTS JEWELRY HANDKERCHIEFS OTHER								
SHOES DRESS CASUAL								

Many customers are warm and naturally outgoing. Approaching them is relatively easy. On the other hand, many others are quiet, reserved, and unfriendly to strangers.

Retail salespeople must meet and greet all kinds of customers—from the most cheerful and agreeable to the most suspicious and difficult. This is why retail selling is so interesting; this is why it is such a challenge.

Purpose of the Approach   While some customers come into a store with very definite needs, seeking a particular item, this is not always the case. The majority of customers—even when they have specific needs—start by browsing. The purpose of the approach is to narrow the customer's focus from broad and generalized interests to specific items.

Elements in an Approach   The approach consists of the following elements: (1) greeting the customer with a genuine smile, (2) introducing yourself by name, (3) developing rapport, and (4) getting the customer to focus his or her attention on a specific area.

Many customers are anxious, particularly when contemplating a major purchase. In addition, customers may feel threatened, thinking a salesperson is going to pounce on them. One approach for reducing this anxiety is to begin the conversation by making a comment about something other than the merchandise they are looking at. For example, an initial comment could be about the weather or a flattering remark about the customer's apparel.

This initial rapport-building phase should continue until the customer's nonverbal and verbal communications indicate he or she is ready to talk about merchandise. Then the sales process should be started by focusing the customer's attention on (1) a product feature, (2) a product application, (3) the manufacturer of the merchandise, and (4) a special value.

Many customers look at merchandise without really seeing. Often the merchandise contains hidden features. By drawing the customer's attention to particular features, the salesperson helps him or her really "see" it.

Some merchandise has multiple uses, some very special uses. A good attention focuser is mentioning application of what the customer is looking at—where and how the apparel can be worn.

Manufacturer reputation, if it is well known to customers, gives the customer a specific thing to think about. This can be especially important when the manufacturer's labels are on the inside of the apparel or can not be easily seen on the product.

Finally, any particular value, such as special price, gives the customer a specific factor to consider.

The following examples illustrate how a customer's attention can be focused using benefit statements and/or questions:

Benefit statement: "There's no better time to consider a raincoat. Prices were never lower." (particular value)

Question: "What member of your family were you considering that shirt for?" (product application)

Benefit statement and question: "The colors in that tie are smart and up to date. What color suit would you be wearing it with?" (product and product application)

The "Just Looking" Customer   Salespeople should avoid using the simple approach, "May I help you?" The answer to this question is almost always, "I'm just looking." But these customers are not just looking. They will buy eventually. The customer is there to buy, but the salesperson has to make a sale.

The key to handling the "just looking" customer is patience. The salesperson needs to convey a desire to help and then give the customer a chance to look at the merchandise alone. Sandie Robbins, a furniture salesperson for J. C. Penney Co. in Anchorage, Alaska, related this looking experience:

> Last August a couple told me they weren't interested in anything in particular when I approached them. I kept an eye on them anyway. A little later I noticed they seemed very interested in one piece. When they started checking the price tag, I approached them again. This time I cracked the shell. Since then, I've been to their home three times to advise them, and they've bought almost $12,000 in furniture from me.[8]

Selecting Merchandise to Show

Retail salespeople are often perplexed as to which merchandise to show first. Some salespeople show the medium-priced merchandise on the theory it is possible to trade up or down from there without too much difficulty. Other salespeople, however, prefer to start with the top of the line; they hope customers will appreciate quality merchandise and see value before price. However, this technique can backfire. Showing a budget-minded customer a $40 perfume will often send the customer out the door.

Salespeople need to do some digging to determine the customer's needs and preferences. It's essential to use questions to get the customer talking. Some basic information a retail salesperson needs to know to select the appropriate merchandise is:

The type of item or items sought.

Financial capacity.

---

[8]*You and a Changing J.C. Penney,* Holiday 1986, p. 2.

Good salespeople
use gentle
persuasion—
responsibly.

© Joel Gordon 1983

How the merchandise will be used.

Lifestyle of customer.

Existing wardrobe, appliances, consumer electronics, and so on.

Preferences for color and style.

Customers often want salespeople to ask them questions and then want the salesperson to answer them. For example, even when customers come in with a specific idea for draperies, they usually want to know the salesperson's opinion. The customers realize salespeople have a lot of experience. They can often suggest a different type or color of draperies, giving customers an opportunity to consider their purchase from a different viewpoint.

Educating customers helps them realize which merchandise is appropriate for them. For example, a customer may not know about the variety of features in televisions or videocassette recorders and so cannot tell the salesperson what they want. Thus, a salesperson might ask if the television is for the living room or bedroom. The answer to this question will tell the salesperson whether a console or portable model is appropriate. By learning that small children are in the household, the salesperson can point out that a less complicated, more rugged television may be appropriate.

Finally, a little gentle persuasion may be needed to make sure customers get what they need. A man who wears a 46 coat and 42 pants may ask for a side-vented suit in those sizes. However, that style suit is not available in larger sizes; even if altered to fit, it will not look very good. Through questioning, the salesperson can learn why the man wants a side-vented suit and direct him to another style that will satisfy his needs for a fashionable suit.

The art of asking questions is discussed in more detail in Chapter 6. The conversation below illustrates how questions are used effectively.

Salesperson: Have you shopped at Wilmont's before?

Customer: I've been in, but haven't bought anything.

Salesperson: To save you some time and to be certain you get the best value, it would be helpful if I could get some information about you. You mentioned a sport coat. How would you be using it?

Customer: Well, as I said, I'm just looking. I wanted something sporty that I could wear around on weekends and after work.

Salesperson: You look to be about a size 40 or 42. Would that be right?

Customer: Yeah, usually a 42. Sometimes 40 long.

Salesperson: They're right over here. Now, what style did you have in mind?

Customer: Nothing in particular. Sporty, modern, but not wild.

Salesperson: Let's try this one here, just to be certain we've got the size.

Customer: OK. I'm not so sure I like that one, though.

Salesperson: That's all right. Let's just check size now. If you'll just stand over there by the mirror. What is it about this one that you don't like?

Customer: The color, to begin with. I don't like this maroon.

Salesperson: What color do you like best?

Customer: Blue.

Salesperson: And what kind of sport coats do you now have?

Customer: I've only two. A navy blue blazer and a knit that has a small pattern. Something like this one, only in blue and gray. They look so dressy and I want something that has a sportier look.

Salesperson: Now, you'd like something not too severe in terms of styling, something that, if not blue, would at least coordinate with blue and would have a very casual look. Would that be about right?

Customer: Yeah, I guess that sums it up.

Salesperson: Based on what you've told me, we've got a couple of jackets you'd be interested in seeing. They're right over here.

Selling Benefits   As discussed in Chapter 5, it is important to sell the benefits of the merchandise, not its features. The differences between selling benefits and features are illustrated below:

Feature

Customer: I like the pants all right, but what makes them cost that much?

Salesperson: Well, Ms. Thomas, there are many factors that work together that make up high-quality clothing.

One of them is the workmanship. On these pants, a good bit of it has been done by hand, and the seams reinforced.

The styling is smart and modern and you can take your choice of six different colors.

Do you see this band of elastic on the inside waistband here?

Customer: Yes.

Salesperson: Well, that's to keep your blouse from popping out. The fabric is a texturized woven.

You've already agreed they're good looking and can be worn in many ways and they could be worn with your new jacket.

Benefit

Customer: I like the pants, but what makes them cost that much?

Salesperson: There is no one single thing that makes for good-quality clothing. It's really the manufacturers' alertness to what customers are looking for.

Workmanship is a key factor; reinforcing the seams so they can withstand rough wear and not split at an embarrassing time. This gives you longer time between replacement so that in effect, these pants cost little more than some that might be less expensive.

The styling is smart and modern. You'll look your best and have others admire your taste. Since you have a choice of six colors, you have the freedom to select the one that suits you best and gives you a well-rounded wardrobe.

See this elastic band around the inside of the waist?

Customer: Yes.

Salesperson: Well, that's to keep your blouse from popping out. It keeps you looking neater. Helps avoid the inconvenience of having to constantly tuck your blouse back in.

This fabric has you participating in the latest trend. This material won't wrinkle, so you always look your best. You avoid the inconvenience of running to the dry cleaners, and as a result save time and money.

You've agreed they're good looking and can be worn in many ways— dress or casual. In fact, they would go well with your new jacket. It's a versatile piece for your wardrobe, saving you money because it can serve so many roles.

Cosmetic salespeople have excellent opportunities to present their merchandise effectively.

Mike Tappin

Presenting the Merchandise

Retail salespeople have an unusual chance to use demonstrations as part of their sales presentations. Through effective planning, merchandise demonstrations can get maximum results from appeals to the senses of sound, touch, sight, taste, and smell. Appropriate lighting and sound effects emphasize the beauty of products and the customer satisfactions they can bring. Retail salespeople should appeal to as many senses as possible in their sales demonstrations. A picture is better than many words, and the action of a demonstration is usually more effective than still pictures or descriptive words alone.

Because customers like to be shown as well as told, demonstrating can be the most effective part of a sales presentation. The demonstration gives the salesperson a chance to make the presentation come alive as customers see the product perform with their own eyes.

A demonstration offers something else—it is an opportunity to generate customer excitement and enthusiasm as customers get hands-on experience with the product and begin to visualize what owning the product will mean to them.

In cosmetics, customer involvement is often the deciding factor in making a sale. When a customer isn't sure which colors will look good on her, a salesperson can try the colors on the customer. Cosmetic salespeople often do a makeover for a customer to show many products from moisturizers and toners to powder. Demonstration of a range of products can get customers to purchase an entire line even when they come in only for blush.

In other areas, demonstrating a limited range of merchandise may be better. For example, customers are often overwhelmed by too many samples in custom decorating. Thus, the decorating salesperson may take only five or six samples that fit the customer's style and price range to the customer's house.

When presenting merchandise salespeople should hedge their bets. For example, if a customer expresses an interest in dressy shoes, the salesperson may include one less formal shoe in the three or four pairs shown to the customer. By seeing the less formal shoe, the customer who really isn't sure will know she has another option. This prevents the customer from leaving because she doesn't think the store has what she wants.

Handling Objections

Chapter 12 describes the skills needed to handle objections. But it may be useful to make a few comments here on how to handle objections in retailing. Retail salespeople may have to reply to many objections for the following reasons: (1) There is a wide range of the products on sale in certain stores; and (2) often customers have little knowledge about the products.

Retail salespeople must keep in mind that objections are a natural part of the sales process. They should respond to them in a way that does not create an argument. One way is to turn the customer's statement into a question. Let's assume a customer says, "These stereo speakers are not adequate for the size of our family room." The salesperson might reply, "Oh, are you really concerned about the speaker's ability to provide the proper sound for your room?" If the customer replies yes, then the salesperson could suggest, "Let's take a look at that point. How large is your room?"

Usually answering an objection with a question is more effective than trying to prove the customer's objection is not valid.

The salesperson's aim should be to soften the objection by getting on the customer's side. This can be done by saying, "I know how you feel—everything seems to cost a lot more these days." Then the salesperson might turn the objection into a question. "What you are really asking is, should you make this kind of investment for a videotape recorder, right?" Then the salesperson should answer the question. If price is the objection, one might translate the price into a low payment per week or per day over a period of time. In this way the expense will not frighten the customer so much. Objections provide the customer with a means to get more justification for buying.

The most common objections are related to price. Some methods of overcoming price objections are:

Stress value, emphasizing unique features such as the warranty offered by the store.

Check to see if the customer is eligible to buy on credit and break the purchase price into monthly payments.

Offer less expensive merchandise such as the cologne instead of the perfume.

Closing

Tips from all-star retail salespeople on closing are shown in Figure 16–3.

Selling Add-ons

Good selling technique requires salespeople to suggest additional related sales before the original sales transaction is completed. It is much easier for a customer to add to a sale than to consummate a separate transaction. Customers like new ideas and suggestions that will "go with" what they have already purchased. Many stores provide salespeople with lists of related products.

Accessories, for example, can add variety and interest to a wardrobe. Good salespeople can point out that adding the right look in scarves, wearing the right shoe, and/or pinning the right piece of jewelry to a scarf will create that special effect customers avidly seek each season. Handbags, belts, gloves, and hosiery can also be suggested to complete a purchase.

Salespeople selling paint to a customer doing a home-decorating or maintenance job might ask if the customer has a paintbrush in good shape. Other items of possible use might be sandpaper and putty. Many customers appreciate this pinpointing of needs because it saves them a return trip to the store.

In suggestion selling, the salesperson should avoid becoming too aggressive. Proposing accessories can only be done if this is acceptable to the customer. The salesperson might mention "specials of the day" with no difficulty. But trying to sell a whole wardrobe to someone who only wants to buy a sweater can be annoying. If additional suggestions are appropriate, they should be made in a positive way. "Anything else?" is not effective compared with "You'll need some tapes to go with your new recorder, won't you?"

Successful suggestion selling has many possibilities. It may relate to buying a higher quality product or buying a larger quantity of the product at a lower unit price. Or it may involve buying tie-in products or quite different products on sale in another department.

In order to succeed in retail selling, salespeople have to know company policies and practices. They need to know the store's merchandise as well as the competitors'. They should develop human relations skills as well as selling and conceptual skills.

FIGURE 16–3
Closing the Sale

I'm enthusiastic. . .

It's important to be enthusiastic about your customers' wants and needs. I become excited with them about their purchase. When I'm showing them merchandise, I listen to their ideas and contribute my own to let them know I'm truly interested. Whether they're redecorating, furnishing a new home, or replacing a piece of furniture, I always try to put myself in their position. As they become more interested in buying, I can feel it. I can tell when they're ready to take the step. Then I just start talking as if the item will definitely be in their home, and, before I know it, I've got the sale. I very rarely have to ask directly.
Ione Nafstad
Furniture

I ask. . .

When I'm after a sale, I forget the meaning of the word "No." First, I find out what the customer's needs and wants are. Then I zero in on the product that fits the bill. After that, you can overcome almost any objection with a little effort. I find out why they're wavering and offer a solution. If they are short on cash, I suggest the lay-away plan. If they want to talk the purchase over with their spouse, I explain our return policy and refer to it as our "Spouse Approval Plan." Once an item goes home with a customer, 99 out of 100 stay there. The idea is to get a commitment, to get the customer off the market. The best way to do it is to ask for the sale, from beginning to end, and to offer the customer as many options as possible until you find the right one.
Bernie East
A.C.E.

I suggest. . .

By offering my customer a wide variety of options, I'm able to get the sale. When people look at window coverings, they're often not sure exactly what they want. They're unsure of how different styles might look in their home. To put them at ease, I discuss many options with them. And it's easy, because I honestly believe that our company offers the best selection. With any given customer, I might go over what we have in stock in the store, what I can help them order from catalog, and what they could get made-to-measure. I emphasize our returns policy. Customers are much more willing to make the purchase if they know they can return or exchange draperies that aren't right for their windows. And, of course, I give them my card so that they know I'm ready to help correct any problems after the sale, too.
Ann Pickrell
Window Coverings

I talk. . .

I sell myself before I sell a suit. It's important that a customer trusts me. While he's trying on jackets to help find the correct cut, I focus on his needs and the benefits a suit will offer him. By letting him know that I want to find the best suit

FIGURE 16–3
(*concluded*)

for him, I can establish a rapport. Once that's there, the rest is easy. By the time we find the correct suit, I know I have the sale.
Adam Jones
Men's Clothing

I offer service. . .

Customers are much more at ease if they feel you're ready and able to help them. I make it a point to wear my customer service award pins. I have about 25 of them on my name tag, and they almost always catch people's attention. Customers are more inclined to buy fine jewelry if they think you know your product. If a customer seems interested, I ask them to sit down. I talk to them about the piece and emphasize that I'm here to help them and answer their questions both before and after the sale. I also tell them that J.C. Penney will always be here, so they are assured of satisfaction. When I feel they are ready to make a purchase, I just ask for their J.C. Penney charge card. And, of course, if they don't have one, I ask them to fill out an application.
Tillie Knepper
Fine Jewelry

Source: *You and a Changing JC Penney,* Fall 1986.

A thorough knowledge of merchandise and how to communicate its features and benefits is imperative. A comparison of products with those of competitors is required.

Greeting customers and determining the customers' needs and wants require a "customer service" attitude. Handling complaints satisfactorily is particularly important to keep customers and to build their goodwill.

General selling skills are much the same in retail selling as in other types of selling. Knowing how to approach a customer, selecting the right merchandise to show, speaking the customer's language, engaging in suggestion selling, providing good demonstrations with customer involvement, answering objections skillfully, closing sales effectively, and trading up when appropriate are all important to success in retail selling.

Selling Several Customers at the Same Time

Handling several customers at a time is a unique problem of the retail salesperson. An industrial products salesperson may have to make a sales presentation to a group. But he or she will normally be presenting a single product and will have a chance to plan the presentation. This is not true with the retail salesperson confronted with several customers who may all have different wants and needs. Some of the customers may be slow, deliberate types; others may be in an extreme hurry and want immediate service; and still others may merely be shoppers who are passing the time of day.

Handling several customers at once is a unique problem of the retail salesperson.

Jack Spratt/Image Works

The retail salesperson must give attention to as many customers as possible without creating ill will. This is not easy. If the salesperson is waiting on a customer who seems to be rather deliberate in making a buying decision, a very aggressive customer who wants immediate attention may come up. The salesperson may continue to serve and give attention to the first customer but at the same time recognize the second customer and indicate that someone will be with him or her in a minute. If other salespeople are near, their assistance should be sought.

Handling several customers at the same time requires a high degree of selling skill that usually comes with much experience.

Working with people is an art; keeping customers happy comes through sensitivity, empathy, and a sincere desire to please. This art *can* be developed.

Developing Goodwill

Especially when big-ticket items are sold, it is wise to reaffirm the customer's good judgment in making the purchase that has just been consummated: "I'm sure you will enjoy your new computer." Or, "You will get a lot of pleasure out of this boat." Or, "Be sure to call me if you need any help. I'm anxious to hear how the people at the dinner liked your dress. Here is my card."

Such aftersale comment is an excellent way to build a clientele or what is sometimes called *personal trade*. It gives evidence that interest in the customer is not lost as soon as the sale has been made. When customers come to the store and ask for you, you know you have built a good

FIGURE 16–4
A Thank-You Card Mailed by One Salesman after a Major Purchase

relationship! Figure 16–4 illustrates a good mail followup after a major purchase.

SUMMARY   Retail selling careers provide many and varied opportunities for men and women with average or unusual abilities. These careers can be attractive to those who seek maximum contact with people. More people are involved in retail selling than any other category of selling. Openings are plentiful.

Advancement for retail salespeople may lead to greater responsibilities in buying, merchandising, and sales promotion or in retail store management positions. Good training courses are available in many stores to help men and women progress. Generally, starting salaries are lower than in other industries. But financial rewards are considerable for capable hard workers. Some men and women use this training and experience to open their own retail businesses.

Retail selling offers a chance to work in a wide variety of selling situations. Almost every consumer product is sold through retail outlets.
The retail salesperson has to provide customers with appropriate goods
and services. Management expects the retail salesperson to represent
store management effectively, and as in any career, the salesperson is
responsible for his or her own personal development.

A demand not usually met in other types of selling is the need to wait
on several customers at the same time. Care must be taken not to alienate
any customers in the process.

Conceptual skills are important for advancement to high positions in
either the selling or managerial fields. Development in this area requires
unusual personal dedication, training, and hard work.

QUESTIONS AND PROBLEMS

1. Assume you are a salesperson in a specialty luggage store. A well-
   dressed young woman about 26 years old comes in and looks at
   several bags in a cursory manner without stopping to examine any
   of them. You walk over to her and say, "Good morning, may I assist
   you?" She replies, "No, thanks, I'm just looking." How would you
   handle this customer? What would you say?

2. Assume you are a salesperson in the toy department of a large
   department store and a woman with two children (ages 6 and 12)
   looks at a number of toys. Apparently she is shopping for a toy
   for the 6-year-old. While she is looking at toys for 6-year-old
   children, the 12-year-old boy wanders over to a counter where
   some pocketknives are displayed. He looks around, picks up a
   knife, and sticks it in his pocket. His mother does not see this, but
   you do. In the meantime, the customer has picked out a children's
   book and brought it over to you to pay for it. Her 12-year-old boy
   has joined her. How would you handle this situation? What would
   you say? To whom? When?

3. What are some opportunities for suggestion selling for the
   following products?
   a. A pipe wrench.
   b. A men's sport coat.
   c. A women's slack suit.
   d. A fishing rod.
   e. A bag of lawn fertilizer.

4. You are working in a shoe department on Saturdays to earn some
   extra money while going to school. You are paid an hourly rate,
   and you can earn extra money by selling the last pair of shoes in
   stock or shoes of an unusual size. You have been instructed by
   your supervisor that when you are unable to sell a customer you
   must "turn the customer over" to another salesperson rather than
   let the customer walk out.

What do you think of this procedure? To be effective, how must the "turnover" take place? What are the hazards of the procedure?

5. If you are using a customer benefits approach, what opening statements might you make when the customer is looking at the following products?
   a. A steel tennis racquet.
   b. A "see-through" umbrella.
   c. An automatic dishwashing machine.
   d. Steel-belted tires.
   e. A digital watch.
   f. A racquetball racquet.
   g. An air-cushioned mattress.
   h. A microwave oven.
   i. A portable typewriter.
   j. A camera.
   k. A videocassette recorder.

6. You are viewing a display of all kinds of plumbing equipment for the do-it-yourselfer, and you remember that you need an ordinary toilet tank float. You cannot find one. A salesperson comes by while you are looking, and you ask:
   Do you have a float?
   No.
   Do you know when you will have some?
   No.
   With the final no, the salesperson walks off into another area of the store!
   Is this an unusual situation? What can be done about it?

7. A customer has just purchased an expensive rug from you. After getting her to *approve* the order (not *sign* it), you want to be sure you perform whatever aftersale amenities are important. What actions or statements might be important at this point? What is your objective?

8. Telephone retail stores promote the sale of many types of telephones to consumers. One frequently promoted item is the cordless telephone. It is easy to use—it can be plugged into a phone jack and a convenient AC outlet. Once charged, the handset works at distances of up to 700 feet from the base. Why would a homeowner buy such an instrument? Identify benefits to the buyer that might be emphasized by a retail salesperson.

9. Some people resent having salespeople attempt to trade up to higher-priced merchandise. Under what conditions would you consider trading up acceptable?

10. What major things should a salesperson remember when an angry customer makes a complaint or returns damaged merchandise?

11. Assume you are selling tires. When a prospective customer comes in, what is the first thing you would do? What additional steps would you take to produce the sale?

12. A woman tries on a $50 pair of shoes in a local retail shoe store. She seems to like the shoes, but hesitates to buy. While one shoe is being tried on, she remarks, "I like the looks of these shoes, but I don't think they are worth $50." About that time, two women shoppers walk by and one says to the other in a loud voice, "You know, the prices in this store are outrageous! I saw some shoes down the street that are just as good, and they sell for $4 or $5 less." You are sure your customer heard the remark. Would you ignore the comment and talk about the value and style of the shoes? Would you try to joke about the remarks "some people make"? Would you attempt to justify the price policy of your store? If you follow none of these procedures, what would you do or say?

13. Merry Chimes has recently obtained a position as salesperson in a local department store. She has been through the company's training program and is beginning to feel more comfortable helping customers buy. Merry is currently working in the women's handbag department.

    A husband comes into the department and starts looking at the bags on display. He has decided to buy his wife a gift for their anniversary. He knows she wants a purse, but he also knows he knows very little about the product he is looking for. He picks up some of the purses on display, opens them, closes them, and appears undecided what to buy. About this time Merry asks, "May I help you?" He picks up one of the purses and says, "Do you think my wife would like something like this?"

    Merry answers, "Oh, I don't know. I like it myself."

    How can Merry improve on this answer? What closing principles are involved?

14. Ten years ago before the Pac-Man craze, young Americans were wild over hi-fi. College students made dorm-room centerpieces out of hi-fi systems, and a generation of young retailers set up shop to minister to the stereo zealots.

    Recently, sales have stagnated, and many of the retailers are in financial trouble—many have gone out of business. Customers seem to prefer stores that offer a variety of products. Also, college students—who were the core of a hi-fi store's business—began, and continue, to spend less money on audio equipment.

    As the assistant manager of a specialized hi-fi store, what recommendations can you make to address the problem?

PROJECTS
1. Visit several retail stores and shop for one of the following products: (1) a Beta or VHS machine, (2) a CB radio, (3) a portable air-conditioning unit, (4) a portable TV set, (5) a carpet, (6) a hot tub, (7) a home computer, (8) a body mitten or a surfboard. Write a report on your experience in terms of the salesperson's knowledge of the store and its policies, knowledge of the merchandise, and human relations and selling skills.

2. Write a report on the advantages and disadvantages of a career in retail selling.

3. Select a person in your class who, you believe, would be an outstanding success in retailing. Without divulging the individual's name, write a one-page report describing why you think this person would be successful.

4. Shop a discount store, a specialty store, and a standard department store for the same item(s). Write a one-page report on the differences in treatment from salespeople or other personnel. Why do customers patronize each type of store?

CASE PROBLEMS

Case 16–1   Winslow's Specialty Shop

Winslow's Specialty Shop is located in a relatively small midwestern city. A large percentage of its customers are students at the college in the city. The store has an excellent reputation for quality merchandise and service. It has been in business since 1930.

The owner, Barbara Winslow, is a graduate of the local college and has been active in alumni and community activities. She has been successful in buying merchandise that fits the needs and desires of the store's clientele.

Winslow's major competition is Miller's Specialty Store, which has been in business since 1975. Bob and Mary Miller, who own and operate the store, are aggressive, and they take particular pride in undercutting Winslow's prices for similar merchandise.

During August 1980, both stores were having sales, and various products were advertised. The merchandise featured by Winslow's included handbags and apparel accessories. A product to which Winslow's gave prominence in its advertising was a South American leather handbag at $27.95. Miller's happened to be offering the same handbag at $32.75. When Bob Miller saw Winslow's ad, he decided to drop his price on the bag to $22. Then he instructed the salespeople to emphasize the price advantage of buying the handbag at Miller's instead of at Winslow's. Miller's did not advertise the bag at $22.

Assume you are a salesperson at Winslow's, and that Mary Cook, who has been a customer of yours for two years, comes in to look at handbags. After you have shown Mary several handbags, she indicates she is interested in the South American bag at $27.95. You describe the product features of the bag to her, and she says, "OK, charge it to my account." (Her credit is good).

Just as Mary says this, Miriam, a friend of hers, happens by. Miriam says, "Hi, Mary, what's new?" Mary responds, "Oh, nothing much. I'm buying a new handbag. My old one is really shot." She shows Miriam the handbag she has just decided to purchase, and Miriam says, "It's beautiful, but I was just looking at this handbag at Miller's this morning, and you can buy the same thing there for $22."

Mary looks at you, and you look at her. Miriam looks at both of you. Mary says, "Why should I be paying $5.95 more for the same handbag just because I'm a good customer of Winslow's?"

Questions:

1. How would you handle this situation if you were the salesperson?
2. What are your options?

Case 16–2   Closing a Sale

Analyze each of the following suggestions on how to close a sale. These suggestions were made by salespeople who sell men's suits.

1. I always have an "ace in the hole" . . . one particular suit in which a customer has shown an interest. Or if I have studied my customer carefully when he first came in (and if I have time I usually have been able to), I go back to the first suit he tried on "for size," and very often it is possible to "close the deal" with that first suit. It is important to keep this suit out of sight and not to bring out this "ace in the hole" until a sale cannot be made on some other garment.

2. When a seemingly successful sale bogs down because the prospect is reluctant to take the final step, I simply tell him, "*Take the coat to the door* (or the window) and see how the daylight brings out the character of the cloth." The psychological reactions are several: It relieves him of the suspicion that any "high pressure" may be applied; his ego is flattered by your apparent confidence in him; the appearance of the fabric is bound to be enhanced by the daylight; the customer is left alone for a minute or so, and with your sales talk bearing fruit, he generally sells himself!

3. There's one technique I've found especially effective with "on-the-fence" buyers: take a tape measure, and as you bend to measure his inseam, ask, "Do you like to wear your trousers pretty well down on your shoe?" Whatever his answer, it usually gives the go-ahead on the purchase, or at least gives the salesperson a lead as to what may be holding the customer back. This works especially well when the wife is along and says, "Yes, I like it, do you?" When that happens, don't wait too long to put the tape on your prospect for complete measurements . . . and the final sale!

4. One of the best ways of helping a customer make up his mind is, surprisingly enough, not to talk about clothing! Discuss current events, sports, his business, or any other

subject unrelated to clothing. A few minutes apparently "wasted" in personal conversation create more customer-confidence in the salesperson, give the customer time to finally make up his mind. In the majority of cases, he will come back to the subject of clothing himself and will be ready to take the garment about which he couldn't make up his mind just a few minutes before.

5. Give your customer a *choice*, for instance, between two colors or two models. Don't hesitate to ask, "Mr. Jones, which model appeals to you, the green or the brown?" Almost invariably he will make a choice, which is your cue to close the sale by taking the trousers from the rack, starting toward the dressing room with the remark, "Step over here and slip the whole suit on." In most cases, the sale will be completed by suggesting that the tailor be called to see if any alterations are necessary.

SELECTED REFERENCES

Berry, Leonard, and Ian H. Wilson. "Retailing: The Next Ten Years." *Journal of Retailing,* Fall 1977, pp. 5–28.

Blyskal, Jeff. "Screws, Bolts . . . and Tighter Competition." *Forbes,* May 24, 1982, pp. 146–49.

"Compu-flor Closes Sales." *Sales & Marketing Management,* December 6, 1982, pp. 18–19.

Culligan, M. J. "What It Takes to Succeed in Sales." *Nation's Business,* April 1982, pp. 42ff.

Duncan, Delbert J.; Stanley C. Hollander; and Ronald Savitt. *Modern Retailing Management: Basic Concepts and Practices.* Homewood, Ill.: Richard D. Irwin, 1983.

"Executive Compensation: What Works?" *Chain Store Age Executive,* October 1979, pp. 19–22.

Hansen, Robert A., and Terry Deutscher. "An Empirical Investigation of Attribute Importance in Retail Store Selection." *Journal of Retailing,* Winter 1977–78, pp. 59–72.

Hirschman, Elizabeth C. "Differences in Consumer Purchase Behavior by Credit Card Payment System." *Journal of Consumer Research,* June 1979, pp. 58–66.

"Industry Profiles—Supermarket, Department Store, Discount Store, Specialty Store, Home Center, General Merchandise, and Drug Store." *Chain Store Age Executive,* August 1982, pp. 18–30.

May, Eleanor G., and Malcolm P. McNair. "Department Stores Face Stiff Challenge in Next Decade." *Journal of Retailing,* Fall 1977, pp. 47–58.

Still, Leonie V. "Part-Time Versus Full-Time Salespeople: Individual Attributes, Organizational Commitment, and Work Attitudes." *Journal of Retailing,* Summer 1983, pp. 55–79.

Sumner, Steven J.; Alan J. Dubinsky; and James H. Donnelly, Jr. "The Use of Social Bases of Power in Retail Sales." *Journal of Personal Selling and Sales Management,* November 1984, pp. 48–56.

Swinyard, William R. "The Appeal of Retailing as a Career." *Journal of Retailing,* Winter 1981, pp. 86–97.

Teas, R. Kenneth. "A Test of a Model of Department Store Salespeople's Job Satisfaction." *Journal of Retailing,* April 1981, pp. 3–23.

"The $100 Million Club." *Chain Store Executive,* August 1982, pp. 35–52.

U.S. Department of Labor, Bureau of Labor Statistics. *Occupational Outlook Handbook,* 1982–83, Bulletin 2200, Retail Trade Sales Workers, Washington, D.C., pp. 249–54.

V Improving the Sales Representative's Personal Effectiveness

This section is devoted to methods salespeople can use to improve their effectiveness and programs companies undertake to improve effectiveness of their salespeople. In Chapter 17, techniques are presented that salespeople can use to improve their performance through better time and territory management. Chapter 18 examines how the effectiveness of face-to-face selling communications is enhanced by other communication vehicles—direct mail and telemarketing. In Chapter 19, the impact of sales management on the salesperson's activities is discussed.

17

Managing Time, Territory, and Self

Some questions addressed in this chapter are:

- Why is time so valuable for salespeople?
- Why should salespeople classify their accounts?
- What should salespeople consider when determining how frequently to call on customers?
- What techniques can salespeople practice to use time effectively?
- How can salespeople increase the number of calls they make per day?
- Why should salespeople analyze their territory coverage, daily activities, and activities during specific sales calls?
- How can salespeople do paperwork efficiently?

Salespeople have more individual freedom than almost any other type of employee. Their success or failure is largely due to their own efforts. A company assigns them to a territory, and then it is up to them to cover the area effectively. Because salespeople work away from the office, they must be self-sufficient. No one tells them when to start working or when to quit for the day.

Because salespeople are allowed so much freedom, they need to be good self-managers. Self-management involves using their scarcest resource, time, so they get the most out of their territory.

THE VALUE OF TIME

The old axiom "Time is money" certainly applies to selling. A salesperson who works 8 hours a day for 240 days a year will work 1,920 hours during a year. If the salesperson earns $20,000, each hour of time would be worth $10.42. An hour of time would be worth $15.63 if a salesman earned $30,000 a year. Looking at it another way, a salesperson working on a 10 percent commission would have to sell $104 worth of products each hour to earn $20,000 for the year.

That is only part of the story. A lot of a salesperson's time is spent on nonproductive activities. The surveys discussed in Chapter 2 (see Figure 2–1) found that salespeople spend less than half of their working day in face-to-face selling. Most of their day is spent traveling, waiting for customers, doing paperwork, and making service calls. Since the typical salesperson only spends 920 hours each year in front of customers, a salesperson on a 10 percent commission would have to sell $217 worth of products during each hour in front of customers to earn $20,000 for the year.

The lesson from this analysis is clear. The successful salesperson must make every hour count. Time management is particularly important in selling because it is so easy for salespeople not to work. They have little supervision. No one really knows how they spend their time. They can easily waste time by playing tennis, taking many coffee breaks, or engaging in social rather than business conversations with customers.

ESTABLISHING GOALS

The first step a salesperson takes in "self-managing" the job is to establish *working goals*. These goals are usually based on the sales quota assigned by the sales manager. They may be expressed in terms of total dollar volume of sales, units of sales, number of customer calls, or number of demonstrations. To meet these goals, the salesperson needs to practice self-discipline by planning and following a working schedule for each day or each week. This will enable him or her to achieve the overall goals or objectives.

The National Society of Sales Training Executives suggests that the speciality salesperson plan a schedule along the following lines:

1. A minimum number of hours of work each day in order to get a given result.
2. A minimum number of demonstrations (or "calls" or "contacts"—or whatever the time spent with prospective buyers may be called).
3. A minimum number of unit sales (or volume in dollars—or whatever other measurement of accomplishment is used).

If a salesperson consistently meets the three requirements set forth above, he or she will have little difficulty realizing the established sales quota.

Achieving minimum goals may limit the salesperson's long-term growth. Sales production records indicate that many salespeople make the mistake of "freezing" their earnings at a certain level. For example, they may establish an earnings goal of $30,000 per year. As soon as their sales are sufficient to realize this income, they begin to ease off. In other words, many salespeople tend to think of themselves as $30,000-a-year or $35,000-a-year salespeople. When they attain this income, they slacken their pace. Salespeople who have this philosophy are seldom promoted to management.

TERRITORY ANALYSIS

Planning is the basis for all time organization. Salespeople need to develop both long-range and short-range plans. Long-range plans help them direct their efforts toward customers and activities that will result in the most sales. A first step in planning is to analyze the territory.

Account Classification and Call Planning

Not all customers have the same potential to buy from a salesperson.[1] The salesperson has to concentrate on the most profitable customers and minimize or eliminate the time spent with customers that offer little opportunity for profitable sales. The proportion of unprofitable accounts is usually greater than one would think. The rule of thumb is that 80 percent of the sales in a territory come from only 20 percent of the customers. Therefore, salespeople should classify customers on the basis of their sales potential.

Sometimes the company will help the salesperson classify accounts, but usually the salesperson has to handle this task. Company sales records are a good source of information about existing accounts. However, information on past sales can be misleading. A customer that has placed small orders in the past may have been placing large orders with a competitor. This is why the salesperson needs to determine the share of business he or she is getting from each customer. Thanks to the information about past sales and share of business, the salesperson can determine the potential sales for each customer. Customers with higher potential will receive a higher classification.

For uncalled-on potential customers, the salesperson will frequently have to estimate their sales potential. Such estimates can be made by comparing the potential customer to a present customer of similar size and in a similar business. If an existing customer that purchases $1,000 or more a month is classified as a major account, then a prospective customer with a similar potential is assigned the same rating.

In a typical classification scheme, each customer might be classified into one of three categories—A, B, or C. A accounts are existing or potential customers that are or might be most profitable for the company.

---

[1]See William J. Tobin, "80–20 or Perish," *Sales & Marketing Management,* August 13, 1984. p. 16.

For example, a copier manufacturer might define A accounts as companies that make over 250,000 copies a month. Customers that are growing rapidly might be classified as A accounts even though they do not meet the required minimum. B accounts are existing customers with a lower potential than A accounts. C accounts are existing or potential customers that are not likely to buy enough to make them highly profitable accounts.

The salesperson should use the classification in determining the frequency and priority of sales calls. A accounts should be developed first and called on most frequently. Prospecting should be directed exclusively to A accounts. As time permits, other customers can be developed systematically.

A national chemical company classifies its customers as shown below. By adhering to the calling schedule, its sales representatives are able to make the best use of their selling time.

Customer Classification	Estimated Annual Purchases	Required Calling Period
1st	$30,000	Every month
2nd	$12,500–$30,000	Every two months
3rd	$ 2,000–$12,500	Every three months
4th	Under $2,000	As time permits

The use of a classification scheme to direct sales efforts helps overcome a natural tendency of new salespeople to concentrate on congenial customers. Research has shown that young salespeople tend to spend most of their time on customers with whom they feel comfortable. Buyers for large companies are often curt and business-oriented, while small customers are willing to talk all day. As a result, new salespeople tend to spend far too much time with a small portion of their territory's sales potential.

Figure 17–1 shows an example of an annual territory sales plan. Notice that the allocation of calls is related to the customer potential. This plan serves as both a sales goal and a method for allocating time.

Sales representatives often use a set of account cards to record customer classifications. Each customer is listed on an index card like the one shown in Figure 17–2. Since the cards are a working tool, information other than the classification is often included. For example, the salesperson may want to list the names of the key buying influences and the hours at which the purchasing agents see vendors.

Grid Analysis for Call Planning

The account classification and sales call levels described in Figure 17–1 are based exclusively on an account's sales potential. Because accounts with the highest potential (Allied Brake and Zebec) are A accounts, they

Figure 17–1 Annual Territory Sales Plan

Salesperson: *Sam Thompson*

Account	Actual Sales ($000) 1985	1986	1987	Estimated Potential	1988 Forecasted Sales	Number of Calls Allocated	Classification
Allied Brake	100	110	160	250	160	48	A
Zebec	75	75	90	300	115	48	A
Wright	40	50	60	175	90	24	B
American Can	20	30	30	150	30	24	B
Tee Products	10	10	25	100	55	18	C
Simmons Mfg.	0	0	30	100	80	18	C
Unilevel	0	0	0	80	75	18	C
Jackright	0	10	20	75	70	18	C
Baker Tool	0	5	12	60	60	12	D
Tool and Die	0	0	10	60	50	12	D
Castmetal, Inc.	10	8	9	50	40	12	D

FIGURE 17–2
Example of Account
Card

```
                                                              Classification: B

        Stoppard Plastics Co.
        53 Culver Blvd.
        Ames, Iowa                                         Tel. 876–2200


        Ms. Susan Blake—Purchasing Agent
        Vendor Hours: 9:00 to 4:00 M/W/Th


        Sales potential: $300/month.
        Buys exclusively from Diamond.
```

are assigned one call a week. Baker Tool, Tool and Die, and Castmetal have the lowest potential. These accounts are classified D and receive only one call a month.

Inefficiencies can develop when annual call rates are determined exclusively by account potential. Let's consider the Allied Brake account. In 1987, Sam Thompson, the salesperson calling on Allied Brake, made $160,000 in sales. Thompson's forecast sales for 1988 are also $160,000. Because of the high potential, he classifies Allied Brake as an A account and plans to make 48 calls during the coming year.

Allied Brake is a satisfied customer that needs little service. In fact, Thompson would be able to sell $160,000 if he called on Allied only once every two weeks. Thus, he is wasting 24 calls a year on Allied. There is no need to spend 24 calls on Allied to make his sales forecast of $160,000.

Where could Thompson use these 24 calls more efficiently? He has never been successful in getting business from American Can. Since this firm's potential sales are only $150,000, it only gets 24 calls a year. At this level of calls, Thompson has not been able to develop the account properly. But if he made an additional 24 calls per year on American Can, he might increase his American Can sales from $30,000 to $80,000.

By shifting calls from a high-potential, satisfied customer—Allied Brake—to a lower-potential customer—American Can—Thompson might increase his 1988 sales volume by $50,000. He would still receive $160,000 from Allied Brake, but he could also get $50,000 from American Can.

This example shows that salespeople need to consider other factors than just sales potential in establishing call levels for an account. In addition to potential, salespeople need to consider the sales that might be gained by increasing the call rate and those that might be lost by decreasing the call rate. In other words, salespeople should consider how hard it is to get more business from an account. The location of an account is another factor to keep in mind. Accounts in out-of-the-way places are expensive to call on. It may take two days to travel back and forth to see a remote customer. Even if the customer has a large potential, it might not be worthwhile to make frequent calls. The salesperson could make more sales calling on smaller customers that are easier to reach.

Professors Raymond LaForge and David Cravens have developed a method called sales call grid analysis for incorporating a number of factors to classify accounts and determine call frequency.[2] Using this method, each account in a salesperson's territory is classified into one of the four segments shown in Figure 17–3. The classification is based on the salesperson's evaluation of the account on the following two dimensions:

1. The *account opportunity dimension* indicates how much the customer needs the product and whether it is able to buy the product. Some factors the salesperson can consider when determining account opportunity are the account's potential, its growth rate, and its financial condition.

2. The *strength of position dimension* indicates how strong the salesperson and his or her company are in selling the account. Some factors that determine strength of position are present share of account's purchases of the product, attitude of account toward company and salesperson, and relationship between the salesperson and the key decision makers in the account.

The appropriate sales call strategy depends on the grid segment in which the account is classified. For example, accounts in Segment 1 are

---

[2]Raymond W. LaForge; Clifford E. Young; and B. Curtis Hamm, "Increasing Sales Productivity through Improved Sales Call Allocation Strategies," *Journal of Personal Selling and Sales Management,* November 1983, pp. 53–59, and Raymond W. LaForge and David Cravens, "Steps in Selling Effort Deployment," *Industrial Marketing Management,* August 1982, pp. 183–94.

FIGURE 17–3
Sales Call Allocation
Grid

Strength of Position

	Strong	Weak
	Segment 1	**Segment 2**

High	Attractiveness:
	    Accounts are very attractive since they offer high opportunity and sales organization has strong position.
	
	Sales call strategy:
	    Accounts should receive a high level of sales calls since they are the sales organization's most attractive accounts.
		Attractiveness:
		    Accounts are potentially attractive since they offer high opportunity, but sales organization currently has weak position with accounts.
		
		Sales call strategy:
		    Accounts should receive a high level of sales calls to strengthen the sales organization's position.

	Segment 3	**Segment 4**

Low	Attractiveness:
	    Accounts are somewhat attractive since sales organization has strong position, but future opportunity is limited.
	
	Sales call strategy:
	    Accounts should receive a moderate level of sales calls to maintain the current strength of the sales organization's position.
		Attractiveness:
		    Accounts are very unattractive since they offer low opportunity and sales organization has weak position.
		
		Sales call strategy:
		    Accounts should receive minimal level of sales calls and efforts made to selectively eliminate or replace personal sales calls with telephone sales calls, direct mail, etc.

Account Opportunity (label at left: Account Opportunity)

Source: Raymond W. LaForge; Clifford E. Young; and B. Curtis Hamm, "Increasing Sales Productivity through Improved Sales Call Allocation Strategies," *Journal of Personal Selling and Sales Management,* November 1983, pp. 53–59.

very attractive. They offer a lot of opportunity and the salesperson is in a good position. Thus, these accounts should receive the highest level of sales calls.

Using Computers for Call Planning

Leonard M. Lodish of the Wharton School has developed a computer program that helps salespeople determine the best call level for each of their accounts.[3] Using this program, salespeople can combine information on travel time, account profitability and potential, and the effects of increasing call frequency to determine the optimal call frequency. To use the program, a salesperson simply answers questions on a computer terminal. Figure 17–4 gives an example of questions asked by the CALL-PLAN computer program. In this example, the CALLPLAN program

_____

[3]Leonard M. Lodish, "CALLPLAN: An Interactive Salesman's Call Planning System," *Management Science,* December 1971, pp. P25–P40; and Leonard M. Lodish, " 'Vaguely Right' Approach to Sales Force Allocation," *Harvard Business Review,* January–February 1974, pp. 119–24.

Figure 17–4   CALLPLAN Computer Program for Sales Calling Planning

When the salesperson first uses the CALLPLAN program, the program asks him or her to divide the territory into geographic regions and list all accounts and prospects in each region. The company also collects information about the travel time between regions. Then the computer asks the following questions about each account:

ACCOUNT NAME: BALFOR   REGION: 3

HOW MANY CALLS DO YOU PRESENTLY MAKE PER YEAR? 32

WHAT SALES DO YOU ANTICIPATE IF PRESENT CALL LEVEL IS CONTINUED? 80,000

WHAT ARE ANTICIPATED SALES IF NO CALLS ARE MADE ON ACCOUNT DURING NEXT YEAR? 0

WHAT ARE ANTICIPATED SALES DURING NEXT YEAR IF ½ PRESENT NUMBER OF CALLS ARE MADE? 50,000

WHAT ARE ANTICIPATED SALES DURING NEXT YEAR IF PRESENT CALL LEVEL IS INCREASED BY 50%? 90,000

WHAT ARE THE MAXIMUM SALES YOU COULD GET FROM THIS ACCOUNT IF YOU SPEND ALL YOUR TIME CALLING ON IT? 100,000

ACCOUNT NAME: CHEMPRO   REGION: 1

HOW MANY CALLS DO YOU PRESENTLY . . . .

The computer outputs a recommended call frequency plus the anticipated effects of the recommended call plan.

Optimal Account Call Frequency Policies

Account	Optimal Calls per Year	Expected Sales Using Optimal Level	Present Calls per Year	Expected Sales Using Present Level
BALFOR	28	75,000	32	80,000
CHEMPRO	12	14,000	24	22,000
CHEMPLST	40	195,000	32	171,000
DILCTX	20	15,000	16	8,000
EMERSON	0	0	4	0
ETHLYN	24	64,000	16	52,000
F/C	20	37,000	20	37,000
M-I	0	0	4	2,000
MICRO	0	0	16	2,000
POLYFIN	4	5,000	12	8,000
.				
.				
.				
MARLOW	0	0	4	1,000

Adapted from *Management Science,* December 1971, pp. 37–39.

recommends increasing the number of calls to CHEMPLST, DILCTX, and ETHLYN, and decreasing the number of calls on all the other accounts. In fact, the program indicates that *no calls* should be made on M-I, MICRO, and MARLOW. Generally, the generated sales call frequencies emphasize the 80–20 rule and indicate salespeople should increase time spent on key accounts and reduce time spent on marginal accounts.

FIGURE 17–5
Form for Key Account Action Plan

| Key account action plan | | SALES STRATEGY | | |

(Left side of form:)

Key account action plan

Customer _____ Area _____
President _____ VP-Opns _____
Chief Engineer _____ Other Exec. _____
Plants   Superintendent

_____   _____
_____   _____
_____   _____

Other people to see   Position

_____   _____
_____   _____
_____   _____

Sales forecast

Product 1	Product 2	Product 3	Product 4	Total

FORECAST

	1983-1988	1988-1993
Projects planned		
Product usage		
Competitive trend		
Environ-mental impact		
Other elements		

(Right side of form:)

SALES STRATEGY

Who to see	Objective	Resource needed

PROGRESS

Date	Person seen	Result and product code

Source: Adapted from *Sales & Marketing Management*, September 1979, p. 60.

Key Account Action Plan

After determining call frequencies, the salesperson needs to devote additional planning efforts to key accounts. For each key account, a set of goals should be established. For each goal, a series of activities should be planned to achieve that goal. Figure 17–5 shows a form for developing a key account action plan.

USING TIME EFFECTIVELY

Figure 17–6 shows the steps involved in using time effectively. The first step is to list the activities that need to be performed during a period of time. A sales representative might make a detailed list for the next day and a more general list for a longer time period, such as a week or a month. After listing the activities, the salesperson determines the priority of each activity on the basis of its importance. Salespeople who make daily or weekly lists soon become aware of self-deception when they find themselves regularly transferring undesirable activities from one list to

FIGURE 17–6
Steps in Using Time
Effectively

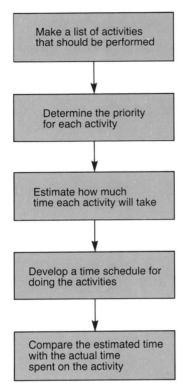

Make a list of activities
that should be performed

Determine the priority
for each activity

Estimate how much
time each activity will take

Develop a time schedule for
doing the activities

Compare the estimated time
with the actual time
spent on the activity

Some hotels now
provide in-room
computer terminals
for guests (in this
case, a salesperson)
to use to consult
airline schedules
and to receive and
send electronic mail.

Courtesy TRAVELHOST

Figure 17–7   List of Activities and Priorities

Activities	Priorities

1. Call on the following prospective customers:
    Flynn Heating and Air Conditioning
    Airtemp Furnaces
    Clayton Plumbing
    Hommell Heating
2. Fill out daily call report form.
3. Submit monthly expense report.
4. Have daily meeting with sales manager.
5. Study new product specification sheet.
6. Check on customers to see if new heat pumps are working properly:
    Cook Plumbing and Heating
    Bryant Furnace
    South Florida Climate Control
7. Be available when first delivery is made to Stephenson Electric.
8. Have lunch with Joe Weller at Miami Heating.
	1. Daily conference with sales manager.
	2. Complete daily call report.
	3. Be available when delivery is made to Stephenson Electric.
	4. Lunch with Joe Weller.
	5. Cook Plumbing and Heating.
	6. Flynn Heating and Air Conditioning.
	7. Hommell Heating.
	8. Clayton Plumbing.
	9. Study new product specification sheet.
	10. Bryant Furnace.
	11. South Florida Climate Control.
	12. Monthly expense report.
	13. Airtemp Furnaces.

the next. A typical list of activities and a priority list for a weekly plan are shown in Figure 17–7.

After developing the priority list, the salesperson estimates how much time will be needed to complete each activity. These estimates plus the priorities are used to make a schedule for the time period. At the end of the period, the salesperson can compare the estimated time with the actual time spent. Such comparisons allow salespeople to schedule their time better in the future and to check on whether their time is being spent on high-priority rather than low-priority activities.

Daily Planning   Each evening, the salesperson should make a plan for the next selling day. The plan should not be limited to where the first call will be made, but should be an entire schedule for the day. Daily plans include spending a maximum amount of time in essential activities. Calls are routed to minimize travel time. Whenever possible, advance arrangements are made for interview appointments and lunch dates.

One company gives its sales representatives the following instructions on the daily sales plan:

1. Select your prospects for tomorrow's calls.
2. List the names and locations of each account.
3. Carefully route those calls to save traveling time.
4. Visualize what is going to take place at each call.
5. Organize your data and exhibits to make each call effective.

FIGURE 17–8
Scheduling Worksheet

Scheduling Worksheet					
Day: _Wednesday_		Date: _June 2, 1987_		Location: _Cincinnati_	
Hours	Appointments and Events	Type of Activity	Deadline	Estimated Time Involvement	Results Anticipated or Required
8:30	Jones Int'l	Sales Call		60 min.	Make presentation to Dave Carey, Vp eng. Demonstrate X35 tester.
10:00	D Square Systems	Service		20 min.	Drop off new catalogue to Sid Jabbar in purchasing.
10:45	Diamond Mfgr.	Sales Call		15 min.	Deliver proposal to Jim O'hara in purchasing. Pick-up order.
11:15	Quad Distributors	Service		15 min.	Get okay to work with new sales people from Jack Conner.
4:15	Write proposal for Wilkes Tool	Paperwork	Due: 6/10/87	60 min.	Have manager review tomorrow morning.
5:15	Get sample for delivery tomorrow to Cube	Paperwork		5 min.	
5:20	Prepare Schedule for tomorrow	Planning		30 min.	

Procedures to use in planning your sales day include the following:

1. First, consult your tickler file for any customer calls due for the next day.
2. Reread the data on each customer card as a refresher. Determine which stage the sale is in.
3. Plan what is to occur on each call. Establish objectives for the call.
4. Determine whether other business can be attended to between calls, such as calling on prospects in the same neighborhood.
5. Consult the prospect file for the case history of each prospect to be called on.
6. Organize the material you will take with you.

7. Arrange your folders in the order you will wish to use them and pack them for carrying in your "hot box."

8. Clip a daily sales activity report to a separate folder and put the folder in the front of your "hot box" so you may fill in the report as you go.

Scheduling Time   Sales calls cannot be made at all hours of the day. Salespeople can call on customers only when the customers are willing to receive them. Many purchasing agents will not see salespeople before 10 A.M., during lunch, or after 4 P.M. Some customers may limit sales calls to a narrow range of time, such as 10 A.M. to noon on Tuesday and Thursday. Even though a customer may not restrict calling hours, a salesperson might find it better to visit during certain hours. For example, a pharmaceutical detail salesperson would want to avoid calling on doctors when they are seeing patients.

In developing a daily plan, salespeople should schedule selling activities first. Sales calls should be scheduled during the prime hours, typically from 9 A.M. to 4 P.M. Time that cannot be spent on selling should be devoted to such activities as servicing accounts (putting up displays, checking out inventories, handling customer complaints), filling out reports, and making phone calls to schedule appointments or get information from the home office.

Salespeople must be realistic in developing a daily plan. If they want to make eight calls during the day, they cannot simply schedule a call each hour. They need to consider driving time and what they want to accomplish during the call. Some calls will need 90 minutes, while others will require only 30 minutes.

Flexibility   Although it is important to work out a daily plan, there are times when the plan should be laid aside. It is impossible to accurately judge the time needed for each call. It would be foolish for a salesperson to hastily conclude a sales presentation just to stick to the schedule. The purpose of making sales calls is to get results. If salespeople believe additional time on a call will yield more results than other scheduled calls, they should revise their schedule accordingly. But such rearrangements should be based on new information received while making the call. Salespeople should not rearrange their schedule just because they are enjoying a conversation with a customer.

To plan for the unexpected, a daily schedule should be arranged so visits are made to the prime prospect first. Then the next best potential customer should be visited. The daily schedule concludes with calls on new prospects. If the day is planned in this manner, unexpected long calls, or emergencies will result in canceling the least important calls—the calls at the end of the day.

"Where am I? Is this a Hyatt or a Ramada? Am I on I-91 or I-95? Sunbelt? Mid-Atlantic? Down East? Where the hell am I?"

©Copyright, Sales & Marketing Management

Reprinted by permission of *Sales & Marketing Management* magazine, January 14, 1985. Copyright 1985.

Routing

Routing plans reduce the nonproductive time spent in going from one sales call to another. Wasting time traveling between customers decreases efficiency and may also increase selling costs through excessive mileage.[4]

There are two basic types of sales call patterns—routine and variable. Routine call patterns are used when a salesperson sees the same customers regularly. For example, when a Procter & Gamble salesperson is assigned a territory, each customer must be contacted regularly. Large grocery stores might be visited once a week; small stores, once a month. After the Procter & Gamble salesperson develops a routing plan, it can be used over and over. Calls are directed toward customers that have a need for a product at a particular time. The routing plan is built around specific customers and specific locations.

The first step in developing a routing plan is to locate customers on a map. Customers often tend to cluster together. Customer clusters reveal obvious ways in which the territory can be divided and the routing plan developed. After the customers are located on a map, the travel time

---

[4]See Wade Ferguson, "A New Method for Routing Salespersons," *Industrial Marketing,* Spring 1980, pp. 171–78.

FIGURE 17–9
Routing for Large Territory

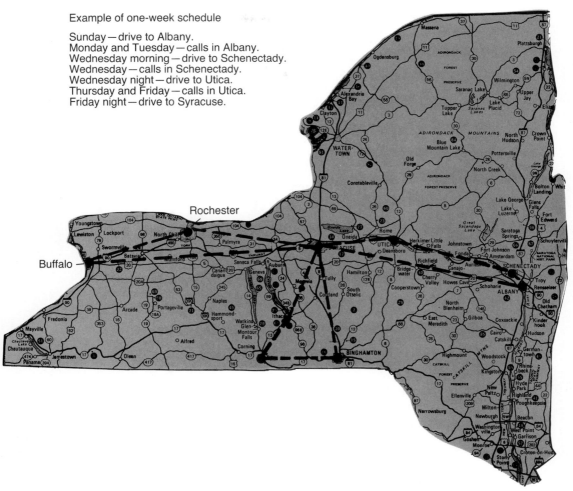

Example of one-week schedule

Sunday—drive to Albany.
Monday and Tuesday—calls in Albany.
Wednesday morning—drive to Schenectady.
Wednesday—calls in Schenectady.
Wednesday night—drive to Utica.
Thursday and Friday—calls in Utica.
Friday night—drive to Syracuse.

between customers is estimated. At what time of day should the salesperson make calls that are a long way from his or her home city? Do the
expected sales justify the travel costs? How much time can he or she
afford to be away from the area?

In planning a sales trip, it is usually best to start working the outlying
areas first and to finish at the home area. Typically, the home area is the
location of the greatest sales potential. If an emergency brings the salesperson back to the home area, he or she will not have to travel as far to
pick up the route again. An example of a four-week itinerary using this
principle is shown in Figure 17–9.

FIGURE 17–10
Routing for
Compact Territory

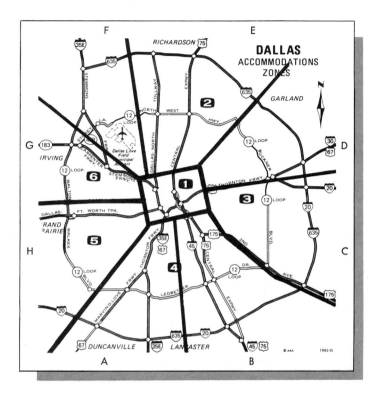

Covering a City or a Small Territory When covering a territory within a two-hour radius of the salesperson's home, it is useful to divide the territory into zones. The zones are worked one at a time. An example of a zone plan is shown in Figure 17–10. The principle of starting with the outermost customer can be used in this situation too. Another way to develop a routing plan for a zone may be to start with a key customer. Suppose the salesperson keys the routing plan for zone B to a customer at location D. If the customer will see the salesperson only at 3:30 P.M., then the route is developed so the customer is the last call for the day.

Salespeople often encounter a conflict between developing an efficient routing plan and making calls on the most profitable customer. Typically the most efficient routing plans will include customers with low sales potentials. One approach to this problem is to develop an efficient routing plan for each customer classification. The salesperson can then use the routing plan for the most profitable customers more frequently than the routing plan for less profitable customers.

ANALYZING THE SALESPERSON'S PERFORMANCE

A careful analysis of sales records and reports provides a salesperson with such information as dollar sales per call, dollar sales by products, number of calls made, number of interviews obtained, number of orders lost, miles traveled per day, number of complaints, and new prospects obtained.

Some sales representatives believe time spent analyzing past records is wasted. In many instances, sales representatives pay little attention to the detailed analyses they receive from the office. This attitude is most prevalent among sales representatives of the "old school," who are reluctant to change their old methods.

The younger and more progressive sales representatives, however, realize the importance of analyzing past accomplishments to improve future operations. Information from past records and reports helps answer the following questions: Am I covering my territory efficiently? Am I concentrating my efforts on customers with the greatest sales potentials? Am I selling a balanced line of products? Am I spending most of my time in actual sales interviews?

Territory Coverage

Many companies require their sales representatives to fill out daily call reports. An example of a call report form is shown in Figure 17–11. Call report forms are useful in analyzing sales activities. From these forms, statistics such as number of calls per day, sales per call, and percentage of calls made on customers in each classification can be calculated. Over time, these statistics might indicate reasons for a sales slump. For example, a salesperson might find that the number of calls made per day has dropped or that too many calls are being made on low-potential accounts.

Table 17–1 provides an analysis of a salesperson's call pattern established on the basis of his or her daily call reports. This analysis demonstrates a common mistake salespeople make in time management: spending too much time on small accounts. Sales from calls on A accounts are 10 times bigger than those on D accounts. Despite the bigger payoff from calls on larger accounts, the salesperson makes more than three times as many calls on D accounts as on A accounts.

Daily Activities

It is also important for salespeople to analyze their activities during the day. To make this analysis, some salespeople carry a pocket notebook ruled by 30-minute periods. During the day, the salesperson writes down what he or she is doing during each 30-minute period. To be effective, the notebook must be filled in after each hour. The salesperson should not rely on memory to complete the record.

FIGURE 17–11
Daily Activity Report

DAILY ACTIVITY REPORT						SALESMAN:		DATE:		
NUMBER OF DEMONSTRATIONS						TOTAL DEMOS	NO. OF PROPOSALS PRESENTED	NO. OF CALLS		
PROD. GR. 1	PROD. GR. 2	PROD. GR. 3	PROD. GR. 5	PROD. GR. 6	PROD. GR. 8				REPEAT	NEW

PROSPECT/CUSTOMER	TRIAL + PLACED – REMOVED DEMONSTRATIONS	COMMENTS
FIRM	TRIAL-STYLE & SER.	
INDIVIDUAL	DEMO-STYLE ONLY	
ADDRESS		
FIRM	TRIAL-STYLE & SER.	
INDIVIDUAL	DEMO-STYLE ONLY	
ADDRESS		
FIRM	TRIAL-STYLE & SER.	
INDIVIDUAL	DEMO-STYLE ONLY	
ADDRESS		
FIRM	TRIAL-STYLE & SER.	
INDIVIDUAL	DEMO-STYLE ONLY	
ADDRESS		
FIRM	TRIAL-STYLE & SER.	
INDIVIDUAL	DEMO-STYLE ONLY	
ADDRESS		
FIRM	TRIAL-STYLE & SER.	
INDIVIDUAL	DEMO-STYLE ONLY	
ADDRESS		
FIRM	TRIAL-STYLE & SER.	
INDIVIDUAL	DEMO-STYLE ONLY	
ADDRESS		
FIRM	TRIAL-STYLE & SER.	
INDIVIDUAL	DEMO-STYLE ONLY	
ADDRESS		

MILEAGE:	EXPENSES:	
TOTAL MILES		
ENDING		
STARTING		

PRINTED IN U.S. AMERICA

1900537 (REV. 9/77)

Table 17–1   Analysis of Call Pattern

Customer Type	Number of Customers Contacted	Number of Calls	Sales Volume	Sales per Call
A	16	121	$212,516	$1,756
B	21	174	116,451	669
C	32	226	78,010	345
D	59	320	53,882	168
	128	841	$460,859	$ 548

Salesperson at a wheat cooperative uses a computer to manage his accounts.

Courtesy IBM

At the end of the week, the salesperson can review the notebook entries and determine how much time was spent seeing customers, waiting to see customers, traveling, planning the day's work, doing paperwork, and so on. This information can help the salesperson improve time management. Perhaps too much time was spent in nonproductive activities, such as having lunch or providing extra services to low-potential customers.

FIGURE 17–12
Postcall Analysis

Customer _____ Date _____ Time _____
  1. Did you meet with the person you planned on seeing? _____
  2. Was the person you met with an important decision maker? _____
  3. Did you get the results you wanted? _____
  4. Were you able to develop a rapport with the person? _____
  5. Did you listen to the person? _____
  6. Were you able to determine the customer's needs? _____
  7. Did you find out who the key decision makers were? _____
  8. Did you establish source credibility as an expert? _____
  9. Did the customer think you were trustworthy? _____
10. Was your presentation effective? _____
11. Did you provide support for your arguments? _____
12. Did you emphasize benefits rather than features? _____
13. Did you watch for nonverbal signals? _____
14. Did you dramatize the presentation? _____
15. Did you hold the customer's interest? _____
16. Were you able to handle objections? _____
17. Did you close at the right time? _____
18. Was your close effective? _____
Considering this postcall analysis, what would you do next time to improve your
selling ability? _____
_____

Postcall Analysis

Salespeople learn how to use their time more efficiently by analyzing their call patterns and daily activities. They can find out how to be more effective during sales calls by analyzing each sales call immediately after it occurs. In addition, a postcall analysis can uncover problems. For example, a review of such analyses might indicate a consistent weakness in closing. The salesperson can then take steps to correct this problem by consulting with other salespeople and the sales training director. He or she might also review training materials and sales textbooks on closing. Figure 17–12 has some questions that are useful for conducting a postcall analysis.

HOW TO MAKE MORE CALLS

Analyzing the territory, making daily plans, and developing efficient routes are important steps toward greater efficiency. Some other techniques for increasing productivity are discussed in this section.

Stretching the Workweek

Many salespeople who cover large territories develop an "out Tuesday, back Friday" complex. They can offer a lot of reasons why they need to work in the office or at home on Monday and Saturday. But this behavior pattern means that the salesperson is making between 20 and 30 percent fewer calls than if he or she spent the whole week on the road.

To get the most out of a territory, the sales representative must use all the available days. For example, the days just before or after a holiday are often slighted. A salesperson might reason that sales effort on these days will be unproductive because the customers are more interested in holiday activities than in business. But it's often easier to get sales interviews on these days because there is less competition. The same reasoning applies to days when the weather is bad. Bad weather reduces competition and makes things easier for the salesperson who doesn't find excuses to take it easy.

Lengthening the Workday

The best and easiest way to see more customers is to work smarter and harder. Many salespeople believe they cannot make calls outside the traditional 9–12 and 2–4 pattern. But many businesses and professionals are available before 9 in the morning and after 4 or 5 in the afternoon. Frequently, people in small industrial and retail businesses work long hours. Many executives pride themselves on being at their desks before their employees arrive in the morning.

These customers are prime candidates for early morning or late afternoon calls. One salesperson brings sweet rolls for his customers so he can make a sales call while sharing the first cup of coffee in the morning.

A salesperson should learn which customers work long hours so he or she can make calls during off-hours. Some customers do not want to talk to salespeople in the early morning. They prefer to use this time to plan their day. However, some early morning calls are possible in almost every sales territory. Once acquainted with their customers' habits, salespeople know where these opportunities exist.

Lunch and dinner offer other opportunities to make sales calls. Customers who are too busy to see salespeople are often willing to take time to eat meals.[5] On such occasions salespeople can talk with customers it might be difficult to see at their place of business. But care must be taken in arranging such appointments. Some customers and companies consider these meetings as entertainment and do not view them favorably. In some situations, the salesperson should refrain from making a presentation during a meal. The meal should be used as an opportunity to develop a better relationship that will be useful in future sales efforts.

Using the Telephone and the Postal Service

The phone is a valuable tool for saving time and covering the territory more effectively. Probably the most important use of the phone in selling is to make, confirm, and reschedule appointments. Making appointments in advance eliminates time wasted waiting in reception rooms or traveling

---

[5] For an interesting assessment of the luncheon meetings between salespeople and buyers, see Paul J. Halvorson and William Rudelius, "Is There a Free Lunch?" *Journal of Marketing,* January 1977, pp. 44–49.

to a customer who will not grant an interview. When making appointments, salespeople should remember that securing an interview is just as important and often as difficult as closing a sale. Salespeople need to prepare for phone calls just as they prepare for personal interviews.

Phone calls can replace more time-consuming sales calls. Although complete sales presentations cannot be made over the phone, some sales can be conducted in this way. For example, the phone can be used to remind regular customers to place routine repeat orders and to inform customers of special discounts and new products. If a salesperson learns that a price increase is anticipated, a phone call to customers will be greatly appreciated. This use of the phone results in customer goodwill and may even lead to sales.

Some customers in a territory may not have the sales potential to warrant personal sales calls. While effective territory coverage means spending the most time with the larger buyers, small buyers can be contacted by phone. The phone is also useful for contacting customers in remote locations that require excessive travel time.

HANDLING PAPERWORK AND REPORTS

Preparing reports for management is part of every sales job. All salespeople complain about such paperwork, but it is important. In general, salespeople are not known for their interest in shuffling paper. They prefer to be out making calls. But if they want to be successful salespeople, and certainly if they want to be promoted to sales management positions, they must learn how to handle paperwork.

Types of Sales Reports

Some typical reports salespeople have to complete are listed below:

1. *Daily work plan.* A list of the customers you plan to see and what you plan to accomplish.
2. *Daily call report.* A daily outline of activities and results. Sales managers can compare the report to the plan to see if you are working effectively.
3. *Weekly summary report.* This report sometimes takes the place of the daily call report. It usually contains a brief recap of activities and results for the week.
4. *Monthly expense report.* This is a list of expenses incurred during the month. The report is used to reimburse salespeople for entertainment and travel costs.
5. *Other reports.* Salespeople may have to complete reports on the status of potential large orders, prospects for future business, dealer inventory levels, lost accounts, or competitive activity in the territory.

FIGURE 17–13
Dictating a Report

Courtesy 3M Company

Doing Paperwork Efficiently

Paperwork is not productive in comparison to the time spent selling to customers. So it's important to get the required paperwork done thoroughly in the least possible time. Some suggestions for handling paperwork follow.

First, salespeople should think positively about paperwork. Even though it's less productive than selling, it can increase productivity by facilitating a detailed review of selling activities.

Salespeople should not let paperwork accumulate. Routine reports should be completed daily. A salesperson should use nonproductive time during the day to complete reports. For example, call reports can be updated while waiting for a customer.

It's a good idea for salespeople to make notes of things to be done and points to remember. If this is not done during the sales interview, it should certainly be done immediately afterward. Many salespeople keep a clipboard in their car for holding cards and notes on calls made during the day. Clipboards are easy to write on. All notes should be dated so the salesperson can place them in the correct time sequence when they are needed to prepare a report.

If a salesperson uses waiting time to work on records and reports, more free time will be available in the evenings for rest or recreation. Some companies provide sales representatives with dictating machines to help them make prompt and descriptive verbal reports. New developments in portable recording units and magnetic discs, records, and belts have simplified the sales representative's reporting (see Figure 17–13).

Finally, salespeople should set aside a block of unproductive time for paperwork. It can be done much quicker if one concentrates on it and avoids interruptions. A specific time should be scheduled each day for writing brief thank-you and followup notes and completing reports.

SUMMARY
Time is a valuable resource for salespeople; it must be managed efficiently. Planning is the key to effective time management. The first step in developing a territory sales plan is to analyze the accounts. This analysis can determine how frequently calls should be made on each account.

Salespeople need to concentrate on the most profitable accounts and minimize the time spent on less profitable accounts. An account's sales potential is a good indicator of its potential profitability. In analyzing accounts, salespeople also need to consider the amount of effort needed to make sales. Some accounts will continue to place orders even if the call frequency is reduced. Computer programs can help salespeople determine the optimal call frequency for each account.

After determining an overall call plan for a territory, salespeople must implement it efficiently. To use time effectively, they need to make daily activity plans. Such plans should be flexible because unforeseen events may arise during the day. In developing daily plans, salespeople ought to make routing plans to minimize travel time.

By analyzing their performance, salespeople can uncover areas for improving their time management and selling skills. An analysis of call frequency can indicate accounts that receive too many or too few calls. Time spent on daily activities should be analyzed in order to minimize nonproductive time. Finally, postcall analysis can help salespeople uncover and correct weaknesses in their selling approach.

Techniques for making more calls include using the entire day and week to make calls; doing such nonproductive activities as paperwork and planning evenings or on weekends; and using the phone and mail to contact remote customers.

QUESTIONS AND PROBLEMS

1. After reading the material in this chapter, a salesperson protests, "That's no fun. I like coffee breaks. If I have to hustle every minute of the day, then forget it. I'll get another job." What would you tell this salesperson?
2. What are the benefits of planning?
3. Distinguish between routing and scheduling. Explain how they may interact to complicate the planning of an efficient day's work.
4. Compare and contrast the special problems of self-management for retail salespeople and outside industrial and trade salespeople.
5. How might a life insurance salesperson increase the number of calls made per day?
6. Sales managers know that making more sales calls results in more sales. Does this mean a salesperson should be encouraged to continually increase the number of calls made each week? Explain your answer.
7. How do sales reports provide useful information for a salesperson?

8. In developing a scheme for classifying customers, which factors would you consider? Why?

9. Recently considerable emphasis has been given to the use of computers and other data processing equipment in the marketing and sales fields. List the kinds of information such equipment might make available to the sales representative in the field.

PROJECTS

1. For a typical 24-hour period, keep as accurate a record as possible of how you spent your waking hours. Compare the amount of time spent on achieving basic objectives with the amount of wasted time.

2. Contact a local company that employs a number of salespeople and make a survey of how the salespeople spend their time during a specific period. Write a report on your findings; break down time utilization by types of activities.

CASE PROBLEMS

Case 17–1 Scheduling Sales Calls

Sue White, an experienced salesperson, explained her system for scheduling calls as follows:

> My years of experience have taught me that the timing of a sales call is critical. It is very important to catch a buyer in the right mood. One buyer is very hard to deal with on Fridays. Another has a staff meeting every Monday afternoon. If I call on him Monday morning, I find it difficult to hold his attention. He always seems to be thinking about the afternoon meeting. If

you study your regular customers closely, you can determine when they will be most receptive to a sales call.

Questions

1. Do you think White has a good system? Why or why not?

2. How can a salesperson determine whether the timing of his or her calls is significant?

Case 17–2 Northern Farm Equipment Company—A Day with a Farm Equipment Salesperson

"We sell a lot of farm equipment throughout this river-bottom area," said Bob Hart, sales representative for Lang Implement Company, the Northern Farm Equipment Company dealer in Quincy, Illinois. Hart's territory lies on both sides of the Mississippi in Illinois and Missouri. He covers it in a Northern pickup truck so he can go right out to his prospects when they are working in the field. Hart often meets his customers in an open-collar shirt, a leather jacket, and a felt hat that he rarely removes. In fact, Hart frequently dresses more like one of his customers than like a sales representative. He knows the problems of his customers, and he talks their language. He is proud of his ability to "run a tractor around a barnyard and tell pretty well by the sound whether or not the rear end is OK."

Some of Hart's ideas on selling farm equipment follow:

The first thing I do is to get around to enough doors and barn lots to find a person who is interested in buying something. During this time of year, there may be weeks when I'm never in the office except in the morning before I start out on my calls. If you expect to sell farm equipment, you have to go out to the customer. And I usually have plenty of customers to call on. I do, however, want to spend some time in the store. If a person tends to business while in the store, he can sell a lot of equipment and get a good many leads for future action.

When you go to some farmers, you can sit and talk all day if you want; and then they'll invite you in for dinner. It's a great temptation to waste time this way when you're out in the country. When I drive into a place, I always assume that the customer is just as busy as I am. So 30 minutes is about as long as I stay. I follow a plan of talking business while I'm there, and when I see it's time to leave, I leave. Often I stop at one place and find that my customer is not going to buy anything. But sometimes the customer will say, "Hart, you ought to go down the road and see Albert Fowler. He's planning on buying a new tractor. Now don't you tell him I told you, but I heard that the John Deere people were out there the other day." When I get a lead like this, instead of going directly to Fowler's place, if he's a next-door neighbor, I go down the road, and then maybe the next morning I stop at the Fowler farm. If he doesn't say anything about the tractor deal, I pass the time of day with him for a while. Then our conversation naturally drifts into a discussion about his tractor.

If customers want to buy something that I don't think they should buy because it doesn't fit their needs, I always try to talk them out of buying it. I may lose an immediate sale by doing this, but in the long run I have found that this procedure pays big dividends. The only time I mention anything about a competitive tractor is when the customer brings the subject up first. I prepare myself for such an occasion by studying up on the literature of all competitive machines.

Whenever you try to talk about everything on a tractor, you get your customer confused. I usually stress one or two major features, such as how the torque amplifier works. When I get the customer sold on the TA, then I mention the hydraulic system, which is a special feature on our tractors.

When I drive from one customer's place to the next, I usually listen to the car radio. This is very helpful, as I always pick up the community news and the market information everybody is talking about. That is because a lot of fellows will tell you that the price of hogs or cattle dropped off yesterday, and they don't know if they ought to buy anything from you. But if you catch that market news, maybe you can answer right back that they went up 50 cents *today*.

By putting such selling techniques as these into practice, Bob Hart helped Lang Implement Company stay in the running with the best of its seven competitors in Quincy.

Bob Hart drove 60 miles on March 4, spending the morning across the river in Missouri and the afternoon in Illinois. He made eight calls and talked to two customers at the store. His efforts bore some fruit, but the day also produced its share of blind alleys and frustrations. Arriving at one stop, he learned that the farmer had gone to Quincy to see *him*.

Efforts to find another farmer at a grain elevator ended in failure. He found Harvey Ireland ringing pigs and had to talk business with him above the pigs' shrill, incessant squealing. Ireland finally decided not to deal.

Right after lunch, Hart drove up to see Glenn Mugdalen, who was in partnership with his brother, Orville, about the possibility of trading for a baler. Glenn's wife, Martha, came out to meet him when she heard the dog bark.

Bob spoke first, "What do you have Glenn doing today?"

"Well, he's sowing clover seed."

"What's he doing sowing clover seed— muddy as it is?"

"Well, I tell you, he looked like a mud turtle. But he's sowing clover seed."

"What have Orville and Glenn decided on that baler?"

"You go over and see Orville. Have you been over there?"

"No, I haven't."

"He has all the statistics, and I think when you get over there, you'll get your answer."

"Thank you a lot, Martha. I'll go right over to see Orville to find out what was decided on the baler."

Hart found Orville preparing to go into the fields with fertilizer. They passed the time of day before Bob got down to business.

"I stopped over at Glenn's and talked with Martha. She said you had all the answers about the baler."

"Yes, sir. Well, I wish I did know all the answers about the baler."

"If you go ahead and trade balers with us now, it'll help us to get rid of the used one."

"After thinking it over, we just kind of thought we'd be better off by having this one fixed."

"You want us to pick it up, then?"

"I believe so."

"We can pick it up any time. That's all right with us if you want to fix it and don't want to trade. And while we've got it down there fixing it, you might take a notion you want to trade."

"That's right. I believe that's about as good a way as any to do it."

"Another thing. I want to see what we can do on that tractor deal. . . ."

But 15 minutes of earnest talk in Orville Mugdalen's barnyard failed to bring the two men to terms on anything but repairing the baler (although a few days later, Orville *did* buy a new Fast-Hitch for his tractor).

Bob Hart's ratio of sales to calls was considerably less than eight for eight on March 4. But every minute he wasn't on the road, he was selling.

Bob made two sales on March 4. Both were corn planters. One of the buyers came to him at the store after he made a sales pitch at the farm. He made the other sale because he went out after it.

Another customer, Bill Adams, owns 400 acres near LaGrange, Missouri, about 12 miles from Quincy. Hart had talked to him before about buying a new four-row planter, using his old John Deere planter as a trade-in. Hart had also agreed to sell Adams' old crawler for him. On the morning of March 4, Hart crossed the river to LaGrange and found Adams at the wheel of his Farmall tractor, hauling feed.

The following conversation ended in a sale:

Hart: You *know* what I stopped for. We're going to trade that John Deere corn planter for that new Northern.

Adams: Just as soon as you sell that crawler.

Hart: They pick it up yet?

Adams: Nope.

Hart: Well, they're *going* to pick it up. Now listen. On that cash part of it. You know we're not worrying about that. But corn planting may be over before we get the crawler sold, and you know you want that new planter. What do you say we trade this morning?

Adams: I have to get some cash—that's all there is to it.

Hart: Your credit is always good.

Adams: You know I never bought anything on time.

Hart: I know you haven't bought anything yet for which you haven't paid cash. But here's our point on the planter. What we're in a hurry for is to get the used one sold because you can wait too long. Then you have to carry it over another year. That's when you lose money. How long would I have to carry you?

Adams: You might have to carry me 'til harvest.

Hart: Aw, I don't think so. You know you're going to buy a planter.

Adams: Oh, I can get by.

Hart: Doggone it, I'd sure like to trade with you. . . . I want to look at that planter of yours again.

At this point, Hart went into a shed to check the trade-in planter. When he came out, Adams waited while Hart returned to his pickup to do some figuring. The conversation began again when Hart finished.

Hart: Well, here's what I'll do. I'll bring that new planter over here for $402.

Adams: $402. Hmm. Let's see how you figured, Bob.

Hart: That's putting a lot of money in *your* planter.

Adams: You're taking that corn sheller in on that, aren't you, Bob—for $100?

Hart: No. Doggone it, I can't.

[*Short pause.*]

Adams: You're still asking a lot of money, Bob.

Hart: But that's giving you an awful good deal on a planter, too, you must remember. If you keep yours, you're going to have to put runners on it. Four of them—that's $32. With this new one you'd be getting a high-speed planter that will plant accurately.

Adams: Is that a good hill-drop planter?

Hart: It sure is. It'll hill-drop 211 hills a minute. In other words, if you're spacing 40 inches apart, it'll hill-drop at 6 miles an hour and put 95 percent of the grains in the size of a silver dollar.

[*Long silence while Bill Adams thinks it over.*]

Adams: That's a lot of money, Bob. It's a good trade, but. . . .

[*Another long pause.*]

Hart: You can see our point. Here it is the fourth day of March, and people are buying this used equipment now. We don't want to wait around too long. . . .

[*Another pause.*]

Adams: Aw, I don't know. You always make me a good deal, Bob. . . .

Hart: Sure I do. Why don't you let me write the order this morning? Let's see, that price is $900. I'm giving you $498 on your planter. That's $402 difference.

Adams: By the time this thaw is over, I'm liable to have to put all that money for a planter into gravel for these roads.

Hart: Well, you don't have to pay for that planter today. Tell me when you *would* pay for it.

[*Pause.*]

Adams: Reckon I can get the job done with that planter?

Hart: I know you can because we'll come out here and start it for you.

Adams: Are you going to get somebody over here to get the governor on this tractor straightened out?

Hart: Sure, I'll get it fixed for you—get somebody out here right away. Can you pay me by the 15th of April? That wouldn't crowd you any, would it?

Adams: Give me 'til the 15th of May. That'll give me a chance to sell some of the bred heifers.

Hart: OK, let me write it up then and you sign the order.

[*At this point, Hart began to write.*]

Adams: Better give me $500 for my planter, Bob.

Hart: I'm *giving* you $498.

Adams: Well, I know, but it looks so much better.

Hart: Well, doggone it, OK. That would make $400 even, wouldn't it? Let's see. March 4. I ought to remember that because I was 49 years old yesterday. I'm getting old. . . .

Adams: I'll say you are.

Hart: Well, there you are. You just sign here. And thanks a lot to you, Bill. I'm sure you will be happy about it.

"The greatest thing we've got to sell is goodwill," Bob Hart says. "If we can keep the customer's goodwill, we'll keep our fair share of the business. Courtesy calls pay

real dividends in this business. About 80 percent of Lang Implement's sales are repeat business. The first sale to a person is a hard one to make. The next one comes easier, and the one after that, even easier. By this time the customers come back because they like the way they are treated."

"Sometimes you can win goodwill by knowing when to walk off a deal." Lang's service manager, Carl Wilson, tells of a case:

> Bob Hart and I were out with a customer, and it got to be 11:30 at night when we got through. The sale we were working on amounted to $9,600. The farmer thought we were completely crazy when we walked off and left it over a $21 difference. He thought we'd take it the next day. The only thing he didn't know was that we'd possibly gone $300 too far already. Another dealer took the deal at the farmer's figures. This happened nearly a year ago, and the other dealer still has the same trade-in on his lot. They've long since fallen out over the deal, and we've taken over the service work and sold the farmer another new tractor. The point is, you can cut a deal so close that you're better off not making it. There's a stopping point someplace.

Bob Hart has learned that goodwill can come from a variety of things, as illustrated in the following experience:

> About three years ago, we stopped in where we thought a man had some work to be done on a baler. We caught him right in the middle of mixing concrete. This was just past noon.
>
> A little after nine that night we finished pushing wheelbarrows, shoveling gravel, and mixing cement. The crew was the farmer, his wife, Carl, and myself. The farmer and his wife would never have finished the job by themselves. They invited us to stay for supper, and she cooked steaks for us. An hour later we had

sold a tractor and were on our way back to town. The tractor deal was never mentioned in any way, shape, or form until the concrete was finished. Since then, this customer has come back with repeat business. He has bought a new hay baler since, and a 350 Diesel. And he's more than 60 miles away from our store. We still do his service work.

Questions

1. What is your reaction to the way Bob Hart utilized his time on March 4?

What, if any, suggestions do you have to improve Hart's sales efforts?

2. If you were Bob Hart, what criteria would you use to evaluate the effectiveness of your sales efforts in your territory?

3. What differences would you expect to find in the planning and controlling of sales efforts for a salesperson who sells heavy construction equipment as compared to a salesperson who sells farm equipment?

Case 17–3   Centerville Sales Territory*

This is the situation:

You are a general-line salesperson for the Great American Corporation. Yours is the Centerville territory. You have worked the territory for several years, and you know it quite well.

You are about to plan your itinerary for the last four weeks of the quarter. Your quota for the quarter is $300,000. Sales for the first two months of the quarter total $280,000, leaving you only $20,000 short of your goal. It is important for you to meet your quota because Great American has big plans for you if you do.

You have 14 regular customers for your products in the Centerville territory. You know that among them they have the potential for an additional $27,500 during the remaining month of the quarter.

You have also identified 10 nonbuying prospects in the territory. They represent an additional $39,800 in potential sales during the remaining month of the quarter. Your job is to plan the itinerary that will generate

the most sales for you during the remaining four weeks of the quarter.

For details of your customers and prospects, identified by name and number, see Exhibit 1. A map of the Centerville territory follows, showing the location of your accounts and the travel time between them.

1. Available Selling Time

Sales time is limited to the period from 8:30 A.M. to 5:00 P.M. for five days, Monday through Friday, during the four-week period for which you are to plan the itinerary. Use a planning form like the one in Exhibit 2. You'll need four copies, one for each week.

Sale time is reduced by the following factors:

Travel—the amount of time it takes to travel from one account to another.

Waiting time—the amount of time you must wait to see a prospect or a

*Adapted from Stewart A. Washburn, "Salesmanship: The Time-Is-Money Game," *Sales & Marketing Management,* March 8, 1976, pp. 43–48.

Exhibit 1 List of Customers and Prospects

Customers	Sales to Date	Remaining Potential	People to See
1. Handwound Coil	$75,000	$3,000	Design engineer* General foreman Foreman Purchasing agent
2. General Dymo	63,000	1,500	Purchasing agent* Design engineer 1 Design engineer 2
3. Superior Electric	34,000	4,000	Purchasing agent* Design engineer
4. Herman Transformer	28,000	1,000	Purchasing agent*
5. Alpha Transformer	24,000	2,000	Purchasing agent* Design engineer
6. Circle D Contrals	9,500	3,000	Purchasing agent* Design engineer
7. Easton Motors	8,000	1,500	Design engineer*
8. Fractional Motors	7,000	3,000	Design engineer* Foreman Purchasing agent
9. Acme Motors	7,000	2,500	Design engineer* Purchasing agent
10. Bartlett Transformer	6,500	1,000	Purchasing agent*
11. Zip Electric	6,000	3,000	Purchasing agent* Design engineer
12. Taft Electric	6,000	500	Purchasing agent* Design engineer
13. Macro Electric	5,000	500	Purchasing agent*
14. Roth Motors	1,000	1,000	Design engineer*

Prospects

15. ABC Transformer	—	3,000	Purchasing agent* Design engineer Foreman
16. Ace Motors	—	1,500	Design engineer* Foreman Purchasing agent
17. Air Conditioning Corp.	—	5,000	Purchasing agent* Design engineer
18. Amp Motors	—	3,500	Design engineer* Foreman Purchasing agent
19. Eastern Windings	—	1,500	Design engineer*
20. Holmes Electric	—	3,000	Design engineer* Purchasing agent
21. Manual Electric	—	1,800	Purchasing agent
22. Micro Electric	—	2,500	Design engineer* Foreman Purchasing agent
23. Twister Coil	—	3,000	Purchasing agent* Design engineer
24. U.S. Lyndon	—	15,000	Design engineer* Foreman 1 Foreman 2 Purchasing agent

*Decision maker.

EXHIBIT 2
Territory Planning Form

TERRITORY PLANNING FORM　　　　　　　　Week ending_____

DAY	MONDAY			TUESDAY			WEDNESDAY			THURSDAY			FRIDAY		
Hours	Account No.	People To See	%	Account No.	People To See	%	Account No.	People To See	%	Account No.	People To See	%	Account No.	People To See	%
8:30–9:00	24	WAIT	–												
9:00–9:30		DE	5												
9:30–10:00		DE	4												
10:00–10:30		DE	3												
10:30–11:00		WAIT	–												
11:00–11:30		PA	4												
11:30–12:00		PA	3												
12:00–12:30	LUNCH	PA	3												
12:30–1:00	"	"	–												
1:00–1:30	APPTS.		–												
1:30–2:00		TRAVEL	–												
2:00–2:30		WAIT	–												
2:30–3:00	21	PA	5												
3:00–3:30		TRAVEL	–												
3:30–4:00		"	–												
4:00–4:30	6	PA	10												
4:30–5:00		PA	7												
Subtotals	32% For #24 / 5% For #21 / 17% For # 6														

customer if you do not have an appointment.

Telephone time—the amount of time you spend on the phone making appointments.

Paperwork—each day of selling activity generates one hour of paperwork, which must be completed before the beginning of the next week.

Lunchtime—unless the lunch hour is used to entertain a customer or a prospect, effective selling time is reduced by a one-hour lunch period sometime between 11:30 and 1:30.

Don't forget holidays—your territory celebrates them all.

2. Travel Time

Travel in the Centerville territory is mostly by car. Facilities for air travel are limited.

North Town Airways has an early morning turnaround flight between Centerville and North Town and a late evening turnaround flight. Service between Easton and North Town and Weston and North Town is quite frequent during the day. The current North Town Airways schedule is shown in Exhibit 3.

If you travel by air, it will take you a half hour after your arrival to rent a car and drive to town. For example, if you fly to Easton, it will take you a half hour to rent a car and drive to Alpha Transformer. However, if your first call after flying to Easton is to be made on the Air Conditioning Corp., it will take you a half hour to rent a car and travel through Easton plus one hour of travel from Easton to the Air Conditioning Corp. Except in the case of air travel to North Town, travel to the first call each day may be completed by 8:30.

EXHIBIT 3
Map of Territory

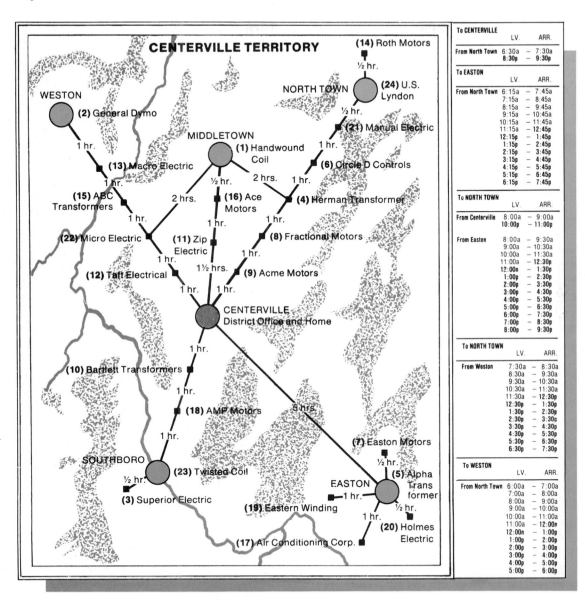

CENTERVILLE TERRITORY

(14) Roth Motors

½ hr.

NORTH TOWN

(24) U.S. Lyndon

WESTON

(2) General Dymo

½ hr.

(21) Manual Electric

MIDDLETOWN

(1) Handwound Coil

1 hr.

1 hr.

(13) Macro Electric

(6) Circle D Controls

1 hr.

½ hr.

2 hrs.

1 hr.

(15) ABC Transformers

2 hrs.

(16) Ace Motors

(4) Herman Transformer

1 hr.

1 hr.

1 hr.

1 hr.

(22) Micro Electric

(11) Zip Electric

(8) Fractional Motors

1 hr.

1½ hrs.

1 hr.

(12) Taft Electrical

(9) Acme Motors

1 hr.

1 hr.

CENTERVILLE
District Office and Home

1 hr.

(10) Bartlett Transformers

1 hr.

(18) AMP Motors

5 hrs.

(7) Easton Motors

½ hr.

(5) Alpha Transformer

SOUTHBORO

EASTON

1 hr.

½ hr.

(23) Twisted Coil

½ hr.

(3) Superior Electric

(19) Eastern Winding

½ hr.

1 hr.

(20) Holmes Electric

(17) Air Conditioning Corp.

To CENTERVILLE		
	LV.	ARR.
From North Town	6:30a	7:30a
	8:30p	9:30p

To EASTON		
	LV.	ARR.
From North Town	6:15a	7:45a
	7:15a	8:45a
	8:15a	9:45a
	9:15a	10:45a
	10:15a	11:45a
	11:15a	12:45p
	12:15p	1:45p
	1:15p	2:45p
	2:15p	3:45p
	3:15p	4:45p
	4:15p	5:45p
	5:15p	6:45p
	6:15p	7:45p

To NORTH TOWN		
	LV.	ARR.
From Centerville	8:00a	9:00a
	10:00p	11:00p
From Easton	8:00a	9:30a
	9:00a	10:30a
	10:00a	11:30a
	11:00a	12:30p
	12:00n	1:30p
	1:00p	2:30p
	2:00p	3:30p
	3:00p	4:30p
	4:00p	5:30p
	5:00p	6:30p
	6:00p	7:30p
	7:00p	8:30p
	8:00p	9:30p

To NORTH TOWN		
	LV.	ARR.
From Weston	7:30a	8:30a
	8:30a	9:30a
	9:30a	10:30a
	10:30a	11:30a
	11:30a	12:30p
	12:30p	1:30p
	1:30p	2:30p
	2:30p	3:30p
	3:30p	4:30p
	4:30p	5:30p
	5:30p	6:30p
	6:30p	7:30p

To WESTON		
	LV.	ARR.
From North Town	6:00a	7:00a
	7:00a	8:00a
	8:00a	9:00a
	9:00a	10:00a
	10:00a	11:00a
	11:00a	12:00n
	12:00n	1:00p
	1:00p	2:00p
	2:00p	3:00p
	3:00p	4:00p
	4:00p	5:00p
	5:00p	6:00p

Hotel or motel accommodations are available within a half hour's travel of all accounts. It is not necessary to return home each night. See the map of the territory (Exhibit 3).

3. Making Appointments

Calls can be made cold or by appointment. Appointments can be made by phone only on the day before the call is scheduled. Three appointments can be made by phone

Exhibit 4   Value of Sales Time

| | **Calls on Present Customers** | | | | | | | | |
| | First Call | | | Second Call | | | Third and Succeeding Calls | | |
	1st ½ Hr.	2nd ½ Hr.	3rd ½ Hr.	1st ½ Hr.	2nd ½ Hr.	3rd ½ Hr.	1st ½ Hr.	2nd ½ Hr.	3rd ½ Hr.
Decision maker	10	7	5	3	5	2	5	3	0
Key buying influence	6	4	2	5	4	3	4	3	2

| | **Calls on Prospects** | | | | | | | | |
| | First Call | | | Second Call | | | Third and Succeeding Calls | | |
	1st ½ Hr.	2nd ½ Hr.	3rd ½ Hr.	1st ½ Hr.	2nd ½ Hr.	3rd ½ Hr.	1st ½ Hr.	2nd ½ Hr.	3rd ½ Hr.
Decision maker	5	4	3	6	7	8	10	11	12
Key buying influence	4	3	2	4	5	6	7	4	3

per half hour. Phone calls to make appointments can be made only during normal selling/business hours, that is, from 8:30 to 5:00. Separate appointments must be made with each individual.

Calls can be made without appointments, but a half hour of waiting time will be used up before the person can be seen.

4. Length of Each Sales Call

No sales call on an individual can exceed 1½ hours. However, if lunch is included, a sales call may be extended to 2½ hours.

5. Value of Sales Time (see Exhibit 4)

Each half hour of sales time with a decision maker or a key buying influence increases the probability of making the sale as follows:

If you make a 1½-hour first call on the design engineer of Handwound Coil and a first call on the general foreman, you will increase the probability of making the sale by 34 percent (10 plus 7 plus 5 plus 6 plus 4 plus 2). You will consume three hours of sales time. However, if you make a one-hour first call on both the design engineer

and the general foreman plus a half-hour second call on each, you will consume the same amount of time—three hours—and you will increase the probability of making the sale to 40 percent (1st calls: 10 plus 7 plus 6 plus 4; 2nd calls: 8 plus 5).

6. Entertainment

You can entertain only one person at a time, only at lunch, and for only one hour. Entertainment increases the probability of making the sale by a percentage equal to the value of the second half hour of the call. You can entertain a prospect or a customer only after spending one-half hour of selling time in his or her office. With entertainment (lunch), a call may extend to 2½ hours, with extra credit for the lunch hour.

7. Scoring

For sales time to count, the probability of making the sale must be greater than 50 percent. To calculate the value of sales time with an account, simply multiply the total probability of making the sale (provided it's greater than 50 percent) by the total remaining potential of the account. Use the scoring sheet in Exhibit 5.

Exhibit 5 Scoring Sheet

Account	(Remaining Potential)	×	(Percent Probability)	=	Sales Income
1. Handwound Coil	$ 3,000	×	_____ %	=	$_____
2. General Dymo	1,500	×	_____	=	_____
3. Superior Electric	4,000	×	_____	=	_____
4. Herman Transformer	1,000	×	_____	=	_____
5. Alpha Transformer	2,000	×	_____	=	_____
6. Circle D. Centrals	3,000	×	_____	=	_____
7. Easton Motors	1,500	×	_____	=	_____
8. Fractional Motors	3,000	×	_____	=	_____
9. Acme Motors	2,500	×	_____	=	_____
10. Bartlett Transformer	1,000	×	_____	=	_____
11. Zip Electric	3,000	×	_____	=	_____
12. Taft Electric	500	×	_____	=	_____
13. Macro Electric	500	×	_____	=	_____
14. Roth Motors	1,000	×	_____	=	_____
15. ABC Transformer	3,000	×	_____	=	_____
16. Ace Motors	1,500	×	_____	=	_____
17. Air Conditioning Corp.	5,000	×	_____	=	_____
18. Amp Motors	3,500	×	_____	=	_____
19. Eastern Windings	1,500	×	_____	=	_____
20. Holmes Electric	3,000	×	_____	=	_____
21. Manual Electric	1,800	×	_____	=	_____
22. Micro Electric	2,500	×	_____	=	_____
23. Twister Coil	3,000	×	_____	=	_____
24. U.S. Lyndon	15,000	×	_____	=	_____
			Total sales volume generated	=	$_____

SELECTED REFERENCES

Allen, Charles C. "A Level-Headed Approach to Increasing Sales Force Productivity." *Sales & Marketing Management,* June 13, 1977, p. 48.

Armstrong, Gary M. "The Schedule Model and Salesman's Effort Allocation." *California Management Review,* Summer 1976, pp. 43–51.

Bliss, Edwin C. *Getting Things Done: The ABC's of Time Management.* New York: Scribner, 1976.

Canning, John, Jr. "Value Analysis of Your Customer Base." *Industrial Marketing Management,* Fall 1982, pp. 89–93.

Dubinsky, Alan J., and Thomas N. Ingram. "A Portfolio Approach to Account Profitability." *Industrial Marketing Management,* Summer 1984, pp. 33–41.

"Fighting the Clock for More Selling Time." *Sales & Marketing Management,* October 10, 1977, p. 27.

Gwin, John W., and William D. Perreault, Jr. "Industrial Sales Call Planning." *Industrial Marketing Management,* Fall 1981, pp. 225–34.

Lahein, Alan. *How to Get Control of Your Time and Your Life.* New York: New American Library, 1973.

Meyer, Paul J. "Make Every Moment Count." *Sales & Marketing Management,* March 17, 1980, pp. 48–49.

Parasuraman, A. "An Approach for Allocating Sales Call Effort." *Industrial Marketing Management,* Winter 1982, pp. 75–79.

Whitty, Thomas A. "Focusing the Sales Effort." *Sales & Marketing Management,* September 17, 1979, pp. 57–60.

18
Supporting the Selling Effort with Advertising, Direct Mail, and Telemarketing

Some questions answered in this chapter are:

- Will direct mail and telemarketing replace salespeople?
- How do telephone selling, direct mail, and advertising complement the personal selling effort?
- How can salespeople use advertising as a sales tool when selling to retailers?
- How should letters be written that convey good news? Disappointing news?
- What is the appropriate structure for a persuasive sales letter?
- How can the telephone be used to increase sales productivity?

Because of the rise in selling costs, companies are interested in increasing the efficiency of their salespeople. A variety of alternative communication approaches are being used to assist salespeople in locating new customers, providing service support, and selling small, remotely located customers. To improve their efficiency, salespeople need to take advantage of these communication techniques.

569

Some companies sell directly to customers without the use of salespeople, retailers, or distributors.

NEW
COMMUNI-
CATION AP-
PROACHES[1]

Over the last 10 years the cost of personal selling has risen dramatically. In 1986, the weekly food, lodging, and automobile expense for a typical salesperson was $748.30. These weekly sales expenses increased 107 percent over the last 10 years.[2]

Stimulated by rising costs, marketers are using alternative methods to communicate with customers, such as advertising, direct mail, demonstration centers, industrial stores, and telemarketing. These new ap-

---

[1]This section is based largely on Benson P. Shapiro and John Wyman, ''New Ways to Reach Your Customers,'' *Harvard Business Review,* July–August 1981, pp. 103–10.

[2]Richard Kevin, ''Survey of Selling Costs: Onward and Ever Upward,'' *Sales & Marketing Management,* February 17, 1986, p. 11.

proaches *do not* replace salespeople. But they help increase the effectiveness of salespeople by allowing them to concentrate their valuable resource—time—on such important activities as selling and servicing key accounts.

Direct Mail

Direct mail is a common method of selling products to consumers. Companies such as Burpee Seeds and L. L. Bean send catalogues directly to consumers. After consumers return the enclosed order form, the company mails the products directly to them. No salespeople, retailers, or distributors are involved.

This traditional approach to consumer marketing is now being used by industrial companies. For example, each quarter Wright Line, Inc., distributes over 10,000 catalogues to computer programmers, analysts, and operators. These catalogues include a description of computer-related supplies sold by the company, forms to place mail orders, and a toll-free 800 number for telephone orders. Wright Line has 140 salespeople calling on large customers and prospects that do not buy from Wright Line. The catalogues and direct-mail brochures are used to fill in for the salesperson between sales calls as well as to sell to customers too small to justify a personal call.

Demonstration Centers and Industrial Stores

Many companies have specially designed showrooms, or demonstration centers, where potential customers can see and try out equipment. These centers enable salespeople to demonstrate complex equipment that is not portable. Often high-level executives who are unavailable for standard sales call presentations are attracted to demonstrations at a center. Union Carbide uses a $100,000 trailer-mounted model to demonstrate how its UNOX system treats waste water from an industrial plant.

IBM, Digital Equipment, and Xerox use industrial stores to sell small business computers. These stores encourage businesspeople to drop in, watch a demonstration of the equipment, and place orders. The stores increase the efficiency of salespeople because salespeople no longer have to spend time traveling to visit small customers. Instead, the customers come to the salespeople.

Satellite communications are frequently used for special demonstrations of new products. For example, 350 record distributors attended a live introduction of Elton John's album, "The Fox." The program originated in Santa Monica, California, and was beamed via satellite to 33 Holiday Inns throughout the United States. The presentation included discussions between Elton John and executives of the album producing and distributing companies. A two-way audio hookup enabled the distributors to talk with Elton John and both see and hear his reactions to questions.

Telemarketing[3]

Telemarketing is the conducting of marketing campaigns directly to the ultimate customer using the telephone. By the early 1980s, companies were spending over $10 billion on telemarketing.[4]

Applications　Telemarketing is very effective in generating sales leads, servicing small accounts, and improving customer service.

The Commander Division of Gulfstream American Corporation uses telemarketing to sell million-dollar business aircraft. Retired business executives employed by the company phone present owners of multiengine aircraft and people who have inquired about the Commander Jetprops. These retired executives understand business at executive levels and can establish a rapport with the prospects. They qualify the prospects over the phone and determine the level of interest in business aircraft. These qualified leads are then turned over to the company sales force. It would be impossible for the salespeople to call on all these potential prospects. In this way the use of telemarketing enables the sales force to focus on the best prospects.

A. B. Dick Company used telemarketing to service over 100,000 small accounts-customers that annually purchased such a small volume of supplies it made little sense to have salespeople assigned to them. In consumer marketing, Montgomery Ward used telemarketing to enroll 300,000 of its own charge customers in a new Ward-sponsored automobile club.

The telephone is particularly effective in providing follow-up services and maintaining customer goodwill. Dissatisfied customers can receive a quick response to their problems.[5] O. M. Scott and Sons Co. uses this approach in its lawn- and garden-care business. Using a toll-free 800 number, factory personnel can quickly handle problems concerning the products or the distribution system. As a result, the salesperson's valuable time is not wasted, and the salesperson has more time to sell new accounts. In addition, the company can use the telephone to get immediate feedback from its salespeople and distributors about how new products are selling and what its competitors are doing.

Types　There are many approaches for communicating with customers by using the telephone. These approaches differ in terms of the type of customer contacted, the originator of the call, and the degree of automation.

---

[3]Based on Kenneth C. Schneider, "Telemarketing As a Promotional Tool—Its Effects and Side Effects," *Journal of Consumer Marketing,* Winter 1985, pp. 29–39.

[4]Bill Gloede, "Growth of 'Telemarketing' could signal opportunity," *Editor and Publisher,* April 17, 1982, p. 16.

[5]See "Good Listener: At Procter & Gamble Success Is Largely Due to Heeding Customers," *The Wall Street Journal,* April 29, 1980, p. 1.

This in-home shopper is ordering products via a videodisc catalog.

Cameramann International, Ltd.

Telemarketing was first used to market products to consumers. Non-store sales (direct mail and telemarketing) are growing 300 to 500 percent faster than retail store sales. Telemarketing has been particularly effective with consumers who do not have the time to shop and no longer view shopping as entertainment. Recently, however, industrial firms such as Gulfstream and A. B. Dick are being pressured to place more emphasis on telemarketing.

The telephone call can originate with either a company representative or the customer. Applications in which the call originates with the customer are referred to as incoming, while applications originating with the firm are called outgoing. Most telemarketing applications are incoming based on AT&T's 800 system.

In outgoing applications, the call varies from a message generated and delivered by a computer to a salesperson making a sales presentation with no external aids. The most common format for outgoing sales calls involves an inside salesperson using an interactive computer to generate a sales presentation based on the customer's responses. Such a system is shown in Figure 18–1.

Advantages   Telemarketing offers several advantages over mass media and magazine advertising. First, telemarketing is more personal than advertising. The telephone messages can be adapted to the customer, and customers tend to pay more attention to people they are talking with than

FIGURE 18–1
Why Telephone
Salespeople Are
Rarely at a Loss for
(the Right) Words

When the Louisiana National Bank (LNB) initiated a telemarketing campaign to find new customers, telephone salespeople guided prospects through the calls by using this flip chart. Provided were several kinds of closes, as well as correct responses to likely questions and objections, all obtained merely by flipping the chart to the appropriate sections of the script.

Panel 1B—Sell TBS/Entree/ Savings to Selected ATM File Communicator Script			Answers to Anticipated Questions/Objections LNB—The Bill System	
Introduction to household		1	"Who can be paid via the bill system?"	16
Introduction to prospect		2		
Introduce tape		3	"How fast will LNB pay?"	17
If hesitant about tape	(1 of 2)	4	"Are there late charges?"	18
If hesitant about tape	(2 of 2)	5	"Is the bill system safe?"	19
After tape	(1 of 2)	6	"Can I add merchants to my list	
After tape	(2 of 2)	7	whenever I want?"	20
Offer		8	"Can I practice before I begin?"	21
If hesitant about the bill system		9	"When can I call?/What are the	
TBS close	(1 of 3)	10	hours?"	22
TBS close	(2 of 3)	11	"Can a business account use the	
TBS close	(3 of 3)	12	bill system?"	23
If not interested		13	"Is there proof of payment, like a	
Entree close		14	cancelled check?"	24
Order termination		15	"What if I make a mistake/have a	
			problem?"	25
			"How do I keep a record before I pay the bills?"	26
			"Do I have to call from my home phone?"	27
			"What if I have a 'one-time' payment?"	28
			"What do you mean by a personal I.D. code?"	29
			"How will I know my payment codes?"	30
			"When is the payment actually made?"	31
			"It sounds so confusing"	32
			"No money/can't afford?"	33
			"No interest/no need/I like the way I pay bills now."	34
			"No hurry/I'll think about it"	35
			"Will I receive my bills each month?"	36
			"I'm no longer with LNB"	37
			"Can I pay bills all at once/one at a time?"	38
			"What happens if overdraft?"	39
			"Why do I need a personal I.D. code?"	40

Source: Excerpted from Murray Roman, *Telemarketing Campaigns That Work* (New York: McGraw-Hill, 1983).

to television commercials. Second, telemarketing campaigns can be developed and implemented more quickly than advertising campaigns. Thus, telemarketing is particularly well suited to promoting seasonal goods, fashion merchandising, and fads.

Limitations   While telemarketing is considerably less expensive than face-to-face sales calls, outgoing telemarketing campaigns cost about $5 per contact, which is considerably more expensive than advertising contacts.

Most products are more effectively sold through visual rather than audio means. Telemarketing is unable to provide the visual information often needed to promote a product. Finally, telemarketing is more intrusive than advertising. This can irritate customers and create an unfavorable image for the company conducting the campaign.

THE ADOPTION PROCESS AND MARKETING COMMUNICATIONS

These new communications approaches, plus the traditional marketing communications vehicles of advertising and sales promotions, help the salesperson move a prospect through the adoption process. The adoption process, which is shown in Figure 18–2, is a sequence of stages a prospect goes through before becoming an adopter. An adopter can be described as a customer that buys the salesperson's product on a repeat basis.

Stages in the Adoption Process[6]

The process begins when potential customers become aware of a product. Then the prospects acquire information or knowledge about the product. This information can be collected from a number of sources, including friends, business associates, magazine articles, and salespeople.

On the basis of the knowledge the prospects have acquired, they next move to the evaluation stage. In this stage, the prospects consider the acquired information and evaluate the product. They determine whether the product satisfies their needs. If they have positive feelings about the product after this evaluation, prospects may make an initial purchase to try the product. If the results of this trial stage are positive, the customer will then become an adopter and make additional purchases of the product.

Salespeople and the Adoption Process

Salespeople can play an important role at each stage of the adoption process. Initially, salespeople introduce people to their products and create awareness. Then they provide the product information needed by prospective customers during the knowledge stage. In the evaluation stage, salespeople demonstrate to customers how the product will satisfy their needs. Next, salespeople provide the aftersale servicing to make sure

---

[6]See Thomas Robertson, *Innovative Behavior and Communication* (New York: Holt, Rinehart & Winston, 1971).

Figure 18–2 The Adoption Process and Marketing Communications

Stage in the Adoption Process	Communication Aids for the Salesperson
Awareness	Advertising Direct mail Telephone selling
↓	
Knowledge	Telephone selling
↓	
Evaluation	Telephone selling
↓	
Trial	Demonstration centers
↓	
Repeat purchase adoption	Catalogue sales Direct mail Telephone servicing

customers have a favorable trial experience. Finally, salespeople continue to make calls on the customers and provide service to get repeat orders.

Salespeople can certainly be used to perform all of these activities. However, some of the activities can be done for less cost by using other methods of communication. For example, advertising may be used to make people aware of products at a very low cost. A sales call costing over $100 is needed to create awareness through the use of a salesperson. But direct mail could be used to perform this same function for less than $1, while an advertisement would cost less than one cent to expose a potential customer to the product.

A customer may buy a new brand of detergent just to try it. Some companies even provide discount coupons to make the purchase less expensive. However, many products are too expensive for people to make a trial purchase. Few small business owners can afford to buy a computer merely to see how it works. This is why demonstration centers and industrial stores play an important role during the trial stage. They give business owners a chance to use the computer, see how it works, and determine whether it will be useful in their applications.

Finally, repeat purchases of a product are often quite routine. Customers only need a quotation for price and delivery. This information can be provided by direct mail, through catalogues, or by telephone. Expensive sales calls are not needed to support purchases made during the adoption phase.

As we see, alternative communication methods free salespeople's time so they can concentrate on the functions they do best. Personal selling is more effective than advertising and telephone selling during the knowledge and evaluation phase. Salespeople can tailor their presentations to each individual customer, provide information the customer wants, and show how the information about the products is related to satisfying the customer's needs.

The effectiveness of direct mail and advertising is very limited. These impersonal sources provide information that satisfies only the needs of typical customers. They are not designed to provide specific information related to individual customer needs. In addition, the communication is one way. An advertisement cannot answer a customer's question or sense when a consumer is confused.

Telephone selling involves two-way communication. However, the telephone salesperson cannot see or be seen by the customer so it is very difficult for telephone salespeople to determine how customers are reacting to their presentations. They cannot tell when something excites a customer or when a customer begins to frown. In addition, telephone salespeople cannot use visual aids to demonstrate the benefits of a product. According to the old saying, "A picture is worth a thousand words." If this is true, then salespeople are not able to use one of the most effective tools of communications.

The following section discusses in more detail the relationship between advertising and personal selling. Then we'll take up the use of advertising as a sales tool in trade selling. The chapter concludes with information on how salespeople can communicate effectively through the mail and over the telephone.

ADVERTISING AND PERSONAL SELLING

Role of Advertising

Advertising plays different roles for industrial and consumer products. Since most industrial products are very complex, buyers need a lot of information before they make a purchase, and they expect to have personal contact with someone from the company. Advertising by itself is not sufficient to move the industrial buyer through the adoption process.

On the other hand, advertising alone can frequently move a consumer through the adoption process from awareness to repeat purchases. Since most consumer products are quite simple, consumers need only a small amount of information before they are willing to try a product.

Even though advertising alone can move consumers through the entire adoption process, salespeople still play an important role in the marketing of consumer products. Advertising stimulates the demand for consumer products, but salespeople work with distributors and retailers to ensure the products are readily available and on the store shelves. Some of the major roles for advertising are discussed in this section.

Preselling Customers and Prospects Advertising lays a foundation for the salesperson's call. It can create a favorable image of the salesperson's

FIGURE 18–3
McGraw-Hill's ''Man-in-the-Chair'' Ad

Advertising lays a foundation for the salesperson's call.
Reprinted with permission from McGraw-Hill Publications Company

company and make the selling task easier. This point is illustrated by the ''Man-in-the-Chair'' ad in Figure 18–3. Advertising is used to answer the questions posed by the buyer in the ad before the salesperson arrives.

This is how advertising makes the salesperson more productive. A study of 26 industrial products found that the amount sold per sales call was much higher when the customers had been exposed to company advertising before the call. In addition, buyers who had seen the company's ads had a much more favorable impression of the company's salespeople. They rated the salespeople higher on product knowledge, service, and enthusiasm.[7]

Reaching Inaccessible Buyers   Often salespeople cannot see people who have important influences on the buying process. Even though these potential customers will not talk to salespeople, they do read trade magazines

[7]John E. Morrill, ''Industrial Advertising Pays Off,'' *Harvard Business Review,* March–April 1970, pp. 4–14.

and can be reached with advertising. In fact, advertising can provide the information the salesperson is unable to present.

Reaching Unknown Buyers Most salespeople do not know all the people involved in purchase decisions. Studies of industrial buying indicate salespeople contact less than 40 percent of the people involved in purchase decisions. The Chilton Company interviewed over 4,000 people who influence buying decisions in their companies for more than four different products. Sixty-one percent of the people had not been called on by a salesperson in *the last six months*.[8]

Advertising provides a method for these unknown customers to identify themselves. By responding to the advertisements, such customers can request additional information. In turn, these requests for information or inquiries become leads for salespeople. The use of advertising to generate leads is discussed in Chapter 8.

Selling between Calls Advertising can reach prospects and customers more frequently than salespeople can. The frequency of personal calls depends on the value placed on each customer, the product sold, and the territory covered. Therefore, it is not uncommon for salespeople to cover their territories only two to four times per year. Between calls, advertising can help make a salesperson's visits more profitable and selling easier.

One advertising executive observed that without the help of advertising, salespeople would have to make more than 60 personal calls a day in order to call on each prospect just once a month.

Advertising and Selling to Retailers

Consumer product salespeople use their company's advertising programs to persuade retailers and wholesalers to buy the company's products. Advertising programs undertaken by companies such as Procter & Gamble and Levi Strauss & Co. provide the following benefits to retailers:

Advertising Increases Turnover Most retailers are interested in securing a maximum turnover of their stock. Any technique that helps them increase this turnover will command their immediate attention.

A retailer can sell a nationally advertised product more quickly than a product that is not nationally advertised because the advertising has acquainted the consumer with the product name and its value before the consumer enters the store. As a result, the retailer invests money in a product for a shorter time and can use the money received from its sale to buy more merchandise. The more often the retailer can use the dollars

---

[8]Richard Manville, "Why Industrial Companies Must Advertise Their Products," *Industrial Marketing,* October 1978, pp. 45–49.

invested in the business, the greater will be the profit. Also, the retailer will need to invest less capital to maintain the volume of business.

If a retailer can sell out a stock of nationally advertised products four times a year and a stock of nonadvertised products only twice a year, the retailer will secure twice as much business from the investment in advertised products as from that in nonadvertised products.

While the margin of profit to the retailer may be less on nationally advertised products than on nonadvertised products, the increase in sales volume brought about by advertising creates a greater total profit. In addition, the retailer receives a higher rate of return on money invested in inventories.

Advertising Builds Greater Store Traffic The retailer is constantly attempting to attract more customers into the store. A well-advertised product can help accomplish this. Selling Scenario 18–1 describes a promotion that was, perhaps, too effective in this regard.

Customers who prefer a particular brand name are likely to trade where they know it is available. When they are attracted to a store to purchase a specific brand name product, the retailer is in a favorable position to sell related products. The customer who prefers Arrow shirts, for example, is also likely to need ties, socks, and handkerchiefs.

Increased store traffic creates greater numbers of impulse purchases. It is not unusual for customers to buy on impulse more than the amount of their planned purchases.

Advertising Builds Store Prestige The manufacturer's trademark or trade name, in many cases, has become synonymous with quality, style, service, or economy. Value is associated with the product.

The value attached to a trademark or trade name is likely to be transferred, in the customer's eyes, to the retail store. The customer's only contact with the manufacturer is through the retailer. If the store stocks well-known brands of merchandise, which are considered "good buys," then it is viewed as a "good" store. Just as individuals are judged by the company they keep, so a store is judged by the merchandise it carries.

Advertising as a Sales Tool

It is important for sales representatives to encourage retailers to tie in with company national or local advertising. The manufacturer customarily agrees to reimburse the retailer for a portion of the cost of local advertising when such advertising supplements the manufacturer's program. One large furniture manufacturer includes an advertising credit in its franchise agreement with retailers. This credit, which is issued by the manufacturer, equals one half of the retailer's advertising and promotional costs. The credit may not exceed 5 percent of the cost of shipments purchased by the retailer during a given period. Such tie-in programs are referred to as

Selling Scenario 18–1

A PROMOTION THAT WAS TOO EFFECTIVE

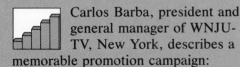 Carlos Barba, president and general manager of WNJU-TV, New York, describes a memorable promotion campaign:

Shortly after I arrived at WNJU, I came up with an idea to increase our prime-time ratings. It all revolved around a soap opera called "Esmeralda," which was on weeknights at 9 P.M. We knew a lot of our viewers were housewives, so we offered them a pair of emerald earrings, delivered to them by the handsome male star of the show. All they had to do was mail in the box top from a package of Bufferin, and the winner's name would be drawn out of a hat. There were also some cash prizes, but the grand prize was the pair of earrings. We got Bristol-Myers, which makes Bufferin, to co-sponsor the contest, and off we went.

Three weeks later, I got a frantic call from our ad agency. They said, "We need you at a meeting right away. You must stop the contest!"

It seems that the folks at Bristol-Myers were receiving hundreds of phone calls from drugstores complaining about customers purchasing 10 to 15 packages of Bufferin apiece. This wasn't so bad,

they said, but people were coming in and taking the packages from the shelves and leaving the bottles behind. The packages were selling like hotcakes—without the product!

I immediately called my lawyer, who told me the contest had to go on, in accordance with FTC and FCC regulations. At about the same time, the Newark post office called the station to tell us it was suspending our mail delivery. The post office was flooded with letters from entrants.

I didn't know what we were going to do next; then I decided to run a bulletin during the show saying that it was no longer necessary to send in the box top—just a three-by-five index card would do.

By the end of the contest's 10-week run, we had received about 789,000 letters—enough to fill a swimming pool, which was exactly where we put them! The contest created such a stir that the *New York Times* picked up the story, and it was called one of the biggest responses to a contest ever run by a television station. Now that's promotion!

Source: Reprinted from "Strange Tales of Sales," *Sales & Marketing Management,* June 3, 1985, p. 46.

co-op advertising since manufacturer and retailer are cooperating on a joint program.[9]

This practice enables retailers to obtain national advertising for their stores by featuring in local advertising the same appeal or theme used in

---

[9]See Ed Crimmons, "A Key Co-Op Issue Between Retailers and Manufacturers: Whose Money Is It?" *Sales & Marketing Management,* September 5, 1979, pp. 57–60, and Martin Everett, "Handling Co-Op With Care," *Sales & Marketing Management,* November 1978, pp. 61–70.

national magazines, newspapers, television, or radio networks. Manufacturers may also use direct mail and other media, and different manufacturers may endorse different media for tie-in purposes.

Manufacturers gain from such tie-in agreements because they help manufacturers to secure more effective local advertising—probably at a lower cost than if it were placed by the head office because newspapers usually quote a lower rate to local advertisers than to national advertisers.

In addition, it is difficult to name local outlets in which a nationally advertised product may be secured unless the local retailer capitalizes on the national advertising. An effective tie-in, then, benefits both the local retailer and the manufacturer. The manufacturer's representative will certainly point out the benefits to the retailer from this form of cooperation in advertising.

USING THE MAIL IN SELLING[10]

Salespeople can improve their productivity by using letters in place of some personal visits. Letters are useful for uncovering prospective customers, making appointments, transmitting information about products, and establishing goodwill. Because customers and prospects receive so much mail, all letters should be written with skill and care. Malcolm Forbes, chairman and editor-in-chief of *Forbes* magazine, believes the ability of marketers to write business letters well will be a key factor in their success in the 1980s.[11]

Types of Letters

Salespeople can use three types of letters. Customers welcome the "good-news letter" because it tells them things they are glad to hear. The "disappointment letter" conveys information customers do not want to hear. The "persuasive letter" seeks to persuade prospects or customers to do something they may not wish to undertake. Different styles should be used for each of these letters.

Good-News Letters   They acknowledge, for example, an order has been shipped, indicate credit has been approved, or comply with a customer request. Since these letters contain good news, the first sentence should say what the customer wants to know. Subsequent sentences can provide any important details. The letter should end with a short line recalling the benefits of the good news to the customer. Such letters should be short and to the point. Figure 18–4 shows a sample good-news letter about the replacement of a machine part damaged in transit.

---

[10]For more information on the material in this section see C. W. Wilkinson, Peter B. Clarke, and Dorothy C. Wilkinson, *Communicating through Letters and Reports,* 8th ed. (Homewood, Ill.: Richard D. Irwin, 1983).

[11]Malcolm Forbes, "Exorcising Demons from Important Business Letters," *Marketing Times,* June 1980, pp. 36–38.

FIGURE 18–4
Good-News Letter Informing Customer of a Delivery

PACKER, INC.
555 Sloan Avenue
Los Angeles, CA 90000
(213) 555-1212

Dear Customer:

Your new lower rack sensor unit, shipped by UPS Blue Service this morning, should be at your door about June 12.

The same kind of thick padding carefully protecting your new sensor unit in the heavy-unit corrugated box will be standard for all our future shipments of fragile articles so that they will arrive in the same perfect condition in which they leave our plant.

And now will you take a moment to assist us in recovering for the sensor unit from the Postal Service? Just sign the enclosed notification forms and return them with the original sensor unit. Of course we will reimburse you for returning it.

Your Cary Can-packer will soon be operating efficiently again-in time for the cherry harvest.

Sincerely,

John Wilson

John Wilson
Customer Service Representative

Source: Adapted from C. W. Wilkinson, Peter B. Clarke, and Dorothy C. Wilkinson, *Communicating through Letters and Reports*, 8th ed. (Homewood, Ill.: Richard D. Irwin, 1983), p. 88. Reprinted with permission.

Disappointment Letters   Letters containing bad news include refusals of credit, indications of delivery delays, and refusals of an order because the product is no longer available or the customer is not an authorized dealer. Such letters should not be as direct as the good-news letters. To soften its effect, the disappointment letter should begin with a buffer that contains something both the salesperson and customer can agree on. The following sentences should tactfully prepare the way by providing some justification before the bad news is presented. The letter in Figure 18–5 shows how to handle an order that cannot be filled for 20 days.

Persuasive Letters   Prospecting for customers, requests for appointments, and soliciting orders are examples of persuasive letters. Although effective persuasive letters lead prospects through the stages in the adoption process shown in Figure 18–2, they should not be too long. The prospect or customer should be able to determine very quickly the purpose of the letter, which should be easy to understand and should tell its story smoothly. Technical jargon and unusual words should be avoided.

The beginning of the letter should get the prospect's attention and interest by *quickly and naturally* indicating what the product can do. Because unusual or tricky openings are usually not relevant to the prospect, they are not effective. The best opening introduces a benefit, relates it to the prospect, and then indicates the company's product provides this benefit.

Next, to win credibility in the eyes of the prospect, the letter must provide specific evidence to back up the claim in the opening statement. Such evidence might include a description of how the product works or testimonials of users, facts and figures on sales, guarantees, free trial offers, or demonstration offers.

Finally, the letter should end with a clear statement of what action the prospect needs to take. Any questions the prospects might have should be answered here. Order blanks or prestamped addressed postcards should be included to make it easy for the prospect to take action. Figure 18–6 contains a sample persuasive letter to a lawn-mower dealer.

Adapting the Letter to the Prospect

All sales letters should be personalized. Prospects are not street addresses but people with unique needs and interests. The theme or emphasis in the letter must be tailored to the individual's needs. For example, the letter to the lawn-mower dealer stresses that the mower will be easy to sell to the dealer's customers. This approach would not be effective in direct selling to homeowners. A sales letter sent to homeowners would need to emphasize such benefits as eliminating hand clipping, trimming, and raking. Figure 18–7 contains a checklist for sales prospecting letters.

FIGURE 18–5
Disappointment Letter Announcing a Shipment Delay

Tennis Unlimited
381 Alamo Drive
San Antonio, TX 53471
(818) 555-1212

Dear Customer:

The women's white tennis dresses you ordered April
7—4 dozen—style no. 16J7 women's tennis dresses,
1 dozen each in sizes 8, 10, 12, and 14 @ $300 a
dozen terms 2/10, N/30

—are leading the summer sportswear sales from Maine
to Hawaii.

We are increasing production on this model and have
booked your tennis dresses for rush shipment by air
express April 27.

The unusual preseason popularity of this trimly cut
tennis dress owes much to its shimmering polyester
and cotton fabric. When we used up our stock of the
genuine combed cotton material, rather than use a
substitute we shut down production on this model.
A large stock of Glachine cotton fabric is already
en route here from Wancrest's famous North Carolina
mills, however; thus we are able to promise your
shipment by April 27.

For this chance to prove once again Tropical's
continuing fashion superiority, we thank you
sincerely.

Joan Monroe

Joan Monroe
Customer Service Representative

Source: Adapted from C. W. Wilkinson, Dorothy C. Wilkinson, and Gretchen N. Vik, *Communicating through Writing and Speaking in Business*, 9th ed. (Homewood, Ill.: Richard D. Irwin, 1986), p. 205. Reprinted with permission.

FIGURE 18–6
A Persuasive Letter for Selling to a Lawn-Mower Dealer

Multimower, Inc.

9999 Broad Street
Philadelphia, PA 19000
(213) 555-1212

Dear Customer:

When you show a customer a Multimower—a lawn mower
completely new in design and principle, which cuts,
trims, and "rakes" a lawn in one operation, you have
a quick sale, a satisfied customer, and a $46.65
profit.

Your customers will like the Multimower because it
gives them more time to spend in enjoyable summer
recreation. It cuts right up to walls, fences,
trees and flower beds and thus eliminates the need
for hand trimming in spots not reached by ordinary
mowers. Its easily adjustable cutting-height
regulator and self-sharpening cutters that slice
down the toughest kinds of grass, dandelions, and
weeds will assure them of having a trim, neat lawn
in half the time they've formerly spent.

Both men and women like the Multimower because its
light weight—only 58 pounds—means easy handling.
The quiet operation of the interlocking cutters has
won approval of 8,000 Multimower users. They like
it, too, because it is permanently lubricated and
self-sharpening. With a minimum of care it's always
ready for use. So normally you just put in the gas
and it's ready to go.

No doubt many of your customers have been reading
about the Multimower in the full-page, four-color
monthly ads that started running in Homeowners and
Vacation magazines in March and will continue through
July. A reprint, along with testimonials and
conditions of our guarantee, appears on the next page.
Note the favorable guarantee and servicing arrangements.

In these days of high prices, the $139.95 retail cost
of the Multimower will be popular with your customers.
Our price to you is only $93.30.

By filling out and returning the enclosed order blank
along with your remittance today, you'll be sure to
have Multimowers on hand when your customers begin
asking for them.

Multimower, Inc.

Source: Adapted from C. W. Wilkinson, Peter B. Clarke, and Dorothy C. Wilkinson, *Communicating through Letters and Reports,*
8th ed. (Homewood, Ill.: Richard D. Irwin, 1983), p. 262. Reprinted with permission.

FIGURE 18–7
Checklist for Sales
Prospecting Letters

1. Get started effectively and concisely.
   a. Suggest or hint at a specific reader need/benefit.
   b. Concentrate on a positive, distinctive central selling point at first.
2. Back up your opening promise with a persuasive description.
   a. Subordinate and interpret physical features in terms of benefits.
   b. Specificity in description is necessary for conviction.
   c. Eliminate challenging superlatives and useless history.
3. Develop the most appropriate central selling point adequately.
   a. Provide adequate conviction through selected methods.
   b. Introduce any enclosure stressing what to do with it or get from it.
   c. Check for any unintentional promises of safety or warranty.
4. Unless using a recognized-bargain appeal, minimize price.
5. Forthrightly ask for appropriate action (and tell why to buy by mail).
   a. Avoid high-pressure bromides: "Why wait?" "Don't delay!"
   b. Refer subordinately to ordering aids (blanks or envelopes).
   c. End with a reminder of what the product will contribute.

Source: C. W. Wilkinson, Dorothy C. Wilkinson, and Gretchen N. Vik, *Communicating through Writing and Speaking in Business,* 9th ed. (Homewood, Ill.: Richard D. Irwin, 1986), p. 224.

There is no substitute for being organized!

"Sorry to keep you waiting . . . I expected to
be put on hold . . ."

From *The Wall Street Journal,* with permission of Cartoon
Features Syndicate.

USING THE TELEPHONE IN SELLING

The telephone is widely used in sales work. Activities that can be done effectively by telephone include locating and qualifying prospective customers, making appointments, handling customer inquiries and questions, and maintaining goodwill. In addition to these traditional uses of the telephone, more and more actual selling is done by telephone.

Advantages of the Telephone

The telephone is an easy way to contact customers quickly and inexpensively. By using the telephone, salespeople can increase the amount of time they are in contact with customers. For example, productivity is increased when salespeople call ahead to make appointments. In this way, salespeople minimize the time spent waiting for unavailable customers. Advance telephoning also improves productivity during the sales call. When salespeople call for appointments, they can ask key questions and get information that will help them plan their sales presentations.

The telephone also provides timely information to customers. Salespeople can promptly advise their customers of delivery problems, changes in price or product availability, product introductions, and new promotional opportunities.

Contact with marginal or remotely located customers can be handled by telephone since it's not economical to make regular personal visits to them. In this way, salespeople can increase the amount of time available to call on key accounts.

Finally, the telephone increases a salesperson's flexibility. If customers cancel an appointment or are tied up when the salesperson arrives, the salesperson may have some "down time" between appointments. But the telephone, which is always at hand, can convert this interval into productive time. For example, the salesperson can make goodwill calls or set up future appointments.

Limitations of Telephoning

There are several drawbacks to using the telephone in selling. First, customers and prospects may find telephone calls an annoying inconvenience. Unexpected calls may interrupt customers involved in meetings or concentrating on their work. In telephoning customers, salespeople need to respect the customer's privacy and not abuse the privilege.

Second, telephone communications are limited to verbal messages. When using the telephone, salespeople cannot show the features and benefits of their products. Because nonverbal communications are restricted, the salesperson cannot see the customer's reactions to the presentation, and the customer cannot see the salesperson's enthusiasm. In this way, the telephone limits communication effectiveness.

Third, it is harder to maintain the attention and interest of customers over the telephone. During face-to-face encounters customers, out of politeness, will concentrate on the person with whom they are talking.

Use of the
telephone increases
a salesperson's
productivity and
flexibility.

Billy E. Barnes

Alan Carey/Image Works

H. Armstrong Roberts

But customers talking on the telephone can engage in other activities; they may even continue to work on a report or read a magazine.

Finally, it is much easier to say no over the telephone than in a face-to-face conversation. Because they cannot see the salesperson, customers are often rude during telephone conversations. It's easy to end a phone conversation by hanging up, but it's harder for a customer to walk away from a face-to-face conversation with a salesperson.

Salespeople need to be aware of these limitations, some of which can be overcome by good telephoning technique. The remaining portion of this section discusses some of the principles of this technique.

Telephone Etiquette

When making a call, salespeople should immediately state their name and the name of their company. Most people do not feel comfortable talking with someone they cannot identify.

It is often appropriate to check the convenience of the call. Customers appreciate the sensitivity of a salesperson who asks, "Did I call at a convenient time, or should I call back later?" Such consideration increases the likelihood of a future appointment if the call took place at a bad time.

Dealing with Subordinates

Frequently customers protect themselves from unwanted calls by having their secretary or an assistant answer the phone. In dealing with subordinates, it is always best to be honest and forthright. Salespeople should identify themselves as sales representatives for their companies. Attempts at disguise are likely to backfire. The salesperson might get around the secretary once, but future interactions will be unpleasant. In addition, subordinates can often be valuable information sources. For this reason salespeople should always be courteous. Instead of looking down on subordinates, the salesperson should compliment them for a good job or when they prove helpful.

An example of an appropriate conversation follows:

Salesperson: Good morning. I am Herb Quinn of Master Supplies. I wonder if you could help me?

Secretary: OK, what can I do for you?

Salesperson: I would like to make an appointment to see the purchasing manager. Do you handle the appointments, or should I speak to the purchasing manager directly?

Encouraging
Two-way
Communica-
tions

Because of the telephone's limitations, it is often hard to maintain a two-way flow of information. When talking face to face with customers, salespeople can encourage them to continue talking by nodding their heads or by positive facial expressions. To encourage conversations over the telephone, salespeople must use such verbal cues as "Uh-huh," "I see," or "That's interesting."

It is useful to pause at times during a conversation. This gives customers the opportunity to ask questions, indicate agreement or disagreement with a point, or relate the points to their circumstances.

Tone of Voice

The lack of nonverbal cues makes it harder to communicate effectively over the telephone. To improve understanding, salespeople should speak clearly and at a moderate rate. In addition, they should use a friendly, enthusiastic tone of voice. Over the phone they should try to make a smile come through in their voice. One technique for achieving this objective is to observe facial expressions by looking in a mirror while talking over the phone.[12]

After the Call

Immediately after a business call, the salesperson should write down the details of the conversation. We all tend to become preoccupied with other activities when a call is over, but this can cause us to forget important information. To avoid such problems, the salesperson should:

1. Write down the time, date, and location of future appointments or followup calls on a calendar.
2. Record significant information in the customer's file.
3. Process orders or paperwork resulting from the phone call.

Examples of
Telephone
Applications

Figures 18–8 and 18–9 show examples of how to use the telephone to revive an inactive account and collect an overdue account. Illustrations of how to prospect and make appointments by telephone are presented in Chapters 8 and 9, respectively.

SUMMARY

Because of the rapid increase in the costs of personal selling, companies are using new approaches for communicating with customers. These new communication tools, which include demonstration centers, industrial stores, and telemarketing, do not replace salespeople. But they do increase the efficiency of the selling effort.

Each of these approaches helps salespeople move customers through the stages of the adoption process. Advertising, direct mail, and telephone

---

[12]See John P. Moncur and Harrison M. Karr, *Developing Your Speaking Voice*, 2nd ed. (New York: Harper & Row, 1972).

FIGURE 18–8
How to Revive an
Inactive Account

Salesperson: Good morning, Mr. Account. This is Joe Sales from the ABC Corp. It's been some time since we've heard from you. *[Pause— Customer realizes why you are calling.]* Mr. Account, I was wondering if there was a problem with the last shipment of Super A's we sent you.

Customer: *[Either voices a complaint or says no.]*

Salesperson: I'm sorry about that, Mr. Account. I'll send a replacement case immediately *[or whatever action is appropriate]*; *[or]* I'm glad there is nothing wrong.

I'm glad you're still using Super A's. We are having a special sale on cases of Super A's this month. You'll save x percent by buying the case. *[pause]*

How many cases will you need? *[pause]* They'll be delivered the day after tomorrow.

Thank you for your order, Mr. Account. I hope we'll hear from you more often from now on.

FIGURE 18–9
How to Collect
Overdue Accounts

Salesperson: Good morning, Mr. Renfro. This is Sam Pearson from ABC Corp. *[Pause—He knows why you're calling.]* Mr. Renfro, according to our records, you received your shipment of widgets on the 10th but we have no record of payment for them. [*Give customer a chance to speak.*]

I was wondering if there was a problem with the shipment. *[pause]*

I'm sorry some of the widgets were damaged, Mr. Renfro. I'll adjust your bill and send you an updated one immediately.

When would it be convenient for you to pay? All right, I'll mark the account that we are to receive payment by next Monday then. Thank you, Mr. Renfro, it was nice to talk with you. *[or]*

By the way, you haven't ordered any whatnots lately. I'll ship you some today, OK? Thanks for your order.

selling are economical and inexpensive ways to advise customers of products and to encourage repeat sales. Demonstration centers and industrial stores provide a handy, economical opportunity for customers to try products. But personal selling still remains the best way to provide information and influence customer evaluations of products.

Advertising plays many roles. For simple consumer products, advertising alone may be enough to sell products. But advertising is also an important sales tool when selling consumer products to retailers. For more complex industrial products, advertising is limited to preselling customers and contacting hard-to-reach or unknown buyers.

Salespeople can use letters and the telephone to increase their productivity. Letters convey information about product delivery and availability and help prospect for new customers. The structure of a letter depends on the information it conveys and its objective.

Some selling activities that can be performed by telephone are selling marginal customers, locating and qualifying customers, making appointments, and maintaining goodwill. The telephone is a flexible, efficient means of communications, but it has drawbacks. Communications over the phone are limited to verbal messages. Nonverbal communication cannot be used to demonstrate key points or determine a customer's reactions. It is harder to maintain a customer's attention and easier for him or her to say no over the telephone.

When using the telephone, salespeople should observe the rules of etiquette; they should state their name at the beginning of a conversation and be courteous with secretaries. In addition, salespeople need to encourage two-way communications with customers.

QUESTIONS AND PROBLEMS

1. Your company wants to encourage its retailers to conduct a direct-mail advertising campaign to supplement the company's national advertising. Yet on your first dealer contact, you get this reply, "Direct-mail pieces are used too often. Customers are getting so they don't pay any attention to them. Besides, what would we use for a mailing list? I'd much rather advertise in our local newspaper. Let's work out a deal on newspaper ads." Assume your company prefers its retailers to use direct mail and is willing to supply the direct-mail pieces for one half the actual printing cost. How would you answer the retailer? Point out five or six advantages of direct-mail advertising.

2. Advertising is said to lower costs to consumers and to force competition. Comment on these statements, and supply illustrations to support your opinions.

3. An advertising executive claims, "We are heading for an economy without personal salespeople!" According to this view, the need for personal selling is declining as advertising slowly takes the place of countless door-to-door salespeople, counter salesclerks, demonstrators, and jobber salespeople. Do you agree with this reasoning? Why or why not? Do you believe personal selling is necessary, even for products sold from vending machines? Illustrate.

4. One of merchandising's most widespread problems today is placing point-of-purchase displays in retail stores so they can do the job they are designed to do. What can management do to win retailer cooperation in scheduling merchandising-promotion

programs through point-of-purchase displays? What can a sales representative do?

5. Develop an opening statement designed to interest a prospect in giving you an appointment next Wednesday.

6. How does telephone selling differ from face-to-face selling?

7. How would you handle a prospect you have contacted by telephone who says, "You lousy peddler! I don't trust you or anyone trying to push something on me over the phone. I've been burned before, and I'm not going to be burned again."

8. What are the advantages in selling by mail or telephone rather than through face-to-face interactions? What are the disadvantages?

9. Name some products that would be better sold by mail or telephone than by personal selling. Why would the mail or telephone be better for these products?

10. Co-op advertising is a mutual effort by the manufacturer and the retailer to sell products. How far should the retailer go in setting guidelines for accepting co-op funds from the manufacturer?

PROJECTS

1. Investigate the current role of cable television in today's marketing. Find out its cost to the user, its popularity in your community, and the bases used for marketing the service. Prepare a brief statement of your conclusions.

2. Collect 10 ads from magazines, newspapers, and/or direct mail. Evaluate the ads in terms of believability. Try to illustrate both good and bad ads with the reasons for your decisions. Summarize your conclusions.

CASE PROBLEMS

Case 18–1   Day Business Equipment

The following telephone conversation took place between Tom Rather, a salesperson for Day Business Equipment, and Kathy Waters, his customer:

Rather: Good morning, Ms. Waters. This is Tom Rather from Day Business Equipment.

Waters: Hello, Mr. Rather. What can I do for you?

Rather: Thank you very much for your order for the Model 8100 slide projector. We just received it yesterday.

Waters: That's quite all right. We think it will do our job and are pleased to do business with you.

Rather: We are shipping the projector tomorrow morning. You should get it late in the afternoon.

Waters: Can't ask for faster delivery.

Rather: If you have any questions or problems when you get the projector, please give me a call.

Waters: Thanks. I certainly will do that.

Rather: I was just thinking. Some of my customers have found that the adjustable stand for the projector is very useful. Often it is difficult to find a place to set up the projector. Also, if the projector is not set up properly, it can fall and get damaged.

Waters: I guess that might be a problem. How much is the stand?

Rather: The price is $109. Shall I send the stand with the projector?

Waters: I better think it over for a while. Thanks for the suggestion.

Questions

1. Evaluate Tom Rather's telephone selling technique.
2. Why wasn't he successful in selling the stand?

Case 18–2   Kingfisher, Inc.*

Kingfisher, Inc., has developed an inflatable boat called the Eaze-fish. The boat has the following characteristics:

1. Made of tough rubber-coated nylon.
2. Lab tests show better weather and ozone resistance as well as 40 percent greater strength than neoprene-coated boats.
3. Wooden transon motor-mount supports motor that attaches with nylon ropes.
4. Plastic oarlocks, nylon sidegrab ropes, plastic grommets.
5. Charcoal gray with blue floor.
6. Two varnished marine plywood, removable seats.
7. Two separate chambers, each able to support the boat's rated weight capacity.
8. Costs $290, measures 11¼ feet, weighs 66 pounds.
9. Certified by boat industry association.
10. Repair kit included.
11. Can be stored in a closet, transported in a car trunk, set up and launched at a beach, riverbank, or dock.
12. Unparalleled stability and load-carrying capability.
13. Safe and seaworthy (avoid possible legal problems).
14. One person can set up the boat in 10 minutes.

Questions

1. The company plans to locate prospects for the boat by direct mail using a mail list of *Sports Illustrated* subscribers. Write a letter that asks readers to fill out and return an enclosed card requesting additional information.
2. Write a letter to sell the Eaze-fish to a marine supply store in your area. The dealer cost is $180.
3. Write a letter selling the Eaze-fish to resort owners in Michigan, Wisconsin,

---

*Adapted from C. W. Wilkinson, Peter B. Clarke, and Dorothy C. Wilkinson, *Communicating through Letters and Reports,* 8th ed. (Homewood, Ill.: Richard D. Irwin, 1983), pp. 271–72.

and Minnesota. Indicate that the boat can be used on lakes other than the one on which the resort is located—saves hauling heavy boats to other lakes in the spring and bringing them back in the fall. Offer a 10 percent price reduction if three or more boats are bought.

SELECTED REFERENCES

Aaker, David, and James Myer. *Advertising Management,* 3rd ed. Englewood Cliffs, N.J.: Prentice-Hall, 1985.

Benchin, Richard L. "Electronic Marketing 1990: How You'll Handle Tomorrow Selling." *Industrial Marketing,* August 1982, pp. 58–61.

Hardy, Michael G. "Take a Letter, Plain and Simple." *Sales & Marketing Management,* June 8, 1981, pp. 37–38.

Lesikar, Raymond V. *Basic Business Communications.* Homewood, Ill.: Richard D. Irwin, 1982.

MacMillion, Bruce B. "Seven Ways to Improve Your Writing Skills." *Sales & Marketing Management,* March 11, 1985, pp. 75–76.

Ojala, John F. "The Media Vehicle Plan: How to Mesh Your Selling and Advertising Efforts." *Industrial Marketing,* September 1982, pp. 68–74.

Roman, Murray. "Reach Out and Sell Someone with Business Direct Mail." *Industrial Marketing,* August 1982, pp. 78–80.

"Special Report/Direct Mail." *Sales & Marketing Management,* January 14, 1985, pp. 39–61.

Swinyard, William R. "How Many Ad Exposures Is a Sales Call Worth?" *Journal of Advertising Research,* February 1979, pp. 17–21.

Taylor, Thayer C. "Special Report/Telemarketing." *Sales & Marketing Management,* June 4, 1984, pp. 44–63.

Vitullo, Ray. "Commonsense Advice on Industrial Direct Mail." *Industrial Marketing,* August 1982, p. 11.

Winga, Chuck. "Telemarketing: A Great Idea Whose Time Has Come." *Industrial Marketing Management,* August 1981, pp. 71–77.

19

The Salesperson and Sales Management

Some questions answered in this chapter are:

- What are line and staff functions in a sales department?
- How are sales departments organized?
- What are the duties of the sales executive and the field sales manager?
- Why are there different types of compensation plans?
- What are the different types of leadership styles used by field sales managers?
- How can a salesperson prepare for a sales management position?

Qualified salespeople can become sales supervisors or sales managers. Eventually they may have the opportunity to become members of top management. Analyses of top management in business concerns throughout the country show that many of these executives began their careers in their companies' sales divisions. It is now more common for successful sales managers to be considered for top leadership positions. Early in the text, we discussed corporation presidents who rose to their positions through successful selling and sales management jobs. It has been estimated that 50 percent of members of top management got their start in sales.

There is a big difference, however, between selling and sales management. Some people would rather sell than be promoted to sales management positions. They earn good money and are happier calling on customers and prospects and closing sales.

The objective of this chapter is to acquaint the salesperson with the field of sales management.

FIGURE 19–1
Organizational Chart for Marketing Department

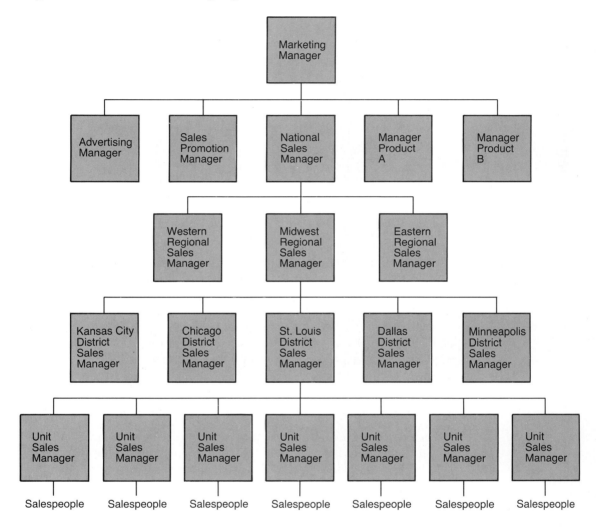

SALES FUNCTIONS IN THE MARKETING ORGANIZATION

The marketing concept presented in Chapter 1 stresses the need for a coordinated marketing program aimed at satisfying customer needs. The marketing executive is responsible for designing and implementing this marketing program. The elements of such a program are product development, pricing, advertising, personal selling, and distribution. A typical organization chart for a marketing department is shown in Figure 19–1.

Product managers are responsible for developing marketing programs for specific products. They coordinate the advertising, selling, and product development efforts. Although they do not have authority over the sales department, they provide support material for salespeople and help train salespeople to sell specific products.

Sales management work is performed at several levels within the organization. The person at the top is either a vice president in charge of sales or a national sales manager. People in intermediate or middle management include divisional, regional, and district sales managers. The first level of sales management includes branch or unit managers. Middle-level sales managers serve as connecting links between policy-making sales executives in the home office and first-level field sales managers.

Line and Staff Functions

The sales department shown in Figure 19–1 is a line organization. All of the authority and responsibility for implementing the sales program in an area lies in the hands of the manager for that area. A complete line of authority can be tracked from the sales executive to each salesperson. Communications up and down the organization take place through this line. Decision-making authority is delegated along this line.

In large firms, the amount of work done by a sales manager is often too much for one person. Specialized skills are often needed to perform some functions. Staff people reporting to the sales managers perform these functions.

Staff people can be used at several levels in the sales organization. A person in charge of sales forecasting may report to the sales executive. This person serves as an assistant to the sales executive. The forecaster may have little or no contact with salespeople. However, even though the forecaster has no direct authority over them, his or her activities can affect them. Other staff people reporting to the sales executive may be responsible for order processing, sales administration, and training. Middle-level sales managers often have staff people who are responsible for hiring and training new salespeople in the field and for providing them with technical support.

Organization of the Sales Department

Most sales departments are organized into geographic regions. Each salesperson is assigned to a specific territory. The salesperson is responsible for selling all of the company's products to each customer in the territory.

Large companies often find it more efficient to have salespeople specialize in specific activities within a territory. Such salespeople are not responsible for selling all of the company's products to each customer in the territory.[1] The specialization can be based on sales activities, products, or customers.

---

[1]See Alton Doody and William Nickels, "Structuring Organizations for Strategic Selling," *MSU Business Topics*, Autumn 1972, pp. 27–35.

Sales Activities   A common form of specialization based on sales activities has some salespeople develop new accounts while others maintain existing accounts. Developing new accounts is normally more difficult and requires a different set of skills than maintaining an account that is already sold. Xerox Data Services, a supplier of computer time-sharing services, has two types of salespeople: marketing representatives and account representatives. Marketing representatives get new customers. After a customer has used Xerox's time-sharing services for six months, the customer is turned over to an account representative. The account representative has to make sure the customer's needs are satisfied and encourage the customer to use additional services.

Products   When companies' products are diverse, salespeople often specialize by types of products. For example, the Johnson & Johnson Baby Products Company has two specialized sales forces: the disposable product sales force and the toiletries product sales force. Hewlett-Packard has separate sales forces that specialize in selling computers, electronic test instruments, electronic components, medical test equipment, and analytical test instruments. Each sales force has its own regional, district, and area sales managers.

In the life insurance field, sales representatives may be grouped by such product categories as individual policies, group policies, business policies, and trusts and estates.

Customers   Customers often have different needs for a company's products. When this occurs, salespeople may be organized by distribution channel, industry, or company function. For example, NCR has different sales forces for manufacturing companies, and retail and financial institutions. Some Procter & Gamble salespeople call on central buying offices for grocery store chains; others call on food wholesalers.

Many companies are organized in a special manner to deal with large national or key accounts. Typically, national accounts centralize all buying activities in a national or regional headquarters. In some cases, an entire sales force is developed to service the national account. In other cases a company executive is assigned to the national account. This executive coordinates all salespeople who call on home offices of the national account.

THE SALES EXECU-TIVE'S JOB

The sales executive plays a vital role in determining what the company's future strategies should be with respect to new products, new markets, sales forecasts, prices, and competition. He or she must determine the size and organization of the sales force, develop annual and long-range plans, and monitor and control the sales efforts. This section discusses specific activities performed by sales executives, including forecasting, budgeting, setting quotas, and designing a compensation program.

A sales executive
must monitor and
control sales efforts
for the company.

Reprinted by permission of *Sales & Marketing Management* magazine, May 13, 1985. Copyright 1985.

Forecasting

In most companies, long-range planning starts with a sales forecast.[2] The first step in preparing a sales forecast is to make a preliminary forecast based on past and present sales. The preliminary forecast is simply an extension of past sales to predict future sales. It is adjusted on the basis of changes anticipated in the company and in the company's environment. For example, the preliminary forecast would be adjusted upward if the company planned to make unusual increases in product introductions, advertising, the number of salespeople, or the number of distribution outlets. The preliminary forecast would be adjusted downward if the economy were deteriorating, or if competitors were unusually active in product introductions and promotions.

A number of techniques are used to arrive at a sales forecast. These techniques can be divided into two categories: judgmental and quantitative.

Judgmental Forecasting Techniques   One of the most widely used forecasting techniques is to combine each salesperson's forecast for his or her territory into a forecast for total company sales. Normally, before

---

[2]See ''Forecasting for Higher Profits,'' *Sales & Marketing Management*, special report, November 17, 1975.

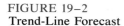

FIGURE 19–2
Trend-Line Forecast

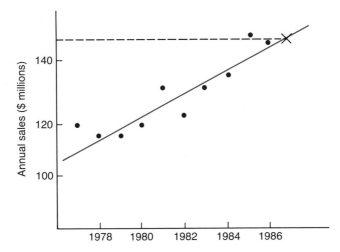

each individual's forecasts are forwarded to headquarters, each level of field sales management makes adjustments based on its greater experience and broader perspective.

One advantage of this forecasting technique is that it is based on information provided by the people closest to the market—the salespeople. Another is that it places responsibility for making the forecast in the hands of the people who are responsible for making the sales. However, the sales executive cannot rely solely on this technique because the composite forecast may be biased. Salespeople tend to be optimistic and might overestimate future sales. On the other hand, if they know their bonuses depend on exceeding their forecasts, they might underestimate future sales.

Other judgmental techniques used by sales executives are collecting expert opinions and surveying customer purchase intentions.

Quantitative Forecasting Techniques   The simplest quantitative forecasting technique is fitting a trend line. This technique is shown in Figure 19–2. The forecaster tries to fit a straight line through the points representing past sales. This can be done by sight or by using statistical techniques such as regression. More sophisticated trend projections, such as those based on the use of a moving average and exponential smoothing, place greater weight on sales in recent years.[3]

The major problem with quantitative forecasting techniques is that they rely on projections of past sales. They do not explicitly consider what changes are planned or might occur in the future. Therefore, the best forecasts combine judgmental and quantitative techniques.

---

[3]See Steven C. Wheelright and Darrel G. Clarke, "Corporate Forecasting: Promise and Reality," *Harvard Business Review*, November–December 1976, pp. 50–58.

Budgeting

A sales budget is a financial planning guide for the future. It contains both forecast sales and the costs of obtaining them. Most companies require that budgets be developed on a monthly basis for at least one year ahead.

Budgets for a sales department typically include forecast sales broken down by territory, product, and salesperson. Expenses are broken down into the following categories:

Salespeople expenses:
Salaries, commissions, and bonuses.
Administrative expenses:
Salaries, commissions, and bonuses for sales managers.
Traveling expenses for sales managers.
Sales trainer and trainee costs.
Secretarial services.
Sales meetings and conventions.
Mailing and telephone expenses.
Recruiting expenses.
Display and showroom expenses.
Moving expenses for salespeople and managers.

Management by Objectives   It is important for sales personnel to participate in development of plans, forecasts, and budgets. Management by objectives (MBO) is a method for securing such participation by developing goals and objectives acceptable to management and salespeople. If middle-level sales managers can be persuaded to set realistic goals, they will have more motivation to achieve the goals and fewer excuses if the goals are not achieved.[4]

Control and Quota Setting

The sales executive is mainly concerned with matching overall performance against predetermined plans and objectives. The challenge of the sales executive is to set up a balanced control system that will encourage each sales manager and each salesperson to maximize results through effective self-control. The sales executive should get involved only when exceptions or major deviations from plans develop.

Quotas are a useful technique for controlling the sales force. There are many types of quotas. Quotas based on sales volume represent a simple breakdown of the company's sales forecast. Thus, the total of all the sales quotas equals the sales forecast. Other types of quotas are discussed below.

---

[4]See Charles M. Futrell, John E. Swan, and Charles W. Lamb, "Benefits and Problems in a Salesforce MBO System," *Industrial Marketing Management*, Fall 1977, pp. 265–72.

Expense quotas are used to control costs. An expense quota or budget may be expressed in dollars or as a percent of sales volume. A regional manager or a salesperson may be awarded a bonus if he or she spends less than the expense budget. However, placing too much emphasis on expenses can lead to lower sales.

Profit or gross margin quotas are used to motivate the sales force to sell more profitable products or to sell to more profitable customers.[5] Some companies assign a point value to each product based on its gross margin. More points are assigned to products with higher gross margins. Each salesperson must meet a point quota during the specified time period. The salesperson can meet this quota by selling a lot of low-margin products or fewer high-margin products.

Activity quotas are used to control the activities of the sales force. Activities for which quotas may be established include number of demonstrations, total customer calls, calls on new customers, displays set up, and sales made.

For quotas to be effective in controlling the sales force, they must be fair, understandable, and attainable. Quotas should be supported by solid information that is accepted by both managers and salespeople. If quotas are unrealistic, people will ignore them.

Compensation and Evaluation

An important task of the sales executive is to establish the company's basic compensation and evaluation system. The compensation system must satisfy the needs of both the salespeople and the company. Salespeople need a system that is equitable, stable, and understandable, and that motivates them to meet their objectives. The system must base rewards on efforts and results. The compensation must be uniform within the company and in line with that received by competitors' salespeople.

The company expects the compensation system to attract and keep good salespeople and to encourage them to do specific things. It should reward outstanding performance and achieve the proper balance between sales results and costs.

Three basic decisions must be made in developing a compensation plan. First, the sales executive must establish the overall or gross level of compensation for each sales job. This decision is based on the experience, education, and ability needed to perform the job; the income of persons holding comparable positions in the company; and the income of salespeople performing comparable jobs for the company.

Next, the sales executive must decide how much income will be based on regular salary versus incentive pay. In other words, what percent of the salesperson's salary will come from straight salary, commissions, and

---

[5]See Douglas J. Dalrymple, P. Ronald Stephenson, and William Cron, "Gross Margin Sales Compensation Plans," *Industrial Marketing Management*, Fall 1981, pp. 219–24.

FIGURE 19–3
Alternative Sales
Compensation and
Incentive Plans,
1986

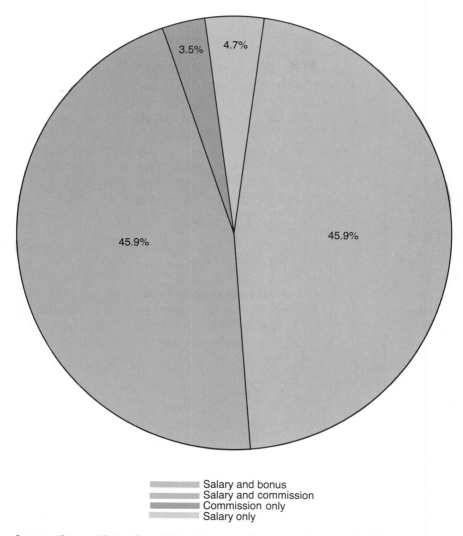

FIGURE 19–3
Alternative Sales
Compensation and
Incentive Plans,
1986

Source: "Survey of Selling Costs," *Sales & Marketing Management*, February 16, 1987, p. 57.

bonuses. Finally, a decision must be made on the criteria for awarding bonuses and commissions. Performance to quotas is normally used to determine the amount of incentive pay each salesperson earns.

The four basic methods of compensating salespeople are: (1) *straight salary*, (2) *straight commission*, (3) *bonus*, and (4) *combination*. Each of these methods is discussed in the following sections. The frequency with which these methods are used is shown in Figure 19–3.

Straight Salary   Under this method, a salesperson is paid a fixed amount of money for work during a specific time. This method assures salespeople of a steady income and helps develop their sense of loyalty to the customer. It also gives the company more control over the salesperson. Since the salesperson's income is not based directly on results, the company can ask the salesperson to do things in the best interest of the company even though they may not lead to immediate sales. The main disadvantage of the method is that it does not provide a financial incentive for salespeople.

Straight salary plans are used when sales require long periods of negotiations (for example, computer sales), when a team of salespeople is involved in making sales, or when other aspects of the marketing mix such as advertising are much more important than the salesperson's efforts in determining sales (trade selling of consumer products). Most sales trainees receive a straight salary.

Commission   The commission plan includes a base and a rate. The base is typically unit sales, dollar sales, or gross margin. The rate is expressed as a percent of the base, such as 10 percent of sales or 8 percent of gross margin.

Commission plans often include a draw. The draw is money paid against future commissions. For example, a salesperson could receive a draw of $1,000 a month. If the salesperson earns less than $1,000 in commissions during the month, the salesperson will still receive $1,000 in compensation. The difference between earned commissions and the draw will be made up by commissions earned in later months. When the draw is guaranteed, the salesperson does not have to make up insufficient commissions.

The commission plan has the advantage of tying the salesperson's salary directly to results, providing more financial incentives. But salespeople under a commission plan have little loyalty for the company. They are basically small entrepreneurs. They are less willing to perform non-selling activities such as writing reports and providing extra services for customers.

Commission plans are typically used by companies that do not emphasize service to customers or anticipate long-term customer relationships (for example, direct selling and life insurance). They are also used when the sales force consists of many part-time employees.

Bonus   Under bonus plans, salespeople are paid a lump sum of money for outstanding performance. Bonuses may be awarded monthly, quarterly, or annually. They are always used in conjunction with salary and/ or commissions, and for this reason will be discussed under combination plans.

Combination Plans   Frequently, two or three of the basic methods are used to create a combination plan. Combination plans offer the greatest flexibility for motivating and controlling the activities of salespeople. They can incorporate the advantages and avoid the disadvantages of salary, commission, and bonus plans.

The main disadvantage of combination plans is their complexity. Since the plans combine several elements, they can be misunderstood by salespeople and misused by sales management.

Salary plus commission plans are used when management wants to motivate salespeople to increase revenues and also to continue to perform nonselling activities. When management wants to develop long-term customer relations, salary plus bonus plans are used. Bonus plans are also used when the sales effort is made by a team of people.

THE SCOPE OF A FIELD SALES MANAGER'S JOB

The field sales manager's job is similar to that of the sales executive. The same management processes are involved—planning, organizing, directing, coordinating, and controlling. However, implementing these processes is quite different in many respects.

Planning

As mentioned before, the company's sales planning often starts at the grass roots—in the field—where the salesperson and the customer meet face to face. The field sales manager is responsible for knowing what is really happening in his or her territory. The field sales manager who has good communication with salespeople throughout the territory is the company's most effective source of information with respect to sales forecasts and planning.

In addition to providing information for the company's overall planning, a field sales manager has to formulate specific plans in terms of sales and profits by product and by customer throughout the territory; establish goals; develop specific sales goals and strategies; and establish policies and procedures to implement those goals and strategies.

Organizing

Field sales managers are in the best position to know what kinds of organization are most productive in their areas. They know and understand each customer's needs. They recognize special problems involving weather, transportation, and local community culture. They are close enough to the salespeople to know what kinds of organization will produce the best results for each of them.

The key to effective results in the territory is a competent field manager. He or she should have enough authority to reorganize the territory with a minimum of red tape.

Directing

The transition from salesperson to sales manager is often traumatic. This is particularly true when the new sales manager has been a successful salesperson. The new sales manager will be strongly tempted to remain too involved in salesperson-customer relations. If the sales manager accompanies a salesperson on a customer call and the salesperson does not appear to be making the sale, the sales manager may succumb to the temptation to take over. This may save the sale, but in the long run it may not be the best way to develop the salesperson.

A new sales manager should realize that his or her main responsibility is not to make individual sales. It is to direct, to motivate, and to train sales representatives to make effective presentations.

Coordinating

The coordinating responsibility of the field sales manager is perhaps not as complex as that of the sales executive. Yet it is extremely important for the field sales manager to perform the coordination within the territory and with the regional or headquarters office.

The field sales manager must see that there is effective communication throughout the territory about changing conditions in the territory, sales made in the territory, new company developments, new actions taken by competition, and new governmental regulations. If sales representatives within the territory are having problems getting delivery or financing sales, the field sales manager should provide coordination with the home office to resolve these problems.

Controlling

The records and reports submitted by sales representatives play an important role in controlling sales activities in a territory. But these reports are not enough. Field sales managers need to make calls with salespeople so they can directly observe their performance. These observations can be used as a basis for recommendations for improving performance or for commending salespeople who are doing a good job.

LEADERSHIP AND THE FIELD SALES MANAGER

Field sales managers encounter "people-centered" problems. This is natural, as salespeople tend to possess somewhat different personal characteristics and traits than production or office workers. Salespeople tend to be individualists who prefer to do things their own way. Their jobs force them to spend a good deal of time alone, away from their homes and families. Extreme emotional reactions may result from closing a large and profitable sale or from losing a sale that might have resulted in a large commission or bonus. The field sales manager is the one the salesperson looks to for guidance and counsel in times of stress or discouragement. It is essential, therefore, for field sales managers to possess knowledge and skills in the area of human behavior.

The field sales manager is a leader of a group of salespeople. The role of a leader is closely related to the role of a salesperson. Salespeople try to influence customers to purchase their products or services. In the same way, leaders try to influence members of the group to work toward a set of goals or objectives.

Dimensions of Behavior	There are two basic dimensions to a leader's behavior: (1) authoritarian versus participative and (2) relations-oriented versus task-oriented.

Authoritarian versus Participative   Authoritarian managers make all decisions for the group. They use the authority of their position to get salespeople to do what the managers think they should be doing.

Participative managers are more democratic. They share information and power with subordinates. Salespeople are treated as equals and are allowed to participate in decision making. But participative managers are not passive. They try to direct salespeople by using influence rather than authority.

Task-Oriented versus Relations-Oriented   Task-oriented managers are mainly concerned with getting sales. Salespeople are important only because they can produce sales. On the other hand, relations-oriented managers are concerned with the welfare of their salespeople. Such managers are considerate of each salesperson's feelings and strive to provide a supportive atmosphere. |
| **Leadership Styles**[6] | Psychologists have identified a number of styles or behavior patterns used by leaders. Some of these styles are shown in Figure 19–4. Each style is related to the amount of authority used by the sales manager and the amount of freedom the salespeople have.

Over the last 50 years, psychologists and managers have searched for the one, best leadership style. Today people realize that there is no one best style. Each leadership style is appropriate in some situations and inappropriate in others. The effective sales manager uses all the styles. For example, a sales manager might be autocratic with a new trainee yet give free rein to an experienced salesperson. The remaining portion of this section discusses each style and the situations for which it is appropriate.

Autocratic   Sales managers who use an autocratic style make all decisions. The results of these decisions are given to the salespeople to implement. The salespeople have no chance to participate in the decision making. The sales manager uses his or her authority, rather than persuasion, to get them to do their jobs.

The autocratic style is most appropriate for new sales representatives and sales representatives who have become complacent and lazy. It is also appropriate when an emergency prevents the use of a more parti- |

---

[6]Adapted from Thomas F. Stroh, *Managing the Sales Force* (New York: McGraw-Hill, 1978), pp. 408–14; and Robert Tannenbaum and Warren H. Schmidt, "How to Choose a Leadership Pattern," *Harvard Business Review*, May–June 1973, pp. 162–80.

FIGURE 19–4
Leadership Styles

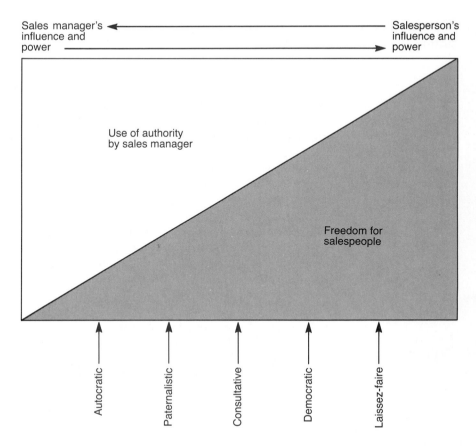

cipative style. The autocratic style is inappropriate with experienced sales-people or in situations requiring teamwork and group effort.

Paternalistic   When using the paternalistic style, the sales manager as-sumes the role of father or big brother. While the sales manager sets the goals, he or she tries to convince the salespeople that the goals are in their best interest. Participation, though not stifled completely, is limited to minor issues.

The paternalistic style works best for managers who are not in a strong position of authority. This may occur when a sales manager is new on the job or when real authority lies with the sales manager's boss. A paternalistic style does not work well with mature and independent sales-people.

Consultative   The consultative sales manager solicits the ideas and beliefs of the salespeople before making a decision. For example, a consultative manager might say: "We are getting a lot of complaints from headquarters about the service we are providing customers. What do you think is going wrong? How do you think this problem can be corrected?'' After getting opinions from the salespeople, the consultative sales manager makes the decision.

This leadership style is useful when salespeople are experienced, mature, and well trained. It is not suitable for independent salespeople who are not interested in working as a group.

Democratic   The democratic style represents a movement toward more freedom for salespeople and less authority for sales managers. Democratic managers are interested in implementing the views of most salespeople who work for them. Such managers encourage discussion and accept the group's decision.

The democratic style is most suitable when dealing with a small group of knowledgeable sales representatives. It is difficult to use this style when the number of salespeople is large, when decisions must be made quickly, or when salespeople do not have enough knowledge or training to participate in decisions.

Laissez-Faire   The laissez-faire or free-rein style is at the passive end of the leadership-style spectrum. It permits expert salespeople to control their own work. The sales manager exercises little control and primarily assists salespeople in achieving their personal goals. This style is very appropriate in dealing with the most experienced salespeople.

SPECIFIC DUTIES AND RESPON- SIBILITIES OF A SALES MANAGER

We have briefly mentioned the types of problems encountered by the sales executive and the field sales manager. The higher the sales manager is in the organizational structure, the more he or she will be concerned with broad management problems. If the sales manager is responsible for sales in a small territory, district, or branch, his or her most immediate concerns will be with such activities as recruiting, training, stimulating, and motivating salespeople. The following pages describe typical problems that arise in working with salespeople. It is impossible to cover more than a few selected activities. But the activities described will give students some insight into sales management.

Recruiting

Most companies have a constant problem recruiting and maintaining a competent sales staff. The major responsibility for replacing and adding salespeople usually rests with the field or district sales managers. Sales managers are becoming aware of the value of developing a recruiting and selection program in cooperation with personnel specialists.

Many large companies with comprehensive staffing plans follow a standard procedure that entails: (1) analyzing the essential elements in the sales job and determining the qualifications necessary to perform the job in a satisfactory manner; (2) analyzing the present sales force to find what distinguishes superior salespeople from inferior ones; (3) setting standards, norms, or profiles based on the characteristics or qualities of successful salespeople; (4) locating sources to provide the types of sales applicants desired; and (5) measuring the qualifications of sales applicants to compare with norms based on the characteristics of the company's successful salespeople.

How to Recruit   While no single technique of recruiting and hiring applies equally well to all types of businesses, certain fundamentals are essential to effective recruiting programs.

Ordinarily, the sales manager recognizes that a well-organized sales structure is built from the bottom. The number of salespeople needed in the future can be estimated only after sales-job descriptions are written and sales forecasts made. The sales manager knows some salespeople will resign, some will be transferred, and some will prove unsatisfactory. In other words, provision must be made for replacements. In addition, in most companies there is a constant need for recruiting new salespeople to sell new products and to cover new territories. After the preparatory steps are taken and the number and types of salespeople to be recruited are determined, the sales manager will proceed with their recruitment.

From company experience, certain standards are determined with regard to such factors as age, education, experience, marital status, and minimum test scores. Critical profiles based on these standards may then be used to evaluate candidates. While the profiles may show the characteristics of ideal employees, the sales manager must recognize that a certain amount of flexibility is desirable in selecting individuals for sales positions.

After acceptable standards are set, the next problem is to locate sources of desirable applicants. An important part of a sales manager's job is to locate and cultivate good sources of competent salespeople.

Where to Recruit   University and college placement offices are excellent sources. Many sales managers contact professors for leads on outstanding graduates before visiting the placement offices.

Present employees of the company are sometimes asked for recommendations. Members of the sales staff may have friends or acquaintances suited for sales work, but sometimes friends may be recommended who do not possess the desired qualifications.

Employees working in another department of the company are sometimes qualified for sales work. An employee currently in accounting, credit, or traffic work, for example, may be interested in sales work.

Customers or clients are often able to recommend qualified applicants. From their dealings with company salespeople, they are in a position to know which types of persons will probably succeed.

Well-prepared ads in newspapers, magazines, and trade publications may bring good results. For sales jobs requiring a minimum of qualifications, newspaper advertising is likely to bring many inquiries. Unless the necessary qualifications are stated, many unqualified candidates may apply. For sales jobs requiring highly qualified individuals, trade publications are likely to reach more acceptable candidates.

Sales representatives for competing companies or sales representatives who are selling related lines are sometimes available for a new sales job. Of course, pirating employees from competitors can work both ways.

Public and private employment agencies can supply qualified sales applicants for certain kinds of work. Influential friends and voluntary applicants are also sources.

The sources for new employees are numerous. The sales manager who wants to maintain an efficient sales staff is always looking for potential sales representatives. No one source can be relied on to supply company needs. Good sales managers constantly evaluate their sources to determine which ones are providing the greatest number of successful candidates. There is no easy way to get good sales representatives; it takes time and an organized plan to attract capable people. However, it is less expensive to take the time and effort to hire good people than to hire subpar candidates who fail after the training investment has been made.

Selecting

In recent years, considerable progress has been made in screening and selecting salespeople. Most companies have discarded the myth there is a "sales type" who will be successful in any type of selling, whether it is routine behind-the-counter sales or creative outside selling of intangibles.

An effective sales recruiting and selection plan should start with development of realistic specifications for the different sales jobs. These job descriptions are used to screen potential recruits. Each applicant's qualifications are matched against requirements in a job description. Some important sources of information about recruits are (1) the application form, (2) references, (3) tests, and (4) personal interviews.

Application Form   This is a preprinted form the candidate completes. The form supplies facts about the candidate and is often useful in structuring a personal interview.

References   Checking with people who know the applicant is a good way to validate the information on the application form. References also can supplement the information with personal observations. The most frequently contacted references are former employers. Other references are co-workers and leaders of social or religious organizations to which the applicant belongs.

An experienced sales manager generally expects to hear favorable comments from an applicant's references. The most useful information is contained in unusual comments or gestures, such as ambiguous remarks, faint praise, hesitant responses, or inconsistent facial expressions.

Tests Intelligence, ability, personality, and interest tests provide information about a potential salesperson that cannot be obtained as readily from other selection tools. The intelligence test, for example, provides information on the individual's native ability. This information can be used to train and supervise a particular salesperson. Tests can also correct misjudgments made by sales managers who think they can spot a good salesperson at first sight.

Most companies attach less importance to test results in the selection process because these results have not been good predictors of sales performance.[7] Candidates can fake responses to personality tests or can "freeze up" when taking ability tests. And many tests discriminate against minorities. Women, blacks, and first- or second-generation Americans often do not share the experiences and values of the white middle-class males who design the tests.[8]

Interviews More attention is now given to using multiple interviews in the selection process. This seems appropriate because selling is based on interpersonal communications. An interview also stresses that the selection process is a two-way street. The sales manager needs to know more about the applicant, and the applicant needs to know more about the company. Figure 19–5 describes typical questions asked in interviews and suggests how to analyze the responses.

Interviews are generally conducted in the later stages of the selection process. Applicants are asked questions about their background, experience, and objectives. The interviewer often poses a hypothetical situation to get the candidate's reactions.

There is no one sales selection plan used by all companies. Selection methods differ, depending on such factors as the following: size of the sales organization, nature of the product, geographic location, status of the labor market, and personal characteristics of management. A sales selection plan tailored to meet the specific needs of a given company will, in the long run, prove to be the most beneficial.

Training

The training program in a large company is devised to educate the beginning salesperson and to provide refresher training for the experienced

---

[7]See Barton A. Weitz, "Effectiveness in Sales Interactions: A Contingency Framework," *Journal of Marketing*, Winter 1981, pp. 16–24.

[8]See Hal Lancaster, "Job Tests Are Dropped by Many Companies Due to Antibias Drive," *The Wall Street Journal*, September 3, 1975, pp. 1, 19.

FIGURE 19–5
How to Answer
Questions Asked in
a Job Interview

Question. Why are you interested in this position and why did you respond to our ad?

Comment. What the interviewer is looking for is an answer that reflects thoughtfulness, preparation and clarification of the applicant's goals, likes and dislikes. It's here that the applicant has a chance to show that he or she has done homework and knows a good bit about the industry as a whole and about the company in particular.

Question. Tell me about your current and previous bosses. What kind of people are they?

Comment. It is a mistake to bad-mouth bosses, and this can turn an interviewer to stone. The basic point in this question is to determine how you get along with superiors, the types of personality with which you mix well and poorly. Do you work better with a boss who gives you plenty of room or with a boss who believes in tight structure? The interviewer is trying to see if there is a match between you and the person who would be your boss in the job for which you are applying. If you can show that you are flexible in dealing with people, you are ahead of the game.

Question. Has your job performance ever been appraised? How were you assessed? What were the pluses and minuses?

Comment. This question is designed to give the interviewer some sense of your honesty. Nobody is expected to reveal major flaws or serious shortcomings, but everybody has some weaknesses, and failure to admit any puts you in a questionable light. But be reasonable in what you share. The more detrimental information you give, the greater risk you run of hurting your chances for the job. So you need to downplay the minuses and play up the pluses. If you're asked about weaknesses, don't say that you're not good at detail if you're applying for a job that requires thoroughness. You want to indicate factors that help you to be more attractive. If you're asked for weaknesses, list minor shortcomings—not something the company is looking for as a strength.

Question. What are the most important factors you require in a job? How should it be structured to provide you with satisfaction?

Comment. These questions are asked before you are given any detailed information about the job. The answers you give—autonomy, security, compensation, responsibilities—help the interviewer to determine how mutually satisfying the job for which you are applying might be. This reinforces the essential nature of interview preparation. Know what the job is all about and if it does not suit your needs, keep looking. Don't try to con the interviewer by telling him what you think he wants to hear—if it doesn't reflect the way you really feel.

Question. What are the most satisfying aspects of your present job? The most frustrating?

Comment. The interviewer is looking for insight into what makes you tick. Are you result-oriented and pleased with attaining specific goals? Or has there been difficulty with interpersonal relationships, personality conflicts that may have stymied efforts to reach objectives?

Question. Describe a time when you felt particularly effective in your job.

Comment. The interviewer is not so much interested in the activity itself as in how it is described and the behavior shown during the explanation. If an applicant says, "I'm not sure what you want," he or she is considered to be

FIGURE 19–5
(*concluded*)

exhibiting a dependent trait—which is not something that interviewers tend to embrace. So jump on this question with both feet.

Question. Where do you want to be in the next 5 years? In the next 10 years?

Comment. This is probably the hardest question to answer, but it is asked because the interviewer is trying to get a handle on how much you have really considered long-term objectives and how to reach them. Answers should be logical. Example: If your education, training and work experience are grossly unsuited to the goals you express, you raise more questions than you answer for the interviewer. So before the interview, give this question some thought. It is a question that is posed in almost every interview.

Source: From Darrell Sifford, "How to Answer Questions Asked at a Job Interview," *Philadelphia Inquirer,* June 19, 1984, p. 4–C.

Table 19–1 Average Cost of Sales Training per Salesperson, 1986

Type of Company	Training Cost* Including Salary		Percent Increase	Median Training Period (weeks)	
	1986	1982	1982–86	1986	1982
Industrial products	$27,525	$22,490	22.4%	17	21
Consumer products	19,320	15,090	28.0	19	20
Services†	20,460	14,720	39.0	14	15

*In addition to salary, covers such items as instructional materials prepared, purchased, and rented for training program; transportation and living expenses incurred during training course; instructional staff; outside seminars and courses; and management time spent with salesperson when it is a part of the training budget.
†Includes insurance, financial, utilities, transportation, retail stores, etc.
Source: "Survey of Selling Costs," *Sales & Marketing Management,* February 16, 1987, p. 62.

salesperson. The sales manager is concerned with what to teach and how to teach. The following discussion will explore some methods used for training salespeople. The amount of money spent on training a salesperson is shown in Table 19–1. Table 19–2 summarizes the amount of time spent on training.

Training the New Salesperson Normally, these programs combine the following: centralized instructional meetings; assignment to production and/or other departments to obtain product and company knowledge; and on-the-job supervised sales practice in a sales territory. The nature and length of the training program for new salespeople vary considerably. Companies in highly technical industries, such as the computer, chemical,

A sales manager
directs training
sessions for sales
representatives.

Jon Feingersh/Click, Chicago

Table 19–2   Length of Training Period for New Salespeople, 1986

	Type of Company		
	Industrial Products	Consumer Products	Services*
0 to 6 weeks	25%	25%	25%
Over 6 weeks to 3 months	8	25	17
Over 3 months to 6 months	42	42	33
Over 6 months to 12 months	17	8	25
Over 12 months	8	0	0
Total	**100%**	**100%**	**100%**
Median training period (weeks)	**17**	**19**	**14**

*Includes insurance, financial, utilities, transportation, retail stores, etc.
Source: "Survey of Selling Costs," *Sales & Marketing Management,* February 16, 1987, p. 62.

and paper industries, usually have very comprehensive training programs
for new salespeople.

IBM, for example, has an educational and training budget as large as
the educational budget of many major universities. The corporation uses
all the most modern tools and techniques to train its new sales representatives.

The Dow Chemical Company also has a very comprehensive training
program for new sales trainees (see Figure 19–6).

FIGURE 19–6
Dow Chemical Sales
Training Program

General training
  Orientation
  Duration   1 week chemistry course
               4 weeks general orientation
  Purpose   to gain knowledge of the chemical industry with emphasis on
                 Dow's products, plants, and people

  Sales office experience
  Duration   1 week in office
               3 weeks traveling with various salesmen
  Purpose   to obtain first-hand information
               to learn the functions of the sales office and its relation to the
                 overall organization
               to learn what the job of a field salesman involves

  Production tours
  Duration   8 to 10 weeks
  Purpose   to acquaint men with our research labs, production facilities, and
                 raw material picture

  Sales clinic
  Duration   4 weeks
  Purpose   to develop actual sales tools to be of use to the salesman—help
                 him gain insight and sharper judgment

Product end-use training
  Duration   1 to 5 months
  Purpose   to give specific information on uses of products, markets,
                 competitive materials, etc.

On-the-job training
  Duration   6 months to 1 year
  Purpose   to increase job skills and to familiarize the salesman with his
                 territory and customers

Source: Adapted Courtesy of Dow Chemical Co.

The Hewlett-Packard Company has a training program as modern as its electronic products. The company maintains a home office school to give Hewlett-Packard sales representatives initial and refresher training.

The new sales representative at Hewlett-Packard attends five weeks of intensive product information classes. After this initial schooling, the sales representative serves a year's apprenticeship as a staff engineer, taking phone orders, handling customers' calls for information, and becoming familiar with the products. Then the new sales trainee works for another year as a field engineer, making sales calls under close supervision before being given a territory.

Personal contacts
help the sales
manager to motivate
the individual
salesperson.

H. Armstrong Roberts

The sales manager's role in training a new salesperson is very important. In developing a selling skill, the practice method is effective. The salesperson can watch a skilled person (the sales manager or the sales supervisor) make a presentation. The salesperson can then practice until he or she has the presentation down perfectly.

The sales manager's function, then, is to train the new sales representative through individual instruction, coaching, and evaluation. One sales manager listed the following "five steps to successful coaching":

1. *Tell* the salesperson what you are going to do on the call. For instance, "I am going to explain three reasons why our transformer runs cooler," or, "I am going to show how we can get by the receptionist into the prospect's office," or, "I am going to tell the buyer why it's to his or her benefit to place an order three times larger than before."

2. *Demonstrate* your plan by making the call in the role of a sales representative, with your associate standing by silently.

3. *Have the sales trainee do it* when he or she feels ready. People learn by doing. This step is where sales training really begins. Let the salesperson handle the call. Don't come to the rescue.

4. *Constructively correct* between calls. Compliment for things done right. Invite analysis of things done wrong or left out.

5. *Habituate*—continue coaching until better performance becomes habitual.

Training the Experienced Salespeople   It's often harder to train experienced salespeople than new trainees. Experienced salespeople may have acquired ineffective techniques or bad habits. They may resent outside advice and may want to "do their own thing." If they are reasonably successful and have reached an economic earnings plateau that is satisfactory for their way of life, additional training is less attractive to them.

The sales manager is responsible for analyzing the training needs of each salesperson in the territory and for taking the necessary steps to jar the experienced, but reluctant, salespeople out of their "comfort zones."

Experienced salespeople may receive refresher training as individuals or in groups. The group method of training has many advantages; the sales manager can choose from several methods when conducting sales training meetings—lectures, demonstrations, practice, or conference or discussions. Any one method or combination of methods may be desirable, depending on the objective.

Stimulating and Motivating

One of the hardest tasks of sales managers is to keep salespeople in a positive frame of mind. Most new sales representatives begin their selling careers with great enthusiasm and a determination to set sales records. But personal problems, failure to meet quotas, changes in economic conditions, and other factors may discourage them. Unhappy sales representatives usually do not represent their companies well.

Motivating cannot be achieved solely through personal contact with the sales manager or through contests and sales promotions. The product must be of high quality and properly priced; the territory must be appropriate; the salesperson must be properly trained and have the proper selling tools; and the company's compensation plan must be fair. Otherwise, maintaining morale is a hard task.

The successful sales manager knows the sales staff is composed of individuals who differ in their likes and dislikes. He or she knows certain methods are effective in stimulating some salespeople and ineffective with others. In other words, individual differences must be considered. In large organizations, it's not practical to develop a different method for each salesperson; hence, a variety of plans are used to interest the greatest possible number of salespeople. Personal contacts with each salesperson, however, help the sales manager take individual differences into account.

FIGURE 19–7
Announcement from
a College Placement
Bureau

> *Sales Management Trainee:* This interview has as its purpose the selection and training of men and women for a sales management career rather than for a purely sales career. Graduates of this program will be placed in the company's sales offices as managers, assistant managers, or supervisors. Training will be in Los Angeles or in an agency city under the supervision of the resident manager. $19,000 to $23,000 to start, annual increases.

The alert sales manager knows how to best motivate each salesperson in his or her territory. Some salespeople can be motivated only through increases in salary, bonuses, or commissions. Others strive for promotion in the company or for public recognition of their performance at a sales meeting. Some salespeople just want a pat on the back from the sales manager. Salespeople have different needs and must be motivated in different ways.

HOW TO PREPARE FOR SALES MANAGEMENT WORK

Opportunities

Opportunities in sales management are available for students who want to train for the responsibility after graduation from college. Such opportunities are also available for experienced sales representatives who prove themselves successful salespeople.

One large life insurance company recruits sales management trainees at colleges. Figure 19–7 shows the announcement one company prepared to recruit college graduates. The company believes some sales experience is necessary but that a particular kind of management skill must be learned. This skill may be exercised, the company believes, by people who have not had many years of top sales production experience.

Other companies will consider candidates who have had considerable experience both in selling and in management work.

Sales management opportunities are available in all types of industries. For the capable salesperson who has the desire to manage and the necessary characteristics, there will always be opportunities to manage a sales force.

How to Prepare for Management Responsibility

Advancement to sales management does not just happen. It is awarded only to salespeople who are qualified and ready when the opportunity arises. Salespeople who desire advancement don't wait until the opportunity arrives to get ready for it—they prepare in advance.

What can the salesperson do to get ready for more responsibility? How far in advance can a salesperson prepare? How long does it take? Obviously, there is no one answer to these questions. However, a few helpful suggestions follow.

While a college education in itself guarantees nothing, it can be helpful in preparing for management work. Education, however, does not end with a college degree—what is learned afterward earns progress and advancement. But a sound education is a good base. And work experience while attending college pays dividends in both getting and keeping a job.

In addition to education and work experience, a student should look for opportunities to be a leader at school. He or she should participate in clubs, sports, and organizations to gain confidence.

On the job, salespeople who want to manage others must first prove they can manage themselves. Answers to the following questions may be a clue to efficient self-management: Is the ratio of sales calls to sales favorable? Are lost accounts replaced with new accounts? Have any ideas for improvement of operations been passed along recently? Are sales calls and territory coverage planned efficiently? These and similar questions help point to good self-management.

Ambitious salespeople also prepare for advancement by trying on the boss's job for size. That is, they attempt, in their own minds, to solve the problems the sales manager faces. The salesperson compares his or her decision with that made by the executive and evaluates the results. Of course, these decisions are not volunteered unless they are requested. Self-confidence is built if the salesperson arrives at conclusions that resemble those of the successful sales executive.

Salespeople can visualize themselves as sales managers. They may ask themselves: "How would I recruit? Where? How would I get more sales? How would I cut expenses in the territory?" A potential sales manager is expected to have ideas on these and other problems.

A good procedure is to try to make a self-evaluation from the viewpoint of the current sales manager. The salesperson may place himself or herself in the sales manager's position and ask: "Is this salesperson doing his or her best? Would I be glad to recommend this salesperson, should an opening occur? Is the salesperson growing or just standing still?" Answers to these questions can help determine a salesperson's fitness for promotion.

It is a good idea to study the decisions made by management at the policy level. How many were good decisions? How many were poor decisions? What caused the poor decisions? What can be done to ensure right decisions most of the time?

Sales management ability is not a gift; it is an ability developed through study, experience, and willingness to work. If salespeople have the right attitude, if they plan and organize their efforts, they can look forward to working in this challenging management field.

SUMMARY

Sales management functions are performed at several levels in the organization. The sales executive is responsible for determining policy and for maintaining financial control over the sales organization.

A major policy decision is the method of compensation for the sales force. The four basic methods are straight salary, straight commission, bonus, or combination plans. Each plan has its advantages and disadvantages. Straight commission plans provide a strong motivation for salespeople, but the company has little control over salespeople's activities. On the other hand, the company has more control over the activities of salespeople under the straight salary plan, but there is less incentive for salespeople to work hard.

Another policy decision concerns organization of the sales force. All sales forces are organized on a geographic basis. But within a geographic area, salespeople might specialize in selling to a particular type of customer or in selling a specific type of product.

The field sales manager performs the same management function as the sales executive—planning and organizing. But the primary emphasis of field sales managers is the motivation, evaluation, and training of salespeople. Field sales managers are leaders of a group of salespeople. There are several leadership styles field sales managers can use. Each of these styles is effective with some type of salespeople and ineffective with others. Good managers use the appropriate style when dealing with each of their salespeople.

Salespeople must first learn to manage themselves and their territory before they can manage other people. In addition to obtaining the appropriate education and work experience, salespeople who aspire to be sales managers should look for opportunities to assume leadership roles. Salespeople can learn management skills by studying the actions of their sales managers.

QUESTIONS AND PROBLEMS

1. Robert R. Smith, director of sales, film department, E. I. du Pont de Nemours and Co., made the following statement on the problem of remotivating older salespeople:

> This is no ordinary day-to-day problem of motivation we're talking about. This is a special case—and it could well be a lasting one. We're talking about the problem of motivating a person who has come face-to-face with a sobering realization that comes to all of us. We're talking about a person who has had to face squarely the knowledge that he or she has gone as far as he or she can go. Depending upon the individual, this can be a bleak and deeply disturbing realization—particularly if the person has lived for years not only with ambition for higher attainments but with an unrealistic appraisal of his or her own potential. It can, and often does, produce a protracted period of rationalizing. It can, and often does, effect a change in a person's personality. It stalls the sales engine, and when the engine stalls, we don't move goods.

What can be done to remotivate older salespeople who have started to coast? How should it be done?

2. Surveys show there is tremendous waste in current methods of hiring and training new salespeople. Make a list of questions a good sales executive should ask to determine whether there is room for improvement in hiring and training techniques.

3. Assume you are the sales manager for the western district of a manufacturer of trucks, tractors, and farm machinery. A dealer in your district is eager to increase the sale of parts for this equipment. He asks you to help him determine the potential market for machine parts in his area. To what sources would you refer him to get the needed data? Justify each source or method recommended.

4. How would you feel about having your sales manager travel with you as a part of your regular evaluation? Do you believe the sales manager has anything to gain *personally* from such visits?

5. Write a job description for a salesperson in the men's clothing department of a department store.

6. Good salespeople do not make good sales managers. Explain why you agree or disagree with this statement.

7. What leadership style would you recommend for sales managers of door-to-door salespeople selling encyclopedias? For managers of computer salespeople? Should the styles be different? Why?

8. To what extent should salespeople be allowed to manage themselves? What are the advantages and disadvantages of self-management?

9. The Emporium is the largest department store in San Francisco. For many years this concern has operated a very successful training program for new employees. An applicant fills out a preliminary application form and is given a screening interview by the supervisor of the trainee program. The trainee supervisor gives the applicant a training program brochure; briefly outlines the training program, store policies, and benefits; and answers questions. If the candidate appears to have good potential, a longer application form is filled out and an appointment is made to return for a battery of aptitude tests and a patterned interview. The tests and interview last about two hours. The applicant is then given some booklets so he or she may learn more about the store before returning for the tests and interview. Assume you are interested in entering the Emporium's training program. What kinds of tests would you expect to take? What kinds of questions would you expect the interviewer to ask you during the patterned interview?

10. Should new salespeople be trained by the sales manager and the regular sales representatives or by specialized company instructors who teach full-time? What are the advantages and disadvantages of each method as far as new salespeople are concerned?

PROJECTS

1. Make a survey of three local sales organizations, and obtain information on the kinds of incentives they use to motivate their salespeople. Evaluate and contrast the incentive plans of each organization.

2. Assume you are a sales manager for a company that sells typewriters and dictating machines. Design a patterned interview blank you could use when interviewing candidates for sales positions.

3. Compare the ads for sales positions that appear in the Sunday classified section of your local newspaper and in "The Mart" (classified advertising) section of *The Wall Street Journal*. Write a report describing the differences in the ads. Explain why these differences exist.

CASE PROBLEMS

Case 19–1   Sawyer's Clothing

Don Moore is a store manager for Sawyer's Clothing, a nationwide chain carrying quality men's clothing and accessories. He is having considerable problems with his salespeople.

Two of the salespeople reporting to the assistant sales manager, Paul Stevens, are Jim Miller and Walter Carter. Moore hired Stevens because he wanted to spend more time on planning and merchandising. He was also interested in developing Stevens into a store manager, so he could have a ready replacement for himself when an opportunity for promotion in the corporation arose.

Unfortunately, Stevens has not turned out the way Moore expected. Stevens, who is in his late 30s, has had considerable difficulty getting along with Miller and Carter. He finds it nearly impossible to give them orders. When he does, they always reply with a sarcastic comment. Miller and Carter are always playing practical jokes on Stevens. They hide his order pad and put tags on his back when he is not looking.

Stevens has not taken these problems to Moore. He is afraid Moore will see the problems as a sign of poor management ability. However, the situation has resulted in a decrease in sales. Customers are being neglected. Some customers have been offended by the practical jokes. When Moore asked Stevens why sales had declined, Stevens responded there were not any customers.

Finally, Moore heard about the situation through complaints from regular customers. When these complaints were presented to Stevens, Stevens blamed Miller and Carter. He said they were immature. Moore said he had never had problems with either Miller or Carter.

Questions

1. What kind of leader is Stevens?
2. What should Moore do about the situation?

Case 19–2   Remember-It

Remember-It produces and sells approximately 1,000 leather, paper, plastic, and metal advertising specialties on a nationwide basis. Most of its advertising specialties are remembrance advertising items, such as calendars, matches, executive datebooks, pencils, pens, and pocket business cards.

The company employs 1,000 salespeople who earn an average income of $19,000 after one year of employment. During 1986, about half of the salespeople earned over $30,000. The top 15 salespeople earn from $60,000 to $80,000 a year. The average order is about $300. The salespeople study the specific needs of their clients and recommend remembrance advertising that will appeal to the customers of each client. Remember-It sales representatives are taught to consider carefully what their prospects need to make them better known, better liked, and better patronized. The sales representatives must be alert to opportunities that others do not see, and they must have very keen imaginations. The company sells remembrance advertising to about 120 different kinds of businesses, so the sales representatives must be flexible and astute.

Past experience shows that many sales representatives fail during the first year with the company because they are not able to sell specialized remembrance advertising. Once the sales representatives become established, however, they seldom leave the company. The company's experience indicates the best sales applicant is about 30 to 35 years of age; is married, with one or two children; and has life insurance, a car, and equity in a home.

The company has always placed major emphasis on recruiting new salespeople through the present field personnel. Sales aptitude tests have never been used because management believes such tests do not meet the needs of Remember-It. The responsibility for recruiting, selecting, and training new sales representatives rests primarily with the district managers.

Questions

1. Assume you are a district manager for Remember-It. What sources would you depend upon in securing sales applicants?
2. If you used newspaper advertising as one of your sources, what kind of advertisement would you run? What kind of copy?
3. What, if any, training aids and help would you expect from the home office in training the salespeople in your district?

Case 19–3   The Barton Company

The Barton Company employs 25 sales representatives who sell office supplies and equipment directly to business and industrial users in the metropolitan Atlanta area. In addition to hundreds of items such as carbon paper, pencils, rubber bands, paper clips, blotters, erasers, ink, and stencils, the company sells typewriters, safes, adding machines, desk lamps, posture chairs, filing cabinets, desks, calculators, and many other office-equipment products.

The company's sales representatives are required to spend one day each week on the floor at the company's downtown retail outlet. The remainder of the workweek is spent outside the store contacting and selling buyers who have a need for almost any type of office supplies or equipment. The sales representatives have small drawing accounts or guarantees to provide them with an adequate minimum income during their learning period, and they are paid on a straight commission basis after the learning period ends.

Each individual is assigned a specific territory, and all sales in this territory are credited to his or her account exclusively for commission purposes. The company's sales representatives are required to concentrate their selling of certain products periodically in order to guarantee that the complete line of office products is merchandised. At some periods the emphasis is on adding machines; at other times, on typewriters; at other times, on checkwriters; and so on.

Quotas are assigned for various families of products, and contests are held frequently to help stimulate sales and meet quotas. New business is important, and detailed records of activity are required. Considerable emphasis is also placed on cultivating old customers.

The company's sales manager plans to award a "Sammy" each year to the company's outstanding sales representative; appropriate ceremonies will accompany presentation of the award. In order to select the outstanding sales representative, the sales manager asks each sales representative to submit a scoring sheet identifying 10 areas in which a rating should be made.

Questions

1. Identify 10 areas and list four or five appropriate questions in each area to point out the important success factors to be considered. For example, areas may be "personal habits and qualities": (*a*) Is the person neat in appearance? (*b*) Can he or she be depended upon to complete what is started? (*c*) Is the person enthusiastic about work? (*d*) Does the person constantly strive to improve selling ability? (*e*) Can the person express himself or herself effectively? Prepare the material in the form of a rating sheet.

2. Which of the areas listed should be given the greatest weight in the total evaluation of the salesperson? The least weight? Why?

Case 19–4 Wisconsin Manufacturing Company*

The increase in the price of gasoline and the problem of its availability are considered by Roy Arnold, Wisconsin's sales manager, to be leading factors in the rising costs of sales. In recent years selling expenses have risen dramatically, especially those associated with travel.

Wisconsin Manufacturing produces a full line of builders' hardware. Corporate objectives indicate sales are to be made

*Reprinted from Gilbert A. Churchill, Jr., Neil M. Ford, and Orville Walker, Jr., *Sales Force Management: Planning, Implementation, and Control* (Homewood, Ill.: Richard D. Irwin, 1981).

Exhibit 1   Number of Calls Made by District

District		Year				
		1982	1983	1984	1985	1986
1		6,326	6,390	6,415	6,383	6,358
2		4,020	4,115	4,110	4,180	4,200
3		5,812	5,750	5,803	5,791	5,876
4		5,581	5,965	6,658	6,837	7,025
5		3,905	4,118	4,150	4,109	4,008
6		7,132	7,100	7,085	7,110	7,145
7		6,028	6,085	6,115	5,990	6,163
8		4,930	4,918	5,112	5,138	5,035
	Totals	43,734	44,441	45,448	45,538	45,810

only to retailers or to retail voluntary chain organizations. Customers range from small hardware stores to large franchised operations such as True Value and Ace Hardware. Occasionally a sales representative has made a sale to a hardware wholesaler, only to have the sale canceled. Wisconsin has settled on this account management strategy to ensure its retailers have access to hardware supplies at reasonable prices. The theory is that this strategy should enable Wisconsin to stay competitive and to stay in business.

To better understand what has happened to sales expenses, Arnold asks his sales analyst, Nancy Lindberg, to bring together information to help isolate the issues. Wisconsin has been collecting information for years pertaining to such things as:

Number of customers.

Orders by customer.

Number of calls by salesperson by customer.

Sales by customer.

Wisconsin's sales force of 48 people is divided into eight districts, with an average of six sales representatives for each district. Depending on location, a sales representative is assigned an entire state, parts of several states, parts of one state, or in some cases, a single metropolitan area. Large metropolitan areas, such as Chicago, are divided into two or more territories. The size of a territory plus the number of accounts are factors in determining territory potential and the need for territory modification. To date, Wisconsin has not developed a market index for determining territory potential.

The first step to be taken by Nancy Lindberg is to compile information on call activity for each sales representative by district for the last five years. Exhibit 1 shows these results.

A cursory analysis of Exhibit 1 shows District 4 had a sizable increase in number of calls from 1982 to 1986. Since selling expenses in District 4, located in the Midwest, have increased above average, Nancy Lindberg decides this is where her detailed analysis should start.

The next step produces a table showing the number of calls for each sales representative for the last five years. As Exhibit 2 indicates, the number of calls has increased since 1982. This is the result of Roy Arnold's insistence that Wisconsin's sales force call on *all* retail hardware and lumber dealers. To meet Arnold's wishes, most sales representatives have paid close attention to their routing patterns. Dramatic improvements have resulted; some sales

Exhibit 2 Calls Made by District 4 Sales Representatives

| Sales Representatives | Year | | | | |
	1982	*1983*	*1984*	*1985*	*1986*
L. Daniel	1,005	1,074	1,198	1,231	1,245
D. Malley	893	954	998	957	1,001
J. Christopher	895	894	965	1,094	1,120
J. Harrison	1,116	1,193	1,332	1,367	1,407
P. Tonneson	1,010	1,104	1,215	1,246	1,267
M. Leary	662	746	950	942	985
Totals	5,581	5,965	6,658	6,837	7,025

Exhibit 3 Sales, Selling Costs, and Number of Sales Calls by Sales Representative for District 4, 1986

Sales Representative	Sales	Number of Calls	Salaries	Commissions	Expenses
L. Daniel	$ 288,840	1,245	$12,430	$ 7,808	$ 8,484
D. Malley	220,220	1,001	11,300	4,166	7,238
J. Christopher	254,240	1,120	10,735	6,707	7,520
J. Harrison	295,470	1,407	13,000	9,658	9,121
P. Tonneson	291,410	1,267	13,560	5,275	9,818
M. Leary	224,580	985	11,860	4,761	8,313
Totals	$1,574,760	7,025	$72,885	$38,375	$50,494

Exhibit 4 Sales and Number of Calls for Harrison's Territory, 1986

Counties	Sales	Number of Calls
Columbia	$ 3,875	9
Crawford	0	0
Dane	32,379	157
Dodge	8,412	55
Fond du Lac	8,387	28
Grant	4,903	17
Green	4,053	17
Green Lake	0	0
Iowa	3,152	10
Jefferson	7,797	52
Kenosha	14,991	80
Lafayette	1,850	19
Manitowoc	789	37
Milwaukee	99,812	403
Ozaukee	8,131	30
Racine	19,894	100
Richland	0	0
Rock	14,772	83
Sauk	4,563	10
Sheboygan	2,206	44
Walworth	7,579	45
Washington	8,223	46
Waukesha	29,702	165
Totals	$285,470	1,407

EXHIBIT 5
Harrison's 23-
County Territory

representatives have increased both calls and sales without a corresponding increase in selling expenses. Some districts, however, have probably increased the number of calls by spending less time on each call. This is what Nancy Lindberg suspects has happened in District 4, where calls have increased substantially but sales have remained fairly constant. Her next step is to examine 1986 sales by sales representative. The results appear in Exhibit 3.

Lindberg calculates sales and calls for each representative relative to the total and discovers that Harrison accounts for 19 percent of the district's sales and makes 20 percent of the district's calls. Although this may seem reasonable, all other sales representatives have a percentage of sales equal to or greater than the percentage of calls. For example, Daniel accounts for 18 percent of both district sales and calls. Lindberg decides a more detailed analysis of Harrison's territory is the logical next step.

With existing data, Lindberg is able to identify calls and sales for Harrison's 23 counties in south central Wisconsin (see

Exhibit 4). Exhibit 5 shows the county breakdown for Harrison. Harrison lives in the district in Beloit (Rock County), a city that borders the state of Illinois.

Before she can complete her analysis, Lindberg is promoted to market research analyst. She has been able to identify several problems or questions that need attention, however.

Questions

1. How effectively is Harrison covering the 23-county territory?

2. Develop an index that can be used as a guide for planning the number of calls that should be made in each territory?

3. Is Wisconsin's sales manager correct in urging the sales force to increase its number of calls?

4. How can the sales analysis program at Wisconsin be improved?

SELECTED REFERENCES

Abernathy, Paul L., Jr. "Setting Performance Objectives Requires Lots of Give and Take." *Sales & Marketing Management*, May 19, 1980, pp. 86–91.

Archibald, Dale. "S&MM Spends a Day at Josten's New Man's Sales School." *Sales & Marketing Management*, April 7, 1980, pp. 46–50.

Churchill, Gilbert A., Jr.; Neil M. Ford; and Orville C. Walker, Jr. *Sales Force Management: Planning, Implementation and Control.* 2nd ed. Homewood, Ill.: Richard D. Irwin, 1985.

Demirdjian, Z. S. "A Multidimensional Approach to Motivating Salespeople." *Industrial Marketing Management*, Winter 1984, pp. 25–32.

Dobbs, John H. "Hiring: Sales Force Turnover Can Make—or Break You." *Sales & Marketing Management*, May 14, 1979, pp. 53–55.

Dubinsky, Alan J., and Richard W. Hansen. "The Sales Force Management Audit." *California Management Review*, Winter 1981, pp. 86–95.

Eckles, Robert W. "The Seven S's of Successful Sales Management." *Business Horizons*, March–April 1983, pp. 14–19.

Falvey, John J. "Myths of Sales Training." *Sales & Marketing Management*, April 3, 1977, pp. 81–83.

Henry, Porter. "Managing Your Sales Force as a System." *Harvard Business Review*, March–April 1979, pp. 85–95.

Patty, C. Robert. *Managing Salespeople.* 2nd ed. Reston, Va.: Reston Publishing, 1982.

Tyagi, Pradeep, and Carl Block. "Monetary Incentives and Salesmen Performance." *Industrial Marketing Management*, Fall 1983, pp. 263–69.

Author Index

Company Index

Subject Index